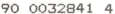

Tolley's
MANUAL OF ACCOUNTING

VOLUME II

Published by
Tolley Publishing Company Limited
Tolley House
2 Addiscombe Road
Croydon Surrey CR9 5AF England
081-686 9141

Typeset by Tek-Art (Typesetting) Ltd, Kent

Printed and bound in Great Britain by
Mackays of Chatham PLC, Chatham, Kent

FOREWORD

By Peter Morgan
Director General of the Institute of Directors

In 1985 the Companies Acts were consolidated into one Act. This consolidation meant that company law was slightly easier to follow than it had been for many years. However, the Companies Act 1989, which represents a major piece of legislation, has made the task of reading, let alone interpreting, company law extremely complex.

Ascertaining which provisions of Company Law now apply to a group's annual report and accounts is a major headache. The position becomes even worse when you try to decipher how accounting standards fit in with the legislation, especially where they seem to conflict. Barry Johnson and Matthew Patient must be congratulated at making eminent sense of what is an accounting and legal minefield. Their clear explanations of the accounting provisions of the Companies Acts and of the innumerable other accounting principles and practices adopted by companies show their breadth of experience and knowledge in this technically complicated area.

The accounting and legal world is becoming more regulated each year and it is difficult for the best of finance directors and accountants to keep abreast of the changes. Consequently, a major work like this is to be commended and the authors informed comment and examples taken from published accounts make what is invariably a dry subject come alive.

'Manual of Accounting' is a major reference work and is an extremely useful comprehensive explanatory text, exploring all aspects of UK GAAP. I am therefore only too pleased to commend it to its readers, as I know they will find it invaluable.

Peter Morgan

March 1990

PREFACE

'Manual of Accounting' is the second (much revised) edition of our very successful book on accounting disclosure and measurement, which was previously entitled 'Accounting Provisions of the Companies Act 1985'. This time, we have published in three volumes. The first two volumes cover similar material to that dealt with in our previous edition, but much expanded. Volume I looks primarily at individual companies, whereas volume II deals with groups (and includes many of the provisions that stem from the Companies Act 1989). Volume III considers the varied accounting and disclosure requirements that apply to a number of specialised businesses.

Both volumes I and II give detailed explanations of the accounting provisions of the Companies Acts 1985 and 1989. They also refer throughout to the additional reporting requirements that limited companies have to comply with and that are set out in Statements of Standard Accounting Practice (including exposure drafts) and The International Stock Exchange's Continuing Obligations for listed companies and its General Undertaking for USM companies. The text of volumes I and II include worked examples and extracts from published financial statements. The financial reporting provisions and Schedules to the Companies Act 1985 (as amended by the Companies Act 1989) are reproduced in the two volumes. The appendices include detailed checklists to those disclosure requirements that apply to company's and to group's financial statements and volume I includes a model set of financial statements.

Volume III is an introduction to the accounting requirements of a number of specialised businesses such as friendly societies, unlimited companies and banking companies. It considers how such entities are incorporated, the different statutes and regulations that apply to them, their filing responsibilities, the accounting requirements that apply to their financial statements and any requirements for audit.

The three volumes of 'Manual of Accounting' also include practical advice and comment we have gained through our work for the Technical Support Section of Coopers & Lybrand Deloitte in advising the Firm's clients, partners and staff.

We hope that finance directors, accountants, legal practitioners, company administrators, financial advisers and auditors will find this manual useful.

We thank Mary Arden, QC (our legal consultant) for her advice once again on the legal content of volumes I and II.

We offer our special thanks to Jyoti Ghosh for his considerable contribution in researching, drafting and checking much of the text. We also thank Eddie Hodgson for his invaluable, voluminous and amusing review comments and William Carver for his contribution and other members of the department for their helpful comments and advice.

Barry Johnson & Matthew Patient

Coopers & Lybrand Deloitte
London
March 1990

CONTENTS

Contents

Paragraph

7. Fair valuing assets and liabilities

x

9. Merger relief and merger accounting

10. Minority interests

11. Associated undertakings and joint ventures

12. Foreign currency translation

ABBREVIATIONS AND TERMS USED

accounts	=	financial statements.
the Act/the 1985 Act	=	the Companies Act 1985 (as amended by the Companies Act 1989).
the 1989 Act	=	the Companies Act 1989.
ACT	=	advance corporation tax.
AER	=	All England Law Reports.
APC	=	Auditing Practices Committee.
ASC	=	Accounting Standards Committee.
CACA	=	Chartered Association of Certified accountants.
CCAB	=	Consultative Committee of Accountancy Bodies Limited.
CC(CP)	=	Companies Consolidation (Consequential Provisions) Act 1985.
Ch	=	Law Reports, Chancery Division.
chapter (1)	=	'Manual of accounting - companies' volume II, chapter (1).
CIMA	=	Chartered Institute of Management Accountants.
CIPFA	=	Chartered Institute of Public Finance and Accountancy.
Cmnd	=	Command Paper.
CO	=	Continuing Obligations, Section 5 of the 'Admission of Securities to listing'.
DP	=	Discussion paper.
EC	=	European Community.
ECU	=	European currency unit.
ED	=	exposure draft.
financial statements	=	accounts.
the 7th Directive	=	EC 7th Directive on Company Law.
GAAP	=	Generally accepted accounting principles (and practices).
GU	=	General Undertaking of the Unlisted Securities Market.
IAS	=	International Accounting Standard.
IAS	=	International Accounting Standards Committee.

ICAEW	=	Institute of Chartered Accountants in England and Wales.
ICAI	=	Institute of Chartered Accountants in Ireland.
ICAS	=	Institute of Chartered Accountants of Scotland.
ICR	=	Industrial Cases Reports.
MR	=	Master of the Rolls.
NASDQ system	=	National Association of Securities Dealers Automated Quotation System.
para(s)	=	paragraph(s) of Schedules to the Companies Acts, or SSAPs, or EDs, or DPs, or text.
QC	=	Queen's Counsel.
RGD	=	Regional development grant.
SC	=	Session Cases
Sch	=	Schedule to the Companies Act 1985 (as amended by the Companies Act 1989) (4A Sch 85 = Schedule 4A, paragraph 85).
Sec(s)	=	Section(s) of the 1985 Act (as amended by the Companies Act 1989).
s	=	section of another Act.
SI	=	statutory instrument.
SOI	=	Statement of Intent.
SORP	=	Statement of Recommended Practice.
SSAP	=	Statement of Standard Accounting practice.
TR	=	Technical release.
UK	=	United Kingdom.
US	=	United States of America
USM	=	Unlisted Securities Market.
VAT	=	value added tax.
volume I, chapter (1)	=	'Manual of accounting - groups' volume I, chapter (1).
volume III, chapter (1)	=	'Manual of accounting - specialised businesses', volume III, chapter (1).
WLR	=	Weekly Law Reports.
Yellowbook	=	The International Stock Exchange's 'Admission of Securities to Listing'.

Chapter 1

INTRODUCTION

1

INTRODUCTION

Manual of accounting

1.1 This 'Manual of Accounting' is the second of three volumes covering many aspects of accounting in the United Kingdom (UK). The books not only cover the accounting provisions included in company law, but also deal with other accounting principles and practices that concern each different entity considered. Each volume covers different aspects of accounting in the UK, and their titles are as follows:

■ Manual of Accounting - volume I - Companies.

■ Manual of Accounting - volume II - Groups.

■ Manual of Accounting - volume III - Specialised businesses.

1.2 This volume of the manual of accounting concerns groups of companies and the accounting provisions that apply to them. Consequently, it considers in detail the requirements for consolidated financial statements which are included in the Companies Act 1989. This legislation, for the most part, reflects existing accounting standards or best practice concerning the preparation of, and the disclosure made in, consolidated financial statement. However, the Companies Act 1989 does make a number of other important changes (for example, the changes to the definitions of subsidiary companies) and these are also dealt with.

1.3 Volume I of the 'Manual of Accounting' deals primarily, as its title suggests, with the provisions of the Acts that apply to individual companies' financial statements. However, many of these provisions are equally applicable to groups of companies and in certain areas the different rules that apply specifically to groups are also explained.

1.4 Furthermore, during 1990 the Companies Acts 1985 and 1989 are to be further supplemented by various statutory instruments (SIs). These will relate to *inter alia* the following matters:

■ Schedule 6 of the Companies Act 1985, which concerns the disclosure of director's loans and transactions, is due to be rewritten.

■ The Overseas (Accounts) (Modifications and Exemptions) Order 1982 (SI 1982/676), has been rewritten. The SI's provisions have not altered significantly. The new SI is considered in 'Manual of Accounting - volume III'

■ A new SI to allow listed companies to send summary financial statements of their shareholders. (This SI is considered in detail in chapter 4.)

■ A new SI to require the disclosure of non-audit fees.

■ A further SI to deal with other sundry matters stemming from the enactment of the Companies Act 1989.

1.5 These changes to company law are expected to be relatively minor in relation to the totality of accounting provisions included in current legislation. However, it is necessary to bear in mind that there may be additional regulations passed since the publication of this book that have a bearing on particular matters discussed in it.

EC company law harmonisation

1.6 By 1990, the UK had included a substantial number of European Community (EC) Company Law Directives on its statute books. The major directives included in UK legislation are as follows:

■ 1st Directive - Publicity requirements, ultra vires and nullity.

■ 2nd Directive - Formation of companies and dividend requirements.

■ 3rd Directive - Mergers.

■ 4th Directive - Company accounts.

■ Directive on listing particulars.

■ Directive on continuing disclosure of information.

■ 6th Directive - 'Scissions'.

■ 7th Directive - Group accounts.

■ 8th Directive - Auditors.

1.7 The Companies Act 1989 introduced into legislation the latter two directives. A copy of the 4th Directive is included as appendix 8 to 'Manual of Accounting - volume I' and a copy of the 7th Directive is included as appendix 2 and a destination table is given in appendix 3. A summary of EC company law directives and their status in March 1990 is given in appendix 3 to 'Manual of Accounting - volume I'. This appendix also indicates where the directives mentioned above are enacted in UK company law.

1.8 The EC company law harmonisation programme is still far from complete and will continue for many years. As a consequence, the Companies Acts 1985 and 1989 will be further amended and supplemented when further EC Directives are implemented in the UK.

The Companies Act 1989

1.9 The Companies Act 1989 received Royal Assent on 16th November 1989. A major proportion of that Act implements the 7th and 8th Directives. In addition, there were a number of changes made to accounting provisions already dealt with in the Companies Act 1985. The Companies Act 1989 also amended other statutes including, the Fair Trading Act 1973 and the Financial Services Act 1986.

1.10 In order to make the changes to the accounting provisions required to comply with the 7th Directive, Parliament has in Part I of the Companies Act 1989 effectively re-enacted Part VII of the Companies Act 1985. Most of the changes to the Companies Act 1985 are of a minor nature and do not alter greatly existing law, but a few other amendments do introduce substantial changes and these are referred to in detail in the text of this book.

Commencement

1.11 The provisions of the Companies Act 1989 come into force at varying dates during 1990 and 1991. The main accounting provisions were brought into force by The Companies Act 1989 (Commencement No. 4) Order 1990 (SI 1990/355) with effect from 1st April 1990 and apply to accounting periods starting on or after 23rd December 1989. There are a number of transitional provisions that apply to companies' accounting periods that begin before 23rd December 1989 where they have not filed their statutory financial statements by 1st April 1990. Basically, these companies may prepare their financial statements under the accounting provisions set out in the old Part VII of the Companies Act 1985. However, certain provisions of Part I of the Companies Act 1989 also apply, but so as not to affect the content of the financial statements prepared under the old Part VII. Reference should be made to the SI to determine the full extent of the provisions that apply during the transitional period.

1.12 In addition, the commencement order No. 4 includes a number of other provisions of a transitional nature that apply to both the disclosure requirements and the accounting requirements of the Companies Act 1989 (for example, how to determine, for disclosure purposes, the gross amount of goodwill written off in a company).

These transitional provisions are mentioned where applicable in the text of volumes I and II of 'Manual of Accounting'. In cases of doubt, reference should be made to the SI.

The accounting provisions of the Act

1.13   Throughout the 'Manual of Accounting' reference is made to 'the Act'. Such references, unless otherwise stated, are to the Companies Act 1985. As explained above, all of the accounting provisions included in the Companies Act 1989 are amendments to the Companies Act 1985. The Companies Act 1985 is split into 27 parts. A summary of these together with the arrangement of sections found in the Act is given on pages 401 to 424. Pages 425 to 536 include a reproduction of the accounting provisions of the Act relating to groups that are considered in this volume of 'Manual of Accounting'. The reproduction is a consolidated version of the Companies Act 1985 as amended by the Companies Act 1989. Volume I of 'Manual of Accounting' includes a reproduction of the accounting provisions of the Act that relate to companies generally, again amended to include the changes made by the Companies Act 1989.

1.14   This volume deals in particular with the following parts of the Companies Act 1985:

■   Part V - Share capital, its increase, maintenance and reduction. In particular the provisions of Chapter III that deals with share premiums. (The other provisions of this part are considered in 'Manual of Accounting - volume I'.)

■   Part VII - Accounts and audit. This includes provisions that apply to the financial statements of groups generally. (Provisions that apply to companies generally are considered in 'Manual of Accounting - volume I' and those that apply to the financial statements of banking and insurance companies are dealt with in 'Manual of Accounting - volume III'.)

■   Schedule 4A - Form and content of group accounts.

■   Schedule 5 - Disclosure of information: related undertakings (as concerns groups).

■   Schedule 24 - Punishment of offences under the Act. (Those sections that relate to the accounting provisions of the Act are reproduced in 'Manual of Accounting - volume I' appendix 4.)

1.15   The Schedules to the Act are introduced (where necessary) into the text when they apply to the provisions of the Act that are being considered.

Other generally accepted accounting principles and practices

1.16   In addition to explaining the accounting provisions of the Companies Acts, the 'Manual of Accounting' summarises also, where appropriate, the other provisions of Generally Accepted Accounting Principles (GAAP) in the UK that are contained in Accounting Standards, exposure drafts, The International Stock Exchange's Continuing Obligations (which apply to listed companies) and The International Stock Exchange's General Undertaking (which applies to companies traded on the Unlisted Securities Market (USM)).

1.17   Accounting Standards are continually being amended and new ones being introduced. In particular, a number of Accounting Standards that relate to consolidations (which include SSAP 1, SSAP 14, SSAP 22 and SSAP 23) are being revised and those revisions will take account of the new provisions introduced into UK law by the Companies Act 1989. Where possible, we have commented in the text on the effects of proposals included in exposure drafts where such documents have been issued at the time of writing, or on statements of intent where exposure drafts on the particular subject have not yet been issued. A full list of the accounting standards and exposure drafts considered in 'Manual of Accounting' is given in appendix 4 of this volume.

1.18   Furthermore, 'Manual of Accounting' also mentions other generally accepted accounting practices that are not covered in specific provisions of the legislation or other accounting regulations, but that are still considered as part of UK GAAP. Consequently, this book serves as a practical guide to applying the accounting provisions of all the major regulations that companies have to consider when they prepare their annual financial statements. Appendix 1 includes a detailed checklist to the measurement and disclosure requirements that make up UK GAAP and that apply specifically to consolidation requirements. A similar checklist that applies to a company's financial statements generally can be found in appendix 1 to volume I. Volume I also includes a model set of consolidated financial statements for GAAP UK plc (see 'Manual of Accounting - volume I' appendix 2).

1.19   'Manual of Accounting' also includes practical comment based on advice given by the Technical Support Group of Coopers & Lybrand Deloitte to the Firm's partners, staff and clients. In order to illustrate matters relating to presentation and disclosure in company financial statements, it includes also extracts from the published financial statements of various companies.

Scope of this book

1.20   Unless otherwise stated, the provisions examined in this book apply to those companies that are defined in section 735 of the Act. The definition in section 735 embraces companies registered under either the Act or a former Companies Act, with an exception for certain Irish companies.

1.21   Companies may be either limited or unlimited. A 'limited' company is a company in which the members' liability is limited by shares or by guarantee. [Sec 1(2)(a)(b)]. An 'unlimited' company is a company that does not limit its members' liability. [Sec 1(2)(c)]. Many of the provisions of this book apply to companies limited by guarantee and to unlimited companies. However, these two types of company are considered further in 'Manual of Accounting - volume III'.

1.22   Limited companies may be either public or private. A 'public' company (plc) is a company limited by shares (or, if incorporated before 22nd December 1980, by guarantee and having a share capital) where its memorandum states that it is a public company. Such a company must also be registered as a public company, and, before it can do business or exercise any borrowing power, it must satisfy the statutory requirements as to its authorised minimum share capital. [Sec 1(3)(4), 117,118]. The current 'authorised minimum' share capital that such a company is required to allot before it can do business or exercise any borrowing power is £50,000, of which a quarter of the nominal values (plus the whole of any premium) has to be paid up. [Sec 118].

1.23   A private company is any company that is not a public company. [Sec 1(3)]. The text of this book draws attention to those requirements of the Act that differ for public companies and private companies respectively.

Chapter 2

THE GROUP AND GROUP ACCOUNTS

THE GROUP AND GROUP ACCOUNTS

Introduction

2.1 Companies have performed consolidations since the early 1900s in the US and they were in evidence in the UK by the 1920s. Since then the methods of consolidation have evolved and will continue to change as European harmonisation takes pace. The first step in the consolidation process remains to decide whether group accounts are required. Before the Companies Act 1989 was enacted, there were different ways of presenting group accounts. For example, the group accounts could be presented as consolidated financial statements, or as a collection of subsidiaries' individual financial statements bound with the holding company's financial statements, or as more than one set of consolidated financial statements each dealing with part of the group. These options have, however, been removed by the Companies Act 1989 which requires that group accounts should be presented in a single set of consolidated financial statements of the company and its subsidiaries.

2.2 Consequently, determining whether group accounts are necessary is an important step in the consolidation process and this chapter considers the rules that govern this area. However, before looking at the various exemptions from the requirement to prepare group accounts the three 'group' concepts are considered briefly.

Concepts of the group

2.3 The 'group' is defined in the Act to mean *"a parent undertaking and its subsidiary undertakings"*. [Sec 262(1)]. However, three concepts have evolved since the first consolidations were made that concern how the group is established and how the financial statements of the companies forming the group are consolidated. The three concepts are the:

■ Proprietary concept.

■ Entity concept.

■ Parent company concept.

2.4 Each of these concepts is explained in the paragraphs that follow.

11

Proprietary concept

2.5   The proprietary concept considers the group as if the parent's members are only concerned with the proportion of the assets and liabilities of the group that they own. Consequently, it takes a very narrow view of the group. The members are, therefore, not concerned with the control they might have over the proportion of assets (and liabilities) that are owned, in effect, by minorities.

2.6   Under this concept the consolidated balance sheet deals only with the proportion of assets and liabilities that the parent owns in a subsidiary. Similarly, the profit and loss account would deal with only an equivalent proportion of revenues and expenses of such a subsidiary. Consequently, no minority interests would be shown in the consolidated financial statements.

2.7   This concept of accounting is not generally used in the UK, although it may be seen as a foundation for the equity method and for proportional consolidation, which is used also in France. Partnerships in the UK are sometimes consolidated on a proportional basis, which similarly takes account only of the parent's share of the assets and liabilities and profits and losses. Proportional consolidation is considered further in chapter 11.

Entity concept

2.8   The entity concept considers the group as a single entity. Consequently, any companies that are controlled by the parent would be consolidated. Therefore, unlike the proprietary concept, this concept requires 100 per cent consolidation of all subsidiaries even if the parent has less than 100 per cent of the shares in the subsidiary. Furthermore, intra-group profits would be eliminated 100 per cent.

2.9   Minority interests are sometimes recognised under this concept, but they are treated as part of the shareholders' funds, thereby emphasising the control that the parent and its shareholders have over a subsidiary. The entity concept is not used in the UK, and minority interests are not treated as part of shareholders' funds. However, this concept has been used in Germany.

Parent company concept

2.10   The parent company concept takes an intermediate view between the two concepts mentioned above. The concept still retains 100 per cent consolidation of all controlled subsidiaries as its base, but recognises that the interest of the parent company's members is limited to the parent's shareholding in subsidiaries. Consequently, minority interests are not recognised as shareholders' funds, but are shown separately either before or after shareholders' funds.

2.11   This concept developed in the UK and stems from the early days of consolidation when the consolidated balance sheet was seen as a supplement to the parent company's balance sheet. The US also uses a similar concept, but in contrast the consolidated balance sheet is seen in the US as a substitute for the parent's balance sheet.

2.12   The basis of consolidation to be used under the Act is made quite clear in section 262(1)(b). The section defines the term 'included in consolidation' to mean the *"undertaking is included in the accounts by the method of full (and not proportional) consolidation"*.

Form of group accounts

2.13   As mentioned above, before the enactment of the Companies Act 1989, a holding company could choose between several options in presenting its group accounts. However in practice, group accounts were normally presented as consolidations. Where a holding company did not prepare group accounts in the form of consolidated financial statements, it still had to give either the same or equivalent information as it would have disclosed if it had prepared consolidated financial statements.

2.14   In addition, SSAP 14 required the directors to state the reasons why they considered the group accounts gave a fairer view of the group's financial position than those statements would have done had they been prepared as consolidated financial statements. [SSAP 14 para 22].

2.15   Section 5 of the Companies Act 1989 substitutes a new section 227 of the Companies Act 1985 to ensure that the parent company directors prepare all group accounts in the form of *consolidated* financial statements. [Sec 227(2)]. These consolidated financial statements should be prepared in addition to the parent company's individual financial statements. [Sec 227(1)]. Consequently, there is now only one form of group accounts. The consolidated financial statements are required to include the following:

■   A consolidated balance sheet that deals with the state of affairs of the parent company and its subsidiary undertakings.

■   A consolidated profit and loss account that deals with the profit and loss of the parent company and its subsidiary undertakings.

[Sec 227(2)].

2.16   These provisions of the Act reflect closely the requirements in SSAP 14 that require a holding company to:

> *"...prepare group accounts in the form of a single set of consolidated financial statements covering the holding company and its subsidiary companies, at home and overseas".*
> [SSAP 14 para 15].

2.17   SSAP 14 also requires that where consolidated financial statements are presented, a description should be given of the bases on which those statements deal with subsidiary companies. [SSAP 14 para 15]. This disclosure would normally form part of the group's accounting policies (see chapter 4).

2.18   Schedule 4A has been added to the Companies Act 1985 which deals with the form and content of consolidated financial statements. [Sec 227(4)]. A company's consolidated financial statements must comply with this schedule in order to give a true and fair view. The schedule provides detailed rules on the form and content of the following:

■   The consolidated balance sheet.

■   The consolidated profit and loss account.

■   Additional information to be given in the notes to the financial statements.

[Sec 227(4)].

True and fair view

2.19   There is an overriding requirement in the Act that a company's consolidated financial statements must give a true and fair view of the state of affairs, as at the end of the financial year, of the undertakings included in the consolidation. [Sec 227(3)].

2.20   Where, however, compliance with the disclosure provisions of the Act (including Schedule 4A to the Companies Act 1985) would not be sufficient to give a true and fair view, then additional information should be given in the notes to the financial statements. [Sec 227(5)]. This additional information needs to be of sufficient detail to ensure that its disclosure enables the financial statements to give a true and fair view.

2.21   There is a further provision concerning the true and fair view, which provides that if in 'special circumstances' compliance with the Act's provisions would be inconsistent with the requirement to give a true and fair view, the directors of the company must depart from the Act's provisions. Where such a departure is necessary, the particulars of the departure, the reasons for it and its effect must be given in a note to the financial statements. [Sec 227(6)].

2.22 These requirements differ from those that operated before the enactment of the Companies Act 1989, because the *special circumstance* provision was previously limited to situations where a company could not give a true and fair view even where it gave additional information. Now it is possible to use the *special circumstance* provision as an alternative in some situations where additional information could be given and would be sufficient to give a true and fair view.

2.23 What is meant by *special circumstances* is not clear, because it is not defined in the Act. Certain businesses because of their special nature (for example, investment trusts or charities) have to depart from the detailed profit and loss account and balance sheet formats set out in the Act. However, this type of departure is specifically provided for by paragraph 3(3) of Schedule 4 to the Act.

2.24 The wording in section 227(6) has been changed from that was used in the original 1985 Act to exclude the words that followed *"special circumstances"*, which were *"in the case of any company"*. Consequently, the term 'special circumstances' can now also be used for particular categories or sectors of industry (for example, the construction industry) in addition to being used for circumstances such as off balance sheet finance, or debt factoring. Table 1 illustrates a situation where this provision has been used to justify consolidating undertakings that are not subsidiaries. See overleaf.

2.25 The meaning of true and fair view and its interaction with SSAPs is considered further in 'Manual of Accounting - volume I' chapter 3.

Parent and subsidiary undertakings

2.26 The Companies Act 1989 introduced important changes to the definition of parent and subsidiary. Although these changes are fundamental in nature, they will not generally affect the composition of most groups.

2.27 The Act refers throughout to 'parent undertaking' and 'subsidiary undertaking'. These terms stem directly from the 7th Directive. The term 'undertaking' is defined in the Act as follows:

> *"... a body corporate or partnership, or an unincorporated association carrying on a trade or business, with or without a view to profit."* [Sec 259(1)].

2.28 Consequently, a *parent undertaking* could be a partnership or an unincorporated business. However, consolidated financial statements have only to be prepared where, at the end of a financial year, an undertaking is a *parent company*. [Sec 227(1)]. Therefore, parent

Table 1: Example of the true and fair override being used in 'special circumstances' to consolidate companies that are not subsidiaries.

Extract from Burnett & Hallamshire Holdings Plc Report & Accounts 31st March 1985.

Balance Sheets

31st March, 1985

	Adjusted Group* 1985 £'000 (Notes 1 and 31)	Note	Group 1985 £'000	Group 1984 £'000	Company 1985 £'000	Company 1984 £'000
Fixed assets						
Intangible assets	718	14	718	2,340	–	–
Tangible assets	113,051	15	73,623	100,163	111	90
Investments	13,591	16	28,682	31,023	91,484	163,014
	127,360		103,023	133,526	91,595	163,104
Current assets						
Assets held for sale (net of borrowings)	3,997	17	3,997	–	896	–
Stocks and work-in-progress	32,754	18	27,497	41,211	–	–
Debtors	32,546	19	23,576	60,953	3,065	5,232
Cash at bank and in hand	2,267	20	2,265	15,877	58	291
	71,564		57,335	118,041	4,019	5,523
Creditors: amounts falling due within one year:						
Borrowings	(67,693)	21	(61,596)	(35,255)	(55,878)	(33,124)
Other creditors	(32,852)	22	(26,320)	(45,006)	(1,634)	(4,464)
Net current (liabilities) assets	(28,981)		(30,581)	37,780	(53,493)	(32,065)
Total assets less current liabilities	98,379		72,442	171,306	38,102	131,039
Creditors: amounts falling due after one year:						
Loans	(38,108)	21	(38,108)	(31,084)	(20,093)	(11,516)
Other creditors	(35,266)	22	(5,108)	(5,802)	–	–
Provisions for liabilities and charges	(25,832)	23	(30,053)	(23,526)	(20,203)	(9)
Accruals and deferred income	(3,411)		(3,411)	(2,542)	(2,044)	(1,204)
Net (liabilities) assets	(4,238)		(4,238)	108,352	(4,238)	118,310
Represented by:						
Capital and reserves						
Called-up share capital	9,675	25	9,675	9,673	9,675	9,673
Reserves	(13,913)	26	(13,913)	98,679	(13,913)	108,637
	(4,238)		(4,238)	108,352	(4,238)	118,310

Table 1 continued

*The adjusted figures are presented in compliance with Section 230 (4) of the Companies Act 1985 (Note 16) because the Balance Sheet of the Group, which complies with Schedule 4 to the Act, does not reflect on its face the substantial liabilities and assets relating to PBS Coals Inc., and Mincorp Shipping & Finance Limited. These companies were related companies at 31st March, 1984 and 31st March, 1985 and they are shown as such in the Group's 1984 and 1985 Balance Sheets above. The Group was responsible under guarantees and otherwise for the substantial liabilities and obligations of these companies (Note 1) which have not been consolidated, and had in consequence to meet their funding requirements and losses.

In the opinion of the Directors, the Balance Sheet of the Group prepared in accordance with Schedule 4 does not provide sufficient information to give a true and fair view. Accordingly an Adjusted Group Balance Sheet has been drawn up to show the substance of the Group's liabilities and obligations and its present 100% Interest in PBS Coals Inc., and Mincorp Shipping & Finance Limited (the balance of which interest has been acquired since the year end) as if those interests had subsisted at 31st March, 1985.

The Group Balance Sheet as at 31st March, 1985 must be read in conjunction with the Adjusted Group Balance Sheet set out above and the notes set out on pages 17 to 39.

The financial statements were approved by the Board of Directors on 20th December, 1985.

T. CARLILE ⎫
A. DODD ⎬ Directors
⎭

undertakings that are not companies are not required by the Act to prepare consolidated financial statements.

2.29 However, *subsidiary undertakings* (including both partnerships and unincorporated associations) will have to be consolidated into the group's consolidated financial statements. This represents a significant change, because before the Companies Act 1989 partnerships, for example, were either treated as associates in accordance with the provisions of SSAP 1, 'Accounting for associated companies' (see chapter 11), or were consolidated on a proportional basis. Proportional consolidation means a line by line consolidation of the company's share of income, expenditure, assets and liabilities of the partnership (see chapter 11). Such entities will normally have to be fully consolidated and any minority interest (see chapter 10) will have to be shown separately in the consolidated balance sheet.

2.30 Another significant change introduced by the Companies Act 1989 is to the definitions of subsidiary undertaking. These changes implement the provisions of the 7th Directive. Previously, the definitions of a subsidiary were based principally on ownership, whereas the new definitions are based more on control. Although the changes in the definitions of a subsidiary undertaking are fundamental, they are unlikely to affect most group structures significantly. However, certain off balance sheet companies will in future require consolidation.

2.31 The Act requires that all subsidiary undertakings should be included in the consolidated financial statements. [Sec 229(1)]. However, there are a number of situations where subsidiary undertakings may be excluded from consolidated financial statements and may be accounted for in some other way. These situations are covered in the provisions of both the Act and SSAP 14.

2.32 The provisions of both the Act and SSAP 14 that relate to the definitions of subsidiary undertakings and the exemptions from the requirement to consolidate certain subsidiary undertakings are considered in detail in chapter 3.

Exemptions from preparing consolidated financial statements

2.33 An intermediate holding company is not required to prepare consolidated financial statements, where it is wholly owned by its immediate parent undertaking that is established under the law of any EC member state. [Sec 228 (1)(a)]. Previously a parent had to be incorporated in Great Britain for this exemption to apply. However, there are a number of conditions that must apply before the exemption can be taken and these are summarised below in paragraph 2.37

2.34 Furthermore, this exemption extends to the situation where the parent (established under the law of any EC member state) holds more than 50 per cent of the shares by number in the company and no notice has been served on the company to prepare consolidated financial statements. Such notice has to be made by either of the following:

■ Shareholders holding in aggregate more than half of the remaining shares in the company.

■ Shareholders holding in aggregate five per cent of the total shares in the company.

[Sec 228(1)(b)].

2.35 The notice has to be served within six months of the end of the previous financial period (that is, normally within the first six months of the financial year for which the consolidated financial statements are being prepared). [Sec 228(1)]. Consequently, in future, the onus will be clearly on the minority shareholders to serve such notice if they require consolidated financial statements to be prepared for a sub-group.

2.36 For the purposes of determining whether the company is wholly-owned or whether the parent holds more than 50 per cent of the shares of the company, the rules below apply:

■ Shares held by directors to comply with their share qualification requirements should be disregarded when determining whether a company is wholly-owned. [Sec 228(4)].

■ In determining whether the parent holds more than 50 per cent of the shares of the company, shares held by a wholly-owned subsidiary should be attributed to the parent undertaking. Also shares held on behalf of the parent or by or on behalf of a wholly-owned subsidiary should be attributed to the parent undertaking. [Sec 228(5)].

2.37 Both the exemptions outlined above in paragraphs 2.33 and 2.34 only apply, however, where the following conditions have been complied with:

■ The company is included by full consolidation in the consolidated financial statements of a larger group drawn up to the same date (or an earlier date in the same financial year) by a parent established (that is, incorporated) in an EC member State. [Sec 228(2)(a)].

■ The financial statements of the company and the consolidated financial statements of the parent must be audited and drawn up in accordance with the provisions of the 7th Directive. [Sec 228 (2)(b)].

■ The exemption must be noted in the company's individual financial statements that it is not required to prepare and deliver to the Registrar of Companies consolidated financial statements. [Sec 228(2)(c)].

■ The name of the parent that prepares the consolidated financial statements must be noted in the company's individual financial statements stating one of the following:

  □ The country of incorporation of the parent, if it is incorporated outside Great Britain.

  □ Whether the parent is registered in England and Wales or in Scotland, if it is incorporated in Great Britain.

  □ The address of the parent's principal place of business, where it is unincorporated.

  [Sec 228(2)(d)].

■ The company must deliver to the Registrar of Companies within the period allowed for delivering its individual financial statements a copy of the group's consolidated financial statements and a copy of the parent undertaking's annual report together with the audit report thereon. [Sec 228(2)(e)].

■ Where any of the documents delivered to the Registrar of Companies in accordance with the previous requirement is not in English, a copy of a translation must be annexed to those documents. The translation has to be certified in the prescribed manner to be a correct translation. [Sec 228(2)(f)].

■ The company cannot have any securities listed on any stock exchange in an EC member state. [Sec 228(3)]. For this purpose, 'securities' include shares and stocks, debentures (including debenture stock, loan stock, bonds, certificates of deposit and other similar instruments), warrants and similar instruments, and certain certificates and other instruments that confer rights in respect of third parties. [Sec 228(6)]. It would appear that companies that only have securities traded on the USM may avail themselves of the exemption.

Small and medium-sized groups

2.38 A parent company need not prepare consolidated financial statements if the group headed by it qualifies as a small group or a medium-sized group, provided it is not an ineligible group. [Sec 248(1)]. An ineligible group includes the following:

■ A public company or a body corporate that is able lawfully to issue shares or debentures to the public.

■ An authorised institution under the Banking Act 1987.

■ An insurance company to which Part II of the Insurance Companies Act 1982 applies.

■ An authorised person under the Financial Services Act 1986.

[Sec 248(2)].

Qualifying conditions

2.39 The qualifying conditions that apply in determining whether a group is a small group or a medium-sized group are different to those that apply to companies wishing to file abbreviated (previously modified) financial statements. To qualify as a small group or a medium-sized group, the group must satisfy two or more of the requirements that follow:

Small group

Aggregate turnover:	Not more than £2 million net (or £2.4 million gross)
Aggregate balance sheet total:	Not more than £1 million net (or £1.2 million gross)
Aggregate number of employees:	Not more than 50

Medium-sized group

Aggregate turnover:	Not more than £8 million net (or £9.6 million gross)
Aggregate balance sheet total:	Not more than £3.9 million (or £4.7 million gross)
Aggregate number of employees: [Sec 249(3)].	Not more than 250

2.40   The figures are ascertained by adding together the relevant figures from each subsidiary. The net figures refer to the relevant amounts after making consolidation adjustments for set-offs and other matters. As an alternative, the gross figures can be applied to the relevant amounts before making such adjustments. [Sec 249 (4)]. In any year, it is possible to mix the use of gross and net figures.

2.41   To determine the balance sheet total for the conditions above, the total for each company included in the group or sub-group has to be aggregated. In this respect, 'balance sheet total' refers in balance sheet Format 1 (included in Schedule 4 to the Act) to the amounts shown in the balance sheet under the headings A to D in the formats. [Sec 247(5)(a)]. That is the total of the following:

■   Called up share capital not paid.

■   Fixed assets.

■   Current assets.

■   Prepayments and accrued income.

2.42   For companies that prepare their balance sheet in accordance with Format 2 of Schedule 4 to the Act, the relevant balance sheet total is the aggregate of amounts shown under the general heading 'Assets'. [Sec 247(5)(b)].

2.43   With regard to the numbers of employees of the company, the figure means the average number employed in the year (determined on a weekly basis). This figure should be calculated in the same way as the figure for the average number of employees required to be disclosed in individual company financial statements prepared under Schedule 4 to the Act. [Sec 247(6)]. Consequently, for most UK companies the figure can be ascertained directly from the disclosure made in the companies' financial statements.

2.44 The subsidiary's financial statements used to ascertain the figures necessary in applying the qualifying conditions are those that are prepared to the same date as the parent's financial statements. [Sec 249(5)(a)]. If the subsidiary does not prepare its financial statements to this date, then its last financial statements ending before those of the parent should be used. [Sec 249(5)(b)]. However, in either situation where the required figures cannot be ascertained without disproportionate expense or undue delay, the latest available figures for the subsidiary can be used instead. [Sec 249(6)].

2.45 Normally, a parent of a small or medium-sized group will not be required to prepare consolidated financial statements if the relevant size criteria are met in the current financial year and in the previous financial year. [Sec 249(1)(b)]. However, where it is the parent's first financial year, it is not required to prepare consolidated financial statements if the group satisfies the criteria in that year. [Sec 249(1)(a)].

2.46 Furthermore, if the group satisfied the criteria in the previous financial year but it does not do so in the current year, the parent is still exempt from preparing consolidated financial statements. [Sec 249(2)(a)]. Where the group then satisfies the criteria again in the next financial year, the parent is exempt once more from preparing consolidated financial statements. [Sec 249(2)(b)].

Illustration of the provisions

2.47 The application of the provisions in the last two paragraphs is complicated and is best illustrated by an example. Consider the following details relating to two groups of companies (A and B). Group A has existed for many years, and in the year immediately before year 1 it qualified as a medium-sized group. Group B's parent is incorporated on the first day of year 2. The figures given below are the aggregated figures for the group (excluding consolidation adjustments) taken from the financial statements of the parent's individual subsidiaries.

Group A	Year 1	Year 2	Year 3	Year 4
Turnover	£10.2m	£11.6m	£10.8m	£9.8m
Balance sheet total	£4.5m	£5.1m	£6.5m	£4.6m
Average number of employees	240	245	250	250

	Year 1	Year 2	Year 3	Year 4
Group B				
Turnover	-	£2.2m	£5.6m	£3.3m
Balance sheet total	-	£1.1m	£4.8m	£4.6m
Average number of employees	-	106	260	260

Group A

In year 1, group A satisfies two out of the three criteria (that is, balance sheet total and average employees) that enable it to be treated as a medium-sized group. Therefore, because it also satisfied the criteria in the previous year, group A is not required to prepare consolidated financial statements for year 1.

In year 2, group A does not satisfy the criteria of a medium-sized group because both its turnover and balance sheet total exceed the criteria. However, the group is still exempted from preparing consolidated financial statements for year 2, because it satisfied the criteria in year 1.

In year 3, group A ceases to qualify as a medium-sized group, because it does not satisfy the criteria for the second year running. Consequently, consolidated financial statements have to be prepared for the group.

In year 4, group A once more satisfies the criteria as a medium-sized group, because both its balance sheet total and its average number of employees are not more than the limits set. However, the group will have to prepare consolidated financial statements for the year, because it did not satisfy the criteria in year 3.

Group B

In year 2, group B is a small group because it satisfies the turnover and balance sheet total criteria. Therefore, group B is not required to prepare consolidated financial statements for year 2 as this is the parent company's first financial year.

In year 3, group B exceeds two of the three criteria of a medium-sized group (that is, balance sheet total and average number of employees). However, because group B satisfied the criteria of a small group in year 2, it is not required to prepare consolidated financial statements for year 3.

In year 4, group B satisfies the criteria of a medium-sized company because both its turnover and its balance sheet total are within the limits. group B is not required to prepare consolidated financial statements because although it did not satisfy the criteria in year 3, it failed to satisfy the criteria for only one year.

Abbreviated financial statements of the parent company

2.48   In certain circumstances the group's parent company may also be able to *file* abbreviated (previously modified) individual financial statements as a small company or a medium-sized company. In this circumstance, abbreviated individual financial statements for a small company can only be *filed* by the parent if the group headed by it qualifies under the rules set out above as a small group. Similarly, such a parent can only *file* abbreviated individual financial statements for a medium-sized company if the group headed by it qualifies under the above rules as a medium-sized group. [Sec 246(5)]. Qualify in this respect means that the group is not required to *prepare* consolidated financial statements in a particular year because of the reasons specified in paragraphs 2.38 to 2.45 above. In contrast, however, to the provisions that exempt a small or medium-sized group from *preparing* consolidated financial statements, the entitlement to *file* small or medium-sized individual financial statements does not relieve the company from the obligation to sent full individual financial statements to its members.

2.49   The following example illustrates how this provision applies to the parents of both group A and group B (company A and company B respectively) using the same information as that given in the example above.

Company A

In year 1, group A qualifies as a medium-sized group and, therefore, company A may be eligible to file abbreviated financial statements as a medium-sized company.

In year 2, although group A does not satisfy the criteria as a medium-sized group, it does qualify as one because it did so in the previous year and, consequently, company A may be eligible to file abbreviated financial statements as a medium-sized company.

In year 3 group A does not qualify as a medium-sized group and, therefore, company A cannot file abbreviated financial statements as a medium-sized company.

In year 4, group A does not qualify as a medium-sized group even though it does fall within the size criteria, because it did not satisfy the criteria in year 3. Consequently, company A is not eligible to file abbreviated financial statements as a medium-sized company.

Company B

In year 2, group B qualifies as a small group and, therefore, company B may be eligible to file abbreviated financial statements as a small company.

In year 3, although group B exceeds the criteria of both a small group and a medium-sized group, it still qualifies as a small group, because it qualified as such in the previous period. Therefore, company B may be eligible to file abbreviated financial statements as a small company.

In year 4, group B is allowed to be treated as a medium sized group, because it only did not satisfy the criteria for one year. Consequently, company B may be eligible to file abbreviated financial statements as a medium-sized company.

2.50   Whether company A or company B can in fact file abbreviated financial statements for a small company or a medium-sized company will also depend on whether they satisfy the criteria to be treated as such. The criteria used to determine whether a company is a small company or a medium-sized company are very similar to those used for groups (explained above). However, although the figures for average number of employees remain the same, the figures for turnover and balance sheet total in each category are smaller than the gross figures given above. The rules concerning the qualification of a company as a small company or as a medium-sized company are considered in detail in 'Manual of Accounting - volume I' chapter 23.

Auditors' responsibilities

2.51 If the directors wish to take advantage of the provisions outlined above and not prepare consolidated financial statements, the parent company's auditors have to report to the directors whether the company is entitled to the exemption. [Sec 248(3)]. The exemption will only apply where such a statement is obtained and a copy of it is attached to the company's individual financial statements. [Sec 248(4)]. The example auditor's statement that follows deals with a report to the company's directors where the company is not required to prepare consolidated financial statements.

Auditors' report to the directors of Blank Limited under section 248(3) of the Companies Act 1985

We have examined the financial statements of the company and each of its subsidiaries for the year ended 31st December 1990. The scope of our work for the purposes of this report was limited to confirming that the company is entitled to the exemptions conferred by section 248 from preparing group accounts.

In our opinion, the company is entitled to the exemption from preparing group accounts conferred by section 248 of the Companies Act 1985.

2.52 The statement should be attached to the parent's full financial statements. In many situations, groups that are not required to prepare consolidated financial statements may also be eligible to file abbreviated financial statements. Auditor's responsibilities with regard to filing abbreviated financial statements for a small company and for a medium-sized company are considered further in 'Manual of Accounting - volume I' chapter 23.

Additional information concerning subsidiaries

2.53 Where consolidated financial statements are not prepared for any of the reasons given in this chapter, additional information has to be given in the parent's individual financial statements concerning subsidiary undertakings. This information is detailed in Schedule 5 to the Act and is considered in detail in 'Manual of Accounting - volume I'.

2.54 However, Schedule 8 to the Act provides that if a small company is not required to produce consolidated financial statements as outlined in paragraphs 2.38 to 2.46 above, but files individual abbreviated financial statements, it will not need to provide some of the additional information about subsidiary undertakings usually required. The exemptions include the following information:

■ The reasons why a subsidiary's year end did not coincide with that of the parent company, and the date on which its financial year ended.

■ Details of any qualifications contained in the auditors' reports of subsidiaries and the aggregate investment in the subsidiary stated by way of the equity method.

■ The number, description and amount of the shares and debentures of the company held by or on behalf of a subsidiary.

■ Details of arrangements receiving merger relief during the current financial year and details of any profit or loss generated from the sale of shares or assets acquired under arrangements receiving merger relief in the current year or in the preceding two years.

[8 Sch 3(2)].

Chapter 3

DETERMINING THE GROUP STRUCTURE

DETERMINING THE GROUP STRUCTURE

Introduction

3.1   Before the parent of a group of companies can start to prepare consolidated financial statements, an important process is to decide exactly which undertakings form the group and should, therefore, be included in the consolidation. In addition, it is important to determine whether any particular subsidiaries should be excluded from the group under the exemptions allowed by the legislation.

3.2   Consequently, determining which undertakings are the parent's subsidiaries and should, therefore, be consolidated is fundamental to the preparation of consolidated financial statements and this chapter considers the rules that govern whether an undertaking is a subsidiary for this purpose. The chapter also considers the rules that apply in determining whether a subsidiary can be excluded from consolidation and details the resulting accounting treatment and disclosure.

Implications of the 7th Directive

3.3   The Companies Act 1989 implements most of the provisions of the EC's 7th Directive with regard to the definitions of subsidiary undertakings. The definitions included in the 7th Directive are based on control, whereas the definitions that applied under the old rules in the Companies Act 1985 were based more on the legal ownership of a company. Although the changes in some of the definitions are fundamental, they do not affect significantly the companies that are consolidated by groups. This is because, for example, the majority of 100 per cent *owned* subsidiaries that were consolidated under the old legislation, are also *controlled* 100 per cent and, consequently, are also consolidated under the provisions in the Companies Act 1989.

3.4   Therefore, in practice in the majority of situations, if a company was a parent's subsidiary before the Companies Act 1989, it will also be a subsidiary under the definitions in the new legislation. However, some undertakings that were previously excluded from consolidation, may now require to be consolidated. Furthermore, some undertakings that were subsidiaries before the new legislation, are not subsidiaries under the new legislation.

3.5   These important changes to the definitions of subsidiaries are explained in the paragraphs that follow.

Meaning of subsidiary undertaking

3.6 As mentioned in chapter 2 only parent undertakings that are companies are required to prepare consolidated financial statements. [Sec 227 (1)]. However, a subsidiary undertaking can mean any of the following undertakings:

■ A body corporate.

■ A partnership.

■ An unincorporated association carrying on a trade or business for profit.

■ An unincorporated association not trading for profit.

[Sec 259(1)].

3.7 Consequently, any undertakings included in the above list may fall to be consolidated with the financial statements of the parent company if they are subsidiary undertakings.

3.8 There are five situations where an undertaking may be a subsidiary of a parent undertaking and these are briefly where the parent:

■ Holds a majority of voting rights.

■ Is a member of the undertaking and can appoint or remove directors having the majority of the votes on the board.

■ Has a right to exercise a dominant influence over the undertaking by virtue of provisions either in its memorandum or articles, or in a 'control contract'.

■ Is a member of the undertaking and operates control via an agreement with other shareholders.

■ Owns a participating interest in the undertaking and actually exercises a dominant influence or operates unified management.

The five situations are considered in detail in the paragraphs that follow.

Majority of voting rights

3.9 An undertaking is a subsidiary where the parent undertaking holds a majority of its voting rights. [Sec 258(2)(a)].

3.10 In this situation, 'voting rights' means the rights conferred on shareholders in respect of their shares to vote at the undertaking's general meetings on all, or substantially all, matters. [10A Sch 2(1)]. Similarly, where an undertaking does not have a share capital, voting rights also mean the rights conferred on members to vote at the undertaking's general meetings on all, or substantially all, matters. [10A Sch 2(1)]. If the undertaking does not have general meetings where matters are decided by exercising voting rights, 'voting rights' will mean having the right under the undertaking's constitution to direct its overall policy, or to alter the terms of its constitution. [10A Sch 2(2)].

3.11 In determining whether an undertaking holds a majority of the voting rights certain common rules apply and these are explained further in paragraphs 3.41 to 3.45.

3.12 In addition, the total voting rights in an undertaking have to be reduced where any rights are exercisable by the undertaking itself. [10A Sch 10]. This means, for example, that where an undertaking holds any of its own shares they should be excluded from the total voting rights taken into account in deciding whether the undertaking is a subsidiary.

3.13 The corresponding provision to determine whether an undertaking was a subsidiary in the old legislation relied on the parent company holding more than half, in nominal value, of the subsidiary's equity share capital. Consequently, the new provision has moved away from *legal ownership* to *effective control*.

3.14 The example that follows illustrates how the changes from the old legislation to the new legislation will affect whether companies are treated as subsidiaries. Company A owns 100 ordinary shares in company B and company C owns 100 five per cent preference shares in company B. Company B has no other share capital.

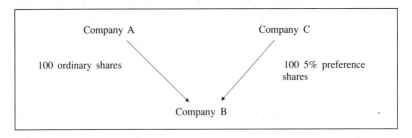

The rights attached to company B's shares are as follows:

☐   Ordinary shares:

   •   100 £1 ordinary shares.

- All dividends after payment of preference dividends.

- Right to all surplus assets on a winding up of the company after repayment of five per cent preference shares.

- Right to vote on all matters at any meetings of the company.

☐ Preference shares:

- 100 £1 preference shares.

- Fixed preference dividend.

- Right on winding up to the repayment of par value and up to 25 per cent of any sum standing to the credit of the share premium account.

- No rights to vote at company meetings.

The ordinary shares carry a right to participate beyond a specified amount in the winding up of the company and are, therefore, 'equity' share capital. In addition, the preference shares are similarly equity because they also carry a right to participate beyond a specified amount in a winding up. The classification of shares between equity share capital and non-equity share capital was crucial in determining whether a company was a subsidiary of another under the old rules. Consequently, in this example, because both types of share rank as equity, company A only owns 50 per cent of the equity share capital of company B. Company B would, therefore, not be a subsidiary of company A under those rules.

Under the new rules, however, the distinction between equity share capital and other share capital is irrelevant in determining whether an undertaking is a subsidiary of another. The new definition looks at who controls the 'voting rights' in the undertaking The preference shares have no voting rights, while the ordinary shares do. Consequently, under the new rules, company B is a subsidiary of company A, but is not a subsidiary of company C. This of course ignores who has the right to appoint the majority of the board of directors.

3.15   Two further examples of the effect of these provisions are given in Tables 2 and 3.

Table 2: Example of a company that was a subsidiary before the introduction of the Companies Act 1989, but that is no longer a subsidiary.

Extract from Trusthouse Forte PLC Report & Accounts 31st October 1988

Accounting policy extract

Basis of consolidation
(c) Subsidiary not consolidated: At 31st October, 1988 the Group owned 69% of the equity of The Savoy hotel PLC ("Savoy") representing 42.3% of the voting rights. The accounts of Savoy have not been consolidated as the Group does not have voting control. However, in view of the significance of the Group's share and the long term nature of its investment, the results have been accounted for on an equity basis.

> **Table 3: Illustration of an investment in a company that will probably not be a subsidiary under the Companies Act 1989, because of lack of control.**
>
> *Extract from John Lewis Partnership plc 28th January 1989.*
>
> **Note extract**
>
> Leckford Estate Limited is a company controlled by its preference shareholders. The whole of the issued ordinary share capital is owned by John Lewis plc. The company made a loss in the year to 30th September 1988 of £8,382 before tax and £25,370 after tax. No dividend was paid on the ordinary shares in 1988 (Nil). The capital and reserves of Leckford Estate Limited at 30th September 1988 were as follows:
>
> | | £ |
> |---|---|
> | Ordinary shares of £1 each | 25 |
> | 6% (now 4.2% plus tax credit) Preference shares | 75 |
> | Deferred Ordinary shares of £1 each | 500,000 |
> | Reserves | (13,922) |
> | | 486,178 |

Appointment or removal of majority of the board

3.16 An undertaking is a subsidiary where the parent is a member of that undertaking and has the right to appoint or remove a majority of its board of directors. [Sec 258(2)(b)].

3.17 In this circumstance, *"the right to appoint or remove the majority of the board of directors"* means the right to appoint or remove directors that have a majority of the voting rights at board meetings (without the need for any other person's consent or concurrence, except in the case where no other person has the right to appoint or, as the case may be, remove in relation to that directorship). In these circumstances, an undertaking should be treated as having the right to appoint a person to a directorship where:

- The person's appointment follows directly from his appointment as a director of the investing undertaking.

- The directorship is held by the investing undertaking itself.

[10A Sch 3].

3.18 Certain common rules apply to the expression 'rights' used above and these are explained further in paragraphs 3.41 to 3.45.

3.19 This provision to determine whether an undertaking is a subsidiary is not the same as the provision that operated before the introduction of the Companies Act 1989. This is because the old legislation merely required control of the *composition* of the board, whereas now the legislation refers to the right to appoint or remove the directors holding a majority of the *votingrights* at meetings of the board.

3.20 The rule is illustrated by the example that follows. In this example, the situation is the same as that described in paragraph 3.14 above and illustrated in the diagram. However, in this example the rights attaching to the two different types of share are as follows:

☐ Ordinary shares:

- All dividends after payment of preference dividends.

- Right to all surplus assets on a winding up of the company after repayment of 5 per cent preference shares.

- Right to vote on all matters at any meetings of the company.

- Power to appoint two directors of the company with one vote each.

☐ Preference shares:

- Fixed preference dividend.

- Right on winding up to the repayment of par value and up to 25 per cent of any sum standing to the credit of the share premium account.

- No rights to vote at company meetings.

- Power to appoint two directors of the company with two votes each.

The rights attached to the ordinary shares and the preference shares are identical to those given in the previous example. However, in this example the ordinary shares have the right to appoint only two directors with one vote each, whereas the preference shareholders can also appoint two directors but they have two votes each. Therefore, company A still holds the majority of the voting rights of company B, but company C now has the right to appoint the directors holding a majority of voting rights at meetings of company B's board.

Consequently, company B is a subsidiary of company A by virtue of section 258(2)(a) (as explained in para 3.14 above) and company B is also a subsidiary of company C by virtue of section 258(2)(b) as it has the right to appoint or remove directors holding a majority of the voting rights at company B's board meetings.

3.21 The situation described in the example is unusual as it is common accounting practice to treat an asset as belonging to only one entity at any particular time. For example, with assets held under a finance lease, although the lessor retains title to the asset, it only recognises a receivable in its books. The lessee, on the other hand, is the party that recognises the asset in its books of account. In the circumstance as described in the example, both company A and company C will have to consolidate company B.

Right to direct operating and financial policies

3.22   An undertaking will be a subsidiary where the parent has the right to exercise a dominant influence in either of the following two ways:

■   By provisions contained in the undertaking's memorandum or articles of association.

■   By a 'control contract' with the undertaking.

[Sec 258(2)(c)].

3.23   The right to exercise dominant influence over another undertaking shall not be regarded as exercisable unless:

"... it has a right to give directions with respect to the operating and financial policies of that other undertaking which its directors are obliged to comply with whether or not they are for the benefit of that other undertaking." [10A Sch 4(1)].

3.24   A 'control contract' is a contract in writing that confers such a right that is authorised by the memorandum or articles of the undertaking in relation to which the right is exercisable and is permitted by the law under which that undertaking is established. [10A Sch 4(2)].

3.25   This provision comes directly from the 7th Directive and, consequently, was not included in the previous legislation. Whether it will affect undertakings in the UK is uncertain, although it could clearly affect foreign subsidiaries of UK parents. Such types of contract do exist in Germany. This provision also emphasises once more the importance of *control* in the definitions of subsidiaries.

Control governed by an agreement

3.26   An undertaking will be a subsidiary where the parent is a member of it and controls alone, following an agreement with other shareholders or members of the undertaking, a majority of its voting rights. [Sec 258(2)(d)]. 'Voting rights' in this circumstance means the same as the term explained in paragraphs 3.10 to 3.12 above.

3.27   This provision also derives from the 7th Directive and was another change introduced into UK law by the Companies Act 1989. It similarly emphasises the importance of control as opposed to ownership in determining which undertakings are subsidiaries.

Dominant influence or unified management

3.28   A further important definition of subsidiary will have a very significant impact on some groups and may bring many off balance sheet companies back onto the balance sheet. A parent is now required to consolidate an undertaking if it, or a subsidiary, has a 'participating interest' in that other undertaking and either of the two situations that follow also apply:

■ The parent or subsidiary actually exercises a 'dominant influence' over the other undertaking.

■ The parent (or subsidiary) and the other undertaking are 'managed on a unified basis'.

[Sec 258(4)].

3.29 Once again, this provision comes straight from the 7th Directive, although its implementation by member States into their national laws was optional. The UK decided to include this provision in the Companies Act 1989 deliberately to reduce the number of off balance sheet finance schemes that use special purpose companies to avoid consolidation.

3.30 A 'participating interest' is defined in the Act in the following way:

"...a 'participating interest' means an interest held by an undertaking in the shares of another undertaking which it holds on a long-term basis for the purpose of securing a contribution to its activities [or the activities of any of its subsidiary undertakings or the group as a whole] *by the exercise of control or influence arising from or related to that interest."* [Sec 260(1)(5)].

3.31 In this respect, a holding of 20 per cent or more of the shares of an undertaking is presumed to be a participating interest, unless the contrary is shown. [Sec 260(2)]. References to 'interest' above include both an interest, which is convertible into an interest in shares and an option to acquire shares (or an option to acquire such an interest, for example a convertible share). Such an interest will exist whether the shares concerned are issued or unissued. [Sec 260(3)]. An interest held on behalf of the parent (or subsidiary) should be taken into account in determining whether the parent (or subsidiary) has a participating interest. [Sec 260(4)]. Similarly, any interest in the undertaking held by any of the parent's subsidiaries should be taken into account as if it were, in effect, being held by the parent. [Sec 260(5)].

3.32 There is no definition, however, within the Act, or the Directive, of the terms 'dominant influence' or 'managed on a unified basis'. Dominant influence clearly means more than the term 'significant influence', which is explained in SSAP 1 as requiring the investing company to have at least board representation and some participation in the operating and financial policy decisions of the undertaking. How much further the meaning of the term 'dominant influence' goes is difficult to determine and will have to be judged on the circumstances of each particular case. That judgment should probably take into account the following:

- The degree of board representation.

- The degree of influence over the operating and policy decisions of the undertaking.

- The degree of participation by the investing company in the risks attached to the undertaking's business.

- The rewards and benefits that the investing company will derive from its investment.

- Whether to exclude the undertaking from consolidation would affect the truth and fairness of the group's consolidated financial statements.

When the Companies Act 1989 was being debated in Parliament, Hansard reported that economic dependence alone was not intended necessarily to indicate 'dominant influence'.

3.33 Similarly, because there is no guidance given in the legislation, it is difficult to determine the meaning of 'managed on a unified basis'. For example, the term could cover some or a combination of the following situations:

- Adopting an overall management strategy for the group, which includes the undertaking in question.

- The group's board treating the undertaking as if it were a subsidiary and determining its strategy (which may be different to the rest of the group).

- Having the same management team for the investing company and the undertaking.

- Using the same accounting systems for the investing company and the undertaking.

- Having the same people work for the undertaking that also work for the investing company.

3.34 The ASC has given some guidance on the meaning of these terms in its proposed revisions of SSAP 14. The exposure draft entitled

'Consolidated accounts' which it is proposed will replace SSAP 1 and SSAP 14 suggests a possible definition for 'dominant influence' as follows:

> *"Dominant influence is effective control with or without the legal rights that normally signify control. The result of dominant influence is that major decisions will be taken in accordance with the wishes of the dominant party whether these are expressed or perceived. Actual exercise of dominant influence is not defined in the Act. Actual exercise implies that the dominant influence should have an effect in practice. It includes both active direction of the operating and financial policies of another enterprise, and the passive influence that can derive from the holding of a legal or effective power of veto."*

In this context a suggested definition of 'control' is given in the following terms:

> *"Control over the enterprise is the power to direct that enterprise. In the context of group accounts control means the power of an enterprise to direct the financial and operating policies of another enterprise so as to gain benefits from its activities."*

The exposure draft also considers what may be meant by 'managed on a unified basis' and proposes the following:

> *"Two or more enterprises are managed on a unified basis if the whole of the operations of the enterprise are completely integrated and they are managed as a single unit. Unified management·does not arise by virtue of an enterprise (an operator) managing another on behalf of one or more third parties."*

Until an accounting standard is issued on consolidated accounts these proposals can only form guidance on the meaning of these terms.

3.35 On the introduction of the new legislation, groups will have to reconsider whether they have undertakings where they do exercise dominant influence, or where they are managed on a unified basis (for example, see Tables 4 and 5 overleaf). If so, they will have to consolidate such undertakings and this could involve a significant amount of work. The effect of the provisions is illustrated in the example that follows.

Example

Company A has an investment in company B of 25 per cent. However, although company A has significant influence over company B it merely has one director on company B's board and, therefore, does not exercise dominant influence. Company A is owned 100 per cent by Mr X who also owns the remaining 75 per cent of company B. Both of the companies occupy the same premises and are in effect managed by Mr X.

Table 4: *Example of the effect of the Companies Act 1989 change in definitions of subsidiary companies.*

Extract from The Burton Group plc Annual Report and Accounts 2nd September 1989.

Financial overview extract

Accounting Issues
The accounting profession has seen significant debate in respect of changes to the existing legislative and regulatory framework. This includes, amongst other things, standardisation of certain aspects of company law within the European Economic Community.

The recently enacted Companies Act 1989 is likely to require consolidation of the Group's financial services activities, which are conducted by Burton group Financial Services (Holdings) Limited. Consideration is also being given to the implications of the Act for the Group's other related company, High Street Property Investments Limited. Details of both related companies are given in Note 25 to the accounts. Consolidation of financial services would increase reported gearing, but it is the Group's intention to continue to break down the activities of its business within the reported results to enable shareholders to understand properly the Group's financial position. The new Companies Act will have no effect on the commercial operations, profitability, cash flow or existing banking arrangements of the Group.

Notes extract

25 Related companies
The principal related companies are:

	Country of Operation	Country of Registration	Shares in Issue	Group's Shareholding
Burton Group Financial Services (Holdings) Limited	UK	England	150 £1 "A" Ordinary	100%
			150 £1 "B" Ordinary	—
			2,000 £1 Preference	100%
High Street Property Investments Limited	UK	England	52 £1 "A" Ordinary	—
			52 £1 "B" Ordinary	100%
			19,948 £1 Preference	100%

Burton Group Financial Services (Holdings) Limited (BGFSH)
BGFSH holds the whole of the issued share capital of BG Holdings Limited, Burton Group Personal Accounts Limited and The First Personal Bank plc (formerly Welbeck Finance plc), the principal companies who provide financial services for the Group.

High Street Property Investments Limited (HSPI)
In August 1986 the Group entered into sale and leaseback arrangements with HSPI, in respect of properties with a book and market value of £100.1 million. HSPI has granted ten year options to certain Group companies to repurchase the individual properties at market value and pre-emptive rights over the properties for a period of 20 years. The Group has no obligations to repurchase the properties or in respect of the repayment of loans made to HSPI by its lending banks. The Group is entitled to, and accounts for, the retained profits of HSPI under the equity method of accounting, including any profits which may arise on the sale of properties to third parties.

Unless the contrary can be shown company A's interest in company B will be presumed to be a participating interest and company B will, therefore, be a subsidiary of company A under the new legislation. This is because company A and company B appear to be managed on a unified basis. The effect on the balance sheets of company A and company B together with the consolidated balance sheet for the group prepared on the basis of the previous legislation (the old basis) and on the basis of the new legislation (the new basis), are shown below:

	Co. A	Co. B	Consolidation Old basis	New basis
	£'000	£'000	£'000	£'000
Investment in company B	25	-	50	-
Other net assets	150	200	150	350
Total net assets	175	200	200	350
Share capital	50	100	50	50
Reserves	125	100	150	150
Minority interest	-	-	-	150
	175	200	200	350

The consolidation prepared on the old basis shows the investment in company B as an associated company. Accordingly, in accordance with SSAP 1 (see chapter 11) the investment is consolidated using the equity method and, consequently, the example shows company A's share of company B's net assets (that is, £200,000 x 25% = £50,000). The consolidation prepared under the new legislation shows company B treated as a subsidiary of company A. Therefore, company B's assets are consolidated with those of company A and a substantial minority interest is disclosed (that is £200,000 x 75% = £150,000).

Table 5: Example of the effect of dominant influence over a company explained in the directors' report.

Extract from the BOC Group plc Report & Accounts 30th September 1989.

Group trading result extract

There are a number of accounting changes planned for 1990.

There will be a change to an average rate for translation of the profit and loss account. This will simplify the reporting process by reducing the number of differences between the information reported under US GAAP and that issued under UK GAAP. It should also reduce some of the volatility in quarterly and annual figures.

There is also a change to reflect the Companies Act 1989. Osaka Sanso, our Japanese associate will, in future, be classified as a subsidiary company. Although the Group does not own a majority of the shares, it exercises a dominant influence.

If these changes were reflected in this year's figures, Group pre-tax profits would increase from £330.5 million to £334.3 million; earnings would reduce marginally from £229.3 million to £226.1 million. Capital employed would increase to £2 133.9 million, up £110.0 million. Borrowings would increase by £15.1 million to £711.0 million. Gearing would decrease from 34.4% to 33.3%.

3.36   The example illustrates that in certain circumstances the effect of the requirement in the Act to consolidate such undertakings is significant. Furthermore, the shareholding in an undertaking of this nature can fall below 20 per cent and the provisions may still apply. That is because a 'participating interest' means any interest held by an undertaking on a long-term basis for the purpose of securing a contribution to its activities by the exercise of that control, but is presumed to exist where a holding exceeds 20 per cent. Generally, however, where a parent has an investment in an undertaking of this nature and exercises only *significant influence* over it (as explained above), it should be accounted for in accordance with the provisions of the Act and SSAP 1 using the equity method. Those provisions of the Act and of SSAP 1 are explained in chapter 11.

Common expressions and interpretations

3.37   In the definitions of subsidiaries explained above there are a number of common expressions and interpretations and these are considered in the paragraphs below.

Parent and subsidiary undertakings

3.38   In the definitions of subsidiaries a parent undertaking is treated as a member of another undertaking if any of the parent's subsidiaries are members of that other undertaking. [Sec 258(3)(a)]. Furthermore, this is also so if any shares in the other undertaking are held by a third party on behalf of the parent or its subsidiaries. [Sec 258(3)(b)]. (These provisions, however, do not extend to the situation where an undertaking is consolidated for the reason that its parent has a participating interest and exercises dominant influence over it, or manages it on a unified basis, although similar attribution provisions can be found in section 260(4)(5).)

3.39   For example, a parent's subsidiary may be a member of another undertaking. In this circumstance, even where the parent is not a member of the undertaking itself (for the purposes of determining whether the undertaking is a subsidiary of the parent), the parent is treated as a member of the undertaking by virtue of section 258(3).

3.40   In addition, where a group has intermediate holding undertakings (which can either be companies or unincorporated undertakings), their subsidiaries will also be regarded as subsidiaries of any parent undertakings further up the group structure. [Sec 258(5)]. Consequently, subsidiaries of all parent undertakings within a group are deemed by this provision to be subsidiaries of the ultimate holding company.

Provisions concerning rights

3.41   There are a number of common provisions that explain how to treat rights in different situations. These rules apply to voting rights (see paras 3.9 and 3.26 above), and rights to appoint or remove the majority of the board of directors (see para 3.16 above).

3.42   In determining whether rights should be attributed to a parent, rights held by a subsidiary undertaking should be treated as if they are held by the parent. [10A Sch 9(1)].

3.43   Rights exercisable in certain circumstances should only be taken into account when those circumstances have arisen and only for as long as they continue. [10A Sch 5(1)(a)]. Furthermore, such rights should also be taken into account where the circumstances are in the control of the person having the rights. [10A Sch 5(1)(b)]. In addition, rights that the undertaking can normally exercise, but that are temporarily incapable of being exercised, should continue to be taken into account. [10A Sch 5(2)].

3.44   Rights should not be treated as held by a person (which includes an undertaking) if they are held in a fiduciary capacity. [10A Sch 6]. Similarly, rights held by a person as nominee should not be treated as held by him. Such rights will be considered held 'as nominee' for another person if they can only be exercised on his instructions or with his consent. [10A Sch 7]. However, this provision cannot be used to require rights held by a parent to be treated as held by any of its subsidiaries. [10A Sch 9(2)].

3.45   Rights that are attached to shares held as security shall be treated as held by the person providing the security where those rights (excluding any right to exercise them to preserve the value of the security, or to realise it) are only exercisable in accordance with his instructions. This rule applies where the shares are held in connection with granting loans in the normal course of business and the rights are exercised only in the interest of the person providing the security. [10A Sch 8]. This provision, however, cannot be used to require rights held by a parent to be treated as held by any of its subsidiaries. [10A Sch 9(2)]. Furthermore, rights should be treated as being exercisable in accordance with the instructions, or the interests of, an undertaking if they are exercisable in accordance with the instructions of, or in the interests of, any group undertaking. [10A Sch 9(3)].

Provisions concerning capital

3.46   References to shares in an undertaking with a share capital are to allotted shares. [Sec 259(2)(a)]. In an undertaking that has capital, but no share capital, shares mean the rights to share in the capital of the undertaking. [Sec 259(2)(b)]. For example, in the case of a partnership, this would mean the relevant partners' share in the capital of the partnership. For an undertaking that has no capital, shares mean an interest conferring any right to share in the profits, or to contribute to the losses, of the undertaking. In this situation, it could also mean an interest giving rise to an obligation to contribute to the debts or expenses on winding up the undertaking. [Sec 259(2)(c)].

Expressions not used by unincorporated undertakings

3.47 Because subsidiaries can now include other unincorporated undertakings such as partnerships, various parts of the legislation use expressions that are common to companies only. Consequently, the Act provides the following provision:

> *"Other expressions appropriate to companies shall be construed, in relation to an undertaking which is not a company, as references to the corresponding persons, officers, documents or organs, as the case may be, appropriate to undertakings of that description."* [Sec 259(3)].

3.48 This provision will apply in a number of situations, but a good example of its effect concerns the expressions used by limited partnerships. A limited partnership is made up of a 'general partner' and a number of 'limited partners'. The general partner manages the business and the limited partners cannot be involved in the day to day business of the partnership. The partnership itself does not have a board of directors, but the equivalent to the board is the general partner himself. Consequently, if a company is a general partner in a limited partnership, then it will control the board of the limited partnership and the partnership will, therefore, be a subsidiary under section 258(2)(b).

3.49 This section is also important because various disclosure provisions concerning subsidiary undertakings detailed in Schedule 5 to the Act are expressed using terms that are only relevant to companies. These disclosure requirements are considered further in paragraphs 3.87 to 3.94.

Meaning of subsidiary used elsewhere in the legislation

3.50 The Companies Act 1989 substituted a new section 736 into the Companies Act 1985 concerning the meaning of 'subsidiary', 'holding company' and 'wholly-owned subsidiary'. This section includes some of the amendments to the definitions outlined above. However, the definitions given above relate to the undertakings to be consolidated in a group and also to various other accounting provisions (for example, disclosure of information concerning subsidiaries), whereas section 736 relates to other provisions of the Act that mention subsidiaries. The definition in section 736 does not include the following parts of the definition used for consolidation purposes that are outlined above:

■ Rights to direct operating and financial policies (see para 3.22).

■ Dominant influence or unified management (see para 3.28).

3.51 As a consequence of these changes, the notion of 'equity share capital', previously used as the main criteria in determining whether a company was a subsidiary of another, has disappeared when determining whether an undertaking is a subsidiary for the purposes of consolidation as well as for other purposes within the Act. However, the term will remain, because it is used elsewhere in the legislation.

3.52 Loan stock deeds often refer to the parent and its subsidiaries as defined by section 736 in determining borrowing restrictions. However, in this particular circumstance, section 736B(6) will allow the old definition to remain in operation for trust deeds executed before the Companies Act 1989 came into effect.

Subsidiaries excluded from consolidation

3.53 As mentioned in chapter 2, the general rule under the Act requires that all subsidiary undertakings should be included in the consolidated financial statements. [Sec 229(1)]. However, there are five exceptions to this rule and these exceptions differ slightly from those given previously in the legislation. The exemptions that allow groups to exclude subsidiaries from consolidation are now very similar to the provisions in SSAP 14 and are briefly as follows:

■ Inclusion not material.

■ Severe long-term restrictions.

■ Disproportionate expense or undue delay.

■ Subsequent resale.

■ Dissimilar activities.

3.54 A subsidiary undertaking *may* be excluded from consolidation for any of the first four reasons summarised above. With regard to the last reason, where it applies, the undertaking *must* be excluded from consolidation. However the equivalent provisions of SSAP 14 *require* subsidiaries to be excluded. Consequently, where a subsidiary comes under one of the reasons for exclusion covered by both the Act and SSAP 14, it *must* still be excluded until such time as SSAP 14 is revised to say otherwise. All of these five circumstances are considered in more detail in the paragraphs that follow. Also detailed below are the accounting treatments that should be followed where subsidiaries are not *consolidated*.

3.55 If the situation should arise where the parent's directors considered that all of the company's subsidiaries should be excluded from the consolidated financial statements for any of the reasons stated above, then they need not prepare consolidated financial statements. [Sec 229(5)].

3.56　SSAP 14 also states that where a subsidiary has been excluded from the group's consolidated financial statements, for any of the reasons outlined in the paragraphs that follow, the reason for the exclusion must be given in the group's financial statements. It also says that where a subsidiary has been excluded in this way, the resulting financial statements will need to be considered to determine whether they give a true and fair view of the position of the group as a whole. [SSAP 14 para 20; Sec 227(3)].

Inclusion not material

3.57　A subsidiary undertaking does not require to be consolidated where its inclusion in the consolidation would be immaterial. Two or more undertakings may only be excluded using this provision where taken together they are still not material to the consolidation. [Sec 229(2)]. See for example Table 6.

Table 6: Example of subsidiaries not consolidated on the grounds of materiality.

Extract from Ford Motor Company Limited Annual Report & Accounts 31st December 1988.

Note extract

Unconsolidated subsidiaries
The accounts of fifteen subsidiary companies have not been consolidated as, in the opinion of the directors, consolidation would be of no real value to members of the Company in view of the insignifcant amounts involved. Details of these subsidiaries will be filed with the Registrar of Companies.

3.58　The explanatory forward to SSAPs states that accounting standards need not be applied to items whose effect is judged to be immaterial to an understanding of the financial statements. Consequently, there is no conflict with the Act, because where such subsidiaries are not material to the consolidation, the provisions of SSAP 14 that require consolidation do not apply.

Severe long-term restrictions

3.59　Consolidation of a subsidiary undertaking is not required where severe long-term restrictions substantially hinder the exercise of the parent company's rights over the assets or over the management of the undertaking. [Sec 229(3)(a)]. In this situation, the 'rights' of the parent company are the rights attributed to it under the definition of a 'parent undertaking' (see para 3.41). This type of situation is illustrated in Table 7.

Table 7: Example of subsidiaries excluded from consolidation probably because severe long-term restrictions hinder the parent's rights.

Extract from Eastern Produce (Holdings) PLC Annual Report 31st December 1988.

Notes extract

12 Fixed assets investments extract

(iii) Three subsidiary companies which previously operated in Sri Lanka and did not trade during the year have not been consolidated.

The accounts of Robert Hudson & Sons (Pty) Limited, the subsidiary controlling the Angolan operations, have not be consolidated and a full provision has been made against the investments in, and amounts due from, that company. Unaudited accounts have been prepared up to 31 December 1987 and disclose capital and reserves amounting to £2,762,000 at the year end exchange rate.

3.60   This exemption is very similarly worded to the exemption given in SSAP 14. The standard states that a subsidiary should be excluded from consolidation where the subsidiary operates under severe restrictions that significantly restrict the holding company's control over the subsidiary's assets and operations for the foreseeable future. [SSAP 14 para 21(c)].

3.61   In this situation, the standard states that the amount of the group's investment in the subsidiary should be stated in the consolidated balance sheet, under the equity method of accounting (see further chapter 11), at its value at the date when the severe restrictions came into force. No further accrual should be made for its profits or losses after that date. However, if the directors consider that there has been a permanent fall in the value of the investment from the value determined under the equity method, then they should provide for the loss through the consolidated profit and loss account. For this purpose, they should consider each investment individually. [SSAP 14 para 25].

3.62   In addition, the consolidated financial statements should give the following information in respect of the subsidiary:

■   The amount of its net assets.

■   The profits or losses for the period.

46

■ Any amounts included in the parent's consolidated profit and loss account for dividends received or for the write-down of the investment.

[SSAP 14 para 26].

Disproportionate expense or undue delay

3.63 Consolidation of a subsidiary is not required where the information necessary to prepare consolidated financial statements cannot be obtained without disproportionate expense or undue delay. [Sec 229(3)(b)].

3.64 This exemption does not specifically appear in SSAP 14, although the standard does refer to subsidiaries excluded from group accounts for the reasons permitted by the Companies Acts. In this circumstance, SSAP 14 requires that the reasons for exclusion should be stated. [SSAP 14 para 20].

3.65 There are no specific requirements in either the Act or SSAP 14 concerning what should be included in the consolidated financial statements with regard to subsidiaries excluded under this exemption. However, it is likely that the lack of information available will inevitably mean that the investment will have to be included in the consolidated financial statements either at cost or under the equity method of accounting at the date the latest information is available. In addition, substantial additional information concerning the reason for the treatment will have to be given in the notes to the financial statements in order for the consolidated financial statements to give a true and fair view.

3.66 The equivalent provisions in the old legislation meant that a parent company did not have to deal with a subsidiary in its group accounts where its inclusion would have involved *"expense or delay out of proportion to the value to its members"*. This exemption differed from that outlined above because the measure for exemption was made by considering the value of including a subsidiary in the group accounts to the benefit derived by the *members* of the parent company. Under the new exemption there is no such measure and, consequently, the new test of disproportionate expense or undue delay is intended to be more restrictive.

3.67 The old exemption was often used by UK intermediate holding companies which were wholly owned by overseas parents. In this situation, such holding companies were normally obliged to prepare consolidated financial statements under the Act because their parent was incorporated outside Great Britain. However, under this exemption, it was normally easy to conclude that inclusion of all subsidiaries in consolidated financial statements (and therefore their preparation) at the Great Britain intermediate holding company level would involve expense or delay out of proportion to the value to the company's members (that is, the overseas holding company). The overseas holding company would normally have little use for such consolidated financial statements as it would generally have obtained equivalent information, perhaps by consolidation returns or board representation and management information.

3.68   The exclusion of this exemption from the new legislation means that even where overseas parents (excluding EC parents) wholly own UK groups, the UK group will have to prepare consolidated financial statements. The reason for tightening the test, and omitting the part that considered the value to the company's members, is that since the original exemption was included in the Companies Act 1948 consolidated financial statements have become more widely used. Accordingly, such sub-groups have become much more accountable and their consolidated financial statements are now used not only by members, but also by creditors (particularly banks), financial analysts, journalists, prospective members and many others. Furthermore, the ASC, in its exposure draft on consolidated accounts, proposes that 'disproportionate expense or undue delay' should not be used in any circumstances to exclude a material subsidiary from consolidation.

Subsequent resale

3.69   Consolidation of a subsidiary undertaking is not required where the interest of the parent company was acquired and is held exclusively with a view to subsequent resale. [Sec 229(3)(c)]. In this situation, the 'interests' of the parent company are the interests attributed to it under the definition of 'parent undertaking' (see para 3.6 *et seq*).

3.70   SSAP 14, in effect, includes this exemption by allowing exclusion where the holding company's directors intend that control of the subsidiary is intended to be temporary. [SSAP 14 para 21(d)]. This provision of SSAP 14 could be read to allow exclusion of a subsidiary that has previously been consolidated as part of the group where the parent has decided to sell it, but has not completed the sale by its year end. However, this possibility was not the intention of this exemption, and it should only be used where a subsidiary has been acquired with the intention of resale. Consequently, that interpretation of paragraph 21(d) of SSAP 14 conforms with the exemption now given in the Act.

3.71   SSAP 14 also states that in this circumstance the investment should be included in the consolidated balance sheet as a current asset at the lower of cost and net realisable value. [SSAP 14 para 27].

Dissimilar activities

3.72   A further exemption from consolidation applies where the activities of
        one or more subsidiaries are so different from those of the other
        undertakings included in the consolidated financial statements that
        their inclusion would be *"incompatible with the obligation to give a true
        and fair view"*. [Sec 229(4)].

3.73   This requirement is mandatory, whereas the old provision in the Act
        was optional. In addition, previously, under the old provision the
        Secretary of State's permission was required if this reason was used to
        exclude a subsidiary from consolidation. His permission is no longer
        necessary.

3.74   SSAP 14 includes a very similar exemption where the subsidiary's
        activities are so different from those of other group companies that
        consolidated financial statements *including* that subsidiary would be
        misleading. [SSAP 14 para 21(a)]. This contrasts with the tighter
        condition in the Act that consolidated financial statements including
        the subsidiaries would have to be *incompatible with the obligation to
        give a true and fair view*, before the particular subsidiaries must be
        excluded from consolidation.

3.75   The provisions in the Act also go on to state that this exemption does
        not apply merely because some of the undertakings are industrial, or
        some are commercial and some provide services, or because they carry
        on industrial or commercial activities involving different products or
        provide different services. [Sec 229(4)]. The intention of this
        paragraph is to restrict significantly the undertakings that the
        exemption applies to and is taken directly from the 7th Directive.

3.76   In the US FASB No 94, 'Consolidation of all majority-owned
        subsidiaries' was issued in October 1987. This statement requires that
        all majority-owned subsidiaries should be consolidated unless control
        is temporary or does not rest with the majority owner. The statement
        requires consolidation of all majority-owned subsidiaries even if they
        have 'nonhomogeneous' operations (that is, dissimilar activities in UK
        terminology). Previously in the US before the introduction of this
        FASB, subsidiaries with dissimilar activities were excluded from
        consolidation. However, there has been a general shift in the views of
        many accountants throughout the world towards consolidation of the
        majority of subsidiaries whether they have dissimilar activities or not
        and this is borne out in the US. Furthermore, this change of views
        coincides with the suggested provision of more detailed segmental
        information on different aspects of a group's businesses (for example
        see Table 8 overleaf). In this respect in the UK ED 45 on segmental
        reporting was published in December 1989 and is considered further
        in 'Manual of Accounting - volume I' chapter 13.

Table 8: Example of activities that might have been dissimilar before the Companies Act 1989, which have been consolidated but have been disclosed separately in the notes.

Extract from Sketchley plc Report and Accounts 31st March 1990.

Note extract

23 ASSET LEASING

A major part of the Group's operations involves providing capital assets to customers on rental contracts. These comprise vending machines and workwear amounting to:

	1989 £000	1988 £000
Tangible assets: machines on rental	2,909	5,165
Circulating inventory	16,435	14,929
Debtors: finance leases	25,091	26,827
	44,435	46,921

The debt drawn by Sketchley Finance Limited under a Multiple Option Facility to finance these assets is secured on the rental contracts. At the year end future income under these rental contracts amounted to £70,200,000 (1988: £72,300,000). This debt, together with finance lease obligations secured directly on rental assets, provides the funding for the Group's leasing activities and is analysed separately below:

	Trading activities		Leasing activities		Group	
	1989 £000	1988 £000	1989 £000	1988 £000	1989 £000	1988 £000
Net assets before net borrowings	53,870	41,840	44,435	46,921	98,305	88,761
Net borrowings	(14,993)	(7,381)	(37,581)	(38,137)	(52,574)	(45,518)
Shareholders' funds	38,877	34,459	6,854	8,784	45,731	43,243
Net gearing	39%	21%	548%	434%	115%	105%

3.77 The wording in section 229(4) also seems to support the view that the majority of subsidiaries should be consolidated. The exemption from consolidation will, therefore, only apply in a minority of situations. The minority will include banking subsidiaries and insurance subsidiaries whose financial statements are drawn up under Schedule 9 to the Act, where their parents prepare their consolidated financial statements in accordance with Schedule 4 and 4A to the Act. As the bases on which their financial statements are drawn up are dissimilar, it is appropriate that such companies should be excluded from consolidation. For the avoidance of doubt, the proposals in the ASC's exposure draft on consolidated accounts confirm that the use of this exemption should be limited to situations where the subsidiary concerned is either a bank or an insurance company that prepares its financial statements in accordance with Schedule 9 to the Act.

3.78   The Act requires the interest of the group in the undertakings excluded under this exemption to be shown in the consolidated financial statements, using the equity method of accounting. [4A Sch 18]. Any goodwill arising from this accounting treatment has to be dealt with in accordance with the Act's provisions (see chapter 8). This will mean in practice that such subsidiaries can be dealt with as a 'one line' item in the balance sheet and the profit and loss account (although taxation and any extraordinary items will have to be shown separately). These 'one line' items would show, respectively, the group's share of assets and liabilities and the group's share of profits and losses of the subsidiaries concerned.

3.79   SSAP 14 also requires that the consolidated financial statements should include the subsidiary under the equity method of accounting. [SSAP 14 para 23(d)]. In addition, the standard requires that the consolidated financial statements should include the subsidiary's separate financial statements. These financial statements may be combined with the financial statements of those other subsidiaries that have similar operations. The subsidiary's financial statements should include the following:

■   Details of the holding company's interest.

■   Details of intra-group balances.

■   The nature of the subsidiary's transactions with the rest of the group.

■   A reconciliation with the amount included in the consolidated financial statements for the group's investment in the subsidiary.

[SSAP 14 para 23].

3.80   The requirements of SSAP 14 go further than is now required by the Act, as the legislation does not require that the financial statements of all subsidiaries excluded from consolidation should be appended to the consolidated financial statements (see further para 3.95 below). However unless SSAP 14 is revised, this requirement will still have to be complied with, although the obligation is often satisfied by giving abbreviated details of a subsidiary's financial statements as a note to the consolidated financial statements. These provisions are illustrated in Table 9 overleaf.

Lack of effective control

3.81   SSAP 14 has one further exemption that is not covered by those exemptions outlined above. This exemption applies where a holding company, although owning directly or through other subsidiaries more than half the equity share capital of a subsidiary, is in either of the two following positions:

- The holding company does not own share capital carrying more than half the votes.

- The holding company has contractual or other restrictions imposed on its ability to appoint the majority of the board of directors.

[SSAP 14 para 21(b)].

Table 9: Illustration of a group that does not consolidate its insurance companies.

Extract from Willis Faber p.l.c. Annual Report 31st December 1988.

Accounting policies extract

BASIS OF CONSOLIDATION

The Group financial statements incorporate those of all subsidiairies made up to 31 December and include the results of associated companies attributable to the Group's interest based on financial statements drawn up to 31 December.

The financial statements include the results of subsidiary and associated companies acquired and disposed of during the year from or to the relevant dates of acquisition or disposal.

The investment in associated companies is shown as the Group's share of net assets less goodwill and provisions.

The net assets of the wholly owned insurance subsidiary companies are included as one figure in the Group balance sheet and the profit before tax is separately disclosed because the nature of their business differs from that of the remainder of the Group.

Purchased goodwill is written off directly against reserves as it arises.

Balance sheet extract

		Group		Company	
		1987	1988	1987	1988
	Notes	£000	£000	£000	£000
Fixed assets:					
Tangible assets	13	66,013	117,609	27,119	72,483
Investments:					
subsidiary companies	14	–	–	300,263	77,158
insurance companies	15	36,366	46,507	–	–
associated companies	16	85,343	77,561	45,631	45,526
other	17	3,539	1,469	2,216	466
		191,261	243,146	375,229	195,633

Table 9 continued

Notes extract

NOTE 3
RESULTS OF INSURANCE COMPANIES

	1987	1988
	£000	£000
Premiums written	69,392	104,983
Reinsurance ceded	(36,421)	(56,669)
Net premiums written	32,971	48,314
Movements in provision for unearned premiums	(564)	(3,126)
Net premiums earned	32,407	45,188
Losses incurred	(26,358)	(33,599)
Underwriting expenses	(7,362)	(12,371)
Underwriting loss	(1,313)	(782)
Investment income	5,229	9,454
Investment profits (note)	–	269
Interest payable	(188)	(226)
Expenses	(566)	(998)
	3,162	7,717

Note:
Realised and unrealised investment profits and losses averaged over five years were included in profit in 1988 for the first time. If they had been included in 1987, pofit before tax would have been higher by approximately £400,000.

NOTE 15
INVESTMENTS IN INSURANCE COMPANIES

	1987	1988
	£000	£000
Fixed assets (note (a))	405	442
Investments (note (b))	80,046	96,770
	80,451	97,212
Current assets:		
Debtors	35,821	39,787
Cash and short term deposits	24,582	34,746
	60,403	74,533
Current liabilities	(20,552)	(26,889)
Net current assets	39,851	47,644
	120,302	144,856
Less: insurance funds (note (c))	(83,936)	(98,349)
Net assets	36,366	46,507

Table 9 continued

Notes:

(a) Fixed assets	Land and buildings	Fixtures, equipment and vehicles	Total
	£000	£000	£000
Cost 1 January 1988	46	551	597
Depreciation 1 January 1988	(30)	(162)	(192)
Additions at cost	32	180	212
Depreciation and other adjustments	(9)	(166)	(175)
Net book value 31 December 1988	39	403	442

(b) Investments are included at market value in 1988. If they had been included at market value in 1987, they would have been shown as £81,565,000.

(c) Insurance funds comprised:

	1987	1988
	£000	£000
Unearned premium provisions	7,062	10,496
Outstanding claims provisions	30,600	38,919
Three year insurance fund	46,274	48,934
	83,936	98,349

3.82 This exemption is now rendered unnecessary by the new legislation, because as explained above, the matter of whether a holding company controls another undertaking is reflected in the new definitions of subsidiaries.

3.83 Consequently, if the undertaking is a subsidiary under the Act it will have to be consolidated under the Act's provisions. However, if the undertaking is not a subsidiary under the Act, but it satisfies all of the criteria in SSAP 1 requiring it to be treated as an associated company, it should be included in the consolidated financial statements under the equity method of accounting (see further chapter 11). If it not an associated company under the Act and SSAP 1, it should be included in the consolidated financial statements as an investment at cost or valuation, less any provision required. [SSAP 14 para 24].

Subsidiaries no longer excluded from consolidation

3.84 There are two reasons for excluding a subsidiary from consolidation that used to appear in the Companies Act 1985, but that are excluded from the new requirements introduced by the Companies Act 1989. These reasons were where including the subsidiary in the group accounts would be *misleading, or harmful* to the business of the company or any of its subsidiaries.

3.85 In effect, the *misleading* part of the exemption is covered in part by three specific situations included in the new legislation. These exemptions from consolidation are discussed in paragraphs 3.59 to 3.80 above and are as follows:

■ Severe long-term restrictions.

■ Subsequent resale.

■ Dissimilar activities.

3.86 With the old legislation the *harmful* part of the exemption required the Secretary of State's permission before exclusion of the subsidiary on this ground was allowed. This exemption was left out of the new legislation because it was not allowed by the 7th Directive.

Disclosure where a subsidiary is excluded from consolidation

3.87 Schedule 5 to the Act sets out certain information about subsidiaries that companies who prepare consolidated financial statements have to give and these general requirements are considered in chapter 4. Also, companies that do not prepare consolidated financial statements have to give information about their subsidiaries and this information is similarly set out in Schedule 5 to the Act. These provisions are considered in detail in 'Manual of Accounting - volume I' chapter 9. The additional disclosure required by Schedule 5 concerning subsidiaries that have been excluded from consolidation where consolidated financial statements are prepared is considered below.

3.88 Where a subsidiary is excluded from consolidation, the notes to the consolidated financial statements must disclose:

■ The reasons why the subsidiary or the subsidiaries are not dealt with in the consolidated financial statements. [5 Sch 15(4); SSAP 14 para 20]. The reason disclosed would have to be one of those explained above.

■ Any qualification contained in the auditors' report on the subsidiaries' financial statements for the relevant financial year. This includes any additional information included in a note to those financial statements to call attention to the matter, which would have otherwise been included in the qualification itself. This applies to the extent that the qualification is not covered by the group's consolidated financial statements, and to the extent that it is material from the point of view of the holding company's shareholders. If the required information is not obtainable, a statement to that effect should be given in the notes to the consolidated financial statements [5 Sch 18].

■ The aggregate amount of the subsidiary's capital and reserves at the end of their relevant financial year and their profit or loss for the period. This information need not be given, however, where either of the following conditions is satisfied:

☐ The group's total investment in its subsidiaries' shares is included in the consolidated financial statements by the equity method of valuation (see chapter 11).

☐ The undertaking is not required under the Act to file its balance sheet with the Registrar of Companies or publish it in Great Britain or elsewhere. Exemption is only allowed under this provision, however, if the group's holding in the undertaking is less than 50 per cent of the nominal value of that undertaking's shares.

[5 Sch 17(1)(2)].

3.89 References to 'relevant financial year' above are to the subsidiary's financial year ending with the parent's year end or the last financial year ending before that date. [5 Sch 17(4)]. The information required by paragraph 17 need not be given if it is not material.

3.90 All or some of the additional information required above need not be disclosed if, in the directors' opinion, its disclosure would be seriously prejudicial to the subsidiary's business or to the business of the parent or any of its subsidiaries. This exemption applies where the particulars relate to a subsidiary that is established under the law of a country outside the UK or where its business is carried on outside the UK. However, the Secretary of State has to agree that the disclosure need not be made and the fact that advantage is taken of this exemption has to be disclosed. [Sec 231(3)(4)].

3.91 An example of an occasion when it would be allowable not to disclose this information would be when a company has trading subsidiaries in two countries, and those two countries are either in conflict, or have trade embargoes between them. In these two situations the disclosure of the UK group's investment in each subsidiary might impair its trading ability in those countries.

3.92 The general exemption explained in chapter 4 paragraph 4.63 where certain information is not required if the number of undertakings is such that the resulting disclosure is excessively lengthy, does not apply to subsidiaries that are excluded from consolidation for the reasons given in paragraph 3.53 above. [Sec 231(5)(b)].

3.93 SSAP 14 requires that the following additional information should be disclosed in the consolidated financial statements in respect of those subsidiaries that are excluded from consolidation in addition to the detailed information required by the Act:

■ The names of the principal subsidiaries excluded.

■ Any premium or discount on acquisition determined by comparing the purchase consideration and the fair value of the assets acquired (see further chapter 8) to the extent that it has not been written off.

[SSAP 14 para 28].

3.94 In addition, where a subsidiary has been excluded from consolidation as outlined in paragraphs 3.53 to 3.80 above, the Act requires that the information outlined in chapter 4 paragraphs 4.42 to 4.53 should be given. Also, where a holding company prepares consolidated financial statements, the information set out in chapter 4 paragraphs 4.12 to 4.17 (details of intercompany balances, etc.) must be given in respect of any subsidiaries that are not consolidated.

Filing of subsidiary financial statements excluded on grounds of dissimilar activities

3.95 Where a subsidiary has been excluded from consolidation in accordance with the exemption described above in paragraph 3.72 concerning dissimilar activities, certain additional provisions of the Act may apply. These provisions apply if the subsidiary is incorporated outside Great Britain and does not have a place of business in Great Britain, or if it is an unincorporated undertaking. In practice in these circumstances, the financial statements of these undertakings are not filed in Great Britain. Consequently, the Act requires that a copy of the undertaking's financial statements should be filed with the Registrar of Companies attached to the parent's financial statements. [Sec 243(1)(2)]. In addition, if the financial statements are audited, a copy of the auditor's report should also be filed. [Sec 243(2)].

3.96 The undertaking's financial statements filed in this way should be its latest individual financial statements, or if the undertaking is itself a parent, its latest group financial statements must be filed. [Sec 243(2)]. The undertaking's financial statements that are filed must be for a period that ends not more than 12 months before the parent's financial year end. [Sec 243(3)]. Furthermore, if the financial statements or the auditor's report is in a language other than English, then the directors must file a translated version, which must be certified to be correct. [Sec 243(4)].

3.97 The undertaking is not required to append financial statements where its financial statements do not satisfy the above requirements, or where financial statements are not prepared. [Sec 243(5)(a)]. In this particular circumstance, therefore, no financial statements would have to be filed with those of the parent.

3.98   In addition, the undertaking's financial statements need not be filed where they are not required to be published or made available for public inspection anywhere in the world. However, if this exemption applies and advantage is taken of it, the reason for not appending the undertaking's financial statements must be stated in a note to the parent's financial statements. [Sec 243(5)(b)].

3.99   Where, for example, the undertaking excluded from consolidation is itself an intermediate holding company, its consolidated financial statements should be filed. Insofar as the undertaking's subsidiaries are included in those consolidated financial statements, their individual financial statements need not also be filed. However, where the undertaking's subsidiaries are excluded from consolidation under section 229(4) (dissimilar activities), their financial statements will have to be filed appended to the ultimate parent's financial statements. [Sec 243(5)(c)].

Chapter 4

FORMAT AND CONTENT OF CONSOLIDATED FINANCIAL STATEMENTS

Chapter 4

FORMAT AND CONTENT OF CONSOLIDATED FINANCIAL STATEMENTS

Introduction

4.1   The formats of consolidated financial statements are substantially similar to those of financial statements prepared by individual companies. Many of the basic rules concerning the formats have little to do with the process of consolidation and, consequently, they are not dealt with in depth here, but are considered in detail in 'Manual of Accounting - volume I' chapter 6. This chapter considers the provisions of the Act that affect the formats of consolidated financial statements. It also considers certain other disclosures that have to be given in the notes to consolidated financial statements.

4.2   The group's consolidated financial statements have to comply as far as practicable with the provisions of Schedule 4 to the Act as if the undertakings included in the consolidation were a single company. [4A Sch 1(1)]. In addition, the consolidated financial statements have to comply with the provisions of Schedule 4A as to their form and content. [Sec 227(4)]. A group's consolidated financial statements will include the following:

■   The directors' report. [Sec 234].

■   The consolidated balance sheet and related notes of the parent company and its subsidiary undertakings. [Sec 227(2)(a)].

■   The consolidated profit and loss account and related notes of the parent company and its subsidiary undertakings. [Sec 227(2)(b)].

■   The parent company's individual balance sheet and related notes. [Sec 226(1)(a)].

■   The parent company's individual profit and loss account, unless advantage is taken of the exemption. [Secs 226(1)(b), 230].

■   The group's statement of source and application of funds. [SSAP 10 para 12].

■   The auditors' report on the statements above other than on the directors' report (although its content would be reported on if it were inconsistent with the rest of the financial statements). [Sec 235; SSAP 10 para 10].

4.3   The contents of the directors' report and the source and application of funds statement are considered in 'Manual of Accounting - volume I'. The other statements mentioned above are considered in the paragraphs below, together with a summary of the rules that apply to the formats.

Summary of format rules

4.4   There are a number of rules that apply to the formats detailed in Schedule 4 to the Act and these are as follows:

■   Items detailed in the formats have to be shown in the order and under the headings and sub-headings set out in the format adopted. [4 Sch 1(1)].

■   Generally, once a group has chosen a format it cannot change it. If it wishes to do so, then special rules apply. [4 Sch 2(2)].

■   An item may be shown in greater detail than the formats require. [4 Sch 3(1)].

■   An item not represented in the formats can be shown separately. [4 Sch 3(2)].

■   The arrangement of headings and sub-headings preceded by Arabic numerals must be adapted if the special nature of the group's business requires this. [4 Sch 3(3)].

■   Items that are preceded in the formats by Arabic numerals may be combined where the items are not material, or where the combination facilitates the assessment of the state of affairs or profit or loss of the group. In the latter case, however, a detailed breakdown must be given in the notes to the financial statements. [4 Sch 3(4)]. Generally, groups make use of this concession to combine items on the face of the consolidated balance sheet and profit and loss account and expand them in the notes.

■   Headings and sub-headings need not be shown where there are no amounts for the current and preceding years. [4 Sch 3(5)]

4.5   A more detailed explanation of these rules is given in 'Manual of Accounting - volume I' chapter 6.

The consolidated balance sheet

4.6   The Act includes two alternative balance sheet formats for individual companies. In Format 1, net assets can be equated with the aggregate of share capital and reserves and this format is normally presented vertically. In comparison, in Format 2, assets appear on right side of the account and capital and liabilities on the other. The group's parent will have to choose one of these formats for its individual balance sheet .and that format would normally also be used to present the consolidated balance sheet. However, there is nothing in the legislation to prevent the parent from adopting a different format for its consolidated balance. sheet, although this is unlikely to happen in practice, unless the group has banking or insurance activities.

4.7   Format 1 is the most common format used by groups to present both the parent's individual balance sheet and the group's consolidated balance sheet. Schedule 4A to the Act includes provisions that modify the formats detailed in Schedule 4, to include certain additional items that require disclosure in the consolidated balance sheet. Set out below is balance sheet Format 1 amended to include those additional items (shown in bold).

CONSOLIDATED BALANCE SHEET - FORMAT 1

A   Called-up share capital not paid

B   Fixed assets

I   Intangible assets

    1   Development costs
    2   Concessions, patents, licences, trade marks and similar
        rights and assets
    3   Goodwill
    4   Payments on account

II   Tangible assets

    1   Land and buildings
    2   Plant and machinery
    3   Fixture, fittings, tools and equipment
    4   Payments on account and assets in course of construction

III   Investments

    1   Shares in group undertakings
    2   Loans to group undertakings
    3   Interests in associated undertakings
    4   Other participating interests
    5   Loans to undertakings in which the company has a
        participating interest
    6   Other investments other than loans
    7   Other loans
    8   Own shares

C   Current assets

I   Stocks
    1   Raw materials and consumables
    2   Work in progress
    3   Finished goods and goods for resale
    4   Payments on account

II   Debtors
1   Trade debtors
2   Amounts owed by group undertakings
3   Amounts owed by undertakings in which the company has a participating interest
4   Other debtors
5   Called-up share capital not paid
6   Prepayments and accrued income

III   Investments
1   Shares in group undertakings
2   Own shares
3   Other investments

IV   Cash at bank and in hand

D   Prepayments and accrued income

E   Creditors: amounts falling due within one year
1   Debenture loans
2   Bank loans and overdrafts
3   Payments received on account
4   Trade creditors
5   Bills of exchange payable
6   Amounts owed to group undertakings
7   Amounts owed to undertakings in which the company has a participating interest
8   Other creditors including taxation and social security
9   Accruals and deferred income

F   Net current assets (liabilities)
G   Total assets less current liabilities
H   Creditors: amounts falling due after more than one year
1   Debenture loans
2   Bank loans and overdrafts
3   Payments received on account
4   Trade creditors
5   Bills of exchange payable
6   Amounts owed to group undertakings
7   Amounts owed to undertakings in which the company has a participating interest
8   Other creditors including taxation and social security
9   Accruals and deferred income

I   Provisions for liabilities and charges
1   Pensions and similar obligations
2   Taxation, including deferred taxation
3   Other provisions

J   Accruals and deferred income
K   **Minority interests** (alternative position M)
L   Capital and reserves
I   Called up share capital
II   Share premium account
III   Revaluation reserve
IV   Other reserves
1 Capital redemption reserve
2 Reserve for own shares
3 Reserves provided for by the articles of association
4 Other reserves
V   Profit and loss account
M   **Minority interests** (alternative position K)

Rules concerning particular items

4.8   There are a number of rules concerning particular items in the balance sheet formats and these cover:

■   Investments by subsidiaries in a parent's own shares.

■   Disclosure of taxation and social security.

■   Payments received on account of work in progress.

4.9   A more detailed explanation of the rules concerning these particular balance sheet items is given in 'Manual of Accounting - volume I' chapter 6.

4.10   The following items may be shown in alternative positions in the formats.

■   Called-up share capital not paid (A and C.II.5).

■   Own shares (B.III.7 and C.III.2).

■   Prepayments and accrued income (C.II.6 and D).

■   Accruals and deferred income (H.9 and J).

■   Minority interests (K and M).

4.11   An illustration of a Format 1 consolidated balance sheet is given in Table 10 overleaf. 'Manual of Accounting - volume I' chapter 6 also includes examples of Format 1 and Format 2 balance sheets.

Investments in and amounts due to and from group undertakings

4.12   The balance sheet format detailed above specifies the place where the aggregate amounts should be shown of any amounts owed to and from, and any interests in, group undertakings. In Format 1 these items can be summarised as follows:

```
B      Fixed assets
III    Investments
       1     Shares in group undertakings
       2     Loans to group undertakings

C      Current assets
II     Debtors
       2     Amounts owed by group undertakings
III    Investments
       1     Shares in group undertakings
```

E	Creditors: amounts falling due within one year
	6 Amounts owed to group undertakings
H	Creditors: amounts falling due after more than one year
	6 Amounts owed to group undertakings

Table 10: Illustration of a consolidated balance sheet prepared in accordance with Format 1.

Extract from Tootal Group plc Report & Accounts 31st January 1989.

CONSOLIDATED BALANCE SHEET

31 January 1989	1989	1988	Notes
	£'000	£'000	
FIXED ASSETS			
Tangible assets	107,321	85,888	13
Investments	11,116	8,568	14
	118,437	94,456	
CURRENT ASSETS			
Stocks	119,728	114,267	15
Debtors	97,129	86,760	16
Cash at bank and in hand	20,678	10,532	
	237,535	211,559	
CREDITORS: AMOUNTS DUE WITHIN ONE YEAR			
Borrowings	25,555	26,124	17
Others	98,633	99,104	18
	124,188	125,228	
NET CURRENT ASSETS	113,347	86,331	
TOTAL ASSETS LESS CURRENT LIABILITIES	231,784	180,787	
CREDITORS AMOUNTS DUE AFTER MORE THAN ONE YEAR			
Borrowings	34,102	34,977	17
Others	7,619	1,505	19
PROVISIONS FOR LIABILITIES AND CHARGES	2,583	4,886	20
	187,480	139,419	
CAPITAL AND RESERVES			
Called-up share capital	77,192	62,684	21
Share premium account	29,497	3,047	24
Revaluation reserve	3,858	3,846	24
Profit and loss account	67,361	51,877	24
	177,908	121,454	
Minority interests	9,572	17,965	25
	187,480	139,419	

Directors J A Craven   A D Webb

4.13   In addition to the disclosure required by the formats, a parent or a subsidiary must disclose separately (either on the face of the balance sheet or in the notes to the financial statements) the amounts detailed above, split between the amounts owed to or from, and any interests in:

■   Any parent or any fellow subsidiary.

■   Any subsidiary.

[4 Sch 59].

4.14   Because amounts owed by and to group undertakings have to be shown in specific positions in the formats, it is not acceptable for undertakings to net these balances off and to disclose the net balance in the balance sheet as 'Investment in subsidiaries'. This applies even where a note to the financial statements gives additional information that explains the net balance. For example, the disclosure that follows is not acceptable:

Investment in subsidiaries	
Shares in subsidiaries	X
Amounts owed by subsidiaries	X
Amounts owed to subsidiaries	(X)
	X

4.15   Moreover, the amounts owed and owing have to be ascertained on an undertaking by undertaking basis. [4 Sch 5]. Consequently, for accounting disclosure purposes in the parent's financial statements, amounts that one subsidiary owes to the parent cannot be offset against amounts the parent owes to another subsidiary. Set-off can be allowed only in circumstances where there is a legal right of set-off between the loans. Such a legal right may exist, for example, if it is included as a clause in a loan agreement.

4.16   Undertakings have to analyse 'amounts owed by (and to) group undertakings' between amounts that will fall due within one year and amounts that will fall due after more than one year. [Notes 5 and 13 on the balance sheet formats]. The results of this analysis will largely depend both on the way in which group undertakings are financed and on the terms of any formal or informal agreements between the undertakings.

4.17   In addition, The International Stock Exchange's Continuing Obligations and the USM's General Undertaking require listed companies and companies that are traded on the USM, respectively, also to analyse amounts due from subsidiary companies between the aggregate amounts repayable:

■   In one year or less, or on demand.

■   Between one and two years.

■   Between two and five years.

■   In five years or more.

[CO 21(f); GU 10(f)].

Consolidated profit and loss account

4.18   There are four formats for the consolidated profit and loss account
given in the Act. Formats 1 and 3 classify expenses by function (for
example, cost of sales, distribution costs and administrative expenses).
Formats 2 and 4 classify expenses by type (for example, raw materials
and consumables, staff costs, and depreciation). Formats 1 and 2 are
presented vertically and Formats 3 and 4 are presented horizontally.
Schedule 4 to the Act sets out the basic formats allowed and Schedule
4A details the additional information that is required to be presented
in a consolidated profit and loss account (the additional requirements
are shown in bold). The consolidated profit and loss accounts that
follow include the requirements of both Schedule 4 and Schedule 4A.
Formats 3 and 4 are not given as they are rarely used and they
replicate the information in formats 1 and 2. Format 1 is given below
and Format 2 is given on the next page.

CONSOLIDATED PROFIT AND LOSS ACCOUNT - FORMAT 1

1   Turnover
2   Cost of sales
3   Gross profit or loss
4   Distribution costs
5   Administrative expenses
6   Other operating income
7   Income from shares in group undertakings
8   Income from interests in associated undertakings
9   Income from other participating interests
10   Income from other fixed asset investments
11   Other interest receivable and similar income
12   Amounts written off investments
13   Interest payable and similar charges
14   Tax on profit or loss on ordinary activities
15   Profit or loss on ordinary activities after taxation
16   Minority interests
17   Extraordinary income
18   Extraordinary charges
19   Extraordinary profit or loss
20   Tax on extraordinary profit or loss
21   Minority interests (in extraordinary items)
22   Other taxes not shown under the above items
23   Profit or loss for the financial year

CONSOLIDATED PROFIT AND LOSS ACCOUNT - FORMAT 2

1   Turnover
2   Changes in stocks of finished goods and in work in progress
3   Own work capitalised
4   Other operating income
5   (a) Raw materials and consumables
    (b) Other external charges
6   Staff costs:
    (a) Wages and salaries
    (b) Social security costs
    (c) Other pension costs
7   (a) Depreciation and other amounts written off tangible and intangible
        fixed assets
    (b) Exceptional amounts written off current assets
8   Other operating charges
9   Income from shares in group undertakings
10 Income from interests in associated undertakings
11 **Income from other participating interests**
12 **Income from other fixed asset investments**
13 Other interest receivable and similar income
14 Amounts written off investments
15 Interest payable and similar charges
16 Tax on profit or loss on ordinary activities
17 Profit or loss on ordinary activities after taxation
18 **Minority interests**
19 Extraordinary income
20 Extraordinary charges
21 Extraordinary profit or loss
22 Tax on extraordinary profit or loss
23 **Minority interests** (in extraordinary items)
24 Other taxes not shown under the above items
25 Profit or loss for the financial year

4.19   There are certain rules that apply to the profit and loss account formats. Generally, all of the items in the profit and loss account formats may be relegated in appropriate situations to the notes. [4 Sch 3(4)]. In addition to the information given in the formats, the consolidated profit and loss account must also show:

■   The group's profit and loss on ordinary activities before taxation. [4 Sch 3(6)].

■   Any amount that has been set aside, or that it is proposed to set aside, to reserves. [4 Sch 3(7)(a)].

■   Any amount that has been withdrawn, or that it is proposed to withdraw, from reserves. [4 Sch 3(7)(a)].

■   The aggregate amount of any dividends paid and proposed. [4 Sch 3(7)(b)].

4.20   These additional items, however, must be shown on the face of the profit and loss account. [4 Sch 3(7)].

4.21   The two items for 'minority interest' in the formats are not alternatives, as the item on line 21 of Format 1 and on line 23 of Format 2 relate to the minority's share of extraordinary items. [4A Sch 17(4)].

4.22   An example of a Format 1 profit and loss account is given in Table 11. Examples of Format 1 and Format 2 profit and loss accounts are also illustrated in 'Manual of Accounting - volume I' chapter 6.

Table 11: Example of a consolidated profit and loss account prepared under Format 1.

Extract from THORN EMI plc Annual Report 31st March 1989.

CONSOLIDATED
PROFIT AND LOSS ACCOUNT
for the year ended 31 March 1989.

	Notes	1989 £m	1989 £m
Turnover	1	3,290.6	3,054.0
Cost of sales		(2,694.9)	(2,539.4)
Gross profit		595.7	514.6
Distribution costs		(128.5)	(110.0)
Administrative expenses		(242.6)	(225.6)
Other operating income		72.0	44.7
Operating profit	2	296.6	223.7
Share of profits less losses of related companies		23.3	20.0
Profit before finance charges	1	319.9	243.7
Finance charges	3	(30.8)	(18.4)
Profit on ordinary activities before taxation		289.1	225.3
Taxation on profit on ordinary activites	4	(96.1)	(79.0)
Profit on ordinary activities after taxation		193.0	146.3
Minority interests		(10.6)	(8.8)
Profit before extraordinary items		182.4	137.5
Extraordinary items less taxation	5	(8.8)	(14.2)
Profit attributable to members of the Holding Company		173.6	123.3
Dividends	6	(77.2)	(64.1)
Transfer to profit and loss reserve	20	96.4	59.2
Earnings per Ordinary Share – basic	7	64.2p	53.1p
– fully diluted	7	60.7p	50.1p

Movements on reserves are set out in Note 20.

Parent's profit and loss account

4.23   When a parent company prepares consolidated financial statements in accordance with the Act, it is not required to include its own profit and loss account and related notes if the financial statements satisfy the following requirements:

■ The notes to the parent company's individual balance sheet show the company's profit or loss for the financial year determined in accordance with the provisions of the Act. [Sec 230(1)(b)].

■ The parent company's board of directors must approve the company's individual profit and loss account in accordance with the rules concerning approval of the company's financial statements. [Sec 230(3)].

■ The notes to the financial statements disclose the fact that the holding company has taken advantage of this exemption. [Sec 230(4)].

4.24 Where the consolidated financial statements do not include the company's profit and loss account, it need not include certain supplementary information when presented to the Board for their approval. [Sec 230(2)]. The information that can be excluded is specified in paragraphs 52 to 57 of Schedule 4 to the Act, which includes the following:

■ Certain items of income and expenditure including:

☐ Interest and similar charges.

☐ Amounts set aside for the redemption of shares and loans.

☐ Income from listed investments.

☐ Rents from land.

☐ Hire of plant and machinery.

☐ Auditor's remuneration.

[4 Sch 53].

■ Detailed particulars concerning tax. [4 Sch 54].

■ Disaggregated information concerning turnover. [4 Sch 55].

■ Particulars of the average number of staff. [4 Sch 56].

■ Certain miscellaneous matters including:

☐ The effect of including any preceding year items in the current year's profit and loss account.

☐ Particulars of extraordinary income or extraordinary charges.

☐   The effect of any exceptional items.

[4 Sch 57].

4.25   Suitable wording for a note to be included in the consolidated
financial statements when the parent's profit and loss account is not
reproduced would be:

> *"As permitted by section 230 of the Companies Act 1985, the
> parent's profit and loss account has not been included in these
> financial statements."*

See also the example given in Table 12.

**Table 12: Example of the disclosure made where no profit and loss
account of the parent is presented.**

Extract from Calor Group plc Annual Report 31st March 1989.

Note extract

As permitted by section 228(7) of the Companies Act 1985, [*now section 230 of the Companies Act
1985*], no profit and loss account of the parent company is presented. The amount of the
consolidated profit for the financial year dealt with in the accounts of the parent company is £34.9m
after including dividends and the management charges to subsidiary companies of £41.6m.

Summary financial statements

4.26   A major change brought about by the enactment of the Companies
Act 1989 is that summary financial statements may in certain
circumstances be sent to members of listed companies instead of the
company's full financial statements. 'Listed' in this respect refers to
public companies that have been admitted to the Official List of The
International Stock Exchange of the United Kingdom and the
Republic of Ireland Limited. [Sec 251(1)]. This provision is, however,
subject to the company not being prohibited from distributing such
accounts by its memorandum or articles of association.

4.27   Obviously, for many groups of companies this concession will reduce
significantly the cost of sending full sets of financial statements to
shareholders. This type of summary has already been used by building
societies, which are allowed to send summary financial statements to
their members under section 76 of the Building Societies Act 1986.

Conditions to be complied with

4.28   The conditions that must be complied with before summary financial
statements can be issued are summarised in separate regulations
detailed in SI 1990/515 as follows:

■ The company must ensure that the member has indicated to the company that he does not wish to continue to receive full financial statements.

■ The period allowed for filing full financial statement must not have expired.

■ The summary financial statement must be approved by the board of directors and signed on its behalf by a director. It must also state the name of the director signing it.

■ Summary financial statements of a company that *is not* required to prepare consolidated financial statements must include the following statement in a prominent position.

> "This summary financial statement does not contain sufficient information to allow for a full understanding of the results and state of affairs of the company. For further information the full annual accounts, the auditors' report on those accounts and the directors' report should be consulted."

■ Summary financial statements of a company that *is* required to prepare consolidated financial statements must include the following statement in a prominent position.

> "This summary financial statement does not contain sufficient information to allow for a full understanding of the results of the group and state of affairs of the company or of the group. For further information the full annual accounts, the auditors' report on those accounts and the directors' report should be consulted."

■ The summary financial statements should disclose in a prominent position the member's right to demand a copy of the company's last full financial statements free of charge.

■ A printed card or form should accompany the summary financial statements and be so worded as to enable the member, by marking a box and returning the card or form, to notify the company that he wishes to receive the full financial statements for the same year dealt with in the summary. In addition, the member should be able to indicate on the card or form if he wishes to receive the full financial statements in subsequent years. Any postage should be borne by the company.

[SI 1990/515 para 5(a) to (h)].

4.29   A member may inform the company in writing in any manner whether or not he wishes to receive full or summary financial statements. However where, in response to a 'relevant consultation', a member is given an opportunity to elect to receive full financial statements and no notification is received, summary financial statements only may in future be sent to that member. [SI 1990/515 para 6(1)]. Any notification given by a member must be made at least 28 days prior to the date on which full financial statements are due to be sent to members. [SI 1990/515 para 6(2)].

4.30   A 'relevant consultation' of the wishes of a member is a notice to the member which complies with the following requirements:

- It states that in future the member will be sent summary financial statement instead of full financial statements, unless he notifies the company he wishes to continue to receive the full financial statements.

- It includes a statement in a prominent position that failure to respond to the notice has important consequences.

- It accompanies a copy of the full financial statements.

- It has attached to it a copy of the summary financial statements and this is identified in the notice as an example of the statement the member will receive in the future, unless he notifies the company otherwise.

- It is accompanied by the printed card or form outlined in the last point in paragraph 4.28 above.

[SI 1990/515 para 3(a) to (e)].

Format and content of summary financial statements

4.31   The Act states that every summary financial statement shall include the following:

- The fact that it is only a summary of the annual financial statements and the directors' report.

- A statement by the company's auditors whether the summary financial statement is consistent with the annual financial statements, including the directors' report, and complies with the requirements of section 251 of the Act and any regulations made under that section.

- Whether the auditors' report on the annual financial statements was qualified or unqualified. If qualified, the report will have to be set out in full, together with any further information needed to understand the qualification.

■   Whether the auditors' report on the annual financial statements includes a statement concerning proper accounting records or inadequate returns under section 237(2), or failure to obtain certain necessary information and explanations under section 237(3). If so, the statement will have to be set out in full.

[Sec 251(4)].

4.32   These provisions will apply to financial statements prepared by a listed company. However, full financial statements must still be prepared for filing purposes and will have to be sent to any member of the company who wishes to receive the company's full financial statements . [Sec 251(2)].

4.33   The regulations specify different formats for summary financial statements that can be prepared by companies in the following situations:

■   Listed public companies *not required* to prepare consolidated financial statements. The format is set out in Schedule 1 to the regulations.

■   Listed public companies *required* to prepare consolidated financial statements. The format is set out in Schedule 1 to the regulations.

■   Listed public *banking and insurance* companies *not required* to prepare consolidated financial statements, who prepare their individual financial statements in accordance with Schedule 9 to the Act. The formats are set out in Schedules 2 and 3 to the regulations respectively.

■   Listed public companies being the parent of *a banking or an insurance group* entitled to prepare consolidated financial statements in accordance with Schedule 9 to the Act. The formats are set out in Schedules 2 and 3 to the regulations respectively.

4.34   The paragraphs that follow outline the format and content of summary financial statements applicable to listed companies that prepare consolidated financial statements. The information required to be included in such summary financial statements includes:

■   A summary of the fair review of the development of the business included in the directors' report, as required by section 234(1)(a).

■   A summary of the particulars of any important post balance sheet events, as required by Schedule 7 paragraph 6(a).

■ A summary of the indication given of likely future developments of the business, as required by Schedule 7 paragraph 6(b).

■ A list of the names of directors as required by section 234(2).

4.35 A Format 1 summary consolidated profit and loss account is illustrated below and indicates references to the items in the full consolidated profit and loss account set out in paragraph 4.18 above some of which are required to be aggregated. Comparative figures are required to be given in the summary profit and loss account for the immediately preceding year. Also as indicated, the aggregate directors' emoluments has to be disclosed. The format will not cast from top to bottom.

SUMMARY CONSOLIDATED PROFIT AND LOSS ACCOUNT
FORMAT 1

Turnover	[1]	X
Income from interests in associated undertakings	[8]	X
Other interest receivable and similar income and interest payable and similar charges	[11+13]	X
Profit or loss on ordinary activities before tax		X
Tax on profit or loss on ordinary activities	[14]	X
Profit or loss on ordinary activities after tax	[15]	X
Minority interests	[16]	X
Extraordinary income and charges after tax and minority interests	[19+20+21]	X
Profit or loss for the financial year	[23]	X
Dividend paid and proposed		X
Directors emoluments	[6 Sch 1(1)]	X

4.36 For the summary consolidated balance sheet the regulations require that the main headings under the formats should be disclosed. For example, the disclosure for a summary consolidated balance sheet under Format 1 would look as set out below. The letters in brackets refer to the full Format 1 balance sheet given in paragraph 4.7 above. Comparative figures are also required.

SUMMARY CONSOLIDATED BALANCE SHEET

Called-up share capital not paid	[A]		X
Fixed assets	[B]		X
Current assets	[C]	X	
Prepayments and accrued income	[D]	X	
Creditors: amounts falling due within one year	[E]	(X)	
Net current assets (liabilities)	[F]		X

Total assets less current liabilities	[G]	X
Creditors: amounts falling due after more than one year	[H]	X
Provisions for liabilities and charges	[I]	X
Accruals and deferred income	[J]	$\frac{X}{\overline{\overline{X}}}$
Capital and reserves	[L]	X
Minority interests	[M]	$\frac{X}{\overline{\overline{X}}}$

4.37 Where there are alternate positions in the formats for particular items, then the summary balance sheet must use the same position used for the item as used in the full balance sheet.

Transitional provisions

4.38 For summary financial statements issued for a financial year beginning prior to 23rd December 1989 the formats set out above should be modified as follows:

■ Summary consolidated profit and loss account.

   □ Item 8 should be replaced by 'income from shares in related companies'.

   □ Item 16 'minority interest' is not required to be shown. This is because this heading does not appear in the profit and loss account formats in Schedule 4 and, therefore, cannot be required to be disclosed. However, it is likely that most groups would wish to give this figure to accord with the spirit of the legislation.

   □ The aggregate of items 19, 20 and 21 does not need to include the minority interests in extraordinary items. However, as mentioned above, groups may wish to comply with the spirit of the legislation and include this amount.

■ The summary consolidated balance sheet is also not required to include the item for 'minority interests' because it does not appear in the Schedule 4 balance sheet formats. However groups should give this information for completeness and in order that the balance sheet should cast.

4.39 There is also a provision in the regulations that allows a company to issue summary financial statements for a period beginning prior to 23rd December 1989, even where its articles of association prohibit such a document. However, in order to issue summary financial statements in any subsequent year, the company will have to alter its articles of association accordingly.

Concessions for private companies

4.40   The Companies Act 1989 also introduced a number of concessions that apply to private companies. These concessions will reduce the administrative burden for groups, because many subsidiaries will be able to take advantage of them. The concessions relate to the areas summarised below:

■   Election to dispense with submitting financial statements to a general meeting.

■   Business may be transacted in most situations by written resolutions, therefore, doing away with the need to hold company meetings.

■   Election to dispense with annual general meetings.

4.41   These provisions of the Act are considered in detail in 'Manual of Accounting - volume I' chapter 25.

Additional disclosure concerning subsidiaries

4.42   Certain additional information has to be given for all subsidiaries and this is detailed in Schedule 5 to the Act. The disclosure requirements are split into the following categories:

■   Information about subsidiaries included in the consolidation. These disclosure requirements are considered below.

■   Information concerning any subsidiaries that are excluded from consolidation. This information is considered in chapter 3 paragraph 3.87.

■   Information required concerning subsidiaries when the parent does not prepare consolidated financial statements. These provisions are considered in detail in 'Manual of Accounting - volume I' chapter 9.

Place of origin and reason for consolidation

4.43   The Act requires disclosure of the following information concerning subsidiary undertakings:

■   Names of each subsidiary undertaking.

- The country of incorporation, if incorporated outside Great Britain.

- If incorporated in Great Britain, whether it is registered in England and Wales or Scotland.

- The address of the principal place of business if the undertaking is unincorporated.

- Whether the subsidiary is included in the consolidation, and if not, the reasons for excluding it.

[5 Sch 15(1) to (4)].

This type of disclosure is illustrated in Table 13 overleaf.

4.44   Furthermore, it is necessary to disclose the particular definition of 'subsidiary undertaking' that makes an undertaking a subsidiary under the provisions of the Act. [5 Sch 15(5)]. However, there is an exemption where the undertaking is a subsidiary because the parent holds a majority of its voting rights and the immediate parent holds the same proportion of shares in the subsidiary as it holds voting rights. This will obviously be the reason for consolidating most subsidiaries and, consequently, disclosure will only be required for other subsidiary undertakings, of which there will be relatively few.

Holdings in subsidiary undertakings

4.45   The following information has to be given separately (where different) concerning the subsidiary's shares held by the parent and the group:

- The identity of each class of shares held.

- The percentage held of the nominal value of each of those classes of shares.

[5 Sch 16].

This type of disclosure is illustrated in Table 13 overleaf.

4.46   Shares that are held on the parent's or group's behalf by any other person should be treated for this purpose as if they are held by the parent. [5 Sch 32(1)(2)(a)(3)]. However, shares held on behalf of a third party other than the parent or the group should be disregarded for this purpose. [5 Sch 32(3)].

Table 13: Illustration of the type of information required to be disclosed concerning principal subsidiaries.

Extract from Reuters Holdings PLC Annual Report 31st December 1988.

Note extract

24 Subsidiary and related companies [*now participating interests*]
The principal trading subsidiary and related [*now participating interests*] companies at 31 December 1988 are shown below. The shares in Reuters Limited were held by Reuters Holdings PLC. The shares in the other companies were held by Reuters Limited or its wholly owned subsidiaries.

	Country of incorporation	Principal country of operation	Percentage of equity shares held
Subsidiary companies			
Supply of general, economic and financial news			
Reuter Nederland BV	Netherlands	Netherlands	100%
Reuter Services SARL	France	France	100%
Reuters AG	West Germany	West Germany	100%
Reuters Australia Pty Limited	Australia	Australia	100%
Reuters Hong Kong Limited	Cook Islands	Hong Kong	100%
Reuters Information Services Inc.	USA	USA	100%
Reuters Italia S.p.A.	Italy	Italy	100%
Reuters Japan Kabushiki Kaisha	Japan	Japan	100%
Reuters Limited	Great Britain	Worldwide	99.4%
Reuters SA	Switzerland	Switzerland	100%
Design of communication and financial trading systems			
Rich Inc.	USA	USA	100%
L.H.W. Wyatt Brothers Limited	Great Britain	Great Britain	100%
Financial markets access networks and databases			
Instinet Corporation	USA	USA	100%
I.P. Sharp Associates Limited	Canada	Worldwide	100%
Television news agency			
Visnews Limited	Great Britain	Worldwide	88.75%
Manufacture of equipment			
IDR Inc.	USA	USA	100%
Related company [*now participating interests under Companies Act 1989*]			
Provision of communications facilities			
AAP Reuters Communications Pty Limited	Australia	Australia	43.8%

The issued share capital of AAP Reuters Communications Pty Limited at 31 December 1988 was 19,639,000 shares of A$ 1 each.
The financial years for the above subsidiary and related companies end on 31 December.

Financial years of subsidiaries

4.47   Where a subsidiary's financial year does not coincide with its parent's financial year, the notes to the consolidated financial statements must disclose:

■   The reasons why the directors consider it inappropriate for the subsidiary's financial year to coincide with the parent's financial year.

■   The balance sheet date of the subsidiaries involved ended last before the balance sheet of the parent or the earliest and the latest of those dates.

[5 Sch 19; SSAP 14 para 18].

4.48   In addition, SSAP 14 requires that the notes should disclose, for each principal subsidiary that has a different accounting date, its name, its accounting date and the reasons for using a different accounting date. If a principal subsidiary's accounting period is of a different length from that of the holding company, this accounting period should also be stated. [SSAP 14 para 18].

4.49   The requirements concerning non-coterminous year ends are considered further in chapter 5.

Company shares and debentures held by subsidiaries

4.50   A subsidiary company cannot generally own shares in its holding company. [Sec 23(1)]. This provision extends to sub-subsidiaries holding shares in their immediate holding companies and also their ultimate holding companies. However, the prohibition does not apply where the subsidiary is acting as a personal representative for a third party, or as a trustee. This exemption only applies, however, where the subsidiary or a holding company is not beneficially interested under the trust. [Sec 23(2)]. The provision also does not extend to market makers. [Sec 23(3)]. This prohibition also includes those shares that might be held on behalf of the subsidiary by another person as its nominee. [Sec 23(7)].

4.51   Where a corporate body becomes a subsidiary company because of the changes in the definition of subsidiaries included in section 736 of the Act, it may retain any shares that it already held in its parent. However, where shares are held in this way, they will carry no right to vote at company meetings. [Sec 23(4)].

4.52   In certain situations a subsidiary may find that it does hold shares in its parent. This may arise, for example, where the parent has recently acquired a subsidiary which owned shares in the parent before it became a group member. Before the introduction of the Companies Act 1989, the effect of section 23(1) of the Act was unclear. Now, section 23 expressly provides that, where a company acquires shares in its parent but before it becomes a subsidiary of the parent, it may retain those shares. In this circumstance also, those shares will carry no right to vote at company meetings. [Sec 23(5)].

4.53 The notes to a parent's financial statements must disclose the number, the description and the amount of any of its shares or debentures that subsidiaries or their nominees hold. [5 Sch 20(1)]. This information is not required, however, where the subsidiary holds the shares or debentures as personal representative or as a trustee. [5 Sch 20(2)]. However, the exemption for a subsidiary acting as a trustee will not be available if the company or any of its subsidiaries is beneficially interested under the trust, unless the beneficial interest is by way of security for the purpose of a transaction entered into by it in the ordinary course of business, which includes the lending of money. [5 Sch 20(3)].

Significant investment holdings of the parent or group

4.54 Where the parent or any of its subsidiaries have *significant holdings* in undertakings, certain additional information has to be given in the consolidated financial statements. A 'significant holding' means one where the investment in the undertaking concerned amounts to ten per cent or more of the nominal value of *any class* of shares in the undertaking. [5 Sch 23(2)(a),26(2)(a)]. (Joint ventures and associated undertakings are considered separately in chapter 11.)

4.55 The disclosure is also required where the holding by the parent or its subsidiaries exceeds ten per cent of the amount of the parent's, or the group's, assets. [5 Sch 23(2)(b),26(2)(b)]. The information to be disclosed is as follows:

■ The name of the undertaking.

■ The country of incorporation of the undertaking, if it is incorporated outside Great Britain,

■ Whether the undertaking is registered in England and Wales or in Scotland, if it is incorporated in Great Britain.

■ The address of its principal place of business, if it is unincorporated.

■ The identity of each class of shares held.

- The percentage held of the nominal value of each of those classes of shares.

[5 Sch 24,27].

4.56 Furthermore, certain additional information is required to be disclosed in the consolidated financial statements where a parent or any of its subsidiaries has a significant holding in an undertaking amounting to 20 per cent or more of the nominal value of the shares in the undertaking. This information is as follows:

- The aggregate amount of the capital and reserves of the undertaking at the end of its 'relevant year'. Relevant year means the year ending with, or last before, that of the company

- Its profit or loss for the year.

[5 Sch 25(1)(4),28(1)(4)].

4.57 This additional information need not be disclosed if the undertaking is not required by the Act to deliver to the Registrar of Companies a copy of its balance sheet and does not otherwise publish it (for example, a partnership). However, this exemption only applies where the company's holding is less than 50 per cent of the nominal value of the undertaking's shares. [5 Sch 25(2),28(2)]. Consequently, this exemption is likely to apply to investments in partnerships that are not subsidiaries. The information is also not required if it is immaterial.

4.58 For investments in unincorporated undertakings with capital, 'shares' for the purposes of the paragraphs above means the rights to share in the capital of the undertaking, by virtue of section 259(2)(b). In respect of an undertaking that does not have capital the term 'shares' refers to any right to share in the profits or liability to contribute to losses of the undertaking, or an obligation to contribute to its debts or expenses on winding up. [Sec 259(2)(c)].

Interpretation of 'shares held by the group'

4.59 In the paragraphs above, reference to shares held by the group are to shares held by the parent company or any of its subsidiaries, or to shares held on their behalf. However, such references do not include shares held on behalf of third parties. [5 Sch 32(3)]. Furthermore, shares held by way of security must be treated as held by the person providing the security where both the following apply:

- The rights attached to the shares are exercisable only in accordance with that person's instructions (apart from the right to exercise them for the purpose of preserving the value of the security or of realising it).

■ The shares are held in connection with granting loans as part of normal business activities and the rights attached to the shares are exercisable only in that person's interest (apart from the right to exercise them for the purpose of preserving the value of the security, or of realising it).

[5 Sch 32(4)].

Disclosure 'seriously prejudicial'

4.60 In certain circumstances, the information required by Schedule 5 concerning subsidiaries and other significant holdings in undertakings (summarised above) need not be given where the undertaking is established under the law of a country outside the United Kingdom, or carries on business outside the United Kingdom. [Sec 231 (3)]. The situations where this exemption will apply are where, in the directors' opinion, disclosing information would be *seriously prejudicial* to the business of that undertaking, or to the business of the parent company, or to any of the parent's subsidiaries. Permission to exclude the information also needs to be obtained from the Secretary of State before advantage can be taken of this exemption.

4.61 The previous legislation had a similar exemption that applied if, in the opinion of the directors, disclosure would be *harmful* to the business of the company or to any of its subsidiaries. The wording in the new legislation has been tightened to apply now only in situations where disclosure would be seriously prejudicial.

4.62 The exemption does not apply, however, to the information required by paragraph 20 of Schedule 5, which is summarised in paragraph 4.53 above.

Disclosure of excessive information

4.63 There is a further relaxation of the disclosure requirements of Schedule 5 that applies if, in the directors' opinion, the resulting disclosure would be excessively lengthy. This will often be the situation where the group has a significant number of subsidiaries. Where this is so, the directors need only give the required information concerning the undertakings whose results or financial position principally affect the figures shown in the company's annual accounts. [Sec 231(5)]. However, the directors are required to give the necessary information that relates to undertakings excluded from consolidation, except where they are excluded on the ground of materiality (see further chapter 3 para 3.87).

4.64 Where the directors take advantage of this exemption, they have to note in the financial statements that the information given is only in respect of principal subsidiaries and significant investments (see for example Table 14). [Sec 231(6)(a)]. In addition, the full information (including that disclosed in the financial statements) has to be annexed to the parent's next annual return. [Sec 231(6)(b)].

Table 14: Example of the reason given to exclude excessive information concerning subsidiaries.

Extract from The RTZ Corporation PLC annual report and accounts 31st December 1988.

1 The RTZ Group comprises a large number of companies but it is not practical to include all of them in this list. The list therefore only includes those companies which principally affect the profit or assets of the Group.

Disclosure of holding company

4.65 Under the Act, a subsidiary has to name its ultimate holding company and indicate where that company was incorporated (or registered if incorporated in Great Britain). In addition, the provisions of the Companies Act 1989 go further and require that where a parent company is itself a subsidiary it should disclose the following information concerning its *ultimate holding company* (which includes any other type of corporate body):

■ Its name.

■ The country of incorporation, if incorporated outside Great Britain.

■ Whether it is registered in England and Wales or in Scotland, if it is incorporated in Great Britain.

[5 Sch 31].

This type of disclosure is illustrated in Table 15.

Table 15: Note disclosing the ultimate holding company.

Extract from Ford Motor Company Limited Annual Report & Accounts 31st December 1988.

Note extract

22	*Ford Motor Company Limited is a wholly owned subsidiary of Ford Motor Company,*
Ultimate	*Dearborn, Michigan, USA.*
holding	
company	

4.66 This provision applies both to companies that prepare consolidated financial statements and to companies that have subsidiaries, but that are not required to prepare consolidated financial statements.

4.67 Furthermore, where the parent company is itself a subsidiary, similar information has to be disclosed for the parent undertaking that heads the following:

- The largest group of undertakings that prepares consolidated financial statements which include the sub-group either by consolidation or by equity accounting.

- The smallest group of undertakings that prepares consolidated financial statements which include the sub-group either by consolidation or by equity accounting.

[5 Sch 30(1)].

4.68 The information to be disclosed in respect of both these undertakings is similar to that required by paragraph 4.65 above:

- The name of the parent undertaking.

- The country of incorporation of the undertaking, if it is incorporated outside Great Britain.

- Whether the undertaking is registered in England and Wales or in Scotland, if it is incorporated in Great Britain.

- The address of its principal place of business, if it is unincorporated.

- If copies of the undertaking's consolidated financial statements are available for the public, then the address where copies of the financial statements can be obtained.

[5 Sch 30(2)(3)(4)].

4.69 Where the ultimate parent company prepares consolidated financial statements, the information in paragraph 4.68 disclosed in the sub-group parent's financial statements need be given only for the ultimate parent and for the smallest group of undertakings that prepare consolidated financial statements which include the sub-group (if such an undertaking exists). [5 Sch 30(1)].

4.70 However, where the ultimate parent does not prepare consolidated financial statements, the information in paragraph 4.65 above has to be disclosed in the sub-group parent's financial statements. In addition, the information set out in paragraph 4.68 may also be required to be

disclosed concerning the largest and smallest group that prepare
consolidated financial statements which include the subgroup.

4.71 These provisions can be very confusing and are best illustrated by an
example. Consider the group structure set out in the diagram below.

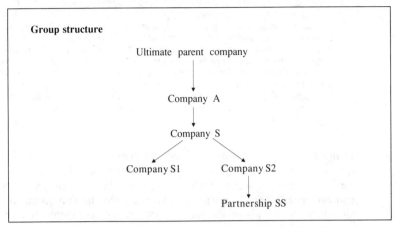

Group structure

Ultimate parent company

Company A

Company S

Company S1   Company S2

Partnership SS

In the situation where the ultimate parent company **does prepare** consolidated financial
statements, the following disclosure applies:

☐   Company A will have to disclose for the ultimate parent company (being the
largest group parent) the information set out in paragraphs 4.65 and 4.68 above by
virtue of paragraphs 31 and 30 of Schedule 5.

☐   Company S will have to disclose for company A the information set out in
paragraph 4.68 above by virtue of paragraph 30 of Schedule 5 (if company A
prepares consolidated financial statements as it is the smallest group parent).
Company S will also have to give for the ultimate parent company (being also the
largest group parent) the information set out in paragraphs 4.65 and 4.68 above by
virtue of paragraphs 31 and 30 of Schedule 5.

☐   Company S2 will have to disclose for the ultimate parent company (being also the
largest group parent) the information set out in paragraph 4.65 and 4.68 above by
virtue of paragraphs 31 and 30 of Schedule 5. If company S prepares consolidated
financial statements, then company S2 will also have to disclose for company S
(being the smallest group parent) the information set out in paragraph 4.68 above
by virtue of paragraph 30 of Schedule 5. Where company S does not prepare
consolidated financial statements, then company S2 has to give the same
information for company A (if company A prepares consolidated financial
statements as it is the smallest group parent)).

In the situation where the ultimate parent company **does not** prepare consolidated
financial statements, the following disclosure applies:

☐   Company A will have to disclose for the ultimate parent company the information
set out in paragraph 4.65 above by virtue of paragraph 31 of Schedule 5.

☐   Company S will have to disclose for company A the information set out in
paragraph 4.68 above by virtue of paragraph 30 of Schedule 5 (if company A
prepares consolidated financial statements as it is the largest group parent).
Company S will also have to give for the ultimate parent company the information
set out in paragraph 4.65 above by virtue of paragraph 31 of Schedule 5.

☐ Company S2 will have to disclose for the ultimate parent company the information set out in paragraph 4.65 above by virtue of paragraph 31 of Schedule 5. If company A prepares consolidated financial statements it is the largest group parent and company S2 will have to disclose for company A the information set out in paragraph 4.68 above by virtue of paragraph 30 of Schedule 5. In addition, the same information will have to be given for company S (if company S prepares consolidated financial statements as it is the smallest group parent). This means that in the situation described, company S2 is required to disclose information concerning three parent companies. Furthermore the situation might arise, for example, where another intermediate holding undertaking exists in the group structure between company S and company A. Even where such an undertaking prepares consolidated financial statements company S2 is still only required to give information concerning company A and company S. This is because the legislation only requires the information concerned to be disclosed for the largest and smallest groups preparing consolidated financial statements and is not concerned with other intermediate parents in between that prepare consolidated financial statements.

4.72 In practice in the majority of situations, these provisions will mean that the information required by paragraph 4.68 above will have to be given for the next holding undertaking in the group that prepares consolidated financial statements that included the sub-group, and will also have to be given for the ultimate parent company that prepares consolidated financial statements.

4.73 As mentioned above, all subsidiaries that do not prepare consolidated financial statements have to disclose the name of the ultimate parent company (which includes any corporate body) in their individual financial statements. [5 Sch 12(2)]. In addition, if known by the subsidiary's directors, the following has to be disclosed concerning the ultimate parent company:

■ Its country of incorporation, if outside Great Britain.

■ Whether it is registered in England and Wales, or in Scotland, if is incorporated in Great Britain.

[5 Sch 12(3)].

Corresponding amounts

4.74 Normally all matters disclosed in the consolidated financial statements require corresponding information to be given for the previous financial year. [4 Sch 4]. However, there are certain areas where corresponding information is not required by Schedule 4 to the Act and these exceptions apply also to consolidated financial statements. The exceptions are as follows:

■ Certain details of the accounting treatment of acquisitions required by paragraph 13 of Schedule 4A (see chapter 6 para 6.48). [4 Sch 58(3)(a)].

■ Details concerning the identity and class of shares held in subsidiary undertakings required by paragraphs 2 and 16 of Schedule 5 (see para 4.45). [4 Sch 58(3)(b)].

■ Details concerning the identity and class of shares held in undertakings where the investment is 10 per cent or more of any class of shares required by paragraphs 8(3), 24(3)(4) and 27(3)(4) of Schedule 5 (see para 4.55). [4 Sch 58(3)(b)].

■ The proportion of capital held in joint ventures required by paragraph 21(1)(d) of Schedule 5 (see chapter 11). [4 Sch 58(3)(b)].

■ The identity and proportion of each class of shares held in associated undertakings required by paragraph 22(4)(5) of Schedule 5 (see chapter 11). [4 Sch 58(3)(b)].

■ Loans and other dealings in favour of directors and others required by Parts II and III of Schedule 6. [4 Sch 58(3)(c)].

■ Movements on fixed assets required by paragraph 42 of Schedule 4. [4 Sch 58(3)(d)].

■ Movements on reserves and provisions required by paragraph 46 of Schedule 4. [4 Sch 58(3)(d)].

Disclosure of directors' emoluments and transactions

4.75 Schedule 6 to the Act sets out the disclosure requirements concerning directors' emoluments. Prior to the Companies Act 1989 an exemption was included in paragraph 63 of Schedule 4 which meant that the disclosure requirements concerning directors' emoluments did not apply to consolidated financial statements. Paragraph 1(2) of Schedule 6 makes it clear, however, that the aggregate emoluments to be disclosed are those received by the directors for their services as directors of the parent and emoluments received in respect of their services as directors of subsidiaries. (See further 'Manual of Accounting - volume I' chapter 17.)

4.76 The rules that the group has to follow concerning disclosing transactions with its directors are dealt with in parts II and III of Schedule 6. The disclosure required concerns primarily the directors of the parent company. The detailed disclosure requirements concerning directors loans and transactions together with the rules concerning directors' emoluments are considered in detail in 'Manual of Accounting - volume I'.

Chapter 5

BASIC CONSOLIDATION RULES

BASIC CONSOLIDATION RULES

Introduction

5.1 Consolidated financial statements must give a true and fair view, so far as they concern the holding company's shareholders, of the state of affairs and the profit or loss of the company and those of its subsidiaries included in the consolidated financial statements as a whole. [Sec 227(3)]. As with individual financial statements, this is an overriding requirement. This overriding requirement is explained in chapter 2 paragraph 2.19.

5.2 In addition to the overriding requirement to give a true and fair view, the Act includes various accounting rules that apply to consolidated financial statements. In general, these provisions correspond to those that apply to an individual company's financial statements. Consequently, consolidated financial statements must comply with the requirements of Schedule 4 to the Act both as to their form and content and as to the information they must disclose in the notes (to the extent that this Schedule applies to consolidated financial statements). The historical cost accounting rules and the alternative accounting rules set out in Schedule 4 to the Act apply equally to consolidated financial statements as they do to individual companies' financial statements. These rules are considered in detail in 'Manual of Accounting - volume I' chapters 4 and 5.

5.3 Furthermore, Schedule 2 to the Companies Act 1989 introduced a new Schedule 4A to the Companies Act 1985. This Schedule details the rules concerning the form and content of consolidated financial statements and introduced into UK company law the majority of the 7th Directive's provisions. One exception to these consolidation rules is that if any member of a group is a banking or an insurance company the Schedule 4 and 4A formats are not appropriate and, consequently, the group may prepare its consolidated financial statements in accordance with Schedule 9 to the Act. Banking and insurance companies are considered in 'Manual of Accounting - volume III'.

5.4 If, at the end of the financial year, a company has one or more subsidiaries, consolidated financial statements must be prepared in addition to the holding company's individual financial statements. The consolidated financial statements should deal with the state of affairs and the profit or loss of the company and its subsidiaries. [Sec 227(2)].

5.5 SSAP 14 specifies additional rules that groups must comply with. It similarly requires that a holding company should prepare group accounts in the form of a single set of consolidated financial statements covering the holding company and its subsidiary companies (both UK and overseas). [SSAP 14 para 15].

5.6   The only exceptions to the general rules outlined in paragraph 5.4 above are considered in chapter 3 paragraphs 3.53 to 3.83.

5.7   The particular provisions in Schedule 4A to the Act and the provisions in SSAP 14 that form the basic consolidation rules are explained below, together with other rules that have become generally accepted accounting principles through their general use in preparing consolidations.

Generally accepted accounting principles

5.8   Consolidated financial statements have to incorporate all of the information contained in the individual financial statements of the undertakings included in the consolidation. [4A Sch 2(1)]. However, this provision is subject to adjustments authorised by the new Schedule 4A and to any adjustments that are necessary in order to accord with "generally accepted accounting principles or practice". Although the term in the Act incorporates the word 'practice', the term is more often referred to by accountants as 'Generally Accepted Accounting Principles' (GAAP). This is the first time that such a term has been recognised in UK law, although the term GAAP is recognised in other countries (for example, in the US and in Canada). The term UK GAAP is one that means generally accepted accounting principles that apply to UK companies and groups and that encompass UK law, accounting standards, The International Stock Exchange accounting requirements (if appropriate) and other generally accepted accounting practices. An illustration of the use of the term UK GAAP is given in Table 16.

5.9   The accounting principles that are used in the consolidation process should be disclosed in the accounting policies note to the consolidated financial statements. This note generally covers the following matters:

■   The methods of accounting used to consolidate subsidiaries, that is either of the following:

☐   Acquisition accounting (see chapter 6).

☐   Merger accounting (see chapter 9).

Different consolidation methods may be used for different subsidiaries and the accounting policy disclosure may also note whether merger relief has been taken by the parent company (see chapter 9).

■ The treatment of any goodwill arising on consolidation, and the treatment of other differences arising on consolidation (see further chapters 6 and 9 respectively).

■ The treatment of purchases and sales of subsidiaries during the financial year (see paras 5.48 and 5.49 below).

■ The translation of overseas subsidiaries' financial statements (see chapter 12).

■ How minority interests are dealt with (see chapter 10).

■ How associated companies and joint ventures are dealt with (see chapter 11).

■ The treatment of intra-group transactions (see para 5.33 below)

Table 16: Example of a statement that the consolidated financial statements are prepared in accordance with UK GAAP.

Extract from Cadbury Schweppes Public Limited Company Annual Report 31st December 1988.

Additional information for US investors – extract

The group prepares its consolidated accounts in accordance with generally accepted accounting principles ("GAAP") applicable in the UK.

The terms and principles used are explained on pages 45 and 46 and differ from those applicable in the US. The effect of such differences and an explanation of the accounting terms and principles are set out below.

| | Per UK GAAP | | Per US GAAP | |
| | 1987 | 1988 | 1987 | 1988 |
EFFECT OF DIFFERENCES	£m	£m	£m	£m
Operating income	180.6	228.8	178.9	277.3
Income before tax	176.1	215.7	177.9	269.7
Net income (as below)	109.3	140.5	123.4	156.1
Shareholders' equity	476.7	486.0	651.0	770.6

Procedure for consolidation

5.10 As mentioned in paragraph 5.8 above, the Act specifies that the consolidated balance sheet and the consolidated profit and loss account should incorporate in full the information contained in the individual financial statements of the undertakings included in the consolidation, subject to certain consolidation adjustments. [4A Sch 2(1)]. However, it does not specify how the aggregation of this information should be undertaken.

5.11 SSAP 14 comments only that the method for preparing consolidated financial statements on an item by item basis, eliminating intra-group balances and transactions and unrealised intra-group profit, is well understood and does not deal further with the matter. [SSAP 14 para 3]. IAS 27, 'Consolidated financial statements and accounting for investments in subsidiaries', mentions that, in preparing consolidated financial statements, the financial statements of the parent and its subsidiaries are combined on a line by line basis by adding together like items of assets, liabilities, income and expenses. [IAS 27 para 13]. IAS 27 then goes on to mention some of the steps in the consolidation process. These are very similar in nature to the matters mentioned in paragraph 5.9 above.

5.12 In practice, there are two methods of preparing consolidated financial statements. The first method takes the individual financial statements of subsidiaries and aggregates the profit and loss account and balance sheet figures on a line by line basis. These aggregate figures are then amended to deal with consolidation adjustments. Such adjustments would be necessary in order to:

■ Adjust individual figures in the financial statements of subsidiaries to bring them onto a common basis for consolidation (see paras 5.15 to 5.21 below).

■ Adjustments to achieve the consolidation (see paras 5.22 to 5.24 below).

5.13 A second method, more suitable for large groups, is for each subsidiary to prepare a consolidation return. The consolidation return is made up from the individual subsidiary's financial statements which are:

■ Adjusted onto a common consolidation basis.

■ Edited into a format and analysis appropriate to produce consolidated figures.

These returns are then aggregated to form the group's consolidated financial statements.

Consolidation adjustments

5.14 There are a number of reasons why a parent may wish to make consolidation adjustments to its subsidiaries' financial statements in preparing the group's consolidated financial statements. Some of these reasons and the rules relating to such adjustments are considered below.

Uniform accounting polices

5.15   When preparing consolidated financial statements, the group should
        follow uniform accounting policies. Where a subsidiary does not follow
        the group's uniform policies in preparing its own financial statements,
        appropriate adjustments should be made in the consolidated financial
        statements. The need for such consolidation adjustments should not
        arise frequently in a group that operates wholly within the UK,
        because all UK companies are expected to follow SSAPs.

5.16   If a new subsidiary is acquired that applies an accounting policy that
        differs from the group's policy, the new subsidiary has a sufficient
        reason to change its policy and to make a prior-year adjustment in
        accordance with SSAP 6 . Alternatively, adjustments can be made on
        consolidation to achieve uniform accounting policies. An illustration is
        given in Table 17.

*Table 17: Accounting policy note illustrating alignment of accounting
policies to those of the group for companies acquired.*

*Extract from MARKS AND SPENCERS p.l.c. Annual Report and
Financial Statements 31st March 1989.*

Goodwill
Goodwill arising on consolidation, which represents the excess of the consideration given over the
fair value of the net tangible assets acquired, is written off on acquisition against reserves. The net
assets of companies acquired are incorporated into the consolidated accounts at their fair values to
the group and after adjustments to bring the acounting policies of companies acquired into
alignment with those of the Group.

5.17   Where it is impracticable to adopt for a subsidiary the same
        accounting policies as the group on consolidation, the group may use
        different policies for that subsidiary, provided that:

■   They are generally acceptable.

■   They are disclosed in the consolidated financial statements.

■   The consolidated financial statements indicate the amounts of
    assets and liabilities involved.

■   The consolidated financial statements indicate, where practicable,
    the effect the different policy has had on the group's results and
    net assets.

■   The consolidated financial statements give the reasons for the
    different treatment.

[SSAP 14 para 16].

5.18   The Act specifically requires consolidation adjustments to be made where a subsidiary undertaking's assets and liabilities have been valued using accounting rules that differ from those used by the group. [4A Sch 3(1)]. For example, the need for such an adjustment would arise where a subsidiary values its stocks using a LIFO method of valuation. In the UK LIFO stock valuations are not allowed for UK corporation tax purposes and are considered in SSAP 9 to be likely to be incompatible with the requirement to give a true and fair view. Such valuations are, however, allowed for both tax and accounting purposes in other countries, for example South Africa and the US, and, consequently, subsidiaries that operate in those countries may value their stocks on that basis. Clearly, when such subsidiaries are consolidated, an adjustment will be required to bring the stock valuations onto a basis acceptable in the UK (for example, FIFO or average cost). Such a situation is illustrated in Table 18.

> **Table 18: Illustration of an accounting policy concerning consolidation adjustments made to bring subsidiaries' financial statements onto a UK GAAP basis.**
>
> *Extract from Grand Metropolitan Public Limited Company Annual Report 30th September 1989.*
>
> ## Accounting policies extract
>
> Overseas subsidiaries
> The financial statements of some overseas subsidiaries do not conform with the group's accounting policies because of the legislation and accouting practices of the countries concerned. Appropriate adjustments are made on consolidation in order to present the group financial statements on a uniform basis.

5.19   However in certain situations, the parent's directors might consider that there are special reasons for retaining the different accounting rules adopted by the subsidiary. Where this is so, the Act's provisions require that particulars of the departure, the reasons for it and its effect should be disclosed in the notes to the consolidated financial statements. [4A Sch 3(2)]. This is, in effect, the information required by SSAP 14 outlined in paragraph 5.17 above.

5.20   Similarly, if the accounting policies used by the parent in its individual financial statements differ from those of the group, these differences are required to be disclosed by the Act in the notes to the consolidated financial statements and the reason for the difference must be given. [4A Sch 4]. For example, this could arise where the parent records the cost of an investment in a subsidiary at its nominal value having taken merger relief (see further chapter 9). In this situation, the group may account for the subsidiary using acquisition accounting and a consolidation adjustment is then necessary to bring the investment's value to fair value in order to calculate the goodwill arising on consolidation.

5.21 Problems can arise with overseas subsidiaries in applying uniform accounting policies. Where the subsidiaries are subject to either company law or tax law that is different from that in the UK, it may not always be practicable for the parent to insist that the subsidiaries change their accounting policies to bring them into line with the group's accounting policies. For example, under the tax law of a number of European countries, provisions for accelerated depreciation and other items have to be incorporated in the statutory financial statements in order to qualify for tax relief. In these circumstances, it would obviously not be in the group's best interests for the UK parent to insist that the foreign subsidiary company should depreciate, in its statutory financial statements, its fixed assets over their estimated useful lives, in accordance with the Act and SSAP 12. Therefore, to comply with the provisions of both the Act and SSAP 14, an appropriate consolidation adjustment should be made.

Other consolidation adjustments

5.22 Consolidation adjustments may be required for a variety of reasons, for example, for any of the reasons given below:

■ To eliminate pre-acquisition reserves (see chapter 6).

■ To set up, or write off, goodwill on consolidation (see chapter 8).

■ To deal with the differences that arise on consolidation when merger accounting is used (see chapter 9).

■ To account for minority interests (see chapter 10).

■ To deal with abnormal transactions that arise between the year end of a subsidiary and the year end of its parent (see para 5.32 below).

■ To eliminate the effects of intra-group trading and indebtedness (see para 5.33 below).

■ To translate the results of overseas subsidiaries (see chapter 12).

5.23 A consolidation adjustment may be necessary also where a material 'subsequent event' occurs in a subsidiary between the date when the subsidiary's directors sign the subsidiary's own financial statements and the date when the holding company's directors sign the consolidated financial statements. If the 'subsequent event' is material to the group and is an 'adjusting event' (as defined in SSAP 17 - see 'Manual of Accounting - volume I' chapter 20), a consolidation adjustment should be made for it in the consolidated financial statements.

5.24 It is debatable, however, whether some other adjustments that are made 'on consolidation' and do not relate to the process of consolidation are permissible. For example, a group could set up a provision on consolidation for redundancies in a subsidiary, which it intends to run down. In this situation, it would be unlikely that the subsidiary's financial statements could give a true and fair view without that provision being reflected in them.

Subsidiary year ends

5.25 The Companies Act 1989 has brought into force a significant change with regard to the financial statements of subsidiaries that can be used for consolidation. Under the previous legislation, the parent's directors had, wherever practicable, to ensure that the financial year end of each of its subsidiaries coincided with the company's own financial year. This applied unless the directors considered that there were good reasons why subsidiaries should not have had coterminous year ends. [CA 1985 Sec 227(4) as originally enacted]. However, where the year ends did not coincide, a parent was allowed to consolidate the financial statements of a subsidiary whose year ended before, or on the same date as, its own year end. [CA 1985 Sec 230(7) as originally enacted]. There was, therefore, no restriction on the period allowed between the subsidiary's year end and that of the parent. For example, an Australian subsidiary could have made up its financial statements to 30th June 1989 and these could have been consolidated with those of a UK parent's made up to 31st December 1989. The parent could have required the subsidiary to make up management accounts for the six months to 31st December 1989, but as the Secretary of State's permission would have been required before those management accounts could be consolidated, few groups chose to do so.

5.26 The Companies Act 1989 requires that the financial statements of a subsidiary may not be consolidated if its accounting period ends more than three months before that of its parent. [4A Sch 2(2)(a)]. If the subsidiary's financial year ends before this period, it has to prepare interim financial statements to coincide with the end of the parent company's financial year. [4A Sch 2(2)(b)]. Where this latter provision is applied, the Secretary of State's permission is no longer required. Table 19 illustrates this type of situation. Consequently in the example given above and if the new rules were to apply in 1990, the subsidiary would have to make up interim financial statements to 31st December 1990 for consolidation purposes. The subsidiary could not, however, make up its interim financial statements to (say) 30th November 1990. Also, as corresponding amounts are required, additional interim financial statements to 31st December 1989 would be needed.

Table 19: Example of a group that consolidates management accounts for certain subsidiaries made up to coincide with the group's year end.

Extract from Ford Motor Company Limited Annual Report & Accounts 31st December 1988.

Note extract

	Beneficial interest	Reference date	Country of incorporation	Principal activity
Subsidiary companies				
Ford Motor Credit Company Limited	100%	31 December	England	Finance company
Automotive Finance Limited	100%	30 June	England	Finance company
Ford Automotive Leasing Limited	100%	30 September	England	Finance company
Ford Financial Trust Limited	100%	31 December	England	Finance company
Ford Lease Financing Limited	100%	31 March	England	Finance company

For commercial reasons certain companies have accounting reference dates other than 31 December as noted above. The profit and loss accounts and balance sheets of these subsidiary companies have been consolidated on the basis of management accounts for the year to 31 December.

5.27 The Act reiterates the content of SSAP 14, which requires that all subsidiaries' financial statements should, wherever practicable, be prepared:

■ To the same accounting date as the holding company.

■ For identical accounting periods as the holding company.

[SSAP 14 para 17].

5.28 The interim financial statements are not required by the Act to be audited. However, they would have to be audited to some extent to satisfy the requirement that the group's consolidated financial statements have to be audited and give a true and fair view. Therefore, some audit work will have to be carried out on those interim financial statements, but it may be less detailed than the work carried out on the subsidiary's financial statements prepared for statutory purposes. This may be, for instance, because the audit work can be carried out based on materiality levels applicable to the group's consolidated financial statements.

5.29 Where a subsidiary's financial year does not coincide with that of its holding company the consolidated financial statements must disclose the following information concerning the subsidiary:

■ Its name.

■ Its accounting date.

■ The reason for using a different accounting date.

■ The accounting period if it is different in length from that of the parent.

[SSAP 14 para 18].

5.30   The last disclosure requirement in paragraph 5.29 above applies whether or not the subsidiary's year end coincides with that of its parent.

5.31   The requirements of the Companies Act 1989 accord with the rules in IAS 27, which requires that the financial statements of subsidiaries included in the consolidation should usually be drawn up to the same date. Where this is impracticable, however, the standard allows financial statements drawn up to another date to be used provided the difference between the year end of the parent and that of its subsidiary is not more than three months. [IAS 27 para 31].

5.32   Where a subsidiary's year end does differ from that of its parent, but it is within the three month limit and, therefore, the subsidiary's normal financial statements are used for consolidation purposes, certain adjustments may be required on consolidation. Consolidation adjustments may be necessary to deal with any abnormal transactions in the intervening period that might take place between, for example, the parent company and the subsidiary. Such adjustments would be required, for example, where the subsidiary pays a dividend to its parent in this period. Another example that would require adjustment is where a parent settles an inter-company transaction that was outstanding in the subsidiary's financial statements at its year end.

Elimination of intra-group transactions

5.33   In the past, there have been no rules concerning the elimination of intra-group transactions. Nevertheless, it has been accepted accounting practice to eliminate transactions between group members in the consolidated financial statements. SSAP 14 states that such eliminations should be made, but does not detail how, apart from stating that the method is well understood. [SSAP 14 para 3]. However, the Act now specifically requires *"debts and claims"* (that is, debts and liabilities) between group undertakings to be eliminated on consolidation. Also, income and expenditure relating to transactions between group undertakings should be eliminated on consolidation. [4A Sch 6(1)].

5.34   Similarly, profits and losses resulting from transactions between group undertakings included in the value of assets retained at the year end should be eliminated. [4A Sch 6(2)]. The Act specifies that the elimination of such profits and losses may be made in proportion to the group's interest in the shares of the undertaking. [4A Sch 6(3)]. Prior to the Companies Act 1989, companies have generally eliminated 100 per cent of such transactions.

5.35   SSAP 14 makes no comment on how the elimination of such transactions should be made, but IAS 27 states that intra-group balances and intra-group transactions should be eliminated in full. [IAS 27 para 30]. The explanation in IAS 27 is more specific and sets out the following steps concerning the elimination of intra-group transactions:

■   Intra-group balances and intra-group transactions, including sales, expenses and dividends, should be eliminated in full. [IAS 27 para 13(b)].

■   Unrealised losses resulting from intra-group transactions that are included in the carrying amount of assets, such as stocks and fixed assets, should be eliminated in full. [IAS 27 para 13(c)].

■   Unrealised losses resulting from intra-group transactions that are deducted in arriving at the carrying amount of assets are also eliminated unless cost cannot be recovered. [IAS 27 para 13(d)].

5.36   With respect to the paragraph 5.34 above, the Act allows elimination in proportion to the group's interest in the shares of the undertaking. An example of how the Act's provisions would work in practice is given below.

Example

A parent owns 60 per cent of a subsidiary. The subsidiary sells some stock to the parent for £70,000 and makes a profit of £30,000 on the sale. Previously, the parent would eliminate the entire profit on consolidation, therefore, excluding the profit of £30,000 and reducing the cost of stock on consolidation to £40,000 (that is, £70,000 - £30,000). Under the new provisions, the parent may eliminate on consolidation only 60 per cent of the profit made on the sale by its subsidiary (that is, £18,000). The group will then show the remaining £12,000 in the consolidated profit and loss account, although this amount will then be deducted as attributable to the minority interest. The stock figure in the balance sheet will be £52,000 (that is, £70,000 - £18,000 or at cost of £42,000 plus share of the profit retained of £12,000).

5.37   It should be noted that this provision of the Act is optional and only applies where profits and losses resulting from transactions between undertakings are included in the book values of assets. Where it is used, any profit taken in the group's consolidated profit and loss account must be attributed to the minority, because it represents the minority's share. Furthermore, it follows that this provision cannot be used where a *parent* sells assets to a partly-owned subsidiary. This is because the parent makes the profit and the group's interest in the parent is 100 per cent. Consequently in this situation, the profit should be completely eliminated on consolidation.

5.38 Whichever method is adopted, it is important that the accounting policy is disclosed in the consolidated financial statements. Furthermore, the ASC in its exposure draft on consolidated accounts has not taken up the Act's alternative method of eliminating intra-group profits in proportion to the group's interest in the subsidiary. Consequently, the exposure draft proposes that all intra-group transactions should be eliminated in full.

Effective date of acquisition or disposal of subsidiaries

5.39 An undertaking can only be consolidated where it is a subsidiary at the balance sheet date. The date upon which a parent should account for either the acquisition or the disposal of a subsidiary should be the earlier of the two dates that follow:

■ The date on which consideration passes.

■ The date on which an offer becomes, or is declared, unconditional.

[SSAP 14 para 32].

5.40 This applies even where the acquiring undertaking has the right, under the agreement, to share in the profits of the acquired business from an earlier date. The ASC's exposure draft on consolidated accounts proposes that the effective date of acquisition should also be *"the date of such other event at which control or significant influence is gained or ceases to exist"* where this is earlier than the two dates mentioned in paragraph 5.39 above. Furthermore, it is proposed that the reference to consideration in the first point in paragraph 5.39 should be to the consideration given for the controlling interest and the reference to the offer in the second point in paragraph 5.39 should be to that which leads to control passing.

5.41 The application of paragraph 32 of SSAP 14 still causes problems in practice. The second point in paragraph 5.39 above reflects the legal (and more usual) position as to when an undertaking either becomes or ceases to be a subsidiary. The first point in paragraph 5.39 covers the more usual situation where the whole of the consideration passes at the time of acquisition. In the latter situation, the acquiring company would almost certainly take effective management control of the acquired company shortly before the consideration passes.

5.42 If there is a provision in a purchase agreement that the acquiring company has a right to share in profits of the acquired business before the effective date of its acquisition, this provision cannot override the accounting treatment required by paragraph 32 of SSAP 14. A company is purchased at a particular date, and the acquirer has the right to the company's net assets at that date. For accounting purposes, the acquired company's retained earnings at the date of the purchase are pre-acquisition to the acquirer. (The treatment of pre-acquisition profits is considered further in chapter 6.) Even where the purchase agreement refers to the net assets at the previous balance sheet date, the acquirer, in arriving at the purchase price, will have taken into account changes in those net assets between that date and the date of acquisition.

5.43   In practice, the effective date of acquisition or disposal, (particularly where an unlisted company is involved) may differ from that originally intended by the management of both the vendor and the purchaser. Negotiations either to purchase or to sell a subsidiary often take place over a considerable period. There can also be a delay between the time when agreement is reached in principle and the time when the formal contracts and other necessary legalities are completed. Conditions, such as the receipt of third parties' consent, may take time to be satisfied. Until such time as agreement is reached and all the conditions are satisfied, the transaction cannot be regarded as 'unconditional'. The date when an agreement in principle is made is often not the date on which the parties become legally bound to buy and sell respectively. This is because their agreement is not legally binding if they contemplate that they should not be bound until various steps have been taken (most commonly the execution of full documentation).

5.44   To a lesser extent, for unlisted companies, the behaviour of the respective parties to the transaction may also give some indication as to the effective date. If they both act as if the control of the company concerned had changed hands, this would normally indicate that the acquisition was effective. However, if there was some major matter that was still unresolved between the parties, or if there was some important condition that had still to be satisfied under the agreement, it is unlikely that the acquirer would become involved in the undertaking's management.

5.45   Paragraph 32 of SSAP 14 does not apply to those situations where the combination is treated as a merger (see further chapter 9).

5.46   So far as acquisition or disposal of associated companies are concerned, SSAP 1 includes a paragraph in respect of the effective date of acquisition or disposal of an interest in an associated company that is similar to paragraph 32 of SSAP 14. SSAP 1 is discussed further in chapter 11.

5.47   Where the effective date of acquisition is after the year end, but before the consolidated financial statements are approved and signed on behalf of the board, the acquisition should be treated as a non-adjusting post balance sheet event. [SSAP 17 para 23]. The nature of the event and its estimated financial effect should be disclosed where practicable (see for example Table 20).

> **Table 20: Example of the acquisition of two subsidiaries after the year end being treated as a non-adjusting post balance sheet event.**
>
> *Extract from Cadbury Schweppes Public Limited Company Annual Report 31st December 1988.*
>
> ### Report of the Directors extract
>
> POST BALANCE SHEET EVENTS
> Cadbury Schweppes Australia Limited
> Your Company is now in the process of completing the purchase of the whole of the ordinary shares held by the 30.3% minority interests in our Australian subsidiary following a sufficient level of acceptances. In 1989 as a result of this transaction your Company will acquire the minority by issuing about 24.2m new ordinary shares in Cadbury Schweppes p.l.c. and paying an estimated A$242.3m (£114.8m) in cash.
>
> Bassett Foods plc
> On 2 February 1989 it was announced that the Boards of Bassett Foods plc and your Company had reached agreement on the terms of a recommended offer for your Company to acquire Bassett. The terms of the offer, which remains open until 3 March 1989, are 8 new ordinary shares in Cadbury Schweppes for every 5 ordinary shares in Bassett or 536p in cash for each ordinary share in Bassett. Preference shareholders in Bassett have been offered 125p per share in cash.
> On 2 February 1989, the Company purchased for cash on the stock market 2,343,087 ordinary shares in Bassett, representing 14.9% of the issued equity. At 2 March 1989, acceptances representing a further 24.6% of the equity had been received.

Acquisition of subsidiaries

5.48 Accounting for the acquisition of a subsidiary is a complex area and there are a number of significant factors that need to be considered. These matters are considered in detail in the following chapters:

■ Chapter 6 - Acquisition accounting.

■ Chapter 7 - Fair valuing assets and liabilities.

■ Chapter 8 - Accounting for goodwill and intangibles.

■ Chapter 9 - Merger relief and merger accounting.

Disposal of subsidiaries

5.49 Disposing of a subsidiary is often as complex as accounting for the acquisition of a subsidiary. Consequently, there are a number of matters that need to be considered when a group sells a subsidiary and these include both how to account for the sale itself and how to account for trading in the period after the implementation of the decision to sell the subsidiary. These matters are considered in the paragraphs that follow.

Accounting for the sale of a subsidiary

5.50   When there is a material disposal, the consolidated profit and loss account should include the following:

■   The subsidiary's results up to the date of disposal.

■   The gain or loss on the sale of the investment. This gain or loss is the difference, at the time of the sale, between the sale proceeds and the holding company's share of the subsidiary's net assets, together with either any premium (less any amounts written off) or any discount on acquisition.

[SSAP 14 para 31].

5.51   The gain or loss on the eventual sale of such a subsidiary should be treated as an extraordinary item. SSAP 6 lists various examples of extraordinary items and specifically includes *"the sale of an investment not acquired with the intention of resale, such as investments in subsidiary and associated companies"*. [SSAP 6 para 4(b)]. Extraordinary items are defined in SSAP 6 as:

> *"...material items which derive from events or transactions that fall outside the ordinary activities of the company and which are therefore expected not to recur frequently or regularly. They do not include exceptional items nor do they include prior year items merely because they relate to a prior year."*   [SSAP 6 para 30].

Such extraordinary items have to be shown separately and suitably described either on the face of the consolidated profit and loss account or in the notes to the consolidated financial statements. [SSAP 6 para 37].

5.52   The calculation of the gain or loss on sale can be illustrated by the following example:

Example

A holding company purchased an 80 per cent interest in a subsidiary for £80,000 during 1990, when the fair value of the subsidiary's net assets was £87,500. Goodwill on consolidation that arose on the acquisition is being amortised over its estimated useful life of ten years, and a full year's charge for amortisation was made in the group accounts to 31st December 1990. The holding company sold its investment in the subsidiary on 31st December 1994 for £100,000. The book value of the subsidiary's net assets on the date of the sale was £112,500.

The holding company's profit and loss account for 1994 would show a gain on the sale of the investment of £20,000 calculated as follows:

	£
Sale proceeds	100,000
Less: Cost of investment in subsidiary	(80,000)
Gain on sale in the parent's accounts	20,000

However, the group's profit and loss account for 1994 would show a gain on the sale of the subsidiary of £4,000 calculated as follows:

	£
Sale proceeds	100,000
Less: Share of net assets at date of disposal (£112,500 x 80%)	(90,000)
Less: Goodwill on consolidation unamortised at date of sale*	(6,000)
Gain on sale to the group	4,000

*The unamortised goodwill on consolidation is calculated as follows:

	£
Fair value of consideration at date of acquisition	80,000
Less: Fair value of net assets of subsidiary at date of acquisition (£87,500 x 80%)	70,000
Goodwill arising on consolidation	10,000
Amortisation (4 years x £1,000)	4,000
Unamortised goodwill at 31.12.1994	6,000

The difference between the gain in the holding company's profit and loss account and the gain reported in the group's consolidated profit and loss account is £16,000 (that is, £20,000-£4,000).

This difference represents the share of post-acquisition profits retained in the subsidiary of £20,000 (that is, (£112,500 - £87,500) x 80%) that have been reported in the group's profit and loss account up to the date of sale, less goodwill of £4,000 that has been written off in the group's profit and loss account.

Disposal of a business segment

5.53 The treatment of the sale of a subsidiary is less clear where it forms part of the decision to close a business segment. A business segment is defined in SSAP 6 as:

> "... a material and separately identifiable component of the business operations of a company or group whose activities, assets and results can be clearly distinguished from the remainder of the company's activities. A business segment will normally have its own separate product lines or markets."
> [SSAP 6 para 32].

5.54 The area of particular difficulty is whether a subsidiary's trading results from the implementation of the decision to close the business segment to the date of sale of the subsidiary can be treated as extraordinary.

5.55 The argument for treating the trading results during this period as extraordinary is that SSAP 6 states that where a decision has been taken to discontinue a business segment, a provision is necessary for the consequences of all decisions taken up to the balance sheet date. [SSAP 6 para 11]. Such a provision would normally include all debits and credits arising from trading after the commencement of implementation. This requirement appears in the standard under the heading 'terminated activities'. The standard states that one example of an extraordinary item is profits or losses arising from the *"discontinuance of a business segment either through termination or disposal"*. [SSAP 6 para 4(a)].

5.56 There is a counter argument which supports the view that such trading results should not be treated as extraordinary. This view is based on the provision in SSAP 14, mentioned above, that the effective date for accounting for the disposal of a subsidiary is the earlier of the date on which consideration passes, or the date on which the offer becomes unconditional. [SSAP 14 para 32]. Furthermore, where there is a material disposal the consolidated profit and loss account should include the subsidiary's results up to the date of disposal. [SSAP 14 para 31]. The gain or loss is the difference at the time of sale between the sale proceeds and the holding company's share of net assets, together with any premium on acquisition is so far as it has not been written off, or discount on acquisition (see para 5.50 above).

5.57 Where the sale of the subsidiary is clearly part of the implementation of the closure of the business segment, that is, it is pursued as an alternative to the closure of the subsidiary itself, then there is an argument for taking the results from the date of implementation as extraordinary. For example see Table 21.

Table 21: Example of an accounting policy concerning terminated activities.

Extract from Ferranti 31st March 1989.

Extraordinary items
Profits and losses on sales of businesses are accounted for as extraordinary items as are the costs of disclosure in respect of terminated activities and their trading results taken from the date of commencement of implementation of the decision to effect termination.

5.58 If, however, the subsidiary being sold forms a substantial and major part of the business segment and other closure costs are incidental to the disposal, then the trading results should not be treated as extraordinary. Furthermore, the trading results should not be treated as exceptional either. This is because the results form part of the normal trading of the group.

Disposal after the year end

5.59 Sometimes a company may decide, before its accounting year end, to sell one of its subsidiaries, but the actual disposal does not take place until early in the next accounting period.

5.60 The question then arises as to how the company's current year's consolidated financial statements should reflect the planned transaction. Under SSAP 17, the disposal of the subsidiary is a non-adjusting event. Consequently, despite the company's decision to sell, the parent should still include the subsidiary in its current year's consolidation. In addition, if material, the fact of the sale and its financial effect should be shown in the notes to the consolidated financial statements by disclosing it as a non-adjusting post balance sheet event.

Disclosure requirements

5.61 The Act requires certain information to be given in the consolidated financial statements relating to disposals of subsidiaries where they significantly affect the figures disclosed in those financial statements. The required information is as follows:

■ The name of the subsidiary, or if a sub-group has been disposed of, the name of its parent.

■ The extent to which the profit or loss shown in the consolidated profit and loss account is attributable to the subsidiary or sub-group.

[4A Sch 15].

5.62 Where the directors consider that disclosure of the above information would be seriously prejudicial to the business of any undertaking in the group and the subsidiary being sold is established, or carries on business, outside the UK, the information is not required to be given. However the Secretary of State's permission is required. [4A Sch 16].

5.63 In addition, SSAP 14 requires that where a group makes a material disposal it should show clearly the results of the group's continuing operations to enable shareholders to appreciate the effect of the sale on the consolidated results. [SSAP 14 para 30]. In order to do this, a group could give the trading results of the subsidiary up to the date of sale more prominence in the consolidated profit and loss account by, for example, showing a separate line for each profit and loss item (such as turnover, operating profit, etc.) headed 'discontinued activities'. For example, see Table 22.

Table 22: An illustration of the results of companies sold or to be sold being shown separately as discontinued activities.

Extract from Budgens plc Report and Accounts 29th April 1989.

Accounting policy extract

Consolidation
The Group accounts consolidate the accounts of the Company and its subsidiaries all of which are made up to 29 April 1989.

Inter-company sales and profits are eliminated on consolidation. The results of companies acquired during the period are dealt with from the effective date of their acquisition. Purchased goodwill, representing the excess of the consideration given over the fair value of assets acquired, is either written off against reserves at the time of acquisition or amortised over its estimated useful life, depending on the amount involved and the circumstances of the acquisition.

The results of companies sold and to be sold *(refer to note 25)* are shown as 'Discontinued activities' in the notes to the accounts. The results of companies sold during the period are included to the date of disposal.

As permitted by section 228(7) of the Companies Act 1985, the profit and loss account of the parent company has not been presented separately in the Group Accounts.

Note extract

	70 weeks to 29.4.89 £000	52 weeks to 26.12.87 £000
2 Turnover		
Food retailing – UK	365,214	243,551
Discontinued activities	16,272	34,237
	381,486	277,788
3 Profit on ordinary activities before interest and taxation		
Food retailing	18,547	11,857
Discontinued activities	836	1,621
Dividends receivable	377	–
Net profit on sale of properties and other fixed assets	2,535	1,866
	22,295	15,344
Less Group central costs	(2,768)	(1,294)
	19,527	14,050

5.64   SSAP 22 also requires the following information to be given where a previously acquired business or business segment is disposed of:

■   The profit or loss on disposal.

■ The amount of goodwill attributable to the business or business segment and an explanation of how it has been dealt with in determining the profit or loss on disposal.

■ The accounting treatment adopted and the amount of the proceeds in situations where no profit is recorded on the disposal because the proceeds have been accounted for as a reduction in the cost of the acquisition.

[SSAP 22 para 52].

5.65   The second disclosure requirement in paragraph 5.64 will ensure that companies show clearly how any goodwill that has been previously written off affects the profit or loss on the sale of the undertaking. This is a particularly important disclosure where a sale follows shortly after an undertaking is acquired and where the goodwill on the acquisition has been written off immediately to reserves (see further chapter 8). Often in this type of situation the profit on sale is inflated because of the goodwill write-off. SSAP 22 does not require such purchased goodwill to be deducted from (or added to) the profit (or loss) on disposal, but merely disclosed. In practice, however, it may sometimes give a fairer view of the profit on sale if goodwill previously written off is taken into account in determining the profit or loss on sale.

5.66   Where the disclosure in paragraph 5.64 relates to acquisitions that took place before 1st January 1989, the implementation date of SSAP 22, it may be impossible or impracticable to ascertain the attributable goodwill on a disposal. Where this is so, this fact should be stated and the reasons for non-disclosure should be given. [SSAP 22 para 53].

5.67   Furthermore, SSAP 10 requires that the statement of source and application of funds should show the effects of additions to, and disposals from, the group. These requirements in SSAP 10 are considered in chapter 6.

Realised and distributable reserves

5.68   Realised and distributable reserves are discussed in detail in 'Manual of Accounting - volume I' chapter 19. The restrictions on distributions contained in the Act apply to individual companies, and not to groups. This is because individual companies make distributions, whereas groups do not. However, users of consolidated financial statements may wish to know the amount the holding company could distribute if all the group's subsidiaries were to pay up their realised profits by way of dividends to the holding company. The figure of consolidated realised reserves gives an approximate indication of this potential distribution. Many groups specifically disclose the amount of consolidated realised reserves. If this information is not disclosed, users of the consolidated financial statements might interpret the consolidated profit and loss account balance and any other reserve balance as representing realised reserves, and the consolidated revaluation reserve balance as representing unrealised reserves. The amount of the consolidated realised reserves can be a very important figure to users of the consolidated financial statements. Also, if it is not disclosed, it may affect the truth and fairness of those financial statements in certain situations.

5.69 In addition, SSAP 14 requires that where there are significant restrictions on the holding company's ability to distribute the group's retained profits (other than those shown as non-distributable) because of statutory, or contractual or exchange control restrictions, the extent of the restrictions should be indicated.

5.70 The holding company's ability to distribute pre-acquisition reserves of its subsidiaries is discussed in chapter 6.

Chapter 6

ACQUISITION ACCOUNTING

ACQUISITION ACCOUNTING

Introduction

6.1   When a parent undertaking acquires an investment in another
undertaking there are a number of ways in which that investment can
be accounted for in consolidated financial statements. The accounting
treatment will depend on both the size of the investment and the
extent of the influence that the parent has over the undertaking. Such
acquisitions are required to be treated in one of the following ways:

■   Valued at cost less any provisions for diminution in value. This
normally applies to investments that are held for the short-term or
where below 20 per cent of the undertaking's voting rights are
controlled. See further 'Manual of Accounting - volume I' chapter
9.

■   Valued at market value or directors' valuation using the
alternative accounting rules. This method of valuation is an
alternative to the first method above. See further 'Manual of
Accounting volume I' chapters 5 and 9.

■   Accounted for on the equity basis. This is normally used when the
parent has a significant influence over the undertaking. For
example, where the investment gives control of greater than 20 per
cent of the undertaking's voting rights and where the investing
company has board representation. Where significant influence is
exerted in this way, the investment is an associate (see chapter
11).

■   Consolidated on a proportional basis where the company's
investment is in an unincorporated undertaking and it manages
the undertaking jointly with one or more other parties.
Proportional consolidation is allowed for partnerships and other
unincorporated joint ventures (see chapter 11).

■   Full consolidation on a line-by-line basis where the investment is a
subsidiary (see chapter 3 paras 3.6 to 3.36). Minority interests are
identified separately (see chapter 10).

6.2   Many investments that end up as subsidiaries start out as much
smaller interests in the undertakings concerned and may be treated in
the group's financial statements in a variety of ways before they
actually become subsidiaries. This chapter considers primarily the
accounting treatment that should be adopted when an undertaking

becomes a subsidiary, and then considers some of the problems that arise with piecemeal acquisitions. It also outlines the disclosure that is required in the year that a company acquires a subsidiary.

Acquisition and merger accounting

6.3   There are two accounting methods that may be applied when a subsidiary is acquired. The group may use either acquisition accounting or merger accounting to account for the new subsidiary. However, there are a number of conditions that must be satisfied before merger accounting may be adopted.

6.4   The Act contains rules on acquisition accounting and merger accounting, an area which had traditionally been left to accounting standards and practices. The Act states that an acquisition should be accounted for by the acquisition method of accounting, unless the conditions for accounting for it as a merger are met and the merger method of accounting is adopted. [4A Sch 8]. Merger accounting is, therefore, optional even where the merger accounting conditions are satisfied. Acquisition accounting is considered in the paragraphs that follow and merger accounting is considered in detail in chapter 9. An illustration of a group that uses both methods of accounting for its acquisitions and its justification for their use is given in Table 23.

Acquisition accounting rules

6.5   The rules concerning acquisition accounting are summarised in SSAP 14, SSAP 22 and SSAP 23. In addition, the Act summarises the general principles of acquisition accounting, and all of these rules are considered in the paragraphs below.

Process of consolidating a new subsidiary

6.6   SSAP 14 says very little about the process of consolidating a new subsidiary into the group's consolidated financial statements. It does state, however, that any difference between the purchase consideration and the value ascribed to the subsidiary's net tangible assets and identifiable intangible assets such as trade marks, patents or development expenditure, will represent a premium or discount on acquisition. [SSAP 14 para 29]. SSAP 23 confirms this treatment and states that any premium arising on consolidation will represent goodwill. [SSAP 23 para 16].

6.7   The Act goes further and details how the initial acquisition of a subsidiary should be dealt with. The Act requires that the interest of the parent and its subsidiaries in the adjusted capital and reserves of the new subsidiary should be off-set against the acquisition cost of the group's interest in the undertaking's shares. [4A Sch 9(4)]. The difference if positive represents goodwill and if negative represents a

Table 23: Example of a group's rationale for using acquisition accounting and merger accounting for different acquisitions.

Extract from 'The Answers' The Dee Corporation PLC

IS DEE'S POLICY ON THE USE OF MERGER OR ACQUISITION ACCOUNTING CONSISTENT AND FAIR?

Present accounting rules permit a choice of merger accounting (pooling) or acquisition accounting (purchase accounting) if the consideration paid for a company is 90% or more in the form of ordinary shares; acquisition accounting is required in all other cases. Under acquisition accounting, profits for the acquired business are included from the date of purchase. Under merger accounting, profits for both businesses are included for the full year; however, this is compensated in the earnings per share calculation by also including for the full year the shares issued in consideration. Moreover, acquisition accounting requires the purchaser to assign fair value to the assets acquired. In the case of merger accounting, substantially no change is made to the opening balance sheet. Where a choice is involved the rules give minimal guidance. Dee has always applied the following tests before merger accounting for any acquisition:

1. Is there a true merger of the managements, identities and physical assets of the two businesses in the layman's sense and is there a clear trading benefit?
2. What is the size of the transaction relative to the existing business?
3. Will the management materially impact the trading and management of the acquired business before the next report and accounts?
4. How can the presentation to shareholders best depict the company's future trading base?

    The accounting treatment of Dee's major acquisitions was as follows:—

Acquisitions	Date	Form of Consideration	Accounting Basis Adopted	Principal Reasons
Key Markets	June 83	Cash	Acquisition	No choice
F A Wellworth	Dec 83	Shares	Merger	Scale—business impacted in 1983/84. Expansion of existing business
Lennons	Oct 84	Shares	Acquisition	Small—substantial part of business sold within 1984/85 year
International Stores	Dec 84	Shares	Merger	Scale—business totally integrated
Herman's	April 86	Shares	Acquisition	New stand alone business: Management not impacted in 1985/86 year
Fine Fare	June 86	Shares	Merger	Scale—business totally integrated
M&H Sporting Goods	Aug 86	Cash	Acquisition	No choice
Medicare	Dec 86	Cash & Shares	Acquisition	No choice

    Dee has treated its acquisitions consistently by applying the tests mentioned above. This has not always given the highest immediate reported results. For instance, if Fine Fare had been acquisition accounted, then Dee's earnings per share for the year to 25 April 1987 would have been marginally higher than the 17.7 pence per share reported.

negative consolidation difference (that is, negative goodwill). [4A Sch 9(5)].

6.8   SSAP 14 also states that the amount to be attributed to purchased goodwill should be the difference between the fair value of the consideration given and the aggregate of the fair value of the separable net assets where this is positive. [SSAP 14 para 29]. Where the difference is negative, it represents negative goodwill.

6.9   Consequently, on acquisition it is necessary to ascertain both the acquisition cost and the adjusted capital and reserves of the undertaking acquired.

Acquisition cost

6.10   Under the Act the 'acquisition cost' incurred in acquiring a subsidiary includes the amount of any cash consideration paid and the fair value of any other consideration (such as shares and debentures), together with fees and other expenses of the acquisition. [4A Sch 9(4)].

6.11   Similarly, SSAP 22 provides that, where a parent acquires another undertaking and it does not use merger accounting, it must include in its own balance sheet the shares in the acquired undertaking at cost based on the fair value of the consideration it gave. [SSAP 22 para 18]. SSAP 22 defines the term 'fair value' as the amount for which an asset or a liability could be exchanged in an arm's length transaction. [SSAP 22 para 30]. However, neither the Act nor SSAP 22 give any guidance on how to ascertain the fair value of the consideration given.

6.12   Where a company acquires another company for cash, the fair value of the consideration will be the cost to the acquiring company of the cash paid. However, when the consideration includes an issue of shares, the fair value of the consideration is more difficult to determine.

6.13   Many of the aspects of fair valuing assets and liabilities are considered in chapter 7. That consideration includes a fuller discussion of how to ascertain the fair value of the 'acquisition cost' of a subsidiary.

6.14   When a company issues shares as part of the consideration to acquire a subsidiary, the difference between the fair value of the consideration and the nominal value of the shares issued has to be credited to the share premium account, unless the company is eligible for merger relief. If the company can obtain merger relief on the issue, then the difference between the fair value of the shares issued and their nominal value can be credited to a merger reserve. Merger relief is considered further in chapter 9. Where the company is unable to obtain merger relief, both the fair value of the shares issued and their nominal value determine the amount credited to the share premium account. Unlike the merger reserve, the share premium account can only be used for the following specific purposes to:

■ Pay up fully paid bonus shares.

■ Write off preliminary expenses.

■ Write off expenses of any issue of shares or debentures.

■ Write off commission paid or discount allowed on any issue of shares or debentures.

■ Provide for the premium on any redemption of debentures.

[Sec 130(2)].

The use of the share premium account is also illustrated in Table 24.

Table 24: Example of the uses made of the share premium account.

Extract from Trafalgar House Public Limited Company Report and Accounts 30th September 1989.

Note extract

23 Share premium account

	1989 £m
As at 30th September 1988	322.2
Premium arising on issues of Ordinary shares	5.6
Utilised for issues of scrip dividend shares	(.3)
Expenses of debenture loan issue	(4.3)
	323.2

6.15   Consequently, the fair value of the consideration has a direct bearing on the amount that has to be treated either as share premium or as a merger reserve.

Fees and expenses of acquisition

6.16   The fees and expenses of acquisition that can be added to the cost of an investment are considered in chapter 7 paragraph 7.36.

Adjusted capital and reserves acquired

6.17   The Act requires that the adjusted capital and reserves is set off against the acquisition cost of the acquired subsidiary in order to ascertain the figure of goodwill (or negative goodwill) arising on the acquisition. In this context 'adjusted capital and reserves' means the subsidiary's capital and reserves at the date of acquisition after adjusting the undertaking's identifiable assets and liabilities to fair values. [4A Sch 9(4)]. Consequently, the subsidiary's adjusted capital and reserves will be made up of its capital and reserves disclosed in its books of account adjusted for any changes in the value of net assets determined in fair valuing its assets and liabilities. The following example illustrates this provision of the legislation.

Example

Company A acquires 80 per cent of company B on 22nd November 1991. The acquisition cost is £500,000 and at the date of acquisition, the reserves of the subsidiary are determined as follows:

Capital and reserves of company B	£
Share capital	20,000
Share premium account	10,000
Revaluation reserve	100,000
Profit and loss account	150,000
Total capital and reserves	280,000

Company B carries out a fair value exercise as at 22nd November 1991 and ascertains that its fixed assets and stocks have values in excess of their book values of £120,000 and £35,000 respectively.

Adjusted capital and reserves of company B	£
Capital and reserves (as above)	280,000
Fair value adjustment	155,000
Total capital and reserves	435,000

Consequently, the difference arising on consolidation (goodwill) would be calculated as follows:

Difference arising on consolidation	£
Acquisition cost	500,000
Adjusted capital and reserves (£435,000 x 80%)	348,000
Goodwill	152,000

Identifiable assets and liabilities

6.18 The Act goes on to require that the subsidiary's identifiable assets and liabilities must be included in the consolidated balance sheet at their fair values, as at the date of acquisition. [4A Sch 9(2)]. For this purpose the Act defines 'identifiable assets and liabilities' to mean the:

> "...assets or liabilities which are capable of being disposed of or discharged separately, without disposing of a business of the undertaking." [4A Sch 9(2)].

6.19   The Act is, in this respect, repeating standard accounting practice under SSAP 22. The standard requires that, on consolidation, a group should attribute the cost of the investment to the acquired company's separable net assets. It should do this by stating them at their fair values. [SSAP 22 para 36]. The term 'identifiable assets and liabilities' comes straight from the 7th Directive, whereas SSAP 22 refers to 'separable net assets'. SSAP 22 defines 'separable net assets' as:

> "...those assets (and liabilities) which can be identified and sold (or discharged) separately without necessarily disposing of the business as a whole. They include identifiable intangibles." [SSAP 22 para 27].

6.20   The test in SSAP 22 to decide whether an asset should be included in the category of separable net assets, is whether the asset can be identified and sold separately without disposing of the business as a whole. In this context, goodwill is clearly not separable from the business as a whole. Such assets, however, may well include other intangible assets (including trade marks and brands) and their valuation is considered in more detail in chapter 7. It should also be noted that the Act talks in terms of disposing of "a business of the undertaking", whereas SSAP 22 talks in terms of "the business as a whole".

6.21   As can be seen from the above, the meaning of the terms 'identifiable assets and liabilities' and 'separable net assets' is in essence the same. Ascertaining the fair values of identifiable assets is very difficult in practice and substantial problems can arise. There is no guidance in the Act or in accounting standards on how to determine the fair values of assets and liabilities. Chapter 7 considers some of the problems of fair valuing identifiable assets and liabilities.

Recording adjustments to fair values

6.22   Where a subsidiary company carries out a fair value exercise as at the date of acquisition, it is not required to record these values in its books of account. [SSAP 14 para 29]. However, there is nothing generally to stop the adjustments being made in the subsidiary's books of account and this may happen in practice. But it is not normally possible for UK subsidiaries to record their stocks at a fair value that exceeds cost, because the Act and SSAP 9 require stocks to be valued at the lower of cost and net realisable value. [4 Sch 23; SSAP 9 para

26]. (This will be so unless the subsidiary prepares current cost accounts.) Consequently, in the previous example in paragraph 6.17 only £120,000 would be able to be recorded in the subsidiary's books of account.

Treatment of goodwill

6.23 Any difference between the total of the subsidiary's acquisition cost (that is, the fair value of the purchase consideration) and the group's share of the subsidiary's adjusted capital and reserves represents purchased goodwill arising on consolidation (or, if negative, a negative consolidation difference). [4A Sch 9(5); SSAP 22 para 36]. The group should eliminate purchased goodwill arising from the acquisition from its consolidated financial statements by either immediate write-off or amortisation. Chapter 8 explains in detail the treatment of both goodwill and negative goodwill arising on consolidation. An example of an accounting policy for acquisitions and for goodwill is given in Table 25.

Table 25: Illustration of an accounting policy relating to the preparation of consolidated financial statements.

Extract from BASS PLC Annual Report 30th September 1989.

Accounting policies extract

BASIS OF ACCOUNTING

i) The accounts have been prepared under the historical cost convention except that certain fixed assets are included at valuation.

ii) The Group accounts deal with the state of affairs and profit of the Company and its subsidiaries, of which the principal are listed on page 8. The results of the United Kingdom trading subsidiaries are for the 53 week period ended 30th September 1989. Where local legislation or practice prevents overseas subsidiaries from complying with the Group's accounting policies, adjustments are made on consolidation to comply with those policies.

iii) On acquisition of a business, the purchase consideration is allocated between the underlying assets and liabilities on the basis of a fair value to the Group in accordance with its accounting policies. Where merger relief is available under the provisions of the Companies Act 1985, the purchase consideration is deemed to be the nominal value of the BASS PLC shares issued therefor.

Any difference between the purchase consideration and the value attributed to the assets and liabilities represents discount or premium on acquisition. Any discount is taken to undistributable reserves. Premiums are taken to the Group's undistributable reserves (if available) or retained earnings in the year of acquisition. To the extent that premiums in foreign currencies (arising on acquisitions of overseas subsidiaries) continue to have value, the amount of premium is adjusted at each balance sheet date.

The parent company's financial statements

6.24 Where one company acquires another company, the separable net assets acquired from the point of view of the acquiring company will be the shares in the acquired company, not the individual assets and liabilities of the acquired company. The fair value of the consideration given will normally equal the fair value to the purchaser of the shares acquired. Consequently, when one company acquires another company, purchased goodwill will normally not arise in the parent's balance sheet.

6.25 Where the fair value of the shares acquired is not the same as the fair value of the acquired company's individual assets and liabilities, goodwill will arise on consolidation.

Example

Company H acquires a listed company S for £10 million, even though the Stock Exchange capitalisation of company S is only £9 million and the value of its adjusted capital and reserves (which equates to its separable net assets) is £8 million. The total market capitalisation is based on the number of shares multiplied by the market price. However, the market's price is the price for only small parcels of shares. The market may put a different value on a controlling interest in the company. Consequently, the £10 million consideration is more likely to represent the fair value of the shares that the holding company has acquired. Therefore, purchased goodwill will not arise in the holding company's financial statements but, in this example, £2 million of goodwill will arise on consolidation.

6.26 The parent's investment in the subsidiary should be recorded in the parent's books at cost. In the example above, the investment would be recorded in the parent's books of account at £10 million. This is so unless merger relief applies (see further chapter 9).

6.27 SSAP 22 does not require an adjustment to be made in the parent's financial statements to the carrying value of the shares in the subsidiary in respect of any consolidation goodwill written off either in the consolidated financial statements or in the subsidiary's own financial statements. The parent company will in normal circumstances only write down the investment's carrying value to reflect any permanent diminution in value. Because of this requirement, it is not unusual to see groups where the reserves of the parent are greater than those of the group, because the latter take into account goodwill write-offs on consolidation.

Pre-acquisition and post-acquisition reserves

6.28 In the past, an important element of consolidations was whether profits of a subsidiary should be treated as pre-acquisition or post-acquisition. In particular, this was important because it had a bearing on how dividends paid by the subsidiary were treated in the parent's financial statements. If, for example, a subsidiary paid a dividend out of pre-acquisition profits to a parent, the parent would reduce its investment in the subsidiary by this amount (assuming that the net worth of the subsidiary had decreased by a similar amount). The parent could not treat this amount as realised and could not distribute it.

6.29 Paragraph 15(5) of the original Schedule 8 to the Companies Act 1948 was amended by the Companies Act 1981. As a result of this change, when a dividend is paid out of pre-acquisition profits by a subsidiary, it need not be applied in reducing the value of the investment in the subsidiary in the parent's books. It can be taken to the profit and loss account. Only if the underlying value of the subsidiary does not support the value of the parent's investment in it following the dividend, does the parent have to make a provision against its investment if that diminution in value is expected to be permanent. This accords with the legal requirements included in Schedule 4, paragraph 19(2), which requires a company to make provision for any permanent diminution in value of any fixed asset. Consider the following example.

Example

Company A has an investment in its subsidiary company B. Company A acquired the subsidiary for £22,000. The net assets of the subsidiary at that time were £18,000. In the following year, the subsidiary's net assets are £20,000 and it decides to pay a dividend to its parent of £1,000. It is unclear whether this dividend is made out of pre-acquisition reserves or post-acquisition reserves. Company A may take the dividend it receives from company B to its profit and loss account. However, company A then has to consider whether it is necessary to make a provision against the carrying value of its investment in company B. This assessment will take into account not only the net asset value of company B (which after the dividend payment has reduced to £19,000), but also any additional value that the shares in company B have. When it was acquired, this additional value was £4,000, which equates to the goodwill arising on consolidation. If company A considers that the value of company B's shares have not diminished, then the worth of company B is in excess of £23,000. On this basis company A does not need to make a provision against its investment in company B and can treat the dividend received as realised and, consequently, distributable.

Date for recognising trading

6.30 The Act states that income and expenditure of the subsidiary should only be brought into the consolidated financial statements from the date of acquisition. [4A Sch 9(3)]. The effective date of acquisition is considered in chapter 5 paragraph 5.39. Similarly, SSAP 23 requires that the results of the acquired company should be brought into the consolidated financial statements from the date of acquisition. [SSAP 23 para 17].

6.31 Before the introduction of the Companies Act 1989 there were two possible ways of complying with the legislation and SSAP 23. The most common practice adopted by companies was to consolidate 100 per cent of the new subsidiary's trading results on a line-by-line basis in the profit and loss account, but only dealing with those results from the date of acquisition. The alternative method less often used was to consolidate the entire results of the subsidiary for the whole of the trading period and then make a deduction at the end of the profit and loss account to eliminate the profits and losses before the effective date of acquisition (that is the pre-acquisition profits).

6.32 The alternative method is not possible under the Companies Act 1989 because the Act, as mentioned above, clearly requires the income and expenditure to be brought into the consolidated financial statements from the date of acquisition. [4A Sch 9(3)].

6.33 It is, therefore, necessary on an acquisition to apportion the results between pre-acquisition and post-acquisition on an accurate basis. In practice, this is often achieved by using the subsidiary's management accounts. However, there may be situations where there is no alternative but to use a time apportionment method. Where such a method is used, however, it will be necessary to identify any profit and loss account items that do not arise evenly over the accounting period. For such items a time apportionment would not be acceptable. For example, this may be the situation with exceptional items and extraordinary items. Such items would, therefore, need to be analysed into the period in which they arose and treated accordingly as either being pre-acquisition or post-acquisition.

6.34 Although the method of consolidating the results in the profit and loss account outlined above has to be adopted, groups may still wish to give their members an idea of what the results of the new group would have looked like for a whole period's trading. Clearly, the shareholders will not be able to ascertain this picture from the consolidated results as presented. In this situation, there in no reason why the group should not also include in its consolidated financial statements a pro-forma consolidated profit and loss account by way of a note showing the combined results of all subsidiaries for the entire period of trading, regardless of when they were acquired. In addition, the group may wish to disclose a pro-forma earnings per share by way of note based on the pro-forma consolidated profit and loss.

6.35 Where the group decides to include this type of additional information in its consolidated financial statements, it should not give the pro-forma accounts more prominence than its statutory accounts. The pro-forma accounts should be clearly titled as such and should indicate whether or not they are audited. In practice, such statements are usually audited, as the auditors have to satisfy themselves that the pro-forma accounts, being information contained in the financial statements, are not misleading.

Piecemeal acquisitions

6.36 Many problems can arise with piecemeal acquisitions. Such acquisitions arise where the investing company starts off with a small stake in an undertaking and gradually increases its investment. Initially the interest in the undertaking is no more than an investment that will be either valued at cost (less any provisions for diminution in value of the investment) or at a valuation (under the alternative accounting rules). As mentioned above, the accounting treatment of such investments is considered in of 'Manual of Accounting - volume I' chapter 9.

6.37　Once the interest in the undertaking becomes 20 per cent or more of the equity voting rights of a company, then the investment may have to be treated in the consolidated financial statements as an associate in accordance with the requirements of SSAP 1. In certain circumstances an interest in an undertaking can be treated as an associate where the investment is below 20 per cent. The accounting treatment of associates is discussed further in chapter 11.

6.38　There is, in addition, another complication, because in special circumstances an investment below 50 per cent might be a regarded as a subsidiary, where control over the undertaking is exercised in some other way (see chapter 3 paragraph 3.28).

6.39　There are three basic situations that might arise with a piecemeal acquisition, as follows:

■　An undertaking has an investment in another undertaking and makes an offer for the undertaking so that it becomes a subsidiary.

■　An undertaking has an investment in an associate and makes an offer for the undertaking so that it becomes a subsidiary.

■　A parent has an investment in a subsidiary and makes an offer to acquire part or all of the minority's interest.

6.40　A reverse situation where an investment in a subsidiary becomes an associate is dealt with in chapter 11. The other situations described above are looked at in turn below.

An investment becomes a subsidiary

6.41　This is the simplest situation to account for. Chapter 5 paragraph 5.39 explains the rules that apply in determining the date upon which an undertaking becomes a subsidiary. Consequently, these rules are not dealt with further here.

6.42　The initial investment will be recorded in the parent's accounting records at either its cost (less provisions) or at a valuation (in accordance with the alternative accounting rules). With creeping acquisitions, up to the date of acquisition the parent will only have accounted for dividend income received from the undertaking. On acquisition, the goodwill arising on the acquisition has to be ascertained and this will be the difference between the fair value of the consideration given for the subsidiary (including the cost of the investment to date, any revaluation being ignored) and the fair value of the parent's share of net assets acquired. Consider the following example:

Example

A group made an investment of 10 per cent in a company in 1985. The investment cost £25,000 and has subsequently been revalued to £50,000. In 1991 it makes a further investment in the company of 50 per cent to bring its total investment to 60 per cent. The fair value of the consideration given for the 50 per cent is £250,000. The net assets of the company acquired stand in its books at the date of acquisition at £200,000. The fair value exercise shows that the company's net assets are worth £350,000. The adjusted capital and reserves of the company are, as a consequence, £50,000 share capital and £300,000 reserves (which includes a £150,000 revaluation reserve). The goodwill on acquisition and minority interest would be calculated in the following way:

	£'000
Cost of acquisition	
Original investment in company (at cost)	25
Fair value of consideration given	250
Total consideration	275
Consolidation goodwill	
Total consideration	275
Adjusted capital and reserves	
(being 60% of £350,000)	210
Goodwill	65
Minority interest	
Share capital (40% of £50,000)	20
Reserves (40% of £300,000)	120
Minority	140

The only additional adjustment that is required in this example, in contrast to a straight acquisition of a subsidiary, is to reduce the value of the original investment from its market value to cost. The entry on consolidation would be to debit the revaluation reserve with £25,000 and credit the investment £25,000. Whether the parent decides to make this adjustment in its books of account might depend on whether the total cost of the subsidiary including the valuation adjustment exceeds the parent's share of the subsidiary's worth (including goodwill). Consequently, in this example the total consideration paid for the subsidiary together with the book value of the original investments is £300,000 (that is, £250,000 + £50,000). If 60 per cent of the subsidiary (including goodwill) is worth more than £300,000, then no provision will have to be made in the parent's books of account against the carrying value of its investment. However, if a provision were necessary, the first £25,000 of it could be debited to the revaluation reserve to offset the previous revaluation surplus on the same asset. Note that it would be incorrect to ascertain the fair value of the net assets of the subsidiary at the date the 10 per cent was acquired and use this to calculate the goodwill arising on that part of the acquisition.

An associate becomes a subsidiary

6.43 When an associate becomes a subsidiary the accounting treatment is not as straightforward as in the previous example. The main difference lies in the fact that a proportion of the associate's results have already been dealt with in the consolidated profit and loss account and consolidated balance sheet. In addition, goodwill will have been calculated on the acquisition of the interest in the associate and will have been either written off to reserves or amortised over its useful economic life.

6.44 Consequently, there are a number of other factors that need to be taken into account when determining the value of goodwill arising on the acquisition and when calculating the minority's interest.

Example

A group made an investment of 20 per cent in a company in 1985. The investment cost £120,000 and the fair value of the associate's net assets at that date was £500,000. In 1991 it makes a further investment in the company of 50 per cent to bring its total investment to 70 per cent. Goodwill on the acquisition of the associate is amortised to the consolidated profit and loss account over ten years, making a full charge in 1985, but no charge in 1991. The net assets of the associate stand in its books at £680,000 on the date it becomes a subsidiary. The associate would be treated as follows up to the date of acquisition:

	£'000
Acquisition of associate	
Original investment in company	120
Fair value of net assets acquired (20% x £500,000)	100
Goodwill arising	20
Consolidation of associate up to date of increased investment	
Share of net assets	
Date of acquisition	100
Post acquisition profits (being (£680,000 - £500,000) x 20%)	36
	136
Goodwill (£20,000 - (20,000 x 5/10))	10
	146

The fair value of the consideration given for the additional 50 per cent is £420,000. The fair value exercise shows that the company's net assets are worth £750,000. The adjusted capital and reserves of the company are, as a consequence, £50,000 share capital and £700,000 reserves (which includes a £70,000 revaluation reserve). The group has decided to include the whole amount of the fair value of the subsidiary's net assets in the consolidated balance sheet. The goodwill on acquisition and minority interest would be calculated as follows:

Further acquisition to subsidiary
Cost of acquisition as shown in the parent's books

	£'000	£'000
Original investment in company		120
Fair value of consideration given for new investment		420
Total investment in subsidiary		540

Consolidation goodwill

Total consideration		540
Adjusted capital and reserves		
being 50% of £750,000	375	
being 20% of £500,000	100	475
Goodwill		65
Goodwill previously amortised		10
Balance of goodwill		55

Minority interest

Share capital (30% of £50,000)	15
Reserves (30% of £700,000)	210
Minority	225

The goodwill on consolidation is made up of the £10,000 remaining on the acquisition of the associate that has still to be amortised and £45,000 that arises on the acquisition of the additional 50 per cent (that is, £420,000 - (£750,000 x 50%)). If the goodwill were to be recalculated at the date the company becomes a subsidiary using the new fair values, this would be wrong because the share of the results of the associate up to that date would be treated as pre-acquisition. The results since the date of acquisition of the associate are clearly earned by the parent and as such should be correctly treated as post-acquisition (see further para 6.28). There is one further adjustment that is required to be made on consolidation in this example. There is a difference of £50,000 between the fair values of the assets consolidated (that is, £750,000) and the adjusted capital and reserves taken into account above (that is, £475,000 + £225,000 = £700,000). The amount relates to two items. Part relates to the post acquisition profits of £36,000 taken into account since the acquisition of the associate (that is 20% x (680,000 - 500,000)). The other part relates to the increase in net assets of £70,000 from their book value of £680,000 to their fair value of £750,000. In the above example 30 per cent of that increase is reflected in the minority's interest and 50 per cent is taken into account in calculating goodwill. The other 20 per cent (that is, £14,000) is the further adjustment that will need to be credited to the consolidated revaluation reserve.

A parent acquires part or all of the minority

6.45 The accounting treatment for an acquisition of a minority interest (or part of the minority interest) can be similar in many respects to the treatment of an associate becoming a subsidiary. This is because the pre-acquisition profits of the subsidiary before the acquisition of the minority should remain pre-acquisition reserves. Consequently, the goodwill that arises on the piecemeal acquisition can be calculated at each separate stage of the acquisition for the new proportion of the acquisition only. The example that follows illustrates one way of accounting for the acquisition of a minority interest and uses, where possible, similar figures to the example above:

Acquisition accounting

Example

A group made an investment of 60 per cent in a company in 1985. The investment cost £320,000 and the fair value of the associate's net assets at that date were £500,000. The fair value of the net assets is represented by adjusted capital and reserves of share capital £50,000 and reserves £450,000. In 1991 it makes a further investment in the company of 30 per cent to bring its total investment to 90 per cent. Goodwill on the original acquisition of the subsidiary is amortised to the consolidated profit and loss account over ten years, making a full charge in 1985, but no charge in 1991. The subsidiary would be treated as follows up to the date of the new investment:

Goodwill arising on first investment	£'000
Original investment in company	320
Fair value of net assets acquired (60% of £500,000)	300
Goodwill arising	20
Minority interest	
Share capital (40% of £50,000)	20
Reserves (40% of £450,000)	180
Minority	200

The fair value of the consideration given for the additional 30 per cent is £250,000. The net assets of the company acquired stand in its books at the date of acquisition at £680,000. The fair value exercise shows that the company's net assets are worth £750,000. The adjusted capital and reserves of the company are as a consequence £50,000 share capital and £700,000 reserves (which includes a £70,000 revaluation reserve). The group has decided to include the whole amount of the fair value of the subsidiary's net assets in the consolidated balance sheet. The goodwill on acquisition and minority interest would be calculated as follows:

Cost of acquisition as shown in the parent's books	£'000	£'000
Original investment in company		320
Fair value of consideration given for new investment		250
Total investment in subsidiary		570
Consolidation goodwill		
Total consideration		570
Adjusted capital and reserves		
being 30% of £750,000	225	
being 60% of £500,000	300	525
Goodwill		45
Goodwill previously amortised		10
Balance of goodwill		35
Minority interest		
Share capital (10% of £50,000)		5
Reserves (10% of £700,000)		70
Minority		75

As in the previous example, the goodwill on consolidation is made up of the £10,000 remaining on the acquisition of the associate that has still to be amortised and the

£25,000 that arises on the acquisition of the additional 30 per cent (that is, 250,000 - (£750,000 x 30%)). Similarly as in the previous example, there is one further adjustment that must be made on consolidation in order to balance the accounts. There is a difference of £150,000 between the fair values of the assets consolidated (that is, £750,000) and the adjusted capital and reserves taken into account above (that is, £525,000 + £75,000 = £600,000). The amount relates to two items. Part relates to the post acquisition profits of £108,000 taken into account since the company first became a subsidiary (that is 60% x (680,000 - 500,000)). The other part relates to the increase in net assets of £70,000 from their book value of £680,000 to their fair value of £750,000. In the above example 10 per cent of that increase is reflected in the minority's interest and 30 per cent is taken into account in calculating goodwill. The other 60 per cent (that is, £42,000) is the further adjustment that will need to be credited to the consolidated revaluation reserve.

6.46   It is also acceptable on the acquisition of a minority not to carry out a fair value exercise and to use the fair values on the date the undertaking first became a subsidiary. This basis is proposed in the ASC's exposure draft on consolidated accounts. It suggests that, where a group increases its stake in an existing subsidiary, no fair value exercise should be carried out and the whole of the difference between the consideration and the book value of assets acquired should be treated as goodwill.

6.47   In the example above, the parent has used acquisition accounting to deal with the acquisition of the subsidiary's minority. However, in certain circumstances, merger relief may be available to the acquiring company. Where this is so, the value of the investment could be recorded in the books of the parent at the nominal value of any shares issued together with the fair value of any other consideration. Generally, however, most companies record such investments at their fair value and show a merger reserve instead of a share premium account. Although merger relief might be available, where the acquisition is accounted for as an acquisition (as opposed to a merger) the result on consolidation will be the same as that set out above. Merger accounting and merger relief are considered in chapter 9.

Disclosure regarding acquisitions

6.48   Certain information that has to be disclosed concerning investments in undertakings and investments in subsidiaries and these requirements are considered in chapter 4 paragraph 4.52 to 4.64. In addition to this information, Schedule 4A sets out various details that have to be disclosed in the consolidated financial statements in the year that a subsidiary is acquired.

6.49   The disclosure requirements concern acquisitions that are accounted for using either acquisition accounting or merger accounting. Those relating to merger accounting are considered in chapter 9. SSAP 22 includes disclosure related to the acquisition itself and disclosure related to goodwill arising from the acquisition. The disclosure relating to the treatment of goodwill is described in chapter 8. The disclosure requirements concerning the acquisition of a subsidiary accounted for as an acquisition are set out in the paragraphs below.

6.50 Some of the disclosure requirements concerning acquisitions included in Schedule 4A to the Act are very similar to the additional disclosure requirements included in SSAP 22 when it was revised in July 1989. The Act's requirements are set out below together with the requirements of SSAP 22 and SSAP 23:

■ The names of undertakings acquired during the financial year, or where a group of companies is acquired, the name of the group's parent. [4A Sch 13 (2)(a)]. This information is also required by SSAP 23 para 21(a).

■ The basis of accounting used for each acquisition (that is, either the acquisition method or the merger method). [4A Sch 13 (2)(b)]. Similarly, this information is also required by SSAP 23 para 21(c).

■ The nature and amount of significant accounting adjustments to achieve uniform accounting policies. [4A Sch 3(1); SSAP 23 para 21(d)].

■ For significant acquisitions, the composition and the fair value of the consideration for the acquisition given by the parent and its subsidiaries. [4A Sch 13 (3)]. In contrast, SSAP 22 merely requires the fair value of the consideration together with the goodwill arising to be shown separately. [SSAP 22 para 47]. Furthermore, SSAP 23 requires the number and class of the securities issued in respect of the acquisition and details of any other consideration. [SSAP 23 para 21(b)].

■ For significant acquisitions, the profit or loss of the undertaking or group acquired for the period from the beginning of its financial year up to the date of acquisition. [4A Sch 13 (4)(a)]. In addition the date on which the undertaking's or group's financial year began should be disclosed.

■ For significant acquisitions, the profit or loss of the undertaking or group acquired for the previous financial year. [4A Sch 13 (4)(b)].

■ In subsequent years, where there are material adjustments to fair values, and therefore to goodwill, such adjustments should be explained and disclosed. [SSAP 22 para 50]. These adjustments have to be shown separately for material acquisitions and have to be shown in total for other acquisitions where they are material in aggregate. [SSAP 22 para 51].

Sometimes the number of acquisitions a group may make in an accounting period can be numerous and there is no exemption from disclosure on the grounds of excessive information. Table 26 shows a group that has numerous acquisitions in a particular accounting period.

Table 26: Disclosure of the acquisitions made by the group during the accounting period.

Extract from Maxwell Communication Corporation plc Report and Accounts 31st March 1989.

Report of the directors (extract)

Acquisitions by the Group
The Group itself made the following acquisitions in the 15 month period to 31st March 1989:
1. January 1988: Alco Gravure, Inc. (renamed Maxwell Graphics Memphis) for $75.5 million in cash.
2. January: The assets of PUB/DATA, Inc. for $4.5 million in cash.
3. March: 91% of the issued share capital of Home and Law Magazines Limited for £17 million in cash.
4. March: The business, assets and liabilities of Armed Forces Journal International, Inc. for $5.2 million in cash.
5. April: 90% of the issued share capital of Patey Doyle (Publishing) Limited for £5.8 million in cash.
6. May: 67% of the issued capital of Imprimerie François SA for £1.8 million in cash and the remaining 33% in January 1989 for £0.9 million in cash.
7. July: The Evan Steadman Communications Group for an initial £8.3 million in cash.
8. July: Science Research Associates, Inc. for $150 million in cash.
9. August: London House, Inc. for $17.5 million in cash.
10. September: 60% of the issued share capital of ORAC Limited for £1.6 million in cash.
11. October:84% of the issued share capital of Panini International SpA. for £60.5 million in cash.
12. January 1989: BRS Europe for £11.9 million in cash.
13. February: Jossey-Bass, Inc. for $8 million in cash.

Table of assets and liabilities acquired

6.51   Furthermore, the Act requires the book values and fair values of each class of assets and liabilities of the undertaking or group acquired to be stated in tabular form. This should include a statement of the amount of goodwill or reserve arising on consolidation, together with an explanation of any significant adjustments made (for example, provisions for reorganisation, see further chapter 7). [4A Sch 13 (5)].

6.52   SSAP 22 requires that a similar table of information should be given showing the book values of each major category of assets and liabilities acquired before making any consolidation adjustments. [SSAP 22 para 48]. The table should also detail the fair values of those same categories of assets and liabilities. An explanation should be given of the reasons for any differences between the book values and the fair values. The requirement suggests that the movement between book values and fair values should be analysed in the table. It also requires that the adjustments should be analysed between the following:

■ Revaluations.

■ Provisions made in respect of future trading losses.

■ Other provisions established in respect of the acquisition.

■ Adjustments to bring accounting polices of the subsidiary onto the same basis as those of the group.

■ Any other major items that cannot be classified into the four categories above.

[SSAP 22 para 48].

6.53 The standard's provisions also require the disclosure of movements on provisions that relate to acquisitions, showing separately amounts used, amounts released unused or applied for another purpose. The information given should be sufficient to indicate whether the provision was necessary. [SSAP 22 para 49]. Provisions of this nature are discussed further in chapter 7.

6.54 The standard includes in appendix 3 an example of the type of disclosure that it envisages should be made in the consolidated financial statements when a subsidiary is acquired during the year. This table is reproduced on the next page, but has been amended to include certain additional information as required by the Act and SSAP 22. The additional information required by the Act is shown in the table in bold and concerns the disclosure of the fair value of the consideration and the resulting goodwill (or negative reserve) arising on consolidation (see point four of paragraph 6.50 above). [4A Sch 13(5); SSAP 22 para 47]. An illustration of the disclosure is also given in Table 27 overleaf.

6.55 The disclosure requirements set out above concerning SSAP 22 have to be given separately for each material acquisition and have to be given in aggregate for those acquisitions that are material when taken together. [SSAP 22 para 51].

Fair value table - acquisition - XYZ Ltd. date 19th February 1989

	Book value £'000	Revalua-tion £'000	Provis-ions for trading losses £'000	Other provis-ions £'000	Account-ing policy align-ment £'000	Other major items £'000	Fair value to the group £'000
Fixed assets							
Intangibles	-	-	-	-	-	80 (f)	80
Tangibles	160	20 (a)	-	-	-	-	180
Investments	20	5 (b)	-	-	-	-	25
Current assets							
Stocks	40	-	(4)(c)	(5)(d)	(2)(e)	-	29
Debtors	35	-	-	-	-	-	35
Investments	10	-	-	-	-	-	10
Cash at bank	12	-	-	-	-	-	12
Total assets	277	25	(4)	(5)	(2)	80	371
Liabilities							
Provisions:							
Pensions	30	-	-	-	-	-	30
Taxation	45	-	-	-	-	10 (g)	55
Other	10	-	8 (c)	-	-	-	18
Creditors							
Debentures	2	-	-	-	-	-	2
Bank loans	15	-	-	-	-	-	15
Trade creditors	30	-	-	-	-	-	30
Other creditors	10	-	-	-	-	-	10
Accruals	5	-	-	-	-	-	5
Total liabilities	147	-	8	-	-	10	165
Net assets acquired	130	25	(12)	(5)	(2)	70	206
Fair value of consideration							**284**
Goodwill							78

ADJUSTMENTS

EXPLANATIONS

1. **Revaluations**

   Note a — Increases in value of freehold properties since last revaluation in 1981.

   Note b — Increases in value of shares of USM investment since purchase in 1983.

2. **Provisions for trading losses**

   Note c — Losses expected to be incurred prior to closing down small tools division.

3. **Other provisions**

   Note d — Write-down following reassessment of realisable value of stock which is more than one year old.

4. **Accounting policy alignment**

   Note e — Change of stock valuation from weighted average cost to FIFO which is used by the group.

5. **Other items**

   Note f — Recognition of intangibles - relating to publishing titles and brands acquired.

   Note g — Adjustment to deferred tax arising from the incorporation of fair values.

Table 27: Example of a table showing net assets acquired, fair value adjustments and the gross goodwill arising on the acquisition.

Extract from Grand Metropolitan Public Limited Company Annual Report 30th September 1989.

Note extract

26 Acquisition of The Pillsbury Company

	Pillsbury balance sheet at 31st December 1988 £m	Accounting policy realignment £m	Revaluation and acquisition adjustments £m	Fair value balance sheet at 3rd January 1989 £m
Fixed assets				
Intangible assets	326	1,437	–	1,763
Tangible assets	801	(38)	(19)	744
Investments	56	–	(5)	51
	1,183	1,399	(24)	2,558
Working capital				
Stocks	375	(2)	4	377
Debtors	416	–	147	563
Investments for resale	187	–	39	226
Creditors and provisions	(737)	(110)	(334)	(1,181)
Deferred tax	3	51	91	145
	1,427	1,338	(77)	2,688
Net borrowings	(746)	–	(3)	(749)
Shareholders' funds	681	1,338	(80)	1,939
Purchase price				(3,221)
Goodwill				(1,282)

The Pillsbury balance sheet at 31st December 1988 is a summarised version of the audited financial statements of The Pillsbury Company, which were filed with the Securities and Exchange Commission in the United States. The balance sheet has been converted at $1.79 = £1, the exchange rate at acquisition. The principal adjustments made to convert this balance sheet to fair values are as follows:

Accounting policy realignment
(i) Intangible assets are replaced by the purchase consideration attributable to significant brands acquired.
(ii) Tangible fixed assets are adjusted to reflect a higher minimum capitalisation level per addition.
(iii) Provisions are increased in respect of liabilities not previously included in the Pillsbury balance sheet, including post employment medical benefits.

Table 27 continued

Revaluation and acquisition adjustments

(i) Tangible fixed assets are adjusted to fair value based on external property valuations and internal reviews of other assets less provisions for closure where appropriate.

(ii) The investments for resale comprise those businesses which the group was committed to selling prior to acquisition – Steak & Ale Restaurant Corp. and Pillsbury Grain Merchandising. The acquisition adjustment is the profit on the sale of those businesses. Subsequently further businesses have been sold and the profit on disposal is included in the adjustment to debtors.

(iii) The acquisition adjustment to creditors and provisions represents the cost of restructuring the business and strategically realigning its operations to acceptable levels of efficiency.

Deferred consideration

6.56   In certain circumstances, mainly where the acquisition consideration includes an element of deferred consideration, it may not be possible to ascertain the eventual cost of the acquisition by the end of the accounting period and, consequently, it has to be determined on a provisional basis. Where this type of situation exists, SSAP 22 requires that the fact that the consideration is based only on a provisional figure should be stated, together with an explanation of the situation. [SSAP 22 para 50]. Deferred consideration is considered in more detail in chapter 7.

Exemption for overseas businesses

6.57   If in the directors' opinion the disclosure of any of the information required by the Act as outlined in paragraphs 6.50 and 6.51 relating to an undertaking established, or one that carries on a business, outside the UK, would be seriously prejudicial to the business of the undertaking or group, it need not be given if the Secretary of State's permission is obtained. [4A Sch 16].

Statements of source and application of funds

6.58   For a group, the statement of source and application of funds should be based on the group's consolidated financial statements. SSAP 10 requires that, where a subsidiary is purchased or sold, the funds statements should reflect the effects on the separate assets and liabilities dealt with in the statement. [SSAP 10 para 5]. Consequently, with an acquisition, the net assets acquired and the consideration given should be summarised in a footnote to the funds statement. The example below illustrates the type of disclosure that is required and is reproduced from the appendix to SSAP 10.

Summary of the effects of the acquisition of Subsidiary Limited

Net assets acquired	£'000	Discharged by	£'000
Fixed assets	290	Shares issued	290
Goodwill	30	Cash paid	60
Stocks	40		
Debtors	30		
Creditors	(40)		
	350		350

6.59 This type of summary should be referenced to the related items in the funds statement, which can show the acquisition in either of the following two ways:

■ Show the individual increases and decreases in assets and liabilities as part of the movement of the total group assets and liabilities, showing separately the goodwill arising on the acquisition. The shares issued would be shown as a separate source of funds and the cash element of the acquisition as a cash movement.

■ Show the purchase of the subsidiary as a one line item equal to the net assets acquired including goodwill. The shares issued would be similarly shown as a separate source of funds and the cash element of the acquisition as a cash movement.

6.60 Table 28 illustrates the disclosure given in a source and application of funds statement concerning both acquisitions and disposals of subsidiaries.

Table 28: Example of the disclosure in a source and application of funds statement of the treatment of acquisitions and disposals.

Extract from Avon Rubber p.l.c. Annual Report 30th September 1989.

Source and application of funds extract

This statement includes the effect of the acquisitions of the assets of TR Sillinger and the entire share capital of the Cadillac group together with the disposals of 70% of Motorway Tyres and Accessories Limited and the whole of Motorway Tyres and Batteries Limited.

	Aquisitions £'000	Disposals £'000		Acquisitions £'000	Disposals £'000
Goodwill	35,855	–	Issue of shares	20,850	–
Fixed assets	9,795	6,331	Cash	20,301	16,421
Stocks	5,153	7,547	Effect on reserves	–	584
Debtors	8,071	12,805	Transfer to investments	–	800
Creditors	(8,958)	(22,248)			
Borrowings	(8,765)	–			
Profit on disposals	–	13,370			
	41,151	17,805		41,151	17,805

Chapter 7

FAIR VALUING ASSETS AND LIABILITIES

FAIR VALUING ASSETS AND LIABILITIES

Introduction

7.1   The ASC published a discussion paper entitled 'Fair valuation in the context of acquisition accounting' in June 1988. The discussion paper came at a time when the accounting profession was deeply divided on how to treat goodwill in acquisition accounting. Until SSAP 22 was published, the problems of fair value accounting had not been properly addressed or highlighted, even though the concept was established much earlier in SSAP 14 and SSAP 1.

7.2   In SSAP 14 the principle of fair valuing is set out as follows:

> *"When subsidiaries are purchased the purchase consideration should be allocated between the underlying net tangible and intangible assets other than goodwill on the basis of the fair value to the acquiring company. Any difference between the purchase consideration and the value ascribed to net tangible assets and identifiable intangible assets such as trademarks, patents or development expenditure, will represent premium or discount on acquisition."* [SSAP 14 para 29].

7.3   In SSAP 1 the investing group's share of net assets other than goodwill of associated companies was stated *"...where possible, after attributing fair values to the net assets at the time of acquisition of the interest in the associated companies"*. [SSAP 1 para 26].

7.4   SSAP 22 also deals, to an extent, with fair values. It states that:

> *"When ascribing fair values to separable net assets at the time of an acquisition a provision may be needed in respect of items which were taken into account in arriving at the purchase price, that is, anticipated future losses or costs of reorganisation."* [SSAP 22 para 14].

7.5   It also states that separable net assets to which fair values are attributed could include identifiable intangibles such as concessions, patents, licences, trade marks and similar rights and assets (such as publishing titles, franchise rights, and customer lists). It goes on to state that *"identifiable intangibles such as these form part of the separable net assets which are recorded in an acquiring company's accounts at fair value, even if they were not recorded in the acquired company's accounts"*. [SSAP 22 para 13].

The 'acquiring company's accounts' presumably means the consolidated financial statements of the acquirer.

7.6   The Act also talks about fair values in Schedule 4A and states that the acquisition cost is the cash consideration given in the acquisition plus the *"fair value of any other consideration, together with such amount (if any) in respect of fees and other expenses of the acquisition as the company may determine"*. [4A Sch 9(4)]. Similarly, the Act uses the term 'identifiable assets and liabilities' (instead of the SSAP 22 term 'separable net assets') and states that these assets and liabilities should *"be included in the consolidated balance sheet at their fair values as at the date of acquisition"*. [4A Sch 9(2)].

7.7   The ASC are proposing to issue an exposure draft that describes the role of fair values in acquisition accounting and merger accounting. The proposed exposure draft will also describes how fair values are relevant to accounting for associated companies and how they affect the recording of investments in subsidiaries in a holding company's financial statements. It will also explain that, where fair values are incorporated in the financial statements of an acquired subsidiary, the alternative accounting rules of the Act apply (see 'Manual of Accounting - volume I' chapter 5). This chapter considers the proposals made in the discussion draft and the proposed exposure draft and how those proposals interact with the requirements of the Act and relevant SSAPs.

Acquisition cost

7.8   As mentioned above, the Act states that the acquisition cost of a subsidiary is made up of some or all of the following elements:

■   Cash consideration.

■   Fair value of other consideration.

■   Expenses of acquisition.

[4A Sch 9(4)].

7.9   Consequently, the objective of determining the fair value of the consideration given is to fix the acquisition cost of the investment. Non-cash consideration may take the form of:

■   Listed securities.

■   Unlisted securities.

■   Consideration in a form other than securities.

7.10 These elements of consideration can be broken down further into the constituent parts of securities, as follows:

■ Ordinary shares.

■ Preference shares (convertible or non-convertible).

■ Loan stock (convertible or non-convertible).

■ Share warrants and other options relating to the securities of the acquiring company.

7.11 The various elements that make up the total consideration are considered further in the paragraphs that follow.

Listed securities

7.12 The most common form of securities given as consideration is ordinary or equity shares. The discussion paper concluded that the fair value of such shares should be the bid price. [DP para 5.4, 5.40(a)]. This price may be more appropriate than the mid-market price, because it is the price that could be obtained by selling the shares in the market. However, there are two related problems that need also to be considered:

■ The use of alternative valuations to a valuation based on the quoted market price.

■ The point in time at which shares should be valued.

7.13 It is proposed that the fair value of ordinary shares given as consideration should be based on the market price of the security on the date on which the final successful bid becomes unconditional. In order to eliminate, so far as possible, any fluctuations in general market conditions, the proposal is that the value should be determined by reference to an average of prices. A period of ten dealing days should normally be adequate for averaging purposes.

7.14 The price should generally be ascertained on the date the final bid becomes unconditional. Consequently, this price takes account of the market's reaction to a bid and movements in the share price of a bidder in determining the fair value of shares issued.

Unlisted securities

7.15 The valuation of unlisted securities causes particularly difficult problems in practice.

7.16 Where no market price is available for ordinary shares, or where the market price is inappropriate for certain reasons, the fair value should be estimated by reference to features such as:

■ The price/earnings ratio.

■ Dividend yield.

■ Expected growth rates of comparable shares of undertakings with similar characteristics.

7.17 Consequently, the values of unlisted securities can be estimated by reference to securities with, and issued by enterprises with, similar characteristics, using one of the methods above, adjusted where necessary for any significant differences in the nature of the security. Furthermore, the reasons for adopting the method used to value such securities, and the method itself, should be disclosed in the notes to the financial statements.

Other securities

7.18 The general principles that apply to determining the fair value of ordinary shares can also be applied to other securities such as preference shares, loan stock, share warrants and other options. Consequently, where there is a market price available the market price on the date on which the bid finally becomes unconditional should be used. Where there is no market price, the same bases as described in the last paragraph above should be used. For convertible securities, such as convertible loan stock or preference shares, the likelihood of conversion should be taken into account in arriving at a fair value. Generally, the greater the likelihood of conversion taking place, the closer the fair value will be to that of the security into which it can convert in the future.

Consideration in a form other than securities.

7.19 Where cash forms part of the consideration, the fair value will be the amount payable in respect of the item, unless settlement is deferred, where it may be necessary to discount it. Where consideration is given in the form of non-monetary assets, the fair value is usually the realisable value at the time of transfer. This applies except where the acquirer intends to replace the asset transferred, in which case the replacement cost of the asset should be used. Where monetary assets other than cash are given as consideration their fair value will usually be the amount of cash payable.

7.20 There are certain forms of 'consideration' that for tax or other reasons are commonly given. These include payments made for an agreement by the directors of the vendor company not to compete with the acquirer for a number of years and bonus payments to vendors who continue as directors of the acquired company. However, there are no laid down general principles on how to account for such arrangements.

Deferred consideration

7.21 One of the most common problems with ascertaining the fair value of the acquisition cost is where deferred consideration is involved. There are a variety of problems that might arise and these are considered below.

7.22 Deferred consideration payable in cash should be taken to be the amount of the cash payable discounted to its present value where appropriate. In addition, any deferred cash consideration should be provided in the acquirer's financial statements as a liability.

7.23 Where such consideration is discounted the proposals suggest it should be discounted to its present value using a discount rate that is equivalent to the cost that the company would pay to raise an additional amount of capital (see further para 7.121 below).

7.24 The value of deferred consideration in a form other than cash should be based on the rules that apply to the other forms of consideration discussed above. Normally with shares, the amount of deferred consideration payable is fixed at the date of acquisition and the number of shares issued to satisfy that consideration varies according to the market price of the shares at the date the consideration is paid.

7.25 Deferred cash consideration can be paid in the form of post-acquisition dividends out of profits accruing prior to the acquisition. The discussion paper proposed that such dividends should only be treated as part of the purchase consideration where it can be demonstrated that the payment was envisaged at the time of the acquisition. [DP para 5.33]. A note to Hanson Trust Plc's financial statements for 1986 illustrates the treatment suggested in the discussion paper and this is reproduced in Table 29 overleaf.

7.26 It is proposed that deferred consideration given in the form of shares should normally be provided as part of the company's shareholders' funds. If this requirement becomes standard it will have a significant impact in practice, because at present many companies do not account for such deferred consideration until it becomes due. Table 30 overleaf, however, shows an example of a situation where deferred consideration has been taken into account in calculating the gross consideration on acquisition.

7.27 Furthermore, it is also proposed that any deferred consideration in the form of securities should be taken into account when calculating the

Table 29: Note illustrating the treatment of dividends suggested in the discussion paper.

Extract from Hanson Trust PLC Annual Report 30th September 1986.

Note extract

8 Dividends (extract)

£18m of the ordinary dividend for the year has been charged to the cost of acquisition of Imperial Group plc. This represents the proportion of the dividends paid to shareholders of Imperial Group relating to the period before that company joined Hanson Trust.

Table 30: Summary of acquisitions and disposals made in the year which shows the make up of the gross consideration paid for the acquisition including deferred instalments.

Extract from Cadbury Schweppes Public Limited Company Annual Report 31st December 1988.

Note extract

22 ANALYSIS OF ACQUISITIONS AND DISPOSALS

	Acquisitions	Disposals
	£m	£m
Net assets:		
Tangible fixed assets	16.4	68.7
Investments	3.8	–
Stock	9.1	31.7
Debtors	35.7	36.0
Creditors and provisions	(48.0)	(10.7)
Taxation	1.2	–
Minority interests	1.5	–
	19.7	125.7
Goodwill		
– attributable to Group	105.3	–
– attributable to minorities	3.1	–
Liabilities assumed by vendor	–	16.9
Gain on disposal	–	99.8
	128.1	242.4
Consideration for acquisitions:		
Shares issued	1.1	
Cash and loan notes	119.6	
Borrowings acquired	2.9	
Deferred instalments	4.5	
	128.1	
Proceeds of disposals:		
Cash and securities		224.6
Borrowings assumed by purchasers		17.8
		242.4

fully diluted earnings per share figure. Where this is so, it should be disclosed clearly in a note to the group's financial statements. However, such deferred consideration should not be taken into account when calculating the normal earnings per share figure.

Contingent consideration

7.28 The most common form of contingent consideration arises where the acquirer agrees to pay additional consideration if the acquired company achieves a certain level of performance. The probable amount of such contingent consideration should normally be included in the cost of the investment.

7.29 With regard to contingent consideration, the discussion paper drew a distinction between what it termed the 'expected amount' and the 'probable amount'. The expected amount is represented by a weighted average of the possible values of the consideration and an example of how this average could be calculated was given in the discussion paper and is reproduced below:

The expected value of an item is represented by a weighted average of its possible values, the weighting being based on the probability of occurrence of each possible outcome. Thus the expected value of contingent consideration would be found by the following calculation:

Probability	Consideration payable £	Sum = the equivalent value £
0.3	100,000	30,000
0.6	140,000	84,000
0.1	180,000	18,000
		132,000

The most probable amount, in the example, is by contrast £140,000.

7.30 The 'probable amount', unsurprisingly, is the amount that will probably have to be paid. This amount will have to be adjusted when the final amount payable is determined. If a minimum sum or guaranteed future amount is offered as deferred consideration, then the fair value should in practice be determined by reference to those figures plus an amount to bring it up to the probable amount payable.

7.31 Present practice is generally to accrue the amount that will probably become payable where this is known. However, in many situations even the probable amount is difficult to estimate. This is so where, for example, the contingent consideration is based on an average of profits achieved for two or three years ahead. Where it is not possible to be reasonably confident as to the amount that will become payable, companies have in the past normally given details of the contingency in a note to the financial statements, together with a range of possibilities. This practice will no longer be possible if the proposals are accepted. It is also proposed that the notes to the financial statements should disclose the nature of any contingent consideration and the basis on which the probable amount has been arrived at.

7.32   In many situations where contingent consideration is to be settled in shares, or where there is an option to issue shares instead of cash, some companies have not considered it necessary to show the shares that may be allotted in the balance sheet. Others have shown such shares as a separate line under share capital. It is likely that the most probable cash consideration will be required to be provided as a liability and the most probable share consideration will be required to be provided as part of shareholders' funds.

7.33   Often with deferred or contingent consideration, either the acquirer or the vendor has the option to take the consideration in the form of shares or cash. Consequently, initially it will not be possible to tell exactly how the deferred consideration will be settled. Where the acquirer has the option, the accounting treatment should normally reflect his intentions. On the other hand, where the vendor has the option, then the acquirer should estimate the most probable outcome and account for the deferred consideration accordingly. These type of options have wider implications than just deferring the value of consideration, because whether the cash or the shares are taken up may affect whether the acquisition can be accounted for as a merger (see further chapter 9).

7.34   When the contingent consideration becomes more certain as the time gets nearer to its payment, the estimated amount may prove to be incorrect. Where this is so, the amount provided should be revised as the outcome becomes more certain until the ultimate amount is known. These amendments will also affect the amount of goodwill recognised on the acquisition, and similar adjustments should be made to the goodwill figure until the deferred consideration is finally determined.

7.35   An example of how a company has accounted for deferred consideration is reproduced in Table 31.

Fees and other expenses of acquisition

7.36   Costs incurred in carrying out the acquisition should normally be added to the cost of the investment. However, section 130(2) of the Act specifically allows a company to write off the expenses of an issue of shares against the share premium account. Consequently, a company might have a choice as to where expenses of an acquisition are charged.

***Table 31: Illustration of a group that has accrued deferred
consideration to be settled in shares and included the
amount set aside under capital and reserves.***

Extract from Charles Barker PLC 31st December 1987.

Consolidated Balance Sheet (extract)

at 31st December 1987

Capital and reserves	Note	1987 £'000s	1986 £'000s
Called up share capital	17	1,086	1,005
Share capital to be allotted	18	167	72
Other reserve	19	(1,293)	93
Profit and loss account	20	3,572	3,015
		3,532	4,185
Minority interest		47	17
		3,579	4,202

Note extract

18 SHARE CAPITAL TO BE ALLOTTED

	Number of ordinary shares £'000s	£'000s
At 1st January 1987	1,434	72
Adjustment on allotment of shares	169	8
Shares allotted in May 1987	(1,603)	(80)
Estimated shares to be allotted in May 1988	3,341	167
At 31st December 1987	3,341	167

On 10th April 1986, the company entered into an agreement to acquire the entire issued share capital of NBI.

The first and second tranche of the consideration for the acquisition of the shares of NBI was satisfied by the allotment, credited fully paid, of 3,711,645 ordinary shares of 5p each in the company. The final tranche of the consideration amounting to £4,009,215 is due to be satisfied by the allotment of ordinary shares in the company in May 1988. The number of ordinary shares of the company to be allotted to satisfy this consideration will depend on the price at the relevant date in May 1988. At a price of 120p for the ordinary shares of 5 p each in the company, the consideration would be satisfied by the allotment of 3,341,013 shares.

Table 31 continued

19 OTHER RESERVE

	Group £'000s	Company £'000s
At 1st January 1987	93	5,137
Adjustment to the surplus arising on allotment of shares to acquire NBI in May 1987 and related costs	(39)	(8)
Estimated surplus arising on the shares to be allotted in May 1988	3,842	3,842
Goodwill arising on the final consideration for the acquisition of NBI	(4,009)	–
Goodwill arising on the acquisition of The Chuter Morgenthau Partnership Limited and Traverse-Healy & Regester Limited, including estimated future consideration	(1,180)	–
At 31st December 1987	(1,293)	8,971

In accordance with S131 Companies Act 1985 the premium arising on the issue of shares to acquire NBI has been credited to reserves and has been applied in partly eliminating the goodwill arising on the acquisition of NBI.

7.37   There are a number of different types of acquisition costs and these might include:

■   Fees of legal, accounting and merchant banking advisers.

■   Stamp duty.

■   Expenses of producing legal documents.

■   Finders' fees.

■   Advertising.

■   Time spent by a company's management on researching and negotiating an acquisition.

7.38   The first three items in the above list can generally be written off against the share premium account if the company wishes to do so (see for example Table 32). With regard to the other items of expenditure listed above, they would generally not be allowed to be written off the share premium account. For example, it would not be acceptable to treat staff costs as an expense of the issue of shares where they would have been paid whether or not there was an issue.

7.39   If the consideration were part shares and part cash or loan stock, the expenses attributable to the shares and capable of being charged to the share premium account would be apportioned. Generally, costs that cannot be, or are not, written off against the share premium account, may be capable of being capitalised as part of the cost of the investment.

Table 32: Illustration of a group writing share issue costs off against the share premium account.

Extract from London & Edinburgh Trust PLC Annual Report 31st December 1988.

23. RESERVES	Share premium account £m	Capital redemption reserve £m	Other reserves (unrealised) £m	Revaluation reserve (unrealised) £m	Capital reserve (realised) £m	Profit and loss account £m
Group:						
At 1st January, 1988	1.3	–	48.0	52.5	4.2	33.6
Premium on shares issued	7.2	–	–	–	–	–
Purchase of own shares	–	0.3	–	–	–	(3.6)
Share issue costs	(0.9)	–	–	–	–	–
Surplus on revaluation of investment properties	–	–	–	63.4	–	–
Sale of investment properties	–	–	–	(2.0)	5.9	–
Surplus on foreign currency translation	–	–	0.3	–	–	–
Acquisition of subsidiary companies	–	–	6.4	–	–	–
Share of related company reserves	–	–	–	2.2	–	–
Goodwill written off	–	–	–	–	–	(13.2)
Sale of London & Metropolitan PLC	–	–	(7.0)	–	–	–
Retained profit for the year	–	–	–	–	–	33.6
At 31st December, 1988	7.6	0.3	47.7	116.1	10.1	50.4

Fair value of identifiable assets and liabilities

7.40   The Act now embodies the term 'identifiable assets and liabilities' and, as explained in chapter 6 paragraph 6.20, this term means the same as 'separable net assets'.

7.41   The fair value of an asset can be defined as the amount that the acquiring company would have been willing to pay for the asset had it acquired it directly. This value would normally be the asset's net current replacement cost and would represent the cost of replacing the asset with one having a similar service potential.

7.42   The process of fair valuing separable net assets can be split into the elements that follow, each of these elements is considered further in the paragraphs below and fair valuing particular assets and liabilities is also considered:

■   Meaning of fair value.

■   Perspective from which the fair value exercise should be carried out.

■   Extent of knowledge on which the exercise should be based.

■ Identifying assets and liabilities acquired.

■ Assigning fair values to fixed assets, stocks, other assets and
  liabilities.

Meaning of fair value

7.43 It is proposed that 'fair value' will be defined as the amount for which
      an asset or liability could be exchanged in an arm's length transaction

7.44 The objective in the fair value exercise is to estimate the cost of the
      individual assets and liabilities acquired. Assets and liabilities should
      be individually identified and fair valued, fair values being based on
      what it would have cost the acquirer to purchase the items had they
      been acquired directly. This method is consistent with the objective of
      consolidated financial statements, which is to show the assets and
      liabilities of the group as if it were a single entity.

7.45 In carrying out the fair value exercise, it would be appropriate to work
      at a fairly detailed level and, therefore, to assign fair values to
      individual assets or small groups of assets. For example, if a property
      portfolio is being fair valued, it would probably be necessary to carry
      out the exercise on individual assets. Clearly, this may not be possible
      where stocks are concerned. Also where, for example, a business
      segment of the acquired company is to be disposed of soon after
      acquisition, it will probably be more appropriate to value the whole
      business segment as a single item (see further para 7.78).

7.46 Some property assets are valued on a basis that has regard to the
      trading potential that attaches to the property. This trading potential is
      sometimes wrongly thought of as goodwill. For such properties,
      valuations on an open market basis that has regard to the properties'
      trading potential will represent their fair value. This basis is clearly
      described in SSAP 22 paragraph 15.

Perspective of the acquirer

7.47 The exposure draft contemplates that fair values should normally be
      attributed from the perspective of the acquirer, rather than that of the
      perspective of the acquired company. The perspective of the acquirer
      is favoured in the proposals because it takes into account the
      acquirer's plans for the future and its style of operation. This basis is
      consistent with SSAP 14 which requires that the purchase
      consideration should be allocated on the basis of *"the fair value to the
      acquiring company"*. [SSAP 14 para 29]. This principle is illustrated in
      the following example.

Example

The management of a company that is acquired may have certain stocks that are slow moving, but which they hope to sell after conducting an advertising campaign. They may, therefore, value these stocks at cost. The management of the acquirer may decide, on investigating the company, that an advertising campaign would not work and that consequently, the stocks are unsaleable. The management of the acquirer would, therefore, attribute a fair value of nil to the stocks.

7.48 Clearly, the perspective of the acquiring company is more appropriate in the example, particularly as the purchaser will have the final say as to whether the stocks will be sold.

Knowledge on which to base fair values

7.49 Many of the problems associated with the fair value exercise derive from the different degrees of knowledge possessed by the aquirer before and after the acquisition. The question arises as to whether the knowledge should only be the knowledge that the acquirer has before he has time to examine the acquisition, or whether it should mean all knowledge relating to the acquisition both before and after it takes place, or a degree of knowledge which is between these two extremes. The conclusion reached in the proposals is that the last of these is to be preferred, because the other two give the acquirer too little or too much opportunity to determine fair values. Generally, the fair values should be based on circumstances existing at the date of acquisition and should not be affected by matters arising after this date.

7.50 The period of hindsight, proposed is the time between the acquisition date and the date when the acquirer first publishes financial information affected by the fair values assigned. However, it may not be possible for companies to ascertain the required fair value information where the acquisition is made shortly before publication of its financial statements. Therefore, where the acquisition takes place within six months of the date of publishing the group's consolidated financial statements, provisional allocations should be made. These provisional figures could then be amended in the next financial statements with a corresponding adjustment made to goodwill arising on the acquisition.

7.51 Where a company publishes interim or preliminary statements, it will be necessary to disclose consolidated information including the effects of acquiring subsidiaries. It is proposed that the time scales for annual financial statements mentioned above will apply also to information published in advance of the annual financial statements.

7.52 Amendments may be necessary to fair values after the hindsight period has ended. These should be accounted for in accordance with SSAP 6. Fundamental errors that are discovered outside the hindsight period should be adjusted for by making prior year adjustments to the previously computed goodwill figure. Normally, however, any amendments will be the result of revisions of estimates and should, therefore, be treated as part of the profit on ordinary activities, shown separately as exceptional items if material. Only where there is a fundamental error should amendments be treated as prior year adjustments.

7.53 An example of where an amendment should be treated as extraordinary is where it involves the release or increase of provisions made for losses in a segment of the acquired business that is being closed.

7.54 Another area that has caused problems in practice is where companies have, as a matter of course, included in extraordinary items the costs of integrating new businesses acquired with their existing businesses. Although such costs are not amendments to fair value, as such, they are the result of the process of assessing the acquisition and deciding on the action needed to integrate the business. Such costs should be charged against trading profits (above the line) if they relate to continuing activities. This is because acquisitions are not normally extraordinary events and amendments made after the hindsight period should, for that reason, normally be treated as part of ordinary activities. See further the examples in paragraph 7.101 below.

Identifying assets and liabilities acquired

7.55 As mentioned above, the Act introduces the term 'identifiable assets and liabilities', whereas SSAP 22 uses the term 'separable net assets'. In practice, they have identical meanings. The definition of separable net assets given in SSAP 22 is as follows:

> "Separable net assets of a company are those assets (and liabilities) which can be identified and sold (or discharged) separately without necessarily disposing of the business as a whole. They include identifiable intangibles" [SSAP 22 para 27].

7.56 Such assets and liabilities should be identified at an early stage. Certain deferred costs and prepayments do not meet the definition of a separable net asset. However, such items should normally be taken into account in the fair value exercise.

7.57 Assets and liabilities that may be recognised by the acquirer in the fair value exercise may not have been recognised in the acquired company's financial statements. Such liabilities can, for example, include provisions for reorganisation costs, unprovided contingent liabilities, unprovided arrears of preference dividends and unprovided post-retirement benefits. Similarly, assets such as patents, licences and pension scheme surpluses may be recognised by the acquirer, but not by the acquired company. Furthermore, not all items recognised by the acquired company will be recognised by the acquirer.

7.58 There is a lack of consistency at present as to when identifiable intangibles that have been acquired should be recognised. Many companies recognise intangibles such as publishing rights and trade marks while others do not. Such intangibles can constitute very significant proportions of a company's consolidated balance sheet. For example over 50 per cent of the capital employed of Reed International comprises publishing rights and titles and exhibition rights, see Table 33 overleaf. SSAP 22 already requires companies to recognise separable intangibles, but the requirement often appears to be overlooked. The relevant paragraph in SSAP 22 is as follows:

> *"The amount attributed to purchased goodwill should not include any value for separable intangibles. The amount of these, if material, should be included under the appropriate heading within intangible fixed assets in the balance sheet."*
> [SSAP 22 para 37].

7.59 Fair valuing intangible assets is considered in paragraph 7.74 below and also in chapter 8.

Fair valuing fixed assets

7.60 For fixed assets the fair value of an asset will normally reflect what the acquirer would have to pay for the item directly, which will normally be its replacement cost. The replacement cost would normally take into account the condition and location of the asset. Professional valuers might be required to value such assets, for example see Table 34 overleaf. Often the replacement cost will be the second hand value of the asset. However, where a second hand value is not available, the gross replacement cost of an asset will then have to be determined by reference to other sources of information such as:

■ Suppliers' quotations and current price lists.

■ Recent purchases of the same or similar assets.

■ Expert knowledge of the market, which might include expert opinion.

■ Relevant specific price indices.

7.61 To arrive at the replacement cost, an appropriate amount of depreciation should be deducted to reflect the age of the asset.

Table 33: *Example showing that over 50 per cent of the group's total
assets are intangible.*

*Extract from Reed International P.L.C. Annual Report 31st March
1989.*

Consolidated balance sheet extract

£ million	1989	
Fixed Assets		
Intangible assets *note 12*	856.0	
Tangible assets *note 13*	128.1	
Investments *note 14*	148.8	
		1,132.9
Current Assets		
Stocks *note 15*	100.5	
Debtors *note 16*	339.8	
Deferred taxation *note 17*	–	
Cash and short term investments *note 18*	680.0	
	1,120.3	
Creditors: Amounts falling due within 1 year *note 19*	650.8	
Net Current Assets		469.5
Total Assets less Current Liabilities		1,602.4

Accounting policy extract

Intangible assets
Publishing rights and titles, exhibition rights and other intangible assets, are stated at fair value on
acquisition. Having no finite economic life, amortisation is not provided. Subject to annual review,
any permanent impairment of value is written off against profit.

On the acquisition of businesses, subsidiary or related companies the purchase consideration is
allocated between the underlying net tangible and intangible assets on a fair value basis. Any excess
cost or goodwill written off against consolidated reserves.

Other acquired intangible assets are amortised over their useful economic life.

7.62 In certain circumstances, where the asset is to be disposed of or is not
worth replacing, its fair value will be its net realisable value or its
recoverable amount respectively.

7.63 Also account should be taken of any grants that might have been
available had assets eligible for grants, such as plant and machinery
and motor vehicles, been acquired directly.

7.64 Where fair values are attributed to fixed assets and these fair values
are not incorporated into the accounts of the acquired company, the
group will need to keep two records of the cost and depreciation of

such assets. This is because, in addition to the records of the acquired company, the group will need to keep records of the fair values of the assets and depreciation charged on the basis of those fair values in the group's consolidated financial statements.

Table 34: Illustration of an accounting policy that explains that the group uses professional values to ascertain certain fair values.

Extract from Cadbury Schweppes Public Limited Company Annual Report 31st December 1988.

(d) Acquisition and disposal of subsidiaries

Results of subsidiary companies acquired during the financial year are included in group profit from the effective date of acquisition and those of companies disposed of up to the effective date of disposal. For this purpose the net tangible assets of newly acquired subsidiaries are incorporated into the accounts on the basis of the fair value to the group as at the effective date of acquisition. Land and buildings are included at values confirmed by professional valuers and treated as being at cost.

Any excess of the consideration over the fair value of the net tangible assets of newly acquired subsidiaries at the effective date of acquisition is written off against reserves on consolidation.

The difference between the sales proceeds and the net assets at the effective date of disposal is taken to profit and loss account.

Fair valuing stocks

7.65   It has been quite normal in the past for an acquirer not to fair value stocks upwards, although often provisions are made against the value of stocks. However, stocks should more correctly be valued at their current replacement cost based on the condition and location of the asset at the date of acquisition. In addition, it will be necessary to take into account during the stockholding period any value added due to the stock maturing or appreciating during that period, because of improvements through work carried out since it was originally acquired.

7.66   The implications of this basis of valuation for raw materials, work in progress and finished goods are as follows:

■   Raw materials should be valued at replacement cost.

■   Work in progress should be the estimated selling price of the finished goods less the cost of completion and disposal and a profit allowance for the effort involved in completing and selling the goods.

This basis is similar to the normal basis of valuation of long-term contracts. However, it may be difficult to apply where a contract is in the early stages and the outcome cannot be foreseen. Applying this basis to such a contract would involve the acquirer in making judgements about the inclusion of profits, which the company acquired would not have been entitled to make under SSAP 9.

■ Finished goods should be valued at estimated selling price less the costs of disposal and an allowance for the profit generated by the selling effort.

It is not entirely clear how the 'profit generated by the selling effort' would to be calculated. However, it is likely that the amount of the profit included in the fair value should be reduced by a certain fraction. This fraction might, at its simplest, be calculated as selling costs over total costs. However, the calculation of such a fraction may vary significantly in practice.

7.67   Clearly, fair valuing stocks may tend to reduce the extent to which acquirers sometimes include in post-acquisition profits the profit element in stocks that they acquire. However, enforcing any fair value proposals in this area may be difficult in practice.

7.68   Another aspect of fair valuing long-term contracts is where contracts are acquired that are similar in nature to contracts already being carried out by the acquirer. If the acquired contracts are less profitable than those of the acquirer, the acquirer may consider that provisions should be made in the fair value exercise so that the contracts acquired will then give similar margins to those of the acquirer.

Example 1

If the selling price of finished goods is £200,000, and the costs to complete are estimated at £50,000 with selling costs to be incurred of £30,000, then the first part of the calculation would be to reduce the figure of £200,000 by £80,000 to give £120,000. If the overall profit earned on such a contract was normally 10 per cent then it would be fair to assume that a profit allowance of £8,000 should also be deducted (being 10 per cent of costs to complete and selling costs).

This would leave a carrying value of £112,000. If the contract was in fact carried in the books of the acquirer at £125,000 a provision would have to be made of £13,000 to reduce the carrying value to fair value.

Example 2

Another way of calculating the fair value might be to add to the carrying value the costs to complete and sell of £80,000. This would give a figure of £205,000 (£125,000 + £80,000). A provision would be made of £5,000 against the loss that would be incurred, and an allowance of £20,000 would also be made for the company's normal profit margin of 10 per cent on the whole contract. This would give a fair value of £100,000 (that is, £205,000 - £80,000 - £25,000).

7.69   This method would, however, not be acceptable as it involves allowing for the company's normal profit margin on the whole cost, including that incurred prior to acquisition. The difference between the fair value of £112,000 in the first example and the fair value of £100,000 in the second example is the difference between 10 per cent of £200,000 being the total value of the contract and 10 per cent of £80,000 being the costs to complete and sell.

7.70 In the same example, assume that the carrying value in the acquired company was £105,000. The expected sales value would, as before, be reduced by costs to complete and selling costs of £80,000 plus the attributable profit of £8,000. This would give a fair value of £112,000 and the contract would be written up to that value in the consolidated financial statements. This recognises that part of the profit earned by the acquired company in bringing the contract to its present condition had not been reflected in the carrying value.

7.71 If fair values are attributed to stocks, and these values are in excess of cost to the acquired company, it would seem that the provisions of SSAP 9 would not allow the fair values to be incorporated in the financial statements of the acquired company. This is because the standard requires that stocks, other than long-term contracts, should be recorded at the lower of cost and net realisable value. [SSAP 9 para 26]. Fair values may be incorporated in the consolidated financial statements because they represent cost to the group, but not in the acquired company's financial statements if they are in excess of cost to that company.

7.72 It will again be necessary for the group to keep separate records of any stocks that are recorded at fair values in excess of cost to the acquired company. A consolidation adjustment will be necessary to adjust the profits and stocks of the acquired company for the effect of the fair value exercise, for so long as the stocks remain unsold.

Fair valuing cash, receivables and prepayments

7.73 The fair value of cash will obviously be its carrying amount in the acquired company's balance sheet. Whereas, the fair value of receivables should be the amount received discounted to present value where appropriate. The fair value of prepayments will need to be recognised at amounts that will ensure proper matching of costs and revenues post-acquisition.

Fair valuing intangible assets

7.74 Although only certain intangibles are specifically mentioned in SSAP 22, others appear in financial statements. These other intangibles include the value of know how, the present value of insurance business in force and even milk quotas. As some of these intangibles are often said to have an infinite useful life they are often not depreciated.

7.75 On the other hand some of the intangibles that are mentioned in SSAP 22 rarely appear in company financial statements. Customer lists is an example of such an intangible.

7.76 Acquisitions in the past have highlighted the extent to which the value of intangibles such as trademarks or brand names have been excluded from company balance sheets in the past. From the point of view of an acquirer, intangibles, such as trademarks, clearly have a real and often high value (see further chapter 8).

Fair valuing liabilities

7.77 Liabilities should generally be valued at the amount that will be disclosed in discharging the liability, discounted to present value if appropriate. Where long-term liabilities are to be discounted, the proposals suggest the rate used should be equivalent to the cost of raising an additional amount of capital (see further para 7.119).

Disposals of business segments

7.78 There have been many examples of acquisitions where the acquirer has subsequently disposed of large unwanted portions of the business, sometimes recouping the major part of his initial outlay in the process. It has also been quite normal for the proceeds of disposals made before the acquirer's year end to be netted off the total consideration in the fair value exercise. Obviously, in this circumstance it would be inappropriate to value the business segment being sold at its replacement cost.

7.79 Where the acquirer has no intention of retaining an asset or business segment the fair value should normally be the net realisable value of the asset. The net realisable value should be used in order to ensure that the post-acquisition results of the group are not distorted by profits earned or losses incurred prior to the acquisition. However, it is questionable whether the acquirer will necessarily always be in a position to know the actual realisable value of the assets or companies that he has acquired as part of a larger acquisition and which he intends to sell. It has been suggested that the realisable value should be the maximum amount the acquiring company would have been willing to pay for this asset had it been acquired directly.

7.80 It is debatable whether this value will always be the same as the amount for which the acquirer hopes to sell the asset, since he is unlikely to have been willing to pay highly for an asset or company that he does not want to keep. If there is a significant difference between the maximum amount the acquiring company would have been willing to pay for such an asset and the actual sale proceeds, such a difference will flow through to the profit and loss account of the acquiring company as a post-acquisition profit or loss. If the expected proceeds were used as the fair value, the effect would be quite different. The difference would reduce the goodwill, if it were a profit and increase the goodwill if it were a loss (see further chapter 8).

7.81 Where a low fair value is placed on assets acquired and these are subsequently sold at a profit it is always tempting to argue that the profit is entirely due to the expertise of the new management. It may, however, be equally valid to argue that in deciding on the total purchase consideration the acquirer took account of the expected sale price of assets rather than the price he would have been prepared himself to pay for them. Consider the example that follows.

Example

A group acquires another company that, at the acquisition date, has in its balance sheet a subsidiary held for sale at the estimated sale proceeds of £500,000. The group subsequently renegotiated the sale price of the subsidiary at a higher value. Should the group take the difference in the selling price as an adjustment to the fair value of assets acquired, or can it be taken as a post-acquisition profit?

If, but only if, it can be established that the increase in the sales price has been achieved by the new management's better negotiating skills, can the additional profit be taken to the consolidated profit and loss account as a post-acquisition item. It should in any event be disclosed as an extraordinary item.

Treatment of contingencies

7.82 The treatment of contingent purchase consideration is considered earlier in paragraph 7.28. The paragraphs that follow consider contingencies that affect the value of separable net assets.

7.83 The first matter to consider with contingencies is whether they should be recognised in the fair value exercise at their full amount or at an expected amount. The expected amount is based on the range of possible amounts weighted by the probability of each of these amounts arising. The proposals are that the full amount should be used (rather than the expected amount) if it is probable that the liability will crystallise. Similarly, SSAP 18, which applies to the post-acquisition financial statements, requires the full amount rather than the expected amount of contingencies to be taken into account. [SSAP 18 para 19].

7.84 Whether contingent liabilities are recognised or not in the fair value exercise depends on the criteria laid down in SSAP 18, which states that:

"... a material contingent loss should be accrued in financial statements where it is probable that a future event will confirm a loss which can be estimated with reasonable accuracy at the date on which the financial statements are approved by the directors." [SSAP 18 para 15].

7.85   Where the contingent liability is recognised in the fair value exercise, it will have to be reconsidered in future periods to ascertain whether it is adequate. Where it is not, an additional provision will have to be made to the post-acquisition profit and loss account.

7.86   SSAP 18 also states that contingent gains should not be accrued in financial statements. [SSAP 18 para 17]. However, the proposals are that contingent gains should be recognised in the fair value exercise, if they meet criteria similar to those that SSAP 18 lays down for the recognition of contingent liabilities. This is because recognition of contingent gains or liabilities in the financial statements has no immediate profit and loss account effect. However, omitting a contingent gain in the fair value exercise will have a profit and loss account effect in succeeding financial statements.

7.87   If such gains were recognised, goodwill would be increased and may be written off to reserves. If gains are recognised, but subsequently they do not materialise, there will be an adverse effect on the profit and loss account. In this respect where a contingent asset is set up on consolidation, it will be necessary to consider in future periods whether there is a reduction in its value. Where there is, the asset should be written down, by providing an amount against post-acquisition profits.

Setting up provisions

7.88   Much public criticism has been made of the methods used to set up provisions when accounting for business combinations. To some extent this criticism led to the revision of SSAP 22, which now requires disclosure of the uses to which provisions are put (see further chapter 6). The paragraphs that follow concentrate first on provisions for reorganisation costs and then on provisions for future losses.

Provisions for reorganisation

7.89   As mentioned above, the fair value exercise should be conducted from the perspective of the acquirer. For this reason, it seems consistent that if provisions for reorganisation costs and provisions for losses need to be made, they should be provided for in the fair value exercise. The fact that decisions about making investments include consideration of the costs involved in 'turning a company around' is further support for this view.

7.90   By setting up provisions a company is able to charge costs that would otherwise be borne by the profit and loss account against those provisions in the post-acquisition period. If the provisions are not set up the costs of reorganisation will flow through to the profit and loss account in the subsequent periods and will, therefore, adversely affect the earnings per share of the combined group.

7.91   Two conditions are proposed for the recognition of provisions for reorganisation, which are that:

- There is a clearly defined programme of reorganisation and those costs for which provisions are to be made must have been specified in reasonable detail.

- There is evidence that the costs were contemplated by the acquirer at the time of acquisition.

7.92   In addition, the group should disclose in its consolidated financial statements the following information:

- Broad details of the purposes to which the provisions are to be put.

- Description of the movements in provisions, showing separately the amounts used and the amounts released unused in sufficient detail to show the purpose for, and the extent to which, the provision proved necessary.

7.93   Guinness in its 1987 financial statements gave details of all fair value adjustments, including provisions, relating to the acquisition of Distillers. This approach has also been adopted more recently by a growing number of companies, see for example Table 35 overleaf. Such tables are now required by both the Act and SSAP 22 (revised). The content of the tables is considered further in chapter 6 overleaf.

7.94   One of the major problems with reorganisation provisions is where the acquirer needs to reorganise not only the business of the company acquired, but also his own business. This is often necessary in order successfully to integrate the new business and achieve economies of scale. The question this raises is whether or not the acquirer is entitled to take account of the costs of reorganising his existing business in the fair value exercise, if that reorganisation is a direct consequence of the acquisition. In practice, it often happens that reorganisation provisions set up as part of the fair value exercise do include an element that relates to the existing business of the acquirer. It can be argued that since the fair value exercise is concerned with the assets and liabilities of the acquired company only, inclusion of costs relating to existing businesses is wrong. However, it is sometimes very difficult in practice to differentiate between costs relating to existing and newly acquired businesses.

7.95   As mentioned in paragraph 7.49 the proposal that there should be evidence that the costs were contemplated at the time of the acquisition, seems to ignore the 'hindsight period'. It seems reasonable that, if an acquirer is to be given a period in which he can amend fair values, this period should also be allowed for deciding what reorganisation costs will have to be incurred in respect of the newly acquired business.

Table 35: Example showing fair value adjustments made on an acquisition.

Extract from Tesco PLC Annual Report and Accounts 27th February 1988.

19. Merger Reserve

	Hillards consolidated accounts at 2nd May, 1987 £m	Acquisition accounting adjust- ments £m	Total £m
Net Assets/(liabilities) acquired			
Goodwill on acquisition	–	193.9	193.9
Fixed Assets	82.0	6.4	88.4
Stocks	16.2	(2.7)	13.5
Debtors	0.8	–	0.8
Cash at bank and in hand	14.6	–	14.6
Creditors falling due within one year	(41.6)	–	(41.6)
Net Current Liabilities	(10.0)	(2.7)	(12.7)
Creditors falling due after more than one year	(21.6)	–	(21.6)
Increase in consolidated reserves from 2nd May, 1987 to 15th May, 1987	–	0.3	0.3
Total net assets acquired	50.4	197.9	248.3
Reorganisation costs, net of taxation (a)	–	(10.3)	(10.3)
	50.4	187.6	238.0
Consideration paid			
Ordinary shares issued (b)			2.1
Cash			2.4
Merger reserve arising on consolidation			233.5
Less: Goodwill written-off			193.9
			39.6

For presentation purposes, the audited Hillards' balance sheet at their 2nd May, 1987 year-end has been used to illustrate the calculation of the merger reserve. The acquisition was made on 15th May, 1987 and the adjustment to reserves reflects this.

(a) Acquisition accounting adjustments
   Adjustments have been made to the book values of the net assets acquired to reflect their fair value to align the accounting policies of Hillards with those of the group and to provide for reorganisation costs subsequent to acquisition. The principal adjustments are as follows:
   (i) Fixed Assets
      Tangible assets have been included at fair value based principally on external professional property valuations and provisions against the disposal of fixtures and fittings arising from store comversions.
   (ii) Stocks
      Stocks have been adjusted mainly by writing down surplus stocks and providing for costs of realisation.

Provisions for future losses

7.96 Setting up reorganisation provisions has been a source of considerable argument since the contentious paragraph 14 of SSAP 22 first appeared. There has sometimes been agreement between acquirer and acquiree in order to achieve a situation where costs to be incurred by the acquirer's business have effectively been transferred to the acquiree. The argument has even been put forward that a general provision can be made where the acquiree's gross margins are lower than those of the acquirer. The provision would have the effect of allowing the acquired company to show the same margins as the acquirer for a number of years into the future, until reorganisation is completed, to improve the acquired company's margins.

7.97 A reason for not permitting such losses to be provided could be the requirement in SSAP 14 that the profit and loss account should deal with the post-acquisition results of the acquired company from the effective date of acquisition. Future trading losses or profits of the acquired company are not liabilities or assets that should be reflected in the fair value exercise.

7.98 One exception to this general rule could be where provision is made for the trading results (profits and losses) of business segments that are to be disposed of following the acquisition. The term 'business segment' is defined in SSAP 6. This treatment is consistent with SSAP 14, which states that subsidiaries acquired with the intention that control will be temporary should be stated as a current asset, at the lower of cost and net realisable value (see further chapter 3 para 3.69). The aim should be to ensure that the disposal of a part of the business, that at the time of acquisition was only acquired as an incidental part of the transaction, has a neutral impact on the consolidated profit and loss account.

7.99 The proposals on provisions for losses should succeed in eliminating a major loophole in SSAP 22, which refers only to *anticipated future losses* without specifying whether such losses related to continuing business segments, or segments that are to be disposed of. [SSAP 22 para 14].

7.100   As a result of these proposals companies may be encouraged to make fuller disclosure in future of the post-acquisition results attributable to companies acquired. This will be particularly so if such results are depressed by losses of continuing activities.

7.101   Examples of the different types of problems that can arise concerning provisions are considered in the examples below:

Example 1

A group acquires another company that is in the same trade. The group's average gross profit is 80 per cent, while the acquired company's gross profit is 70 per cent. Can a provision be made for 10 per cent of budgeted sales for the next two years, as the group hopes to have increased the gross profit percentage of the subsidiary over that time?

This type of provision would not be allowed under the proposals. It should not be made, because there is no loss now or in the future. Its sole effect it to produce higher margins in the future.

Example 2

A group acquires a new subsidiary and wishes to know whether it can provide for reorganising the group after the acquisition as well as providing for reorganising the subsidiary acquired.

Generally, the costs of providing for reorganising the existing group should be treated as an exceptional item in the consolidated financial statements. However, it might be possible to provide certain reorganisation costs in the reorganisation provision made as part of the fair value exercise of the subsidiary.

Example 3

A group acquired a company some years ago and provisions for reorganisation were made at the time. The group now realises that a substantial part of these provisions is not required. Can they be written back to the consolidated profit and loss account?

To accord with the proposals, subsequent amendments to fair values should generally be dealt with through the profit and loss account and fully disclosed. However, if a fundamental error in fair valuing has occurred at the time the fair values were first established, then the amount should be treated as a prior year adjustment in accordance with SSAP 6.

Example 4

A company purchases a partnership and agrees to reduce the consideration it pays in order to pay the partners a pension. The company has purchased an annuity and proposes to charge the cost to the profit and loss account.

This treatment would be incorrect and the company should treat the cost of the annuity as a liability that it acquired on purchasing of the partnership. Therefore, this will have the effect of increasing the goodwill recognised on the partnership's acquisition.

Example 5

A group acquired a subsidiary last year and included it in its consolidated financial statements. In the current year, the group incurred substantial reorganisation costs

---

that were not provided for as part of the fair value exercise. The group wishes to adjust the goodwill figure that arose on the acquisition last year.

If under the proposals, the subsidiary was acquired in the six month period prior to publishing the group's financial statements and it was not possible to ascertain the provision for reorganisation in the time available, then an adjustment could be made to the goodwill figure. If, however, this is not the situation and it was just an oversight that no provision was made, then it might be possible to treat the adjustment as a fundamental error and make a prior year adjustment. However, where it is not considered a fundamental error, it should be charged to the consolidated post-acquisition profit and loss account.

Pension schemes

7.102 A large number of companies have taken advantage of pension scheme surpluses in recent years to reduce their pension contributions, or on occasions to take a cash refund. In many situations, this has had a material effect on earnings per share.

7.103 Defined contribution schemes do not pose the same accounting problem as defined benefit schemes and are, therefore, not considered further below. With defined contribution schemes a liability will exist in the company's accounts if all contributions due by it have not been paid to the scheme and an asset will exist where excess contributions have been paid.

7.104 The accounting principle in SSAP 24 requires that, for defined benefit schemes, variations from regular costs should usually be allocated over the expected average remaining service lives of the employees in the scheme. The discussion paper considered three alternative approaches to fair valuing a defined benefit scheme as follows:

■ Continue with the existing funding rate.

■ Commission an up-to-date valuation using the actuarial assumptions and methods of the acquired company. Then recognise the resulting surplus or deficiency at the acquisition date.

■ Carry out an actuarial valuation using the assumptions and methods of the acquiring company and recognise the resulting surplus or deficiency at the acquisition date.

7.105 The first option described above is dismissed in the discussion paper, because the method ignores the fact that the acquisition has occurred. Similarly, the second alternative is also rejected in favour of the third, which is consistent with the other proposals that the acquirer's perspective should be used. Generally, therefore, the acquirer should determine the fair value of the pension scheme from its own perspective, employing the assumptions and methods of its own actuary to perform the valuation, recognising the resulting surplus or deficit at the acquisition date and thereafter charging the regular cost to the profit and loss account.

7.106 Another problem is whether changes to a pension scheme resulting from an acquisition should be reflected in the fair value exercise. Such changes might include upgrading the pension rights of employees in a newly acquired subsidiary. In addition, adjustments might be necessary due to a change in the number of employees following an acquisition. However, the proposal is not to set up such provisions for changes in benefits following the acquisition. The reason for not allowing such provisions is that they relate to a post-acquisition decision that should rightly be reflected in the post-acquisition consolidated profit and loss. Adjustments should also not be made for changes in the number of employees, unless provision has been made for the costs of closure of a business segment as a result of the acquisition and such costs include redundancies. In such a situation, the effect on pension scheme costs relating to the redundant employees should be accounted for in the fair value exercise.

7.107 It seems rather inconsistent that the proposals allows that provisions may be made for reorganisation costs of continuing activities in the fair value exercise, but then does not consider that the effects of such a reorganisation should be reflected in the fair value of the pension scheme. If there are redundancy costs included in the provisions, it can be argued that it is correct to take account of the resultant saving in pension contributions when making the provisions.

7.108 It also seems inconsistent that decisions to upgrade pension benefits of employees should not be reflected in the fair value exercise. After all, there is a reasonable amount of time allowed in the hindsight period for decisions on this to be taken and for an actuarial valuation to be obtained.

Taxation implications

7.109 A distortion to the tax charge in the post-acquisition consolidated profit and loss account will occur if account is not taken of the tax effects of the fair value exercise carried out on assets and liabilities. This distortion will arise where any assets acquired are subsequently sold. This is because the profit for the post-acquisition period will be the difference between the proceeds of sale and the fair values of assets sold, but the tax charge will be based on the difference between proceeds and the book value of the assets in the acquired company's books. If the tax charge is not adjusted it will be unrelated to the profit figure based on proceeds less the fair value of assets.

7.110 An adjustment should be generally be made, therefore, to deferred tax in the fair value exercise in order to avoid such distortions. The differences between fair values and book values are not dealt with in SSAP 15 as timing differences, because the standard does not deal specifically with fair values in the context of an acquisition. However, such differences should probably be treated as timing differences and deferred tax should be provided as if the timing differences were covered by SSAP 15.

7.111 Adjusting the deferred tax balance in the fair value exercise may or may not have real significance for companies. Distortions are generally created by the effect of fair valuing plant and machinery and stocks and in the past these are two types of asset that have not been valued upwards in most fair value exercises. For plant this may be because of the difficulties of obtaining replacement costs. In relation to stocks the tendency has been to make provisions against the book value rather than to revalue upwards. If, as a result of the exposure draft, companies are more ready in the future to revalue plant and machinery and stocks upwards, then the tax effects will become more significant.

7.112 In general, companies already take account of tax when making fair value provisions. The provision for deferred tax should be viewed from the overall position of the group. This treatment is consistent with the concept that the acquirer's view is taken when considering fair values. The following situations could, therefore, arise.

Example 1

An acquirer can demonstrate that it will be able to use tax losses in the future to group relieve any tax liabilities arising in the acquired company.

In this situation, if there is a deferred tax liability in the acquired subsidiary's financial statements it can be reduced by the unusable losses in the fair value exercise.

Example 2

The acquirer has provided for a deferred tax liability, but the acquired company expects to have net originating timing differences in the future, which can be used to reduce the acquirer's tax liability.

In this situation, a deferred tax asset should be recognised in the fair value exercise, being the value of the relief that the group will obtain from the acquired company's expected future timing differences.

7.113 Normally, tax losses brought forward in the acquiring company will not be able to be group relieved and so will not benefit the acquiring company. However, where there are circumstances where such losses can be used, a deferred tax asset should be set up as part of the fair values.

7.114 In its 1985 accounts, CH Beazer (Holdings) PLC included a deferred asset in respect of tax losses of a newly acquired company. This disclosure reflected the value of losses to be used up within a limited period of two years, with the value of remaining losses not being recognised. The deferred tax asset in Beazers' accounts was £2,162,000 and is explained in Table 36.

Table 36: Example of a deferred tax asset recognised on acquisition.

Extract from C H Beazer (Holdings) PLC Report and Accounts 30th June 1988.

Note extract

15. Deferred taxation (extract)

The acquired deferred tax losses reflect the value attributed at the time of acquisition to the tax losses of William Leech and its subsidiary companies to the extent that they are expected to be utilised in the period to 30th June 1987. This amount is taken into account in arriving at the goodwill written off on this acquisition

Certain group companies have further tax losses of some £12,800,000 (1984—£4,000,000), in aggregate, which are available for set off against those companies' future taxable profits. Of this sum a total of approximately £11,400,000 relates to losses of Leech and its subsidiaries which were acquired during the year, the utilisation of which is not anticipated prior to 30th June 1987.

7.115 There are a number of situations where the tax consequences of an acquisition can have significant effects. For example, if a loss making company is acquired during an accounting period it does not always follow that tax losses are apportioned in the same way as losses for accounting purposes. Therefore, a situation can arise where losses incurred by an acquired company before acquisition may be group relieved against the profits of the acquiring company in the post-acquisition period. When such losses are significant the effect on the tax charge and earnings per share in the post-acquisition consolidated financial statements can be very material.

7.116 In the past, it has not been the practice to recognise a deferred asset in respect of losses such as these, because there is a general reluctance to recognise deferred tax assets. However, the Act requires details to be given of significant factors that affect the tax charge for current and future periods, and because of this, disclosure has usually been made of the circumstances leading to the reduction to the group tax charge. [4 Sch 54(2)].

7.117 This is an example of a situation where the losses are certain to be of value and, therefore, should presumably be recognised. However, there are other examples where there is no certainty that there will be a tax benefit to the acquiring company. Sometimes, acquisitions are structured in such a way that certain elements of the consideration may be allowable for tax. For example, 'non competition covenant payments' may be allowable in certain countries. If such a payment is made as part of the consideration it will generally be treated as part of the cost of investment in the acquiring company's books. If, however, there is uncertainty as to whether such a payment will be allowed for tax, or if the benefit arises over a period of years, it may be argued that the tax benefit should not be set up as an asset, but instead should flow through to the profit and loss of the group as it arises.

7.118 The discussion paper appeared to rule out the treatment of possible tax benefits as contingent assets. However, the above example and similar situations show there is an argument for not dismissing the possibility of treating tax benefits as contingent assets rather than recorded assets in some situations. There may be examples where the potential tax benefits should be treated as contingent assets, rather than as recorded assets and, therefore, no asset is recorded at the time of the fair value exercise.

Using discounted amounts

7.119 The proposals outline two situations where discounting may be appropriate as follows:

- In fair valuing long-term receivables and payables.

- In calculating the amount recoverable from the further use of a fixed asset.

Long-term receivables and payables

7.120 The discounted value of most receivables and payables is usually not significantly different from the face value since a market rate of interest is charged or received on most long-term payables and receivables and for short-term items the discount would be insignificant. Consequently, discounting of long-term receivables and payables should only be necessary where the interest rates the instruments bear are significantly different from the rate the company can obtain when raising additional finance.

7.121 One of the few examples of discounting is contained in the financial statements of Ultramar PLC. This example does not relate to a fair value exercise on acquisition, but demonstrates how discounting might be used for long-term payables and is shown in Table 36A overleaf.

Fixed assets

7.122 Where fixed assets are valued at their recoverable amount, there can be practical difficulties in identifying and quantifying the future cash flows for the purpose of discounting. It may, nevertheless, be appropriate to discount the recoverable amount where assets are valued in this way.

Table 36A: Illustration of a group that discounts long-term debt.

Extract from Ultramar PLC Annual Report 31st December 1988.

Note extract

22 Long term debt

	1988 £ million	1987 £ million
a) Long term debt consists of:		
Debt finally repayable after 1993:		
Unsecured 6% convertible bonds maturing 2002 (Note 29)	38.0	38.0
Unsecured 5⅛% Sw.Fr. 150 million public bond issue maturing 1996	55.4	–
Unsecured loans totalling Sp. Ptas 15,484 million due for final repayments in 1995 (Note 22(b))	75.7	74.9
Unsecured loans of US$51.2 million due for final repayment in 1995 (Note 22(b))	28.3	26.3
Unsecured facility ofUS$140.0 million (to a maximum of US$175.0 million) due for final repayment in 1993 (currently 10⅛%)	77.3	51.6
Unsecured facility of Can$250.0 million due for final repayment in 1999 (currently 10⅝%)	116.3	–
Other loans due to 2007 at interest rates to 10½%, secured on fixed assets	0.4	2.7
Loan of Can$141.0 million, secured on fixed assets, due for final repayment in 1993 prepaid during the year	–	57.8
Debt repayable before 1994:		
Unsecured facility of US$32.5 million due for final repayment in 1992 (currently 10⅜%)	18.0	22.6
Non recourse loan of £4.8 million due for final repayment in 1990 (currently 10⅛%)	4.8	–
Other loans at interest rates to 11%, secured on fixed assets	0.2	0.3
Unsecured loans due for final repayment in 1992 prepaid during the year	–	18.6
Unsecured loan of Can$100 million with repayment in 1991 prepaid during the year	–	41.0
	414.4	333.8
Less: Amounts due within one year included in current creditors	25.6	23.0
	£388.8	£310.8

b) Unsecured loans with a face amount at 31st December 1988 of US$65.1 million and Sp. Ptas 19,379 million bear interest at the average favourable rates of 3⅛% and 8% respectively. In the table above the loans are stated at the present values of US$51.2 million and Sp. Ptas 15,484 million having been discounted at the appropriate market rate of interest (averages of 10⅜% and 15¾% respectively) pertaining at the date of assumption of each loan. The difference is being amortised, and treated as additional interest expense, in line with the principal outstanding. Ultramar PLC has issued guarantees in connection with these loans (Note 27(a) (ii)).

7.123   If the discounted amounts of assets and liabilities that are acquired are not reflected back into the accounts of the acquired company, it will be necessary to make a consolidation adjustment each year until the asset or the liability crystallises. This would be done by determining the discounted amount of the asset or liability by reference to market rates of interest at the date of acquisition. It would not usually be necessary to adjust these market rates and thus the discount each year. The interest charge in the group's consolidated profit and loss account would then be diminished or increased by the amount of the discount over the life of the asset or liability respectively. The asset or liability would be correspondingly increased until the full value is shown on maturity.

Technical Release 773

7.124 The Technical Committee of the Institute of Chartered Accountants in England & Wales issued Technical Release 773 (TR 773) entitled 'The Use of Discounting in Financial Statements' in January 1989. The recommendations and the guidance it gives are considered in the following paragraphs.

7.125 The TR briefly explains that there are three principal variables in applying discounting techniques. These are:

■   Cash flow.

■   Cost or present value.

■   Interest rate.

7.126 Where two of these are known it is possible to calculate a value for the third. For instance, where a deep discounted bond has been issued, it is possible to determine the present value as the initial cash inflow, the future cash outflows will be stipulated in the contract, and therefore the issuer can calculate the rate of interest, which, when used to discount the future cash outflows, will equal the present value.

7.127 TR 773 deals with the application of discounting in financial statements, and illustrates this by taking the example of an expense that is incurred immediately, but that is payable over an extended period. In such a situation, depending on the length of the credit period relative to rates of interest, there may be a benefit to the business. If so, only the present value of the future amount payable should be allocated to the financial statements of the first accounting period.

7.128 Similarly, where an acquisition takes place and deferred consideration is payable, the credit period may be a significant benefit that should be recognised by stating the asset at a cost less than the aggregate of the total eventual cash outflow.

7.129 TR 773 states that the interest rate to be used where cash flows and present value are both known is the Internal Rate of Return (IRR). This rate equates the initial outlay (or proceeds) of an asset (or liability) with the present value of the future inflows (or outflows) discounted at that rate.

7.130 In circumstances where discounting is used to derive a present value (either as a cost or as a valuation) the TR states that the rate to be used should normally be a current rate that takes account of the riskiness of the asset and the costs of available finance.

7.131 TR 773 addresses the legal point in that the Act requires assets to be held at purchase price or production cost. It could be argued that it is, therefore, not acceptable to show an asset at a discounted amount. However, TR 773 adopts the approach that deferred consideration represents the purchase of two separate assets, the item acquired and the right to pay over an extended period. Accordingly, the discounted amount is considered by the technical release to represent the purchase price of the asset.

7.132 TR 773 makes the point that where discounting is applied to liabilities it may be necessary in certain circumstances to record the ultimate liability under creditors and the discount as an asset. This will depend on the terms of the contract giving rise to the liability. For example, if the contract were to be terminated early and the company would still have to pay the full amount, then the full liability should be recorded with the discount shown as an asset. If under the contract the liability gradually increases over the period to maturity then it would be acceptable to show the liability net of the discount in the financial statements.

7.133 The discounted value of most receivables and payables is usually not significantly different from the face value since a market rate of interest is charged or received on most long-term payables and receivables and for short-term items the discount would be insignificant. Discounting of long-term receivables and payables should only be necessary where their interest rates are significantly different from prevailing rates.

7.134 In relation to provisions or other items involving estimates of future events, such items are normally valued at today's prices in practice. If they were valued at prices expected to prevail when the item crystallises and then a discount was applied, no material difference from today's prices would normally arise.

Chapter 8

ACCOUNTING FOR GOODWILL AND OTHER INTANGIBLES

ACCOUNTING FOR GOODWILL AND OTHER INTANGIBLES

Introduction

8.1 Before 1978 there was no accounting standard in the UK that dealt with consolidations or the treatment of the premium or discount arising on the acquisition of subsidiaries. Although there was no official standard, the calculation of the premium or discount on acquisition (that is, goodwill or negative goodwill respectively) and its treatment were well established.

8.2 SSAP 14 was introduced in 1978 and comments that the preparation of consolidated financial statements is well understood and, therefore, it does not elaborate further on the subject. [SSAP 14 para 3]. However, it does confirm that the premium or discount on acquisition will be the difference between the purchase price and the value ascribed to net tangible assets and identifiable intangible assets such as trade marks, patents or development expenditure. [SSAP 14 para 29].

8.3 Just after SSAP 14 was published, the ICAEW survey of published accounts for the year 1979-80 showed that 195 companies chose to write goodwill off immediately, whereas only 30 companies amortised it.

8.4 Until SSAP 22 was approved by the ASC in March 1984, there were no rules about how to treat the premium or discount on acquisition. The development of SSAP 22 was started by the ASC issuing a discussion paper in June 1980, which considered the possible accounting treatments for goodwill. The discussion paper concluded that purchased goodwill should be eliminated by amortising it through the profit and loss account. However, by the time ED 30 was published in October 1982, the ASC had taken account of commentators' views on the discussion paper, which were split between immediate write off and amortisation. Consequently, ED 30 allowed a choice of methods, and this choice remains in SSAP 22, except that the immediate write-off option is preferred.

8.5 The debate on whether goodwill should be allowed to be written off immediately continues. The ASC's presently intends to revise SSAP 22 further. The proposed revision set out in ED 47 would require in the future that goodwill arising on consolidation should be recognised as an asset in the balance sheet and amortised. The maximum period of amortisation would be 40 years but any period in excess of 20 years would have to be justified (see further para 8.122 below).

8.6 SSAP 22 was partially revised in July 1989 to include certain additional disclosure requirements concerning the acquisition of subsidiaries. There additional requirements are considered in chapter 6 paragraphs 6.48 to 6.60.

General principles

8.7 The revised SSAP 22 is intended to be consistent with the Act, and deals with both goodwill arising in a company's individual financial statements and goodwill arising on consolidation. The paragraphs that follow consider goodwill arising on consolidation, although many of the principles apply equally to goodwill that arises when a company purchases an unincorporated business and the goodwill arises in the company itself. Goodwill in an individual company's financial statements is dealt with in 'Manual of Accounting - volume I' chapter 7.

Purchased goodwill

8.8 Goodwill may be shown as an asset only if it was acquired for valuable consideration. [Note 3 on the balance sheet formats].

8.9 This means that companies cannot capitalise goodwill if, for example, it is internally generated. This accords with the requirement in SSAP 22 that groups may recognise goodwill in their financial statements only if it has arisen from a purchase transaction. [SSAP 22 para 35].

Non-purchased goodwill

8.10 Paragraph 4 of the standard acknowledges that non-purchased goodwill may exist, because the value of a business as a going concern may be either worth more or worth less than the sum of the fair values of its separable net assets. However, even though non-purchased goodwill may exist, it should not be included in the balance sheet.

Definition of goodwill

8.11 The Act does not specifically define goodwill, but it does say that the difference between the acquisition cost and the acquirer's interest in the adjusted capital and reserves of the undertaking acquired shall, if positive, be treated as goodwill and, if negative, as a negative consolidation difference (see further chapter 6 para 6.17). [4A Sch 9(4)(5)]. SSAP 22 defines goodwill as the difference between the value of a business as a whole and the aggregate of the fair values of its separable net assets. [SSAP 22 para 26].

Treatment of goodwill

8.12 SSAP 22 requires a company or a group to adopt one of the following two policies with regard to purchased goodwill:

■ It should be eliminated from the financial statements by immediate write-off against reserves (not as a charge in the profit and loss account). [SSAP 22 para 39].

■ It should be carried as an intangible fixed asset in the balance sheet, and amortised to the profit and loss account over its useful economic life. [SSAP 22 para 41].

8.13 SSAP 22 comments that the first method outlined above is the standard's preferred treatment.

8.14 These requirements accord with those of the Act, because the Act states that where goodwill is treated as an asset, it should be reduced by provisions for depreciation calculated to write off the amount systematically over a period chosen by the company's directors, which must not exceed its useful economic life. [4 Sch 21(2)(3)]. Furthermore, where there is a permanent diminution in the value of any goodwill held as an asset which is expected to be permanent, a provision should be made in the profit and loss account. [4 Sch 19(2)]. If the reasons for such a provision no longer apply, then the provision should be written back to the extent that it is no longer necessary. [4 Sch 19(3)]. Where paragraphs 19(2) or (3) apply, the amounts concerned should be disclosed in the profit and loss account or in a note to the financial statements.

8.15 SSAP 22 paragraph 41(a) states that purchased goodwill should not be revalued. This prohibition seems to apply to revaluation above original cost, and consequently, it would appear that a provision for permanent diminution could be written back, to the extent that such a write back would not take the value of goodwill above its original cost. Provisions for permanent diminution in value are considered further in 'Manual of Accounting - volume I' chapter 4.

Revaluation of purchased goodwill

8.16 As mentioned above, SSAP 22 states that a group should not revalue purchased goodwill. [SSAP 22 para 41(a)]. This accords with the legal requirements, because Schedule 4, paragraph 31(1) does not permit goodwill to be revalued.

Characteristics of goodwill

8.17 As mentioned above, goodwill is ascertained by taking the value of the business as a whole from the value of the aggregate of the fair value of the undertaking's separable net assets. [SSAP 22 para 26]. The resultant difference can be positive or negative. This definition means that purchased goodwill cannot be realised separately from the business as a whole. Consequently, goodwill cannot be sold without selling part of the business. The amount of goodwill recognised will depend on a number of factors, for example, the location of the business, the loyalty of its staff, its product range and customer loyalty. The characteristic that goodwill cannot be realised separately distinguishes it from all other items in the financial statements.

8.18   Furthermore, SSAP 22 identifies certain other characteristics of goodwill as outlined in the paragraphs that follow:

- The value of goodwill has no reliable or predictable relationship to any costs that the company may have incurred. [SSAP 22 para 2(a)].

  Consequently, goodwill cannot be derived by, for example, applying a formula to the costs a company incurs over a number of years.

- It is impossible to value reliably individual factors that may contribute to goodwill. [SSAP 22 para 2(b)].

  Many factors can contribute to goodwill's value. For example, in some businesses (such as, estate agents) the businesses' location may be of prime importance and this might add to the value of goodwill. Similarly in other businesses, for example football clubs, the people working for the company might generate the goodwill. In other businesses (for example, retailing businesses) the customer base might be a large factor in the goodwill that it generates. Similarly other undertakings might generate goodwill via strong product lines (for example, the confectionery industry). Such strong product lines may generate goodwill in excess of brand values (see further para 8.65).

- The value of goodwill may fluctuate widely according to internal and external circumstances over relatively short periods of time. [SSAP 22 para 2(c)].

  In the examples given above, it can be seen that differing factors might make goodwill fluctuate widely within a short period of time. For example, with an estate agent it might lose its valuable high street location, because of excessive rent reviews. Similarly, the football club might suddenly lose one of its star players through injury and this might have a distinct affect on the success of the club and the goodwill it generates.

- The assessment of the value of goodwill is highly subjective. [SSAP 22 para 2(d)].

  Ascertaining the amount of a company's goodwill at any point in time is extremely difficult and as can be seen from the above examples there are many factors that might have a bearing on its value.

8.19   Consequently, according to the standard, any amount attributable to goodwill is unique to the valuer and to the specific date of measurement, and is valid only at that time and in the circumstances then prevailing.

Determining the value of purchased goodwill

8.20   On consolidation, the cost of the acquisition is attributed to the fair value of the separable net assets acquired. [SSAP 22 para 19]. Any difference between the total of these fair values and the fair value of the purchase consideration represents goodwill (or negative goodwill) arising on consolidation. [SSAP 22 para 36]. The principles of determining the value of goodwill are explained in chapter 6 and the principles of determining the fair value of the consideration given for a business and the fair value of the separable net assets acquired are considered in detail in chapter 7.

Difference between goodwill and other intangible assets

8.21   In the definition of goodwill, separable net assets include intangible assets. Groups often try to identify intangible assets when they acquire a business so that the figure of goodwill that arises on consolidation is kept to a minimum. Intangible assets include concessions, patents, licences, trade marks and similar rights and assets. [4 Sch formats; SSAP 22 para 13]. Other examples include brands, publishing titles, franchise rights and customer lists (see Tables 37, and 38 overleaf).

Table 37: Extract from a group's accounting policies that shows its treatment of music publishing copyrights.

Extract from THORN EMI plc Annual Report 31st March 1989.

Music Publishing Copyrights purchased up to and including 31 March 1989 have been written off to reserves on acquisition. Copyrights acquired on or after 1 April 1989 will be treated as an intangible asset in the Group balance sheet. The capitalised amount of such copyrights, being their purchase cost, will only be subject to amortisation to the extent that royalty income generated by the total music publishing copyright portfolio is insufficient to support its book value. No significant music publishing copyrights were purchased in the year to 31 March 1989; the purchase of the important SBK portfolio of music publishing copyrights was completed on 2 June 1989.

Table 38: Example of a group that capitalises publishing rights, titles and benefits.

Extract from Maxwell Communication Corporation plc Report and Accounts 31st March 1989

Accounting policy extract

Intangible fixed assets
Publishing rights, titles and benefits
  Publishing rights, titles and benefits are stated at fair value on acquisition and are carried forward in the balance sheet. No amortisation charge is made unless there is a permanent diminution in value as, in the opinion of the directors, these assets do not have a finite economic life. Subject to annual review, any permanent diminution in value is charged to the profit and loss account.

8.22   Where a group identifies intangible assets (excluding purchased goodwill) on the acquisition of a subsidiary, it should incorporate them in its consolidated balance sheet at their fair value and depreciate them. [SSAP 22 para 37]. In subsequent years, groups may revalue these intangible assets to their current cost. Some groups revalue as many of their intangible assets as possible in order to strengthen their consolidated balance sheet. Such groups ensure that they identify all intangible assets when they acquire a subsidiary. In this respect, recognising brands is becoming increasingly important and this is explored further in paragraphs 8.64 to 8.102 below. Two examples of the differences between goodwill and intangible assets follow:

Example 1

A group acquires a company which has a franchise to sell a certain well known product in its shops. The purchase price is £5 million, which is represented by recorded net assets of £1 million and, therefore, goodwill of £4 million.

In this situation, it might be possible that the amount of goodwill of £4 million actually represents the cost to the group of the franchise. If so, the value of the franchise can be separately identified as an intangible asset and amortised over its useful life.

Example 2

A publishing group acquires a publishing company and the consideration it pays is £1 million greater than the acquired company's net assets. Is it possible to attribute £1 million of the value to the publishing rights that it has acquired?

Capitalisation of publishing rights is permitted under SSAP 22 (revised), but it is necessary to distinguish in this example between the value of the rights or titles and the value of goodwill.

Methods of eliminating goodwill arising on consolidation

8.23 The ways in which groups should deal with goodwill arising on consolidation once they have attributed a value to it are dealt with in SSAP 22 in paragraphs 38 to 42. The group should not carry goodwill arising on consolidation in its consolidated balance sheet as a permanent item. [SSAP 22 para 38]. As mentioned above consolidation goodwill may be eliminated using either the immediate write-off method or the amortisation method.

The immediate write-off method

8.24 Groups should normally eliminate goodwill arising on consolidation (other than negative goodwill) from their consolidated financial statements immediately on acquisition against reserves. [SSAP 22 para 39]. The standard refers to this method as the 'immediate write-off method'. The immediate write off of purchased goodwill arising on consolidation is consistent with the accepted practice of not including non-purchased goodwill in the financial statements.

8.25 The immediate write off of consolidation goodwill should be made against reserves, and not as a charge in the consolidated profit and loss account. This treatment should be adopted for two reasons. First, purchased goodwill is written off as a matter of accounting policy (that is, in order to achieve consistency of treatment with non-purchased goodwill), rather than because it has suffered a permanent diminution in value. Secondly, the write off is not related to the results of the year in which the acquisition is made. The reserves that can be used to write goodwill off against are considered below in paragraphs 8.36 to 8.58.

The amortisation method

8.26 SSAP 22 describes the immediate write-off method as the *"preferred treatment"*, and says that groups should normally adopt that method. [SSAP 22 para 10]. However, the standard recognises that there is an alternative way of considering positive goodwill, which is that, although goodwill is intangible, it nevertheless exists. And when a group purchases a company, the price it pays includes an amount attributable to purchased goodwill. Consequently, the group has expended resources in exchange for an asset (namely, goodwill) and the alternative view of goodwill considers that the group should recognise that asset and treat it in the same way as it treats any other asset. SSAP 22 allows a group, therefore, to carry consolidation goodwill as an asset and to amortise it through the consolidated profit and loss account on a systematic basis over its useful economic life. [SSAP 22 para 41]. The useful economic life of goodwill is considered in paragraphs 8.59 to 8.64.

8.27   A question that arises from this treatment is whether it is possible to amortise goodwill through the profit and loss account as an extraordinary item or amortise goodwill direct to reserves. These types of treatments conflict with both SSAP 6 and SSAP 22. Goodwill on consolidation arises out of the continuing activities of the group and as such its amortisation should be treated as a deduction from the profits and losses a group makes on its ordinary activities and should not be included as an extraordinary item. [SSAP 22 para 41]. Furthermore, the Schedule 4 Formats include specific positions for depreciation included within ordinary activities, which should include the amortisation of goodwill.

Acceptability of using both elimination methods

8.28   A group's circumstances may require it to adopt different policies in relation to goodwill that arises on different acquisitions. For example, a group may generally follow the preferred policy of immediate write-off, but it may need to adopt the policy of amortising goodwill on an unusually large acquisition because of the effect that an immediate write-off would have on its reserves.

8.29   This treatment is acceptable under SSAP 22 and, therefore, a group may use the immediate write-off treatment for the goodwill that arises from one acquisition, and the amortisation treatment for the goodwill that arises from another. [SSAP 22 para 42]. The standard adds the proviso that whatever accounting policy the group chooses, it must provide for consolidation goodwill to be eliminated on a basis consistent with the standard. Once the group has chosen an accounting policy for the goodwill arising from a particular acquisition, the group should apply that policy consistently thereafter to the goodwill arising on consolidation. For example, a group should not amortise consolidation goodwill arising from a particular acquisition for a number of years and then write the remaining balance off direct to reserves.

8.30   Where a group does use different elimination methods for a number of acquisitions, it will need to explain clearly the treatments adopted (see further para 8.109).

Treatment of negative goodwill

8.31   Groups should credit 'negative goodwill' direct to reserves. [SSAP 22 para 40]. 'Negative goodwill' is the term used for any excess of the aggregate of the fair values of the separable net assets acquired over the fair value of the consideration given. Negative goodwill is the mirror image of positive goodwill. However, where negative goodwill arises, the amounts attributed to the relevant separable net assets will need to be reviewed particularly carefully to ensure that the fair values ascribed to them are not overstated. [SSAP 22 para 8]. The standard does not require a group to set up a separate reserve for negative goodwill. However, where a group does set up a separate reserve, an appropriate description in the financial statements would be 'negative goodwill' or 'reserve arising on consolidation'. This item should be included under 'other reserves' in the balance sheet format.

Write off to reserves

8.32 Where a *company* as opposed to a group writes goodwill off immediately against reserves, the write-off may be initially to a suitable unrealised reserve. [SSAP 22 appendix 2 para 2]. However, the revaluation reserve may not be a suitable reserve for this purpose (see further para 8.46 below). If a *company* does write goodwill off initially to a suitable unrealised reserve, then it should transfer the amount written off from unrealised reserves to realised reserves over its useful economic life so as to reduce realised reserves on a systematic basis in the same way as if the company had amortised goodwill (see further 'Manual of Accounting - volume I' chapter 7). However, in the case of goodwill arising on consolidation, the distinction between realised and unrealised reserves is not relevant, because it is individual companies, not groups, that make distributions. [SSAP 22 appendix 2 para 1].

8.33 Although it is individual companies, not groups, that make distributions, users of consolidated financial statements may wish to know how much the parent could distribute if all the subsidiaries in the group were to pay up their realised profits by way of dividends to the parent. Many groups specifically disclose the amount of consolidated realised reserves. In the absence of such disclosure, users of the consolidated financial statements might mistakenly interpret the profit and loss account reserve as representing realised reserves and the revaluation reserve as representing unrealised reserves. So, although appendix 2 to SSAP 22 is correct in saying that it is individual companies, not groups, that make distributions, the amount of consolidated realised reserves can be an important figure to users of the consolidated financial statements.

8.34 If a group writes off consolidation goodwill immediately to reserves, the write-off will not affect the distributable profits of any individual company and, therefore, it will not affect the amount of the total potential distributable profits of the group. Consequently, a group may write off consolidation goodwill either to consolidated realised reserves or to certain consolidated unrealised reserves. Furthermore, a group does not need to transfer any amounts from unrealised reserves to realised reserves over the estimated useful economic life of goodwill.

8.35 One consequence of the immediate write off option in SSAP 22 is that it is possible that the reserves of the company (which have not borne the consolidation goodwill write off) may be larger than those of the group. For example, see Table 39 below.

Table 39: Illustration showing the company's reserves exceeding the group's reserves caused partly by the write-off of consolidation goodwill to reserves.

Extract from Saatchi & Saatchi Company PLC Annual Report and Accounts 30th September 1988.

BALANCE SHEETS (extract)

As at 30th September	Note:	GROUP 1988 £ million	GROUP 1987 £ million	COMPANY 1988 £ million	COMPANY 1987 £ million
CAPITAL AND RESERVES					
Called up share capital	14	115.1	115.1	115.1	115.1
Share premium	15	1.9	–	1.9	–
Special reserves	15	–	–	565.8	565.8
Goodwill reserve	15	(320.9)	(160.3)	–	–
Revaluation reserve	15	–	0.5	–	–
Profit and loss account	15	127.4	84.9	61.6	47.0
		(76.5)	40.2	744.4	727.9
Called up Preference share capital issued by a subsidiary	14	176.5	–	–	–
Minority interests		7.6	6.7	–	–
		107.6	46.9	744.4	727.9

Reserves used for write offs

8.36 Groups have the option to write goodwill off against a variety of reserves. A group may have any of the following reserves and accounts in its consolidated balance sheet:

■ Profit and loss account reserve.

■ Share premium account.

■ Capital redemption reserve.

■ Revaluation reserve.

■ Merger reserve.

■ Other non-distributable reserves.

■ Goodwill write-off reserve.

8.37 Some of the reserves and accounts listed above have specific uses and are, therefore, not available to write off goodwill even on consolidation. Each of the reserves and accounts is considered further in the paragraphs that follow.

Profit and loss account reserve

8.38 Consolidation goodwill can be written off direct to the profit and loss account reserve, and the write-off can be made as a reserve movement. Consequently, unless the group adopts a policy of amortising consolidation goodwill the goodwill write-off can be made direct to the profit and loss account reserve and does not have to be shown in the consolidated profit and loss account itself.

Share premium account

8.39 The use of the share premium account is governed by the Act and, consequently, it can only be used for specific purposes. Therefore, share premium accounts can only be used to:

■ Pay up fully paid bonus shares.

■ Write-off preliminary expenses.

■ Write-off expenses of any issue of shares or debentures.

■ Write-off commission paid or discount allowed on any issue of shares or debentures.

■ Provide for the premium payable on any redemption of debentures.

[Sec 130(2)].

8.40 However, although the share premium account can only be used for specific purposes, it does form part of a company's capital and, as such, can be reduced under section 135 of the Act by application to the court. Where groups make large acquisitions by issuing shares (or a mixture of shares and other forms of consideration) the parent, unless it is eligible for merger relief, has to credit the difference between the fair value of the shares issued and their nominal value to its share premium account. The parent company may then take steps to reduce its share premium account by a certain amount and that amount would in the consolidated financial statements be redesignated as another reserve to be used specifically to write off consolidation goodwill. A special resolution for the reduction is required and all of the relevant facts about the proposal must be set out in the documentation sent to shareholders (for example see Table 40 overleaf).

> **Table 40: Example of a resolution proposed to reduce the company's share premium account in order that consolidation goodwill can be written off the new reserve created.**
>
> **Extract from Metal Box p.l.c. Notice to shareholders of annual general meeting 27th July 1988.**
>
> **vi Cancellation of share premium account**
> The acquisitions made by the Group in the year to 31st March 1988 have given rise to goodwill (namely the difference between the fair value of the net tangible assets acquired and the price paid) in the consolidated balance sheet of the Group totalling £71 million.
>
> Statement of Standard Accounting Practice 22 requires that goodwill be either written off immediately against reserves (which is the recommended treatment), or amortised through the profit and loss account over the useful economic life of the goodwill. Your Board has considered it more appropriate to write off goodwill in the year in which it arises against reserves, rather than charge the profit and loss account over a period of years.
>
> The amount standing to the credit of the Company's share premium account has grown over a number of years as a result of various share issues, and the balance of this account now amounts to some £77.4 million.
>
> The uses to which a share premium account can be put are severely restricted by law. However, with the consent of the High Court, it is possible to cancel the share premium account of the Company and to apply the reserve which arises on such cancellation in writing off goodwill arising on consolidation. Therefore, in line with action taken by other major listed companies and after consultation with the Company's auditors, your Board proposes the cancellation of the balance of this account. It is proposed that the balance will be transferred to a new special capital reserve in the Company's accounts. On consolidation there can be deducted from this reserve, with the consent of the Court, goodwill which has arisen in the year to 31st March 1988 and/or goodwill arising on future acquisitions. This proposal will not affect the tangible assets of the Group.
>
> Resolution No. 10 will be proposed as a Special Resolution to approve the cancellation of the balance on the share premium account.
>
> If this Resolution is passed, it will be necessary to obtain the Court's confirmation of the cancellation which is expected to be given by the end of this year. For this purpose the Company will give an undertaking to the Court for the protection of creditors at the date of the cancellation to the effect that the credit arising from the proposed cancellation will be treated as a special capital reserve which will not be available for distribution by way of dividend for as long as any liabilities to the Company at the effective date of the cancellation remain undischarged, unless the persons to whom such liabilities are owed shall otherwise agree.

8.41   Once the shareholders have passed the necessary special resolution, an application has to be made to the court to obtain its confirmation. Such confirmation is required by the Act and the court will be concerned in particular to ensure that the parent company's creditors are not prejudiced.

8.42   Share premium reductions of this nature are now very common (for example see Table 41) and companies have been permitted in appropriate situations to reduce their share premium accounts to create reserves in excess of the goodwill that they wish to write off. Consequently, in this type of situation, the excess reserve would be available to write off goodwill in the future.

Table 41: *Extract from a directors' report explaining a share premium reduction.*

Extract from THORN EMI plc Annual Report 31st March 1989.

Share Premium Account
With the sanction of an order of the High Court of Justice dated 20 July 1988, the share premium account of the Company was reduced by £282m in order to create a special reserve account against which goodwill may be written off.

8.43   The reserve that is created from the share premium account is in most cases initially not available for distribution by the parent. It remains undistributable until certain conditions required by the court have been satisfied, for instance, that the creditors that exist at the date of the reduction have been paid. Once these conditions have been fulfilled, the reserve becomes distributable.

8.44   It must be remembered that the share premium account in such situations is that of the parent company. However, for the reasons mentioned in paragraph 8.33, whether the reserve arising on the reduction is distributable or not is not relevant for consolidation purposes. Consequently, consolidation goodwill can be written off to the reserve created out of the parent's share premium account whether or not it is distributable by the parent.

Capital redemption reserve

8.45   Capital redemption reserves are set up for a specific purpose and will be utilised at some future date. Therefore, their use is restricted. Furthermore, the normal provisions that apply to the reduction of share capital also apply to the capital redemption reserve. [Sec 170(4)]. Consequently, except where there has been a reduction confirmed by the court, this reserve is not available to write off goodwill arising on consolidation.

Revaluation reserve

8.46   In practice, the most common unrealised reserve is the revaluation reserve, which arises when a company revalues some or all of its fixed assets. The Act similarly specifies what the revaluation reserve can be used for and states that:

"*An amount may be transferred from the revaluation reserve-*

(a) to the profit and loss account, if the amount was previously charged to that account or represents a realised profit, or

(b) on capitalisation;

*and the revaluation reserve shall be reduced to the extent that
the amounts transferred to it are no longer necessary for the
purposes of the valuation method used.*

*In sub-paragraph (b) 'capitalisation', in relation to an amount
standing to the credit of the revaluation reserve, means applying
it in wholly or partly paying up unissued shares in the company
to be allotted to members of the company as fully or partly paid
shares.*

*The revaluation reserve shall not be reduced except as
mentioned in this paragraph."* [4 Sch 34(3)(3A)(3B)].

8.47   The wording of paragraph 34 has been changed by the Companies Act
1989 specifically to ensure that goodwill arising on consolidation
cannot be written off against the consolidated revaluation reserve. In
the past, the Act (by reference to the EC 4th Directive) prohibited
goodwill arising in a company's individual financial statements from
being written off against the company's revaluation reserve. However,
this restriction did not extend to goodwill arising on consolidation,
because the provisions of the 4th Directive did not cover consolidated
financial statements. Consequently, in the past many groups have in
practice written consolidation goodwill off against the consolidated
revaluation reserve. As mentioned above, this treatment is no longer
allowed by the Act.

8.48   However, the commencement order introducing Part I of the
Companies Act 1989 into the UK's legislation includes certain
transitional provisions. One of these provisions concerns those
companies that have in the past written off consolidation goodwill to
their consolidated revaluation reserve. Where a group has previously
written consolidation goodwill off against the revaluation reserve, it
will not have to reverse this treatment (for example see Table 42).
However, for any new acquisitions that the group makes this treatment
will no longer be possible. In addition, where an undertaking becomes
a subsidiary because of the changes to the definitions of subsidiary
contained in the Companies Act 1989 (see chapter 3 paras 3.6 to 3.36),
any goodwill arising on the consolidation of the new subsidiary will
have to be treated under the new rules. Therefore, such goodwill will
not be able to be written off against the consolidated revaluation
reserve.

8.49   Where the consolidated revaluation reserve has been used in the past
to write off goodwill arising on consolidation, problems might arise
where the revaluation reserve is subsequently used by the parent
company for another purpose. For example, the revaluation reserve

can be used wholly or partly to pay up unissued shares in the parent to be allotted to its members as fully paid shares in a bonus issue. In this situation, it might be necessary to transfer amounts from another reserve to make up any deficiency on consolidation.

Table 42: Example of a group writing consolidation goodwill off its revaluation reserve.

Extract from Grand Metropolitan Public Limited Company Annual Report 30th September 1989.

23 Reserves

	Share premium account £m	Revaluation and special reserves £m	Related companies' reserves £m	Profit and loss account £m	Total £m
Group					
At 30th September 1988	7	931	16	2,010	2,964
Exchange adjustments	–	1	–	(82)	(81)
Retained profit for the year	–	–	8	893	901
Premiums on share issues, less expenses	429	–	–	–	429
Goodwill acquired during the year	–	(1,909)	–	–	(1,909)
Transfer of goodwill on disposal	–	185	–	(185)	–
Other transferes between reserves	–	(152)	(14)	166	–
At 30th September 1989	436	(944)	10	2,802	2,304

Merger reserve

8.50   A merger reserve arises on consolidation where a company acquires another for shares and it takes merger relief on the issue of those shares. The provisions of merger relief are explained fully in chapter 9. Where such a reserve exists, it can be used to write off goodwill that arises on the acquisition that gave rise to the reserve, and it can also be used to write off any other goodwill (for example see Table 43 overleaf).

Other non-distributable reserves

8.51   Neither SSAP 22 nor the Act restrict groups from writing off goodwill arising on consolidation against any other non-distributable reserves. However, it may not be sensible to write consolidation goodwill off to a reserve that has been set up for a particular purpose.

Table 43: Example of goodwill being written off to the merger reserve.

Extract from Granada Group PLC Annual Report 31st December 1988.

Note extract

Reserves Group	Share premium £m	Merger reserve £m	Revaluation reserve £m	Profit and loss account £m
Balance at 3 October 1987	20.8	–	153.0	162.4
Share issues in the period	3.0	241.8	–	–
Retained profit for the period	–	–	–	60.7
Revaluation of fixed assets	–	–	120.8	–
Currency adjustments	–	–	–	(1.8)
Goodwill written off	–	(407.6)	–	–
Transfers arising from the sale of properties at revalued amounts	–	–	(5.2)	–
Transfers and other movements	5.5	–	(0.3)	(5.5)
At 1 October 1988	29.3	(165.8)	268.3	215.8

Goodwill write-off reserve

8.52   Before the introduction of SSAP 22, some groups used to show goodwill as a permanent deduction from reserves, rather than writing it off to reserves. This treatment was known as the 'dangling debit'. However, SSAP 22 states that a group should not carry purchased goodwill as a permanent item in its consolidated balance sheet. [SSAP 22 para 38]. The 'dangling debit' treatment in effect means that goodwill is carried as a permanent asset that is deducted from reserves. Furthermore, the prescribed formats in Schedule 4 to the Act and the off-set provision in paragraph 5 of Schedule 4 also prohibit groups from using the 'dangling debit' method.

8.53   However, there is nothing in the legislation or in SSAP 22 that prohibits a group from writing off goodwill arising on consolidation against a reserve set up for the purpose that initially has a nil balance. For example, see Tables 44 and 45 overleaf. The consequence of this write-off means that the reserve created would be negative and would equal the figure of goodwill written off. It can be seen that this reserve is very similar, therefore, to the 'dangling debit' mentioned above. The only difference is that the group has adopted a policy of writing off goodwill and, therefore, it is no longer carried in the balance sheet as a permanent asset, as it is deducted from reserves.

8.54   Many people consider the use of negative reserves in this way to be sleight of hand, but the DTI has confirmed that it can see nothing that is against the provisions of the Act with this treatment, with the reservation that to confirm this view it would have to be tested in a court of law.

Table 44: Example of a negative goodwill write off reserve.

Extract from Saatchi & Saatchi Company PLC Annual Report and Accounts 30th September 1988.

Note extract

15. RESERVES

	Share premium £ million	Special reserves £ million	Goodwill reserve £ million	Revaluation reserve £ million	Profit and loss account £ million
GROUP					
At beginning of year	–	–	(160.3)	0.5	84.9
Premium on Ordinary shares issued, less expenses	1.9	–	–	–	–
Goodwill arising in the year written off	–	–	(166.8)	–	–
Transfer of revaluation reserve	–	–	–	(0.5)	0.5
Expenses of Convertible Preference share issue	–	–	–	–	(5.7)
Exchange translation	–	–	–	–	3.9
Amortisation of goodwill reserve	–	–	6.2	–	(6.2)
Transfer from profit and loss account	–	–	–	–	50.0
At end of year	1.9	–	(320.9)	–	127.4

8.55   Where a group adopts the policy of writing off goodwill to a negative reserve an appropriate caption in the consolidated balance sheet would be 'goodwill write-off reserve'. The reserve should be included in the consolidated balance sheet under the item 'other reserves'.

Treatment of negative goodwill

8.56   Where negative goodwill arises, a company should credit it initially to an unrealised reserve. [SSAP 22 appendix 2 para 3]. The company may then transfer the negative goodwill from that unrealised reserve to realised reserves. This transfer should be in line with the depreciation or the realisation of the assets acquired in the business combination that gave rise to the goodwill in question. However, the distinction between distributable and undistributable reserves is not relevant for negative consolidation goodwill. As mentioned above, the reason for this is that it is individual companies, not groups, that make distributions. Therefore, negative goodwill arising on consolidation may be credited to either unrealised or realised consolidation reserves (excluding statutory reserves of the group).

**Table 45: *Illustration of goodwill written off to the profit and loss
account reserve, creating a negative reserve.***

*Extract from Hanson PLC Report and Accounts 30th September
1989.*

Note extract

17 Reserves

	Group	Company
	£ million	
Share premium account		
At October 1, 1988	145	145
Premium on shares issued	111	111
At September 30, 1989	256	256
Revaluation reserve		
At October 1, 1988	218	
Revaluations during year	2	
Transfer in respect of subsidiaries sold	(55)	
At September 30, 1989	165	–
Profit and loss account		
At October 1, 1988	872	743
Retained profit for the year	764	1,434
Transfer in respect of subsidiaries sold	55	–
Exchange fluctuation	36	–
Goodwill arising on acquisitions during year	(2,086)	–
At September 30, 1989	(359)	2,177

8.57   Often, groups set up a specific reserve for negative goodwill entitled
'reserve arising on consolidation'. This specific reserve would be
classified under the item 'other reserves' in the consolidated balance
sheet.

Examples of reserve write offs

8.58   The examples that follow explain how goodwill should be treated in
various circumstances and consider in particular the reserves that
goodwill may be written off against.

Example 1

A company acquires a subsidiary during the year and substantial goodwill arises on
consolidation. It acquires another subsidiary just after its year end and substantial
negative goodwill arises on that acquisition. Can the company defer writing off goodwill
in the current year so that it can eliminate negative goodwill on the acquisition that
arises in the next year?

There seems to be no justification in this example not to amortise or write off the goodwill at the year end. There may be further acquisitions next year that will absorb the negative goodwill, for example. However, if the company amortises the goodwill in the current year, there is nothing to preclude them from changing their accounting policy next year to write off new purchased goodwill immediately, if the directors consider this gives a fairer view.

Example 2

A parent company receives a capital contribution from its ultimate parent company during the year, which has been credited to a separate reserve. The company wishes to write goodwill off against this reserve.

Although, as mentioned above, goodwill cannot legally be written off against the share premium account, or the revaluation reserve, there are no legal restrictions on the use of a reserve created by a capital contribution. Therefore, goodwill can be written of against such a reserve.

Example 3

A group has goodwill on acquisition that it wishes to write off against a merger reserve. However, the goodwill exceeds that reserve and the group has no other reserves that it can make the write off to. The group wants to capitalise the excess and amortise it.

The proposed treatment is not acceptable because SSAP 22 requires that one policy, either the immediate write off of goodwill or amortisation of goodwill should be adopted for each acquisition. It is not acceptable to write off part of the goodwill on acquisition and amortise the balance. However, it is acceptable to write goodwill off to the merger reserve (see further chapter 9).

Example 4

A group makes several acquisitions in a year and the first three acquisitions give rise to goodwill. The last acquisition has been treated as a merger (see further chapter 9) and a large merger reserve is created. The group proposes that the goodwill arising on the acquisitions will be set off against the merger reserve that arises at a later date, but within the same accounting period.

There is nothing in the Act or in SSAP 22 to prevent a group setting goodwill arising on earlier acquisitions against a merger reserve arising from a later acquisition in the same accounting period. This treatment would not be acceptable if the acquisitions took place in different accounting periods.

Example 5

An unlimited company issues shares at a large premium to acquire a partnership. Consequently, a substantial amount of goodwill arises on the acquisition.

It is possible for an unlimited company to repay capital of the company to its members without restriction. However, the share premium account is still restricted to the uses set out in section 130 of the Act (see para 8.39). But because an unlimited company can reduce its share capital without court permission (provided it has the power to do so in its Articles of Association) it is possible for the company to reduce its share premium and create another reserve in a similar way as if it had entered into a capital reduction scheme (see para 8.40 above). The goodwill arising on the acquisition can then be written off against the reserve created.

Useful economic life

8.59   The Act makes no attempt to define the 'useful economic life' of goodwill. SSAP 22 provides that the useful economic life should be estimated at the time of acquisition. In addition, it should not include any allowance for the effects of subsequent expenditure or other circumstances subsequently affecting the company since these would have the effect of creating non-purchased goodwill. [SSAP 22 para 41(b)]. Furthermore the standard states that the estimated useful life of goodwill many be shortened, but cannot be increased. [SSAP 22 para 41(c)]. However, guidance on how to determine the useful economic life of purchased goodwill is given in SSAP 22, appendix 1.

8.60   Although the standard does not specify either a minimum or a maximum amortisation period, appendix 1 says that the useful economic life of purchased goodwill is the period over which benefits may reasonably be expected to accrue from that goodwill. In the period following the acquisition, the value of the purchased goodwill is considered to diminish, although it may be replaced by non-purchased goodwill. The total goodwill (both purchased and non-purchased) may either remain constant or increase or decrease. The purchased goodwill whose useful life is being determined is only that which existed and was recognised at the time of the acquisition.

8.61   Several factors may be relevant in determining the useful economic life of purchased goodwill, and a group should assess these factors at the time it makes the acquisition. They include the following:

- ■   Expected changes in products, markets or technology.

  For example, a high technology company that only has one main product might have considerable goodwill while that product is leading the market, but as soon as a competitor produces a better product, then the company's goodwill can diminish rapidly.

- ■   The expected period of future service of certain employees.

  A merchant bank's goodwill may be very dependent on key employees and the bank's goodwill may depend significantly on the retention period of certain employees.

- ■   Expected future demand, competition or other economic factors that may affect current advantages.

  For example, when the economy is booming, the sales of luxury goods will flourish, while when the economy is in recession spending on such goods reduces considerably, and so does the goodwill of companies producing them.

8.62 It is not possible to specify general rules regarding the useful economic life over which purchased goodwill should be written off. The ASC considered that it is inappropriate to indicate a maximum number of years for the amortisation period. Furthermore, a company or group may select different useful economic lives for the goodwill that arises on its different acquisitions.

8.63 In the US, the maximum period allowed to write off goodwill is 40 years and many corporations use that period. Similarly, many UK groups with US links (such as, those owned by US corporates) also use 40 year write-off periods. However, examples of groups using such periods are uncommon in the UK, but it is quite common for UK groups to use periods up to 20 years. The ASC issued ED 47 in February 1990 which proposes to revise SSAP 22 and suggests that goodwill should be capitalised and amortised by all groups. It also proposes that a maximum write-off period should be specified in a future standard as 40 years, but where a group uses a period over 20 years, it should explain in its consolidated financial statements the reason for using such a period (see further para 8.122 below).

8.64 The discussion paper that preceded SSAP 22 and ED 30 (referred to in the introduction to this chapter) suggested a formula for the maximum period of goodwill amortisation. The formula was $2\frac{1}{2}$ times the estimated P/E ratio. Appendix 4 of the discussion paper provided some mathematical support for this formula. The figure for P would be the fair value of the business acquired, and the figure for E would be the acquiring company's best estimate of the expected annual distributable earnings of the acquired business. Consequently, if P was £600,000 and E was £100,000, then the formula would give a P/E ratio of 6 and a maximum amortisation period of 15 years (that is, $2\frac{1}{2}$ x 6). However, ED 30, SSAP 22 and ED 47 do not refer to the discussion paper's suggested formula.

Brands and other intangibles

8.65 The identification and valuation of brands is an important example of an intangible asset that has seldom in the past been incorporated in companies' balance sheets. Recent takeover bids have highlighted the fact that significant values are placed by bidders on brand names and other intangibles (for example see Table 46 overleaf). Many companies, whether involved in takeover bids or not, have considered strengthening their balance sheets by including the value of their brand names.

8.66 The growing interest in attributing values to brand names and other intangibles derives mainly from the realisation that bidders are prepared to pay substantial amounts for companies which own valuable brand names.

Table 46: Illustration of a group changing its accounting policy to record the capitalisation of own brands.

Extract from Grand Metropolitan Public Limited Company Annual Report 30th September 1988.

Accounting policy extract

Goodwill and other intangible assets

On the acquisition of a business, including an interest in a related company, fair values are attributed to the group's share of net tangible assets and significant owned brands acquired. Where the price paid exceeds the values attributable to such net assets, the difference is treated as goodwill and is written off direct to reserves in the year of acquisition.

Significant owned brands acquired after 1st January 1985, the value of which is not expected to diminish in the foreseeable future, are recorded in the balance sheet as fixed intangible assets. No amortisation is provided on these assets but their value is reviewed annually and the cost written down as an exceptional item where permanent diminution in value has occurred.

Note extract

24 Reserves

	Share premium account £m	Revaluation and special reserves £m	Related companies' reserves £m	Profit and loss account £m	Total £m
Group					
At 30th September 1987 as previously reported	425.8	(651.9)	14.2	1,508.1	1,296.2
Capitalisation of brands	–	630.0	–	(22.0)	608.0
As restated	425.8	(21.9)	14.2	1,486.1	1,904.2
Exchange adjustments	–	(5.8)	–	(13.3)	(19.1)
Retained profit for the year	–	–	2.2	570.4	572.6
Premiums on share issues, less expenses	7.1	–	–	–	7.1
Goodwill acquired during the year	–	(143.7)	–	–	(143.7)
Surplus on revaluation of property	–	643.1	–	–	643.1
Transfer of goodwill on disposal	–	62.0	–	(62.0)	–
Share premium transfer	(425.7)	425.7	–	–	–
Other transfers between reserves	–	(29.0)	–	29.0	–
At 30th September 1988	7.2	930.4	16.4	2,010.2	2,964.2

The ASC's view on valuing intangible assets

8.67   The ASC issued a technical release TR 780 in February 1990, that sets out the ASC's views on accounting for intangible assets which it intends to include in a future exposure draft. The ASC propose that intangible fixed assets should only be recognised where the following apply:

■   The historical costs incurred in creating the intangible are known or where it can be clearly demonstrated that they are readily ascertainable.

■ The intangible's characteristics can be clearly distinguished from those of goodwill and other assets.

■ The intangible's cost can be measured independently of goodwill, of other assets and of the earnings of the relevant business or business segment. The Technical Release further comments that there will normally need to be an active market in an intangible asset of the same kind, which is independent of the purchase and sale of the business or business segment.

8.68 The Technical Release further proposes that intangible fixed assets should only be carried at historical cost less provisions for depreciation and, where applicable, provisions for permanent diminutions in value. Provisions for depreciation should be made to write off the intangible asset over its useful economic life. The suggestion is that this period should not exceed 20 years, unless there are exceptional circumstances. Where such circumstances exist, the useful life should not exceed 40 years. These proposals are identical to those propose in ED 47 (see para 8.122 below).

8.69 The ASC suggest that intangible fixed assets should only be carried at a valuation where both the following apply:

■ The carrying amount is based on the depreciated replacement cost of the asset and this figure can be measured with reasonable certainty.

■ The depreciated replacement cost represents the current cost of the asset.

8.70 The ASC believe that many intangible fixed assets, particularly internally created ones will fail to meet the criteria for recognition as an asset in the balance sheet. Furthermore, the ASC suggest that intangibles should not be allowed to be revalued where their historical cost cannot be ascertained.

8.71 The ASC also believe that if the characteristics of an intangible fixed asset cannot be clearly distinguished from goodwill, it will not be possible to identify it individually. In addition, the characteristics of an intangible might be so closely associated with the business as a whole that they cannot be recognised separately form goodwill and should be subsumed within it.

8.72 With regard to brands, the ASC state that the term 'brand' is used to describe what is generally regarded for accounting purposes as goodwill. They go on to state that goodwill is a combination of factors expected to produce enhanced earnings in the future and that often the expectation of enhanced future earnings is based on a past history of such earnings. The ASC, therefore, conclude that for accounting purposes, brands are subsumed within goodwill and should be accounted for accordingly (see further para 8.78 below).

8.73   The ASC's proposals are controversial and may well change before a final exposure draft is published on intangible assets.

London Business School's findings

8.74   The ASC's proposals are based on a study undertaken by the London Business School in the Summer of 1989 entitled 'Accounting for brands'. There appears to be little evidence that incorporating brand values into a company's balance sheet actually enhances its value. The study indicated that analysts had no interest in brand valuations unless by disclosing them they gave new information. The study looked at the following aspects of brand accounting:

■   The accounting background, including the extent of intangibles found in balance sheets and the differences between brands and goodwill.

■   Brands as separable net assets, considering longevity as well as separability.

■   The effect of brand information on the capital markets.

■   The different valuation methods and approaches.

■   The implications for developing an accounting standard.

8.75   The study concluded that if goodwill were to be carried on the balance sheet, much of the immediate pressure to capitalise brands would disappear. The study identified major problems with establishing the value of brands and believed that in most situations the value of a brand is impossible to separate from the company's other business. With regard to valuation methods, the researchers were concerned that there was no general agreement on the method used. Also, the available methods were likely to fail the test of 'reasonable certainty' mentioned in a report by Professor Solomons entitled 'Guidelines for financial reporting standards'. It said that *"an item should be recorded in the financial statements if ... its magnitude ... can be measured and verified with reasonable certainty"*. It went on to state that to allow brands, whether acquired or internally generated, to be included in the balance sheet would be highly unwise.

The Stock Exchange's view on intangible assets

8.76   The International Stock Exchange circulated a note of change in practice in January 1989 concerning the values of brands and other intangibles in company balance sheets. The circular concerned specifically the assets that should be taken into account on an acquisition or disposal of a company to determine the class that the transaction falls into. The Admission of Securities to Listing states that for the purpose of determining the class of a transaction (that is, classes 1 to 4 and super class 1), the assets of the acquiring or disposing company mean the book value of the net assets, excluding capital and amounts set aside for future taxation. The International Stock Exchange has relaxed this rule and has amended its definition of assets to include all tangible and intangible assets.

8.77 Intangible assets for this purpose are likely to include purchased goodwill, brand values, newspapers and magazine titles, publishing rights and other intellectual property rights. However, to be treated in this way, intangible assets have to be specifically included in the company's audited financial statements.

Treatment and valuation of brands

8.78 Although TR 780 suggests that brands should be subsumed within goodwill and the London Business School's report came out against valuing brands and the discourages revaluing intangibles, brands (both acquired and internally generated) have been valued and included in certain companies' balance sheets and those valuations have been audited. In particular, brands have been capitalised in a number of food groups. Other brands, such as publishing rights, have been capitalised by some companies for many years. It is likely for the time being that companies will still wish to continue to value their brands in certain situations. The following paragraphs, therefore, set out some of the factors that may be taken into account when considering a valuation of brand names or other intangibles.

Establishing whether brands are separable net assets

8.79 With many brand names there should be little difficulty in establishing that they could be sold separately from the business as a whole. Many well known names are already exploited by granting licences or franchises to third parties. For example, a name associated with a particular type of footwear may be exploited by granting a licence for a third party manufacturer of sports clothes to use the name. Another example is where a fast food chain grants franchises to third parties to use the name for their restaurants.

8.80 Many brand names are identified with single products which form only part of a company's business. For example, a particular detergent may have a well known brand name, but the name could be sold and the company would still carry on making the product, even though that product might generate lower profits, because it was no longer 'branded'.

8.81   Where a brand name is the same as that of the company itself it is still conceivable that the name could be sold separately from the business, and this would probably be done by granting a licence for the use of the name. Even if there is no intention to sell or license a brand name there would appear to be no objection to regarding it as a separable asset (for example see Table 47). A name might be either specific to one product or it might cover a range of products or services. An example of the latter might be the name of a subsidiary company that supplies a range of products and is well known for quality and attracts business for that reason. There may, of course, be many examples where it is not possible to demonstrate the 'separability' of a brand name. This may be because the name is associated with a particular service or product, but is not otherwise well known, and there are, therefore, very limited opportunities for exploiting the name by licensing it or selling it separately from the business.

Table 47: Illustration of the capitalisation of a brand name.

Extract from Ladbroke Group PLC Annual Report 31st December 1988.

Note extract

10 Intangible assets	£m	£m	£m	£m
	Total	Licences	Brand name	Publishing copyrights
Cost or valuation				
At 31st December 1987 (as reported)	293.4	291.3	–	2.1
Hilton International brand name	276.7	–	276.7	–
At 31st December 1987 (as restated) (a)	570.1	291.3	276.7	2.1
Exchange rate movements	(4.7)	(4.7)	–	–
Newly acquired subsidiaries	3.4	3.4	–	–
Revaluation surplus	27.3	27.3	–	–
Additions at cost	6.3	6.3	–	–
Disposals	(2.3)	(0.2)	–	(2.1)
At 31st December 1988	600.1	(b) 323.4	276.7	–

(a) Intangible assets at 31st December 1987 have been restated to include the amount attributed to the Hilton International brand name as at 14th October 1987, the date of acquisition of Hilton International Co. This attributed value has been limited to the amount of goodwill that arose in respect of the acquisition and was deducted from reserves in the 1987 accounts. No account has been taken of the full value of the brand (see page 51, note 24).

(b) UK betting office licences for shops opened in 1983 and earlier years have been restated by the directors at their estimated current cost. The amount of licences determined according to the historical cost accounting rules at 31st December 1988 is £150.8m (1987 £146.0m).

8.82   Both the Act and SSAP 22 permit the value of brands to be recognised in a company's balance sheet. This applies provided that the brand is a separable net asset. Separable intangibles in the form of brands should be capitalised if they are acquired for value, and internally generated brands that meet the separability test may be included at their cost or their current cost. Although as mentioned above, it should be remembered that the ASC discourages companies from incorporating revaluations of intangibles (such as, brands) in the balance sheet

Valuation principles

8.83   There are a number of methods of valuing brands at present and as yet no definitive rules can be laid down. The paragraphs below set out some of the factors that may be taken into account when considering a valuation and they describe briefly some of the methods that have been suggested.

8.84   One method is that the value of the brand should be measured by reference to the total earnings from the branded products. Another method is that only the marginal benefit is relevant to a valuation. The marginal benefit would be the difference between the earnings of the branded product and the earnings of a similar unbranded product.

8.85   The problem with the former method is that it undoubtedly would include in the valuation factors that apply to non-branded as well as to branded products and would lead to inflated values. This method attributes a value to the whole of the business segment represented by the brand (that is, it values the business including goodwill as well as the brand name). Consequently, this method is not considered acceptable. The problem with the latter method is that it is often extremely difficult to find a comparable unbranded product with which to compare the branded product.

8.86   These difficulties may be overcome by adopting an approach that is based on an assessment of what it would cost a third party to purchase a licence to use the brand name. This approach and other alternative methods of valuation are briefly discussed in the paragraphs below.

8.87   In determining the value of a brand various factors may be considered, which include the following:

■   The market sector.

    Brands that are established in a business sector that generates high sales, margins, or both, will clearly have a higher value than those in markets that are restricted in terms of total sales volume or profit margins. Expanding markets for a product will enhance the prospects for exploiting the brand name and will, therefore, increase its value.

■ Durability.

If a brand name has lasted for many years, it is likely to have considerable customer loyalty and will, therefore, support a higher valuation than a name that may be fashionable, but that is in a business sector where fashions change rapidly and brand names are less durable.

■ Overseas markets.

A brand name that is also known in overseas markets and which, therefore, has a larger potential customer base will usually be worth more than a brand that can be sold only in the domestic market.

■ Market position.

A brand that is a market leader will be worth more than one that is not recognised as a leader.

■ Advertising support.

This could be either a negative or a positive factor in valuing a brand. If a brand requires substantial advertising to maintain its place in the market, this could be a sign that the value of the brand is declining. If however, advertising spend increases sales and/or margins significantly, so that the brand is better known, the value of the brand itself could be enhanced.

■ Existing licences or franchises.

Where a company has granted licences to use the brand name of its products or its own company name, the latest prices paid by third parties provide evidence of the current value of the brand name.

■ Changes or prospective changes in legislation, or technological advances.

Many brands are vulnerable to changes in legislation or environmental factors. However, if a brand name has survived such changes, the fact that it is able to adapt to new conditions may enhance its value.

■ Competition.

The introduction of alternatives to the branded product or indications that competitors are likely to increase spending on rival products could also affect the value of brands.

8.88 The factors listed above are not comprehensive and are intended only as an indication of the difficulties involved in brand valuation. There is no professional body, accounting or other, that has yet issued guidance on how brands should be valued. Until such guidance is issued, a number of different approaches may be adopted. It is important however that, whatever approach is adopted, the assumptions and bases on which a valuation is made should be clearly explained.

8.89 As stated above in paragraph 8.22, the Act permits intangible assets to be included at current cost. Although current cost is not defined in the Act, the ASC's handbook entitled 'Accounting for the effects of changing prices', includes an appendix on determining current costs. The appendix states that the current cost of an asset is the lower of:

■ Its net current replacement cost.

■ Its recoverable amount, that is the higher of the following:

   □ Its net realisable value.

   □ The amount recoverable from its future use (that is, its economic value).

8.90 It may be useful to refer to the detailed considerations set out in that appendix if current cost valuations of brands are being contemplated. Although the principles of current cost valuations are well described in the appendix, it does not provide detailed guidance on the specific question of valuing intangibles and merely states that:

> "The same principles apply to the determination of the current cost of these assets (intangibles) as for any other assets. However it is not uncommon for it to be impracticable to estimate their current cost."

8.91 The appendix states that, if it is impracticable to estimate the current cost of an intangible, it will be necessary to consider alternatives such as the application of a broad based index. However, unless a company is able to establish the original cost of a brand name (which is unlikely) that solution may be impracticable.

Valuation methods

8.92 Two methods for valuing brands that have been suggested are described below:

■ Earnings method.

The earnings attributable to a branded product are multiplied by a factor that is estimated after taking into account the considerations listed above (that is, durability, market sector etc.). This method attempts to predict what a third party might pay to acquire the brand name. It has the disadvantage of being highly subjective and of taking into account the whole earnings of a branded product and not just the marginal earnings attributable to the brand name. A similar method, but one that takes into account only such marginal earnings, is preferable.

■ Royalty method.

In this method an attempt is made to determine the value that could be obtained by licensing the name to a third party. The factors that would have to be considered are:

☐ The sales that a third party could generate through using the name.

☐ The nature of the licence. For example, whether it would be an exclusive licence or whether it would include the benefit of future research and development.

☐ How the royalty is expressed. If it was expressed as a percentage of sales, whether it reflects the 'normal' percentage for the industry.

☐ The 'multiplier' that should be used to arrive at a capitalised value for the royalty.

8.93 Whatever method is chosen, the value attributed to a brand name should be based on the marginal earnings attributable to the brand name, not on the total earnings attributable to the branded product. Alternatively, the royalty basis could be used. Both of the above methods are, however, highly subjective and it is important that the assumptions and bases used are well documented.

Brands acquired but not recognised in past years

8.94 Where a company has made acquisitions in the past, but has failed to identify and capitalise separable net assets in the form of brands, it is acceptable (at present) to reassess those acquisitions. If fair values are attributed to such brand names, a prior year adjustment will be necessary to reverse the element of goodwill that has now been allocated to the fair value of brands (for example see Table 48).

Table 48: *Illustration of the capitalisation of brands.*

Extract from Guinness PLC Report and Accounts 31st December 1988.

Accounting policy extract

Brands

The fair value of businesses acquired and of interests taken in related companies includes brands, which are recognised where the brand has a value which is substantial and long term. Acquired brands are only recognised where title is clear, brand earnings are separately identifiable, the brand could be sold separately from the rest of the business and where the brand achieves earnings in excess of those achieved by unbranded products.

No amortisation will be provided except where the end of the useful economic life of the acquired brand can be foreseen. The useful economic lives of brands and their carrying value will be subject to annual review and any amortisation or provision for permanent impairment will be charged against the profit for the period in which they arise.

Note extract

11. Acquired brands at cost

Acquired brands represent the historical cost of brands acquired on the purchase of businesses. The cost of the attributable share of LVMH's brands, taken into account in arriving at the amount at which the investments in related companies are stated, amounts to £320m.

22. Reserves

	Share premium account £m	Revaluation reserve £m	Capital redemption reserve £m	Merger reserve £m	Retained earnings £m	Related companies £m	Goodwill reserve £m	Total £m
At 1 January 1988	4	48	–	–	442	21	–	515
Prior year adjustment	–	–	–	–	–	–	1,375	1,375
Transfers	–	–	–	1,781	88	–	(1,869)	–
As restated	4	48	–	1,781	530	21	(494)	1,890
Issue of shares	374	–	–	–	–	–	–	374
Purchase of own shares	–	–	11	–	(136)	–	–	(125)
Retained earnings	–	–	–	–	233	6	–	239
Revaluation of properties	–	40	–	–	–	–	–	40
Goodwill during the year	–	–	–	–	–	–	(60)	(60)
Transfers	–	(2)	–	–	4	(2)	–	–
Exchange adjustments	–	(3)	–	–	(20)	(2)	–	(25)
At 31 December 1988	378	83	11	1,781	611	23	(554)	2,333

The prior year adjustment relates to the cost of acquired brands recognised as an intangible fixed asset.

8.95 If goodwill is carried as an asset in the balance sheet the prior year adjustment will mean that part of that asset will be reclassified as a separable intangible and an adjustment may have to be made to reverse any amortisation charged against the goodwill that has now been reclassified. Whether a further adjustment will be necessary in respect of accumulated depreciation on the brand name since acquisition will depend on an assessment of the useful life of the brands (see para 8.100 below).

8.96 If the goodwill has been written off, the adjustment will be made by crediting the reserve against which the write off was made and debiting the fair value of brands to the asset account. Again further adjustments to reflect accumulated depreciation since the date of acquisition may be necessary.

8.97 If acquisitions are re-assessed as described above and fair values are attributed to brands, it is preferable that comparative figures are restated. Where this would be impracticable, the reasons for not adjusting the comparative figures should be disclosed.

8.98 Restatement of fair values of assets acquired in the past is very unusual, and can only be justified by strong arguments for recognising such brand names. Consequently, there should be full disclosure of the circumstances and adjustments made in such situations, and this disclosure should be made prominently in the financial statements (for example, in the directors' report). Some companies may not have sufficient records of past acquisitions to enable them to reassess the fair value of brands acquired. In such circumstances, it is preferable not to reassess past acquisitions, but instead to have a policy that will recognise the value of brands only on future acquisitions.

Internally created brands

8.99 Where a company adopts a policy of valuing internally created brands the policy should be consistently applied to all, and not just some, of its brands. But as mentioned in paragraph 8.72 above, the ASC proposes to prohibit companies from incorporating brands in the balance sheet.

Depreciation

8.100 The Act requires that depreciation should be provided on any fixed asset that has a useful economic life and where an asset has suffered a permanent diminution in value provision for this should be made. [4 Sch 18, 19].

8.101 Where a brand has been acquired, the fair value will be reflected in the consolidated balance sheet and that value is regarded as cost to the group. Where the fair value of brands has been established and recognised on acquisition or by reassessing previous acquisitions, it may be decided in later years to revalue these brands. Any surplus above fair value that arises as a result of such a revaluation will be transferred to a revaluation reserve under the Act's alternative accounting rules. [4 Sch 29 to 34]. Where internally created brands are valued for the first time the surplus arising will also be transferred to the revaluation reserve. [4 Sch 34].

8.102 Whether brands are acquired or internally generated, companies are required to estimate the useful lives of these assets. If the lives are finite the assets should be depreciated to their residual values, over their useful lives. The ASC believes that there is a rebuttable presumption that intangibles, including brands, have a limited useful economic life and that internally generated brands should not be capitalised.

8.103 Therefore, depreciation should be provided on brands. There are two arguments that have been advanced to demonstrate that in certain circumstances such depreciation would be negligible.

8.104 Some companies that have included brands in their balance sheets have stated that the lives of the brands are infinite and, therefore, no depreciation charge is made (for example, see Table 38). Others take the view that expenditure on advertising and other brand support costs mean that the brands' residual value is always equal to or greater than cost, and this is put forward as an alternative reason for not providing depreciation.

8.105 Whether or not these arguments apply, it will still be necessary for companies to review the values of brands annually in order to determine whether there has been a permanent diminution in any brand's value. Such a review might be made by the directors or by an external valuer.

8.106 A permanent diminution in value may be indicated by any one of a number of factors, that could include a fall in the volume of sales, a fall in the profit margins attainable from sales, or the need for increased advertising costs to support the existing levels of sales and margins.

8.107 Where there has been a permanent diminution in the value of an asset that is carried at cost, provision has to made in the profit and loss account for the diminution in value. However, where a previously revalued brand has suffered a permanent diminution in value the provision should first be set against the previous revaluation surplus on the same brand and then the balance should be charged against the profit and loss.

Goodwill disclosure

8.108 The requirements concerning the disclosure of the acquisition of a subsidiary, including some aspects of disclosure that relate to goodwill, are considered in chapter 6 paragraphs 6.48 to 6.60. The paragraphs that follow detail the disclosure requirements of both the Act and SSAP 22 that apply to goodwill arising on consolidation.

Accounting policy

8.109 The note to the consolidated financial statements should explain the accounting policy the group follows in respect of goodwill. [SSAP 22 para 43]. This accords with the general requirement in SSAP 2 and the requirement in paragraph 36 of Schedule 4 to the Act that groups should disclose all relevant accounting polices.

8.110 The following examples show how different groups could disclose their accounting policies for goodwill. Example 1 discloses how the group defines purchased goodwill. This could form the first paragraph of an accounting policy on goodwill. The standard does not allow groups any element of choice in how to define purchased goodwill. Consequently, the principles contained in example 1 will not vary much from group to group. Examples 2 to 4 disclose how different groups could eliminate purchased goodwill from their consolidated financial statements. As explained above, the standard does allow groups an element of choice in how they eliminate purchased goodwill. Consequently, any one of examples 2 to 4 could form the second paragraph of a group's accounting policy for goodwill.

Example 1

Purchased goodwill arising on the acquisition of a new subsidiary represents the excess of the fair value of the consideration given over the aggregate of the fair values of the separable net assets acquired. Negative goodwill represents the excess of the aggregate of the fair values of the separable net assets acquired over the fair value of the consideration given.

Example 2

The group eliminates goodwill arising on consolidation (other than negative goodwill) from the consolidated financial statements by immediate write-off against reserves (other than the revaluation reserve). The group credits negative goodwill arising on consolidation direct to reserves.

Example 3

The group eliminates goodwill arising on consolidation (other than negative goodwill) from the consolidated financial statements by amortisation through the consolidated profit and loss account. The group amortises such goodwill by equal annual instalments over the estimated useful economic life of the consolidation goodwill of X years. The group credits negative goodwill arising on consolidation direct to reserves.

Example 4

The group eliminates goodwill arising on consolidation (other than negative goodwill) from the consolidated financial statements on different acquisitions either directly by immediate write-off against reserves (other than the revaluation reserve), or by amortisation through the consolidated profit and loss account. Where the group amortises consolidation goodwill, it does so by equal annual instalments over the estimated useful economic life of the consolidation goodwill of X years. The group credits negative goodwill arising on consolidation direct to reserves.

Other disclosure

8.111 The additional requirements concerning the disclosure of goodwill that the Act and SSAP 22 contain are set out in the paragraphs below.

8.112 Where a group makes any acquisitions during the year, it should show the amount of goodwill arising on consolidation and, where this is material, it should be shown separately for each acquisition. [4A Sch 13(5); SSAP 22 para 44].

8.113 Where a group selects the amortisation method, it should show goodwill arising on consolidation as a separate item under intangible fixed assets in the consolidated balance sheet until it is fully written off. [SSAP 22 para 45]. The disclosure requirement in paragraph 45 accords with the Schedule 4 formats, which require a group to show purchased goodwill (to the extent that it has not been written off) separately under the heading of 'intangible fixed assets'. For a group, purchased goodwill may include goodwill arising on consolidation. It may also include any goodwill that exists in a subsidiary's financial statements which arose when that subsidiary acquired another business.

8.114 SSAP 22 requires the group also to show the movement on the goodwill account during the year. [SSAP 22 para 45(a)]. Paragraph 42 of Schedule 4 contains a similar requirement. A group should show the cost, the accumulated amortisation and the net book value of goodwill both at the beginning and the end of the year.

8.115 In addition, a group must show in respect of goodwill:

■ The effect that any acquisitions, any disposals and any transfers have had on cost during the year.

■ The amount of goodwill amortised during the year.

■ The amount of any provision against goodwill during the year.

■ The amount of any adjustments to accumulated amortisation that have arisen from any disposals.

■ The amount of any other adjustments to accumulated amortisation.

[4 Sch 42].

8.116   Furthermore, paragraph 21(4) of Schedule 4 and paragraph 45(b) of SSAP 22 both require a group to disclose the period it has selected for amortising the consolidation goodwill relating to each of its major acquisitions. Paragraph 21(4) of Schedule 4 to the Act requires the group also to disclose its reasons for choosing that period.

8.117   As noted in paragraph 8.62, the standard permits a group to select different useful economic lives for the goodwill that arises on different acquisitions. Consequently, a group may need to disclose several amortisation periods, with each one relating to different elements of the goodwill total.

8.118   The Act requires that the cumulative amount of goodwill written off that results from acquisitions in the current year and in earlier years to be disclosed. [4A Sch 14(1)]. The amount disclosed should also be stated net of any goodwill attributed to an undertaking that has subsequently been sold. [4A Sch 14(2)]. It appears that this requires the aggregate of amounts written off directly to reserves and amounts amortised through the profit and loss account, to be disclosed. The reason for this requirement is unclear, but in order to be able to give the required disclosure, groups will have to maintain detailed records of goodwill even when it has been written off.

8.119   The Act, however, does not require the gross amount of goodwill written off to be disclosed in certain circumstances where an undertaking that is established outside the UK or that carries on its business outside the UK has obtained the permission of the Secretary of State (see also chapter 6 para 6.57). [4A Sch 16]. Similarly the transitional provisions on the introduction of the Companies Act 1989 do not require the amount to be disclosed in certain circumstances. This would be where it is not possible to ascertain the figure for goodwill written off that has arisen on acquisitions made prior to the introduction of the new legislation and to do so would cause unreasonable expense or delay. In this situation the financial statements must state that the gross figure disclosed does not include an amount on these grounds.

8.120   ED 44 issued in September 1988 proposed that where goodwill is amortised, the earnings per share before any charge for amortisation should be shown on the face of the profit and loss account. This disclosure would have been in addition to that required by SSAP 3, 'Earnings per share'. However, this proposal was not adopted in SSAP 22 and, consequently, is not required.

8.121 The following example shows how a group might comply with the disclosure requirements of both the Act and SSAP 22.

Balance sheet (extract)

	Note	1989 £'000	1988 £'000
Fixed assets			
Intangible assets			
Concessions and patents		5	5
Goodwill	10	93	81
		98	86

Note 10 - Goodwill

	£000
Cost at 1st January 1989	115
Elimination of fully amortised goodwill	(15)
Goodwill arising from acquisition during the year	20
Cost at 31st December 1989	120
Accumulated amortisation at 1st January 1989	34
Charge to profit and loss account	8
Elimination of accumulated amortisation on fully amortised goodwill	(15)
Accumulated amortisation at 31st December 1989	27
Net book value at 31st December 1989	93
Net book value at 31st December 1988	81

Gross amount of goodwill written off to reserves:

At 31st December 1989	42
At 31st December 1988	34

(a) Goodwill of £100,000 arose from the acquisition of XYZ Ltd in 1986. The economic life of this goodwill has been estimated at 20 years, and the goodwill is being amortised over that period, commencing in 1986.

(b) Goodwill of £20,000 arose from the acquisition of three subsidiaries in 1989. This goodwill is being amortised over its estimated useful economic life of ten years, commencing in 1989.

(c) Goodwill of £15,000 arose from the acquisition of ABC Ltd in 1973. That goodwill was amortised over 15 years, and so has now reached the end of its useful economic life. Consequently, the cost and the accumulated amortisation have been eliminated from the financial statements.

Note that in this example, the figures in note 10 have been arrived at by combining the three separate elements of the goodwill account as follows:

	(a) £'000	(b) £'000	(c) £'000	Total £'000
Cost at 1st January 1989	100	-	15	15
Elimination	-	-	(15)	(15)
Addition	-	20	-	20
Cost at 31st December 1988	100	20	-	120
Accumulated amortisation at 1st January 1989	20	-	14	34
Charge	5	2	1	8
Elimination	-	-	(15)	(15)
Accumulated amortisation at 31st December 1989	25	2	-	27
Net book value at 31st December 1989	75	18	-	93
Net book value at 31st December 1988	80	-	1	81

Provisions of ED 47

8.122 As mentioned above, ED 47 was issued in February 1990 and, if adopted unaltered, it will change the way in which many groups account for goodwill arising on consolidation. In contrast to SSAP 22's preferred treatment of immediate write off to reserves, ED 47 proposes to make capitalisation and amortisation standard accounting practice. However, the disclosure requirements proposed in the exposure draft are identical to those required in SSAP 22, except that those relating to acquisitions (for example, the table of book values and fair values) can be found in ED 48.

8.123 The ED's proposals have aroused considerable controversy particularly among listed companies. There is a consensus of opinion that where the 'amortisation method' is used, the effect of amortisation has been to depress reported profits by a figure that is often arbitrary, as the useful economic life of goodwill cannot be accurately determined. It remains, therefore, to be seen whether the proposals will eventually become standard accounting practice. The proposals in the exposure draft are summarised in the paragraphs that follow.

Purchased goodwill

8.124 The exposure draft recognises that purchased goodwill is an asset of the business that is real and has a measurable cost. It goes on to state that *"to show goodwill at a cost-based amount will provide information on the resources that have been deployed in acquisitions on the shareholders' behalf and can, therefore, help provide a basis for assessing management's performance".* [ED 47 para 10]. Consequently, it proposes that purchased goodwill (which includes goodwill arising on consolidation) should be recognised as a fixed asset and recorded in the balance sheet. [ED 47 para 47].

8.125 Once capitalised, purchased goodwill should be amortised through the profit and loss account. [ED 47 para 51]. The amortisation period to be used should equate to the useful economic life of the goodwill. [ED 47 para 51]. However, unlike SSAP 22, ED 47 then sets a maximum period for the useful economic life of purchased goodwill. It states that this should not exceed 20 years except in rare circumstances. [ED 47 para 52]. Realising that a 20 year period would cause a conflict with the US requirements (which have a maximum write-off period of 40 years), the exposure draft then sets an absolute maximum period of 40 years to be used even in rare circumstances.

8.126 Furthermore, the directors should review the value of goodwill for each acquisition at the end of each year and if they consider its carrying value is excessive, they should provide for any permanent diminution in value. [ED 47 paras 53, 54].

8.127 The exposure draft makes it quite clear that charges for amortisation and charges for permanent diminutions in value should be made to the profit and loss account. In addition for amortisation, the exposure draft is quite specific and proposes that such charges should be made before arriving at the profit or loss on ordinary activities before tax. [ED 47 para 50].

Negative goodwill

8.128 Where negative goodwill arises on consolidation, the exposure draft states that the fair values ascribed to the assets and liabilities should be reviewed to ensure that those values are appropriate. The negative goodwill balance should be credited to the profit and loss account over an appropriate period on a systematic basis. [ED 47 para 56]. The exposure draft indicates that the average life of the fixed assets may provide a suitable period.

Disposals of subsidiaries

8.129 ED 47 proposes that where there is a material disposal of a previously acquired business any remaining goodwill related to it included in the balance sheet should be written off against the proceeds of the disposal. [ED 47 para 58]. (See also chapter 5 para 5.49).

Transitional provisions

8.130 The exposure draft includes a paragraph concerning transitional provisions, which states that it is not intended to make the amortisation proposal retrospective. However, it leaves it up to the directors whether they wish to reinstate goodwill previously written off. Where such goodwill is reinstated it should be at an amount calculated as if the exposure draft had been in force from the subsidiary's date of acquisition. [ED 47 para 65]. In the year of change additional information will have to be disclosed concerning the reinstatement.

Chapter 9

MERGER RELIEF AND MERGER ACCOUNTING

MERGER RELIEF AND MERGER ACCOUNTING

Introduction

9.1   Chapter III of Part V of the Act sets out rules that relate to the creation of share premium on an issue of shares, and also to the way in which that premium may be used. The basic rule is detailed in section 130(1), and it says that, where a company issues shares at a premium (whether for cash or otherwise), a sum equal to the aggregate amount or value of the premium must be transferred to a share premium account. This section is derived from section 56 of the Companies Act 1948 and, until the Companies Act 1981 came into effect, there was no relief from the provisions of that section. The Companies Act 1981 introduced certain merger relief provisions that modified the effect of section 56 of the Companies Act 1948. These merger relief provisions are currently set out in sections 131 and 132 of the Companies Act 1985.

9.2   Chapters 6, 7 and 8 consider various matters concerning acquisition accounting. This chapter looks at the alternative accounting method a company may use in certain circumstances when preparing consolidated financial statements, namely merger accounting. However, before this method is considered, the provisions of the Act that relate to share premiums are examined.

Share premium account

9.3   Where a company issues shares at a value that exceeds their nominal value, a sum equal to the difference between the issue value and the nominal value must be transferred to a share premium account. [Sec 130(1)]. For example, if a company issues 100,000 £1 shares at £1.50 each, then it must credit £50,000 to a share premium account.

9.4   Once a share premium account has been established, it may only be used for certain specified purposes as outlined in paragraph 6.14 of chapter 6. Apart from these specific uses, the share premium account has to be treated as if it were part of the paid-up share capital of the company. Consequently, the provisions of the Act that apply to the reduction of share capital apply also to the share premium account. [Sec 130(3)].

Implications of Shearer v Bercain Ltd.

9.5 The tax case of *Shearer v Bercain Ltd. [1980] 3 AER 295* questioned the construction of section 56 of the Companies Act 1948, which is now section 130 of the Companies Act 1985.

9.6 Before *Shearer v Bercain Ltd.*, it was widely thought that there were two legally acceptable methods of accounting for certain types of business combinations, as discussed below:

■ The first method, the acquisition method, which the majority of companies used, required that the shares transferred to the purchasing company should be recorded in that company's books at their fair value. Where that value exceeded the nominal value of the shares issued in exchange, the excess had to be recorded as a share premium (in accordance with the requirements of section 56 of the 1948 Act). This treatment had the effect of treating the acquired company's reserves as pre-acquisition and, therefore, as undistributable.

■ The second method, the merger method, which few companies used, required that the shares transferred to the purchasing company as part of a merger should be recorded in the purchasing company's books at the nominal value of the shares that it issued in exchange. Consequently, the only difference that had to be dealt with on consolidation was the difference between the nominal value of the shares issued as consideration and the nominal value of the shares transferred to the purchasing company. With the exception of any adjustment required to account for this difference, the distributable reserves of all the companies involved in the merger remained distributable, provided they could be passed up to the parent by way of dividend.

9.7 The merger method was seldom used in practice, because its legality was uncertain. However, it was more attractive than acquisition accounting because it gave companies freedom to distribute, in effect, both companies' distributable reserves (subject to the rules concerning distributions contained in the Act - see 'Manual of Accounting - volume I' chapter 19).

9.8 In *Shearer v Bercain Ltd.*, the court had to consider whether company law permitted companies to use the 'merger' method as an alternative to the 'acquisition method'.

9.9 The court held that where shares were issued at a premium, whether for cash or otherwise, section 56 of the 1948 Act required the premium to be carried into a share premium account in the issuing company's books, and the premium could be distributed only if the

procedure for reducing capital was carried through (see further
chapter 8 para 8.40).

9.10   This judgment gave authority to the interpretation of section 56 of the
1948 Act that required a company to set up a share premium account
in any transaction where it acquired another company's shares in
return for the allotment of its own shares, and the fair value to it of
the shares it acquired exceeded the nominal value of the shares it
issued.

9.11   *Shearer v Bercain Ltd.* was not directly concerned with the actual
accounting treatment of acquisitions. But the effect of requiring that a
share premium account should be set up in such circumstances was to
legally prohibit the merger method of accounting. It meant that it was
also not lawful for the acquiring company to distribute the acquired
company's pre-acquisition profits paid to it by a dividend.
Consequently, companies that had previously used merger accounting,
and had then regarded the acquired company's pre-acquisition profits
as distributable, had contravened the law.

9.12   Following the court's decision, the Government made it known that it
considered that there were certain circumstances in which a
company's failure to set up a share premium account was
unobjectionable. Accordingly, the Government introduced legislation
that relieved companies, in certain circumstances, from the obligation
to carry any share premium to a share premium account. The
provisions that give this relief appear in sections 131 and 132 of the
1985 Act.

Merger relief

9.13   The essence of merger relief is that, where appropriate conditions are
met, section 130 of the 1985 Act does not apply.

9.14   The situations in which companies can obtain merger relief are those
in which the transaction satisfies the following three conditions:

■   A company (known either as the issuing company or the acquiring
company) secures at least 90 per cent of the nominal value of each
class of the equity share capital of another company (the acquired
company) as a result of an arrangement.

■   The arrangement provides for the allotment of equity shares in
the issuing company. (Such allotment will normally be made to the
acquired company's shareholders.)

■   The consideration for the shares so allotted is either the issue or
the transfer to the issuing company of equity shares in the
acquired company or the cancellation of those of the equity shares

in the acquired company that the issuing company does not already hold.

[Sec 131(1)(5)].

9.15 In determining whether a particular merger satisfies the above conditions, the following rules apply:

- Any shares in the acquired company that are held by other companies in the same group (other than associates) as the issuing company, or their nominees, should be treated as being held by the issuing company. [Sec 131(6)].

- An 'arrangement' means any agreement, scheme or arrangement, including an arrangement that is sanctioned under either section 425 of the Act (company compromise with creditors and members) or section 110 of the Insolvency Act 1986 (liquidator accepting shares, etc., as consideration for the sale of the company's property). [Sec 131(7)].

- A company will be treated as having secured a 90 per cent holding in another company as part of an arrangement, irrespective of whether or not it actually acquired, under that arrangement, all the equity shares that it holds. [Sec 131(4)]. This rule means that, in determining whether or not a company has obtained a 90 per cent holding in another company, prior holdings can be taken into account.

- 'Company' includes any body corporate, except where reference is made to the issuing company (or the acquiring company). [Sec 133(4)].

- In any provisions that relate to a company's acquisition of shares in another company, shares that a nominee of a company acquired are to be treated as having been acquired by the company itself. Similarly, the issue, or the allotment or the transfer of any shares to or by a company's nominee is to be regarded as if the shares were issued, or allotted or transferred to or by the company itself. [Sec 133(2)].

- 'Equity share capital' is a company's issued share capital, excluding any part that (as regards dividends and capital) does not carry a right to participate beyond a specified amount in a distribution. [Sec 744, 131(7)]. 'Non-equity shares' are all other shares. In particular, preference shares will generally not form part of a company's 'equity share capital'. (See further 'Manual of Accounting - volume I' chapter 12.)

■ The transfer of a company's shares includes the transfer of a right to be included in the company's register of members in respect of those shares. [Sec 133(3)].

9.16 The examples that follow illustrate the application of these provisions:

Example 1

Company A acquires 90 per cent of company B's equity shares in a share-for-share exchange. This is the most obvious application of the provisions. In these circumstances, company A is entitled to the relief from section 130 of the Act.

Example 2

Company C owns 60 per cent of company D's equity shares. The members of company D agree to a cancellation of the equity shares that company C does not hold, in return for the allotment to them of equity shares in company C. In this situation, also, company C is entitled to the relief from section 130. There are two reasons for this:

☐ The effect of cancelling the remaining shares is to increase company C's 60 per cent holding to a 100 per cent holding (and so over the 90 per cent threshold).

☐ The consideration for the allotment of company C's equity shares is the cancellation of those of company D's shares that it does not already hold.

For this purpose, it is irrelevant that the acquiring company did not acquire the original 60 per cent holding as part of the arrangement. To be entitled to the relief, a company (whether newly formed or otherwise) needs only to acquire shares sufficient to either secure or increase its holding to at least 90 per cent. However, company C is entitled to the relief only on the shares it is now issuing in consideration for the cancellation of the shares in company D that it does not hold. It cannot retrospectively write back any share premium that it set up on any shares it issued when it acquired the 60 per cent holding.

Example 3

Company E acquires all of company F's 'A' equity shares. Company F also has 'B' equity shares in issue, but company E holds none of these. In this situation, company E is not entitled to the relief from section 130 of the Act, because section 131 requires a 90 per cent holding of each class of equity shares in the acquired company. This applies even if the 'B' shares represent in total only 10 per cent or less of the nominal value of company F's equity share capital.

Example 4

Company G acquires 95 per cent of company H's equity shares. The consideration for these shares is, in equal proportions, equity shares in company G and cash. In this situation, company G is entitled to the relief from section 130. This is because there is no 'cash limit' criterion in the merger conditions. The section states only that the consideration for the shares allotted should be equity shares. It does not stipulate any minimum proportion of the consideration that should consist of shares.

Application of merger relief

9.17 Where an issue of shares satisfies the conditions referred to in paragraph 9.14, the Act provides relief from the application of section 130. In these circumstances, section 130 will not apply to any premium that attaches to the shares that the issuing company allots as part of the arrangement. [Sec 131(2)].

9.18   In addition, where a merger satisfies the conditions referred to in paragraph 9.14, the relief will extend to shares issued for either the acquisition, or the cancellation, of non-equity shares. The relief extends to cover an arrangement that provides for the allotment of any shares in the issuing company in return for either of the following:

■   The issue or the transfer to the issuing company of non-equity shares in the acquired company.

■   The cancellation of any such shares that the issuing company does not hold.

In such circumstances, section 130 will not apply to any premium that attaches to the shares that the issuing company allots for this purpose. [Sec 131(3)].

9.19   In this connection, it is important to note that where a merger satisfies those conditions, the issuing company can allot any of its shares in return for either the acquisition or the cancellation of non-equity shares in the acquired company. This means that the issuing company may itself allot non-equity shares for the acquisition or cancellation of non-equity shares and still take the relief, but only if the consideration it receives includes non-equity shares.

9.20   Merger relief can be used where either acquisition accounting or merger accounting is used. Consequently, where a company decides to acquisition account for a subsidiary, but can take merger relief on the issue of its shares, a merger reserve (instead of a share premium account) and goodwill arise on consolidation. It is then acceptable to write off the goodwill to the merger reserve. See for example Table 49.

Relief in respect of group reconstructions

9.21   The decision in *Shearer v Bercain Ltd.* made it clear also that the issuing company should transfer any premium on the issue of its shares to a share premium account, not only where a 'third party' acquisition occurs, but also where a group reconstruction occurs. The Act provides some relief from this requirement. But it does not dispense altogether with the requirement to set up a share premium account. The merger relief provisions of section 131 (which have been discussed in paragraphs 9.13 to 9.20 above) are not available for group reconstructions. [Sec 132(8)]. The relief in respect of group reconstructions is contained in section 132 of the Act. The group reconstructions to which the Act applies are those that satisfy the following conditions:

- A wholly-owned subsidiary (the issuing company) allots some of its shares either to its holding company or to another wholly-owned subsidiary of its holding company.

- The allotment is in consideration for the transfer to it of any assets (other than cash) of its holding company or of another wholly-owned subsidiary of its holding company.

[Sec 132(1)].

Table 49: Illustration of disclosure given where merger relief is taken and acquisition accounting is used on consolidation.

Extract from Fletcher King Plc Annual Report & Accounts 30th April 1989.

Note extract

8 *Investments – Company*

(b) On 9 May 1988 the company acquired the whole of the issued share capital of Ernest Howard Limited. The consideration for the purchase was the issue of 350,000 ordinary shares of 10p each in the company, credited as fully paid on completion, together with £330,000 cash and £28,000 convertible redeemable loan stock 1991. The loan stock is redeemable in accordance with the provisions set out in note 13.

In accordance with the merger relief provisions of the Companies Act 1985, the company's investment in Ernest Howard Limited has been stated as the aggregate of the nominal value of the shares issued, the cash consideration and the nominal value of the loan stock issued, together with associated acquisition costs. The fair value of the consideration, including associated acquisition costs but excluding the fair value of shares to be converted from the loan stock, is £1,194,000.

Included in the consolidated profit on ordinary activities after taxation is an amount of £203,000 relating to Ernest Howard Limited.

16 *Reserves – Group*

	Share premium account	Merger reserve	Profit and loss account
	£000	£000	£000
At 1 May 1988	49	(133)	994
Premium on shares issued	–	1,142	–
Goodwill written off	–	(1,464)	–
Retained profit for the year	–	–	920
At 30 April 1989	49	(455)	1,914

9.22 For example, the allotment may be in consideration for the transfer to the issuing company of shares in another subsidiary (which is not necessarily wholly-owned) that the holding company holds. Diagrammatically, the situation before and after such a reconstruction would be as shown below.

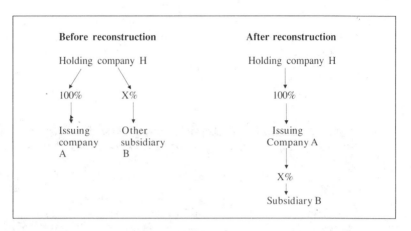

9.23 In practice, the holding company, company H, will often be liquidated after the reconstruction has taken place.

9.24 Where those shares in the issuing company that relate to the transfer are issued at a premium, the issuing company need only transfer to the share premium account an amount equal to the 'minimum premium value'. [Sec 132(2)].

9.25 For this purpose, the following definitions apply:

■ The 'minimum premium value' is the amount, if any, by which the base value of the consideration that the issuing company receives exceeds the aggregate nominal value of the shares that it allots in consideration for the transfer. [Sec 132(3)].

■ The 'base value' of the consideration that the issuing company receives is the amount by which the base value of the assets transferred to it exceeds the base value of any liabilities that the issuing company assumes as part of that consideration. [Sec 132(4)].

■ The 'base value of the assets transferred' is the lower of:

☐ The cost to the transferor company of those assets.

☐ The amount at which the assets are stated, immediately before the transfer, in the transferor company's accounting records.

[Sec 132(5)(a)].

■ The 'base value of the liabilities' assumed is the amount at which those liabilities are stated, immediately before the transfer, in the transferor company's accounting records. [Sec 132(5)(b)].

9.26 The following two examples illustrate the method of calculating the relief available:

Example 1

An issuing company (company Y) allots 1,200 £1 ordinary shares (the consideration being valued at the equivalent of £5 per share) to its holding company (company X). In consideration of this allotment, company X agrees to transfer to company Y its 75 per cent holding in a fellow-subsidiary (company Z). Company X originally paid £3,000 for its 75 per cent holding in company Z. Immediately before the reconstruction, the amount at which that holding was stated in company X's accounting records was £2,000.

In these circumstances, the base value of the shares in company Z is £2,000. This amount is the lower of the cost of the shares to company X (that is, £3,000) and the amount at which the shares are stated in company X's accounting records (that is, £2,000). The nominal value of the shares that company Y allots in respect of the transfer is £1,200. Therefore, the minimum premium value is £800. This amount is calculated as the base value of the shares in company Z (that is, £2,000) less the nominal value of the shares company Y allots (that is, £1,200). Consequently, the amount of £800 must be transferred to Company Y's share premium account. (Without the relief given by section 132, the company would have had to transfer £4,800 to its share premium account. This amount is calculated as the difference between the value of £5 and the nominal value of £1 for each of the 1,200 shares.)

Example 2

A holding company (company H) has a wholly-owned subsidiary (company S). Company H has, as part of its assets, land that originally cost £110,000. This land has subsequently been revalued, and it is currently included in the company's accounting records at £175,000. In addition, the purchase of the land was partly financed by a loan of £40,000 that is secured on the land and is still outstanding. The land is currently valued at £200,000. It is proposed that company S allots to company H 25,000 of its ordinary £1 shares in consideration for the transfer to it of the land that company H currently owns. In addition, company S will assume the liability for the loan of £40,000 that is secured on the land.

If the Act did not provide relief from section 130 in respect of group reconstructions such as the above, company S would need to transfer £135,000 to a share premium account. This premium is calculated as follows:

	£	£
Nominal value of shares allotted		25,000
Fair value of the consideration received:		
Current value of the land	200,000	
less: liability assumed	40,000	
		160,000
Premium on the shares allotted		135,000

However, because of the relief from section 130 that section 132 of the Act gives, the company needs only to transfer £45,000 (which is the 'minimum premium value') to a share premium account. This minimum premium value is calculated as follows:

	£
Base value of the land transferred	110,000
(being the lower of the original cost of £110,000 and	
the amount at which it currently stands in company	
H's books, £175,000).	
Base value of the liability that company S assumes	40,000
Base value of the consideration that company S receives for	
the shares it allots	70,000
Nominal value of the shares that company S allots	25,000
'Minimum premium value'	45,000

9.27   The principal difference between the relief that relates to group reconstructions and the relief that relates to mergers is that, with group reconstructions, the need may arise to set up a share premium account; with mergers, there is no such requirement.

Accounting treatment of the investment in an acquired company

9.28   The Companies Act 1985 clarifies the accounting treatment of an investment in an acquired company that should be used in an issuing company's balance sheet where there is:

■   A merger under section 131.

■   A group reconstruction under section 132.

9.29   In these circumstances, the cost of the issuing company's investment in the acquired company that has to be shown in the issuing company's balance sheet does not need to include an amount corresponding to the premium (or the part of the premium) that the issuing company has not credited to its share premium account. [Sec 133(1)]. The value of the investment to be shown in the holding company's balance sheet is considered further in paragraph 9.64 below.

9.30   Although the Act says that the value of the investment shown in the balance sheet need not include the premium, it is debatable whether the investment should be described as being at cost, because the amount shown in the balance sheet may be quite different from the actual cost. It could be argued that the 'true' cost of the shares issued is their fair value, and not their nominal value. Consequently, the company may need to choose some appropriate wording other than 'cost' to describe the investment (for example, 'at nominal value of shares issued').

Example

A company owns 40 per cent of another company that it acquired for cash several years ago. It decides to acquire the remaining 60 per cent in an exchange for shares. Merger accounting does not apply, but merger relief is available. The company wonders how it should record its investment in the parent company's financial statements.

Even though merger accounting is not available, the parent can record its investment at the nominal value of the shares it issues in exchange for the 60 per cent interest, plus the existing cost of the investment. Alternatively, the fair value of the shares issued can be added to the previous investment cost. The difference between the fair values of the shares issued and their nominal value would then be shown as a merger reserve (as opposed to share premium). If the company adopts the former treatment then the total investment could be revalued using the alternative accounting rules. If this is done, then the difference between the carrying value of the investment and the new valuation should be credited to the revaluation reserve.

Other provisions

9.31 The Secretary of State has the power to make regulations for the following purposes:

■ To make provision for further relief from section 130 in respect of premiums other than cash premiums.

■ To modify or to restrict any relief from section 130 that sections 131 to 133 give.

[Sec 134(1)].

9.32 Any regulations that the Secretary of State makes under section 134 may make either different provisions for different companies or different provisions for different classes of company. They may also include any incidental and supplementary provisions that he believes are necessary. [Sec 134(2)]. However, both Houses of Parliament must approve any such regulation. [Sec 134(3)].

Merger accounting

9.33 In April 1985, the ASC issued SSAP 23 which was the result of a long debate on acquisition and merger accounting that had taken place since the ASC originally published ED 3, 'Accounting for acquisitions and mergers', in 1971. The ASC published ED 3 to try to standardise the method of merger accounting that was developing at the time. However, some people believed at that time that merger accounting might conflict with the requirement in section 56 of the Companies Act 1948 to set up a share premium account (see paras 9.5 to 9.12 above). On the grounds that there was insufficient agreement on the legal implications of merger accounting, the ASC decided not to convert ED 3 into an accounting standard.

9.34 During consideration at the Committee Stage of the merger relief provisions that were incorporated into the Companies Act 1981, the Government indicated that a future accounting standard should prescribe the accounting treatment that companies should adopt where they obtained merger relief. In response to the Government's comments, the ASC issued ED 31, 'Accounting for acquisitions and mergers', in October 1982. In drafting ED 31, the ASC took into account the merger relief provisions in the Companies Act 1981.

9.35 It is important to remember that the Companies Act 1985 originally contained provisions where merger relief applies to companies and did not specify any accounting provisions concerning mergers. SSAP 23, on the other hand, deals with merger accounting in consolidated financial statements, and does not apply to individual companies' financial statements. There is, however, a significant overlap between the concept of merger relief and merger accounting.

9.36 SSAP 23 lays down certain rules that determine whether a holding company should use acquisition accounting or merger accounting in its consolidated financial statements. These rules have been further supplemented by the provisions of the Companies Act 1989. The new provisions have been incorporated into Schedule 4A to the Companies Act 1985 and include certain conditions that must apply to an acquisition before it can be accounted for as a merger. These conditions differ from those in SSAP 23. Furthermore, Schedule 4A to the Act includes certain additional disclosure requirements that apply where an acquisition is accounted for as a merger. The provisions of both the Act and SSAP 23 are considered in detail in the paragraphs that follow. SSAP 23 is, however presently being revised and ED 48 is considered in paragraphs 9.109 to 9.114 below.

Merger accounting conditions

9.37 If a business combination satisfies the conditions outlined in the Act and SSAP 23, then the group may use either acquisition accounting or merger accounting to account for a business combination. If the business combination fails to satisfy the conditions for merger accounting, then the group must use acquisition accounting for the business combination. [4A Sch 10, SSAP 23 para 15]. The conditions contained in the Act are often more restrictive than those in SSAP 23. Situations might still arise where the Act's conditions are satisfied, but those of SSAP 23 are not. Until SSAP 23 is amended (see further para 9.105), where this type of situation arises, merger accounting should not be used. This is because the Act says the adoption of the merger method of accounting must accord with generally accepted accounting principles or practice (for example the conditions contained in SSAP 23). [4A Sch 10(1)(d)]. Similarly, if SSAP 23's conditions are satisfied, but those of the Act are not, merger accounting should not be used. The conditions contained in the Act and SSAP 23 fall under certain tests as follows:

■ Offer to shareholders test.

■ Ninety per cent holding test.

- Prior holding test.

- Ten per cent cash limit test.

9.38   Each of these tests is considered in the paragraphs that follow and the provisions of the Act and SSAP 23 are contrasted.

Offer to shareholders test

9.39   The Act requires that the shares acquired as a result of the acquisition, must be obtained by an arrangement providing for the issue of equity shares by the parent or any of its subsidiaries. [4A Sch 10(1)(b)]. Furthermore, SSAP 23 requires that the business combination must result from an offer both to the holders of all those equity shares that the offeror does not already hold, and to the holders of all those voting shares that the offeror does not already hold. [SSAP 23 para 11(a)].

9.40   To accord with the requirement in SSAP 23, a group may use merger accounting only if the business combination arises from, in effect, a single offer. 'Step-by-step' business combinations (in which the offeror acquires an increasing percentage of the offeree's share capital as a result of several separate offers) will normally not qualify for merger accounting under SSAP 23. One exception to this rule is where the first few offers a company makes result in the company acquiring less than 20 per cent of the offeree's share capital (but see para 9.47), and the final offer secures a holding of at least 90 per cent. Another exception is where the separate offers are effectively a single composite transaction.

9.41   References to 'the offeror' in SSAP 23's merger conditions include not just the offeror itself, but also the following:

- A holding company of the offeror.

- A subsidiary of the offeror.

- A fellow subsidiary of the offeror.

- A nominee or nominees of either the offeror or any of those undertakings mentioned in the three points directly above.

[SSAP 23 para 13].

9.42   References in SSAP 23's merger conditions to voting shares relate to full voting shares. They do not include shares that carry votes only in special circumstances (for example, when dividends are in arrears). [SSAP 23 para 14].

9.43   The examples that follow illustrate some of the problems that can
        arise in this area:

Example 1

A company issues convertible preference shares (which are convertible into ordinary
shares) in an acquisition. Can the company merger account for the acquisition?

Both the Act and SSAP 23 require that the arrangement should provide for the issue of
equity shares by the acquiring company in order for merger accounting to be available.
Equity shares are defined in section 744 of the Act. If the convertible preference shares
satisfy the definition of equity shares then merger accounting might be available.
However, the fact that the preference shares are convertible into ordinary shares would
not in itself make them equity share capital, although it is often possible to vary the
terms of preference shares to make them equity.

Example 2

A company wishes to merger account for an acquisition where it proposes to issue
shares. However, it will issue 10,000 equity shares this year and up to 30,000 additional
equity shares next year. The 30,000 additional shares are conditional on the subsidiary's
next year's profits.

Although some of the consideration is deferred, because it is intended to satisfy all of
the consideration in equity shares merger accounting can be used. The treatment of the
such deferred consideration is considered in chapter 7 paragraph 7.21.

Ninety per cent holding test

9.44   The Act requires that at least 90 per cent of the nominal value of the
        'relevant shares' in an undertaking acquired as a result of an
        arrangement must be held on or behalf of the parent and its
        subsidiaries. [4A Sch 10(1)(a)]. In this context, 'relevant shares' means
        those shares in the acquired company that carry unrestricted rights to
        participate both in its distributions and in its assets upon liquidation.
        [4A Sch 10(2)]. This is in effect 'super-equity', and would include most
        ordinary share capital, but would exclude most other forms of
        participating preference shares (although these shares are often equity
        shares).

9.45   The equivalent requirement in SSAP 23 is that as a result of the offer,
        the offeror must secure a holding of at least 90 per cent of *each class*
        of the offeree's *equity shares*, and must secure at least 90 per cent of
        the offeree's *votes*. [SSAP 23 para 11(b)]. This condition is more
        restrictive than that in the Act. Consequently, it would be possible for
        a company to acquire 90 per cent of the super-equity and, therefore,
        comply with the Act's requirements, but not to have acquired 90 per
        cent of any remaining equity. In this situation, although the conditions
        in the Act would have been complied with, the group would be
        prohibited from merger accounting, because the conditions currently
        in SSAP 23 would not have been fulfilled. The conditions in SSAP 23,
        however, are likely to be revised (see further para 9.109).

9.46   In addition, an offer that secures at least 90 per cent of the total equity shares might not satisfy the merger condition in SSAP 23, because the offeror must secure at least 90 per cent of each class of equity shares (see also para 9.14). Alternatively, the offeree might have voting non-equity shares, and so the offeror might not satisfy the requirement that it must secure at least 90 per cent of the offeree's votes.

Prior holdings test

9.47   The Act states that 90 per cent of the nominal value of the relevant shares must be attained pursuant to an arrangement providing for the issue of equity shares. [4A Sch 10(b)]. However, this does not mean that, in order to merger account, the parent and its subsidiaries cannot hold more that ten per cent of the nominal value of the relevant shares before the acquisition. It merely means that as a result of the offer the company must have acquired at least 90 per cent of the relevant shares (taking into account any prior holdings). For this purpose, 'relevant shares' has the same meaning as explained in paragraph 9.44 above.

9.48   This provision of the Act contrasts with that of SSAP 23, which states that immediately before the offer, the offeror must not hold 20 per cent or more of any class of the offeree's equity shares, and also must not hold 20 per cent or more of the offeree's votes. [SSAP 23 para 11(c)]. Consequently, in situations where there are prior holdings, the condition in SSAP 23 will apply.

Ten per cent cash limit test

9.49   In order to merger account, the consideration given for the relevant shares can include other consideration such as debentures and cash. However, the provisions of the Companies Act 1989 restrict significantly the other consideration that can be given in an acquisition where the merger accounting method is to be used. The fair value of such other consideration given by the parent and its subsidiaries cannot exceed more then ten per cent of the *nominal value* of the equity shares issued as part of the consideration pursuant to the arrangement. [4A Sch 10(c)].

9.50   The provisions of the Act contrast with the requirement included in SSAP 23 where the following two conditions must apply:

- ■ Equity share capital must form not less than 90 per cent of the fair value of the total consideration that the offeror gives for the offeree's equity share capital.

- ■ Equity share capital and/or voting non-equity share capital must form not less than 90 per cent of the fair value of the total consideration that the offeror gives for the offeree's voting non-equity share capital.

9.51 Under these requirements in SSAP 23, the fair value of the total consideration that the offeror gives should include also the fair value of the consideration that the offeror gave for shares that it held before the offer. [SSAP 23 para 11(d)]. (In contrast, it is not necessary to take prior-holdings into account in calculating the Act's limit mentioned in paragraph 9.49.) Consequently, the provisions in the Act may be more restrictive than those in SSAP 23. But, consider the following example.

Example

Company B has share capital of 1,000 £1 ordinary shares. Company A has previously acquired 100 shares in company B for £5,000 (that is, £50 per share). These shares were acquired entirely for cash before the stock market 'crash'. Company A now wishes to acquire the remaining 900 shares in company B. Because of the 'crash' the value of company B has decreased since company A acquired its previous holding, and the 900 shares are valued at £45 per share. The consideration for these 900 shares is to be given entirely by an issue of company A's ordinary shares.

The fair value of the total consideration that company A will have given is:

	£
Cash	5,000
Fair value of shares	
(namely, 900 x £45)	40,500
Total consideration	45,500

Company A makes its offer for 90 per cent of the relevant shares of company B and because this offer is wholly for shares, the Act's provisions on the cash limit explained above do not apply. However, because the cash element of the previous acquisition represents 10.9 per cent of the fair value of the total consideration given in the acquisition, the limit set in SSAP 23 is exceeded and merger accounting cannot be used.

9.52 The fair value of the shares issued will, however, generally no longer have a significant effect on whether or not the business combination satisfies the merger conditions. For example, if the total consideration consists of equity shares with a nominal value of £100,000 plus cash of £15,000, then the merger conditions of the Act are not satisfied as the cash represents more than ten per cent of the nominal value of the shares issued. Merger accounting will then not be available. This will also be the situation even if the shares' fair value is £150,000, and the business combination satisfies SSAP 23's condition that the equity share capital's fair value is not less than 90 per cent of the total of the issued shares' fair value plus the cash element of the consideration.

9.53 Any convertible stock that is outstanding at the time of the offer should not normally be regarded as equity for the purposes of satisfying the merger conditions. The only exception to this is where the convertible stock is converted into equity as a result of, and at the time of, the business combination. [SSAP 23 para 12].

9.54 The examples that follow illustrate situations that can arise in this area.

Example 1

Company A acquires company B and the consideration for the acquisition is entirely
equity shares for equity shares. Consequently, the companies wish to merger account.
However, as part of the consideration, company A agrees to lend company B some
funds to pay off certain of its liabilities.

This funding is not part of the consideration, because it is merely a loan and as such
should be recorded as an inter-company liability in company B's books of account.
Consequently, this element of the transaction would not affect company A's ability to
merger account for the acquisition.

Example 2

A company acquires a new subsidiary and there is deferred consideration that can be
satisfied at the acquirer's option in either shares or cash. If the share option route is
taken, then merger accounting will be available. However, if the deferred consideration
is settled in cash then acquisition accounting will have to be used.

Where it is the intention of the acquiring company to settle the deferred consideration
in shares it would be acceptable to merger account provided the board minuted its
intention. Where they have minuted such an intention and merger accounting is initially
used for the acquisition, but subsequently the deferred consideration is settled in cash,
a prior year adjustment would have to be made in order to account for the combination
as an acquisition.

Differences between merger accounting conditions and merger relief conditions

9.55   There are several differences between the merger accounting
conditions in the Act and SSAP 23 and the conditions for merger
relief in section 131 of the Act (outlined in paragraph 9.14 above).
These differences are:

■   Ninety per cent holding test:

  □   Under the Act to merger account, the offeror must secure 90
per cent of the undertaking's *relevant shares*.

  □   Under SSAP 23, the offeror must secure a holding of at least
90 per cent of *each class of equity shares*, and it must also
secure a holding of the shares that carry at least 90 per cent
of the offeree's *votes*.

  □   To qualify for merger relief under section 131, the issuing
company must secure a holding of at least 90 per cent of *each
class of equity shares*.

■   Ten per cent cash limit test:

  □   Under the Act to merger account, the fair value of other
consideration given as part of the arrangement must not

exceed more than 10 per cent of the *nominal value of the equity shares* issued.

☐ Under SSAP 23, at least 90 per cent of the *fair value of the total consideration* that the issuing company gives for equity shares must itself be in the form of equity shares.

☐ The Act imposes no such condition for merger relief.

■ Prior holding test:

☐ SSAP 23 stipulates that the offeror's prior holding in the offeree must not exceed 20 per cent or more of *any class of* the offeree's *equity shares*, or 20 per cent or more of the offeree's *votes*.

☐ The Act imposes no such condition for merger accounting or for merger relief.

9.56 The conditions for merger accounting in both the Act and SSAP 23 are more restrictive than are the Act's conditions for merger relief. There may be occasions, therefore, where a parent qualifies for merger relief, but the group must use acquisition accounting on consolidation. In these circumstances, the company may record its investment in the subsidiary at nominal value. But SSAP 14 and the Act both require the group to use fair values on consolidation. [4A Sch 9; SSAP 14 para 29].

9.57 Where the parent is entitled to merger relief, it is also acceptable for the parent to record its investment in the subsidiary at the fair value of the consideration given, instead of at cost. However, where the parent adopts this treatment, the difference between the fair value of the shares issued and the nominal value of those shares should not be credited to a share premium account. Instead, it can be credited to a special merger reserve.

Merger accounting principles

9.58 The principles of acquisition accounting are explained in chapters 6, 7 and 8 and the principles of merger accounting are considered in greater detail below.

9.59 When a group uses merger accounting to account for a business combination, the group does not need to incorporate into its consolidated financial statements the fair values of the subsidiary's assets and liabilities. [SSAP 23 para 18]. Therefore, the group should incorporate into its consolidated financial statements the assets and liabilities at the amounts at which the subsidiary recorded them in its books before the combination. [4A Sch 11(2)].

9.60   One exception to this principle is that a group should adopt uniform
        accounting policies for consolidation purposes throughout the group
        in accordance with the Act and SSAP 14. Consequently, if the
        acquired company's accounting policies are not the same as the
        acquiring company's, then adjustments should be made to achieve
        uniformity. One way of doing this might be for the subsidiary to make
        these adjustments in its own records. It could restate the amount of its
        assets and liabilities in its books to reflect the change in accounting
        policy. Alternatively, if it is not practicable for the acquired company
        to change its accounting policies, adjustments may be made on
        consolidation to the values of the acquired company's assets and
        liabilities that are stated in its books. See further chapter 5 paragraph
        5.15.

9.61   The group's consolidated financial statements for the period in which
        the business combination takes place should include the subsidiary's
        income and expenditure for the entire period. [4A Sch 11(3); SSAP 23
        para 19]. That is to say, they should include the subsidiary's results for
        the part of the period before the business combination, as well as the
        results of the subsidiary for the part of the period after the business
        combination consolidated on a line by line basis in the profit and loss
        account. In addition, the corresponding amounts in the consolidated
        financial statements should reflect the position that would have arisen
        if the companies had been combined throughout the previous period
        and also at the previous balance sheet date. [4A Sch 11(4)]. For
        example, see Table 50.

Table 50: Illustration of an accounting policy for merger accounting.

Extract from EMAP plc Annual Report and Accounts 1st April 1989.

Basis of Consolidation
The Group Accounts consolidate the accounts of the Company and is Subsidiaries, prepared to 1st
April 1989. The turnover and results of subsidiary companies are included in the Group Accounts
from the date of acquisition, except where merger accounting principles are employed, in which case
the turnover and results of the companies being merged are included for a full year. In the case of
disposals, turnover and results are included up to the date of disposal. Where merger accounting is
adopted, the cost of investment in the Company's books is recorded as the nominal value of shares
issued together with the costs associated with the merger.

9.62   The aim of the consolidated financial statements in merger accounting
        is to show the combined companies' results and financial positions as
        if they had always been combined, but see further paragraph 9.73.
        Consequently, even the share capital issued during the year for the
        acquisition has to be shown as if it had always been issued (for
        example, see Table 51 overleaf).

Table 51: Illustration of the restatement of share capital where merger accounting is used.

Extract from Cray Electronics Holdings P.L.C. Report and Accounts 31st March 1989.

Accounting policy extract

(a) Basis of consolidation
The group accounts comprise the consolidation of the accounts of the company and its subsidiaries as at 29th April, 1989. No profit and loss account is presented for the Company as provided by s.228(7) of the Companies Act 1985.

Goodwill arising on consolidation has been written off to Reserves.

The purchase of Executive Action Ltd on 1st July, 1988, Ultranet Ltd and its subsidiaries Ultranet Marketing Ltd, Ultranet Services Ltd, Ultranet Manufacturing Ltd and Taunton Software Development Ltd on 8th February, 1989 have been accounted for on an acquisition basis.

The acquisition of GRP Material Supplies Ltd on 11th January, 1989; Beatcan Ltd and its subsidiary Peatgrange (IVD) Ltd on 10th March, 1989 and Crown Graphics Sales Ltd on 28th April, 1989 have been accounted for on a merger basis, and accordingly comparatives have been restated.

Note extract

Allotted, called up and fully paid:	Ordinary Shares 10p each	£000	Deferred Redeemable Shares £1 each	£000
As at 1st May, 1988	79,416,093	7,942	50,000	50
Allotted during year in respect of current mergers:				
11th January, 1989, GRP Material Suppliers Ltd	1,626,513	163		
10th March, 1989–Beatcan Ltd	514,078	51		
28th April, 1989, Crown Graphics Sales Ltd	209,515	21		
Opening share capital as adjusted for merger accounting	81,766,199	8,177	50,000	50

9.63 The examples that follow illustrate some of the problems that can arise with the principles of merger accounting.

Example 1

Company A acquires company B during the year and merger accounts for the acquisition. Company A has large tax losses and has never had a tax charge. Company B paid tax last year and it is proposed that the two companies results should be combined and the tax charge of company B excluded from the comparatives on the basis that if the companies had always been combined, this tax charge would never have arisen.

In this type of situation, it would be carrying the principles of merger accounting too far to eliminate the tax charge. The tax has been paid and cannot be recovered now that company B has joined the group. Consequently, the tax charge should be shown as a comparative in the merged profit and loss account. Company A could of course add a note to explain why the tax charge has arisen.

Example 2

A company acquires another and proposes to merger account. The company's year end is 31st December and the subsidiary's year end is 30th June. The company wishes to know how to deal with the difference in year ends.

The company should consolidate the results of the subsidiary for the 12 months ended 31st December. It should take six months from the year to 30th June and add the following six months of trading. This treatment is necessary to comply with the Act's requirements concerning the accounting period of the subsidiary that must be consolidated (see further chapter 5 para 5.25).

Example 3

A listed company with a December year end acquires a target company with a June year end. Merger accounting is to be used. The target company had a subsidiary that made losses to June, but it disposes of its loss-making subsidiary before the acquisition date which is in November.

The results of the loss-making subsidiaries should be included in the consolidation, because, although technically they never become subsidiaries of the listed company, the spirit of SSAP 23 requires that the merged companies should incorporate the unaltered results of the two companies for the full year. If necessary, the results of the subsidiaries that are sold could be shown separately and disclosed as discontinued operations, but they should still be included in the consolidated profit and loss account of the merged companies.

9.64   In merger accounting, the parent's balance sheet will generally show the holding company's investment in the subsidiary at the nominal value of the shares that the holding company issued as consideration, plus the fair value of any additional consideration, together with any fees and expenses of acquisition. (Alternatively, the parent could also show its investment at fair value and disclose the difference between the nominal value of the shares issued and their fair value as a merger reserve.)

9.65   A difference may then arise on consolidation between the value at which the parent carries its investment in the subsidiary, and the nominal value of the subsidiary's shares that the parent acquires. The value of the investment will represent the aggregate of the following:

■   The nominal value of the 'qualifying shares' issued by the parent in consideration for the acquisition of the shares in the subsidiary. [4A Sch 11(5)(a)]. 'Qualifying shares' means those shares where merger relief is obtained and, consequently, no share premium has to be recorded on them. [4A Sch 11(7)].

**Merger relief and
merger accounting**

■ The fair value of any other consideration given for the acquisition determined at the date of acquisition. [4A Sch 11(5)(b)].

9.66 Normally the nominal value of the subsidiary's shares alone is set off against the value of the investment, but it is becoming increasingly common for any share premium of the subsidiary to be set off against the investment also. This will mean that on consolidation only the share premium of the parent will be disclosed.

9.67 The group should adjust these differences on consolidation against the consolidated reserves. [4A Sch 11(6); SSAP 23 para 20].

9.68 Where the investment's carrying value is less than the nominal value of the shares that the holding company has acquired, the group should treat the difference as a reserve that arises on consolidation. Where the investment's carrying value is greater than the nominal value of the shares acquired, the difference represents the extent to which the group has effectively capitalised its reserves as a result of the merger. Consequently, the group should reduce its reserves by the amount of the difference.

9.69 The two examples that follow show how these consolidation differences arise and how they should be treated:

Example 1 - Where the carrying value is less than nominal value

Company A acquires all of company B's £200,000 nominal share capital. The purchase consideration consists of new shares that company A issues, and these have a nominal value of £190,000. The business combination satisfies all the merger conditions, and the group uses merger accounting. The respective balance sheets, after the merger, of the individual companies and the group are as follows:

	Co. A £'000	Co. B £'000	Group £'000
Net tangible assets	1,500	200	1,700
Investment in subsidiary	190	-	-
	1,690	200	1,700
Share capital	1,190	200	1,190
Profit and loss account	500	-	500
Difference on consolidation	-	-	10
	1,690	200	1,700

The difference on consolidation of £10,000 is calculated as follows:

	£'000
Nominal value of shares acquired	200
Holding company's carrying value of investment	190
Difference on consolidation	10

242

The group should treat the difference on consolidation as a reserve that arises on consolidation, because the investment's carrying value is less than the nominal value of the shares acquired.

Example 2 - Where the carrying value is greater than nominal value

The facts in this example are the same as those in example 1 above, except that the purchase consideration consists of new shares with a nominal value of £250,000. In this example, the respective balance sheets, after the merger, of the individual companies and the group are as follows:

	Co. A £'000	Co. B £'000	Group £'000
Net tangible assets	1,500	200	1,700
Investment in subsidiary	250	-	-
	1,750	200	1,700
Share capital	1,250	200	1,250
Profit and loss account	500	-	500
Difference on consolidation	-	-	(50)
	1,750	200	1,700

The difference on consolidation of £50,000 is calculated as follows:

	£'000
Nominal value of shares acquired	200
Holding company's carrying value of investment	250
Difference on consolidation	(50)

The investment's carrying value is greater than the nominal value of the shares acquired, and so the group should reduce its reserves by the amount of the difference.

9.70 Where the difference on consolidation arises because the investment's carrying value is less than the nominal value of the shares that the parent and its subsidiaries have acquired, paragraph 20 of SSAP 23 says that the group should treat the difference as a reserve that has arisen on consolidation. Where the difference is material, the group should treat the difference as a separate reserve, in order to give a true and fair view. The most appropriate place to disclose the difference is under 'other reserves'. Where the difference is not material, the group may treat the difference by adjusting any of its consolidated reserves (except the share premium account or a capital redemption reserve).

9.71 However, where the difference on consolidation arises because the investment's carrying value is greater than the nominal value of the shares that the parent and its subsidiaries have acquired, paragraph 20 of SSAP 23 says that the group should reduce its reserves by the amount of the difference on consolidation.

9.72   The standard does not specify the reserves against which the group should adjust this type of difference. However, because of the restrictions on the uses of a share premium account detailed in paragraph 9.4, a group may not write such a difference off against a share premium account. It appears also that a group may not write such a difference off against a revaluation reserve. The uses of the revaluation reserve are discussed in chapter 8, paragraphs 8.45 to 8.48.

Comparison of acquisition accounting to merger accounting

9.73   SSAP 23 highlights the following three main differences between acquisition accounting and merger accounting:

■   In acquisition accounting, the consolidated financial statements reflect the acquired company's results from the date of acquisition only. However, in merger accounting, the consolidated financial statements incorporate the combined companies' results as if the companies had always been combined. Consequently, under merger accounting, the consolidated financial statements reflect both companies' full year's results, even though the business combination may have occurred part of the way though the year. Under merger accounting, the corresponding amounts in the consolidated financial statements for the previous year should reflect the results of the combined companies, even though the business combination did not occur until the current year.

■   In acquisition accounting, the acquiring group should account for the assets it acquired at the cost to the acquiring group. The acquiring group determines that cost by attributing a fair value to the assets and liabilities that it acquires. However, in merger accounting, the group does not restate any assets and liabilities at their fair values. Instead, the group incorporates the assets and liabilities at the amounts recorded in the books of the combined companies. As in the first point above, merger accounting shows the position of the combined companies as if the companies had always been combined.

■   Acquisition accounting may give rise to goodwill on consolidation. However, goodwill does not arise in merger accounting. Merger accounting may lead to differences in values on consolidation. For example, in merger accounting, there may be a difference between the nominal value of the shares issued together with the fair value of any additional consideration given, and the nominal value of the other company's shares that have been acquired (see para 9.65). However, such differences are not goodwill as defined in SSAP 22 (revised), because they are not based on the fair values of both the consideration given and the separable net assets acquired.

9.74 The following example illustrates the difference between acquisition accounting and merger accounting:

Company H (the issuing company) acquires the whole of company A's equity share capital. The effect of the acquisition will be to merge the interests of company H and company A.

Company A's shareholders accept an offer from company H of one share in company H for each share in company A as at 31st December 1990. The value at 31st December of the 400,000 of company H's £1 shares that are offered to company A's shareholders is £6,400,000, (that is, £16 per share). The fair value of company A's net assets is £6,100,000 (that is, £100,000 above their net book value). The difference of £300,000 is attributable to goodwill. On 31st December 1990, before the acquisition, the summarised balance sheets of the two companies are as follows:

	Co. H £'000	Co. A £'000
Net assets	5,000	6,000
Share capital (shares of 1 each)	500	400
Reserves	4,500	5,600
	5,000	6,000

The summarised consolidated balance sheets of the issuing company and its subsidiary under the two methods of accounting are as follows:

	Acquisition accounting £'000	Merger accounting £'000
Goodwill on consolidation	300(a)	-
Net assets	11,100(b)	11,000(b)
	11,400	11,000
Share capital	900(c)	900(c)
Distributable reserves	4,500(d)	10,100(e)
Merger reserve	6,000(d)	-
	11,400	11,000

Notes to the example above:

(a) Goodwill on consolidation is the amount by which the purchase consideration (that is, 400,000 shares at £16, or £6,400,000) exceeds the fair value of the underlying net assets acquired (that is, £6,100,000) (see further chapter 8 para 8.11).

(b) Net assets are the two companies' total net assets. In acquisition accounting, the assets are included at their fair value, as required by the Act and SSAP 14 (see further chapters 6 and 7).

(c) The share capital consists of the 500,000 shares originally in issue, together with the 400,000 shares allotted when company H combined with company A.

(d)   The amount credited to the merger reserve taking merger relief under section 131 of the Act is £6,000,000 (that is, 400,000 shares issued at a premium of £15 per share).

(e)   Under merger accounting there is no requirement to transfer to a merger reserve the premium on the shares allotted to the acquired company's shareholders. Consequently, both companies' distributable reserves are pooled. In accordance with the Act and paragraph 18 of SSAP 23, the excess of the fair value of company A's net assets over their book value (that is, £100,000) need not be incorporated into the consolidated financial statements.

Disclosure

9.75   The acquiring company or the issuing company should disclose certain information in respect of all material mergers. The parent must disclose this information in the consolidated financial statements that deal with the period in which the merger occurs. For all acquisitions, the parent must disclose its accounting policy (for example see Table 52) and must give the following information:

- The names of the merging companies. [4A Sch 13(2)(a); SSAP 23 para 21(a)]. The Act goes on to add that where a group of companies is acquired, only the name of the group's parent needs to be disclosed.

- That the company adopted merger accounting for the acquisition. [4A Sch 13(2)(b); SSAP 23 para 21(c)].

Table 52: Example of an accounting policy where the group mainly uses merger accounting.

Extract from Calor Group plc Annual Report 31st March 1989.

(b) Principles of consolidation
The group accounts consolidate the financial statements of the subsidiaries following merger accounting principles (with the exception of Century Power and Light Limited which was accounted for under acquisition accounting principles for the year ended 31 March, 1988).

9.76   In addition, additional information is required to be disclosed for acquisitions that significantly affect the figures shown in the consolidated financial statements. These requirements are as follows:

- The composition and the fair value of the consideration for acquisition given by the parent and its subsidiaries. [4A Sch 13(3); SSAP 23 para 23(a)]. This information should include:

  □   The number and the class of the securities that the company issued in respect of the merger.

☐   Details of any other consideration that the company gave in
respect of the merger.

[SSAP 23 para 21(b)].

■   An explanation of any major adjustments made to the assets and
liabilities of the undertaking acquired. This should include a
statement of any resulting adjustment to the consolidated reserves
(including a restatement of opening consolidated reserves). [4A
Sch 13(6)].

■   The nature and the amount of any significant accounting
adjustments that the merged companies made to achieve
consistent accounting policies. [SSAP 23 para 21(d)].

9.77   If in the directors' opinion the disclosure of any of the information
above that is required by the Act (relating to an undertaking
established under the law of a country, or one that carries on a
business, outside the UK) would be seriously prejudicial to the
business of the undertaking, its parent or its fellow subsidiaries, it
need not be given if the Secretary of State's permission is obtained.
[4A Sch 16].

9.78   In addition in respect of a material merger, the issuing company
should disclose the following information in its financial statements
that deal with a year in which a merger occurs:

■   The amount of the current year's attributable profit before
extraordinary items that relates to the part of the year before the
merger, and also the amount that relates to the part of the year
after the merger.

■   An analysis of the attributable profit before extraordinary items of
the current year up to the effective date of the merger between
that of the issuing company and that of the subsidiary.

■   An analysis of the attributable profit before extraordinary items of
the previous year between that of the issuing company and that of
the subsidiary.

■   An analysis of extraordinary items between those extraordinary
items that relate to the period before the merger's effective date,
and those extraordinary items that relate to the period after the
merger's effective date.

■   An analysis of extraordinary items that indicates to which party to
the merger the extraordinary items relate. It is likely that the

group should analyse the current year's extraordinary items in this way, and should also analyse the previous year's extraordinary items in this way, in order to show a true and fair view.

[SSAP 23 para 23].

9.79   In comparison, the Act requires the following disclosure concerning the profit or loss of the undertaking or group acquired:

■   The profit or loss from the beginning of the undertaking's financial year (or the parent's financial year if it is a group) up to the date of acquisition.

■   The profit or loss for the previous financial year of the undertaking or group.

■   The date on which the financial year referred to in the first point began.

[4A Sch 13(4)].

The figures above should be disclosed after taking into account the consolidation adjustments required by Schedule 4A to the Act. [4A Sch 13(7)]. This would include for example adjustments to achieve uniform accounting policies.

9.80   An illustration of the type of information required to be disclosed is given in Table 53. Further disclosure requirements that may apply if a merger has occurred are set out in paragraphs 9.86 to 9.93.

Accounting for group reconstructions

9.81   SSAP 23 refers mainly to business combinations in which either an acquiring company or an issuing company issues shares in consideration for the transfer to it of another company's shares. Paragraph 24 of SSAP 23 says that the standard applies also to any other arrangements that achieve similar results to the above-mentioned business combination. Such an arrangement might set up a new holding company that issues shares to the shareholders of two other companies, as consideration for the transfer to it of shares in both those other companies.

9.82   Whatever the nature of the arrangement, the group may account for the business combination as a merger only if the business combination complies with all of the merger accounting conditions that are outlined in paragraphs 9.37 to 9.54 above.

9.83   Consequently, where a group reconstruction is eligible for the relief that section 132 of the Act gives in respect of group reconstructions (as discussed in paras 9.21 to 9.30 above), it may also be possible to use merger accounting. But this will be possible only if the reconstruction complies with all of the merger accounting conditions.

Table 53: Illustration of the type of disclosure required when a group uses merger accounting.

Extract from The Bestwood Plc 31st December 1987.

Note extract

25 Subsidiaries acquired

The Furlong companies

a) During the year, the company acquired Furlong Brothers (Construction) Limited and Furlong Brothers (Chingford) Limited for a maximum consideration of £15,430,000, subject to warrented profit levels being achieved up to the year ended 31 December 1989.

The consideration is being satisfied as follows:

On completion 3 September 1987	£1,430,000	by payment in cash
	£6,000,000	by issue of 4,696,394 ordinary shares of 5p
30 June 1989	£4,000,000 ⎱	subject to warranted profit levels and
30 June 1990	£4,000,000 ⎰	by issue of ordinary shares at prevaling market values.

No material accounting adjustments were required by these companies to achieve consistency of accounting policies.

b) In accodance with Section 131 Companies Act 1985, no share premium has been accounted for on the shares allotted as consideration for the acquisition of these companies.

c) Details of the shares acquired are as follows:

Furlong Brothers (Construction) Limited	430,100 ordinary shares of £1
Furlong Brothers (Chingford) Limited	15,300 ordinary shares of £1

d) The results of the subsidiaries dealt with under merger accounting have been included for the full year. The profit after tax of these companies in 1987 was £1,531,000 (1986 - £552,000). Approximately £472,000 of this profit was earned after the actual date of acquisition. There were no extraordinary items in their results for 1987 or 1986.

9.84 The example that follows illustrates the differences between using acquisition accounting and using merger accounting in a group reconstruction:

In 1985, company A acquired all of company C's issued share capital (100,000 £1 shares) for £390,000. Company C had no reserves at that time. On 31st December 1990, another wholly-owned subsidiary (company B) allots 100,000 £1 shares to company A. In return for the allotment, company A transfers to company B the shares in company C that it owns. Subsequently, company A is to be liquidated, and its shareholders will receive shares in company B. At the time of the reconstruction, company B's shares that are issued to company A are worth £400,000 (that is, £4 per share), and the fair value of company C's recorded net assets is £360,000 (the difference of £40,000 being attributed to goodwill). The fair value of company A's and company B's net assets is equal to their book value.

Diagrammatically, the reconstruction is as follows:

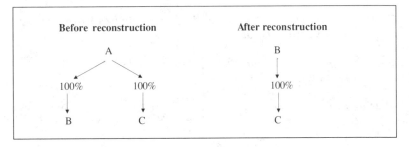

The individual balance sheets of the three companies as at 31st December 1990 before the reconstruction are as follows:

	Co. A £'000	Co. B £'000	Co. C £'000
Investment in B*	210	-	-
Investment in C*	320	-	-
Net assets	-	700	350
	530	700	350
Share capital (shares of 1 each)	150	200	100
Reserves	380	500	250
	530	700	350

*The investments are stated at the cost of shares to company A, reduced for company A's investment in company C by a write-down of £70,000 made in 1988.

After the reconstruction, the summarised consolidated balance sheet of company B and its subsidiary company C is as follows:

	Acquisition accounting £'000	Merger accounting £'000
Goodwill on consolidation	40(a)	-
Net assets	1,060(b)	1,050
	1,100	1,050
Share capital	300(c)	300(c)
Share premium account	300(d)	220(e)
Other reserves	500(d)	530(f)
	1100	1,050

Notes to the example above:

(a) Goodwill on consolidation is the amount by which the purchase consideration (that is, 100,000 shares at £4, or £400,000) exceeds the fair value of the underlying assets acquired (that is, £360,000). Under merger accounting, goodwill does not arise, because the net assets' fair value need not be incorporated in the consolidated financial statements (see para 9.59 above).

(b) Company C's net assets are included at their fair value when they are accounted for as an acquisition. But when they are accounted for as a merger, they are included at their book value.

(c) The share capital consists of the 200,000 shares originally in issue, together with the 100,000 shares allotted on company B's acquisition of company C.

(d) The amount credited to the share premium account in accordance with section 130 of the Act is £300,000 (that is, 100,000 shares issued at a premium of £3 per share).

(e) Under section 132 of the Act, the issuing company is required to transfer to the share premium account only an amount equal to the minimum premium value (see para 9.24). The minimum premium value is calculated as the amount by which the base value of the shares in company C that are transferred from company A to company B exceeds the aggregate nominal value of the shares that company B allots in consideration for the transfer. The amount of the transfer to the share premium account is calculated as follows:

	£'000	£'000
The base value of shares in company C is the lower of:		
The cost of those shares to company A	390	
The amount at which those shares are stated in company A's accounting records immediately before the transfer	320	
		320
Less: Nominal value of the shares company B allotted in respect of the transfer		100
Transfer to the share premium account		220

(f) Under acquisition accounting, the amount to be included in other reserves is the amount of company B's reserves (that is, £500,000). Under section 132 of the Act (which gives the relief in respect of group reconstructions), other reserves are made up as follows:

	£'000
Reserves of company B	500
Reserves of company C less minimum premium value (that is, £250,000 - £220,000)	30
	530

9.85 The main effect of the provisions of section 132 of the Act is to reduce the amount of the premium that must be taken to the share premium account.

The holding company's financial statements

9.86 Although the appendix to SSAP 23 does not form part of the standard, it does provide guidance on how an offeror should normally

account for a merger in its own financial statements. The appendix
states that the offeror should record its investment in the new
subsidiary at the nominal value of the shares that it issues, plus the fair
value of any consideration other than shares.

9.87   Cash is probably the most common form of consideration other than
shares, and loan stock is another form. For example, part of the
consideration may be loan stock that bears an interest rate above the
current market rate. Or it may be loan stock that can be subsequently
converted into shares. The fair value of either type of loan stock may
differ from its nominal value (see further chapter 7).

9.88   Where a parent company takes advantage of the merger relief
provisions in the Act, in either an acquisition or a merger, it must
disclose in its financial statements:

■   The name of the other company.

■   The number, the nominal value and the class of shares allotted.

■   The number, the nominal value and the classes of shares of the
other company that were either issued, or transferred or
cancelled.

■   Details of the accounting treatment the parent has adopted in
both its financial statements and the parent's consolidated
financial statements.

■   If the parent prepares consolidated financial statements,
particulars of how and to what extent the group's profit or loss for
the year as shown in the consolidated financial statements is
affected by the other company's (or any of its subsidiaries') profit
or loss that arose before the merger or acquisition.

[5 Sch 29(2)].

9.89   Where the parent has used merger accounting on consolidation, most
of the information to be disclosed above is also required by SSAP 23
(see para 9.75 above).

9.90   If the parent has, during the financial year or during either of the two
preceding financial years, allotted shares in the circumstances
described above, then the notes to the financial statements may need
to disclose further information in the following two circumstances:

■   The parent company or any of its subsidiaries disposes of either of
the following:

☐   Shares in the 'acquired company'.

□ Fixed assets that, at the time of the merger, were assets of
either the 'acquired company' or any of its subsidiaries.

If the parent company or any of its subsidiaries realises a profit or
loss on such a disposal, and that profit or loss is included in the
consolidated profit and loss account (or in the parent's profit and
loss account if it has not prepared a consolidated profit and loss
account), the amount of that profit or loss has to be disclosed. [5
Sch 10(3)a,29(3)(a)].

■ The parent company or any of its subsidiaries disposes of shares
in any company (other than the 'acquired company'), and the
profit or loss it makes on this disposal is to some extent
attributable to the fact that the company whose shares have been
sold (or one of its subsidiaries) owned as assets either of the
following:

□ Shares in the 'acquired company'.

□ Fixed assets that, at the time of the merger, were assets of
either the 'acquired company' or any of its subsidiaries.

In this situation, the net profit or loss attributable to the sale of
those assets that is included in the parent's consolidated profit
and loss account (or its own profit and loss account - if it has not
prepared a consolidated profit and loss account) has to be
disclosed. [5 Sch 10(3)b,29(3)(b)].

9.91 In both the above situations, the notes to the financial statements must
give an explanation of the transaction. These provisions are explained
by the example that follows:

Company A has two subsidiaries, company B and company C. Company C also owns a
minority interest in company B. In 1990, company A merged with another company,
company D. At the time of the merger, company D owned a particular fixed asset.
Consider the following two situations:

Situation 1

After the merger, company D transferred the asset to company A. In 1991, company A
sells the asset for a profit of £50,000. This profit of £50,000 will be included in the
consolidated profit and loss account that company A prepares for the year ended 31st
December 1991. The notes to these financial statements must disclose the profit of
£50,000 and explain how it has arisen. This is because of the requirement in the first
point in paragraph 9.90 above.

Situation 2

After the merger, company D transferred the asset to company B. In 1991, company C
sells its minority interest in company B, and realises a profit of £200,000. Company A's
directors consider that £30,000 of this profit is attributable to the fact that company B
owned the asset. The profit of £200,000 will be included in the consolidated profit and

loss account of company A for the year ended 31st December 1991. The notes to these financial statements must disclose the fact that £30,000 is attributable to the asset. They must also explain what has happened. This is because of the requirement in the second point in paragraph 9.90 above.

9.92   This type of disclosure alerts those shareholders who have acquired shares in a new company in exchange for their shares in another company, of any substantial disposals of the assets of the company that they originally owned. This type of disclosure may also alert shareholders to situations where a group's management are pursuing a policy of 'asset stripping'. Such a policy would conflict with the basic concept of a merger. An illustration of the disclosure is given in Table 54.

Table 54: Example of the disclosure required where a group disposes of assets previously acquired by shares issued taking advantage of merger relief.

Extract from MEPC PLC Report & Financial Statements 30th September 1989.

Note extract

Particulars required by Para 75 (2) Sch 4 Companies Act 1985: Oldham Estate Company plc group assets with a book value of £13.8m (*£19.7m*) have been disposed of during the year realising a surplus of £11.8m (*£6.5m*) over book value, of which £11.0m (*£5.5m*) is included in profit on ordinary activities before taxation.

9.93   These provisions of the Act apply from the time of the arrangement, which is as follows:

■   Where as a result of the arrangement the other company becomes a subsidiary, the time is the date on which it becomes a subsidiary or if the arrangement becomes binding on fulfilment of a condition, the date on which the condition is fulfilled.

■   Where the company is already a subsidiary, the first day on which shares are allotted.

[5 Sch 29(4)].

Pre-combination profits

9.94   Paragraph 15(5) of the pre-1981 Schedule 8 to the Companies Act 1948 provided that a subsidiary's pre-acquisition profits were not to be treated as the holding company's profits. However, the Companies Act 1981 repealed this requirement so that a company that wishes to claim the benefit of the merger relief provisions is able to distribute to its shareholders the subsidiary's pre-combination profits. If the 1981 Act had not repealed this requirement, one of the principal advantages of merger relief would have been lost, because the distributability of the subsidiary's pre-combination profits would still have been restricted.

9.95 In merger accounting, the subsidiary's pre-combination profits are normally available for eventual distribution to the parent company's shareholders. However, in some circumstances, the subsidiary's pre-combination profits may not be available for distribution to the parent company's shareholders. For example, where the new subsidiary pays a dividend out of its pre-combination profits, the holding company may have to apply the dividend to reduce the carrying value of its investment to the extent that it is necessary in order to provide for a diminution in that carrying value. [SSAP 23 appendix para 3]. The following example illustrates the way in which companies that use merger accounting should apply this rule:

The abbreviated balance sheets of company H and company S before the merger are as follows:

	Co. H £'000	Co. S £'000
Net tangible assets	1,000	135
Share capital	800	10
Profit and loss account	200	125
	1,000	135

Company H issues shares with a nominal value of £100,000 in exchange for the shares in company S. The abbreviated balance sheets of company H, company S and the group after the merger are as follows:

	Co. H £'000	Co. S £'000	Group £'000
Net tangible assets	1,000	135	1,135
Investment	100	-	-
	1,100	135	1,135
Share capital	900	10	900
Profit and loss account	200	125	235*
	1,100	135	1,135

*The group profit and loss account balance is made up as follows:

		£'000
Profit and loss account balance of company H		200
Profit and loss account balance of company S		125
		325
Excess of carrying value of investment over		
nominal value of shares acquired		
(that is, £100,000 - £10,000)		(90)
		235

Suppose that company S pays all of its profit and loss account balance (that is, £125,000) to company H. Then company S is left with share capital of £10,000 and net tangible assets of £10,000.

If the £10,000 of net tangible assets represents the value of company H's investment in company S, then company H should reduce the carrying value of its investment in company S to £10,000. Paragraph 3 of the appendix to SSAP 23 indicates that company H should use £90,000 of the dividend that it receives, in order to provide for the diminution in the carrying value of its investment in company S. The remaining £35,000 of the dividend represents realised profits to company H. The abbreviated balance sheets of company H, company S and the group after the distribution are then as follows:

	Co. H £'000	Co.S £'000	Group £'000
Net tangible assets	1,120	10	1,135
Investment	10	-	-
	1,135	10	1,135
Share capital	900	10	900
Profit and loss account	235	-	235
	1,135	10	1,135

However, the £10,000 of net tangible assets might not represent the value of company H's investment in company S, because company S may have substantial hidden reserves. For example, company S's fixed assets might have a net book value of £5,000 but a current value of £35,000. Company S would then have a hidden reserve of £30,000, and the value of company H's investment in company S would be £40,000 - not £10,000. Consequently, company H need use only £60,000 of the dividend that it receives, in order to provide for the diminution in the carrying value of its investment in company S. The remaining £65,000 of the dividend represents realised profits to company H. The abbreviated balance sheets of company H, company S and the group are then as follows:

	Co. H £'000	Co. S £'000	Group £'000
Net tangible assets	1,120	10	1,135
Investment	40	-	-
	1,165	10	1,135
Share capital	900	10	900
Profit and loss account	265	-	235*
	1,165	10	1,135*

*Company H's profit and loss account is greater than the group's profit and loss account. The group profit and loss account balance is made up as follows:

	£'000
Profit and loss account balance of company H	265
Profit and loss account balance of company S	-
	365
Excess of carrying value of investment over nominal value of shares acquired (that is, £40,000 - £10,000)	(30)
	235

9.96 The above example illustrates the fact that, when the investment's carrying value exceeds the nominal value of the shares that the parent company acquires, some pre-combination profits may not be distributable to parent company shareholders in merger accounting.

9.97 The same principles apply on acquisition accounting, except that the parent would record the investment in its subsidiary at its fair value. Consequently, the parent's investment is recorded at a figure greater than it would have been if merger accounting could be used. Therefore, when the subsidiary pays a dividend to its parent, the parent's investment is more likely to require to be provided against if the value of the investment is not substantiated by the underlying worth of the subsidiary.

9.98 It is also common, where merger accounting cannot be used, for the acquiring company to take merger relief on the shares it issues to acquire a subsidiary. Although under the acquisition rules the shares issued have then to be recorded at their fair value, the premium on the issue can be treated as a merger reserve rather than share premium. In this situation, where a dividend is paid to the parent by its subsidiary an equivalent amount of the merger reserve becomes realised. If there is a need to write down the carrying value of the investment this write down should similarly be made to the profit and loss account. However, an equivalent amount can be transferred from the merger reserve to the profit and loss account reserve.

Vendor placing

9.99 In a business combination, some or all of the target company's shareholders may prefer to receive cash, rather than shares in the acquiring company. However, the acquiring company may want to use merger accounting on consolidation. Consequently, it may prefer to pay for the target company by issuing shares, rather than by paying cash. In these circumstances, a vendor placing can reconcile the apparently conflicting objectives of the target company's shareholders and the acquiring company.

9.100 A vendor placing normally works as follows. The acquiring company will offer its shares to the target company's shareholders in exchange for their shares in that company. If there are any shareholders of the target company who do not wish to retain the consideration shares of the acquiring company, then the acquiring company will arrange for its financial adviser (for example, a merchant bank) to place those consideration shares. The financial adviser will put together a placing list (that will normally include institutions such as pension funds and insurance companies) so that the target company shareholders may dispose of their consideration shares in the acquiring company for cash.

9.101 So after the vendor placing has occurred, cash has been transferred from the institutions, via the financial adviser (acting in his capacity as a broker) to some or all of the target company's shareholders. In return, the institutions now own shares in the acquiring company, and the acquiring company now owns the target company. The acquiring company has issued shares, rather than paying cash, for the target company, and, as long as the offer complies with both the Act's and SSAP 23's merger conditions, the acquiring company can use merger accounting on consolidation.

9.102 On the grounds that the substance of a vendor placing is a cash takeover, there is an argument that vendor placings do not comply with the spirit of SSAP 23. If this were the case, the acquiring company would have to account for the business combination as an acquisition, rather than as a merger. However, SSAP 23's main criterion for merger accounting is whether material resources leave one or other of the combining companies. In a vendor placing, the acquiring company issues shares, and so material resources do not leave the group. Consequently, SSAP 23 allows a group, in this situation, to use merger accounting to account for the business combination.

Vendor rights

9.103 The vendor rights method of financing a business combination is a variation of a vendor placing (see paras 9.99 to 9.102 above). In a vendor placing, the financial adviser normally arranges to place the consideration shares in the acquiring company to institutional investors. Consequently, the acquiring company's other shareholders find that their shareholding becomes diluted. However, the vendor rights method limits the dilution of the shareholder's interests in the acquiring company.

9.104 The vendor rights method should work as follows. The acquiring company will offer its shares to the target company's shareholders in exchange for their shares in that company. If any shareholders of the target company do not wish to retain their consideration shares of the acquiring company, then the acquiring company will arrange for its financial adviser to place those consideration shares. Up to this point, the vendor rights method is the same as a vendor placing. However, as part of the placing agreement, the acquiring company's shareholders will have an option to buy ('claw back') some of the consideration shares from the placees. They will be entitled to buy back at the placing price a certain proportion of the placed shares on a pro-rata basis.

9.105 Therefore, after the vendor rights method is completed, cash has been transferred from the acquiring company's shareholders, via the financial adviser, to some or all of the target company's shareholders. In return, the acquiring company's shareholders now have a stake in a larger group, because the acquiring company now owns the target company. The acquiring company has issued shares, rather than paying cash, for the target company, and so it can use merger accounting on consolidation.

9.106 The method is referred to as 'vendor rights' because it is similar to a rights issue. In both the vendor rights method and a rights issue, the existing shareholders pay cash to acquire more shares in the company. The shares are issued on a pro-rata basis. However, although there are similarities between vendor rights and a rights issue, there are significant differences in the accounting implications. If a company finances a business combination both by making a rights issue and then using the cash to buy the target company, then it must use acquisition accounting on consolidation. However, if a company finances a business combination by using the vendor rights method, then as long as the offer complies with both the Act's and SSAP 23's merger conditions, it may use merger accounting on consolidation.

9.107 As with vendor placings, there is an argument that the vendor rights method does not comply with the spirit of the Act and SSAP 23.

9.108 However, currently the main criterion for merger accounting in SSAP 23 is whether material resources leave one or other of the combining companies. In the vendor rights method, the acquiring company issues shares, and so material resources do not leave the group. Consequently, SSAP 23 allows the group to use merger accounting in accounting for the business combination.

Provisions of ED 48

9.109 The proposals in the ED 48 'Accounting for acquisitions and mergers' issued in February 1990 will, if adopted unchanged, fundamentally affect when a business combination can be accounted for as a merger. No longer will a group have the choice to adopt either acquisition accounting or merger accounting for the purchase of a subsidiary. As explained above, under the present standard where a parent acquiring a subsidiary satisfies the conditions outlined in paragraphs 9.37 to 9.54 it may choose whether to use merger accounting or acquisition accounting. Under the provisions in the exposure draft, this choice will no longer be available.

9.110 The exposure draft proposes that merger accounting should be used only in those situations where the enterprises come together to form a business combination, which both meets the definition of a merger and fulfils all the detailed conditions that reinforce the definition. In addition, the merger will also have to fulfil the Act's conditions outlined in paragraphs 9.37 to 9.54 above.

9.111 The exposure draft defines an acquisition as *"the expenditure of resources by an enterprise to obtain ownership or control of another enterprise. It is a transaction requiring both acquiror and acquiree"*. Although this is the first time that an 'acquisition' has been defined, it is likely to have little impact in practice. However, the exposure draft also defines a merger and, if accepted, the new definition will restrict significantly the number of business combinations that will be able to be accounted for using merger accounting. A merger in the context of a business combination is defined as:

> *"The coming together of two or more enterprises for the mutual sharing of the risks and rewards, of the combined enterprise, where no party to the combination can be identified as acquiror or acquiree. There must be a substantially equal partnership, with the pre-combination enterprises sharing influence in the new economic unit. If a dominant partner (i.e. an acquiror) or a subordinate partner (i.e. an acquiree) can be identified, then the combination will be an acquisition regardless of the form by which the combination was transacted."* [ED 48 para 34].

9.112 There are a number of detailed additional conditions that will have to be complied with if the combination is to be accounted for as a merger. The combination together with any related arrangements will have to comply with the following requirements before it can be treated as a merger:

- None of the parties to the combination must see themselves as acquiror or acquiree.

- None of the parties to the combination must dominate the management of the combined entity.

  In this context, the membership of the board and the chairman or managing director will be relevant, but so will the identity of any persons or group of persons that make key decisions or are involved in actively running the combined entity.

■ None of the parties can have equity shareholders that have, or
could have, disposed of any material part of their shareholdings,
directly or indirectly, for shares carrying significantly reduced
rights in the combined entity or any other non-equity
consideration (which includes cash).

This condition will prohibit certain schemes that have been used
to overcome the conditions in SSAP 23 (such as, vendor placings
and vendor rights).

■ No minority of greater than 10 per cent can remain in any of the
enterprises to which the offer is made.

■ None of the combined parties can be more than 50 per cent larger
that any other enterprise which is a party to the combination. This
is unless there are special circumstances that prevent the larger
entity from dominating the others.

■ The share of the equity in the combination allocated to one or
more parties must not depend on the post-combination
performance of any of the business previously controlled by that
party or parties.

[ED 48 para 51].

9.113 Where a business combination complies with the conditions set out
above and with the conditions of the Act it will have to be accounted
for using merger accounting. [ED 48 para 52].

9.114 The majority of the other provisions in the exposure draft (in
particular the accounting and disclosure requirements) are the same
or similar to those in SSAP 23. However, the exposure draft proposes
that expenses incurred in the combination should be charged to the
profit and loss account of the combined enterprise in the period in
which they are incurred, unless they are charged to the share premium
account in accordance with the Act. [ED 48 para 48]. At present it is
possible to debit such charges to the cost of the investment (see para
9.64).

Chapter 10

MINORITY INTERESTS

MINORITY INTERESTS

Introduction

10.1 'Minority interests' is the term used to describe outside interests in the share capital and reserves of the subsidiaries that are included in the group's consolidated financial statements. It is now defined in the Act to mean *"the amount of capital and reserves attributable to shares in subsidiary undertakings included in the consolidation held by or on behalf of persons other than the parent company and its subsidiary undertakings"*. [4A Sch 17(2)]. For example, where a parent owns 70 per cent of a subsidiary, it will have to consolidate 100 per cent of the subsidiary's capital and reserves, results and net assets and show a minority interest of 30 per cent.

10.2 Before the introduction of the Companies Act 1989 the term was not found in either of the balance sheet formats detailed in Schedule 4 to the Companies Act 1985, because that schedule was drafted for individual companies' financial statements. Consequently, before the enactment of the Companies Act 1989, minority interests could be disclosed in a variety of positions in the balance sheet formats, although paragraph 34 of SSAP 14 states that they should not be shown as part of shareholders' funds. Consequently in the past, minority interests have been generally disclosed in practice in one of two positions: either as a deduction from net assets, or as an additional item below capital and reserves.

10.3 In contrast, Article 21 of the 7th Directive on group accounts states that minority interests should be shown as a separate item (with an appropriate heading 'shares held by persons outside the group') in the company's capital, reserves and results brought forward. The Companies Act 1989 brought this requirement into UK law by incorporating the item 'minority interests' into the legislation, and the Act specifies where minority interests should be shown in both the consolidated balance sheet formats and the consolidated profit and loss account formats.

Position in the formats

10.4 As mentioned above there are now specific positions where 'minority interests' must be shown in the formats. In the balance sheet Format 1 'minority interests' should be shown either directly above or below 'capital and reserves'. In Format 2 the disclosure of 'minority interests' should be made under 'liabilities' between the headings 'capital and reserves' and 'provisions for liabilities and charges'. [4A Sch 17(1)(2)].

Chapter 4 includes a summary of Format 1 which shows the positioning of 'minority interests' (see chapter 4 para 4.7). Table 55 shows an example where minority interests are included before capital and reserves.

Table 55: Example of a consolidated balance sheet where the minority interests are deducted from total assets less liabilities.

Extract from Stakis Public Limited Company Report and Accounts 1st October 1989.

BALANCE SHEETS

At 1 October 1989

| | | Group | | Company | |
	Notes	1989 £'000	1988 £'000	1989 £'000	1988 £'000
Fixed Assets					
Tangible assets	12	379,938	309,180	257,738	285,488
Investments	14	—	—	15,014	12,991
		379,938	309,180	272,752	298,479
Current Assets					
Stocks	15	3,703	2,610	2,814	2,329
Property development projects	16	12,642	8,638	5,319	5,449
Debtors	17	17,760	24,783	72,812	40,014
Investments	18	7,052	5,333	1,131	354
Cash and short term deposits		8,791	2,674	82	113
		49,948	44,038	82,158	48,259
Prepayments and Accrued Income					
Deferred taxation recoverable	19	1,393	1,080	1,393	1,080
Creditors: Within One Year	20	(87,977)	(60,135)	(72,012)	(62,011)
Net Current (Liabilities) Assets		(36,636)	(15,017)	11,539	(12,672)
Total Assets Less Current Liabilities		343,302	294,163	284,291	285,807
Creditors: After More Than One Year					
Loans	21	(57,788)	(32,608)	(57,788)	(32,608)
Minority Interests		(392)	—	—	—
Net Assets Employed		285,122	261,555	226,503	253,199
Capital and Reserves					
Called up share capital	22	26,760	25,858	26,760	25,858
Share premium account	25	23,442	21,910	23,442	21,910
Revaluation reserve	25	133,994	137,767	89,131	138,961
Merger relief reserve	25	4,491	1,460	—	—
Profit and loss account	25	96,435	74,560	87,170	66,470
Shareholders' Funds		285,122	261,555	226,503	253,199

Approved by the Board on 18 January 1990

Reo Stakis, Director
Andros R. Stakis, Director

10.5 For the profit and loss account formats the Act requires two additional lines to be added for minority interests. The first line requires the disclosure of minority interests in the profit or loss excluding extraordinary items and in Format 1 and Format 2 this item should be included between 'profit or loss on ordinary activities after taxation' and 'extraordinary income'. In addition, the Act specifies that the item should be described 'minority interests'. For Format 3 and Format 4 minority interests should be included under 'charges' or 'income' as appropriate, in the same position between 'profit or loss on ordinary activities after taxation' and 'extraordinary charges' or 'extraordinary income'. [4A Sch 17(3)]. The disclosure requirement in SSAP 14 also requires that the minority's share of profits or losses should be either deducted from or added to the group's profit or loss after tax, but before extraordinary items. [SSAP 14 para 35].

10.6 The second line required to be disclosed by the legislation is the minority's share of any extraordinary items. Again this line should be described as 'minority interests' and should be included in the profit and loss account Format 1 and Format 2 between 'tax on extraordinary profit and loss' and 'other taxes not shown under the above items'. For Format 3 and Format 4 if the item is a debit, then it should be shown under 'charges' between tax on extraordinary profit and loss' and 'other taxes not shown under the above items'. However, if the item is a credit then it should appear under 'income' between 'extraordinary income' and 'profit or loss for the financial year'. [4A Sch 17(4)].

10.7 The disclosure above, although more specific, accords with that required by SSAP 14 which states that the minority interest in extraordinary items should be either deducted from or added to the related amounts in the consolidated profit and loss account. [SSAP 14 para 35].

10.8 The consolidated profit and loss account disclosure for 'minority interests' under Format 1 is illustrated in chapter 4 paragraph 4.18.

Power to adapt or combine

10.9 In determining how the disclosure of minority interests can be changed or adapted in the consolidated balance sheet, the Act states that the item should be treated in the same way as if a letter were assigned to it. [4A Sch 17(5)(a)]. Consequently, this means in practice that there is little scope to adapt this item in the consolidated balance sheet, because the Act requires that such items should be shown in the order and under the headings given in the formats.

10.10 There is, however, more scope to adapt and combine the two minority interest disclosures in the consolidated profit and loss account. This is because the Act states that these items shall be treated as if they have been assigned an Arabic number. [4A Sch 17(5)(b)]. This means that the items can be adapted where the special nature of the group's business requires such adaptation, although it is difficult to imagine when this particular provision would apply. [4 Sch 3(3)]. Of more use is the provision that allows such items to be combined where either the individual amounts to be combined are not material or the combination facilitates the assessment of the consolidated profit and loss account. [4 Sch 3(4)]. Many companies use the latter provision to justify giving only minimal information on the face of the consolidated profit and loss account itself, thereby relegating the other disclosure items to the notes.

Calculation of minority interests

10.11 As mentioned in the introduction, 'minority interests' included in the consolidated balance sheet should represent the total amount of capital and reserves attributable to shares in the subsidiary held by or on behalf of persons other than the parent and its other subsidiaries. [4A Sch 17(2)]. Similar wording is also used to indicate how to calculate both of the profit and loss account items of minority interests. [4A Sch 17(3)(4)]. In practice, the calculation of minority interests is fraught with complications. These complications can arise because of the payment of dividends, changes in stake, different rights attaching to shares in the subsidiary and the treatment of losses. Examples 1 to 5 that follow illustrate each of these difficulties in detail.

10.12 There is one further matter that often causes concern when minority interests are calculated and that is how to deal with indirect holdings in subsidiaries. Before the minority interests can be calculated it is first necessary to establish whether the company is a subsidiary of the holding company and, therefore, should be consolidated. For example, consider the following group structure:

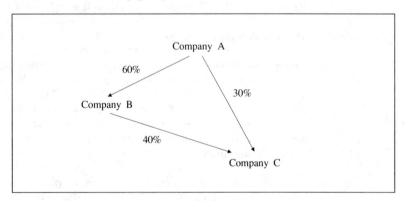

10.13 A number of factors have to be considered in determining whether company C is a subsidiary of company A. These matters are fully discussed in chapter 3. However, in the example it is assumed that company A owns 60 per cent of the equity of company B and also controls 60 per cent of its votes. Consequently, company B is a subsidiary of company A. Company A has an indirect shareholding in company C of 54 per cent (that is, 30% + (60% x 40%)). However, company C will not be a subsidiary of company A unless company A controls more than 50 per cent of the votes of company C or controls the appointment of removal of directors having a majority of votes on the board (there are also certain other less usual reasons for treating a company as a subsidiary see further chapter 3).

In this example, it is assumed that company A controls more than 50 per cent of the votes of company C's shares and it is, therefore, a subsidiary. If it were not, then company A would consolidate company B, but treat the investment in company C as an associate and equity account for 54 per cent. The summarised balance sheets of each of the group companies is given below:

Summarised balance sheets	Co. A £'000	Co. B £'000	Co. C £'000
Investment in subsidiaries*	36	8	-
Net assets	114	192	100
	150	200	100
Share capital	50	50	20
Profit and loss reserve	100	150	80
	150	200	100

* In this example, the investment in subsidiaries represents the investment in company B and company C which were acquired for their nominal value.

The balance sheet minority interests can be ascertained in two ways either by considering the minority interest arising when company C is consolidated with company B and then consolidating that result with company A, or by considering company A's indirect holdings in its subsidiaries. Both arrive at the same result. The latter calculation is considered first. As mentioned above, the indirect holding that company A has in company C is 54 per cent. Therefore, the indirect minority interest in company C is 46 per cent (that is, 100% - 54%). The total minority interests to be disclosed in company A's consolidated financial statements can be calculated as follows:

Minority interests in group - indirect calculation method	£'000
Minority's share of net assets of company C net assets x indirect minority interest (£100,000 x 46%)	46.0
Minority's share of net assets of company B net assets x direct minority interest (£192,000 x 40%)	76.8
	122.8

The direct method of calculating the minority interests in the group is set out below:

```
┌─────────────────────────────────────────────────────────────────┐
│                                                                   │
│  Minority interests in group - direct calculation method         │
│                                                         £'000     │
│  Company C consolidated with company B                            │
│       Share capital of company C (£20,000 x 60%)         12.0     │
│       Reserves of company C (£80,000 x 60%)              48.0     │
│  Minority interests in group B                           60.0     │
│                                                                   │
│  Group B consolidated with company A                              │
│       Share capital of company B (£50,000 x 40%)         20.0     │
│       Reserves of company B (£150,000 x 40%)             60.0     │
│       Reserves of company C ((£80,000 - £48,000) x 40%)* 12.8     │
│  Adjustment to eliminate 30% of company C owned                   │
│    directly by company A                                          │
│       Share capital of company C (£20,000 x 30%)         (6.0)    │
│       Reserves of company C (£80,000 x 30%)             (24.0)    │
│                                                         122.8     │
│                                                                   │
└─────────────────────────────────────────────────────────────────┘
```

* The minority in group B will take their proportion of the reserves of company C that have been consolidated with company B's reserves.

Treatment of minority on acquisition

10.14 When a subsidiary is acquired it is necessary to allocate to the minority its share of the net assets of the subsidiary. This is normally done in the consolidation process by allocating to the minority its share of the capital and reserves of the subsidiary. As a check on the minority figure disclosed in the consolidated balance sheet, it is useful to apply the minority percentage to the subsidiary's net assets, adjusting as necessary for any dividends which have been accrued but not paid. This check can be applied to any year end balance sheet in order to calculate the minority interest, but may be complicated in certain situations where the minority holds preference shares. The example that follows illustrates these principles.

Example 1

At the end of year 1, company H acquires company S. Immediately before the acquisition the summarised balance sheets of both companies are as follows:

Summarised balance sheets	Co. H	Co. S
	£'000	£'000
Net assets	50	10
Share capital	20	2
Share premium account	-	-
Profit and loss reserve	30	8
	50	10

On the acquisition company H issues 1,000 £1 shares to the shareholders of company S to acquire 80 per cent of its issued capital. The fair value of the consideration is valued at £15,000 and the fair value of the net assets of company S are determined to be

£16,000. Consequently, the companies' balance sheets will look as follows after the acquisition:

Summarised balance sheets	Co. H £'000		Co. S £'000	
Investment in subsidiary		15		-
Net assets	50		10	
Fair value adjustment	-	50	6	16
		65		16
Share capital		21		2
Share premium account		14		-
Profit and loss reserve		30		8
Revaluation reserve		-		6
		65		16

The goodwill arising on acquisition and the minority interests are calculated as follows:

Cost of control account/goodwill

Investment	15,000	Share capital (80% x £2,000)	1,600	
		P&L reserve (80% x £8,000)	6,400	
		Revaluation reserve		
		(80% x 6,000)		4,800
				12,800
		Balance, viz goodwill		2,200
	£15,000			£15,000

Minority interests account

Balance	3,200	Share capital (20% x £2,000)	400	
		P&L reserve (20% x £8,000)	1,600	
		Revaluation reserve		
		(20% x 6,000)		1,200
	£3,200			£3,200

The consolidated balance sheet for the group immediately after the acquisition would be as follows:

Summarised consolidated balance sheet		Group £'000
Net assets (£50,000 + £16,000)		66.0
Share capital		21.0
Share premium account		14.0
Profit and loss reserve	30.0	
Goodwill write off	(2.2)	27.8
Shareholders funds		62.8
Minority interests		3.2
		66.0

Profit and loss account and dividend treatment

10.15 Even where there is a minority interest, the group's consolidated profit
and loss account should include all of the profits and losses that are
attributable to a subsidiary. The minority's share of these profits and
losses is then either deducted from or added to the group's
consolidated profit or loss. Where the subsidiary has paid or proposed
a dividend, whether or not this has been accounted for as received or
receivable in the holding company, certain adjustments will have to be
made on consolidation. Consider the following example, which builds
on the information given in example 1 above.

Example 2

Company H acquires company S at the year end and the facts for year 1 remain the
same as in example 1. However, in year 2 company H makes a profit of £15,000, which
includes a dividend receivable from company S of £1,600. Company S has made a profit
of £10,000 during the year and has provided a dividend payable of £2,000, giving a
retained profit of £8,000. The summarised balance sheets of both companies at the end
of year 2 are set out below:

Summarised balance sheets	Co. H £'000		Co. S £'000
Investment in subsidiary		15.0	-
Net assets		63.4	26
Dividend receivable/(payable)		1.6	(2)
		80.0	24
Share capital		21.0	2
Share premium account		14.0	-
Profit and loss reserve	30.0		8
Profit for the year	15.0	45.0	8 16
Revaluation reserve		-	6
		80.0	24

The goodwill arising on acquisition and the minority interests are calculated as follows:

Minority interests account

Balance	5,200	Share capital (20% x £2,000)	400
		P&L reserve (20% x £16,000)	3,200
		Revaluation reserve	
		(20% x 6,000)	1,200
		Dividend payable to minority*	400
	£5,200		£5,200

Cost of control account/goodwill

Investment	15,000	Share capital (80% x £2,000)	1,600
		P&L reserve (80% x £8,000)	6,400
		Revaluation reserve	
		(80% x 6,000)	4,800
			12,800
		Balance, viz goodwill	
		written off	2,200
	£15,000		£15,000

* A dividend payable of £400 arises on consolidation, which represents the difference between the dividend payable in company S's accounts of £2,000 and the amount shown as receivable in company H's accounts of £1,600. The balance of £400 is the amount still due to the minority and could either be added to the minority interest balance as shown in the example, or it could be included under creditors.

The consolidated profit and loss account would be arrived at in the following way:

Extract from profit and loss accounts	Co. H £'000	Co. S £'000	Group £'000
Trading profit	13.4	10	23.4
Dividend received	1.6	-	-
Profit for the year	15.0	10	23.4
Minority interest (£10,000 x 20%)	-	-	(2.0)
Dividend receivable/payable	-	(2)	-
Retained profit	15.0	8	21.4

The consolidated balance sheet for the group at the end of year 2 would be as follows:

Summarised consolidated balance sheet		Group £'000
Net assets (£63,400 + £26,000)		89.4
Share capital		21.0
Share premium account		14.0
Profit and loss reserve	27.8	
Profit for the year	21.4	49.2
Shareholders funds		84.2
Minority interests (including £400 creditor)		5.2
		89.4

Reduction in minority interests

10.16 Where a holding company acquires more shares in a subsidiary either by buying them from the minority or by subscribing for a fresh issue of shares in the subsidiary itself, the goodwill arising on the acquisition will change (for example see Table 56). It is debatable whether a new fair value exercise should be undertaken when part of the minority is acquired, because the requirements of SSAP 22 (revised) only apply to situations where a company acquires another and not specifically to the acquisition of minority interests (see also chapter 6 para 6.45). Table 57 overleaf shows the movement on the minority interests account where part of the minority has been acquired during the year.

Table 56: Example that illustrates that goodwill has arisen on the acquisition of a minority interest and how it has been dealt with.

Extract from The RTZ Corporation PLC annual report and accounts 31st December 1988.

24 Reserves (extract)

	Other reserves	Profit and loss account	1988 Total £m	1987 Total £m
The Group				
At 1 January	192.3	1,021.5	1,213.8	1,230.0
Adjustment on currency translation	18.1	80.4	98.5	(194.9)
Retained profit for year	–	664.5	664.5	191.5
Other movements				
– goodwill written off	–	(346.4)	(346.4)	(15.1)
– miscellaneous movements	(15.0)	17.1	2.1	2.3
	(15.0)	(329.3)	(344.3)	(12.8)
At 31 December	195.4	1,437.1	1,632.5	1,213.8
RTZ and subsidiaries	37.1	1,136.7	1,173.8	920.4
Related companies	158.3	300.4	458.7	293.4
	195.4	1,437.1	1,632.5	1,213.8

The amount of goodwill written off in the year includes £185.0 million and £81.6 million in respect of the acquisitions of MK Electric and the minority interest in Indal.

10.17 The example below is a continuation of the two previous examples and considers how to account for a reduction in the minority interests.

Example 3

On the first day of year 3 company H subscribes for a further 2,000 £1 shares in company S for cash amounting to £4,000. The minority interest in the subsidiary is, therefore, reduced from 20 per cent to 10 per cent. During the year company H makes a profit of £20,000, which includes a dividend receivable from company S of £900. In the same period company S makes a loss of £2,000 and as a consequence reduces its dividend to £1,000, which is provided for in its accounts.

Table 57: Example showing the effect of acquiring part of the minority interest in the period.

Extract from Reuters Holdings PLC Annual Report 31st December 1988.

19 Capital and reserves

Group	Called up share capital £ million	Share premium account £ million	Other reserves £ million	Profit and loss account £ million	Investments by subsidiaries in shares of Reuters Holdings PLC £ million	Minority interest £ million	Total £ million
31 December 1987:							
As previously reported	42.1	50.9	(105.1)	230.3	–	0.9	219.1
Reclassification	–	–	2.2	–	(6.3)	–	(4.1)
As reclassified	42.1	50.9	(102.9)	230.3	(6.3)	0.9	215.0
Shares issued during the year	0.1	1.1	0.2	–	–	–	1.4
Purchased goodwill written off	–	–	(2.0)	–	–	–	(2.0)
Translation differences	–	–	–	1.4	–	–	1.4
Additions	–	–	–	–	(32.1)	–	(32.1)
Increase in shareholders' equity arising on minority conversions	–	–	–	0.6	–	(0.1)	0.5
Retained for the year	–	–	–	88.8	–	0.5	89.3
31 December 1988	42.2	52.0	(104.7)	321.1	(38.4)	1.3	273.5

The balance sheets of company H and company S at the end of year 3 are as follows:

Summarised balance sheets	Co. H £'000		Co. S £'000	
Investment in subsidiary		19.0		-
Net assets		80.1		26
Dividend receivable/(payable)		.9		(1)
		100.0		25
Share capital		21.0		4
Share premium account		14.0		2
Profit and loss reserve	45.0		16	
Profit for the year	20.0	65.0	(3)	13
Revaluation reserve		-		6
		100.0		25

The goodwill arising on acquisition and the minority interests are calculated below:

Cost of control account/goodwill			
Investment		Share capital (80% x £2,000)	1,600
(£15,000 + £4,000)	19,000	Acquired in year	2,000
		Total capital (90% x £4,000)	3,600
		P&L reserve	
		(80% x £8,000)	6,400
		(10% x £16,000)*	1,600 8,000
		Revaluation reserve	
		(80% x £6,000)	4,800
		(10% x £6,000)*	600 5,400
		Share premium	
		(90% x £2,000)	1,800
			18,800
Reserve arising on		Balance, viz goodwill	
consolidation	2,000	written off	2,200
	£21,000		£21,000

* It is only necessary to bring into the cost of control account pre-acquisition reserves. Consequently, the additional percentage acquired need only be applied to the reserve balances at the date of acquisition, which in the example is the first day of the year. Therefore, the balances at the previous year end date have been used (see example 2).

Minority interests account			
Balance	2,600	Share capital (10% x £4,000)	400
		Share premium (10% x £2,000)	200
		P&L reserve (10% x £13,000)	1,300
		Revaluation reserve	
		(10% x 6,000)	600
		Dividend payable to minority*	100
	£2,600		£2,600

* As in the previous example, a balance of £100 arises on consolidation, which represents the difference between the dividend payable in company S's accounts of £1,000 and the amount shown as receivable in company H's accounts of £900. The balance of £100 is the amount still due to the minority and could either be added to the minority interest balance as shown in the example, or it could be included under creditors.

The consolidated profit and loss account would be arrived at in the following way:

Extract from profit and loss accounts	Co. H	Co. S	Group
	£'000	£'000	£'000
Trading profit	19.1	(2)	17.1
Dividend received	.9	-	-
Profit for the year	20.0	(2)	17.1
Minority interest (£2,000 x 10%)	-	-	0.2
Dividend payable	-	(1)	-
Retained profit	20.0	(3)	17.3

The consolidated balance sheet for the group at the end of year 3 would be as follows:

Summarised consolidated balance sheet		Group £'000
Net assets (£80,100 + £26,000)		106.1
Share capital		21.0
Share premium account		14.0
Profit and loss reserve	49.2	
Profit for the year	17.3	66.5
Other reserves*		2.0
Shareholders funds		103.5
Minority interests		2.6
		106.1

* The other reserves figure is made up of the reserve arising on consolidation, which arises as a result of acquiring the new issue of shares.

Minority acquires shares with differing rights

10.18 When a minority acquires shares that have different rights to other shares in the subsidiary, then the calculation of minority interests is complicated by the fact that those shares may have different rights concerning the distribution of capital. This situation arises often where the minority holds preference shares in the subsidiary. Such shares do not generally carry any rights to participate in the capital of the subsidiary on winding up beyond the amount of preference capital itself. In this type of situation the rights attached to the minority's share capital have to be considered very carefully before it is possible to calculate the minority interests. Consider the example that follows which again progresses from the previous example.

Example 4

On the first day of year 4, company S issues £4,000 10 per cent preference shares to its minority shareholders for cash of £6,000. The rights attached to the preference shares are that they carry a fixed dividend payable in one instalment after the year end of the company and on a liquidation the preference shareholders are only entitled to a return of their capital (that is, £4,000). During year 4, company H makes a profit of £30,000 which includes a dividend payable from company S of £1,800. Company S returns to profit in the year and makes a profit of £5,000 from which it proposes an ordinary dividend of £2,000 and a preference dividend of £400. The balance sheets of company H and company S at the end of year 4 are given below:

Minority interests

Summarised balance sheets	Co. H		Co. S
		£'000	£'000
Investment in subsidiary		19.0	-
Net assets		109.2	36.0
Dividend receivable/(payable)		1.8	(2.4)
		130.0	33.6
Share capital		21.0	8.0
Share premium account		14.0	4.0
Profit and loss reserve	65.0		13.0
Profit for the year	30.0	95.0	2.6 15.6
Revaluation reserve		-	6.0
		130.0	33.6

The goodwill arising on acquisition remains the same as in the previous example and is
calculated as follows:

Cost of control account/goodwill

Investment		Share capital (80% x £2,000)		1,600
(£15,000 + £4,000)	19,000	Acquired in year		2,000
		Total capital (90% x £4,000)		3,600
		P&L reserve		
		(80% x £8,000)	6,400	
		(10% x £16,000)	1,600	8,000
		Revaluation reserve		
		(80% x £6,000)	4,800	
		(10% x £6,000)	600	5,400
		Share premium		
		(90% x £2,000)		1,800
				18,800
Reserve arising on		Balance, viz goodwill		
consolidation	2,000	written off		2,200
	£21,000			£21,000

The minority interest will change in order to take account of the issue of the preference
share capital and also to take account of the dividend payable to the minority which is
still outstanding, which as explained in example 2 can be included in either creditors or
minority interests.

Minority interests account

Balance	7,560	Share capital (10% x £4,000)	400
		Preference shares *	4,000
		Share premium	
		(10% x £4,000)*	400
		P&L reserve (10% x £15,600)	1,560
		Revaluation reserve	
		(10% x 6,000)	600
		Dividend payable to minority	600
	£7,560		£7,560

* The minority are allocated all of the preference share capital, although this capital does not entitle them to a greater share of the reserves of the subsidiary. Furthermore, even though the increase in the share premium account is as a direct result of the issue of the preference shares, the minority is only allocated a share of the reserve in proportion to the ordinary share capital that they hold.

The consolidated profit and loss account would be arrived at in the following way:

Extract from profit and loss accounts	Co. H £'000	Co. S £'000	Group £'000
Trading profit	28.2	5.0	33.20
Dividend received	1.8	-	-
Profit for the year	30.0	5.0	33.20
Minority interests*	-	-	(0.86)
Dividend payable	-	(2.4)	-
Retained profit	30.0	2.6	32.34

* The minority's share of the profit for the year is calculated by applying the minority interest to the profit for the year of company S after deducting the preference dividend paid to the minority and then adding back that preference dividend (that is, [(£5,000 - £400) x 10%] + £400 = £860).

The consolidated balance sheet for the group at the end of year 4 would be as follows:

Summarised consolidated balance sheet		Group £'000
Net assets (£109,200 + £36,000)		145.20
Share capital		21.00
Share premium account		14.00
Profit and loss reserve	66.50	
Profit for the year	32.34	98.84
Other reserves *		3.80
Shareholders funds		137.64
Minority interests		7.56
		145.20

* The other reserves include both the reserve arising on consolidation of £2,000 brought forward from the previous example and the group's share of the share premium account that arises in the subsidiary's accounts on the issue of the preference shares of £1,800. Although the premium arose on the issue of the preference shares, it is not attributable to the preference shareholders on winding up the company.

10.19 Certain types of preference shares issued only to the minority can be subject to mandatory redemption and carry a dividend rate that is comparable with the rate of interest charged on equivalent loan finance. The minority shareholder usually retains the redemption initiative. Such shares are consequently, very similar in nature to loan capital. However, on consolidation the shares are shown in the balance sheet as minority interests (as part of capital) rather than as a loan (which would be included in borrowings). Also in the consolidated profit and loss account, the cost of finance would be treated as a dividend (charged after profit or loss for the financial year) rather than as loan interest (charged before profit or loss for the financial year). At present there is no requirement to disclose the substance of such minority interests as borrowings. However, additional disclosure of the rights attaching to the shares should be made in order to give a true and fair view. For example see Table 58.

Table 58: Example of a minority interest note.

Extract from THORN EMI PLC Annual Report 31st March 1989.

21 Minority Interests

	1989	1988
	£m	£m
Preference shares in subsidiaries:		
5¾ per cent Guaranteed Redeemable Convertible Preference Shares 2004	103.0	–
Auction Preferred Stock	118.3	105.8
Other	7.8	19.8
	229.1	125.6

THORN EMI America Finance Inc., a wholly-owned subsidiary registered in Delaware, USA has in issue 200 shares of Auction Preferred Stock of US$1m each. The dividend rate varies (predominantly with prevailing interest rates) and is set every 7 weeks at an "auction" at which the shares are also traded. Funds raised from this issue have been loaned to other Group subsidiaries. Repayment of the loans is guaranteed by the Company.

The 5¾ per cent Guaranteed Redeemable Convertible Preference Shares 2004 are redeemable at par at the preference shareholders' option on either 2 February 1994 or 2 February 1999 and are also redeemable by the issuer in specified circumstances prior to final redemption date; in these instances the rate of preference dividend would be retrospectively increased with effect from issue date so as to provide the preference shareholders with an enhanced return (set at 10.5 per cent per annum for the period to 2 February 1994). No provision for the enhanced rate of preference dividend is made in the profit and loss account for the year because conversion of these preference shares into the Ordinary Shares of the Company is anticipated; however a transfer has been made from Group profit and loss reserve as described in Note 20 to ensure that such reserve is not overstated. Any preference shares which are neither converted into the Company's Ordinary Shares nor redeemed prior to final redemption will be redeemed at par on 2 February 2004.

The preferred element of the share capitals of THORN EMI America Finance Inc. and THORN EMI Capital NV are included as minority interests in the Group balance sheet. Dividends payable on these two classes of preference share are charged to minority interests in the profit and loss account.

Excess of liabilities over assets

10.20 A situation may arise where the minority interest in a subsidiary's net assets becomes a debit balance. This will occur where the company's liabilities (after including holding company loans) exceed its assets. In this situation, the group should include a debit minority interest in the consolidated financial statements only if there is a binding obligation on the minority shareholders to make good the losses incurred. Where there is no such agreement, the consolidated profit and loss account should provide for the minority's share (in addition to the group's share) of the losses the subsidiary made beyond the amount of the minority's share capital. Consequently, no amount should be added back in the profit and loss account for the minority interest. [SSAP 14 para 34]. The above process should be reversed when profits attributable to the minority start to make good the losses that were made earlier. The example below shows a situation where the minority is not given its share of the losses of the subsidiary and these are reflected wholly in the group's consolidated financial statements.

Example 5

During year 5, company S makes a substantial loss of £100,000 and company H makes a profit of £30,000. The group decides that it should account for the entire loss of its subsidiary beyond the amount of the minority's share capital, because it has given an undertaking to the subsidiary to continue to finance it. The group also anticipates buying out the minority in the next financial year.

The balance sheets of the two companies at the end of year 5 are noted below:

Summarised balance sheets	Co. H		Co. S	
	£'000		£'000	
Investment in subsidiary		19		-
Net assets		141		(66.4)
		160		(66.4)
Share capital		21		8.0
Share premium account		14		4.0
Profit and loss reserve	95		15. 6	
Profit/(loss) for the year	30	125	(100.0)	(84.4)
Revaluation reserve		-		6.0
		160		(66.4)

There is no change in the goodwill arising on consolidation from the previous example, and the goodwill balance of £2,200 and the reserve arising on consolidation of £2,000 are calculated in the same way as in example 4.

The minority interests are now calculated in the following way:

Minority interests account			
P&L account	2,560	Share capital (10% x £4,000)	400
Balance	4,400	Preference shares	4,000
		Share premium	
		(10% x £4,000)	400
		P&L reserve (10% x £15,600)	1,560
		Revaluation reserve	
		(10% x 6,000)	600
	£6,960		£6,960

Minority interests

The consolidated profit and loss account would be arrived at in the following way:

Extract from profit and loss accounts	Co. H £'000	Co. S £'000	Group £'000
Trading profit/(loss)	30	(100)	(70.00)
Dividend received	-	-	-
Profit for the year	30	(100)	(70.00)
Minority interests*	-	-	2.56
Dividend payable	-	-	-
Retained profit	30	(100)	(67.44)

* The minority interests credited in the consolidated profit and loss account represent the minority's share of reserves at the beginning of the period that have now been eliminated. The minority interests share of reserves have been eliminated because the example assumes that the group will bear all of the losses of the subsidiary. In future years should the company revert to a positive net asset position, then the minority interests in the consolidated balance sheet would reflect their share of those net assets.

The consolidated balance sheet for the group would be as follows:

Summarised consolidated balance sheet		Group £'000
Net assets (£141,000 - £66,400)		74.60
Share capital		21.00
Share premium account		14.00
Profit and loss reserve	98.84	
Loss for the year	(67.44)	31.40
Other reserves		3.80
Shareholders funds		70.20
Minority interests*		4.40
		74.60

* The minority interests recorded in the balance sheet represents the minority's share in the capital of the subsidiary of £4,400 (that is, £4,000 + £400). If there was an agreement with the minority to fund the net liabilities of the subsidiary, the whole minority interests, which would be a debit, should be recognised in the balance sheet. If this were the situation in the example, the minority interests balance would be calculated by adding their interest at the end of year 4 of £6,960 plus their share of the loss for the year of £10,000. Consequently, the minority interests would be recorded as a debit balance of £3,040.

Minority or majority interests

10.21 Under the new definitions of subsidiary brought into company law by the Companies Act 1989, a company has to be treated as a subsidiary where its parent has a participating interest in its shares and either exercises dominant influence over it or manages it on a unified basis (see further chapter 3 para 3.28). Consequently, it is quite possible for a parent to own only (say) 20 per cent of the equity of an undertaking and exercise dominant influence over it or manage it on a unified basis. Where this is so, it is also quite possible that the minority shareholders will hold (say) 80 per cent of the equity of the undertaking. Accordingly, the minority interests shown in the consolidated financial statements will be calculated using this percentage. This could result, for example, with the group consolidating 100 per cent of the assets and liabilities of the subsidiary, but showing also minority interests of 80 per cent of those assets and liabilities. A similar situation could arise where the parent owns a majority of the voting rights, but owns (say) only 20 per cent of the total equity.

10.22 Where these types of situation arise, it is unlikely that this is a good enough reason for the term 'minority interests' to be amended to (say) 'majority interests'. Furthermore, it is doubtful that circumstances would exist where using the term 'minority interests' would affect the true and fair view and, therefore, justify using another term. In the situation described above, the minority although owning the majority of capital will be in a minority position with regard to controlling the company and, consequently, the term 'minority interests' still describes the outside interest fairly. However, it will be necessary in this type of situation to explain the relationship with the subsidiary fully in the consolidated financial statements in order that they should give a true and fair view.

Chapter 11

ASSOCIATED UNDERTAKINGS AND JOINT VENTURES

ASSOCIATED UNDERTAKINGS AND JOINT VENTURES

Introduction

11.1   Many companies now conduct important parts of their businesses through undertakings in which they control less than 50 per cent of the voting rights. SSAP 1 was introduced in 1971 in order to take into account the opinion held by many accountants and others that to disclose only the dividend income of such a part of a group's activities was unlikely to be sufficient to give an idea of the level of trading of associated undertakings. Consequently, a different basis of accounting known as 'equity accounting' was developed for associated companies.

11.2   In equity accounting, the investing group's share of the associate's profits and losses are reflected in the group's consolidated profit and loss account. The investing group's share of the associate's post-acquisition net assets and premium or discount arising on acquisition are included in the group's consolidated balance sheet as a one line item, which is then expanded in the notes.

11.3   The Companies Act 1981 introduced another term 'related companies', which was very similar to the term 'associated companies' defined in SSAP 1. However, it was possible to have a related company that was not an associate and *vice versa*. The term 'related companies' has been replaced in the Companies Act 1989 by the term 'undertakings in which the company has participating interests'. In addition, on consolidation, this item is further split between 'interests in associated undertakings' and 'other participating interests'. Consequently, the legislation still envisages that there could be situations where a participating interest may be held in an undertaking that is not an associated undertaking. The meaning of the term 'participating interest' is considered further in paragraph 11.6 below.

11.4   For associated undertakings, the Act makes various provisions concerning their accounting treatment and disclosure. This chapter looks at those provisions and compares them with the requirements of SSAP 1. It is likely that SSAP 1 will in due course be revised to take account of the provisions of the Companies Act 1989.

11.5   An area of accounting that has not previously been dealt with in legislation is that of joint ventures. In certain situations, groups can, if they wish to, account for any joint ventures which are in the form of *unincorporated undertakings* on a proportional consolidation basis.

Proportional consolidation is the consolidation on a line by line basis of the parent's proportionate share of the undertaking's individual assets and liabilities as well as its profits and losses. This chapter also considers these provisions and looks at how proportional consolidation will affect groups' consolidated financial statements.

Associated undertakings

Definition

11.6   An 'associated undertaking' is defined in the Act in the following terms:

> "...an undertaking in which an undertaking included in the consolidation has a _participating interest_ and over whose operating and financial policy it exercises a _significant influence_, and which is not-
>
> (a) a subsidiary undertaking of the parent company, or
> (b) a joint venture dealt with in accordance with paragraph 19."
> [4A Sch 20(1)].

11.7   Paragraph 19 of Schedule 4A to the Act gives the option to treat unincorporated joint ventures on a proportional consolidation basis (see further para 11.60 below). Generally otherwise, such undertakings would be treated as associates, in which case they would be equity accounted.

11.8   'Participating interest' is defined in section 260(1) of the Act to mean:

> "...an interest held by an undertaking in the shares of another undertaking which it holds on a long-term basis for the purpose of securing a contribution to its activities by the exercise of control or influence arising from or related to that interest."

11.9   The meaning of 'shares' in the definition is explained in section 259(2) of the Act. This explanation is considered further in chapter 3 paragraph 3.46. This definition is also applicable to other 'participating interests' that the group might have and furthermore applies to the definition of subsidiary for consolidation purposes where the group exercises dominant influence or manages the undertaking on a unified basis (see further chapter 3 para 3.30).

11.10 The definition of 'associated undertakings' in the Act is now very similar to that given in SSAP 1 for an 'associated company', except that the definition has been expanded to include unincorporated undertakings. It can be seen from SSAP 1's definition, given below, that 'significant influence' is an important aspect of both the definitions:

*"A company not being a subsidiary of the investing group or
company in which:*

(a) *the interest of the investing group or company is effectively
that of a partner in a joint venture or consortium and the
investing group or company is in a position to exercise a
significant influence over the company in which the
investment is made; or*

(b) *the interest of the investing group or company is for the
long-term and is substantial and, having regard to the
disposition of the other shareholdings, the investing group
or company is in a position to exercise a significant
influence over the company in which the investment is
made."* [SSAP 1 para 13].

11.11 The definitions in both the Act and SSAP 1 exclude subsidiaries and,
as mentioned above, the Act also excludes unincorporated joint
ventures where they are treated on a proportional consolidation basis.
Also, SSAP 1 comments that in certain situations, partnerships and
unincorporated joint ventures can have features that justify accounting
for them on a proportional consolidation basis. [SSAP 1 para 10].

11.12 It is often difficult in practice to determine whether there is an
associate relationship with an undertaking. SSAP 1 indicates that
significant influence over a company essentially involves participation
in the financial and operating policy decisions of that company (which
would also include its dividend policy). It also confirms that it is not
necessary to control those polices for an associate relationship to exist.
However, it does suggest that representation on the board of directors
is indicative of the relevant degree of participation for the undertaking
to be an associate. [SSAP 1 para 13]. Consequently, it can be seen that
the Act's definition of 'associated undertakings' uses similar terms to
those of SSAP 1.

11.13 In addition, the Act states that where the group holds more than 20
per cent of the voting rights in another undertaking, it is presumed to
exercise a significant influence and, therefore, should be treated as an
'associated undertaking', unless the contrary is shown. [4A Sch 20(2)].
Again this reiterates what is stated in SSAP 1 and the standard agrees
that there will be circumstances where the presumption can be
rebutted. For example, even where the investing group holds more
than 20 per cent of the voting rights, one or more other large
shareholders could prevent the group exercising 'significant influence'.
[SSAP 1 para 14]. Furthermore, where it is the intention of an
investing group to treat an undertaking as an associate when it
controls less than 20 per cent of the votes, it will need to clearly
demonstrate that influence. Generally, this demonstration should
include a statement from the potential associate that it accepts that

the investing group is in a position to exercise significant influence over it. [SSAP 1 para 15]. For example see Table 59.

Table 59: Illustration of an associate relationship existing where the share holding is less than 20 per cent.

Extract from Pearsons plc Annual Report and Accounts 31st December 1988.

Note extract

The cross holdings of shares together with the representation on each other's board, evidence that Pearson and Elsevier have significant influence over each other through, *inter alia*, participation in financial and operating policy decisions and hence each is an associated company of the other. Accordingly Pearson and Elsevier each equity accounts for its share of the other's earnings. Consequently, the profits shown include £0.6m arising from the inclusion of 8.7% of Person's profits in the profits of Elsevier.

Example 1

A group has a 30 per cent investment in an associated company at the beginning of the year. It has previously been treated as an associated company in the group's financial statements. Another shareholder increases his shareholding in the company during the year from 40 per cent to 60 per cent. The group no longer wishes to treat its investment in the undertaking as an associate.

Normally as explained above, where the investment in another undertaking is greater than 20 per cent, it will be presumed that the undertaking is an associate. However, in this situation, if the group can demonstrate that it no longer has a significant influence over the undertaking then it may treat the investment as a trade investment rather than as an associate.

Example 2

A holding company has a 17 per cent share in a partnership and wishes to equity account for the holding in its consolidated financial statements.

The investment in the partnership may be treated as an associate even where the investing company holding is below 20 per cent. However, in this situation, the company would have to show that it does have significant influence over the undertaking. Normally under SSAP 1 this would involve the partnership confirming that the company has such influence. Furthermore, if the investment in the partnership is in the nature of a joint venture, then the company could, if it wished to, account for its investment in the partnership on a proportional consolidation basis in the group's consolidated financial statements (see further para 11.60 below). If the investment was in a limited partnership, then it may have to be treated as a subsidiary and consolidated 100 per cent, see further chapter 3 paragraph 3.48.

Treatment of voting rights

11.14 The Act gives a significant amount of guidance on when to take into account voting rights in order to determine whether an associated relationship exists between two undertakings. The paragraphs that follow summarise the guidance given in the Act.

11.15 For the purposes of the definition of an associated undertaking, 'voting rights in the undertaking' means the rights conferred on the shareholders in respect of their shares to vote at general meetings of the undertaking on all, or substantially all, matters. It can also mean, in a situation where the undertaking has no share capital, any other rights conferred on members to vote at general meetings of the undertaking on all, or substantially all, matters. [4A Sch 20(3)].

11.16 Voting rights should not be treated as held by a person (which includes an undertaking) if they are held in a fiduciary capacity. [4A Sch 20(4), 10A Sch 6]. Similarly, voting rights held by a person as nominee should not be treated as held by him. Such voting rights will be considered held 'as nominee' if they can only be exercised on the instructions or with the consent of another person. [4A Sch 20(4), 10A Sch 7(2)]. However, it is not possible to treat voting rights held by a parent undertaking as held by a subsidiary by using nominee holdings. [4A Sch 20(4), 10A Sch 9(2)].

11.17 Voting rights that are attached to shares held as security shall be treated as held by the person providing the security where those voting rights (excluding any right to exercise them to preserve the value of the security, or to realise it) are only exercisable in accordance with his instructions. This rule applies where the shares are held in connection with granting loans in the normal course of business and the rights are exercised only in the interest of the person providing the security. [4A Sch 20(4), 10A Sch 8]. This provision, however, cannot be used to require voting rights held by a parent to be treated as held by any of its subsidiaries. [4A Sch 20(4), 10A Sch 9(2)]. Furthermore, voting rights should be treated as being exercisable in accordance with the instructions, or the interests of, an undertaking if they are exercisable in accordance with the instructions of, or in the interests of, any group undertaking. [4A Sch 20(4), 10A Sch 9(3)].

11.18 The voting rights in an undertaking have also to be reduced by any voting rights held by the undertaking itself. [4A Sch 20(4), 10A Sch 10].

Position in formats

11.19 The Act indicates the position in the balance sheet and the profit and loss account formats where associated undertakings should be dealt with. In the balance sheet formats shown in Schedule 4 to the Act the item 'shares in related companies' under the heading 'investments' is replaced by 'interests in associated undertakings' and 'other participating interests'. [4A Sch 21(2)]. Chapter 4 paragraph 4.7

includes an updated version of a consolidated balance sheet under Format 1, which indicates where these items should now be disclosed.

11.20 In the profit and loss account formats shown in Schedule 4 to the Act, the item 'income from shares in related companies' is replaced by 'income from interests in associated undertakings' and 'income from other participating interests'. [4A Sch 21(3)]. Chapter 4 paragraph 4.18 also reproduces amended versions of consolidated profit and loss accounts under Format 1 and Format 2 and shows the position where these items should be included.

11.21 The rules governing the disclosure of these items, which also covers the circumstances when they can be combined with other items in the Formats, are summarised in chapter 4. For this purpose, the consolidated profit and loss account items should be treated as if they are preceded by Arabic numerals and the consolidated balance sheet items discussed above should be treated as if they are preceded by a letter.

Equity method of accounting

11.22 The Act stipulates that associated undertakings should be accounted for by the 'equity method' of accounting, which confirms the requirement in SSAP 1. [4A Sch 22(1); SSAP 1 para 18(b),26]. In equity accounting, the investing group's share of the associate's profits and losses are reflected in the group's consolidated profit and loss account. The investing group's share of the associate's post-acquisition net assets and premium or discount arising on acquisition are included in the group's consolidated balance sheet as a one line item, which is then expanded in the notes. The basis used should be disclosed in an accounting policy, for example see Table 60.

Table 60: Illustration of an accounting policy that explains the treatment of associated companies.

Extract from Cadbury Schweppes Public Limited Company Annual Report 31st December 1988.

(n) Associated companies
All companies in which the Group owns, or holds options to take its holding to, at least 20% of the equity on a long term basis and in which, in the opinion of the directors, it also exercises a significant influence in the management, are treated as associated companies. Accordingly, the Group's share of the profits or losses of those companies is included in the profit and loss account and the investments are stated at the value of the Group's share of the underlying net assets.
    All related companies [*now termed participating interests*] as defined in the Companies Act 1985 are included as associated companies.

11.23 Where the associated undertaking is a group of undertakings, the Act requires that the net assets and the profits or losses that should be taken into account on equity accounting the associate should be those of the associate consolidated with its subsidiary undertakings. [4A Sch 22(2)]. This requirement is added to by SSAP 1 which requires that the net assets and profits or losses to be dealt with should include the associate's share of the net assets and profits or losses of investments it may itself have in associated undertakings. [SSAP 1 para 42].

Profit and loss account disclosure

11.24 SSAP 1 requires that income from a company's investments in associates should be brought into account on the following basis:

■ The investing company's own financial statements should show dividends received and receivable.

■ The investing group's consolidated financial statements should show the investing group's share of the profits less losses of associated companies.

[SSAP 1 para 18].

11.25 The consolidated profit and loss account should include, in the profit or loss on ordinary activities before taxation, the investing group's share of the profits less losses of associated undertakings before taxation. SSAP 1 also states that this item should be shown separately and that it should be suitably described. [SSAP 1 para 19]. Now, as mentioned in paragraph 11.20 above, the description of this item is prescribed by the Act as 'income from interests in associated undertakings' and its position is also determined.

11.26 In addition, SSAP 1 requires that the consolidated financial statements should disclose also the following items that relate to the results of associated companies:

■ The tax attributable to the share of the associated companies' profits. This should be included, and should be shown separately within the group's tax charge.

■ The group's share of the extraordinary items dealt with in the associates' financial statements. They should be included with the group's extraordinary items, but only to the extent that they are extraordinary to the group.

■ The group's share of the aggregate of the net profits less losses retained by associated companies.

[SSAP 1 paras 20,21,22].

11.27 SSAP 1 does not require that the group's financial statements should include the group's share of the associated undertaking's turnover or depreciation within the items disclosed in the profit and loss account. If, on the other hand, the results of one or more associated companies are so material in the context of the group's financial statements, more-detailed information about them may need to be disclosed in order that the group's financial statements give a true and fair view. Where this applies, the total turnover, the total depreciation and the total profit and loss on ordinary activities before taxation of the material associated undertakings should be disclosed. In addition, the share of those profits or losses on ordinary activities that are attributable to the investing group should be disclosed. [SSAP 1 para 23]. See for example Table 61.

Table 61: Illustration of more detailed profit and loss account information given regarding a material associate.
Extract from the RTZ Corporation PLC annual report and accounts 31st December 1988.

Note extract

Group's share of net assets of related companies

Listed shares			
CRA Limited	278,422,859 ordinary shares of $A2 each	636.3	459.7
London & Scottish Marine Oil PLC (LASMO)		–	96.9
Non-listed shares			
Minera Escondida Limitada	30 per cent interest in the capital of the company	39.5	26.9
Sociedade Minerade Neves-Corvo S.a.r.l.	7,178,500 shares of Esc 1,000 each	133.8	117.8
Miscellaneous		10.1	4.5
		819.7	705.8

	1988	1988	1987	1987
CRA	$A m	£m	$A m	£m
The pro forma consolidated profit and loss account of CRA Limited for the year ended 31 December 1988, stated in accordance with RTZ accounting policies, was as follows:				
Sales revenue	5,314		5,030	
Cost of sales	4,114		4,272	
Operating profit	1,200		758	
Share of profits less losses of related companies	96		56	
Net interest	(97)		(133)	
Profit before tax	1,199		681	
Taxation	504		279	
Outside shareholders' interests	213		122	
Net profit on ordinary activities	482		280	
RTZ share		111.6		52.7

Balance sheet disclosure

11.28 Unless it is shown at a valuation, the amount at which the investing company's interest in associates should be shown in the investing company's own financial statement is the cost of the investment less any amounts written off. [SSAP 1 para 25].

11.29 The amount at which the investing group's interests in associated companies should be shown in the consolidated balance sheet is the value under the 'equity method' of accounting being the total of:

■ The investing group's share of the net assets (other than goodwill) of the associated undertakings, stated, where possible, after attributing fair values to the net assets at the time the interests in the associated companies were acquired.

■ The investing group's share of any goodwill in the associated companies' own financial statements.

■ The premium paid (or discount received) on the acquisition of the interests in the associated companies, insofar as it has not already been written off or amortised.

[SSAP 1 para 26].

11.30 The standard requires the first point above to be disclosed separately, but the last two items may be aggregated. [SSAP 1 para 26]. For example see Table 62.

Table 62: Illustration of the disclosure of the group's investment in associates.

Extract from Pearsons plc Annual Report and Accounts 31st December 1988.

Note extract

Summary of movements

	Equity £m	Share of retained profit £m	Loans £m	Total £m
31 December 1987	49.8	35.6	1.4	86.8
Additions	172.5	–	1.6	174.1
Disposals	(2.9)	–	–	(2.9)
Writedown of investment	(0.7)	–	–	(0.7)
Retained profit for year	–	11.7	–	11.7
Goodwill written off	(155.9)	–	–	(155.9)
Goodwill written off by associate	–	(5.1)	–	(5.1)
Exchange differences	(0.1)	(0.1)	–	(0.2)
31 December 1988	62.7	42.1	3.0	107.8

11.31   In addition, the Act requires that any goodwill arising on the acquisition of the associated undertaking should be dealt with in accordance with the rules in Schedule 4. [4A Sch 22(1)]. Similarly, the rules in the Act and SSAP 22 also apply to goodwill that arises on the acquisition of an associate. Consequently, under SSAP 22 the preferred treatment would be to write off such goodwill arising on consolidation directly to reserves. Alternatively, the goodwill can be amortised over its useful economic life. Similarly, any goodwill that is shown in the balance sheet of the associated undertaking should be dealt with by that associate in accordance with the provisions of the Act and SSAP 22. Consequently, this should mean that, if goodwill remains in the associate's balance sheet, the alternative treatment has been adopted by the associate and its goodwill is being amortised (or it is an overseas undertaking). The provisions of the Act relating to goodwill and SSAP 22 are considered in more detail in chapter 8.

11.32   Where an investing group's interest in an associated undertaking is material to the investing group's financial statements, more detailed information about that associate's assets and liabilities may need to be given in the group's financial statements in order to give a true and fair view. [SSAP 1 para 30]. For example see Table 63 overleaf.

Deficiency of net assets

11.33   A problem may arise where an associate starts to make losses, particularly where those losses are such that the undertaking has net liabilities. Where this is so, the investing group should normally reflect in its consolidated balance sheet its share of any deficiency in an associated undertaking. [SSAP 1 para 33]. This would apply, for example, where the investment is still regarded by the group as long-term. In addition, there may also be other factors that justify this treatment, for example, where the associate's shareholders intend to continue to support the undertaking. Such a factor could be evidenced by the existence of a binding support agreement. However, where there is no intention to support the undertaking, then only the liabilities that the group will incur if the undertaking should cease to trade would need to be provided for in full in the consolidated financial statements.

11.34   Often where an associate is making losses, there may be a significant diminution in the associate's value. Where there is any permanent diminution in value of the associated undertaking, a provision must be made against the carrying value of the investment in the investing undertaking's financial statements to reflect that decrease in value. [4 Sch 19(2); SSAP 1 para 32]. A similar adjustment would not generally be required in the group's consolidated financial statements, because such an impairment in value would normally be reflected in the associate's net asset value. Where there is such a decrease in value that is provided for in the holding company's financial statements,

SSAP 1 requires that the amount written off the investment in the period should be separately disclosed. [4 Sch 19(2); SSAP 1 para 32].

Table 63: Illustration of more detailed balance sheet information given regarding a material associate. This illustration is a continuation of Table 61.

Extract from the RTZ Corporation PLC annual report and accounts 31st December 1988

Note extract

The pro forma consolidated balance sheet of CRA Limited at 31 December 1988, stated in accordance with RTZ accounting policies, was as follows:

Intangible assets	181	220
Tangible assets	3,460	3,761
Investments	548	462
Working capital	669	977
Net cash less current debt	(91)	40
	4,767	5,460
Less: long term debt	920	1,821
provisions	366	503
outside shareholders' interests	733	697
CRA shareholders' funds	2,748	2,439
RTZ share	636.3	459.7

Adjustment is made to the reserves reported by CRA Limited to reflect RTZ accounting policies. A reconciliation is shown below:

CRA shareholders' funds, as reported	3,621	3,300
Elimination of unrealised asset revaluation reserve	(557)	(512)
Goodwill arising on consolidation written off	(310)	(324)
Other	(6)	(25)
CRA shareholders' funds, as adjusted	2,748	2,439

Joint and several liability

11.35 SSAP 1 makes the important point that, where unincorporated undertakings are treated as associates, a liability could arise in excess of that taken into account when accounting for the group's share of the associate. The example given in the standard is that of joint and several liability in a partnership. [SSAP 1 para 34]. Where such a potential liability exists (or a similar type of support agreement exists) it is necessary to consider whether a provision should be made for the possibility that the other party to the agreement may be unable to meet its obligations under that agreement. Where a provision is required it will be necessary to invoke the 'true and fair' override.

11.36 In circumstances where it is clear that the other party is able to honour such an agreement, it is still necessary for the group to disclose the existence of its potential commitment as a contingent liability under SSAP 18 and clearly explain the circumstances in which the liability might crystallise.

Financial statements used

11.37 The financial statements used for the purpose of including the results of associated companies should be either coterminous with those of the group or made up to a date that is either not more than six months before, or shortly after, the date of the investing group's financial statements. Where non-coterminous financial statements are used, and the effect is material to the group's results, the facts and the dates of the year ends should be disclosed. [SSAP 1 paras 36,37].

11.38 If an associated company is listed on a recognised stock exchange, only published information should be disclosed in the group's financial statements. [SSAP 1 para 36] This can cause particular problems in practice where, for example, there is more than six months between the year end of the associate and that of the group. Where this is so, it may be possible to take the financial statements of the associate and adjust its year end results for any published interim information.

11.39 Care should be taken where the associate's year end does not coincide with that of the investing undertaking to ensure that there are no material events that have occurred since the associate's year end. Where such events have taken place, then it may be necessary to make adjustments to the results and net assets of the associate before they are consolidated with the group's financial statements. [SSAP 1 para 37].

Consolidation adjustments

11.40 Adjustments similar to those required for the purposes of including subsidiaries in the consolidated financial statements should be made when the associated companies are incorporated into the group's consolidated financial statements. The type of adjustments that may be necessary cover the following matters:

■ To achieve consistency of accounting policies.

   The standard states that adjustments should be made to achieve reasonable consistency of accounting policies between the group and its associates. However, in practice, such adjustments will not always be possible, because the information necessary to make them will not necessarily be available. Where this situation arises, the standard offers no guidance. However, where the accounting policy used by the associate is different from the rest of the group and it is thought to have a material effect on the results of the group, then this would have to be clearly explained in the notes to the group's consolidated financial statements.

■ To set up, or write off, goodwill arising on the acquisition of the associate and to deal with fair value adjustments.

■ To deal with abnormal transactions that arise between the year end of an associate and the year end of its parent.

■ To eliminate the effects of intra-group trading.

■ To translate the results of overseas associates.

11.41 These types of adjustments are considered in respect of consolidations of subsidiaries in detail in chapter 5. Those principles can equally be applied to the consolidation adjustments that are required when equity accounting for associated undertakings.

11.42 The method used to eliminate intra-group trading with an associate may be different from that adopted for a company. The normal method of adjustment for a company would be to eliminate profits and losses fully. However, the Act now specifies that the elimination of profits and losses resulting from transactions between group undertakings which have been included in the value of assets may be eliminated in proportion to the group's interest in the shares of the undertaking. [4A Sch 6(3)]. The implications of this method of elimination are considered further in chapter 5 paragraphs 5.33 to 5.38. Although only brought into the legislation by the introduction of the Companies Act 1989, this method of eliminating profits has been used in the past when equity accounting for associated undertakings. Consider the following example.

Example

Company H prepares its consolidated financial statements to the 31st December 1990. It has a 25 per cent investment in an associate partnership. During the year company H purchased an investment from the partnership for £120,000. The partnership made £50,000 profit on the sale. On consolidation, using the equity method of accounting, the profit of the associate should be reduced to the extent of the group's investment in it (that is, reduced by 25%). Consequently, the share of the associate's profit consolidated with the group would be reduced by £12,500 (that is, 25% x £50,000), thereby, reducing the group's share of that profit completely. In addition, to complete the double entry, the value of the investment shown in the group's consolidated balance sheet should be reduced by £12,500 to £107,500.

11.43 This type of adjustment is logical for an associate because the consolidated financial statements only include the group's share of the profits and losses of the associate and, consequently, it would be wrong to eliminate a greater proportion of the profit. Furthermore, in the situation where a group member makes a sale to an associated undertaking, then a profit will arise in the group. Similarly, the associate's asset will also in this situation be overstated by the profit element. Consequently, a similar adjustment will be required on consolidation to reduce the group's share of the associate's assets by the same amount.

Effective date of acquisition or disposal

11.44 The effective date of acquisition and disposal of an associated undertaking is established in the same way as for a subsidiary company. That is, the effective date for dealing with the acquisition or disposal of an interest in an associated company should be the earlier of the following two dates:

■ The date on which the consideration for the acquisition or sale passes.

■ The date on which an offer becomes unconditional.

[SSAP 1 para 44].

11.45 In a similar way to the rules that govern subsidiaries, these rules above apply even if the acquiring company has the right under the acquisition or sale agreement to share in the profits of the acquired business from an earlier date. Those provisions are considered in more detail with regard to the acquisition and sale of subsidiaries in chapter 5 paragraphs 5.39 to 5.47. These paragraphs apply equally to the acquisition and disposal of associated undertakings.

An investment or a subsidiary becomes an associate

11.46 Chapter 6 deals with piece-meal acquisitions of subsidiaries and describes in paragraphs 6.36 to 6.47 various situations that might arise. One of those situations is where an investment in an undertaking is increased such that it becomes an associate. An undertaking might become an associate in a number of ways, for example:

■ The investing group acquires an additional investment in the undertaking to bring its voting rights to over 20 per cent.

■ The investing group has an investment of over 20 per cent, but previously did not have board representation or any influence over the financial or operating policy decisions of the undertaking. It has now gained that influence.

■ The investing group has sold a share of a subsidiary company, which has reduced the group's shareholding to below 50 per cent of the undertaking's voting rights and, accordingly, it is now an associate.

■   A subsidiary issues shares to a third party such that the investing
group's shareholding reduces below 50 per cent of the
undertakings voting rights.

11.47 The treatments of both an investment becoming an associate and a
subsidiary becoming an associate are illustrated in the two examples
that follow.

Example 1 - An investment becomes an associate

A group made an investment of 10 per cent in a company in 1985. The investment cost
£25,000 and has subsequently been revalued to £50,000. It makes a further investment
of 15 per cent to bring its total investment to 25 per cent. The fair value of the
consideration given for the additional investment is £250,000. The net assets of the
investee stand in its own books at the date of the second acquisition at £800,000. A fair
value exercise has been undertaken at the date of acquisition which shows a fair value
of net assets of £1M. The adjusted capital and reserves of the associate are, as a
consequence, £200,000 share capital and £800,000 reserves (which includes a £200,000
revaluation reserve). The associate has no goodwill recognised in its balance sheet as its
policy is to write off goodwill direct to reserves in the year of acquisition. The goodwill
arising on acquisition and the balance sheet treatment in the group would be as follows:

	£'000
Cost of acquisition	
Original investment (reduced to cost)	25
Fair value of consideration given	250
Total consideration	275
Consolidation goodwill	£'000
Total consideration	275
Adjusted capital and reserves	
(being, 25% x £1M)	250
Goodwill	25
Balance sheet extract	£'000
Interests in associated undertakings	
Share of net assets (being, 25% x £1M)	250
Goodwill on acquisition	25
	275

The only adjustment that is required in this example, in contrast to a straight
acquisition of an associate, is to reduce the value of the original investment from its
market value to cost. The entry on consolidation would be to debit the revaluation
reserve with £25,000 and credit the investment £25,000. The premium on acquisition of
£25,000 will have to be dealt with in accordance with SSAP 22 and either written off
immediately to reserves or amortised over its useful economic life.

Example 2 - A subsidiary becomes an associate

A group has had an investment of 80 per cent in a subsidiary for a number of years. At
the beginning of the accounting period, the balance sheets of the group excluding the
subsidiary and the group including the subsidiary are as follows:

Summarised balance sheets

	Group excluding Sub. £'000	Sub. £'000	Group including Sub. £'000
Fixed assets	500	230	730
Investment in subsidiary	220	-	-
Current assets	300	150	450
Current liabilities	(250)	(80)	(330)
	770	300	850
Share capital	250	100	250
Share premium	220	50	220
Profit and loss reserve	150	100	190
Other reserves	100	50	80
Minority interest	50	-	110
	770	300	850

The goodwill that arose on the original acquisition of the subsidiary is £20,000 and is calculated as set out below. The goodwill was written off to other reserves on the acquisition of the subsidiary to give a balance on other reserves of £80,000.

Cost of control account/goodwill

Investment	220,000	Share capital (80% x 100,000)	80,000
		Share premium (80% x 50,000)	40,000
		Pre-acq. profit and loss reserve (80% x 50,000)	40,000
		Other reserves (80% x 50,000)	40,000
		Balance, viz goodwill	20,000
	£220,000		£220,000

The minority interests at the beginning of the year are calculated as follows:

Minority interests account

Minority interests	110,000	Group balance	50,000
		Share capital (20% x 100,000)	20,000
		Share premium (20% x 50,000)	10,000
		Profit and loss reserve (20% x 100,000)	20,000
		Other reserves (20% x 50,000)	10,000
	£110,000		£110,000

The group's profit and loss reserve is made up of £150,000 plus the subsidiary's post-acquisition reserves of £40,000 (that is, £50,000 x 80%).

During the year the group disposes of 40 per cent of its investment in the subsidiary. The proceeds received on the sale are £140,000 and the net asset value of the subsidiary at the date of sale is £320,000. Consequently, up to the date of sale of part of the group's investment in the subsidiary, it made a profit of £20,000. The subsidiary, therefore, becomes an associate part way through the year. The profit and loss accounts of the group excluding the associate, the associate and the group including the associate using the equity method of accounting are given below:

Summarised profit and loss accounts

	Group excluding Assoc. £'000	Assoc. £'000	Group including Assoc. £'000
Ordinary profit (note (a))	40	30	60
Profit on sale of interest in subsidiary (note (b))	30	-	12
	70	30	72
Income from interests in associated undertakings (note (c))	-	-	4
Profit on ordinary activities	70	30	76
Minority interests (note (d))	-	-	4
	70	30	72
Reserve brought forward	150	100	190
Reserve carried forward	220	130	262

(a) The ordinary profit for the group of £60,000 represents the profit of the group excluding the associate of £40,000 plus the profit of the subsidiary up to the date of sale of the 40 per cent interest (which is, £20,000).

(b) The profit on the sale of the subsidiary in the company selling the interest is £30,000, which is calculated by deducting the sale proceeds of £140,000 from the cost of the investment of £110,000 (that is, £220,000 x 50%). The profit on sale to the group is £12,000, which is calculated by deducting from the sale proceeds of £140,000 the group's share of the subsidiary's net assets consolidated up to the date of sale of £128,000. The net assets of the subsidiary are made of the net assets at last balance sheet date of £300,000 plus the profit on ordinary activities to date of sale of £20,000. The group's share of those assets is £128,000 (that is, £320,000 x 40%).

The profit to the group on the sale of the investment, however, does not take into account the share of goodwill that has been written off to other reserves in previous years of £10,000. In certain situations, where for example such goodwill has only been written off in the previous period, it may be necessary to credit other reserves with this amount and to debit the profit on sale in order to show the true profit or loss on the sale of the investment.

(c) The income from interests in associated undertakings of £4,000 is the group's share of the results of the undertaking after it became an associate (that is, 40% x £10,000).

(d) The minority interest figure of £4,000 is the minority's share of the profits of the subsidiary up to the date of sale of the 40 per cent interest and is calculated by applying the minority's share of 20% to the profits recognised of the subsidiary in the period (that is, £20,000).

At the group's year end, the balance sheets of the group and the subsidiary, which is now an associate, are set out below:

303

Summarised balance sheets

	Group excluding Assoc. £'000	Assoc. £'000	Group including Assoc. £'000
Fixed assets	530	250	530
Investment in subsidiary	110	-	-
Interests in associated undertaking	-	-	132
Current assets	460	170	460
Current liabilities	(260)	(90)	(260)
	840	330	862
Share capital	250	100	250
Share premium	220	50	220
Profit and loss reserve	220	130	262
Other reserves	100	50	80
Minority interest	50	-	50
	840	330	862

Note extract

Interests in associated undertaking

Share of associated undertaking's net assets   132

The other reserves figure is made up of the group's reserves excluding the associate of £100,000, less goodwill of £20,000 written off on the original acquisition of the subsidiary investment. The investment in the associate of £132,000 also represents the cost of the investment in the associate of £110,000, adjusted for the group's share of the post acquisition reserves of the associate of £32,000 (that is, (130,000 - 50,000) x 40%). The difference of £10,000 is the goodwill arising on the acquisition of the 40% investment, which has been written of to other reserves in previous years.

Disposal of an associate

11.48 Where an associate ceases to qualify as an associated undertaking, the investing group's consolidated balance sheet should include the investment at the aggregate value (outlined in para 11.29 above) on the date that its status changed. If the investment's carrying value then suffers a permanent diminution in value, provision should be made against it.

Example

A group decides to sell its investment in an associated company. They intend to show the investment in the year end consolidated financial statements as a current asset investment, but still representing the group's share of the net assets of the company.

The investing company could if it wished to show its investment in the company at its current cost as this is permitted by paragraph 31(4) of Schedule 4 to the Act. However, on consolidation, the group may need to make a provision against the net asset value of the company where its current value is lower. This provision would have to be made through the consolidated profit and loss account.

Minority interests

11.49 Where the associated undertaking is held by a subsidiary that is partly
held by a minority, the minority's share of the associated undertaking's
results should be shown as part of minority interests in the
consolidated financial statements. [SSAP 1 para 41].

Additional disclosure

11.50 Schedule 5 to the Act includes certain additional information that has
to be disclosed in the consolidated financial statements about an
undertaking's investments in its associates. Some of this information is
also required to be given by SSAP 1. Such undertakings have to give
the following information:

■   The name of the associated undertaking. [5 Sch 22(2); SSAP 1
    para 49].

■   If the undertaking is incorporated outside Great Britain, the
    country of its incorporation. [5 Sch 22(3)(a)].

■   If the undertaking is incorporated in Great Britain, whether it is
    registered in England and Wales, or in Scotland. [5 Sch 22(3)(b)].

■   Where the undertaking is unincorporated, the address of its
    principal place of business. [5 Sch 22(3)(c)].

■   In respect of shares held by the company or by other members of
    the group:

    ☐   The identity of each class of shares.

    ☐   The proportion held of the nominal value of each class.

    This information has to be disclosed separately for shares held by
    the company and by the other group members. [5 Sch 22(4)(5);
    SSAP 1 para 49(a)].

    This type of information is illustrated in Table 64.

11.51 Furthermore, SSAP 1 requires that the investing group's financial
statements should indicate the nature of the associated companies'
businesses. [SSAP 1 para 49(b)]. In addition, certain information is
required concerning the trading balances with the associate. This
includes the information below, which has to be disclosed separately in
the consolidated financial statements:

■   The total of loans to associates from the group.

■ The total of loans from associates to the group.

[SSAP 1 paras 27,28].

Table 64: Illustration of the type of information required to be disclosed for associated companies.

Extract from Avon Rubber p.l.c. Annual Report 30th September 1989.

Note extract

5 Associated companies extract

Name of Company	Share Capital	Held by the group	Accounting Date	Basis of Consolidation
Ames-Avon Industries USA	2,000 shares of no par value	49%	31st December	Audited accounts for 1988. Unaudited accounts to September 1989
Avon Rubber Company (Kenya) Limited Kenya	586,300 shares of 20 shillings each	36%	30th September	Audited accounts for 1989
Avon Marketing Services (Kenya) Limited Kenya	130,000 shares of 20 shillings each	33%	30th September	Audited accounts for 1989
Avon Export Services Limited Kenya	1,760 shares of 20 shillings each	32%	30th September	Audited accounts for 1989
Avonride Limited England	100,000 shares of £1 each	25%	31st December	Audited accounts for 1988

11.52 In addition, balances that arise from unsettled normal trading between the associate and other group members, should be included under current assets and current liabilities and disclosed separately if material to the group. [SSAP 1 para 29].

11.53 The International Stock Exchange also requires certain information to be given concerning each company in which the group's interest in the equity capital amounts to 20 per cent or more. The required information is as follows:

■ The principal country of operation.

■ Particulars of its issued capital and debt securities.

■ The percentage of each class of debt securities attributable to the company's interest (whether it is direct or indirect).

[CO 21(e)].

11.54 The group's share of post-acquisition reserves of the associate should also be disclosed in the group's consolidated financial statements. This disclosure should also include a summary of movements on those reserves. Furthermore, where for example those reserves arise in a foreign country and they are subject to further tax on distribution, this should be made clear. [SSAP 1 para 31].

11.55 If there are any restrictions on an associated undertaking's ability to distribute its retained profits, the extent of the restrictions should be indicated. [SSAP 1 para 40]. This type of situation could arise where, for example, the associate is situated in a county where there are exchange control restrictions, which restrict the associate's ability to pay dividends out of that country.

Joint ventures

11.56 The Companies Act 1989 included provisions that determine how groups can account for joint ventures. These rules stem directly from the 7th Directive and allow certain joint ventures to be accounted for in the consolidated financial statements on a proportional basis. These provisions, however, only apply to unincorporated undertakings that are joint ventures and do not apply to joint ventures that are undertaken through limited companies.

Meaning of joint ventures

11.57 Although there is no specific definition of the term 'joint venture' in the Act, paragraph 19(1) of Schedule 4A to the Act refers to a situation where an undertaking manages another undertaking jointly with one or more other undertakings that are not included in the consolidation. Consequently, the Act places emphasis on the *joint management* of the undertaking. The provisions do not apply as mentioned above, where the joint venture undertaking is a limited company. They also do not apply where the undertaking is a subsidiary for consolidation purposes under the definitions in the Act (see further chapter 3 paragraphs 3.6 to 3.36). [4A Sch 19(1)].

11.58 There is little published guidance on what might constitute a joint venture, but Accounting Digest No. 126 on associated companies mentions that 'significant influence' rather than 'control' will exist where an investment is made in a joint venture. Consequently, an investment in a joint venture means that the venture is also an associate under SSAP 1. In addition, investors in a joint venture will jointly influence the management policy decisions of the venture. Therefore, for the investment to be a true 'joint venture' no one investor should be in a position to dominate the policy of the venture.

11.59 The digest also states that there is no limit to the number of venturers that can invest and be party to a joint venture. Similarly, there is no limit set in the Act on the number of people that can be party to a joint venture. An important difference between a joint venture and other forms of undertaking, however, is that the parties to a joint venture must both jointly control and influence the undertaking. Similarly, the parties to the joint venture should each receive an adequate share of the profits of the joint venture, which may vary depending on each venturer's contribution to the venture.

Accounting treatment

11.60 Where the group has an investment in an unincorporated joint venture, it *may* consolidate the results and assets and liabilities of the joint venture on a 'proportional basis'. [4A Sch 19(1)]. The basis of proportional consolidation is not described in the legislation, but SSAP 1 does refer to the method as accounting for a proportionate share of the undertaking's individual assets and liabilities as well as its profits and losses. [SSAP 1 para 10]. An illustration of such a basis is described in Table 65.

Table 65: Illustration of an accounting policy used where joint ventures are consolidated on a proportional basis.

Extract from Laing Properties plc Annual Report 31st December 1988.

Accounting policy extract

JOINT VENTURES

The Company's interests in property development joint ventures are incorporated into the consolidated financial statements on the proportional consolidation basis. Under this convention, the Company's shares of joint venture assets and liabilities are included in the consolidated balance sheet in the proportions in which the Company shares joint venture profits. Where the Company has contributed to joint venture capital in excess of its pro-rata share, the excess is treated as an advance to the joint venture partner, and included in debtors as a current asset whilst the joint venture project remains a development property.

Where the joint venture development is subsequently retained as an investment, the property is valued externally and the Company's proportional share of the valuation transferred to investment properties in the consolidated balance sheet. The resulting surplus or deficit on comparison with book value is added to or charged against property revaluation reserve. Any capital contribution by the Company in excess of its pro-rata share is transferred to other investments in the consolidated balance sheet, and shown as advances to joint venture partners in the notes forming part of the financial statements.

The Company's share of turnover and profits or losses of joint ventures is included in the consolidated profit and loss account under investment income or trading surplus as appropriate.

11.61 Proportional consolidation was used before the introduction of the Companies Act 1989 to consolidate a group's interests in partnerships, generally where their investment was between 20 per cent and 50 per cent of the partnership's capital. The basis means a line by line consolidation of the investor's share of the assets and liabilities and also a line by line consolidation of its share of the undertaking's revenues and expenses (including turnover). The example that follows illustrates the principles of proportional consolidation on the acquisition of an interest in a joint venture.

Example

A group acquires a 40 per cent investment in an unincorporated joint venture half way through the group's year. The group paid £100,000 for the interest and the joint venture's net assets at the date of acquisition were £200,000. The summarised balance sheets of the group excluding the joint venture and the group including the joint venture at the group's year end are as follows:

Summarised balance sheets

	Group excluding JV £'000	JV £'000	Memo 40% of JV £'000	Group including JV £'000
Fixed assets	500	180	72	572
Goodwill	-	-	-	20
Investments	100	-	-	-
Current assets	300	150	60	360
Current liabilities	(250)	(80)	(32)	(282)
	650	250		670
Share capital	100	-		100
JV capital	-	100	40	-
Share premium	150	50	20	150
Profit and loss reserve	250	100	40	270
Other reserves	100	-	-	100
Minority interest	50	-	-	50
	650	250		670

The goodwill arising on the acquisition of the joint venture interest is calculated as follows:

Cost of control account/goodwill			
Investment	100,000	Share capital (40% x 100,000)	40,000
		Share premium (40% x 50,000)	20,000
		Pre-acq. profit and loss reserve (40% x 50,000)	20,000
		Balance, viz goodwill	20,000
	£100,000		£100,000

It may be difficult to persuade the joint venture to carry out a full fair value exercise on the acquisition of an interest of 40 per cent. Consequently, no fair value adjustments have been made on consolidation in this example and the group's share of the net book value at the date of acquisition is taken to the cost of control account. Therefore, the group's consolidated profit and loss reserve of £170,000 represents the group's reserves before consolidating the joint venture plus the group's share of the post-acquisition reserves of the joint venture (that is, £150,000 + (£50,000 x 40%)).

11.62 Under the Act, proportional consolidation is an option. Consequently, a group might decide to account for its investment in an unincorporated joint venture as an associated company in accordance with SSAP 1 (as described previously in this chapter). Because it is possible for groups to adopt either method it is desirable that the basis of consolidation is clearly spelt out in an accounting policy. For example see Table 66.

Table 66: Example of an accounting policy for joint ventures which now only allowed if they are unincorporated.

Extract from The RTZ Corporation PLC annual report and accounts 31st December 1988.

1 Basis of Group accounts

The accounts consist of the consolidation of the account of all subsidiary and sub-subsidiary companies, prepared on the historical cost basis, which does not include the revaluation of fixed assets. Joint ventures are accounted for by consolidation of the Group's share of assets, liabilities, revenues and expenses. The Group's share of post-acquisition earnings and reserves of related companies, other than those arising on the revaluation of fixed assets, is included.

Details of the principal subsidiary and related companies are given on pages 48 and 49.

Consolidation adjustments

11.63 With the consolidation of subsidiaries and associated companies, there are a number of matters that have to be dealt with by adjusting the figures that are consolidated into the group's consolidated financial statements. These adjustments equally apply to the proportional consolidation of joint ventures and are as follows:

■ To achieve consistency of accounting policies.

■ To set up, or write off, goodwill arising on the acquisition of the joint venture and to deal with fair value adjustments.

■ To deal with abnormal transactions that arise between the year end of the joint venture and the year end of its parent.

■ To eliminate the effects of intra-group trading.

■ To translate the results of overseas joint ventures.

11.64 These types of adjustments are discussed further in paragraphs 11.40 to 11.43 above concerning associates and in chapter 5 for subsidiaries.

Additional information

11.65 Schedule 5 to the Act includes the additional information that has to be given in the consolidated financial statements about the company's investment in joint ventures, where those investments are included in the consolidated financial statements on a proportional consolidation basis. In this respect, the company has to disclose the following information about its investments in joint ventures:

- The name of the joint venture undertaking.

- The address of the undertaking's principal place of business.

- The factors on which the undertaking's joint management is based.

- The proportion of the undertaking's capital held by the undertakings included in the consolidation.

- The date of the undertaking's last year end if it does not coincide with that of the parent company.

[5 Sch 21(1)(2)].

Chapter 12

FOREIGN CURRENCY TRANSLATION

FOREIGN CURRENCY TRANSLATION

Introduction

12.1   The Act does not include any provisions that deal with either the translation of foreign currency transactions or the translation of foreign currency financial statements, other than to require the basis on which such sums are translated into sterling to be stated. [4 Sch 58(1)]. However, SSAP 20, 'Foreign currency translation', does cover these matters. The intention of the standard is that translation should ensure that the financial statements give a true and fair view.

12.2   The standard deals separately with the translation of foreign currency transactions by individual companies and with the translation of foreign currency financial statements for consolidation purposes. The standard also contains a number of disclosure requirements. This chapter explains the provisions of SSAP 20 that affect consolidations. The provisions of SSAP 20 that relate to individual companies are considered in chapter 18 of 'Manual of Accounting - volume I'.

12.3   Translation of foreign currency financial statements is necessary so that the financial statements of overseas subsidiaries may be consolidated with the holding company's sterling financial statements. SSAP 20 also covers the translation of the results of overseas associated companies and foreign branches. The standard requires that normally, a company should use the 'closing rate/net investment' method for such translations. [SSAP 20 para 52].

Closing rate/net investment method

12.4   The 'closing rate/net investment' method recognises that a company's investment is in the net worth of its foreign undertaking, rather than being a direct investment in that undertaking's individual assets and liabilities. The net investment that a company has in a foreign undertaking is its effective equity stake, and it comprises its proportion of that undertaking's net assets. In appropriate circumstances, intra-group loans and deferred balances may be regarded as part of that effective equity stake. [SSAP 20 para 43].

12.5   Under the 'closing rate/net investment' method, a company should use the closing rate of exchange when translating the amounts in the balance sheets of its overseas undertaking. The company should record, as a movement on consolidated reserves, the exchange differences that arise when it retranslates its opening net investment in a foreign undertaking to the closing rate (see for example Table 67). [SSAP 20 para 53]. However, SSAP 20 does not require companies or groups to maintain a separate reserve for exchange differences, but some companies do so.

> **Table 67: Example of an accounting policy for foreign currency.**
>
> *Extract from Delta plc Annual Report and Accounts 31st December 1988.*
>
> **5 FOREIGN CURRENCY**
>
> The accounts of overseas companies and the overseas assets and liabilities of UK companies are translated into sterling at the rates ruling on the last day of the financial year. The difference arising from the translation of the opening net assets of overseas companies is taken directly to reserves.

12.6   Under the 'closing rate/net investment' method, a company should translate the profit and loss accounts of its foreign undertakings either at the closing rate or at an average rate for the period. Where the average rate has been used, the company should record, as a movement on consolidated reserves, the difference between translating the profit and loss account at the average rate and translating it at the closing rate. [SSAP 20 para 54].

Illustration of closing rate/net investment method

12.7   The closing rate/net investment method is illustrated by the following example.

Example

A UK company has a wholly-owned subsidiary in France. At 31st March 1990, the UK company's net investment (share capital and reserves) in the French subsidiary amounted to FF 1,250,000 and the exchange rate was £1 = FF 10.7. During the year ended 31st March 1991, the French subsidiary made a profit of FF 75,000. The subsidiary made no distribution to the holding company during the year.

At 31st March 1991, the net investment in the French subsidiary amounted to FF 1,325,000 (FF 1,250,000 + FF 75,000) and the exchange rate was £1 = FF 10.8. The loss on the retranslation of the opening net investment is:

	£
FF 1,250,000 at 10.7	116,822
FF 1,250,000 at 10.8	115,741
Loss on retranslation	1,081

The UK company would include the loss on the retranslation of the opening net investment as a movement on its consolidated reserves. The French subsidiary's profit for the year ended 31st March 1991 at the closing rate would be £6,944 (that is FF 75,000 at 10.8). The UK company's net investment in the French subsidiary at 31st March 1991 can be reconciled as follows:

	£
At 31st March 1990	
FF 1,250,000 at 10.7	116,822
Loss on retranslation at closing rate	(1,081)
Profit for the year	6,944
At 31st March 1991	
FF 1,325,000 at 10.8	122,685

If the UK company had used a weighted average rate of £1 = FF 10.75 to translate the profit and loss account of its French subsidiary, it would have had an additional movement on its consolidated reserves. This additional movement would represent the difference between the use of the closing rate and the use of an average rate to translate the French subsidiary's profit for the year. The difference is:

	£
FF 75,000 at 10.8	6,944
FF 75,000 at 10.75	6,977
Difference	33

The net investment in the French subsidiary at 31st March 1991 could then be reconciled as follows:

	£
At 31st March 1990	
FF 1,250,000 at 10.7	116,822
Loss on retranslation at closing rate:	
of opening net investment *	(1,081)
of profit for the year *	(33)
Profit for the year	6,977
At 31 March 1991	
FF 1,325,000 at 10.8	122,685

* Both of these retranslation amounts would be treated as reserve movements.

Calculating closing rate

12.8   SSAP 20 defines the closing rate as the exchange rate for spot transactions that was ruling at the balance sheet date. It is the mean of the buying rate and the selling rate at the close of business on the day for which the rate is to be ascertained. [SSAP 20 para 41]. Where the balance sheet date of an overseas subsidiary differs from that of the holding company, the closing rate for the purposes of preparing consolidated financial statements is the rate ruling at the overseas subsidiary's balance sheet date.

12.9   However, where the rate ruling at the holding company's balance sheet date would give significantly different figures, the holding company will need to consider whether (in accordance with the provisions of SSAP 17) to disclose, or to adjust for, that difference in the consolidated financial statements.

Example

A group expects its overseas subsidiaries to generate profits of $60 million in the year. At an exchange rate of $1.5 = £1 this will generate profits of £40 million, but if the rate changes to $2 = £1 by the year end the contribution will by only £30 million. To guard against this shortfall the group decides to take out an option contract costing £1 million to entitle it to convert $60 million into £40 million at the year end. If the rate moves to $2 = £1 then the contract will generate £10 million.

Whatever the rate happens to be at the year end, the group has locked itself into a rate of $1.5 = £1 at the year end and, consequently, any gain on or loss on the option contract (including its cost) should be reported as part of the profit or loss on ordinary activities.

Calculating average rate

12.10 Where a company uses an average rate, it should calculate it by the method it considers is most appropriate to the foreign undertaking's circumstances. [SSAP 20 para 54]. It can use any reasonable method, but the objective of the method must be to calculate a weighted average that reflects changes both in exchange rates and in the volume of business. The profit or loss for the year translated at the average rate then has to be translated to the year end rate and the difference arising is taken to reserves (see for example Table 68).

> **Table 68: Example of an accounting policy that explains how the difference between translating the profit and loss account at the average rate and year end rates is dealt with.**
>
> *Extract from Calor Group plc Annual Report 31st March 1989.*
>
> (d) Foreign currencies
> The assets and liabilities of the foreign subsidiary companies are translated into sterling at the rates of exchange ruling at the year end. Gains or losses resulting from the realignment of opening foreign currency balances to the year end rates are treated as movements on reserves.
>
> The results of the foreign subsidiary companies are translated into sterling at the average rates of exchange for the accounting period. Gains or losses resulting from the translation of these results from the average to the year end rates are treated as movements on reserves.
>
> Gains or losses arising from the realignment to the year end sterling exchange rate of foreign currency borrowings which finance equity investment in foreign subsidiaries or certain other foreign currency assets are treated as movements on reserves.
>
> All other exchange differences are dealt with through the profit and loss account.

12.11 There are a number of ways in which the average rate of exchange can be calculated. However, companies normally calculate the average on a monthly basis, although there is nothing in the standard to prevent a company using another period if this gives an acceptable result. The following methods of averaging are used in practice:

■ The average of the rate ruling at the end of each month.

- The average of the rate ruling at the beginning of each month.

- The average of each business day of the month.

- The average of the beginning or the end of each week in the month.

12.12 There is no reason why a company should not adopt a more complicated method, for example, by using an average of month one opening and closing rates for month one; an average of month one opening, month one closing and month two closing for month two; an average of month one opening, month one closing, month two closing and month three closing for month three, etc. An illustration of a method is given in Table 69.

Table 69: Example of a method of averaging exchange rates.

Extract from The Boots Company PLC Report and Accounts 31st March 1989.

Accounting policy extract

Foreign Currencies
The results of overseas companies are translated into sterling on an average exchange rate basis, weighted by the actual results of each month.
Assets and liabilities of overseas subsidiaries are translated into sterling at the rates of exchange ruling at the date of the group balance sheet.
Translation differences are taken to reserves. Other exchange gains or losses are taken to trading profit. Overseas investments are stated at the rate of exchange in force at the date each investment was made.

12.13 The number of companies that used the closing rate to translate the results of their overseas subsidiaries' profit and loss accounts used to be greater than those that used the average rate. However, in recent years many companies have moved from using the closing rate to using an average rate. Where this is done, it represents a change of accounting policy and, as a consequence, a prior year adjustment is required in accordance with SSAP 6. It may be reasonably easy for a company to justify changing its accounting policy to move to an average rate of exchange, however, it would generally be much harder for such a company to justify a move back to year end rates, especially where the move to an average rate has only occurred recently.

Using the temporal method

12.14 Where the foreign undertaking's trade depends more on the economic environment of the investing company's currency than on its own reporting currency, the company should use the temporal method of translation. [SSAP 20 para 55]. The mechanics of the temporal method are in most respects identical to those that an individual company uses when preparing its financial statements. For example, the foreign undertaking's fixed assets are translated at the rates ruling at the date when it acquired each asset. As a result, the foreign undertaking's financial statements are included in the consolidated financial statements as if the investing company itself had entered into the undertaking's transactions in its own currency. As a consequence, any translation differences go through the profit and loss account.

12.15 It is often difficult in practice to decide the situations where the temporal method should be used. The standard gives some guidance as to the factors that need to be considered in determining whether the currency of the investing company is the dominant currency in the economic environment in which the foreign undertaking operates. The factors are as follows:

■ The extent to which the cash flows of the undertaking have a direct impact on those of the investing company.

■ The extent to which the function of the undertaking is dependent directly on the investing company.

■ The currency in which the majority of the trading transactions are denominated.

■ The major currency to which the operation is exposed in its financial structure.

[SSAP 20 para 23].

12.16 In practice, however, there will be few occasions when companies should use the temporal method. One example of a situation where the temporal method might be appropriate is where a foreign undertaking acts as a selling agency that receives stocks of goods from the investing company and remits the proceeds back to the investing company. Another example of a situation where the temporal method might be appropriate is where a foreign undertaking is located overseas for tax, or exchange control or similar reasons, or to act as a means of raising finance for, or for holding surplus funds on behalf of, other group companies. A third example is where the foreign entity produces raw materials, or manufactures parts, or manufactures sub-assemblies that are then shipped to the investing company for inclusion in its own products. [SSAP 20 para 24].

Foreign branches

12.17 SSAP 20 extends the definition of a foreign branch to include a group of assets and liabilities that a company accounts for in foreign currencies. [SSAP 20 para 37]. Where such a foreign branch operates as a direct extension of the investing company's business and as such, its cash flows directly affect that business, then the temporal method of translation should be used. However, where this is not the situation and the branch operates as a separate business, then the closing rate/net investment method should be used for translation purposes. [SSAP 20 para 25].

12.18 An example of such a 'foreign branch' is an aircraft a company purchases in US dollars, with an associated loan in US dollars, where the aircraft earns revenues and incurs expenses in US dollars. In this example, the company would account for the aircraft as a dollar asset. It would retranslate the carrying amount at the closing rate each year for inclusion in its financial statements and would, therefore, not use the temporal method of translation.

12.19 Where an investing company treats, as a foreign branch, a group of assets and liabilities that it accounts for in foreign currencies, it will be able to use the offset procedure as explained in paragraphs 12.20 to 12.33 below.

Hedging equity investments

12.20 Where a company has used foreign currency borrowings either to finance, or to provide a hedge against, its foreign equity investments, and where, also, similar conditions to those set out below apply, the group may denominate its equity investments in the appropriate foreign currency. This means that the investment will be regarded as a currency investment and the company will need to translate the carrying amount at the closing rate each year for inclusion in its financial statements. Where a company treats investments in this way, it should take to reserves any exchange differences that arise when the investments are retranslated. It should also take the exchange differences on the related foreign currency borrowings to reserves. It would then offset the exchange differences as a net increase or a net decrease to unrealised reserves. (See further 'Manual of Accounting - volume I').

12.21 The offset procedure described above is available also in consolidated financial statements. Within a group, foreign currency borrowings are often used either to finance, or to provide a hedge against, equity investments in foreign undertakings. Where this is so and also the conditions set out below have been complied with, exchange differences on the borrowings may be offset, as a movement on consolidated reserves against exchange differences that arise when the opening capital and reserves of the subsidiary are retranslated for consolidation purposes. For example, see Table 70.

12.22 The conditions for offset, all of which must apply, are as follows:

■ The relationship between the investing company and the foreign undertakings concerned must justify the use of the closing rate/net investment method of translation for consolidation purposes, rather than the temporal method.

■ In any accounting period, exchange differences on the borrowings may be offset only to the extent of the exchange differences that arise when the net investments are retranslated.

■ The borrowings must not exceed, in aggregate, the total amount of cash that the net investments are expected to be able to generate from profits or otherwise.

■ A company should apply consistently the accounting treatment it adopts.

[SSAP 20 para 57].

Table 70: Example of an accounting policy that explains the group's treatment of borrowings that hedge overseas investments.

Extract from Cadbury Schweppes Public Limited Company Annual Report 31st December 1988.

(c) Foreign currencies

The accounts include borrowings by United Kingdom companies (to finance or hedge overseas investments) and the results and net assets of overseas group companies, which are denominated in foreign currencies. Such amounts are translated into sterling at the middle market rates ruling at the end of the financial year. As a result unrealised exchange differences arise when the new values are compared with their former recorded values. These former values were based on exchange rates at the end of the previous year, except for new loans or the net assets of new subsidiaries, which were based on the exchange rates ruling at the date of their acquisition. The resulting exchange gains or losses are dealt with as a movement on reserves.

Where amounts denominated in a foreign currency are converted into sterling by remittance, a realised exchange difference arises in comparison with the recorded values. Such gains or losses are included in trading profit.

Where overseas investments are financed by borrowings in foreign currencies the cost of those investments in the Company's balance sheet is adjusted to reflect exchange rate movements up to the date of repayment.

Offset restriction

12.23 To illustrate the second condition in paragraph 12.22 above, consider the following example:

Example

Some years ago, company A (incorporated in the UK) raised a loan for US$ 7,500,000 to provide a hedge against an equity investment made by a subsidiary, company B, in a French company, company C (a sub-subsidiary of company B). The net assets of company C amount to FF 36,800,000. The relevant rates of exchange are:

		At 31st March 1990	At 31st March 1991
£1	=	US$ 1.7	US$ 1.6
£1	=	FF 10.3	FF 10.0

The loss on exchange on the loan for the year ended 31st March 1991 is:

	£
US$ 7,500,000 at 1.7	4,411,765
US$ 7.500,000 at 1.6	4,687,500
	£ 275,735

The gain on exchange on the retranslation of the net investment in company C for the year ended 31st March 1991 is:

	£
FF 36,800,000 at 10.3	3,572,816
FF 36,800,000 at 10.0	3,680,000
	£ 107,184

In this example, the amount of the exchange loss on the loan that company A can offset as a reserve movement on consolidation against the exchange gain on the net investment in company C is limited to £107,184. It must include the balance of the exchange loss on the loan (that is, £168,551) in the group's consolidated profit or loss on ordinary activities for the year.

12.24 If, in the example, there had been a gain on exchange on the loan for the year ended 31st March 1991 of, say, £250,000 and a loss on exchange on the net investment of, say, £100,000, the amount of the exchange gain on the loan that company A could have offset as a reserve movement against the exchange loss on the net investment would have been limited to £100,000. The group would have had to include the balance of the exchange gain on the loan (that is, £150,000) in the group's consolidated profit or loss on ordinary activities for the year.

12.25 On the other hand, if in the example there had been a loss on exchange on the retranslation of the French franc net investment as well as a loss on exchange on the loan, the group would have had to include the whole of the loss on exchange on the loan in its consolidated profit or loss on ordinary activities for the year. The group would still treat, as a reserve movement, the loss on exchange on the retranslation of the opening net investment in the French subsidiary.

12.26 Furthermore, if in the example there had been a gain on the loan as well as a gain on exchange of the French franc net investment, the group would have included the gain on exchange on the loan in its consolidated profit or loss on ordinary activities. The group would still treat, as a reserve movement, the gain on exchange on the retranslation of the opening net investment in the French subsidiary.

Borrowing restriction

12.27 The third condition outlined in paragraph 12.22 above states that the borrowings must not exceed, in aggregate, the total amount of cash that the net investments are expected to be able to generate from profits or otherwise. The condition does not specify a time scale that the foreign undertaking is given to generate sufficient profits. The condition should not cause a problem where a borrowing that is invested in a profitable subsidiary is sufficiently long-term to enable that foreign company to generate sufficient profits to cover the group's borrowing. In borderline situations, however, it may be difficult for a group to quantify cash flows and so ensure that it has complied with the condition. Problems may arise also where the borrowing is for a significantly shorter term than the expected useful life of the investment to the group.

12.28 The next example illustrates the operation of the third condition.

Example

In 1985, company A, incorporated in the UK, raised a DM loan to provide a hedge against a DM investment made by a subsidiary, company B, in a German sub-subsidiary company C. Both at 31st March 1990 and at 31st March 1991, the loan amounted to DM 15,000,000. The opening net investment in the German sub-subsidiary (that is. its capital and reserves) amounted to DM 17,000,000. The group, however, considers that the total amount of cash that the subsidiary will be able to generate will be DM 12,000,000.

At 31st March 1990, the exchange rate is £1 = DM 3.0, and at 31st March 1991 the exchange rate is £1 = DM 2.8. In the year ended 31st March 1991, the amount of the exchange loss on the loan that the group can offset as a reserve movement against the exchange gain on the net investment is calculated as follows:

	£
DM 12,000,000 at 3.0	4,000,000
DM 12,000,000 at 2.8	4,285,715
	£285,715

The group must report the exchange loss on the remaining DM 3,000,000 of the loan as part of the group's consolidated profit or loss on ordinary activities for the year.

Consistent accounting treatment

12.29 The fourth condition outlined in paragraph 12.22 above is that a group should apply consistently the accounting treatment it adopts. The objective of the condition is to prevent a group from changing its accounting treatment depending on the way in which exchange rates move. Where exchange rate movements give rise to exchange losses on borrowings, and the first two conditions apply, it is obviously advantageous for a group to be able to use the offset procedure. If, however, in a subsequent year, exchange rate movements give rise to exchange gains on those borrowings, and the first two conditions still apply, the group must still use the offset procedure. It cannot include the exchange gains in its consolidated profit on ordinary activities. Also where a group sells a foreign currency investment it should apply the offset procedure up to the date of sale and not stop at the previous year end. This applies in particular where the related loan has made an exchange gain between the previous accounting year end and the date of sale.

General guidance

12.30 Because it may not be advantageous for a group to adopt the offset procedure, the use of the procedure is optional under the standard.

12.31 SSAP 20 does not require a company to designate the purpose for which each foreign loan is raised at the commencement of the loan. Consequently, provided that the conditions apply, a group could apply the offset procedure to aggregate foreign currency borrowings that either finance, or provide a hedge against, aggregate foreign equity investments. Where, however, there is an economic link between certain loans and certain investments, it is best practice for a group to apply the offset procedure separately, rather than in aggregate.

12.32 The net investment that a company has in a foreign undertaking is its effective equity stake. In appropriate circumstances, intra-group loans and other deferred balances may be regarded as part of the effective equity stake. [SSAP 20 para 20]. The standard states that, where such loans are intended to be as permanent as equity, they should be treated as part of the investing company's net investment in the foreign undertaking. The requirement in Schedule 4 to the Act for a company to analyse amounts owed by or to group companies between amounts that will fall due within one year of the balance sheet date and other amounts may well indicate intra-group loans and other deferred balances that it should properly treat as part of its effective equity stake. For consolidation purposes, where long-term loans are included as part of the equity investment, an adjustment will have to be made to the opening net investment to include such loans. The translation difference that arises on the adjusted opening net investment can then be used to off set the translation difference arising on the foreign currency loan.

12.33 In addition, as shown in the examples above, on consolidation SSAP 20 does not confine the offset procedure to those situations where the holding company raises the currency loan. Any company in the group can raise the finance and the equity investment can also be made by any group company. Furthermore, the investment and the loan do not have to arise in the same company to allow the offset procedure to be applied on consolidation.

Hyper-inflation

12.34 A major difficulty can arise where a group has a foreign subsidiary that operates in a country where a very high rate of inflation exists. If the historical cost financial statements of such a subsidiary are merely translated without further adjustment, those financial statements are unlikely to present fairly the results and the position of that undertaking. The standard proposes that in this type of situation, the foreign subsidiary's financial statements should first be adjusted to reflect current price levels in the foreign country before the translation process in undertaken. [SSAP 20 para 26]. An illustration of such a situation is given in Table 71.

> *Table 71: Extract from an accounting policy that explains that indexation adjustments are made in certain countries.*
>
> *Extract from Davy Corporation plc Annual Report 31st March 1989.*
>
> Foreign Currencies
> Results and assets and liabilities denominated in foreign currencies are translated into sterling at the rates of exchange ruling at the end of the financial year. The net difference arising from the restatement of the net assets of overseas subsidiary and related companies at the beginning of the financial year, using the exchange rates prevailing at the end of the financial year, is taken directly to reserves. Exchange differences on foreign currency loans are also taken directly to reserves where there is an appropriate offset.
> It is the practice in certain South American countries to make indexation adjustments in statutory accounts based on official indices. These adjustments are taken directly to reserves.

12.35 Therefore, such a foreign company's financial statements should first be adjusted either on to a current cost basis or on to a current purchasing power basis before translation. Both the current cost method and the purchasing power method are explained in the ASC's handbook, 'Accounting for the effects of changing prices'.

Example

A group has a subsidiary in an overseas country where the currency has moved from 1.5 = £1 to 2 = £1 in the first six months of the year and at the year end is 7 = £1, and it is now dealt with on an auction basis. The group normally use average exchange rates to translate the results of overseas subsidiaries.

The normal averaging process does not extend to a realignment of a currency and, consequently, the closing rate of exchange should be used after the financial statements of the subsidiary are adjusted to eliminate the effects of price changes.

Examples of other consolidation problems

12.36 The examples that follow illustrate various problems that can arise in translating the results of overseas subsidiaries for consolidation with the rest of the group.

Example 1

An overseas subsidiary has sterling loans on its balance sheet. Exchange differences on these loans are taken to the subsidiary's profit and loss account in its financial statements prepared in the foreign currency. On consolidation, when the financial statements of the subsidiary are retranslated into sterling, the group wish to transfer the exchange difference on the sterling loans to reserves on the grounds that the liability remains a sterling liability.

The sterling loans are repayable out of profits denominated in the foreign currency. Consequently, the differences will affect the actual currency cash flows of the group and, therefore, should be included in the group's consolidated profit and loss account and not taken to reserves.

Example 2

A group wishes to take out a forward contract to sell dollars at the group's year end. The amount to be sold equates to the budgeted profits of the group's US division. In this type of situation, any gain or loss on translating the subsidiary's results for the year should be off-set against the matched gain or loss on the forward contract.

Example 3

A group's parent is a UK company, which has issued shares in US dollars. Because the majority of the group's business is conducted in the US and, consequently, the majority of its cash flows are in US dollars, it wishes to prepare its consolidated financial statements in US dollars.

There is no reason why such a company should not report in US dollars, especially if it has a significant number of US investors. The Registrar of Companies has indicated that he has no objection to financial statements being filed that are expressed in overseas currencies provided that the rate of exchange to the pound is given as at the group's year end date.

Example 4

A group has two overseas subsidiaries. One subsidiary has lent money to the UK parent which has in turn invested in the other subsidiary. At the year end the parent is showing an exchange loss on the loan from the first subsidiary. It wishes to know whether it can offset this loss against the gain on exchange resulting from the translation of the investment in the other subsidiary.

The loan is intercompany as is the investment in the second subsidiary. Therefore, from the group's point of view such intercompany amounts should be netted off and, consequently, the gain and the loss on the investment and the loan may be offset.

Example 5

A group takes out a currency option to hedge against losses arising from the retranslation of the net investment in subsidiaries. It wishes to know how to deal with any profits that arise from the exercise of the option.

The profit on the currency option could be taken to the profit and loss account, or, alternatively, could be taken to reserves by applying the 'hedging' concept in SSAP 20. However, as the option is taken out specifically to act as a hedge it seems logical that the preferable treatment would be to match the profit on the hedge with the loss on the investment taken to reserves.

Disclosure requirements

12.37 The extent of the disclosure requirements depends on whether the group is an exempt group. An exempt group is a group where the holding company or one of its subsidiaries is a banking company, or an insurance company and the group chooses not to prepare its consolidated financial statements in accordance with section 227 of, and Schedule 4A to, the Act.

12.38 However, all groups to which SSAP 20 applies must disclose the translation methods they have used and also the way in which they have treated the resulting exchange differences. [SSAP 20 para 59]. They must disclose also the net movement on reserves that has arisen from exchange differences. [SSAP 20 para 60(b)].

12.39 In addition, groups that are not exempt groups (as outlined in para 12.37) must disclose the net amount of their exchange gains and losses on their foreign currency borrowings less deposits, and they must separately identify the following:

- The amount they have offset in reserves under the offset procedure explained in paragraphs 12.20 to 12.34.

- The net amount they have charged or credited to the profit and loss account.

[SSAP 20 para 60(a)].

12.40 Where a company departs from the historical cost rules, Schedule 4 to the Act requires it to make certain additional disclosures on a historical cost basis. Translation at closing rates does not, however, constitute a departure from the historical cost rules in Schedule 4. Consequently, a company is not required under the provisions of the Act to make additional disclosures on a historical cost basis.

CHECKLIST TO THE REQUIREMENTS OF UK GAAP PART II - GROUPS

This is the second part of the checklist to the requirements of UK GAAP. Part I is reproduced as appendix 1 of 'Manual of Accounting - volume I'. The checklist is designed to assist a company incorporated in the UK or a group whose parent is incorporated in the UK to ensure that the statutory measurement and disclosure requirements of the Companies Act 1985 (as amended by the Companies Act 1989) have been complied with. The checklist also covers the measurement and disclosure requirements of all SSAPs, the International Stock Exchange's Continuing Obligations for listed companies, and the International Stock Exchange's General Undertaking for companies traded on the USM.

Whilst every effort has been made to make the checklist comprehensive, reference should be made to the source documents on any point of doubt or difficulty.

The checklist is not applicable to banking companies or insurance companies or groups who choose to prepare their financial statements under the rules set out in Schedule 9 to the Act. Also, the checklist does not cover special provisions for investment companies that are laid down by Part V of Schedule 4 to the Act.

The accounting provisions of the Companies Act 1989 dealt with in this checklist apply to financial statements starting on or after 23rd December 1989. Consequently, the checklist also does not apply to companies or groups whose financial statements start prior to 23rd December 1989.

To comply with the Act, a company or group must adopt one of the balance sheet formats and one of the profit and loss account formats that are set out in Schedule 4 (as amended by Schedule 4A for groups) to the Act. Unless additional disclosures are required, an item that appears in those formats is not specifically referred to in this checklist.

Reference should be made also to the company's articles of association for any special requirements regarding the presentation of financial statements. Furthermore, a company or group may be subject to other legislation that contains accounting requirements.

Each step in the checklist is accompanied by a reference to the appropriate provisions or regulation. The content of the complete checklist is given below, of which only that shown under Part II is reproduced in this appendix.

The contents of the checklist are divided into the eight sections shown below:

Part I - companies

1. General requirements
2. Directors' report
3. Accounting policies
4. Profit and loss account and related notes
5. Balance sheet and related notes
6. Statement of source and application of funds

Part II - groups

7. Group accounts and accounting for business combinations

7.1 Undertakings included in consolidation
7.2 Subsidiaries excluded from consolidation
7.3 General consolidation rules
7.4 Year ends of subsidiaries
7.5 Accounting policies
7.6 Elimination of intra-group transactions
7.7 Merger relief
7.8 Acquisition of subsidiaries
7.9 Acquisition accounting
7.10 Merger accounting
7.11 Disposal of subsidiaries
7.12 Minority interests
7.13 Associated undertakings
7.13 Joint ventures
7.15 Details of parents
7.16 Foreign currency translation

8. Summary financial statements

7. GROUP ACCOUNTS AND ACCOUNTING FOR BUSINESS COMBINATIONS

Introduction

(a) If the company has subsidiary undertakings, the financial statements must include consolidated financial statements.

Sec 227(1) SSAP 14 paras 15, 19-22

(b) Consolidated financial statements are not required, however, where the company is itself a subsidiary undertaking and its immediate parent is established under the law of an EC Member State where either of the following apply:

(i) The company is a wholly-owned subsidiary of that parent.

Sec 228(1)(a) SSAP 14 para 19

(ii) The parent holds more than 50 per cent of the shares in the company and notice requesting the preparation of consolidated financial statements has not been served on the company by its minority shareholders.

Sec 228(1)(b)

(c) A parent company need not prepare group accounts for a financial year in which the group headed by that company qualifies as a small or medium-sized group and is not an ineligible group. A small or medium-sized group is one where two or more of the following conditions are satisfied:

Sec 248(1)(2)(3) (4)

(i) Aggregate turnover is not more than £8 million net or £9.6 million gross.
(ii) Aggregate balance sheet total is not more than £3.9 million net or £4.7 million gross.
(iii) Aggregate number of employees in not more than 250.

The gross figures relate to the relevant figures before consolidation adjustments and the net figures relate to the relevant figures after consolidation adjustments. An ineligible group is one where any of the group's members is:

(i) A public company or a body corporate that has the power under its constitution to offer its shares or debentures to the public and may lawfully exercise that power.
(ii) An authorised institution under the Banking Act 1987.
(iii) An insurance company to which Part II of the Insurance Companies Act 1982 applies.
(iv) An authorised person under the Financial Services Act 1986.

(c) Consolidated financial statements should cover the parent and all its subsidiaries at home and overseas unless one, or more, of the circumstances in step 7.2.1 apply.

Sec 229(1)

(d) Where all of the company's subsidiaries fall to be excluded for any of the reasons included in step 7.2.1 consolidated financial statements need not be prepared.

Sec 229(5)

7.1 Undertakings included in consolidation

7.1.1 Have the following undertakings been included in the consolidated financial statements, where the parent:

(a) Holds a majority of the undertaking's voting rights?

Sec 258(2)(a)
SSAP 14 para 21(b)

(b) Is a member of the undertaking and has the right to appoint or remove a majority of its board of directors?

Sec 258(2)(b)

(c) Has the right to exercise a dominant influence over the undertaking by virtue of provisions contained in the undertaking's memorandum or articles?

Sec 258(2)(c)(i)

(d) Has the right to exercise a dominant influence over the undertaking by virtue of a control contract?

Sec 258(2)(c)(ii)

(e) Is a member of the undertaking and controls alone, pursuant to an agreement with other shareholders or members, a majority of the undertaking's voting rights?

Sec 258(2)(d)

(f) Has a participating interest in the undertaking and actually exercises a dominant influence over it?

Sec 258(4)(a)

(g) Has a participating interest in the undertaking and it and the subsidiary undertaking are managed on a unified basis?

Sec 258(4)(b)

Notes:

(a) Voting rights in 7.1.1(a) and (e) refer to the rights conferred on shareholders in respect of their shares or, in the case of an undertaking not having a share capital, on members, to vote at general meetings of the undertaking on all, or substantially all, matters.

10A Sch 2(1)

(b) The reference in 7.1.1(b) to the right to appoint or remove a majority of the board of directors is to the right to appoint or remove directors holding a majority of the voting rights at meetings of the board on all, or substantially all, matters.

10A Sch 3(1)

(c) For the purposes of 7.1.1(c) and (d) an undertaking shall not be regarded as having the right to exercise a dominant influence over another undertaking unless it has a right to give directions with respect to the operating and financial policies of that other undertaking which its directors are obliged to comply with whether or not they are for the benefit of that other undertaking.

10A Sch 4(1)

(d) In 7.1.1(d) a 'control contract' means a contract in writing conferring such a right which is of a kind authorised by the memorandum or articles of the undertaking in relation to which the right is exercisable, and is permitted by the law under which that undertaking is established.

10A Sch 4(2)

(e) A 'participating interest' in 7.1.1(f) and (g) means an interest held by an undertaking in the shares of another undertaking which it holds on a long-term basis for the purpose of securing a contribution to its activities by the exercise of control or influence arising from or related to that interest. A holding of 20 per cent or more of the shares (i.e. by number) in an undertaking shall be presumed to be a participating interest unless the contrary is shown. Interests in shares for this purpose includes an interest that is convertible into an interest in shares and options to acquire shares or any such interest.	Sec 260(1) (2)(3)
(f) The right to exercise a dominant influence in note (d) above does not apply to the expression 'actually exercises a dominant influence' in 7.1.1(f).	10A Sch 4(3)

7.1.2	Do the consolidated financial statements deal with all subsidiary undertakings including the following where they fall to be treated as subsidiaries under 7.1.1 above:	Sec 259(1)
	(a) Bodies corporate?	
	(b) Partnerships?	
	(c) Unincorporated associations carrying on a trade or business, with or without a view to profit?	

Notes:	
(a) For undertakings with share capital (such as bodies corporate), references to shares in 7.1.1 are to allotted shares.	Sec 259(2)(a)
(b) In relation to an undertaking with capital but no share capital (such as partnerships), references to shares in 7.1.1 are to rights to share in the capital of the undertaking.	Sec 259(2)(b)
(c) In relation to an undertaking without capital, references to shares in 7.1.1 are to interests either conferring any right to share in the profits or liability to contribute to the losses of the undertaking, or giving rise to an obligation to contribute to the debts or expenses of the undertaking in the event of winding-up.	Sec 259(2)(c)
(d) Other expressions appropriate to companies that are used in 7.1.1 shall be construed, in relation to an undertaking that is not a company, as references to the corresponding persons, officers, documents or organs, as the case may be, appropriate to undertakings of that description.	Sec 259(3)

7.1.3	Do the consolidated financial statements include all undertakings that are subsidiaries of undertakings that are themselves subsidiaries of the parent (i.e. sub-subsidiaries)?	Sec 258(5)
7.1.4	Where an undertaking is consolidated for the first time because of the change in definitions of subsidiaries (outlined in steps 7.1.1 to 7.1.3) have the previous year's figures been adjusted to consolidate the subsidiary?	4 Sch 4(1)

Note: Where an investment in an undertaking has to be consolidated for the first time as a result of the changes in the definitions of subsidiaries, certain information concerning the fair values of assets acquired or other information needed for the 'set-off' calculation to ascertain the goodwill arising on the acquisition may not be available. Where this is so, the calculation may be based on the earliest known values, but a note must disclose the date of the valuation or other 'set-off' information used.	SI 1990/355 2 Sch 8

Disclosure requirements

Note: (a) The information required by 7.1.5 and 7.1.6 need not be given in respect of an undertaking which is established under the law of a country outside the UK, or which carries on business outside the UK, if in the directors' opinion such disclosure would be seriously prejudicial to the business of the undertaking, or to the business of the parent or any of its subsidiaries, and the Secretary of State agrees that the information need not be disclosed. Where advantage is taken of this exemption, it should be stated in a note to the financial statements.	Sec 231(3) (4)
(b) Where disclosure of the information required by 7.1.5 and 7.1.6 would lead in the directors' opinion to disclosure of excessive length, the information need only be given in respect of (i) the undertakings whose results or financial position, in the directors' opinion principally affect the figures shown in the company's financial statements and (ii) undertakings excluded from consolidation. Where advantage is taken of this provision, the notes to the company's financial statements should state that the information is only given for those subsidiaries that in the directors' opinion principally affect the figures shown in the financial statements. Furthermore, the full information including that given in the financial statements must be annexed to the next annual return.	Sec 231(5) (6)

7.1.5 Is the following information given in respect of each subsidiary that is a subsidiary at the end of the financial year (including those excluded from consolidation):

(a) The name of each subsidiary and an indication of the nature of its business?	5 Sch 15 SSAP 14 para 33(b)
(b) The proportion of the nominal value of the issued shares of each class held by the group?	SSAP 14 para 33(a)
(b) One of the following, where the undertaking is:	5 Sch 15

(i) Incorporated outside Great Britain, its country of incorporation?
(ii) Incorporated in Great Britain, whether it is registered in England and Wales or in Scotland?
(iii) Unincorporated, the address of its principal place of business?

(c) Whether the subsidiary is included in the consolidation and, if not, the reasons for excluding it from consolidation (see further 7.2.1)?	5 Sch 15
(d) The condition set out in 7.1.1 by which the undertaking is a subsidiary where the condition is one other than that specified in 7.1.1(a)?	5 Sch 15

7.1.6 Is the following information given separately with respect to the shares   5 Sch 16
of a subsidiary held by the parent and with respect to those held by the
group, if different:

(a) The identity of each class of shares held?

(b) The proportion of the nominal value of the shares of that class
represented by those shares?

7.2   Subsidiaries excluded from consolidation

7.2.1 Has a subsidiary been excluded from the consolidated financial
statements where one (or more) of the following reasons apply:

(a) Inclusion of the subsidiary is not material for the purpose of giving   Sec 229(2)
a true and fair view?

> Note: Two or more such undertakings may be excluded only if taken
> together they are not material.

(b) Severe long-term restrictions substantially hinder the parent's   Sec
exercise of its rights over the assets or the management of the   229(3)(a)
undertaking?   SSAP 14
para 21(c)

(c) The information necessary for preparing consolidated financial   Sec
statements cannot be obtained without disproportionate expense or   229(3)(b)
undue delay?

(d) The interest is held by the parent exclusively with a view to   Sec
subsequent resale and the undertaking has not previously been included   229(3)(c)
in the consolidation?   SSAP 14
para 21(d)

(e) The activities of one or more subsidiaries are so different from   Sec 229(4)
those of other undertakings included in the consolidation that their   SSAP 14
inclusion would be incompatible with the obligation to give a true and   para 21(a)
fair view?

> Notes:
> (a) This exclusion does not apply, however, merely because some of   Sec 229(4)
> the undertakings are industrial, some commercial and some provide
> services, or because they carry on industrial or commercial activities
> involving different products or provide different services.
> (b) The exclusions outlined in 7.2.1(b), (d) and (e) are mandatory   SSAP 14
> under SSAP 14. The other exclusions are optional under the Act.   para 21

Disclosure requirements

7.2.2 Where a subsidiary is excluded from consolidation because of severe   SSAP 14
restrictions (step 7.2.1(b)), is the amount of the group's investment in   para 25
the subsidiary stated in the consolidated balance sheet at the amount at
which it would have been included under the equity method of
accounting at the date the restrictions came into force?

7.2.3 In respect of the type of subsidiary described in step 7.2.1(b) have no   SSAP 14
further accruals been made for its profits or losses?   para 25

7.2.4	If the amount at which the investment in step 7.2.1(b) is stated has been impaired by a permanent diminution in value of the investment, has provision for the loss been made through the consolidated profit and loss account?	SSAP 14 para 25
7.2.5	When determining any necessary provision for step 7.2.4, were investments considered individually and not in aggregate?	SSAP 14 para 25

7.2.6   Where a subsidiary is excluded from consolidation because of severe restrictions (step 7.2.1(b)), are the following disclosed in the group accounts: **SSAP 14 para 26**

(a) Its net assets?
(b) Its profits or losses for the period?
(c) Any amounts included in the consolidated profit and loss account in respect of:

     (i) Dividends received?
     (ii) Writing down of the investment?

7.2.7   Where a subsidiary is excluded from consolidation because control is intended to be only temporary (step 7.2.1(d)), is the temporary investment in the subsidiary stated in the consolidated balance sheet as a current asset at the lower of cost and net realisable value?   **SSAP 14 para 27**

7.2.8   Where a subsidiary is excluded from consolidation because of dissimilar activities (step 7.2.2(e)), do the consolidated financial statements include:

(a) The group's interest and the amount of profit and loss attributable to that interest by the equity method of accounting?   **4A Sch 18**

(b) Separate financial statements for that subsidiary?   **SSAP 14 para 23**

7.2.9   Do these separate financial statements required in 7.2.8(b) include the following: **SSAP 14 para 23**

(a) A note of the parent's interest?
(b) Particulars of intra-group balances?
(c) The nature of transactions with the rest of the group?
(d) A reconciliation with the amount included in the consolidated financial statements for the group's investment in the subsidiary (which should be stated under the equity method of accounting)?

Note: Separate financial statements of subsidiaries with similar operations may be combined if appropriate.

7.2.10   In respect of subsidiaries excluded from consolidation, are the following disclosed in the group accounts:

(a) The reasons for excluding the subsidiaries?   **SSAP 14 para 28(a) 5 Sch 15(4)**

(b) The names of the subsidiaries excluded?   **SSAP 14 para 28(b) 5 Sch 15(2)**

(c) Any goodwill or negative goodwill arising on acquisition (see step 7.9.5) to the extent that it is not written off?   SSAP 14 para 28(c)

(d) Where the group's investment in such an undertaking is not included in the consolidated financial statements by way of the equity method of accounting, the aggregate amount of its capital and reserves as at the end of its relevant financial year and its profit or loss for that year?   5 Sch 17(1)(2)

(e) A statement of any qualifications in the auditors' reports on the subsidiary's financial statements for the year ending with or during the year of the company that are material from the point of view of members of the parent company and that are not covered in the consolidated financial statements?   5 Sch 18(2)

(f) If the information required by 7.2.10(e) is not obtainable, a statement to that effect?   5 Sch 18(3)

Note:

(a) The information in 7..2.10(d) is not needed where the undertaking is not required by any provisions of the Act to deliver a copy of its balance sheet for its relevant financial year and does not otherwise publish that balance sheet in Great Britain or elsewhere and the group's holding is less than 50 per cent of the nominal value of the shares in the undertaking.   5 Sch17(2)

(b) For the purpose of 7.2.10(d), 'relevant financial year' means the undertaking's financial year that ends with that of the parent, or its financial year that ends last before the end of the parent's financial year.   5 Sch 17(4)

(c) The information required in 7.2.10(e) above should include details of any notes to the subsidiaries' financial statements calling attention to a matter without which the auditors' report would have referred to that matter in the qualification.   5 Sch 18(2)

(d) The information required by 7.2.10 need not be given in respect of an undertaking which is established under the law of a country outside the UK, or which carries on business outside the UK, if in the directors' opinion such disclosure would be seriously prejudicial to the business of the undertaking, or to the business of the parent or any of its subsidiaries, and the Secretary of State agrees that the information need not be disclosed. Where advantage is taken of this exemption, it should be stated in a note to the financial statements.   Sec 231(3)

7.3   General consolidation rules

7.3.1   Do the consolidated financial statements comply so far as practicable with the provisions of Schedule 4 as if the undertakings included in consolidation were a single company (see Part I of the checklist)?   4A Sch 1(1)

7.3.2   Do the consolidated financial statements incorporate in full the information contained in the separate financial statements of the parent company and the subsidiaries consolidated with such adjustments as authorised as required by Schedule 4A and such adjustments (if any) as may be appropriate to accord with generally accepted accounting principles or practice?   4A Sch 2(1)

7.4 Year ends of subsidiaries

7.4.1 Wherever practicable for the purposes of consolidated financial statements, have the financial statements of all subsidiaries been prepared:	SSAP 14 para 17 Sec 223(5)

(a) To the same accounting date as the parent?
(b) For identical accounting periods as the parent?

7.4.2 If a subsidiary does not prepare its financial statements to the same date as its parent, because its financial year differs from that of its parent, are the consolidated financial statements made up from either:	4A Sch 2(2)

(a) The financial statements of the subsidiary for its financial year ending not more than three months before the year end of the parent?
(b) Interim financial statements prepared by the subsidiary as at the end of the parent's financial year?

7.4.3 In the situation in 7.4.2(a), have appropriate adjustments been made to the consolidated financial statements for any abnormal transactions in the period between the subsidiary's year end and that of its parent?	SSAP 14 para 18
7.4.4 In addition, where the financial year of any subsidiary does not coincide with that of its parent, are the following disclosed:	5 Sch 19 SSAP 14 para 18

(a) The names of the principal subsidiaries that have different year ends?

(b) The date on which the year of each such subsidiary ended, or where there are a number of such subsidiaries, the earliest and latest of those dates?

(c) The reasons why the company's directors consider that the financial year of such a subsidiary should not end with that of the parent?

Notes:	
(a) This disclosure is required whether or not the subsidiary is dealt with in the consolidated financial statements.	5 Sch 19
(b) The information required by 7.4.4 need not be given in respect of an undertaking which is established under the law of a country outside the UK, or which carries on business outside the UK, if in the directors' opinion such disclosure would be seriously prejudicial to the business of the undertaking, or to the business of the parent or any of its subsidiaries, and the Secretary of State agrees that the information need not be disclosed. Where advantage is taken of this exemption, it should be stated in a note to the financial statements.	Sec 231(3) (4)
(c) Where disclosure of the information required by 7.4.4 would lead in the directors' opinion to disclosure of excessive length, the information need only be given in respect of (i) the undertakings whose results or financial position, in the directors' opinion principally affect the figures shown in the company's financial statements and (ii) undertakings excluded from consolidation. Where advantage is taken of this provision, the notes to the company's financial statements should state that the information is only given for those subsidiaries that in the directors' opinion principally affect the figures shown in the financial statements. Furthermore, the full information including that given in the financial statements must be annexed to the next annual return.	Sec 231(5) (6)

7.4.5   Where the accounting period of a principal subsidiary is of a different   SSAP 14
         length from that of the holding company, is the accounting period   para 18
         involved stated?

7.5   Accounting policies

7.5.1   Is there a description of the bases on which subsidiaries have been   SSAP 14
         dealt with in the consolidated financial statements?   para 15

7.5.2   When preparing the consolidated financial statements has the holding   SSAP 14
         company used uniform accounting policies?   para 16

7.5.3   Where group accounting policies have not been adopted in the financial   4A Sch 3(1)
         statements of a subsidiary, have appropriate adjustments been made in   SSAP 14
         the consolidated financial statements?   para 16

7.5.4   Where it is impracticable to make appropriate adjustments and the   4A Sch 3(2)
         directors' consider that there are special reasons for using different   SSAP 14
         accounting rules: para 16

         (a) Are those policies used generally acceptable?

         (b) Is there disclosure of:

              (i) Particulars of the different policies used and reasons for their
              use?
              (ii) An indication of the amounts of the assets and liabilities
              involved?
              (iii) Where practicable, an indication of the effect on results and
              net assets of the adoption of different policies?
              (iv) The reasons for using different policies?

7.5.5   If there are any differences of accounting rules between those used in   4A Sch 4
         the parent's individual financial statements and those used in the group
         financial statements are the following disclosed in the group's
         consolidated financial statements:
         (a) The nature of the differences?
         (b) The reasons for the differences?

7.6   Elimination of intra-group transactions

7.6.1   Have debts and liabilities between undertakings included in the   4A Sch 6(1)
         consolidation and income and expenditure relating to transactions
         between such undertakings, been eliminated?

7.6.2   Where profits and losses resulting from transactions between   4A Sch 6(2)
         undertakings included in the consolidation are included in the book
         value of assets, have they been eliminated in the consolidated financial
         statements?

7.6.3   Where the elimination in 7.6.2 has been made in proportion to the
         group's interest in the shares of the undertaking, does the resulting
         position give a true and fair view?

7.6.4　Is the extent of any significant restrictions on the ability of the holding company to distribute the retained profits of the group (other than those shown as non-distributable) disclosed?　SSAP 14 para 36

7.7　Merger relief

> Note: The information required by 7.7 need not be given in respect of an undertaking which is established under the law of a country outside the UK, or which carries on business outside the UK, if in the directors' opinion, such disclosure would be seriously prejudicial to the business of the undertaking, or to the business of the parent or any of its subsidiaries, and the Secretary of State agrees that the information need not be disclosed. Where advantage is taken of this exemption, it should be stated in a note to the financial statements.
>
> Sec 231(3) (4)

7.7.1　If during the year the company entered into an arrangement to which section 131(2) (merger relief) applied, are the following disclosed:　5 Sch 29(2)

(a) The name of the company acquired?

(b) The number, the nominal value and the class of shares allotted for the acquisition?

(c) The number, the nominal value and the class of shares the acquired company issued or transferred to the company, or cancelled, as part of the arrangement?

(d) Particulars of the accounting treatment that the company adopted in its own financial statements and in its consolidated financial statements in respect of the issue, transfer or cancellation referred to in 7.7.1(c)?

(e) Particulars of the extent to which, and the manner in which, the consolidated profit or loss for the year is affected by any profit or loss of the acquired company (and any of its subsidiaries) that arose before the allotment?

> Note: The time of the arrangement should be determined as follows:
> (a) Where as a result of the arrangement the other company becomes a subsidiary, the date on which it does so or, if the arrangement in question becomes binding only on the fulfilment of a condition, the date on which that condition is fulfilled.
> (b) Where the other company is already a subsidiary when the arrangement is proposed, the date on which the shares are allotted or, if they are allotted on different days, the first day.
>
> 5 Sch 29(4)

7.7.2　If during the year, or during either of the two immediately preceding years, the company entered into an arrangement to which section 131(2) (merger relief) applied, is there disclosure of the following amounts that are included in the consolidated profit and loss account:　5 Sch 29(3)

(a) The net amount of any profit or loss that the company (or any of its subsidiaries) realised on the disposal of shares in the acquired company?

(b) The net amount of any profit or loss that the company (or any of its subsidiaries) realised on the disposal of any assets that were fixed assets of the acquired company (or any of its subsidiaries) at the date of the acquisition and that were subsequently transferred to the company (or any of its subsidiaries)?

(c) Any net profit or loss (or part thereof) that the company (or any of its subsidiaries) realised on the disposal of shares in a company (X) other than the acquired company where the profit or loss was attributable to the fact that, at the time of the disposal, the assets of X (or any of its subsidiaries) included one or both often following:

(i) Shares in the acquired company?

(ii) Assets that had been fixed assets of the acquired company (or any of its subsidiaries) at the date of the acquisition but which had been subsequently transferred to X (or one of its subsidiaries)?

7.7.3	Where any amount is disclosed under steps 7.7.1 to 7.7.2 is there an explanation of the transaction that gave rise to the amount?	5 Sch 29(3)

7.8   Acquisition of subsidiaries

7.8.1	Are acquisitions accounted for by the acquisition method of accounting unless the conditions for merger accounting are met and the merger method of accounting is adopted?	4A Sch 8
7.8.2	Has the effective date for the acquisition of a subsidiary been taken as the earlier of the date on which consideration passes and the date on which an offer becomes or is declared unconditional?	SSAP 14 para 32

Note: This applies irrespective of whether the acquiring company has the right under the agreement to share in profits of the acquired business from an earlier date.	SSAP 14 para 32

7.9   Acquisition accounting

7.9.1	Where an undertaking becomes a subsidiary, have the identifiable assets and liabilities of the undertaking acquired been included in the consolidated balance sheet at their fair values as at the date of acquisition?	4A Sch 9(2) SSAP 14 para 29 SSAP 23 para 16

Note: 'Identifiable assets and liabilities' of an undertaking acquired are the assets and liabilities that are capable of being disposed of or discharged separately, without disposing of a business of the undertaking.	4A Sch 9(2)

7.9.2	If the adjustment in 7.9.1 is not done by means of adjusting the values in the books of the acquired company, has it been done on consolidation?	SSAP 14 para 29
7.9.3	Is the income and expenditure of the undertaking acquired brought into the consolidated financial statements only from the date of acquisition?	4A Sch 9(3) SSAP 23 para 17

7.9.4   On consolidation, has the acquisition cost of the interest in the undertaking's shares held by the parent and its other subsidiaries been set off against the group's interest in the adjusted capital and reserves of the undertaking acquired?   4A Sch 9(4)

> Notes:
> (a) Any difference between the purchase consideration and the fair value ascribed to net tangible assets and identifiable intangible assets (e.g. trade marks, patents, development expenditure) will represent goodwill or a negative consolidation difference.   4A Sch 9(5) SSAP 14 para 29 SSAP 23 para 16
>
> (b)For the purpose of 7.9.4 above: 4A Sch 9(4)
>
> (i) 'The acquisition cost' means the amount of any cash consideration and the fair value of any other consideration, together with such amount (if any) in respect of fees and other expenses of the acquisition as the company may determine.
> (ii) 'The adjusted capital and reserves' of the undertaking acquired means its capital and reserves at the date of the acquisition after adjusting the identifiable assets and liabilities of the undertaking to fair values as at that date.

Consolidation goodwill

7.9.5   Is the amount attributed to purchased goodwill the difference between the fair value of the consideration given and the aggregate of the fair values of the identifiable assets and liabilities acquired?   SSAP 22 para 36 4A Sch 9(5)

7.9.6   Does the amount of purchased goodwill exclude any value attributable to identifiable intangibles?   SSAP 22 para 37 4A Sch 9(2)

7.9.7   Has goodwill arising on consolidation been treated in either of the following ways:
(a) Eliminated from the consolidated financial statements immediately on acquisition against reserves?   SSAP 22 para 39

(b) Amortised through the profit and loss account in arriving at the profit or loss on ordinary activities on a systematic basis over a period chosen by the directors that should not exceed its useful economic life?   4 Sch 21 SSAP 22 para 41

> Notes:
> (a) The useful economic life of goodwill should be estimated at the time of acquisition. It should not include any allowance for the effects of subsequent expenditure or other circumstances subsequently affecting the company since these would have the effect of creating non-purchased goodwill.   SSAP 22 para 41(b)
> (b) It is acceptable to use both the immediate write-off treatment and the amortisation treatment in respect of goodwill that relates to different acquisitions, as long as the accounting policies provide for the elimination of goodwill on a basis consistent with the provisions above.   SSAP 22 para 42

7.9.8   Is goodwill arising on consolidation shown at its historical amount less amortisation and not revalued?   4 Sch 31(1)
SSAP 22
para 41(a)

7.9.9   Where there is a permanent diminution in the value of goodwill included in the consolidated balance sheet has it been written down immediately?   4 Sch 19(2)
SSAP 22
para 41(a)

7.9.10   Have any revisions to the useful economic life of goodwill only been to shorten its estimated life and not to increase it?   SSAP 22
para 41(c)

7.9.11   Have negative consolidation differences (i.e. negative goodwill) been credited directly to reserves?   SSAP 22
para 40

7.9.12   Has only goodwill arising on acquisitions that took place prior to the introduction of the Companies Act 1989 been written off direct to the revaluation reserve?   SI 1990/355
2 Sch 6

> Note: For 7.9.12 the relevant provisions of the Companies Act 1989 apply to accounting periods starting on or after 23rd December 1989. Consequently, goodwill on acquisitions made in prior periods can remain written off to the revaluation reserve if it was originally written off to that reserve.   SI 1990/355
> 2 Sch 6

Disclosure requirements

7.9.13   Do the consolidated financial statements that deal with the period in which an acquisition takes place disclose the following:

(a) The names of the undertakings acquired (where a group was acquired the name of its parent is sufficient)?   4A Sch 13(2)(a)
SSAP 23
para 21

(b) That the combination has been accounted for by the acquisition method of accounting?   4A Sch 13(2)(b)
SSAP 23
para 21

(c) The number and class of the securities issued in respect of the acquisition?   SSAP 23
para 21

(d) Details of any other consideration given?   SSAP 23
para 21

(e) The nature and amount of significant accounting adjustments by the combining companies to achieve consistency of accounting policies?   SSAP 23
para 21

> Note: The information required in 7.9.13(a) and (b) need not be given in respect of an undertaking that is either established under the law of a country outside the UK or carries on business outside the UK, if in the parent directors' opinion the disclosure would be seriously prejudicial to the business of that undertaking or to the business of the parent or any of its subsidiaries and the Secretary of State agrees that the information should not be disclosed.   4A Sch 16

7.9.14 Do the consolidated financial statements disclose the following in respect of all acquisitions that significantly affect the figures in the consolidated financial statements:

(a) The profit or loss of the undertaking or group acquired for the period from the beginning of the financial year of the undertaking (or parent if it is a group) up to the date of acquisition (after making any necessary consolidation adjustments)? — 4A Sch 13(4)(a)(7)

(b) The date on which the financial year referred to in 7.9.14(a) began? — 4A Sch 13(4)

(c) The profit or loss of the undertaking or group acquired for the previous financial year (after making any necessary consolidation adjustments)? — 4A Sch 13(4)(b)(7)

(d) The date from which the results of major acquisitions have been brought into the accounts (that is, the effective date of those acquisitions)? — SSAP 23 para 22

> Note: The information required in 7.9.14(a), (b) and (c) need not be given in respect of an undertaking that is either established under the law of a country outside the UK or carries on business outside the UK, if in the parent directors' opinion the disclosure would be seriously prejudicial to the business of that undertaking or to the business of the parent or any of its subsidiaries and the Secretary of State agrees that the information should not be disclosed. — 4A Sch 16

7.9.15 In the case of material additions to the group, do the consolidated financial statements contain sufficient information about the results of the subsidiaries acquired to enable shareholders to appreciate the effect on the consolidated results? — SSAP 14 para 30 SSAP 23 para 22

> Note: The information required in 7.9.16, 7.9.17 and 7.9.18 need not be given in respect of an undertaking that is either established under the law of a country outside the UK or carries on business outside the UK, if in the parent directors' opinion the disclosure would be seriously prejudicial to the business of that undertaking or to the business of the parent or any of its subsidiaries and the Secretary of State agrees that the information should not be disclosed. — 4A Sch 16

7.9.16 Do the financial statements disclose separately, where material, the composition and fair value of the consideration given by the parent and its subsidiaries and the amount of goodwill arising from each acquisition made during the period? — 4A Sch 13(3) SSAP 22 paras 44, 47

7.9.17 For each material acquisition is a table provided that shows the book values recorded in the undertaking's books immediately prior to the acquisition and the fair values at the date of acquisition of each class of assets and liabilities of the undertaking or group acquired (after making any necessary consolidation adjustments)? — 4A Sch 13(5)(7) SSAP 22 para 48

7.9.18 Does the table include the amounts of any goodwill or negative goodwill arising on the acquisition?

4A Sch
13(5)

7.9.19 Is an explanation given of the reasons for differences between the values given in 7.9.17 above for each major category of assets and liabilities analysed between:
(a) Revaluations?
(b) Provisions for future trading losses?
(c) Other provisions?
(d) Bringing accounting policies into line with those of the acquiring group?
(e) Any other major item?

SSAP 22
para 48
4A Sch
13(5)

7.9.20 Are movements on the provisions in 7.9.19 disclosed and analysed between amounts used and amounts released unused or applied for another purpose?

SSAP 22
para 49

> Note: Sufficient details should be given to identify the extent to which the provisions have proven unnecessary.

SSAP 22
para 49

7.9.21 To the extent that the fair value of the assets and liabilities, or the consideration, can only be determined on a provisional basis at the end of the accounting period is this stated and the reasons given?

SSAP 22
para 50

7.9.22 Where there are subsequent material adjustments to provisional fair values, with a consequent adjustment to goodwill, are those adjustments disclosed and explained?

SSAP 22
para 50

7.9.23 Are the disclosures in 7.9.17 to 7.9.22 given separately for each material acquisition and in aggregate for other acquisitions where these are material in total although not so individually?

SSAP 22
para 51

7.9.24 For each acquisition made during the period, is the method of dealing with goodwill arising on consolidation disclosed, showing whether it has been set off against the merger reserve or other reserves or has been carried forward as an intangible asset?

SSAP 22
para 47

7.9.25 Where the group treats purchased goodwill as an asset, does the company or group show purchased goodwill as a separate item under intangible fixed assets in the balance sheet or in the notes until the group has fully written off the purchased goodwill?

4 Sch
formats
SSAP 22
para 45

> Notes:
> (a) A group may combine goodwill with another intangible asset sub-heading in either of the two following circumstances:
>
> (i) Where the individual amounts combined are not material to an assessment of the state of affairs of the group.
> (ii) Where the combination facilitates the assessment of the state of affairs of the group. (A note to the financial statements must disclose the individual amounts of any items combined in this way.)
>
> (b) SSAP 22 does not specifically permit a company or group to combine goodwill with another item in either of these two circumstances. However, the preliminary paragraph of SSAP 22 says that a company or group need not apply the Standard to immaterial items.

4 Sch 3(4)

7.9.26 Where the group treats purchased goodwill as an asset, does the group disclose the movement on the goodwill account during the year? Does this disclosure including the following:

4 Sch 42
SSAP 22
para 45(a)

(a) The cost of goodwill at the beginning and at the end of the year?

(b) The accumulated amortisation at the beginning and at the end of the year?

(c) The net book value of goodwill at the beginning and at the end of the year?

(d) The amount of goodwill that the company or group has amortised through the profit and loss account during the year?

7.9.27 Where the group treats purchased goodwill as an asset, does the group disclose the period it has selected for amortising the goodwill that relates to each major acquisition?

4 Sch 21(4)
SSAP 22
para 45(b)

7.9.28 Where the group treats goodwill as an asset, does the group disclose the reasons for choosing the period it has selected for amortising the goodwill?

4 Sch 21(4)

7.9.29 Does the group disclose the cumulative amount of goodwill written off in the current and earlier financial years net of any amounts attributable to subsidiaries disposed of?

4A Sch 14

Notes:
(a) The information required in 7.9.29 need not be given in respect of an undertaking that is either established under the law of a country outside the UK or carries on business outside the UK, if in the parent directors' opinion the disclosure would be seriously prejudicial to the business of that undertaking or to the business of the parent or any of its subsidiaries and the Secretary of State agrees that the information should not be disclosed.

4A Sch 16

(b) Where it is not possible to ascertain the cumulative amount of past goodwill written off on a particular acquisition made prior to 23rd December 1989 or where to do so would cause unreasonable expense or delay, that amount does not have to be shown in the cumulative figure. However, the notes to the consolidated financial statements must disclose that an amount has not been included in the cumulative figure on those grounds.

SI 1990/355
2 Sch 9

7.9.30 Where a group's accounting treatment of goodwill that existed at the time that SSAP 22 came into effect differs from the policy it has followed in respect of all other goodwill, does the company or group disclose the following:

SSAP 22
para 46

(a) The accounting treatment of goodwill that existed at the time the Standard came into effect?

(b) The amounts involved?

Note: SSAP 22 was originally effective in respect of financial statements relating to accounting periods beginning on or after 1st January 1985.

7.10   Merger accounting

7.10.1 Is merger accounting only used where the following conditions are satisfied:

(a) At least 90 per cent of the nominal value of the relevant shares in the undertaking acquired is held by or on behalf of the parent company and its subsidiary undertakings?	4A Sch 10(1)(a)

> Note: The reference to 'relevant shares' in 7.10.1(a) is to those shares carrying unrestricted rights to participation both in distributions and in the assets of the undertaking upon liquidation.   4A Sch 10(2)

(b) The proportion in 7.10.1(a) was attained pursuant to an arrangement providing for the issue of equity shares by the parent company or one or more of its subsidiary undertakings?	4A Sch 10(1)(b)
(c) The fair value of any consideration other than the issue of equity shares given pursuant to the arrangement by the parent and its subsidiaries did not exceed 10 per cent of the nominal value of the equity shares issued?	4A Sch 10(1)(c)
(d) The combination results from an offer to the holders of all equity shares and the holders of all voting shares which are not already held by the offeror?	SSAP 23 para 11(a) 4A Sch 10(d)
(e) The offeror has secured, as a result of the offer, a holding of at least 90 per cent of all equity shares of the offeree (taking each class separately)?	SSAP 23 para 11(b) 4A Sch 10(d)
(f) The offeror has secured, as a result of the offer, a holding of at least 90 per cent of the votes of the offeree?	SSAP 23 para 11(b) 4A Sch 10(d)
(g) Immediately prior to the offer, the offeror does not hold 20 per cent or more of all equity shares of the offeree (taking each class of equity separately)?	SSAP 23 para 11(c) 4A Sch 10(d)
(h) Immediately prior to the offer, the offeror does not hold shares carrying 20 per cent or more of the votes of the offeree?	SSAP 23 para 11(c) 4A Sch 10(d)
(i) Not less than 90 per cent of the fair value of the total consideration given for the equity share capital (including that given for shares already held) is in the form of equity share capital?	SSAP 23 para 11(d) 4A Sch 10(d)
(j) Not less than 90 per cent of the fair value of the total consideration given for voting non-equity share capital (including that given for shares already held) is in the form of equity and/or voting non-equity share capital?	SSAP 23 para 11(d) 4A Sch 10(d)

> Note: Where an acquisition has been consolidated using merger accounting in an accounting period beginning before 23rd December 1989, it may continue to be accounted for on that basis in subsequent periods even though the conditions outlined above may not have been complied with.
>
> SI 1990/355
> 2 Sch 7

7.10.2 Are the assets and the liabilities of the undertaking acquired brought into the consolidated financial statements at the figures at which they stand in the undertaking's financial statements, subject to any necessary consolidation adjustment as outlined above?

4A Sch
11(2)
SSAP 23
para 18

7.10.3 Is the income and expenditure of the undertaking acquired included in the consolidated financial statements for the entire period, including the period before the acquisition?

4A Sch
11(3)
SSAP 23
para 19

7.10.4 Do the consolidated financial statements show corresponding amounts relating to the previous financial year as if the undertaking acquired had been included in the consolidation throughout that year?

4A Sch
11(4)
SSAP 23
para 19

7.10.5 Is the nominal value of the issued share capital of the undertaking acquired set off against the aggregate of the following two items:

4A Sch
11(5)

(a) The 'appropriate amount' of the qualifying shares issued by the parent or its subsidiaries in consideration for the acquisition of shares in the undertaking acquired?

(b) The fair value of any other consideration for the acquisition of the shares in the undertaking acquired, determined as at the date when those shares were acquired?

> Note: In relation to 7.10.5(a) 'qualifying shares' means either of the following:
> (a) For shares in relation to which merger relief applies, the appropriate amount is the nominal value (see further 7.7 regarding the provisions of merger relief).
> (b) For shares in relation to which group reconstruction relief applies, the appropriate amount is the nominal value together with any minimum premium value within the meaning of section 132 (see further 7.7 regarding the provisions of merger relief).
>
> 4A Sch
> 11(7)

Disclosure requirements

7.10.6 Is the difference in 7.10.5 shown as an adjustment to the consolidated reserves?

4A Sch
11(6)
SSAP 23
para 20

7.10.7 Do the consolidated financial statements that deal with the period in which the merger takes place disclose the following:

(a) The names of the undertakings acquired (where a group was acquired the name of its parent is sufficient)?

4A Sch
13(2)(a)
SSAP 23
para 21

(b) The combination has been accounted for by the merger method of accounting?
4A Sch 13(2)(b)
SSAP 23 para 21

(c) That the number and class of the securities issued in respect of the merger?
SSAP 23 para 21

(d) Where the acquisition significantly affects the figures in the consolidated financial statements, the composition and fair value of the consideration for the merger given by the parent and its subsidiaries?
4A Sch 13(3)
SSAP 23 para 21,23

(e) The nature and amount of significant accounting adjustments made in relation to the amounts of assets and liabilities of the undertaking or group acquired, together with a statement of any resulting adjustment to the consolidated reserves (including restatement of opening consolidated reserves)?
4A Sch 13(6)
SSAP 23 para 21

> Note: The information required in 7.10.7(a)(b)(d) and (e) need not be given in respect of an undertaking that is either established under the law of a country outside the UK or carries on business outside the UK, if in the parent directors' opinion the disclosure would be seriously prejudicial to the business of that undertaking or to the business of the parent or any of its subsidiaries and the Secretary of State agrees that the information should not be disclosed.
> 4A Sch 16

7.10.8 Do the consolidated financial statements disclose the following in respect of all material mergers during the year:

(a) The profit or loss of the undertaking or group acquired for the period from the beginning of the financial year of the undertaking (or parent if it is a group) up to the date of merger (after making any necessary consolidation adjustments)?
4A Sch 13(4)(a)(7)

(b) The date on which the financial year referred to in 7.10.8(a) began?
4A Sch 13(4)

(c) The profit or loss of the undertaking or group acquired for the previous financial year (after making any necessary consolidation adjustments)?
4A Sch 13(4)(b)(7)

(d) Sufficient information about the results of subsidiaries acquired to enable shareholders to appreciate the effect on the consolidated results?
SSAP 23 para 22

(b) The date from which the results of major mergers have been brought into the accounts (that is, the effective date of those mergers)?
SSAP 23 para 22

> Note: The information required in 7.10.8(a)(b) and (c) need not be given in respect of an undertaking that is either established under the law of a country outside the UK or carries on business outside the UK, if in the parent directors' opinion the disclosure would be seriously prejudicial to the business of that undertaking or to the business of the parent or any of its subsidiaries and the Secretary of State agrees that the information should not be disclosed.
> 4A Sch 16

7.10.9 Do the financial statements of the acquiring or issuing company which deal with the period in which the merger takes place disclose the following: SSAP 23 para 23

(b) An analysis of the current year's attributable profit before extraordinary items between that before and that after the effective date of the merger?

(c) An analysis of the attributable profit before extraordinary items of the current year up to the effective date of the merger between that of the issuing company and that of the subsidiary?

(d) An analysis of the attributable profit before extraordinary items of the previous year between that of the issuing company and that of the subsidiary?

(e) An analysis of extraordinary items so as to indicate:

   (i) Whether each individual extraordinary item relates to pre-merger or post-merger?
   (ii) To which party to the merger the item relates?

7.10.10 In the case of material additions to the group, do the consolidated financial statements contain sufficient information about the results of the subsidiaries merged to enable shareholders to appreciate the effect on the consolidated results?   SSAP 14 para 30

7.11 Disposal of subsidiaries

7.11.1 Where there is a disposal which significantly affects the figures in the consolidated financial statements of an undertaking or group during the period are the following disclosed:
(a) The name of the undertaking (or the name of the parent if it is a group)?   4A Sch 15(a)

(b) The extent to which the profit or loss shown in the consolidated financial statements is attributable to the profit or loss of the undertaking or group disposed of?   4A Sch 15(b)

> Note: The information required in 7.11.1 need not be given in respect of an undertaking that is either established under the law of a country outside the UK or carries on business outside the UK, if in the parent directors' opinion the disclosure would be seriously prejudicial to the business of that undertaking or to the business of the parent or any of its subsidiaries and the Secretary of State agrees that the information should not be disclosed.   4A Sch 16

7.11.2 Where there is a material disposal, does the consolidated profit and loss account include: SSAP 14 para 31

(a) The subsidiary's results up to the date of disposal?

(b) The gain or loss on the sale of the investment (that is, the difference, at the time of the sale, between the proceeds of the sale and the group's share of the subsidiary's net assets together with any premium (less any amounts written off) or discount on acquisition)?

7.11.3 Has the effective date for the disposal of a subsidiary been taken as the earlier of the date on which consideration passes and the date on which an offer becomes or is declared unconditional?

SSAP 14
para 32

> Note: This applies irrespective of whether the acquiring company has the right under the agreement to share in profits from an earlier date.

SSAP 14
para 32

7.11.4 Are the following disclosed in respect of each material disposal of a subsidiary:

SSAP 22
para 52

(a) The profit or loss on disposal?
(b) The amount of purchased goodwill attributable to the subsidiary disposed of and how it has been treated in determining the profit or loss on disposal?
(c) The accounting treatment adopted and the amount of the proceeds in situations where no profit or loss is recorded on a disposal because the proceeds have been accounted for as a reduction in the cost of acquisition?

> Note: The provisions in 7.11.4 should apply to all disposals where the relevant information is obtainable and in all cases where disposals relate to acquisitions made after 1st January 1989. Where, in relation to acquisitions made prior to that date, it is impossible or impracticable to ascertain the attributable goodwill on disposal, this should be stated and the reasons given.

SSAP 22
para 53

7.11.5 In the case of material disposals from the group, do the consolidated financial statements contain sufficient information about the results of the subsidiaries sold to enable shareholders to appreciate the effect on the consolidated results?

SSAP 14
para 30

7.12 Minority interests

7.12.1 Have outside or minority interests in the share capital and reserves of subsidiaries consolidated been disclosed as a separate amount in the consolidated balance sheet, either before or after 'capital and reserves'?

4A Sch
17(2)
SSAP 14
para 34

7.12.2 Is the figure disclosed under 7.12.1 above the amount of capital and reserves attributable to shares in subsidiaries included in the consolidation that are held on behalf of persons other than the parent and its subsidiaries?

4A Sch
17(2)

7.12.3 Have the profits and losses attributable to minority interests been shown separately in the consolidated profit and loss account after arriving at the group profit or loss after tax but before extraordinary items, and shown after 'profit or loss on ordinary activities after taxation'?

4A Sch
17(3)
SSAP 14
para 35

7.12.4 Have minority interests in extraordinary items been deducted from the related amounts and been shown after 'tax on extraordinary profit or loss' in the profit and loss account formats?

4A Sch
17(4)
SSAP 14
para 35

7.12.5 Are debit balances recognised only if there is a binding obligation on minority shareholders to make good losses incurred, and they are able to meet this obligation?

SSAP 14
para 34

7.13   Associated undertakings

7.13.1 Where the investing group has a 'participating interest' in an undertaking (which is not a subsidiary or a joint venture, see 7.1 and 7.14 respectively) and the group exercises a significant influence over it, is it accounted for as an associate in the consolidated financial statements?

4A Sch 20(1)

> Notes:
> (a) A 'participating interest' means an interest held by an undertaking in the shares of another undertaking which it holds on a long-term basis for the purpose of securing a contribution to its activities by the exercise of control or influence arising from or related to that interest.
>
> Sec 260(1)
>
> (b) Where an undertaking holds 20 per cent or more of the voting rights in another undertaking, it is presumed to exercise a significant influence over it unless the contrary is shown.
>
> 4A Sch 20(2)
>
> (c) 'Voting rights' in an undertaking means the rights conferred on shareholders in respect of their shares or, in the case of an undertaking not having a share capital, on members, to vote at general meetings of the undertaking on all, or substantially all, matters.
>
> 4A Sch 20(3)

7.13.2 Where the interest of the investing group is not effectively that of a partner or a joint venture or consortium and it amounts to 20 per cent or more of the equity voting rights, but it is not treated as an associate, are the accounting treatment adopted and the reasons for adopting this treatment stated?

SSAP 1 para 38

> Note: The standard specifies that "in those cases where disclosure of the reason would be harmful to the business, the directors may omit the information, after consultation with their auditors".
>
> SSAP 1 para 38

7.13.3 Where the interest of the investing group amounts to less than 20 per cent of the equity voting rights, but the interest is treated as an associate, is the basis on which significant influence is exercised stated?

SSAP 1 para 38

7.13.4 In respect of each of the associated undertakings, are the following disclosed:

(a) Its name?

5 Sch 22(2)
SSAP 1
para 49

(b) Where it is:

5 Sch 22(3)

   (i) Incorporated outside Great Britain, its country of incorporation?
   (ii) Incorporated in Great Britain, whether it is registered in England and Wales or in Scotland?
   (iii) Unincorporated, the address of its principal place of business?

(c) The following information split between shares held by the parent and shares held by the group:

5 Sch 22(4)
(5)
SSAP 1
para 49(a)

(i) The identity of each class of shares held?

(ii) The proportion of the nominal value of the shares of that class represented by those shares?

(c) An indication of the nature of its business? — SSAP 1 para 49(b)

Notes: (a) The information required by 7.13.4 need not be given in respect of an undertaking which is established under the law of a country outside the UK, or which carries on business outside the UK, if in the directors' opinion such disclosure would be seriously prejudicial to the business of the undertaking, or to the business of the parent or any of its subsidiaries, and the Secretary of State agrees that the information need not be disclosed. Where advantage is taken of this exemption, it should be stated in a note to the financial statements.	Sec 231(3) (4)
(b) Where disclosure of the information required by 7.13.4 would lead in the directors' opinion to disclosure of excessive length, the information need only be given in respect of (i) the undertakings whose results or financial position, in the directors' opinion principally affect the figures shown in the company's financial statements and (ii) undertakings excluded from consolidation. Where advantage is taken of this provision, the notes to the company's financial statements should state that the information is only given for those subsidiaries that in the directors' opinion principally affect the figures shown in the financial statements. Furthermore, the full information including that given in the financial statements must be annexed to the next annual return.	Sec 231(5) (6)

7.13.5 Is the interest in associated undertakings shown in the investing group's consolidated financial statements by the equity method of accounting (described in paras 17.13.13 to 17.13.35 below)? — 4A Sch para 22(1)

7.13.6 Do associates prepare their financial statements either to the same date as, or to a date that is not more than six months before, or shortly after, the date of the investing group's financial statements? — SSAP 1 para 36

7.13.7 If financial statements not coterminous with those of the investing group are used and the effect is material, are the facts and the dates of the year ends disclosed? — SSAP 1 para 37

7.13.8 If the investing group has used financial statements issued by the associate before the completion of the group's financial statements, has it ensured that later information has not materially affected the view shown by those financial statements? — SSAP 1 para 37

Note: If the associated company is listed on a recognised stock exchange, only published financial information should be disclosed.	SSAP 1 para 36

7.13.9 Where the effect is material, has the investing group made consolidation adjustments to exclude such items as unrealised profits on stocks transferred to or from associated companies and to achieve reasonable consistency with group accounting policies? — SSAP 1 para 39

7.13.10 Where an associated company has subsidiaries or associates, is the investing group's share of the results and net assets based on the group financial statements of the associate? — 4A Sch 22(2) SSAP 1 para 42

7.13.11 Where the investment in an associate is held by a subsidiary in which there are minority interests, do the minority interests in the investing group's consolidated financial statements include the minority share of the subsidiary's interest in the results and net assets of its associates? — SSAP 1 para 41

7.13.12 Has the effective date for both the acquisition and the disposal of an interest, or part interest, in an associate been taken as the earlier of either the date on which consideration passes or the date on which an offer becomes unconditional? — SSAP 1 para 44

Profit and loss account disclosure

7.13.13 Is the investing group's share of profits less losses of associates shown before tax under the heading of 'income from interests in associated undertakings' in the consolidated profit and loss account? — 4A Sch 21(2) SSAP 1 para 19

7.13.14 Is 'income from other participating interests', that are not associates, shown separately? — 4A Sch 21(2)

7.13.15 Does turnover exclude the investing group's share of any turnover of associates? — SSAP 1 para 23

> Note: The associate's turnover should not be aggregated with the group's turnover, but where it is material, it should be disclosed separately. — SSAP 1 para 23

7.13.16 Does depreciation exclude the investing group's share of any depreciation of associated companies? — SSAP 1 para 23

7.13.17 Is income from investments in associates brought into account in the consolidated financial statements on the basis of the group's share of profits less losses of associates? — SSAP 1 para 18

> Note: These bases need not be applied to those interests in partnerships and non-corporate joint ventures where it is appropriate to account for a proportionate share of individual assets and liabilities as well as profits or losses (see further step 7.14).

7.13.18 Does the investing group's consolidated profit and loss account disclose, in taxation, the tax attributed to its share of profits of associates? — SSAP 1 para 20

7.13.19 Do extraordinary items in the consolidated profit and loss account include the investing group's share of the aggregate extraordinary items of associates (unless this amount would not be classified as extraordinary in the context of the investing group)? — SSAP 1 para 21

7.13.20 Where material, is the amount included in step 7.13.19 separately disclosed? — SSAP 1 para 21

7.13.21 Is the investing group's share of the aggregate net profits less losses retained by associates separately disclosed? — SSAP 1 para 22

7.13.22 If the results of one or more associates are very material in the context of the investing group, is there separate disclosure of items such as total turnover, total depreciation charges and total profits less losses before taxation of the associates concerned? — SSAP 1 para 23

> Note: When judging materiality, regard should also be had to the scale of the associates' operations in relation to those of the investing group. — SSAP 1 para 23

Balance sheet disclosure

7.13.23 Is the interest in associates shown under the heading of 'interests in associated undertakings' in the consolidated balance sheet? — 4A Sch 21(2)

7.13.24 Are 'other participating interests' that are not associates shown separately? — 4A Sch 21(2)

7.13.25 Is the interest in associates shown as the total of: — SSAP 1 para 26

(i) Its share of the net assets other than goodwill of associates stated, where possible, after attributing fair values to the net assets at the time each interest was acquired?
(ii) Its share of any goodwill in the associates' own financial statements?
(iii) The premium paid, or discount, on the acquisition of the interest (to the extent that it has not been written off)?

> Note: Item (i) must be disclosed separately, but items (ii) and (iii) may be combined. — SSAP 1 para 26

7.13.26 Where amounts exist in respect of items (ii) and (iii) in step 7.13.25, are these amounts being amortised? — SSAP 22 para 41

7.13.27 Where there has been a permanent impairment in the value of items (ii) and (iii) in step 7.13.25 , have they been written down and is the amount written off in the period separately disclosed? — SSAP 1 para 32

7.13.28 Are outstanding balances between the group and associates included under debtors and creditors and disclosed separately if they are material? — SSAP 1 para 29

7.13.29 Do the consolidated financial statements disclose separately the total of loans from associates to the group and loans to associates from the group? — SSAP 1 para 27,28

7.13.30 Do the consolidated financial statements disclose the following in respect of associates:

(a) The investing group's share of the post-acquisition accumulated reserves of the associates and any movements on those reserves (including amounts that have not passed through the profit and loss account)? — SSAP 1 para 31

(b) Where applicable, the fact that the accumulated reserves of overseas associates would be subject to further tax on distribution? — SSAP 1 para 31

(c) The extent of any significant restrictions on the ability of an associate to distribute its retained profits (other than those shown as non-distributable) because of statutory, contractual or exchange control restrictions?

SSAP 1
para 31,40

7.13.31 Where there are restrictions on the ability of an associate to distribute its retained profits, is the extent of the restrictions indicated?

SSAP 1
para 40

7.13.32 Where an associate has a deficiency of net assets but is still regarded as a long-term investment and is supported in some way by its shareholders, is the investing group's share of the deficiency of net assets reflected in the consolidated financial statements?

SSAP 1
para 33

7.13.33 Where an investment is made in an unincorporated entity and a liability could arise in excess of that resulting from taking account only of the investing group's share of net assets (for example, as a result of joint and several liability in a partnership), has the investing group considered whether it would be prudent either to include an additional provision or to recognise a contingent liability for this excess?

SSAP 1
para 34

7.13.34 If the interests in associates are very material in the context of the group, is more detailed information given about the associate's tangible assets, intangible assets and liabilities?

SSAP 1
para 30

7.13.35 When an investment in a company ceases to fall within the definition of an associate, is it stated in the consolidated balance sheet at the carrying amount at the date it ceases to be an associate under the equity method?

SSAP 1
para 43

> Note: The carrying amount should be adjusted if dividends are subsequently received out of profits earned prior to the change of status or if there is any impairment in value.

SSAP 1
para 43

7.14   Joint ventures

7.14.1 Where any undertakings are included in the consolidated financial statements on the basis of proportional consolidation, are they unincorporated joint ventures?

4A Sch
19(1)

> Note: A joint venture exists where an undertaking included in the consolidation manages another undertaking jointly with one or more undertakings not included in the consolidation.

4A Sch
19(1)

7.14.2 Where the method of proportional consolidation is used for unincorporated undertakings, is the group's share of each item in the profit and loss account and balance sheet of the undertaking consolidated with the group's financial statements?

7.14.3 Is the following information given concerning an undertaking where it is consolidated on a proportional basis:

5 Sch 21

(a) Its name?
(b) The address of its principal place of business?
(c) The factors on which its joint management is based?
(d) The proportion of its capital held by undertakings included in the consolidation?
(e) Where the financial year of the undertaking did not end with that of the parent, the date on which its financial statements last ended before that date?

Notes:
(a) The information required by 7.14.3 need not be given in respect of an undertaking which is established under the law of a country outside the UK, or which carries on business outside the UK, if in the directors' opinion such disclosure would be seriously prejudicial to the business of the undertaking, or to the business of the parent or any of its subsidiaries, and the Secretary of State agrees that the information need not be disclosed. Where advantage is taken of this exemption, it should be stated in a note to the financial statements.   Sec 231(3) (4)

(b) Where disclosure of the information required by 7.14.3 would lead in the directors' opinion to disclosure of excessive length, the information need only be given in respect of (i) the undertakings whose results or financial position, in the directors' opinion principally affect the figures shown in the company's financial statements and (ii) undertakings excluded from consolidation. Where advantage is taken of this provision, the notes to the company's financial statements should state that the information is only given for those subsidiaries that in the directors' opinion principally affect the figures shown in the financial statements. Furthermore, the full information including that given in the financial statements must be annexed to the next annual return.   Sec 231(5) (6)

7.15 Details of parents

Notes:
(a) The information required by 7.15.1 and 7.15.2 need not be given in respect of an undertaking which is established under the law of a country outside the UK, or which carries on business outside the UK, if in the directors' opinion such disclosure would be seriously prejudicial to the business of the undertaking, or to the business of the parent or any of its subsidiaries, and the Secretary of State agrees that the information need not be disclosed. Where advantage is taken of this exemption, it should be stated in a note to the financial statements.   Sec 231(3) (4)

(b) Where disclosure of the information required by 7.15.1, 7.15.2 and 7.14.3 would lead in the directors' opinion to disclosure of excessive length, the information need only be given in respect of (i) the undertakings whose results or financial position, in the directors' opinion principally affect the figures shown in the company's financial statements and (ii) undertakings excluded from consolidation. Where advantage is taken of this provision, the notes to the company's financial statements should state that the information is only given for those subsidiaries that in the directors' opinion principally affect the figures shown in the financial statements. Furthermore, the full information including that given in the financial statements must be annexed to the next annual return.   Sec 231(5) (6)

7.15.1 Where the parent is itself a subsidiary is the following information given with respect to the parent that heads the largest group of undertakings for which consolidated financial statements are prepared **and** the parent that heads the smallest such group of undertakings: 5 Sch 30

(a) The parent's name?

(b) If the parent is incorporated outside Great Britain, the country in which it is incorporated?

(c) If the parent is incorporated in Great Britain, whether it is registered in England and Wales or in Scotland?

(d) If the parent is unincorporated, the address of its principal place of business?

(e) Where the parent's consolidated financial statements are available to the public, the address from which copies can be obtained?

7.15.2 Where the parent is itself a subsidiary, is the following information given in respect of the body corporate (if any) that is regarded by the directors as the ultimate parent: 5 Sch 31

(a) Its name?

(b) If the ultimate parent is incorporated outside Great Britain, the country in which it is incorporated (if known)?

(b) If the ultimate parent is incorporated in Great Britain, whether it is registered in England and Wales or in Scotland (if known)?

Shares and debentures held by subsidiaries

7.15.3 Are the number, description and amount of the shares in and debentures of the parent company held by or on behalf of its subsidiaries disclosed?   5 Sch 20(1)

> Notes:
>
> (a) This disclosure requirement does not apply in relation to shares or debentures where the subsidiary is concerned as personal representative, or as trustee.   5 Sch 20(2)
>
> (b) The exemption regarding holding shares as a trustee does not apply if the parent or any of its subsidiaries is beneficially interested under the trust, otherwise than by way of security only for the purposes of a transaction entered into by it in the ordinary course of a business which includes the lending of money.   5 Sch 20(3)

7.16   Foreign currency translation

7.16.1 If the trade of a foreign enterprise (that is, subsidiary, associate or branch) is more dependent on the economic environment and currency of the investing company than that of its own reporting currency, have that foreign enterprise's financial statements been translated using the temporal method?   SSAP 20 para 55

7.16.2 In all other circumstances, have foreign enterprises' financial statements been translated using the closing rate/net investment method?   SSAP 20 para 52

7.16.3 Has the method of translating each foreign enterprise's financial statements been applied consistently from year to year unless there has been a change in its financial and other operational relationships with the investing company?   SSAP 20 para 56

7.16.4 Where the closing rate/net investment method is used, has the foreign enterprise's profit and loss account been translated at either the closing rate or an average rate for the year?   SSAP 20 para 54

7.16.5 If an average rate is used, has it been calculated by the method considered most appropriate to the circumstances of the foreign enterprise?   SSAP 20 para 54

7.16.6 Where an average rate is used, has the difference between translating the profit and loss account at that rate and translating it at the closing rate been recorded as a movement on reserves?   SSAP 20 para 54

7.16.7 Have exchange differences that arise from retranslating the opening net investment in a foreign enterprise at the closing rate been recorded as a movement on reserves?   SSAP 20 para 53

7.16.8 Where foreign currency borrowings have been used to finance, or to provide a hedge against, group equity investments in foreign enterprises, is the offset procedure used only where all of the following conditions are met:

SSAP 20
para 57

(a) The relationship between the investing company and the foreign enterprises concerned justifies the use of the closing rate method for consolidation purposes?

(b) In any year, exchange gains and losses on the foreign currency borrowings are offset as a reserve movement only to the extent of exchange differences arising on the net investments in foreign enterprises?

(c) The foreign currency borrowings used in the offset process do not exceed in aggregate the total amount of cash that the net investments are expected to be able to generate from profits or otherwise?

7.16.9 If the group has chosen to use the offset procedure, has it applied it consistently from year to year unless the above three conditions cease to apply?

Notes:
(a) Under the offset procedure, exchange losses/gains on the translation of the foreign currency borrowings are offset as a movement on consolidated reserves against exchange gains/losses on the translation of the net investments in the foreign enterprises.
(b) If, in an investing company's financial statements, the offset procedure has been applied to a foreign equity investment that is neither a subsidiary nor an associated company, the same offset procedure may be applied in the consolidated financial statements.

SSAP 20
para 58

Disclosure requirements

7.16.10 Are the following disclosed:

(a) The methods of translating the financial statements of foreign enterprises and the treatment of resulting exchange differences?

SSAP 20
para 59

(b) The net movement on reserves that arises from exchange differences?

SSAP 20
para 60

7.16.11 If the group is not an exempt group, are the following disclosed:

SSAP 20
para 60

(a) The net amount of exchange gains and losses on foreign currency borrowings less deposits?
(b) The amount of (a) that is offset in reserves under the offset procedure?
(c) The net amount of (a) that is charged or credited to the profit and loss account?

Note: An exempt group is one that does not prepare its financial statements in accordance with section 227 of the Act.

SSAP 20
para 35

---

8. SUMMARY FINANCIAL STATEMENTS

Conditions

8.1	Where a group has sent a summary financial statement to its members is it listed and does it have the power to do so in its articles of association?	Sec 251(1)

> Notes:
> (a) 'Listed' in 8.1 means admitted to the Official List of The International Stock Exchange of the United Kingdom and the Republic of Ireland Limited. Sec 251(1)
> (b) Any provision in the articles of association that requires a full set of financial statements to be sent to members can be ignored for summary financial statements that relate to a period commencing prior to 23rd December 1989, where the parent is incorporated prior to 1st July 1985 and it has a provision in its articles equivalent to article 127 of Table A. SI 1990/515 reg 4(2)

8.2	Has the parent ascertained that the member does not wish to continue to receive the group's full financial statements?	SI 1990/515 reg 5(a)
8.3	Has the period allowed for filing the group's full financial statements not expired?	SI 1990/515 reg 5(b)
8.4	Has the summary financial statement been approved by the board of directors and the original statement signed on their behalf by one director, stating the name of the director who signs it?	SI 1990/515 reg 5(c)(d)
8.5	Does the summary financial statement include the following statement in a prominent position:	SI 1990/515 reg 5(f)

"This summary financial statement does not contain sufficient information to allow for a full understanding of the results of the group and state of affairs of the company or of the group. For further information the full annual accounts, the auditors' report on those accounts and the directors' report should be consulted."

8.6	Does the summary financial statement contain a conspicuous statement of a member's right to demand free of charge a copy of the group's last full financial statements?	SI 1990/515 reg 5(g)
8.7	Is the summary financial statement accompanied by a printed card or form (postage paid) so worded to enable a member, by marking a box and returning the card or form, to notify the company of either or both of the following:	SI 1990/515 reg 5(h)

(a) That the member wishes to receive full financial statements for the financial year covered by the summary?
(b) That the member wishes to receive full financial statements for future years?

Disclosure

8.8	Does the summary financial statement derive from the full financial statements of the group?	Sec 251(3)

8.9   Is the fact stated that it is only a summary of the group's full financial statements?

Sec
251(4)(a)

8.10   Does the summary include a statement by the parent's auditors whether it is consistent with the group's full financial statements and complies with section 251 of the Act and the regulations?

Sec
251(4)(b)

8.11   Does the summary state whether the auditor's report on the group's full financial statements was qualified or unqualified?

Sec
251(4)(c)

8.12   Where the auditor's report on the group's full financial statements is qualified, is the report set out in full in the summary financial statement together with any further material needed to understand the qualification?

Sec
251(4)(c)

8.13   Does the summary financial statement state whether the auditor's report on the group's full financial statements contains a statement relating to:

Sec
251(4)(d)

(a) Inadequate accounting records or returns or accounts not agreeing with records and returns?
(b) Failure to obtain necessary information and explanations?

8.14   If the auditor's report does include a statement outlined in 13, is that statement set out in full?

Sec
251(4)(d)

8.15   Does the summary financial statement include the following information taken form the parent's directors' report:

SI 1990/515
1 Sch 2

(a) A summary of the fair review of the development of the business?
(b) A summary of the particulars of any important post balance sheet events?
(c) A summary of the indication given of likely future developments?
(d) A list of the directors' names?

8.16   Does the summary consolidated profit and loss account disclose the following items:

SI 1990/515
1 Sch 3

(a) Turnover?
(b) Income from interests in associated undertakings?
(c) Other interest receivable and similar income and interest payable and similar charges?
(d) Profit or loss on ordinary activities before tax?
(e) Tax on profit or loss on ordinary activities?
(f) Profit or loss on ordinary activities after tax
(g) Minority interests?
(h) Extraordinary income and charges after tax?
(i) Profit or loss for the financial year?
(j) Dividends paid and proposed?
(k) Directors' emoluments?

Notes:
(a) For summary financial statements issued for a financial year beginning prior to 23rd December 1989 item 8.16(b) should be replaced by 'income from shares in related companies'.

SI 1990/515
4 Sch 1

(b) Directors' emoluments in 8.16(k) excludes pensions of directors and past directors, emoluments waived, compensation for loss of office and sums paid to third parties.

SI 1990/515
1 Sch 3(3)

8.17 Does the summary consolidated balance sheet disclose the following items:

    SI 1990/515
    1 Sch 4

    (a) Called-up share capital not paid?
    (b) Fixed assets?
    (c) Current assets?
    (d) Prepayments and accrued income?
    (e) Creditors: amounts falling due within one year?
    (f) Net current assets (liabilities)?
    (g) Total assets less current liabilities?
    (h) Creditors: amounts falling due after more than one year?
    (i) Provisions for liabilities and charges?
    (j) Accruals and deferred income?
    (k) Capital and reserves?
    (l) Minority interests?

Notes:
(a) Where 8.17 (d) and (j) are included in current assets or creditors in the full financial statements they should not be shown separately in the summary.
(b) 'Minority interests' should be shown in the same position as in the group's full financial statements.

SI 1990/515
1 Sch 4(a)

SI 1990/515
1 Sch 4(a)

8.18 Are corresponding amounts shown for the immediately preceding year in respect of each item in 8.16 and 8.17 above?

    SI 1990/515
    1 Sch 3(4),
    4(3)

8.19 If any additional information is given in the summary financial statements is it consistent with the information published in the full financial statements?

EC 7TH COMPANY LAW DIRECTIVE

Seventh Council Directive

of 13 June 1983

based on the Article 54 (3) (g) of the Treaty on consolidated accounts

(83/349/EEC)

The Council of the European Communities,

Having regard to the Treaty establishing the European Economic Community, and in particular Article 54(3)(g)thereof,

Having regard to the proposal from the Commission[1],

Having regard to the opinion of the European Parliament[2],

Having regard to the opinion of the Economic and Social Committee[3],

Whereas on 25 July 1978 the Council adopted Directive 78/660/EEC[4] on the coordination of national legislation governing the annual accounts of certain types of companies; whereas many companies are members of bodies of undertakings; whereas consolidated accounts must be drawn up so that financial information concerning such bodies of undertakings may be conveyed to members and third parties; whereas national legislation governing consolidated accounts must therefore be coordinated in order to achieve the objectives of comparability and equivalence in the information which companies must publish within the Community;

Whereas on 25 July 1978 the Council adopted Directive 78/660/EEC[4] on the coordination of national legislation which the power of control is based on a majority of voting rights but also those in which it is based on agreements, where these are permitted; whereas, further-

---

1.   OJ No C 121, 2.6.1976, p. 2.
2.   OJ No C 163, 10.7.1978, p. 60.
3.   OJ No C 75, 26.3.1977, p. 5.
4.   OJ No L 222, 14.8.1978, p. 11.

more Member States in which the possibility occurs must be permitted to cover cases in which in certain circumstances control has been effectively exercised on the basis of a minority holding; whereas the Member States must be permitted to cover the case of bodies of undertakings in which the undertakings exist on an equal footing with each other;

Whereas the aim of coordinating the legislation governing consolidated accounts is to protect the interests subsisting in companies with share capital; whereas such protection implies the principle of the preparation of consolidated accounts where such a company is a member of a body of undertakings, and that such accounts must be drawn up at least where such a company is a parent undertaking; whereas, furthermore, the cause of full information also requires that a subsidiary undertaking which is itself a parent undertaking draw up consolidated accounts; whereas, nevertheless, such a parent undertaking may, and, in certain circumstances, must be exempted from the obligation to draw up such consolidated accounts provided that its members and third parties are sufficiently protected;

Whereas, for bodies of undertakings not exceeding a certain size, exemption from the obligation to prepare consolidated accounts may be justified; whereas, accordingly, maximum limits must be set for such exemptions; whereas it follows therefrom that the Member States may either provide that it is sufficient to exceed the limit of one only of the three criteria for the exemption not to apply or adopt limits lower than those prescribed in the Directive;

Whereas consolidated accounts must give a true and fair view of the assets and liabilities, the financial position and the profit and loss of all the undertakings consolidated taken as a whole; whereas, therefore, consolidation should in principle include all of those undertakings; whereas such consolidation requires the full incorporation of the assets and liabilities and of the income and expenditure of those undertakings and the separate disclosure of the interests of persons outwith such bodies; whereas, however, the neccesary corrections must be made to eliminate the effects of the financial relations between the undertakings consolidated;

Whereas a number of principles relating to the preparation of consolidated accounts and valuation in the context of such accounts must be laid down in order to ensure that items are disclosed consistently, and may readily be compared not only as regards the methods used in their valuation but also as regards the periods covered by the accounts;

Whereas participating interests in the capital of undertakings over which undertakings included in a consolidation exercise significant influence must be included in consolidated accounts by means of the equity method;

Whereas the notes on the consolidated accounts must give details of the undertakings to be consolidated;

Whereas certain derogations originally provided for on a transitional basis in Directive 78/660/EEC may be continued subject to review at a later date,

Has adopted this Directive

Section 1

Conditions for the preparation of consolidated accounts

Article 1

1. A Member State shall require any undertaking governed by its national law to draw up consolidated accounts and a consolidated annual report if that undertaking (a parent undertaking);

(a) has a majority of the shareholders' or members' voting rights in another undertaking (a subsidiary undertaking); or

(b) has the right to appoint or remove a majority of the members of the administrative, management or supervisory body of another undertaking (a subsidiary undertaking) and is at the same time a shareholder in or member of that undertaking; or

(c) has the right to exercise a dominant influence over an undertaking (a subsidiary undertaking) of which it is a shareholder or member, pursuant to a contract entered into with that undertaking or to a provision in its memorandum or articles of association, where the law governing that subsidiary undertaking permits its being subject to such contracts or provisions. A Member State need not prescribe that a parent undertaking must be a shareholder in or member of its subsidiary undertaking. Those Member States the laws of which do not provide for such contracts or clauses shall not be required to apply this provision; or

(d) is a shareholder in or member of an undertaking, and:

  (aa) a majority of the members of the administrative, management or supervisory bodies of that undertaking (a subsidiary undertaking) who have held office during the financial year, during the preceding financial year and up to the time when the consolidated accounts are drawn up, have been appointed solely as a result of the exercise of its voting rights; or

  (bb) controls alone, pursuant to an agreement with other shareholders in or members of that undertaking (a subsidiary undertaking), a majority of shareholders' or members' voting rights in that undertaking. The Member States may introduce more detailed provisions concerning the form and contents of such agreements.

The Member States shall prescribe at least the arrangements referred to in (bb) above.

They may make the application of (aa) above dependent upon the holdings representing 20% or more of the shareholders' or members' voting rights.

However, (aa) above shall not apply where another undertaking has the rights referred to in subparagraphs (a), (b) or (c) above with regard to that subsidiary undertaking.

2. Apart from the cases mentioned in paragraph 1 above and pending subsequent coordination, the Member States may require any undertaking goverened by their national law to draw up consolidated accounts and a consolidated annual report if that undertaking (a parent undertaking) holds a participating interest as defined in Article 17 of Directive 78/660/EEC in another undertaking (a subsidiary undertaking), and:

(a) it actually exercises a dominant influence over it; or

(b) it and the subsidiary undertaking are managed on a unified basis by the parent undertaking.

Article 2

1. For the purposes of Article 1 (1)(a), (b) and (d), the voting rights and the rights of appointment and removal of any other subsidiary undertaking as well as those of any person acting in his own name but on behalf of the parent undertaking or of another subsidiary undertaking must be added to those of the parent undertaking.

2. For the purposes of Article 1(1)(a), (b) and (d), the rights mentioned in paragraph 1 above must be reduced by the rights:

(a) attaching to shares held on behalf of a person who is neither the parent undertaking nor a subsidiary thereof; or

(b) attaching to shares held by way of security, provided that the rights in question are exercised in accordance with the instructions received, or held in connection with the granting of loans as part of normal business activities, provided that the voting rights are exercised in the interests of the person providing the security.

3. For the purposes of Article 1(1)(a) and (d), the total of the shareholders' or members' voting rights in the subsidiary undertaking must be reduced by the voting rights attaching to the shares held by that undertaking itself by a subsidiary undertaking of that undertaking or by a person acting in his own name but on behalf of those undertakings.

Article 3

1. Without prejudice to Articles 13, 14 and 15, a parent undertaking and all of its subsidiary undertakings shall be undertakings to be consolidated regardless of where the registered offices of such subsidiary undertakings are situated.

2. For the purposes of paragraph 1 above, any subsidiary undertaking of a subsidiary undertaking shall be considered a subsidiary undertaking of the parent undertaking which is the parent of the undertakings to be consolidated.

Article 4

1. For the purposes of this Directive, a parent undertaking and all of its subsidiary undertakings shall be undertakings to be consolidated where either the parent undertaking or one or more subsidiary undertakings is established as one of the following types of company:

(a) *in Germany:*

die Aktiengesellschaft, die Kommanditgesellschaft auf Aktien, die Gesellschaft mit beschränkter Haftung;

(b) *in Belgium:*

la société anonyme / de naamloze vennootschap – la société en commandite par actions / de commanditaire vennootschap op aandelen – la société de personnes à responsabilité limitée / de personenvennootschap met beperkte aansprakelijkheid;

(c) *in Denmark:*

aktieselskaber, kommanditaktieselskaber, anpartsselskaber;

(d) *in France:*

la société anonyme, la société en commandite par actions, la société à responsabilité limitée;

(e) *in Greece:*

η ανώνυμη εταιρία, η εταιρία περιορισμένης ευθύνης, η ετερόρρυθμη κατά μετοχές εταιρία;

(f) *in Ireland:*

public companies limited by shares or by guarantee, private companies limited by shares or by guarantee;

(g) *in Italy:*

la società per azioni, la società in accommandita per azioni, la società a responsabilità limitata;

(h) *in Luxembourg:*

la société anonyme, la société en commandite par actions, la société à responsabilité limitée;

(i) *in the Netherlands:*

de maamloze vennootschap, de besloten vennootschap met beperkte aansprakelijkheid;

(j) *in the United Kingdom:*

public companies limited by shares or by guarantee, private companies limited by shares or by guarantee.

2. A Member State may, however, grant exemption from the obligation imposed in Article 1 (1) where the parent undertaking is not established as one of the types of company listed in paragraph 1 above.

Article 5

1. A Member State may grant exemption from the obligation imposed in Article 1 (1) where the parent undertaking is a financial holding company as defined in Article 5 (3) of Directive 78/660/EEC, and:

(a) it has not intervened during the financial year, directly or indirectly, in the management of a subsidiary undertaking;

(b) it has not exercised the voting rights attaching to its participating interest in respect of the appointment of a member of a subsidiary undertaking's administrative, management or supervisory bodies during the financial year or the five preceding financial years or, where the exercise of voting rights was necessary for the operation of the administrative, management or supervisory bodies of the subsidiary undertaking, no shareholder in or member of the parent undertaking with majority voting rights or member of the administrative, management or supervisory bodies of that undertaking or of a member thereof with majority voting rights is a member of the administrative, management or supervisory bodies of the subsidiary undertaking and the members of those bodies so appointed have fulfilled their functions without any interference or influence on the part of the parent undertaking or of any of its subsidiary undertakings;

(c) it has made loans only to undertakings in which it holds participating interests. Where such loans have been made to other parties, they must have been repaid by the end of the previous financial year; and

(d) the exemption is granted by an administrative authority after fulfilment of the above conditions has been checked.

2. (a) Where a financial holding company has been exempted, Article 43 (2) of Directive 78/660/EEC shall not apply to its annual accounts with respect to any majority holdings in subsidiary undertakings as from the date provided for in Article 49 (2).

   (b) The disclosures in respect of such majority holdings provided for in point 2 of Article 43 (1) of Directive 78/660/EEC may be omitted when their nature is such that they would be seriously prejudicial to the company, to its shareholders or members or to one of its subsidiaries. A Member State may make such omissions subject to prior administrative or judicial authorization. Any such omission must be disclosed in the notes on the accounts.

Article 6

1. Without prejudice to Articles 4 (2) and 5, a Member State may provide for an exemption from the obligation imposed in Article 1 (1) if as at the balance sheet date of a parent undertaking the undertakings to be consolidated do not together, on the basis of their latest annual accounts, exceed the limits of two of the three criteria laid down in Article 27 of Directive 78/660/EEC.

2. A Member State may require or permit that the set-off referred to in Article 19 (1) and the elimination referred to in Article 26 (1)(a) and (b) be not effected when the aforementioned limits are calculated. In that case, the limits for the balance sheet total and net turnover criteria shall be increased by 20%.

3. Article 12 of Directive 78/660/EEC shall apply to the above criteria.

4. This Article shall not apply where one of the undertakings to be consolidated is a company the securities of which have been admitted to official listing on a stock exchange established in a Member State.

5. For 10 years after the date referred to in Article 49 (2), the Member States may multiply the criteria expressed in ECU by up to 2,5 and may increase the average number of persons employed during the financial year to a maximum of 500.

Article 7

1. Notwithstanding Articles 4 (2), 5 and 6, a Member State shall exempt from the obligation imposed in Article 1 (1) any parent undertaking governed by its national law which is also a subsidiary undertaking if its own parent undertaking is governed by the law of a Member State in the following two cases:

(a) where that parent undertaking holds all of the shares in the exempted undertaking. The shares in that undertaking held by members of its administrative, management or supervisory bodies pursuant to an obligation in law or in the memorandum or articles of association shall be ignored for this purpose; or

(b) where that parent undertaking holds 90% or more of the shares in the exempted undertaking and the remaining shareholders in or members of that undertaking have approved the exemption.

In so far as the laws of a Member State prescribe consolidation in this case at the time of the adoption of this Directive, that Member State need not apply this provision for 10 years after the date referred to in Article 49 (2).

2. Exemption shall be conditional upon compliance with all of the following conditions:

(a) the exempted undertaking and, without prejudice to Articles 13, 14 and 15, all of its subsidiary undertakings must be consolidated in the accounts of a larger body of undertakings, the parent undertaking of which is governed by the law of a Member State;

(b)   (aa) the consolidated accounts referred to in (a) above and the consolidated annual report of the larger body of undertakings must be drawn up by the parent undertaking of that body and audited, according to the law of the Member State by which the parent undertaking of that larger body of undertakings is governed, in accordance with this Directive;

(bb) the consolidated accounts referred to in (a) above and the consolidated annual report referred to in (aa) above, the report by the person responsible for auditing those accounts and, where appropriate, the appendix referred to in Article 9 must be published for the exempted undertaking in the manner prescribed by the law of the Member State governing that undertaking in accordance with Article 38. That Member State may require that those documents be published in its official language and that the translation be certified;

(c) the notes on the annual accounts of the exempted undertaking must disclose:
    (aa) the name and registered office of the parent undertaking that draws up the consolidated accounts referred to in (a) above; and
    (bb) the exemption from the obligation to draw up consolidated accounts and a consolidated annual report.

3. A Member State need not, however, apply this Article to companies the securities of which have been admitted to official listing on a stock exchange established in a Member State.

Article 8

1. In cases not covered by Article 7 (1), a Member State may, without prejudice to Articles 4 (2), 5 and 6, exempt from the obligation imposed in Article 1 (1) any parent undertaking governed by its national law which is also a subsidiary undertaking, the parent undertaking of which is governed by the law of a Member State, provided that all the conditions set out in Article 7 (2) are fulfilled and that the shareholders in or members of the exempted undertaking who own a minimum proportion of the subscribed capital of that undertaking have not requested the preparation of consolidated accounts at least six months before the end of the financial year. The Member States may fix that proportion at not more than 10% for public limited liability companies and for limited partnerships with share capital, and at not more than 20% for undertakings of other types.

2. A Member State may not make it a condition for this exemption that the parent undertaking which prepared the consolidated accounts described in Article 7 (2)(a) must also be governed by its national law.

3. A Member State may not make exemption subject to conditions concerning the preparation and auditing of the consolidated accounts referred to in Article 7 (2)(a).

Article 9

1. A Member State may make the exemptions provided for in Articles 7 and 8 dependent upon the disclosure of additional information, in accordance with this Directive, in the consolidated accounts referred to in Article 7 (2)(a), or in an appendix thereto, if that

information is required of undertakings governed by the national law of that Member State which are obliged to prepare consolidated accounts and are in the same circumstances.

2. A Member State may also make exemption dependent upon the disclosure, in the notes on the consolidated accounts referred to in Article 7 (2)(a), or in the annual accounts of the exempted undertakings, of all or some of the following information regarding the body of undertakings, the parent undertaking of which it is exempting from the obligation to draw up consolidated accounts:

– the amounts of the fixed assets,

– the net turnover,

– the profit or loss for the financial year and the amount of the capital and reserves,

– the average number of persons employed during the financial year.

Article 10

Articles 7 to 9 shall not affect any Member State's legislation on the drawing up of consolidated accounts or consolidated annual reports in so far as those documents are required:

– for the information of employees or their representatives, or

– by an administrative or judicial authority for its own purposes.

Article 11

1. Without prejudice to Articles 4 (2), 5 and 6, a Member State may exempt from the obligation imposed in Article 1 (1) any parent undertaking governed by its national law which is also a subsidiary undertaking of a parent undertaking not governed by the law of a Member State, if all of the following conditions are fulfilled:

(a) the exempted undertaking and, without prejudice to Articles 13, 14 and 15, all of its subsidiary undertakings must be consolidated in the accounts of a larger body of undertakings;

(b) the consolidated accounts referred to in (a) above and, where appropriate, the consolidated annual report must be drawn up in accordance with this Directive or in a manner equivalent to consolidated accounts and consolidated annual reports drawn up in accordance with this Directive;

(c) the consolidated accounts referred to in (a) above must have been audited by one or more persons authorized to audit accounts under the national law governing the undertaking which drew them up.

2. Articles 7 (2)(b)(bb) and (c) and 8 to 10 shall apply.

3. A Member State may provide for exemptions under this Article only if it provides for the same exemptions under Articles 7 to 10.

Article 12

1. Without prejudice to Articles 1 to 10, a Member State may require any undertaking governed by its national law to draw up consolidated accounts and a consolidated annual report if:

(a) that undertaking and one or more other undertakings with which it is not connected, as described in Article 1(1) or (2), are managed on a unified basis pursuant to a contract concluded with that undertaking or provisions in the memorandum or articles of association of those undertakings; or

(b) the administrative, management or supervisory bodies of that undertaking and of one or more other undertakings with which it is not connected, as described in Article 1 (1) or (2), consist for the major part of the same persons in office during the financial year and until the consolidated accounts are drawn up.

2. Where paragraph 1 above is applied, undertakings, related as defined in that paragraph together with all of their subsidiary undertakings shall be undertakings to be consolidated, as defined in this Directive, where one or more of those undertakings is established as one of the types of company listed in Article 4.

3. Articles 3, 4 (2), 5, 6, 13 to 28, 29 (1), (3), (4) and (5), 30 to 38 and 39 (2) shall apply to the consolidated accounts and the consolidated annual report covered by this Article, references to parent undertakings being understood to refer to all the undertakings specified in paragraph 1 above. Without prejudice to Article 19 (2), however, the items 'capital', 'share premium account', 'revaluation reserve', 'reserves', 'profit or loss brought forward', and 'profit or loss for the financial year' to be included in the consolidated accounts shall be the aggregate amounts attributable to each of the undertakings specified in paragraph 1.

Article 13

1. An undertaking need not be included in consolidated accounts where it is not material for the purposes of Article 16 (3).

2.   Where two or more undertakings satisfy the requirements of paragraph 1 above, they must nevertheless be included in consolidated accounts if, as a whole, they are material for the purposes of Article 16 (3).

3.   In addition, an undertaking need not be included in consolidated accounts where:

(a) severe long-term restrictions substantially hinder:
    (aa) the parent undertaking in the exercise of its rights over the assets or management of that undertaking; or
    (bb) the exercise of unified management of that undertaking where it is in one of the relationships defined in Article 12 (1); or

(b) the information necessary for the preparation of consolidated accounts in accordance with this Directive cannot be obtained without disproportionate expense or undue delay; or

(c) the shares of that undertaking are held exclusively with a view to their subsequent resale.

Article 14

1.   Where the activities of one or more undertakings to be consolidated are so different that their inclusion in the consolidated accounts would be incompatible with the obligation imposed in Article 16 (3), such undertakings must, without prejudice to Article 33 of this Directive, be excluded from the consolidation.

2.   Paragraph 1 above shall not be applicable merely by virtue of the fact that the undertakings to be consolidated are partly industrial, partly commercial, and partly provide services, or because such undertakings carry on industrial or commercial activites involving different products or provide different services.

3.   Any application of paragraph 1 above and the reasons therefor must be disclosed in the notes on the accounts. Where the annual or consolidated account of the undertakings thus excluded from the consolidation are not published in the same Member State in accordance with Directive 68/151/EEC[1], they must be attached to the

---

1.   OJ No L 65, 14.3.1968, p. 8.

consolidated accounts or made available to the public. In the latter case it must be possible to obtain a copy of such documents upon request. The price of such a copy must not exceed its administrative cost.

Article 15

1.   A Member State may, for the purposes of Article 16 (3), permit the omission from consolidated accounts of any parent undertaking not carrying on any industrial or commercial activity which holds shares in a subsidiary undertaking on the basis of a joint arrangement with one or more undertakings not included in the consolidated accounts.

2.   The annual accounts of the parent undertaking shall be attached to the consolidated accounts.

3.   Where use is made of this derogation, either Article 59 of Directive 78/660/EEC shall apply to the parent undertaking's annual accounts or the information which would have resulted from its application must be given in the notes on those accounts.

Section 2

The preparation of consolidated accounts

Article 16

1.   Consolidated accounts shall comprise the consolidated balance sheet, the consolidated profit-and-loss account and the notes on the accounts. These documents shall constitute a composite whole.

2.   Consolidated accounts shall be drawn up clearly and in accordance with this Directive.

3.   Consolidated accounts shall give a true and fair view of the assets, liabilities, financial position and profit or loss of the undertakings included therein taken as a whole.

4.   Where the application of the provisions of this Directive would nto be sufficient to give a true and fair view within the meaning of paragraph 3 above, additional information must be given.

5.   Where, in exceptional cases, the application of a provision of Articles 17 to 35 and 39 is incompatible with the obligation imposed in paragraph 3 above, that provision must be departed from in order to give a true and fair view within the meaning of paragraph 3. Any such departure must be disclosed in the notes on the accounts together with an explanation of the reasons for it and a statement of

its effect on the assets, liabilities, financial position and profit or loss. The Member States may define the exceptional cases in question and lay down the relevant special rules.

6. A Member State may require or permit the disclosure in the consolidated accounts of other information as well as that which must be disclosed in accordance with this Directive.

Article 17

1. Articles 3 to 10, 13 to 26 and 28 to 30 of Directive 78/660/EEC shall apply in respect of the layout of consolidated accounts, without prejudice to the provisions of this Directive and taking account of the essential adjustments resulting from the particular characteristics of consolidated accounts as compared with annual accounts.

2. Where there are special circumstances which would entail undue expense a Member State may permit stocks to be combined in the consolidated accounts.

Article 18

The assets and liabilities of undertakings included in a consolidation shall be incorporated in full in the consolidated balance sheet.

Article 19

1. The book values of shares in the capital of undertakings included in a consolidation shall be set off against the proportion which they represent of the capital and reserves of those undertakings:

(a) That set-off shall be effected on the basis of book values as at the date as at which such undertakings are included in the consolidations for the first time. Differences arising from such set-offs shall as far as possible be entered directly against those items in the consolidated balance sheet which have values above or below their book values.

(b) A Member State may require or permit set-offs on the basis of the values of identifiable assets and liabilities as at the date of acquisition of the shares or, in the event of acquisition in two or more stages, as at the date on which the undertaking became a subsidiary.

(c) Any difference remaining after the application of (a) or resulting from the application of (b) shall be shown as a separate item in the consolidated balance sheet with an appropriate heading. That item, the methods used and any significant changes in relation to the preceding financial year must be explained in the notes on the accounts. Where the offsetting of positive and negative differences is authorized by a Member State, a breakdown of such differences must also be given in the notes on the account.

2. However, paragraph 1 above shall not apply to shares in the capital of the parent undertaking held either by that undertaking itself or by another undertaking included in the consolidation. In the consolidated accounts such shares shall be treated as own shares in accordance with Directive 78/660/EEC.

Article 20

1. A Member State may require or permit the book values of shares held in the capital of an undertaking included in the consolidation to be set off against the corresponding percentage of capital only, provided that:

(a) the shares held represent at least 90% of the nominal value or, in the absence of a nominal value, of the accounting par value of the shares of that undertaking other than shares of the kind described in Article 29 (2)(a) of Directive 77/91/EEC[1];

(b) the proportion referred to in (a) above has been attained pursuant to an arrangement providing for the issue of shares by an undertaking included in the consolidation; and

(c) the arrangement referred to in (b) above did not include a cash payment exceeding 10% of the nominal value or, in the absence of a nominal value, of the accounting par value of the shares issued.

2. Any difference arising under paragraph 1 above shall be added to or deducted from consolidated reserves as appropriate.

3. The application of the method described in paragraph 1 above, the resulting movement in reserves and the names and registered offices of the undertakings concerned shall be disclosed in the notes on the accounts.

Article 21

The amount attributable to shares in subsidiary undertakings included in the consolidation held by persons other than the undertakings included in the consolidation shall be shown in the consolidated balance sheet as a separate item with an appropriate heading.

Article 22

The income and expenditure of undertakings included in a consolidation shall be incorporated in full in the consolidated profit-and-loss account.

Article 23

The amount of any profit or loss attributable to shares in subsidiary

1. OJ No L 26, 31.1.1977, p. 1.

undertakings included in the consolidation held by persons other than the undertakings included in the consolidation shall be shown in the consolidated profit-and-loss account as a separate item with an appropriate heading.

Article 24

Consolidated accounts shall be drawn up in accordance with the principles enunciated in Articles 25 to 28.

Article 25

1. The methods of consolidation must be applied consistently from one financial year to another.

2. Derogations from the provisions of paragraph 1 above shall be permitted in exceptional cases. Any such derogations must be disclosed in the notes on the accounts and the reasons for them given together with an assessment of their effect on the assets, liabilities, financial position and profit or loss of the undertakings included in the consolidation taken as a whole.

Article 26

1. Consolidated accounts shall show the assets, liabilities, financial positions and profits or losses of the undertakings included in a consolidation as if the latter were a single undertaking. In particular:

(a) debts and claims between the undertakings included in a consolidation shall be eliminated from the consolidated accounts;

(b) income and expenditure relating to transactions between the undertakings included in a consolidation shall be eliminated from the consolidated accounts;

(c) where profits and losses resulting from transactions between the undertakings included in a consolidation are included in the book values of assets, they shall be eliminated from the consolidated accounts. Pending subsequent coordination, however, a Member State may allow the eliminations mentioned above to be effected in proportion to the percentage of the capital held by the parent undertaking in each of the subsidiary undertakings included in the consolidation.

2. A Member State may permit derogations from the provisions of paragraph 1 (c) above where a transaction has been concluded according to normal market conditions and where the elimination of the profit or loss would entail undue expense. Any such derogations must be disclosed and where the effect on the assets, liabilities,

financial position and profit or loss of the undertakings, included in the consolidation, taken as a whole, is material, that fact must be disclosed in the notes on the consolidated accounts.

3. Derogations from the provisions of paragraph 1 (a), (b) or (c) above shall be permitted where the amounts concerned are not material for the purposes of Article 16 (3).

Article 27

1. Consolidated accounts must be drawn up as at the same date as the annual accounts of the parent undertaking.

2. A Member State may, however, require or permit consolidated accounts to be drawn up as at another date in order to take account of the balance sheet dates of the largest number or the most important of the undertakings included in the consolidation. Where use is made of this derogation that fact shall be disclosed in the notes on the consolidated accounts together with the reasons therefor. In addition, account must be taken or disclosure made of important events concerning the assets and liabilities, the financial position or the profit or loss of an undertaking included in a consolidation which have occurred between that undertaking's balance sheet date and the consolidated balance sheet date.

3. Where an undertaking's balance sheet date precedes the consolidated balance sheet date by more than three months, that undertaking shall be consolidated on the basis of interim accounts drawn up as at the consolidated balance sheet date.

Article 28

If the composition of the undertakings included in a consolidation has changed significantly in the course of a financial year, the consolidated accounts must include information which makes the comparison of successive sets of consolidated accounts meaningful. Where such a change is a major one, a Member State may require or permit this obligation to be fulfilled by the preparation of an adjusted opening balance sheet and an adjusted profit-and-loss account.

Article 29

1. Assets and liabilities to be included in consolidated accounts shall be valued according to uniform methods and in accordance with Articles 31 to 42 and 60 of Directive 78/660/EEC.

2. (a) an undertaking which draws up consolidated accounts must apply the same methods of valuation as in its annual accounts. However, a Member State may require or permit the use in consolidated accounts of other methods of valuation in

accordance with the abovementioned Articles of Directive 78/660/EEC.

(b) Where use is made of this derogation that fact shall be disclosed in the notes on the consolidated accounts and the reasons therefor given.

3.   Where assets and liabilities to be included in consolidated accounts have been valued by undertakings included in the consolidation by methods differing from those used for the consolidation, they must be revalued in accordance with the methods used for the consolidation, unless the results of such revaluation are not material for the purposes of Article 16 (3). Departures from this principle shall be permitted in exceptional cases. Any such departure shall be disclosed in the notes on the consolidated accounts and the reasons for them given.

4.   Account shall be taken in the consolidated balance sheet and in the consolidated profit-and-loss account of any difference arising on consolidation between the tax chargeable for the financial year and for preceding financial years and the amount of tax paid or payable in respect of those years, provided that it is probable that an actual charge to tax will arise within the foreseeable future for one of the undertakings included in the consolidation.

5.   Where assets to be included in consolidated accounts have been the subject of exceptional value adjustments solely for tax purposes, they shall be incorporated in the consolidated accounts only after those adjustments have been eliminated. A Member State may, however, require or permit that such assets be incorporated in the consolidated accounts without the elimination of the adjustments, provided that their amounts, together with the reasons for them, are disclosed in the notes on the consolidated accounts.

Article 30

1.   A separate item as defined in Article 19 (1)(c) which corresponds to a positive consolidation difference shall be dealt with in accordance with the rules laid down in Directive 78/660/EEC for the item 'goodwill'.

2.   A Member State may permit a positive consolidation difference to be immediately and clearly deducted from reserves.

Article 31

An amount shown as a separate item, as defined in Article 19 (1)(c), which corresponds to a negative consolidation difference may be transferred to the consolidated profit-and-loss account only:

(a) where that difference corresponds to the expectation at the date of acquisition of unfavourable future results in that undertaking, or to the expectation of costs which that undertaking would incur, in so far as such an expectation materializes; or

(b) in so far as such a difference corresponds to a realized gain.

Article 32

1. Where an undertaking included in a consolidation manages another undertaking jointly with one or more undertakings not included in that consolidation, a Member State may require or permit the inclusion of that other undertaking in the consolidated accounts in proportion to the rights in its capital held by the undertaking included in the consolidation.

2. Articles 13 to 31 shall apply *mutatis mutandis* to the proportional consolidation referred to in paragraph 1 above.

3. Where this Article is applied, Article 33 shall not apply if the undertaking proportionally consolidated is an associated undertaking as defined in Article 33.

Article 33

1. Where an undertaking included in a consolidation exercises a significant influence over the operating and financial policy of an undertaking not included in the consolidation (an associated undertaking) in which it holds a participating interest, as defined in Article 17 of Directive 78/660/EEC, that participating interest shall be shown in the consolidated balance sheet as a separate item with an appropriate heading. An undertaking shall be presumed to exercise a significant influence over another undertaking where it has 20% or more of the shareholders' or members' voting rights in that undertaking. Article 2 shall apply.

2. When this Article is applied for the first time to a participating interest covered by paragraph 1 above, that participating interest shall be shown in the consolidated balance sheet either:

(a) at its book value calculated in accordance with the valuation rules laid down in Directive 78/660/EEC. The difference between that value and the amount corresponding to the proportion of capital and reserves represented by that participating interest shall be disclosed separately in the consolidated balance sheet or in the notes on the accounts. That difference shall be calculated as at the date as at which that method is used for the first time; or

(b) at an amount corresponding to the proportion of the associated undertaking's capital and reserves represented by that participating interest. The difference between that amount and the book value calculated in accordance with the valuation rules laid down in directive 78/660/EEC shall be disclosed separately in the consolidated balance sheet or in the notes on the accounts. That difference shall be calculated as at the date as at which that method is used for the first time.

(c) A Member State may prescribe the application of one or other of (a) and (b) above. The consolidated balance sheet or the notes on the accounts must indicate whether (a) or (b) has been used.

(d) In addition, for the purposes of (a) and (b) above, a Member State may require or permit the calculation of the difference as at the date of acquisition of the shares or, where they were acquired in two or more stages, as at the date on which the undertaking became an associated undertaking.

3. Where an associated undertaking's assets or liabilities have been valued by methods other than those used for consolidation in accordance with Article 29 (2), they may, for the purpose of calculating the difference referred to in paragraph 2 (a) or (b) above, be revalued by the methods used for consolidation. Where such revaluation has not been carried out that fact must be disclosed in the notes on the accounts. A Member State may require such revaluation.

4. The book value referred to in paragraph 2 (a) above, or the amount corresponding to the proportion of the associated undertaking's capital and reserves referred to in paragraph 2 (b) above, shall be increased or reduced by the amount of any variation which has taken place during the financial year in the proportion of the associated undertaking's capital and reserves represented by that participating interest; it shall be reduced by the amount of the dividends relating to that participating interest.

5. In so far as the positive difference referred to in paragraph 2 (a) or (b) above cannot be related to any category of assets or liabilities it shall be dealt with in accordance with Articles 30 and 39 (3).

6. The proportion of the profit or loss of the associated undertakings attributable to such participating interests shall be shown in the consolidated profit-and-loss account as a separate item under an appropriate heading.

7. The eliminations referred to in Article 26 (1)(c) shall be effected in so far as the facts are known or can be ascertained. Article 26 (2) and (3) shall apply.

8. Where an associated undertaking draws up consolidated accounts, the foregoing provisions shall apply to the capital and reserves shown in such consolidated accounts.

9. This Article need not be applied where the participating interest in the capital of the associated undertaking is not material for the purposes of Article 16 (3).

Article 34

In addition to the information required under other provisions of this Directive, the notes on the accounts must set out information in respect of the following matters at least:

1. The valuation methods applied to the various items in the consolidated accounts, and the methods employed in calculating the value adjustments. For items included in the consolidated accounts which are or were originally expressed in foreign currency the bases of conversion used to express them in the currency in which the consolidated accounts are drawn up must be disclosed.

2. (a) The names and registered offices of the undertakings included in the consolidation; the proportion of the capital held in undertakings included in the consolidation, other than the parent undertaking, by the undertakings included in the consolidation or by persons acting in their own names but on behalf of those undertakings; which of the conditions referred to in Articles 1 and 12 (1) following application of Article 2 has formed the basis on which the consolidation has been carried out. The latter disclosure may, however, be omitted where consolidation has been carried out on the basis of Article 1 (1)(a) and where the proportion of the capital and the proprtion of the voting rights held are the same.
   (b) The same information must be given in respect of undertakings excluded from a consolidation pursuant to Articles 13 and 14 and, without prejudice to Article 14 (3), an explanation must be given for the exclusion of the undertakings referred to in Article 13.

3. (a) The names and registered offices of undertakings associated with an undertaking included in the consolidation as described in Article 33 (1) and the proportion of their capital held by undertakings included in the consolidation or by persons acting in their own names but on behalf of those undertakings.
   (b) The same information must be given in respect of the associated undertakings referred to in Article 33 (9), to-

gether with the reasons for applying that provision.

4. The names and registered offices of undertakings proportionally consolidated pursuant to Article 32, the factors on which joint management is based, and the proportion of their capital held by the undertakings included in the consolidation or by persons acting in their own names but on behalf of those undertakings.

5. The name and registered office of each of the undertakings, other than those referred to in paragraphs 2, 3 and 4 above, in which undertakings included in the consolidation and those excluded pursuant to Article 14, either themselves or through persons acting in their own names but on behalf of those undertakings, hold at least a percentage of the capital which the Member States cannot fix at more than 20%, showing the proportion of the capital held, the amount of the capital and reserves, and the profit or loss for the latest financial year of the undertaking concerned for which accounts have been adopted. This information may be omitted where, for the purposes of Article 16 (3), it is of negligible importance only. The information concerning capital reserves and the profit or loss may also be omitted where the undertaking concerned does not publish its balance sheet and where less than 50% of its capital is held (directly or indirectly) by the abovementioned undertakings.

6. The total amount shown as owed in the consolidated balance sheet and becoming due and payable after more than five years, as well as the total amount shown as owed in the consolidated balance sheet and covered by valuable security furnished by undertakings included in the consolidation, with an indication of the nature and form of the security.

7. The total amount of any financial commitments that are not included in the consolidated balance sheet, in so far as this information is of assistance in assessing the financial position of the undertakings included in the consolidation taken as a whole. Any commitments concerning pensions and affiliated undertakings which are not included in the consolidation must be disclosed separately.

8. The consolidated net turnover as defined in Article 28 of Directive 78/660/EEC, broken down by categories of activity and into geographical markets in so far as, taking account of the manner in which the sale of products and the provision of services falling within the ordinary activities of the undertakings included in the consolidation taken as a whole are organized, these categories and markets differ substantially from one another.

9. (a) The average number of persons employed during the finan-

cial year by undertakings included in the consolidation broken down by categories and, if they are not disclosed separately in the consolidated profit-and-loss account, the staff costs relating to the financial year.

(b) The average number of persons employed during the financial year by undertakings to which Article 32 has been applied shall be disclosed separately.

10. The extent to which the calculation of the consolidated profit or loss for the financial year has been affected by a valuation of the items which, by way of derogation from the principles enunciated in Articles 31 and 34 to 42 of Directive 78/660/EEC and in Article 29 (5) of this Directive, was made in the financial year in question or in an earlier financial year with a view to obtaining tax relief. Where the influence of such a valuation on the future tax charges of the undertakings included in the consolidation taken as a whole is material, details must be disclosed.

11. The difference between the tax charged to the consolidated profit-and-loss account for the financial year and to those for earlier financial years and the amount of tax payable in respect of those years, provided that this difference is material for the purposes of future taxation. This amount may also be disclosed in the balance sheet as a cumlative amount under a separate item with an appropriate heading.

12. The amount of the emoluments granted in respect of the financial year to the members of the administrative, managerial and supervisory bodies of the parent undertaking by reason of their responsibilities in the parent undertaking and its subsidiary undertakings, and any commitments arising or entered into under the same conditions in respect of retirement pensions for former members of those bodies, with an indication of the total for each category. A Member State may require that emoluments granted by reason of responsibilities assumed in undertakings linked as described in Article 32 or 33 shall also be included with the information specified in the first sentence.

13. The amounts of advances and credits granted to the members of the administrative, managerial and supervisory bodies of the parent undertaking by that undertaking or by one of its subsidiary undertakings, with indications of the interest rates, main conditions and any amounts repaid, as well as commitments entered into on their behalf by way of guarantee of any kind with an indication of the total for each category. A Member State may require that advances and credits granted by undertakings linked as described in Article 32 or 33 shall also be included with the information specified in the first sentence.

Article 35

1. A Member State may allow the disclosures prescribed in Article 34 (2), (3), (4) and (5):

(a) to take the form of a statement deposited in accordance with Article 3 (1) and (2) of Directive 68/151/EEC; this must be disclosed in the notes on the accounts;

(b) to be omitted when their nature is such that they would be seriously prejudicial to any of the undertakings affected by these provisions. A Member State may make such omissions subject to prior administrative or judicial authorization. Any such omission must be disclosed in the notes on the accounts.

2. Paragraph 1 (b) shall also apply to the information prescribed in Article 34 (8).

Section 3

The consolidated annual report

Article 36

1. The consolidated annual report must include at least a fair view of the development of business and the position of the undertakings included in the consolidation taken as a whole.

2. In respect of those undertakings, the report shall also give an indication of:

(a) any important events that have occurred since the end of the financial year;

(b) the likely future development of those undertakings taken as a whole;

(c) the activities of those undertakings taken as a whole in the field of research and development;

(d) the number and nominal value or, in the absence of a nominal value, the accounting par value of all of the parent undertaking's shares held by that undertaking itself, by subsidiary undertakings of that undertaking or by a person acting in his own name but on behalf of those undertakings. A Member State may require or permit the disclosure of these particulars in the notes on the accounts.

Section 4

The auditing of consolidated accounts

Article 37

1.   An undertaking which draws up consolidated accounts must have them audited by one or more persons authorized to audit accounts under the laws of the Member State which govern that undertaking.

2.   The person or persons responsible for auditing the consolidated accounts must also verify that the consolidated annual report is consistent with the consolidated accounts for the same financial year.

Section 5

The publication of consolidated accounts

Article 38

1.   Consolidated accounts, duly approved, and the consolidated annual report, together with the opinion submitted by the person responsible for auditing the consolidated accounts, shall be published for the undertaking which drew up the consolidated accounts as laid down by the laws of the Member State which governs it in accordance with Article 3 of Directive 68/151/EEC.

2.   The second subparagraph of Article 47 (1) of Directive 78/660/ EEC shall apply with respect to the consolidated annual report.

3.   The following shall be substituted for the second subparagraph of Article 47 (1) of Directive 78/660/EEC: 'It must be possible to obtain a copy of all or part of any such report upon request. The price of such a copy must not exceed its administrative cost'.

4.   However, where the undertaking which drew up the consolidated accounts is not established as one of the types of company listed in Article 4 and is not required by its national law to publish the documents referred to in paragraph 1 in the same manner as prescribed in Article 3 of Directive 68/151/EEC, it must at least make them available to the public at its head office. It must be possible to obtain a copy of such documents upon request. The price of such a copy must not exceed its administrative cost.

5.   Articles 48 and 49 of Directive 78/660/EEC shall apply.

6.   The Member States shall provide for appropriate sanctions for failure to comply with the publication obligations imposed in this Article.

Section 6

Transitional and final provisions

Article 39

1.   When, for the first time, consolidated accounts are drawn up in accordance with this Directive for a body of undertakings which was already connected, as described in Article 1 (1), before application of the provisions referred to in Article 49 (1), a Member State may require or permit that, for the purposes of Article 19 (1), account be taken of the book value of a holding and the proportion of the capital and reserves that it represents as at a date before or the same as that of the first consolidation.

2.   Paragraph 1 above shall apply *mutatis mutandis* to the valuation for the purposes of Article 33 (2) of a holding, or of the proportion of capital and reserves that it represents, in the capital of an undertaking associated with an undertaking included in the consolidation, and to the proportional consolidation referred to in Article 32.

3.   Where the separate item defined in Article 19 (1) corresponds to a positive consolidation difference which arose before the date of the first consolidated accounts drawn up in accordance with this Directive, a Member State may:

(a)   for the purposes of Article 30 (1), permit the calculation of the limited period of more than five years provided for in Article 37 (2) of Directive 78/660/EEC as from the date of the first consolidated a counts drawn up in accordance with this Directive; and

(b)   for the purposes of Article 30 (2), permit the deduction to be made from reserves as at the date of the first consolidated accounts drawn up in accordance with this Directive.

Article 40

1.   Until expiry of the deadline imposed for the application in national law of the Directives supplementing Directive 78/660/EEC as regards the harmonization of the rules governing the annual accounts of banks and other financial institutions and insurance undertakings, a Member State may derogate from the provisions of this Directive concerning the layout of consolidated accounts, the methods of valuing the items included in those accounts and the information to be given in the notes on the accounts:

(a)   with regard to any undertaking to be consolidated which is a bank, another financial institution or an insurance undertaking;

(b) where the undertakings to be consolidated comprise principally banks, financial institutions or insurance undertakings.

They may also derogate from Article 6, but only in so far as the limits and criteria to be applied to the above undertakings are concerned.

2. In so far as a Member State has not required all undertakings which are banks, other financial institutions or insurance undertakings to draw up consolidated accounts before implementation of the provisions referred to in Article 49 (1), it may, until its national law implements one of the Directives mentioned in paragraph 1 above, but not in respect of financial years ending after 1993:

(a) suspend the application of the obligation imposed in Article 1 (1) with respect to any of the above undertakings which is a parent undertaking. That fact must be disclosed in the annual accounts of the parent undertaking and the information prescribed in point 2 of Article 43 (1) of Directive 78/660/EEC must be given for all subsidiary undertakings;

(b) where consolidated accounts are drawn up and without prejudice to Article 33, permit the omission from the consolidation of any of the above undertakings which is a subsidiary undertaking. The information prescribed in Article 34 (2) must be given in the notes on the accounts in respect of any such subsidiary undertaking.

3. In the cases referred to in paragraph 2 (b) above, the annual or consolidated accounts of the subsidiary undertaking must, in so far as their publication is compulsory, be attached to the consolidated accounts or, in the absence of consolidated accounts, to the annual accounts of the parent undertaking or be made available to the public. In the latter case it must be possible to obtain a copy of such documents upon request. The price of such a copy must not exceed its administrative cost.

Article 41

1. Undertakings which are connected as described in Article 1 (1)(a), (b) and (d)(bb), and those other undertakings which are similarly connected with one of the aforementioned undertakings, shall be affiliated undertakings for the purposes of this Directive and of Directive 78/660/EEC.

2. Where a Member State prescribes the preparation of consolidated accounts pursuant to Article 1 (1)(c), (d)(aa) or (2) or Article 12 (1), the undertakings which are connected as described in those

Articles and those other undertakings which are connected similarly, or are connected as described in paragraph 1 above to one of the aforementioned undertakings, shall be affiliated undertakings as defined in paragraph 1.

3. Even where a Member State does not prescribe the preparation of consolidated accounts pursuant to Article 1 (1)(c), (d)(aa) or (2) or Article 12 (1), it may apply paragraph 2 of this Article.

4. Articles 2 and 3(2) shall apply.

5. When a Member State applies Article 4 (2), it may exclude from the application of paragraph 1 above affiliated undertakings which are parent undertakings and which by virtue of their legal form are not required by that Member State to draw up consolidated accounts in accordance with the provisions of this Directive, as well as parent undertakings with a similar legal form.

Article 42

The following shall be substituted for Article 56 of Directive 78/660/EEC:

'*Article 56*
1. The obligation to show in annual accounts the items prescribed by Articles 9, 10 and 23 to 26 which relate to affiliated undertakings, as defined by Article 41 of Directive 83/349/EEC, and the obligation to provide information concerning these undertakings in accordance with Articles 13 (2), and 14 and point 7 of Article 43 (1) shall enter into force on the date fixed in Article 49 (2) of that Directive.

2. The notes on the accounts must also disclose:
    (a) the name and registered office of the undertaking which draws up the consoldiated accounts of the largest body of undertakings of which the company forms part as a subsidiary undertaking;
    (b) the name and registered office of the undertaking which draws up the consolidated accounts of the smallest body of undertakings of which the company forms part as a subsidiary undertaking and which is also included in the body of undertakings referred to in (a) above;
    (c) the place where copies of the consolidated accounts referred to in (a) and (b) above may be obtained provided that they are available.'

Article 43

The following shall be substituted for Article 57 of Directive 78/660/ EEC:

'*Article 57*
Notwithstanding the provisions of Directives 68/151/EEC and 77/91/EEC, a Member State need not apply the provisions of this Directive concerning the content, auditing and publication of annual accounts to companies governed by their national laws which are subsidiary undertakings, as defined in Directive 83/ 349/EEC, where the following conditions are fulfilled:
(a) the parent undertaking must be subject to the laws of a Member State;
(b) all shareholders or members of the subsidiary undertaking must have declared their agreement to the exemption from such obligations; this declaration must be made in respect of every financial year;
(c) the parent undertaking must have declared that it guarantees the commitments entered into by the subsidiary undertaking;
(d) the declarations referred to in (b) and (c) must be published by the subsidiary undertaking as laid down by the laws of the Member State in accordance with Article 3 of Directive 68/151/EEC;
(e) the subsidiary undertaking must be included in the consoli- dated acocunts drawn up by the parent undertaking in accordance with Directive 83/349/EEC;
(f) the above exemption must be disclosed in the notes on the consolidated accounts drawn up by the parent undertaking;
(g) the consolidated accounts referred to in (e), the consolidated annual report, and the report by the person resonsible for auditing those accounts must be published for the subsidiary undertaking as laid down by the laws of the Member State in accordance with Article 3 of Directive 68/151/EEC.'

Article 44

The following shall be substituted for Article 58 of Directive 78/660/ EEC:

'*Article 58*
A Member State need not apply the provisions of this Directive concerning the auditing and publication of the profit-and-loss account to companies governed by their national laws which are parent undertakings for the purposes of Directive 83/349/EEC where the following conditions are fulfilled:
(a) the parent undertaking must draw up consolidated accounts in accordance with Directive 83/349/EEC and be included in the consolidated accounts;
(b) the above exemption must be disclosed in the notes on the

annual accounts of the parent undertaking;
(c) the above exemption must be disclosed in the notes on the consolidated accounts drawn up by the parent undertaking;
(d) the profit or loss of the parent company, determined in accordance with this Directive, must be shown in the balance sheet of the parent company.'

Article 45

The following shall be substituted for Article 59 of Directive 78/660/EEC:

'Article 59
1. A Member State may require or permit that participating interests, as defined in Article 17, in the capital of undertakings over the operating and financial policies of which significant influence is exercised, be shown in the balance sheet in accordance with paragraph 2 to 9 below, as sub-items of the items "shares in affiliated undertakings" or "participating interests", as the case may be. An undertaking shall be presumed to exercise a significant influence over another undertaking where it has 20% or more of the shareholders' or members' voting rights in that undertaking. Article 2 of Directive 83/349/EEC shall apply.

2. When this Article is first applied to a participating interest covered by paragraph 1, it shall be shown in the balance sheet either:
(a) at its book value calculated in accordance with Articles 31 to 42. The difference betweeen that value and the amount corresponding to the proportion of capital and reserves represented by the particpating interest shall be disclosed separately in the balance sheet or in the notes on the accounts. That difference shall be calculated as at the date as at which the method is applied for the first time; or
(b) at the amount corresponding to the proportion of the capital and reserves represented by the participating interest. The difference between that amount and the book value calculated in accordance with Articles 31 to 42 shall be disclosed separately in the balance sheet or in the notes on the accounts. That difference shall be calculated as at the date as at which the method is applied for the first time.
(c) A Member State may prescribe the application of one or other of the above paragraphs. The balance sheet or the notes on the accounts must indicate whether (a) or (b) above has been used.
(d) In addition, when applying (a) and (b) above, a Member State may require or permit calculation of the difference as at the date of acquisition of the participating interest referred to in paragraph 1 or, where the acquisition took place in two or

more stages, as at the date as at which the holding became a participating interest within the meaning of paragraph 1 above.

3. Where the assets or liabilities of an undertaking in which a participating interest within the meaning of paragraph 1 above is held have been valued by methods other than those used by the company drawing up the annual accounts, they may, for the purpose of calculatingthe difference referred to in paragraph 2 (a) or (b) above, be revalued by the methods used by the company drawing up the annual accounts. Disclosure must be made in the notes on the accounts where such revaluation has not been carried out. A Member State may require such revaluation.

4. The book value referred to in paragraph 2 (a) above, or the amount corresponding to the proportion of capital and reserves referred to in paragraph 2 (b) above, shall be increased or reduced by the amount of the variation which has taken place during the financial year in the proportion of capital reserves represented by that participating interest; it shall be reduced by the amount of the dividends relating to the participating interest.

5. In so far as a positive difference covered by paragraph 2 (a) or (b) above cannot be related to any category of asset or liability, it shall be dealt with in accordance with the rules applicable to the item "goodwill".

6. (a) The proportion of the profit or loss atrributable to participating interests within the meaning of paragraph 1 above shall be shown in the profit-and-loss account as a separate item with an appropriate heading.

   (b) Where that amount exceeds the amount of dividends already received or the payment of which can be claimed, the amount of the difference must be placed in a reserve which cannot be distributed to shareholders.

   (c) A Member State may require or permit that the proportion of the profit or loss attributable to the participating interests referred to in paragraph 1 above be shown in the profit-and-loss account only to the extent of the amount corresponding to dividends already received or the payment of which can be claimed.

7. The eliminations referred to in Article 26 (1)(c) of Directive 83/349/EEC shall be effected in so far as the facts are known or can be ascertained. Article 26 (2) and (3) of that Directive shall apply.

8. Where an undertaking in which a participating interest

within the meaning of paragraph 1 above is held draws up consolidated accounts, the foregoing paragraphs shall apply to the capital and reserves shown in such consolidated accounts.

9. This Article need not be applied where a participating interest as defined in paragraph 1 is not material for the purposes of Article 2 (3).'

Article 46

The following shall be substituted for Article 61 of Directive 78/660/EEC:

'*Article 61*
A Member State need not apply the provisions of point 2 of Article 43 (1) of this Directive concerning the amount of capital and reserves and profits and losses of the undertakings concerned to companies governed by their national laws which are parent undertakings for the purposes of Directive 83/349/EEC:
(a) where the undertakings concerned are included in consolidated accounts drawn up by that parent undertaking, or in the consolidated accounts of a larger body of undertakings as referred to in Article 7 (2) of Directive 83/349/EEC; or
(b) where the holdings in the undertakings concerned have been dealt with by the parent undertaking in its annual accounts in accordance with Article 59, or in the consolidated accounts drawn up by that parent undertaking in accordance with Article 33 of Directive 83/349/EEC.'

Article 47

The Contact Committee set up pursuant to Article 52 of Directive 78/660/EEC shall also:

(a) facilitate, without prejudice to Articles 169 and 170 of the Treaty, harmonized application of this Directive through regular meetings dealing, in particular, with practical problems arising in connection with its application;

(b) advise the Commission, if necessary, on additions or amendments to this Directive.

Article 48

This Directive shall not affect laws in the Member States requiring that consolidated accounts in which undertakings not falling within their jurisdiction are included be filed in a register in which branches of such undertakings are listed.

Article 49

1.   The Member States shall bring into force the laws, regulations and administrative provisions necessary for them to comply with this Directive before 1 January 1988. They shall forthwith inform the Commission thereof.

2.   A Member State may provide that the provisions referred to in paragraph 1 above shall first apply to consolidated accounts for financial years beginning on 1 January 1990 or during the calendar year 1990.

3.   The Member States shall ensure that they communicate to the Commision the texts of the main provisions of national law which they adopt in the field covered by this Directive.

Article 50

1.   Five years after the date referred to in Article 49 (2), the Council, acting on a proposal from the Commission, shall examine and if need be revise Articles 1 (1)(d) (second subparagraph), 4 (2), 5, 6, 7 (1), 12, 43 and 44 in the light of the experience acquired in applying this Directive, the aims of this Directive and the economic and monetary situation at the time.

2.   Paragraph 1 above shall not affect Article 53 (2) of Directive 78/660/EEC.

Article 51

This Directive is addressed to the Member States.

Done at Luxembourg, 13 June 1983.

For the Council

The President

H. TIETMEYER

Appendix III

TABLE OF EC 7TH
DIRECTIVE DESTINATIONS

Relating the provisions of the 7th Council Directive 83/348/EEC to the corresponding provisions of the Companies Act 1989 and the equivalent provisions of the Companies Act 1985 shown in square brackets.

Article of 7th Directive	Destination in the Companies Act 1989 [1985]
1	Sec 5 [Sec 227]; Secs 21, 22 [Secs 258, 259, 260]
2	9 Sch [10A Sch]
3	Sec 5(3) [Sec 229]; Sec 21(1) [Sec 258(5)]
4	Sec 5(1) [Sec 227(1)]
5	–
6	Sec 13 [Secs 246–249]
7	Sec 5(3) [Sec 228]
8	Sec 5(3) [Sec 228]
9	Sec 5(3) [Sec 228]
10	–
11	Sec 5(3) [Sec 228]
12	Sec 21 [Sec 258(4)(b)]; 3 Sch [5 Sch]
13	Sec 5(3) [Sec 229(2)(3)]
14	Sec 5(3), Sec 11 [Secs 229(4), 243]; 2 Sch [4A Sch 1(2), 18]
15	–
16	Sec 5 [Sec 227(2)–(6)]
17	2 Sch [4A Sch 1]
18	2 Sch [4A Sch 2]
19	2 Sch [4A Sch 9]
20	2 Sch [4A Sch 10, 11]
21	2 Sch [4A Sch 17(1)(2)]
22	2 Sch [4A Sch 2]
23	2 Sch [4A Sch 17(3)(4)]
24	2 Sch [4A Sch 1]
25	1 Sch 5 [4 Sch 11]
26	2 Sch [4A Sch 1(1)(6)]
27	2 Sch [4A Sch 2(2)]; 3 Sch [5 Sch 4, 19]
28	2 Sch [4A Sch 13–16]
29	2 Sch [4A Sch 3]; 1 Sch 8 [4 Sch 47]
30	2 Sch [4A Sch 9(5)]

31	2 Sch [4A Sch 9(5)]
32	2 Sch [4A Sch 19, 20(1)]
33	2 Sch [4A Sch 20, 21, 22]
34	2 Sch [4A Sch 19]; 3 Sch [5 Sch 21–28] Sec 6 [Sec 231(3)(4)]
35	Sec 6 [Sec 231(2)]
36	Sec 8 [Sec 234]; 5 Sch [7 Sch]
37	Sec 9 [Sec 235]
38	Sec 10 [Secs 238, 239]; Sec 11 [Secs 241, 242]
39	Transitional provisions
40	Sec 18 [Secs 255, 255A]
41	Sec 21 [Sec 258]; Sec 22 [Sec 259]
42	3 Sch [5 Sch 30]
43	–
44	Sec 5(4) [Sec 230]
45	2 Sch [4A Sch 20–22]
46	–
47	–
48	–
49	Implementation
50	Possible revision of certain Articles in five years

STATEMENTS OF ACCOUNTING PRACTICE AND EXPOSURE DRAFTS

SSAP 1	Accounting for associated companies	Revised April 1982
SSAP 2	Disclosure of accounting policies	Issued Nov. 1971
SSAP 3	Earnings per share	Revised Aug. 1984
SSAP 4	The accounting treatment of government grants	Issued April 1974
SSAP 5	Accounting for value added tax	Issued April 1974
SSAP 6	Extraordinary items and prior year adjustments	Revised Aug. 1986
SSAP 8	The treatment of taxation under the imputation system in the accounts of companies	Revised Dec. 1977
SSAP 9	Stocks and long-term contracts	Revised Sept. 1988
SSAP 10	Statements of source and application of funds	Revised June 1978
SSAP 12	Accounting for depreciation	Revised Jan. 1987
SSAP 13	Accounting for research and development	Revised Jan. 1989
SSAP 14	Group accounts	Issued Sept. 1978
SSAP 15	Accounting for deferred taxation	Revised May 1985
SSAP 17	Accounting for post balance sheet events	Issued Aug. 1980
SSAP 18	Accounting for contingencies	Issued Aug. 1980
SSAP 19	Accounting for investment properties	Issued Nov. 1981

SSAP 20	Foreign currency translation	Issued April 1983
SSAP 21	Accounting for leases and hire purchase contracts	Issued Aug. 1984
SSAP 22	Accounting for goodwill	Revised July 1989
SSAP 23	Accounting for acquisitions and mergers	Issued April 1985
SSAP 24	Accounting for pension costs	Issued May 1988
ED 42	Accounting for special purpose transactions	Issued March 1988
ED 43	The accounting treatment of government grants	Issued June 1988
ED 45	Segmental reporting	Issued Nov. 1988
ED 46	Disclosure of related party transactions	Issued April 1989
ED 47	Accounting for goodwill	Issued Feb. 1990
ED 47	Accounting for acquisitions and mergers	Issued Feb. 1990

Tolley's Companies Legislation

Extracts of accounting provisions

Those sections of, and Schedules to, the Act that are reproduced in full are indicated on the Arrangement of Sections by an asterisk.

The first edition of Tolley's Companies Legislation incorporates all relevant companies legislation (excluding insolvency) up to and including the Companies Act 1989, together with statutory instruments. It not only includes current provisions but also superseded provisions to the extent that these have applied at some time since the Companies Act 1985 came into force. Amending or repealing legislation is both given effect to in the original legislation and referred to in the text of the Act or statutory instrument where it occurs. This includes the Commencement Orders up to and including No 4 (SI 1990 No 355) issued on 26 February 1990.

Free of charge supplements will be issued to subscribers with details of commencement dates of the Companies Act 1989 provisions if these are not known at the time of publication.

TOLLEY PUBLISHING CO. LTD.

Abbreviations

BNA	=	Business Names Act 1985
CA 1989	=	Companies Act 1989
CC(CP)A	=	Companies Consolidation (Consequential Provisions) Act 1985
CDDA	=	Company Directors Disqualification Act 1986
CS(ID)A	=	Company Securities (Insider Dealing) Act 1985
FSA	=	Financial Services Act 1986
FTA	=	Fair Trading Act 1973
Pt	=	Part
Reg	=	Regulation
s	=	Section
Sch	=	Schedule
4 Sch 10	=	4th Schedule, paragraph 10
Sec	=	Section
SI	=	Statutory Instrument

Companies Act 1985

1985 Chapter 6 — Royal Assent 11 March 1985 incorporating Companies Act 1989, Chapter 40 — Royal Assent 16 November 1989

ARRANGEMENT OF SECTIONS

CHAPTER III   A COMPANY'S CAPACITY; FORMALITIES OF CARRYING ON BUSINESS

Part II   Re-registration as a Means of Altering a Company's Status

Private company becoming public

Limited company becoming unlimited

Unlimited company becoming limited

Public company becoming private

Part III   Capital Issues

CHAPTER I   ISSUES BY COMPANIES REGISTERED, OR TO BE REGISTERED, IN GREAT BRITAIN

The prospectus

Registration of prospectus

Liabilities and offences in connection with prospectus

Supplementary

CHAPTER II   ISSUES BY COMPANIES INCORPORATED, OR TO BE INCORPORATED, OUTSIDE GREAT BRITAIN

Part IV   Allotment of Shares and Debentures

General provisions as to allotment

Companies Act 1985

CHAPTER VIII   MISCELLANEOUS PROVISIONS ABOUT SHARES
AND DEBENTURES

Share and debenture certificates, transfers and warrants

Debentures

Part VI   Disclosure of Interests in Shares

Individual and group acquisitions

Registration and investigation of share acquisitions and disposals

Companies Act 1985

Companies Act 1985

Part IX   A Company's Management; Directors and Secretaries; their Qualifications, Duties and Responsibilities

Officers and registered office

Provisions governing appointment of directors

Disqualification

Removal of directors

Other provisions about directors and officers

Part X   Enforcement of Fair Dealing by Directors

Restrictions on directors taking financial advantage

Companies Act 1985

Part XI   Company Administration and Procedure

CHAPTER I   COMPANY IDENTIFICATION

CHAPTER II   REGISTER OF MEMBERS

Companies Act 1985

CHAPTER V   AUDITORS

Part XII   Registration of Charges

Companies Act 1985

Companies Act 1985

Companies Act 1985

SCHEDULES

PART I FORMATION AND REGISTRATION OF COMPANIES; JURIDICAL STATUS AND MEMBERSHIP

CHAPTER I COMPANY FORMATION

Memorandum of association

1 Mode of forming incorporated company

(1) Any two or more persons associated for a lawful purpose may, by subscribing their names to a memorandum of association and otherwise complying with the requirements of this Act in respect of registration, form an incorporated company, with or without limited liability.

(2) A company so formed may be either—

(a) a company having the liability of its members limited by the memorandum to the amount, if any, unpaid on the shares respectively held by them ("a company limited by shares");

(b) a company having the liability of its members limited by the memorandum to such amount as the members may respectively thereby undertake to contribute to the assets of the company in the event of its being wound up ("a company limited by guarantee"); or

(c) a company not having any limit on the liability of its members ("an unlimited company").

(3) A "public company" is a company limited by shares or limited by guarantee and having a share capital, being a company—

(a) the memorandum of which states that it is to be a public company, and

(b) in relation to which the provisions of this Act or the former Companies Acts as to the registration or re-registration of a company as a public company have been complied with on or after 22nd December 1980;

and a "private company" is a company that is not a public company.

(4) With effect from 22nd December 1980, a company cannot be formed as, or become, a company limited by guarantee with a share capital.

23 Membership of holding company

[(1) Except as mentioned in this section, a body corporate cannot be a member of a company which is its holding company and any allotment or transfer of shares in a company to its subsidiary is void.

(2) The prohibition does not apply where the subsidiary is concerned only as personal representative or trustee unless, in the latter case, the holding company or a subsidiary of it is beneficially interested under the trust.

For the purpose of ascertaining whether the holding company or a subsidiary is so interested, there shall be disregarded—

(a) any interest held only by way of security for the purposes of a transaction entered into by the holding company or subsidiary in the ordinary course of a business which includes the lending of money;

(b) any such interest as is mentioned in Part I of Schedule 2.

(3) The prohibition does not apply where the subsidiary is concerned only as a market maker.

Companies Act 1985

For this purpose a person is a market maker if—

(a) he holds himself out at all normal times in compliance with the rules of a recognised investment exchange other than an overseas investment exchange (within the meaning of the Financial Services Act 1986) as willing to buy and sell securities at prices specified by him, and

(b) he is recognised as so doing by that investment exchange.

(4) Where a body corporate became a holder of shares in a company—

(a) before 1st July 1948, or

(b) on or after that date and before the commencement of section 129 of the Companies Act 1989, in circumstances in which this section as it then had effect did not apply,

but at any time after the commencement of that section falls within the prohibition in subsection (1) above in respect of those shares, it may continue to be a member of that company; but for so long as that prohibition would apply, apart from this subsection, it has no right to vote in respect of those shares at meetings of the company or of any class of its members.

(5) Where a body corporate becomes a holder of shares in a company after the commencement of that section in circumstances in which the prohibition in subsection (1) does not apply, but subsequently falls within that prohibition in respect of those shares, it may continue to be a member of that company; but for so long as that prohibition would apply, apart from this subsection, it has no right to vote in respect of those shares at meetings of the company or of any class of its members.

(6) Where a body corporate is permitted to continue as a member of a company by virtue of subsection (4) or (5), an allotment to it of fully paid shares in the company may be validly made by way of capitalisation of reserves of the company; but for so long as the prohibition in subsection (1) would apply, apart from subsection (4) or (5), it has no right to vote in respect of those shares at meetings of the company or of any class of its members.

(7) The provisions of this section apply to a nominee acting on behalf of a subsidiary as to the subsidiary itself.

(8) In relation to a company other than a company limited by shares, the references in this section to shares shall be construed as references to the interest of its members as such, whatever the form of that interest.][1]

[1] Substituted by CA 1989, s 129 with effect from a date to be appointed.

PART V   SHARE CAPITAL, ITS INCREASE, MAINTENANCE AND REDUCTION

CHAPTER I   GENERAL PROVISIONS ABOUT SHARE CAPITAL

117   Public company share capital requirements

(1)   A company registered as a public company on its original incorporation shall not do business or exercise any borrowing powers unless the registrar of companies has issued it with a certificate under this section or the company is re-registered as a private company.

(2)   The registrar shall issue a company with such a certificate if, on an application made to him by the company in the prescribed form, he is satisfied that the nominal value of the company's allotted share capital is not less than the authorised minimum, and there is delivered to him a statutory declaration complying with the following subsection.

(3)   The statutory declaration must be in the prescribed form and be signed by a director or secretary of the company; and it must—

(a)   state that the nominal value of the company's allotted share capital is not less than the authorised minimum;

(b)   specify the amount paid up, at the time of the application, on the allotted share capital of the company;

(c)   specify the amount, or estimated amount, of the company's preliminary expenses and the persons by whom any of those expenses have been paid or are payable; and

(d)   specify any amount or benefit paid or given, or intended to be paid or given, to any promoter of the company, and the consideration for the payment or benefit.

(4)   For the purposes of subsection (2), a share allotted in pursuance of an employees' share scheme may not be taken into account in determining the nominal value of the company's allotted share capital unless it is paid up at least as to one-quarter of the nominal value of the share and the whole of any premium on the share.

(5)   The registrar may accept a statutory declaration delivered to him under this section as sufficient evidence of the matters stated in it.

(6)   A certificate under this section in respect of a company is conclusive evidence that the company is entitled to do business and exercise any borrowing powers.

(7)   If a company does business or exercises borrowing powers in contravention of this section, the company and any officer of it who is in default is liable to a fine.

(8)   Nothing in this section affects the validity of any transaction entered into by a company; but, if a company enters into a transaction in contravention of this section and fails to comply with its obligations in that connection within 21 days from being called upon to do so, the directors of the company are jointly and severally liable to indemnify the other party to the transaction in respect of any loss or damage suffered by him by reason of the company's failure to comply with those obligations.

Companies Act 1985

118   The authorised minimum

(1)   In this Act, "the authorised minimum" means £50,000, or such other sum as the Secretary of State may by order made by statutory instrument specify instead.

(2)   An order under this section which increases the authorised minimum may—

    (a)   require any public company having an allotted share capital of which the nominal value is less than the amount specified in the order as the authorised minimum to increase that value to not less than that amount or make application to be re-registered as a private company;

    (b)   make, in connection with any such requirement, provision for any of the matters for which provision is made by this Act relating to a company's registration, re-registration or change of name, to payment for any share comprised in a company's capital and to offers of shares in or debentures of a company to the public, including provision as to the consequences (whether in criminal law or otherwise) of a failure to comply with any requirement of the order; and

    (c)   contain such supplemental and transitional provisions as the Secretary of State thinks appropriate, make different provision for different cases and, in particular, provide for any provision of the order to come into operation on different days for different purposes.

(3)   An order shall not be made under this section unless a draft of it has been laid before Parliament and approved by resolution of each House.

CHAPTER III   SHARE PREMIUMS

130   Application of share premiums

(1)   If a company issues shares at a premium, whether for cash or otherwise, a sum equal to the aggregate amount or value of the premiums on those shares shall be transferred to an account called "the share premium account".

(2)   The share premium account may be applied by the company in paying up unissued shares to be allotted to members as fully paid bonus shares, or in writing off—

(a)   the company's preliminary expenses; or
(b)   the expenses of, or the commission paid or discount allowed on, any issue of shares or debentures of the company,

or in providing for the premium payable on redemption of debentures of the company.

(3)   Subject to this, the provisions of this Act relating to the reduction of a company's share capital apply as if the share premium account were part of its paid up share capital.

(4)   Sections 131 and 132 below give relief from the requirements of this section, and in those sections references to the issuing company are to the company issuing shares as above mentioned.

Cross references. See Sec 131(2); Sec 132(2); Sec 134; CC(CP)A 1985, s 12 (share premiums—retrospective relief).

131   Merger relief

(1)   With the exception made by section 132([8]²) (group reconstruction) this section applies where the issuing company has secured at least a 90 per cent. equity holding in another company in pursuance of an arrangement providing for the allotment of equity shares in the issuing company on terms that the consideration for the shares allotted is to be provided—

(a)   by the issue or transfer to the issuing company of equity shares in the other company, or
(b)   by the cancellation of any such shares not held by the issuing company.

(2)   If the equity shares in the issuing company allotted in pursuance of the arrangement in consideration for the acquisition or cancellation of equity shares in the other company are issued at a premium, section 130 does not apply to the premiums on those shares.

(3)   Where the arrangement also provides for the allotment of any shares in the issuing company on terms that the consideration for those shares is to be provided by the issue or transfer to the issuing company of non-equity shares in the other company or by the cancellation of any such shares in that company not held by the issuing company, relief under subsection (2) extends to any shares in the issuing company allotted on those terms in pursuance of the arrangement.

Companies Act 1985

(4) Subject to the next subsection, the issuing company is to be regarded for purposes of this section as having secured at least a 90 per cent. equity holding in another company in pursuance of such an arrangement as is mentioned in subsection (1) if in consequence of an acquisition or cancellation of equity shares in that company (in pursuance of that arrangement) it holds equity shares in that company (whether all or any of those shares were acquired in pursuance of that arrangement, or not) of an aggregate nominal value equal to 90 per cent. or more of the nominal value of that company's equity share capital.

(5) Where the equity share capital of the other company is divided into different classes of shares, this section does not apply unless the requirements of subsection (1) are satisfied in relation to each of those classes of shares taken separately.

(6) Shares held by a company which is the issuing company's holding company or subsidiary, or a subsidiary of the issuing company's holding company, or by its or their nominees, are to be regarded for purposes of this section as held by the issuing company.

(7) In relation to a company and its shares and capital, the following definitions apply for purposes of this section—

(a) "equity shares" means shares comprised in the company's equity share capital; and
(b) "non-equity shares" means shares (of any class) not so comprised;

and "arrangement" means any agreement, scheme or arrangement (including an arrangement sanctioned under section 425 (company compromise with members and creditors) or section [110 of the Insolvency Act][1] (liquidator accepting shares etc. as consideration for sale of company property)).

(8) The relief allowed by this section does not apply if the issue of shares took place before 4th February 1981.

[1] Substituted by IA 1986, s 439(1), 13 Sch Part I with effect from 29 December 1986 (see IA 1986, s 443 and SI 1986 No 1924).
Previously '582'.

[2] Substituted by CA 1989, 19 Sch 1 with effect from 1 March 1990 (SI 1990 No 142) but deemed always to have had effect.
Previously '4'.

Cross references. See Sec 132(8); Sec 133 (supplementary provisions).

132 Relief in respect of group reconstructions

(1) This section applies where the issuing company—

(a) is a wholly-owned subsidiary of another company ("the holding company"), and
(b) allots shares to the holding company or to another wholly-owned subsidiary of the holding company in consideration for the transfer to the issuing company of assets other than cash, being assets of any company ("the transferor company") which is a member of the group of companies which comprises the holding company and all its wholly-owned subsidiaries.

(2)   Where the shares in the issuing company allotted in consideration for the transfer are issued at a premium, the issuing company is not required by section 130 to transfer any amount in excess of the minimum premium value to the share premium account.

(3)   In subsection (2), "the minimum premium value" means the amount (if any) by which the base value of the consideration for the shares allotted exceeds the aggregate nominal value of those shares.

(4)   For the purposes of subsection (3), the base value of the consideration for the shares allotted is the amount by which the base value of the assets transferred exceeds the base value of any liabilities of the transferor company assumed by the issuing company as part of the consideration for the assets transferred.

(5)   For the purposes of subsection (4)—

   (a)   the base value of the assets transferred is to be taken as—
      (i)   the cost of those assets to the transferor company, or
      (ii)   the amount at which those assets are stated in the transferor company's accounting records immediately before the transfer,
      whichever is the less; and

   (b)   the base value of the liabilities assumed is to be taken as the amount at which they are stated in the transferor company's accounting records immediately before the transfer.

(6)   The relief allowed by this section does not apply (subject to the next subsection) if the issue of shares took place before the date of the coming into force of the Companies (Share Premium Account) Regulations 1984 (which were made on 21st December 1984).

(7)   To the extent that the relief allowed by this section would have been allowed by section 38 of the Companies Act 1981 as originally enacted (the text of which section is set out in Schedule 25 to this Act), the relief applies where the issue of shares took place before the date of the coming into force of those Regulations, but not if the issue took place before 4th February 1981.

(8)   Section 131 does not apply in a case falling within this section.

Cross references. See Sec 133 (supplementary provisions).

133   Provisions supplementing ss 131, 132

(1)   An amount corresponding to one representing the premiums or part of the premiums on shares issued by a company which by virtue of sections 131 or 132 of this Act, or section 12 of the Consequential Provisions Act, is not included in the company's share premium account may also be disregarded in determining the amount at which any shares or other consideration provided for the shares issued is to be included in the company's balance sheet.

(2)   References in this Chapter (however expressed) to—

   (a)   the acquisition by a company of shares in another company; and

   (b)   the issue or allotment of shares to, or the transfer of shares to or by, a company,

include (respectively) the acquisition of any of those shares by, and the issue or allotment or (as the case may be) the transfer of any of those shares to or by, nominees of that company; and the reference in section 132 to the company transferring the shares is to be construed accordingly.

(3) References in this Chapter to the transfer of shares in a company include the transfer of a right to be included in the company's register of members in respect of those shares.

(4) In sections 131 to 133 "company", except in references to the issuing company, includes any body corporate.

134 Provision for extending or restricting relief from s 130

(1) The Secretary of State may by regulations in a statutory instrument make such provision as appears to him to be appropriate—

    (a) for relieving companies from the requirements of section 130 in relation to premiums other than cash premiums, or

    (b) for restricting or otherwise modifying any relief from those requirements provided by this Chapter.

(2) Regulations under this section may make different provision for different cases or classes of case and may contain such incidental and supplementary provisions as the Secretary of State thinks fit.

(3) No such regulations shall be made unless a draft of the instrument containing them has been laid before Parliament and approved by a resolution of each House.

CHAPTER IV   REDUCTION OF SHARE CAPITAL

135   Special resolution for reduction of share capital

   (1)   Subject to confirmation by the court, a company limited by shares or a company limited by guarantee and having a share capital may, if so authorised by its articles, by special resolution reduce its share capital in any way.

   (2)   In particular, and without prejudice to subsection (1), the company may—

      (a)   extinguish or reduce the liability on any of its shares in respect of share capital not paid up; or

      (b)   either with or without extinguishing or reducing liability on any of its shares, cancel any paid-up share capital which is lost or unrepresented by available assets; or

      (c)   either with or without extinguishing or reducing liability on any of its shares, pay off any paid-up share capital which is in excess of the company's wants;

and the company may, if and so far as is necessary, alter its memorandum by reducing the amount of its share capital and of its shares accordingly.

   (3)   A special resolution under this section is in this Act referred to as "a resolution for reducing share capital".

Companies Act 1985

CHAPTER VII   REDEEMABLE SHARES; PURCHASE BY A COMPANY OF ITS OWN SHARES

Redemption and purchase generally

170   The capital redemption reserve

(1)   Where under this Chapter shares of a company are redeemed or purchased wholly out of the company's profits, the amount by which the company's issued share capital is diminished in accordance with section 160(4) on cancellation of the shares redeemed or purchased shall be transferred to a reserve, called "the capital redemption reserve".

(2)   If the shares are redeemed or purchased wholly or partly out of the proceeds of a fresh issue and the aggregate amount of those proceeds is less than the aggregate nominal value of the shares redeemed or purchased, the amount of the difference shall be transferred to the capital redemption reserve.

(3)   But subsection (2) does not apply if the proceeds of the fresh issue are applied by the company in making a redemption or purchase of its own shares in addition to a payment out of capital under section 171.

(4)   The provisions of this Act relating to the reduction of a company's share capital apply as if the capital redemption reserve were paid-up share capital of the company, except that the reserve may be applied by the company in paying up its unissued shares to be allotted to members of the company as fully paid bonus shares.

PART VII   ACCOUNTS AND AUDIT

CHAPTER I   PROVISIONS APPLYING TO COMPANIES GENERALLY

[*Annual accounts*

226   Duty to prepare individual company accounts

   (1)   The directors of every company shall prepare for each financial year of the company—

      (a)   a balance sheet as at the last day of the year, and

      (b)   a profit and loss account.

      Those accounts are referred to in this Part as the company's 'individual accounts'.

   (2)   The balance sheet shall give a true and fair view of the state of affairs of the company as at the end of the financial year; and the profit and loss account shall give a true and fair view of the profit or loss of the company for the financial year.

   (3)   A company's individual accounts shall comply with the provisions of Schedule 4 as to the form and content of the balance sheet and profit and loss account and additional information to be provided by way of notes to the accounts.

   (4)   Where compliance with the provisions of that Schedule, and the other provisions of this Act as to the matters to be included in a company's individual accounts or in notes to those accounts, would not be sufficient to give a true and fair view, the necessary additional information shall be given in the accounts or in a note to them.

   (5)   If in special circumstances compliance with any of those provisions is inconsistent with the requirement to give a true and fair view, the directors shall depart from that provision to the extent necessary to give a true and fair view.

      Particulars of any such departure, the reasons for it and its effect shall be given in a note to the accounts.][1]

---

[1] Inserted by CA 1989, s 4 with effect from 1 April 1990 (SI 1990 No 355) subject to the transitional and saving provisions in Arts 6 to 9 of that Order.

[**227   Duty to prepare group accounts**

   (1)   If at the end of a financial year a company is a parent company the directors shall, as well as preparing individual accounts for the year, prepare group accounts.

   (2)   Group accounts shall be consolidated accounts comprising—

      (a)   a consolidated balance sheet dealing with the state of affairs of the parent company and its subsidiary undertakings, and

      (b)   a consolidated profit and loss account dealing with the profit or loss of the parent company and its subsidiary undertakings.

   (3)   The accounts shall give a true and fair view of the state of affairs as at the end of the financial year, and the profit or loss for the financial year, of the undertakings included in the consolidation as a whole, so far as concerns members of the company.

   (4)   A company's group accounts shall comply with the provisions of Schedule 4A as to the form and content of the consolidated balance sheet and consolidated

profit and loss account and additional information to be provided by way of notes to the accounts.

(5) Where compliance with the provisions of that Schedule, and the other provisions of this Act, as to the matters to be included in a company's group accounts or in notes to those accounts, would not be sufficient to give a true and fair view, the necessary additional information shall be given in the accounts or in a note to them.

(6) If in special circumstances compliance with any of those provisions is inconsistent with the requirement to give a true and fair view, the directors shall depart from that provision to the extent necessary to give a true and fair view.

Particulars of any such departure, the reasons for it and its effect shall be given in a note to the accounts.][1]

---

[1] Inserted by CA 1989, s 5 with effect from 1 April 1990 (SI 1990 No 355) subject to the transitional and saving provisions in Arts 6 to 9 of that Order.

[228 Exemption for parent companies included in accounts of larger group

(1) A company is exempt from the requirement to prepare group accounts if it is itself a subsidiary undertaking and its immediate parent undertaking is established under the law of a member State of the European Economic Community, in the following cases—

   (a) where the company is a wholly-owned subsidiary of that parent undertaking;
   (b) where that parent undertaking holds more than 50 per cent. of the shares in the company and notice requesting the preparation of group accounts has not been served on the company by shareholders holding in aggregate—
      (i) more than half of the remaining shares in the company, or
      (ii) 5 per cent. of the total shares in the company.

Such notice must be served not later than six months after the end of the financial year before that to which it relates.

(2) Exemption is conditional upon compliance with all of the following conditions—

   (a) that the company is included in consolidated accounts for a larger group drawn up to the same date, or to an earlier date in the same financial year, by a parent undertaking established under the law of a member State of the European Economic Community;
   (b) that those accounts are drawn up and audited, and that parent undertaking's annual report is drawn up, according to that law, in accordance with the provisions of the Seventh Directive (83/349/EEC);
   (c) that the company discloses in its individual accounts that it is exempt from the obligation to prepare and deliver group accounts;
   (d) that the company states in its individual accounts the name of the parent undertaking which draws up the group accounts referred to above and—
      (i) if it is incorporated outside Great Britain, the country in which it is incorporated,
      (ii) if it is incorporated in Great Britain, whether it is registered in England and Wales or in Scotland, and
      (iii) if it is unincorporated, the address of its principal place of business;

(e)   that the company delivers to the registrar, within the period allowed for delivering its individual accounts, copies of those group accounts and of the parent undertaking's annual report, together with the auditors' report on them; and

(f)   that if any document comprised in accounts and reports delivered in accordance with paragraph (e) is in a language other than English, there is annexed to the copy of that document delivered a translation of it into English, certified in the prescribed manner to be a correct translation.

(3)   The exemption does not apply to a company any of whose securities are listed on a stock exchange in any member State of the European Economic Community.

(4)   Shares held by directors of a company for the purpose of complying with any share qualification requirement shall be disregarded in determining for the purposes of subsection (1)(a) whether the company is a wholly-owned subsidiary.

(5)   For the purposes of subsection (1)(b) shares held by a wholly-owned subsidiary of the parent undertaking, or held on behalf of the parent undertaking or a wholly-owned subsidiary, shall be attributed to the parent undertaking.

(6)   In subsection (3) "securities" includes—

(a)   shares and stock,

(b)   debentures, including debenture stock, loan stock, bonds, certificates of deposit and other instruments creating or acknowledging indebtedness,

(c)   warrants or other instruments entitling the holder to subscribe for securities falling within paragraph (a) or (b), and

(d)   certificates or other instruments which confer—

    (i)   property rights in respect of a security falling within paragraph (a), (b) or (c),

    (ii)   any right to acquire, dispose of, underwrite or convert a security, being a right to which the holder would be entitled if he held any such security to which the certificate or other instrument relates, or

    (iii)   a contractual right (other than an option) to acquire any such security otherwise than by subscription.][1]

---

[1]   Inserted by CA 1989, s 5 with effect from 1 April 1990 (SI 1990 No 355) subject to the transitional and saving provisions in Arts 6 to 9 of that Order.

[229   Subsidiary undertakings included in the consolidation

(1)   Subject to the exceptions authorised or required by this section, all the subsidiary undertakings of the parent company shall be included in the consolidation.

(2)   A subsidiary undertaking may be excluded from consolidation if its inclusion is not material for the purpose of giving a true and fair view; but two or more undertakings may be excluded only if they are not material taken together.

(3)   In addition, a subsidiary undertaking may be excluded from consolidation where—

(a)   severe long-term restrictions substantially hinder the exercise of the rights of the parent company over the assets or management of that undertaking, or

(b)   the information necessary for the preparation of group accounts cannot be obtained without disproportionate expense or undue delay, or

(c) the interest of the parent company is held exclusively with a view to subsequent resale and the undertaking has not previously been included in consolidated group accounts prepared by the parent company.

The reference in paragraph (a) to the rights of the parent company and the reference in paragraph (c) to the interest of the parent company are, respectively, to rights and interests held by or attributed to the company for the purposes of section 258 (definition of "parent undertaking") in the absence of which it would not be the parent company.

(4) Where the activities of one or more subsidiary undertakings are so different from those of other undertakings to be included in the consolidation that their inclusion would be incompatible with the obligation to give a true and fair view, those undertakings shall be excluded from consolidation.

This subsection does not apply merely because some of the undertakings are industrial, some commercial and some provide services, or because they carry on industrial or commercial activities involving different products or provide different services.

(5) Where all the subsidiary undertakings of a parent company fall within the above exclusions, no group accounts are required.][1]

[1] Inserted by CA 1989, s 5 with effect from 1 April 1990 (SI 1990 No 355) subject to the transitional and saving provisions in Arts 6 to 9 of that Order.

[230 Treatment of individual profit and loss account where group accounts prepared

(1) The following provisions apply with respect to the individual profit and loss account of a parent company where—

(a) the company is required to prepare and does prepare group accounts in accordance with this Act, and
(b) the notes to the company's individual balance sheet show the company's profit or loss for the financial year determined in accordance with this Act.

(2) The profit and loss account need not contain the information specified in paragraphs 52 to 57 of Schedule 4 (information supplementing the profit and loss account).

(3) The profit and loss account must be approved in accordance with section 233(1) (approval by board of directors) but may be omitted from the company's annual accounts for the purposes of the other provisions below in this Chapter.

(4) The exemption conferred by this section is conditional upon its being disclosed in the company's annual accounts that the exemption applies.][1]

[1] Inserted by CA 1989, s 5 with effect from 1 April 1990 (SI 1990 No 355) subject to the transitional and saving provisions in Arts 6 to 9 of that Order.

[231 Disclosure required in notes to accounts: related undertakings

(1) The information specified in Schedule 5 shall be given in notes to a company's annual accounts.

(2) Where the company is not required to prepare group accounts, the information specified in Part I of that Schedule shall be given; and where the company is required to prepare group accounts, the information specified in Part II of that Schedule shall be given.

Companies Act 1985

(3) The information required by Schedule 5 need not be disclosed with respect to an undertaking which—

(a) is established under the law of a country outside the United Kingdom, or

(b) carries on business outside the United Kingdom,

if in the opinion of the directors of the company the disclosure would be seriously prejudicial to the business of that undertaking, or to the business of the company or any of its subsidiary undertakings, and the Secretary of State agrees that the information need not be disclosed.

This subsection does not apply in relation to the information required under paragraph 5(2), 6 or 20 of that Schedule.

(4) Where advantage is taken of subsection (3), that fact shall be stated in a note to the company's annual accounts.

(5) If the directors of the company are of the opinion that the number of undertakings in respect of which the company is required to disclose information under any provision of Schedule 5 to this Act is such that compliance with that provision would result in information of excessive length being given, the information need only be given in respect of—

(a) the undertakings whose results or financial position, in the opinion of the directors, principally affected the figures shown in the company's annual accounts, and

(b) undertakings excluded from consolidation under section 229(3) or (4).

This subsection does not apply in relation to the information required under paragraph 10 or 29 of that Schedule.

(6) If advantage is taken of subsection (5)—

(a) there shall be included in the notes to the company's annual accounts a statement that the information is given only with respect to such undertakings as are mentioned in that subsection, and

(b) the full information (both that which is disclosed in the notes to the accounts and that which is not) shall be annexed to the company's next annual return.

For this purpose the "next annual return" means that next delivered to the registrar after the accounts in question have been approved under section 233.

(7) If a company fails to comply with subsection (6)(b), the company and every officer of it who is in default is liable to a fine and, for continued contravention, to a daily default fine.][1]

---

[1] Inserted by CA 1989, s 6 with effect from 1 April 1990 (SI 1990 No 355) subject to the transitional and saving provisions in Arts 6 to 9 of that Order.

Cross references. See 4 Sch 63.

[232 Disclosure required in notes to accounts: emoluments and other benefits of directors and others

(1) The information specified in Schedule 6 shall be given in notes to a company's annual accounts.

(2) In that Schedule—

Part I relates to the emoluments of directors (including emoluments waived), pensions of directors and past directors, compensation for loss of office to directors and past directors and sums paid to third parties in respect of directors' services,

Part II relates to loans, quasi-loans and other dealings in favour of directors and connected persons, and

Part III relates to transactions, arrangements and agreements made by the company or a subsidiary undertaking for officers of the company other than directors.

(3) It is the duty of any director of a company, and any person who is or has at any time in the preceding five years been an officer of the company, to give notice to the company of such matters relating to himself as may be necessary for the purposes of Part I of Schedule 6.

(4) A person who makes default in complying with subsection (3) commits an offence and is liable to a fine.][1]

---

[1] Inserted by CA 1989, s 6 with effect from 1 April 1990 (SI 1990 No 355) subject to the transitional and saving provisions in Arts 6 to 9 of that Order.

[*Approval and signing of accounts*

233 Approval and signing of accounts

(1) A company's annual accounts shall be approved by the board of directors and signed on behalf of the board by a director of the company.

(2) The signature shall be on the company's balance sheet.

(3) Every copy of the balance sheet which is laid before the company in general meeting, or which is otherwise circulated, published or issued, shall state the name of the person who signed the balance sheet on behalf of the board.

(4) The copy of the company's balance sheet which is delivered to the registrar shall be signed on behalf of the board by a director of the company.

(5) If annual accounts are approved which do not comply with the requirements of this Act, every director of the company who is party to their approval and who knows that they do not comply or is reckless as to whether they comply is guilty of an offence and liable to a fine.

For this purpose every director of the company at the time the accounts are approved shall be taken to be a party to their approval unless he shows that he took all reasonable steps to prevent their being approved.

(6) If a copy of the balance sheet—

(a) is laid before the company, or otherwise circulated, published or issued, without the balance sheet having been signed as required by this section or without the required statement of the signatory's name being included, or

(b) is delivered to the registrar without being signed as required by this section,

the company and every officer of it who is in default is guilty of an offence and liable to a fine.][1]

Inserted by CA 1989, s 7.

(a)   in respect of subsections (1)-(4)(6) with effect from 1 April 1990 (SI 1990 No 355) subject to the transitional and saving provisions in Arts 6 to 9 of that Order.

Cross references. See 4 Sch 63.

[*Directors' report*

234   Duty to prepare directors' report

(1)   The directors of a company shall for each financial year prepare a report—

(a)   containing a fair review of the development of the business of the company and its subsidiary undertakings during the financial year and of their position at the end of it, and

(b)   stating the amount (if any) which they recommend should be paid as dividend and the amount (if any) which they propose to carry to reserves.

(2)   The report shall state the names of the persons who, at any time during the financial year, were directors of the company, and the principal activities of the company and its subsidiary undertakings in the course of the year and any significant change in those activities in the year.

(3)   The report shall also comply with Schedule 7 as regards the disclosure of the matters mentioned there.

(4)   In Schedule 7—

Part I relates to matters of a general nature, including changes in asset values, directors' shareholdings and other interests and contributions for political and charitable purposes,

Part II relates to the acquisition by a company of its own shares or a charge on them,

Part III relates to the employment, training and advancement of disabled persons,

Part IV relates to the health, safety and welfare at work of the company's employees, and

Part V relates to the involvement of employees in the affairs, policy and performance of the company.

(5)   In the case of any failure to comply with the provisions of this Part as to the preparation of a directors' report and the contents of the report, every person who was a director of the company immediately before the end of the period for laying and delivering accounts and reports for the financial year in question is guilty of an offence and liable to a fine.

(6)   In proceedings against a person for an offence under this section it is a defence for him to prove that he took all reasonable steps for securing compliance with the requirements in question.]¹

Inserted by CA 1989, s 8 with effect from 1 April 1990 (SI 1990 No 355) subject to the transitional and saving provisions in Arts 6 to 9 of that Order.

Cross references. See 4 Sch 63.

Companies Act 1985

[234A Approval and signing of directors' report

(1)   The directors' report shall be approved by the board of directors and signed on behalf of the board by a director or the secretary of the company.

(2)   Every copy of the directors' report which is laid before the company in general meeting, or which is otherwise circulated, published or issued, shall state the name of the person who signed it on behalf of the board.

(3)   The copy of the directors' report which is delivered to the registrar shall be signed on behalf of the board by a director or the secretary of the company.

(4)   If a copy of the directors' report—

(a)   is laid before the company, or otherwise circulated, published or issued, without the report having been signed as required by this section or without the required statement of the signatory's name being included, or

(b)   is delivered to the registrar without being signed as required by this section,

the company and every officer of it who is in default is guilty of an offence and liable to a fine.]¹

---

¹   Inserted by CA 1989, s 8 with effect from 1 April 1990 (SI 1990 No 355) subject to the transitional and saving provisions in Arts 6 to 9 of that Order.

[Auditors' report

235   Auditors' report

(1)   A company's auditors shall make a report to the company's members on all annual accounts of the company of which copies are to be laid before the company in general meeting during their tenure of office.

(2)   The auditors' report shall state whether in the auditors' opinion the annual accounts have been properly prepared in accordance with this Act, and in particular whether a true and fair view is given—

(a)   in the case of an individual balance sheet, of the state of affairs of the company as at the end of the financial year,

(b)   in the case of an individual profit and loss account, of the profit or loss of the company for the financial year,

(c)   in the case of group accounts, of the state of affairs as at the end of the financial year, and the profit or loss for the financial year, of the undertakings included in the consolidation as a whole, so far as concerns members of the company.

(3)   The auditors shall consider whether the information given in the directors' report for the financial year for which the annual accounts are prepared is consistent with those accounts; and if they are of opinion that it is not they shall state that fact in their report.]¹

---

¹   Inserted by CA 1989, s 9 with effect from 1 April 1990 (SI 1990 No 355) subject to the transitional and saving provisions in Arts 6 to 9 of that Order.

[236   Signature of auditors' report

(1)   The auditors' report shall state the names of the auditors and be signed by them.

(2) Every copy of the auditors' report which is laid before the company in general meeting, or which is otherwise circulated, published or issued, shall state the names of the auditors.

(3) The copy of the auditors' report which is delivered to the registrar shall state the names of the auditors and be signed by them.

(4) If a copy of the auditors' report—

(a) is laid before the company, or otherwise circulated, published or issued, without the required statement of the auditors' names, or

(b) is delivered to the registrar without the required statement of the auditors' names or without being signed as required by this section,

the company and every officer of it who is in default is guilty of an offence and liable to a fine.

(5) References in this section to signature by the auditors are, where the office of auditor is held by a body corporate or partnership, to signature in the name of the body corporate or partnership by a person authorised to sign on its behalf.][1]

---

[1] Inserted by CA 1989, s 9 with effect from 1 April 1990 (SI 1990 No 355) subject to the transitional and saving provisions in Arts 6 to 9 of that Order.

[237 Duties of auditors

(1) A company's auditors shall, in preparing their report, carry out such investigations as will enable them to form an opinion as to—

(a) whether proper accounting records have been kept by the company and proper returns adequate for their audit have been received from branches not visited by them, and

(b) whether the company's individual accounts are in agreement with the accounting records and returns.

(2) If the auditors are of opinion that proper accounting records have not been kept, or that proper returns adequate for their audit have not been received from branches not visited by them, or if the company's individual accounts are not in agreement with the accounting records and returns, the auditors shall state that fact in their report.

(3) If the auditors fail to obtain all the information and explanations which, to the best of their knowledge and belief, are necessary for the purposes of their audit, they shall state that fact in their report.

(4) If the requirements of Schedule 6 (disclosure of information: emoluments and other benefits of directors and others) are not complied with in the annual accounts, the auditors shall include in their report, so far as they are reasonably able to do so, a statement giving the required particulars.][1]

---

[1] Inserted by CA 1989, s 9 with effect from 1 April 1990 (SI 1990 No 355) subject to the transitional and saving provisions in Arts 6 to 9 of that Order.

[*Publication of accounts and reports*

238 Persons entitled to receive copies of accounts and reports

(1) A copy of the company's annual accounts, together with a copy of the directors' report for that financial year and of the auditors' report on those accounts, shall be sent to—

      (a)   every member of the company,
      (b)   every holder of the company's debentures, and
      (c)   every person who is entitled to receive notice of general meetings,

      not less than 21 days before the date of the meeting at which copies of those documents are to be laid in accordance with section 241.

  (2)   Copies need not be sent—

      (a)   to a person who is not entitled to receive notices of general meetings and of whose address the company is unaware, or
      (b)   to more than one of the joint holders of shares or debentures none of whom is entitled to receive such notices, or
      (c)   in the case of joint holders of shares or debentures some of whom are, and some not, entitled to receive such notices, to those who are not so entitled.

  (3)   In the case of a company not having a share capital, copies need not be sent to anyone who is not entitled to receive notices of general meetings of the company.

  (4)   If copies are sent less than 21 days before the date of the meeting, they shall, notwithstanding that fact, be deemed to have been duly sent if it is so agreed by all the members entitled to attend and vote at the meeting.

  (5)   If default is made in complying with this section, the company and every officer of it who is in default is guilty of an offence and liable to a fine.

  (6)   Where copies are sent out under this section over a period of days, references elsewhere in this Act to the day on which copies are sent out shall be construed as references to the last day of that period.][1]

---

[1] Inserted by CA 1989, s 10 with effect from 1 April 1990 (SI 1990 No 355) subject to the transitional and saving provisions in Arts 6 to 9 of that Order.

[239 Right to demand copies of accounts and reports

  (1)   Any member of a company and any holder of a company's debentures is entitled to be furnished, on demand and without charge, with a copy of the company's last annual accounts and directors' report and a copy of the auditors' report on those accounts.

  (2)   The entitlement under this section is to a single copy of those documents, but that is in addition to any copy to which a person may be entitled under section 238.

  (3)   If a demand under this section is not complied with within seven days, the company and every officer of it who is in default is guilty of an offence and liable to a fine and, for continued contravention, to a daily default fine.

  (4)   If in proceedings for such an offence the issue arises whether a person had already been furnished with a copy of the relevant document under this section, it is for the defendant to prove that he had.][1]

---

[1] Inserted by CA 1989, s 10 with effect from 1 April 1990 (SI 1990 No 355) subject to the transitional and saving provisions in Arts 6 to 9 of that Order.

[240 Requirements in connection with publication of accounts

  (1)   If a company publishes any of its statutory accounts, they must be accompanied by the relevant auditors' report under section 235.

(2)   A company which is required to prepare group accounts for a financial year shall not publish its statutory individual accounts for that year without also publishing with them its statutory group accounts.

(3)   If a company publishes non-statutory accounts, it shall publish with them a statement indicating—

(a)   that they are not the company's statutory accounts,

(b)   whether statutory accounts dealing with any financial year with which the non-statutory accounts purport to deal have been delivered to the registrar,

(c)   whether the company's auditors have made a report under section 235 on the statutory accounts for any such financial year, and

(d)   whether any report so made was qualified or contained a statement under section 237(2) or (3) (accounting records or returns inadequate, accounts not agreeing with records and returns or failure to obtain necessary information and explanations);

and it shall not publish with the non-statutory accounts any auditors' report under section 235.

(4)   For the purposes of this section a company shall be regarded as publishing a document if it publishes, issues or circulates it or otherwise makes it available for public inspection in a manner calculated to invite members of the public generally, or any class of members of the public, to read it.

(5)   References in this section to a company's statutory accounts are to its individual or group accounts for a financial year as required to be delivered to the registrar under section 242; and references to the publication by a company of "non-statutory accounts" are to the publication of—

(a)   any balance sheet or profit and loss account relating to, or purporting to deal with, a financial year of the company, or

(b)   an account in any form purporting to be a balance sheet or profit and loss account for the group consisting of the company and its subsidiary undertakings relating to, or purporting to deal with, a financial year of the company,

otherwise than as part of the company's statutory accounts.

(6)   A company which contravenes any provision of this section, and any officer of it who is in default, is guilty of an offence and liable to a fine.][1]

---

[1]   Inserted by CA 1989, s 10 with effect from 1 April 1990 (SI 1990 No 355) subject to the transitional and saving provisions in Arts 6 to 9 of that Order.

[*Laying and delivering of accounts and reports*

241   Accounts and reports to be laid before company in general meeting

(1)   The directors of a company shall in respect of each financial year lay before the company in general meeting copies of the company's annual accounts, the directors' report and the auditors' report on those accounts.

(2)   If the requirements of subsection (1) are not complied with before the end of the period allowed for laying and delivering accounts and reports, every person who immediately before the end of that period was a director of the company is guilty of an offence and liable to a fine and, for continued contravention, to a daily default fine.

Companies Act 1985

(3) It is a defence for a person charged with such an offence to prove that he took all reasonable steps for securing that those requirements would be complied with before the end of that period.

(4) It is not a defence to prove that the documents in question were not in fact prepared as required by this Part.][1]

---

[1] Inserted by CA 1989, s 11 with effect from 1 April 1990 (SI 1990 No 355) subject to the transitional and saving provisions in Arts 6 to 9 of that Order.

Cross references. SI 1985 No 854 (translation of documents into English).

[242 Accounts and reports to be delivered to the registrar

(1) The directors of a company shall in respect of each financial year deliver to the registrar a copy of the company's annual accounts together with a copy of the directors' report for that year and a copy of the auditors' report on those accounts.

If any document comprised in those accounts or reports is in a language other than English, the directors shall annex to the copy of that document delivered a translation of it into English, certified in the prescribed manner to be a correct translation.

(2) If the requirements of subsection (1) are not complied with before the end of the period allowed for laying and delivering accounts and reports, every person who immediately before the end of that period was a director of the company is guilty of an offence and liable to a fine and, for continued contravention, to a daily default fine.

(3) Further, if the directors of the company fail to make good the default within 14 days after the service of a notice on them requiring compliance, the court may on the application of any member or creditor of the company or of the registrar, make an order directing the directors (or any of them) to make good the default within such time as may be specified in the order.

The court's order may provide that all costs of and incidental to the application shall be borne by the directors.

(4) It is a defence for a person charged with an offence under this section to prove that he took all reasonable steps for securing that the requirements of subsection (1) would be complied with before the end of the period allowed for laying and delivering accounts and reports.

(5) It is not a defence in any proceedings under this section to prove that the documents in question were not in fact prepared as required by this Part.][1]

---

[1] Inserted by CA 1989, s 11 with effect from 1 April 1990 (SI 1990 No 355) subject to the transitional and saving provisions in Arts 6 to 9 of that Order.

[242A Civil penalty for failure to deliver accounts

(1) Where the requirements of section 242(1) are not complied with before the end of the period allowed for laying and delivering accounts and reports, the company is liable to a civil penalty.

This is in addition to any liability of the directors under section 242.

(2) The amount of the penalty is determined by reference to the length of the period between the end of the period allowed for laying and delivering accounts and reports and the day on which the requirements are complied with, and whether the company is a public or private company, as follows:—

Length of period	Public company	Private company
Not more than 3 months.	£500	£100
More than 3 months but not more than 6 months.	£1,000	£250
More than 6 months but not more than 12 months.	£2,000	£500
More than 12 months.	£5,000	£1,000

(3) The penalty may be recovered by the registrar and shall be paid by him into the Consolidated Fund.

(4) It is not a defence in proceedings under this section to prove that the documents in question were not in fact prepared as required by this Part.][1]

---

[1] Inserted by CA 1989, s 11 with effect from a date to be appointed.

[243 Accounts of subsidiary undertakings to be appended in certain cases

(1) The following provisions apply where at the end of the financial year a parent company has as a subsidiary undertaking—

(a) a body corporate incorporated outside Great Britain which does not have an established place of business in Great Britain, or

(b) an unincorporated undertaking,

which is excluded from consolidation in accordance with section 229(4) (undertaking with activities different from the undertakings included in the consolidation).

(2) There shall be appended to the copy of the company's annual accounts delivered to the registrar in accordance with section 242 a copy of the undertaking's latest individual accounts and, if it is a parent undertaking, its latest group accounts.

If the accounts appended are required by law to be audited, a copy of the auditors' report shall also be appended.

(3) The accounts must be for a period ending not more than twelve months before the end of the financial year for which the parent company's accounts are made up.

(4) If any document required to be appended is in a language other than English, the directors shall annex to the copy of that document delivered a translation of it into English, certified in the prescribed manner to be a correct translation.

(5) The above requirements are subject to the following qualifications—

(a) an undertaking is not required to prepare for the purposes of this section accounts which would not otherwise be prepared, and if no accounts satisfying the above requirements are prepared none need be appended;

(b) a document need not be appended if it would not otherwise be required to be published, or made available for public inspection, anywhere in the world, but in that case the reason for not appending it shall be stated in a note to the company's accounts;

(c)   where an undertaking and all its subsidiary undertakings are excluded from consolidation in accordance with section 229(4), the accounts of such of the subsidiary undertakings of that undertaking as are included in its consolidated group accounts need not be appended.

(6)   Subsections (2) to (4) of section 242 (penalties, etc. in case of default) apply in relation to the requirements of this section as they apply in relation to the requirements of subsection (1) of that section.]¹

---

¹   Inserted by CA 1989, s 11 with effect from 1 April 1990 (SI 1990 No 355) subject to the transitional and saving provisions in Arts 6 to 9 of that Order.

[244   Period allowed for laying and delivering accounts and reports

(1)   The period allowed for laying and delivering accounts and reports is—

    (a)   for a private company, 10 months after the end of the relevant accounting reference period, and
    (b)   for a public company, 7 months after the end of that period.

This is subject to the following provisions of this section.

(2)   If the relevant accounting reference period is the company's first and is a period of more than 12 months, the period allowed is—

    (a)   10 months or 7 months, as the case may be, from the first anniversary of the incorporation of the company, or
    (b)   3 months from the end of the accounting reference period,

whichever last expires.

(3)   Where a company carries on business, or has interests, outside the United Kingdom, the Channel Islands and the Isle of Man, the directors may, in respect of any financial year, give to the registrar before the end of the period allowed by subsection (1) or (2) a notice in the prescribed form—

    (a)   stating that the company so carries on business or has such interests, and
    (b)   claiming a 3 month extension of the period allowed for laying and delivering accounts and reports;

and upon such a notice being given the period is extended accordingly.

(4)   If the relevant accounting period is treated as shortened by virtue of a notice given by the company under section 225 (alteration of accounting reference date), the period allowed for laying and delivering accounts is that applicable in accordance with the above provisions or 3 months from the date of the notice under that section, whichever last expires.

(5)   If for any special reason the Secretary of State thinks fit he may, on an application made before the expiry of the period otherwise allowed, by notice in writing to a company extend that period by such further period as may be specified in the notice.

(6)   In this section "the relevant accounting reference period" means the accounting reference period by reference to which the financial year for the accounts in question was determined.]¹

---

¹   Inserted by CA 1989, s 11 with effect from 1 April 1990 (SI 1990 No 355) subject to the transitional and saving provisions in Arts 6 to 9 of that Order.

[Revision of defective accounts and reports

245 Voluntary revision of annual accounts or directors' report

(1) If it appears to the directors of a company that any annual accounts of the company, or any directors' report, did not comply with the requirements of this Act, they may prepare revised accounts or a revised report.

(2) Where copies of the previous accounts or report have been laid before the company in general meeting or delivered to the registrar, the revisions shall be confined to—

(a) the correction of those respects in which the previous accounts or report did not comply with the requirements of this Act, and

(b) the making of any necessary consequential alterations.

(3) The Secretary of State may make provision by regulations as to the application of the provisions of this Act in relation to revised annual accounts or a revised directors' report.

(4) The regulations may, in particular—

(a) make different provision according to whether the previous accounts or report are replaced or are supplemented by a document indicating the corrections to be made;

(b) make provision with respect to the functions of the company's auditors in relation to the revised accounts or report;

(c) require the directors to take such steps as may be specified in the regulations where the previous accounts or report have been—

(i) sent out to members and others under section 238(1),

(ii) laid before the company in general meeting, or

(iii) delivered to the registrar,

or where a summary financial statement based on the previous accounts or report has been sent to members under section 251;

(d) apply the provisions of this Act (including those creating criminal offences) subject to such additions, exceptions and modifications as are specified in the regulations.

(5) Regulations under this section shall be made by statutory instrument which shall be subject to annulment in pursuance of a resolution of either House of Parliament.][1]

[1] Inserted by CA 1989, s 12 with effect from a date to be appointed.

[245A Secretary of State's notice in respect of annual accounts

(1) Where copies of a company's annual accounts have been sent out under section 238, or a copy of a company's annual accounts has been laid before the company in general meeting or delivered to the registrar, and it appears to the Secretary of State that there is, or may be, a question whether the accounts comply with the requirements of this Act, he may give notice to the directors of the company indicating the respects in which it appears to him that such a question arises, or may arise.

(2) The notice shall specify a period of not less than one month for the directors to give him an explanation of the accounts or prepare revised accounts.

(3) If at the end of the specified period, or such longer period as he may allow, it appears to the Secretary of State that no satisfactory explanation of the accounts has been given and that the accounts have not been revised so as to comply with the requirements of this Act, he may if he thinks fit apply to the court.

(4) The provisions of this section apply equally to revised annual accounts, in which case the references to revised accounts shall be read as references to further revised accounts.][1]

---

[1] Inserted by CA 1989, s 12 with effect from a date to be appointed.

[245B Application to court in respect of defective accounts

(1) An application may be made to the court—

    (a) by the Secretary of State, after having complied with section 245A, or
    (b) by a person authorised by the Secretary of State for the purposes of this section,

for a declaration or declarator that the annual accounts of a company do not comply with the requirements of this Act and for an order requiring the directors of the company to prepare revised accounts.

(2) Notice of the application, together with a general statement of the matters at issue in the proceedings, shall be given by the applicant to the registrar for registration.

(3) If the court orders the preparation of revised accounts, it may give directions with respect to—

    (a) the auditing of the accounts,
    (b) the revision of any directors' report or summary financial statement, and
    (c) the taking of steps by the directors to bring the making of the order to the notice of persons likely to rely on the previous accounts,

and such other matters as the court thinks fit.

(4) If the court finds that the accounts did not comply with the requirements of this Act it may order that all or part of—

    (a) the costs (or in Scotland expenses) of and incidental to the application, and
    (b) any reasonable expenses incurred by the company in connection with or in consequence of the preparation of revised accounts,

shall be borne by such of the directors as were party to the approval of the defective accounts.

For this purpose every director of the company at the time the accounts were approved shall be taken to have been a party to their approval unless he shows that he took all reasonable steps to prevent their being approved.

(5) Where the court makes an order under subsection (4) it shall have regard to whether the directors party to the approval of the defective accounts knew or ought to have known that the accounts did not comply with the requirements of this Act, and it may exclude one or more directors from the order or order the payment of different amounts by different directors.

(6) On the conclusion of proceedings on an application under this section, the applicant shall give to the registrar for registration an office copy of the court order or, as the case may be, notice that the application has failed or been withdrawn.

(7) The provisions of this section apply equally to revised annual accounts, in which case the references to revised accounts shall be read as references to further revised accounts.][1]

---

[1] Inserted by CA 1989, s 12 with effect from a date to be appointed.

[245C Other persons authorised to apply to court

(1) The Secretary of State may authorise for the purposes of section 245B any person appearing to him—

   (a) to have an interest in, and to have satisfactory procedures directed to securing, compliance by companies with the accounting requirements of this Act,

   (b) to have satisfactory procedures for receiving and investigating complaints about the annual accounts of companies, and

   (c) otherwise to be a fit and proper person to be authorised.

(2) A person may be authorised generally or in respect of particular classes of case, and different persons may be authorised in respect of different classes of case.

(3) The Secretary of State may refuse to authorise a person if he considers that his authorisation is unnecessary having regard to the fact that there are one or more other persons who have been or are likely to be authorised.

(4) Authorisation shall be by order made by statutory instrument which shall be subject to annulment in pursuance of a resolution of either House of Parliament.

(5) Where authorisation is revoked, the revoking order may make such provision as the Secretary of State thinks fit with respect to pending proceedings.

(6) Neither a person authorised under this section, nor any officer, servant or member of the governing body of such a person, shall l liable in damages for anything done or purporting to be done for the purposes of or in connection with—

   (a) the taking of steps to discover whether there are grounds for an application to the court,

   (b) the determination whether or not to make such an application, or

   (c) the publication of its reasons for any such decision,

unless the act or omission is shown to have been in bad faith.][1]

---

[1] Inserted by CA 1989, s 12 with effect from a date to be appointed.

Companies Act 1985

[CHAPTER II   EXEMPTIONS, EXCEPTIONS AND SPECIAL PROVISIONS

Small and medium-sized companies and groups

246   Exemptions for small and medium-sized companies

(1)   A company which qualifies as a small or medium-sized company in relation to a financial year—

    (a)   is exempt from the requirements of paragraph 36A of Schedule 4 (disclosure with respect to compliance with accounting standards), and

    (b)   is entitled to the exemptions provided by Schedule 8 with respect to the delivery to the registrar under section 242 of individual accounts and other documents for that financial year.

(2)   In that Schedule—

Part I relates to small companies,

Part II relates to medium-sized companies, and

Part III contains supplementary provisions.

(3)   A company is not entitled to the exemptions mentioned in subsection (1) if it is, or was at any time within the financial year to which the accounts relate—

    (a)   a public company,

    (b)   a banking or insurance company, or

    (c)   an authorised person under the Financial Services Act 1986,

or if it is or was at any time during that year a member of an ineligible group.

(4)   A group is ineligible if any of its members is—

    (a)   a public company or a body corporate which (not being a company) has power under its constitution to offer its shares or debentures to the public and may lawfully exercise that power,

    (b)   an authorised institution under the Banking Act 1987,

    (c)   an insurance company to which Part II of the Insurance Companies Act 1982 applies, or

    (d)   an authorised person under the Financial Services Act 1986.

(5)   A parent company shall not be treated as qualifying as a small company in relation to a financial year unless the group headed by it qualifies as a small group, and shall not be treated as qualifying as a medium-sized company in relation to a financial year unless that group qualifies as a medium-sized group (see section 249).][1]

---

[1]   Inserted by CA 1989, s 13 with effect from 1 April 1990 (SI 1990 No 355) subject to the transitional and saving provisions in Arts 6 to 9 of that Order.

[247   Qualification of company as small or medium-sized

(1)   A company qualifies as small or medium-sized in relation to a financial year if the qualifying conditions are met—

    (a)   in the case of the company's first financial year, in that year, and

    (b)   in the case of any subsequent financial year, in that year and the preceding year.

(2) A company shall be treated as qualifying as small or medium-sized in relation to a financial year—

(a) if it so qualified in relation to the previous financial year under subsection (1); or

(b) if it was treated as so qualifying in relation to the previous year by virtue of paragraph (a) and the qualifying conditions are met in the year in question.

(3) The qualifying conditions are met by a company in a year in which it satisfies two or more of the following requirements—

Small company

1. Turnover	Not more than £2 million
2. Balance sheet total	Not more than £975,000
3. Number of employees	Not more than 50

Medium-sized company

1. Turnover	Not more than £8 million
2. Balance sheet total	Not more than £3.9 million
3. Number of employees	Not more than 250.

(4) For a period which is a company's financial year but not in fact a year the maximum figures for turnover shall be proportionately adjusted.

(5) The balance sheet total means—

(a) where in the company's accounts Format 1 of the balance sheet formats set out in Part I of Schedule 4 is adopted, the aggregate of the amounts shown in the balance sheet under the headings corresponding to items A to D in that Format, and

(b) where Format 2 is adopted, the aggregate of the amounts shown under the general heading "Assets".

(6) The number of employees means the average number of persons employed by the company in the year (determined on a weekly basis).

That number shall be determined by applying the method of calculation prescribed by paragraph 56(2) and (3) of Schedule 4 for determining the corresponding number required to be stated in a note to the company's accounts.][1]

---

[1] Inserted by CA 1989, s 13 with effect from 1 April 1990 (SI 1990 No 355) subject to the transitional and saving provisions in Arts 6 to 9 of that Order.

[248 Exemption for small and medium-sized groups

(1) A parent company need not prepare group accounts for a financial year in relation to which the group headed by that company qualifies as a small or medium-sized group and is not an ineligible group.

(2) A group is ineligible if any of its members is—

(a) a public company or a body corporate which (not being a company) has power under its constitution to offer its shares or debentures to the public and may lawfully exercise that power,

(b) an authorised institution under the Banking Act 1987,

(c) an insurance company to which Part II of the Insurance Companies Act 1982 applies, or

(d)   an authorised person under the Financial Services Act 1986.

(3)   If the directors of a company propose to take advantage of the exemption conferred by this section, it is the auditors' duty to provide them with a report stating whether in their opinion the company is entitled to the exemption.

(4)   The exemption does not apply unless—

(a)   the auditors' report states that in their opinion the company is so entitled, and

(b)   that report is attached to the individual accounts of the company.]¹

---

¹   Inserted by CA 1989, s 13 with effect from 1 April 1990 (SI 1990 No 355) subject to the transitional and saving provisions in Arts 6 to 9 of that Order.

[249   Qualification of group as small or medium-sized

(1)   A group qualifies as small or medium-sized in relation to a financial year if the qualifying conditions are met—

(a)   in the case of the parent company's first financial year, in that year, and

(b)   in the case of any subsequent financial year, in that year and the preceding year.

(2)   A group shall be treated as qualifying as small or medium-sized in relation to a financial year—

(a)   if it so qualified in relation to the previous financial year under subsection (1); or

(b)   if it was treated as so qualifying in relation to the previous year by virtue of paragraph (a) and the qualifying conditions are met in the year in question.

(3)   The qualifying conditions are met by a group in a year in which it satisfies two or more of the following requirements—

Small group

1. Aggregate turnover	Not more than £2 million net (or £2.4 million gross)
2. Aggregate balance sheet total	Not more than £1 million net (or £1.2 million gross)
3. Aggregate number of employees	Not more than 50

Medium-sized group

1. Aggregate turnover	Not more than £8 million net (or £9.6 million gross)
2. Aggregate balance sheet total	Not more than £3.9 million net (or £4.7 million gross)
3. Aggregate number of employees	Not more than 250.

(4)   The aggregate figures shall be ascertained by aggregating the relevant figures determined in accordance with section 247 for each member of the group.

In relation to the aggregate figures for turnover and balance sheet total, "net" means with the set-offs and other adjustments required by Schedule 4A in the case of group accounts and "gross" means without those set-offs and other adjustments; and a company may satisfy the relevant requirement on the basis of either the net or the gross figure.

(5) The figures for each subsidiary undertaking shall be those included in its accounts for the relevant financial year, that is—

(a) if its financial year ends with that of the parent company, that financial year, and

(b) if not, its financial year ending last before the end of the financial year of the parent company.

(6) If those figures cannot be obtained without disproportionate expense or undue delay, the latest available figures shall be taken.][1]

---

[1] Inserted by CA 1989, s 13 with effect from 1 April 1990 (SI 1990 No 355) subject to the transitional and saving provisions in Arts 6 to 9 of that Order.

Cross references. See SI 1986 No 1865 (transitional provisions—small and medium-sized companies).

[*Dormant companies*

250 Resolution not to appoint auditors

(1) A company may by special resolution make itself exempt from the provisions of this Part relating to the audit of accounts in the following cases—

(a) if the company has been dormant from the time of its formation, by a special resolution passed before the first general meeting of the company at which annual accounts are laid;

(b) if the company has been dormant since the end of the previous financial year and—

(i) is entitled in respect of its individual accounts for that year to the exemptions conferred by section 246 on a small company, or would be so entitled but for being a member of an ineligible group, and

(ii) is not required to prepare group accounts for that year,

by a special resolution passed at a general meeting of the company at which the annual accounts for that year are laid.

(2) A company may not pass such a resolution if it is—

(a) a public company,

(b) a banking or insurance company, or

(c) an authorised person under the Financial Services Act 1986.

(3) A company is "dormant" during a period in which no significant accounting transaction occurs, that is, no transaction which is required by section 221 to be entered in the company's accounting records; and a company ceases to be dormant on the occurrence of such a transaction.

For this purpose there shall be disregarded any transaction arising from the taking of shares in the company by a subscriber to the memorandum in pursuance of an undertaking of his in the memorandum.

(4) Where a company is, at the end of a financial year, exempt by virtue of this section from the provisions of this Part relating to the audit of accounts—

(a) sections 238 and 239 (right to receive or demand copies of accounts and reports) have effect with the omission of references to the auditors' report;

(b) no copies of an auditors' report need be laid before the company in general meeting;

(c) no copy of an auditors' report need be delivered to the registrar, and if none is delivered, the copy of the balance sheet so delivered shall contain a statement by the directors, in a position immediately above the signature required by section 233(4), that the company was dormant throughout the financial year; and

(d) the company shall be treated as entitled in respect of its individual accounts for that year to the exemptions conferred by section 246 on a small company notwithstanding that it is a member of an ineligible group.

(5) Where a company which is exempt by virtue of this section from the provisions of this Part relating to the audit of accounts—

(a) ceases to be dormant, or

(b) would no longer qualify (for any other reason) to make itself exempt by passing a resolution under this section,

it shall thereupon cease to be so exempt.]¹

---

¹ Inserted by CA 1989, s 14 with effect from 1 April 1990 (SI 1990 No 355) subject to the transitional and saving provisions in Arts 6 to 9 of that Order.

[Listed public companies

251 Provision of summary financial statement to shareholders

(1) A public company whose shares, or any class of whose shares, are listed need not, in such cases as may be specified by regulations made by the Secretary of State, and provided any conditions so specified are complied with, send copies of the documents referred to in section 238(1) to members of the company, but may instead send them a summary financial statement.

In this subsection "listed" means admitted to the Official List of The International Stock Exchange of the United Kingdom and the Republic of Ireland Limited.

(2) Copies of the documents referred to in section 238(1) shall, however, be sent to any member of the company who wishes to receive them; and the Secretary of State may by regulations make provision as to the manner in which it is to be ascertained whether a member of the company wishes to receive them.

(3) The summary financial statement shall be derived from the company's annual accounts and the directors' report and shall be in such form and contain such information as may be specified by regulations made by the Secretary of State.

(4) Every summary financial statement shall—

(a) state that it is only a summary of information in the company's annual accounts and the directors' report;

(b) contain a statement by the company's auditors of their opinion as to whether the summary financial statement is consistent with those accounts and that report and complies with the requirements of this section and regulations made under it;

(c) state whether the auditors' report on the annual accounts was unqualified or qualified, and if it was qualified set out the report in full together with any further material needed to understand the qualification;

(d) state whether the auditors' report on the annual accounts contained a statement under—

     (i)   section 237(2) (accounting records or returns inadequate or accounts not agreeing with records and returns), or

     (ii)   section 237(3) (failure to obtain necessary information and explanations),

and if so, set out the statement in full.

(5)   Regulations under this section shall be made by statutory instrument which shall be subject to annulment in pursuance of a resolution of either House of Parliament.

(6)   If default is made in complying with this section or regulations made under it, the company and every officer of it who is in default is guilty of an offence and liable to a fine.

(7)   Section 240 (requirements in connection with publication of accounts) does not apply in relation to the provision to members of a company of a summary financial statement in accordance with this section.][1]

---

[1]   Inserted by CA 1989, s 15 with effect from 1 March 1990 (SI 1990 No 142) but subject to the notes below.

Notes

(a)   The provisions above inserted by CA 1989, s 15 apply with respect to a financial year for which a company's accounts are prepared under the provisions of the unamended Part VII (see below) as if

    (i)   the references in subsections (1) and (2) above to section 238(1) were references to section 240(1) of the unamended Part VII;

    (ii)   the references therein to the company's annual accounts were references to the documents referred to in section 239(a) and (d) of the unamended Part VII;

    (iii) the reference in subsection (4)(d) thereof to section 237(3) was a reference to section 237(4) of the unamended Part VII; and

    (iv) the reference in subsection (7) thereof to section 240 was a reference to section 255 of the unamended Part VII.

(b)   The repeal of the existing section 251 by CA 1989, s 15 does not affect the continued operation of any regulations previously made thereunder.

(SI 1990 No 142, Art 8).

(c)   The provisions in (a) and (b) above are revoked with effect from 1 April 1990 (SI 1990 No 355) and superceded by the transitional and saving provisions reproduced above Sec 221 above.

Regulations. The Companies (Modified Accounts) Amendment Regulations 1986 (SI 1986 No 1865).

Companies Act 1985

[CHAPTER III   SUPPLEMENTARY PROVISIONS

Accounting standards

256   Accounting standards

    (1)   In this Part "accounting standards" means statements of standard accounting practice issued by such body or bodies as may be prescribed by regulations.

    (2)   References in this Part to accounting standards applicable to a company's annual accounts are to such standards as are, in accordance with their terms, relevant to the company's circumstances and to the accounts.

    (3)   The Secretary of State may make grants to or for the purposes of bodies concerned with—

        (a)   issuing accounting standards,

        (b)   overseeing and directing the issuing of such standards, or

        (c)   investigating departures from such standards or from the accounting requirements of this Act and taking steps to secure compliance with them.

    (4)   Regulations under this section may contain such transitional and other supplementary and incidental provisions as appear to the Secretary of State to be appropriate.][1]

---

[1]   Inserted by CA 1989, s 19 with effect from 1 April 1990 (SI 1990 No 355) subject to the transitional and saving provisions in Arts 6 to 9 of that Order.

[*Power to alter accounting requirements*

257   Power of Secretary of State to alter accounting requirements

    (1)   The Secretary of State may by regulations made by statutory instrument modify the provisions of this Part.

    (2)   Regulations which—

        (a)   add to the classes of documents required to be prepared, laid before the company in general meeting or delivered to the registrar,

        (b)   restrict the classes of company which have the benefit of any exemption, exception or special provision,

        (c)   require additional matter to be included in a document of any class, or

        (d)   otherwise render the requirements of this Part more onerous,

    shall not be made unless a draft of the instrument containing the regulations has been laid before Parliament and approved by a resolution of each House.

    (3)   Otherwise, a statutory instrument containing regulations under this section shall be subject to annulment in pursuance of a resolution of either House of Parliament.

    (4)   Regulations under this section may—

        (a)   make different provision for different cases or classes of case,

        (b)   repeal and re-enact provisions with modifications of form or arrangement, whether or not they are modified in substance,

        (c)   make consequential amendments or repeals in other provisions of this Act, or in other enactments, and

(d)   contain such transitional and other incidental and supplementary provisions as the Secretary of State thinks fit.

(5)   Any modification by regulations under this section of section 258 or Schedule 10A (parent and subsidiary undertakings) does not apply for the purposes of enactments outside the Companies Acts unless the regulations so provide.][1]

---

[1]   Inserted by CA 1989, s 20 with effect from 1 April 1990 (SI 1990 No 355) subject to the transitional and saving provisions in Arts 6 to 9 of that Order.

[*Parent and subsidiary undertakings*

258   Parent and subsidiary undertakings

(1)   The expressions "parent undertaking" and "subsidiary undertaking" in this Part shall be construed as follows; and a "parent company" means a parent undertaking which is a company.

(2)   An undertaking is a parent undertaking in relation to another undertaking, a subsidiary undertaking, if—

(a)   it holds a majority of the voting rights in the undertaking, or

(b)   it is a member of the undertaking and has the right to appoint or remove a majority of its board of directors, or

(c)   it has the right to exercise a dominant influence over the undertaking—
    (i)   by virtue of provisions contained in the undertaking's memorandum or articles, or
    (ii)   by virtue of a control contract, or

(d)   it is a member of the undertaking and controls alone, pursuant to an agreement with other shareholders or members, a majority of the voting rights in the undertaking.

(3)   For the purposes of subsection (2) an undertaking shall be treated as a member of another undertaking—

(a)   if any of its subsidiary undertakings is a member of that undertaking, or

(b)   if any shares in that other undertaking are held by a person acting on behalf of the undertaking or any of its subsidiary undertakings.

(4)   An undertaking is also a parent undertaking in relation to another undertaking, a subsidiary undertaking, if it has a participating interest in the undertaking and—

(a)   it actually exercises a dominant influence over it, or

(b)   it and the subsidiary undertaking are managed on a unified basis.

(5)   A parent undertaking shall be treated as the parent undertaking of undertakings in relation to which any of its subsidiary undertakings are, or are to be treated as, parent undertakings; and references to its subsidiary undertakings shall be construed accordingly.

(6)   Schedule 10A contains provisions explaining expressions used in this section and otherwise supplementing this section.][1]

---

[1]   Inserted by CA 1989, s 21 with effect from 1 April 1990 (SI 1990 No 355) subject to the transitional and saving provisions in Arts 6 to 9 of that Order.

Cross references. See 10A Sch (parent and subsidiary undertakings (supplementary provisions)).

Companies Act 1985

259   Meaning of "undertaking" and related expressions

(1)   In this Part "undertaking" means—

(a)   a body corporate or partnership, or

(b)   an unincorporated association carrying on a trade or business, with or without a view to profit.

(2)   In this Part references to shares—

(a)   in relation to an undertaking with a share capital, are to allotted shares;

(b)   in relation to an undertaking with capital but no share capital, are to rights to share in the capital of the undertaking; and

(c)   in relation to an undertaking without capital, are to interests—

(i)   conferring any right to share in the profits or liability to contribute to the losses of the undertaking, or

(ii)   giving rise to an obligation to contribute to the debts or expenses of the undertaking in the event of a winding up.

(3)   Other expressions appropriate to companies shall be construed, in relation to an undertaking which is not a company, as references to the corresponding persons, officers, documents or organs, as the case may be, appropriate to undertakings of that description.

This is subject to provision in any specific context providing for the translation of such expressions.

(4)   References in this Part to "fellow subsidiary undertakings" are to undertakings which are subsidiary undertakings of the same parent undertaking but are not parent undertakings or subsidiary undertakings of each other.

(5)   In this Part "group undertaking", in relation to an undertaking, means an undertaking which is—

(a)   a parent undertaking or subsidiary undertaking of that undertaking, or

(b)   a subsidiary undertaking of any parent undertaking of that undertaking.][1]

---

[1]   Inserted by CA 1989, s 22 with effect from 1 April 1990 (SI 1990 No 355) subject to the transitional and saving provisions in Arts 6 to 9 of that Order.

[260   Participating interests

(1)   In this Part a "participating interest" means an interest held by an undertaking in the shares of another undertaking which it holds on a long-term basis for the purpose of securing a contribution to its activities by the exercise of control or influence arising from or related to that interest.

(2)   A holding of 20 per cent. or more of the shares of an undertaking shall be presumed to be a participating interest unless the contrary is shown.

(3)   The reference in subsection (1) to an interest in shares includes—

(a)   an interest which is convertible into an interest in shares, and

(b)   an option to acquire shares or any such interest;

and an interest or option falls within paragraph (a) or (b) notwithstanding that the shares to which it relates are, until the conversion or the exercise of the option, unissued.

(4)   For the purposes of this section an interest held on behalf of an undertaking shall be treated as held by it.

(5)   For the purposes of this section as it applies in relation to the expression "participating interest" in section 258(4) (definition of "subsidiary undertaking")—

(a)   there shall be attributed to an undertaking any interests held by any of its subsidiary undertakings, and

(b)   the references in subsection (1) to the purpose and activities of an undertaking include the purposes and activities of any of its subsidiary undertakings and of the group as a whole.

(6)   In the balance sheet and profit and loss formats set out in Part I of Schedule 4, "participating interest" does not include an interest in a group undertaking.

(7)   For the purposes of this section as it applies in relation to the expression "participating interest"—

(a)   in those formats as they apply in relation to group accounts, and

(b)   in paragraph 20 of Schedule 4A (group accounts: undertakings to be accounted for as associated undertakings),

the references in subsections (1) to (4) to the interest held by, and the purposes and activities of, the undertaking concerned shall be construed as references to the interest held by, and the purposes and activities of, the group (within the meaning of paragraph 1 of that Schedule).][1]

[1]   Inserted by CA 1989, s 22 with effect from 1 April 1990 (SI 1990 No 355) subject to the transitional and saving provisions in Arts 6 to 9 of that Order.

[261   Notes to the accounts

(1)   Information required by this Part to be given in notes to a company's annual accounts may be contained in the accounts or in a separate document annexed to the accounts.

(2)   References in this Part to a company's annual accounts, or to a balance sheet or profit and loss account, include notes to the accounts giving information which is required by any provision of this Act, and required or allowed by any such provision to be given in a note to company accounts.][1]

[1]   Inserted by CA 1989, s 22 with effect from 1 April 1990 (SI 1990 No 355) subject to the transitional and saving provisions in Arts 6 to 9 of that Order.

[262   Minor definitions

(1)   In this Part—

"annual accounts" means—

(a)   the individual accounts required by section 226, and

(b)   any group accounts required by section 227,

(but see also section 230 (treatment of individual profit and loss account where group accounts prepared));

"annual report", in relation to a company, means the directors' report required by section 234;

"balance sheet date" means the date as at which the balance sheet was made up;

"capitalisation", in relation to work or costs, means treating that work or those costs as a fixed asset;

"credit institution" means an undertaking carrying on a deposit-taking business within the meaning of the Banking Act 1987;

"fixed assets" means assets of a company which are intended for use on a continuing basis in the company's activities, and "current assets" means assets not intended for such use;

"group" means a parent undertaking and its subsidiary undertakings;

"included in the consolidation", in relation to group accounts, or "included in consolidated group accounts", means that the undertaking is included in the accounts by the method of full (and not proportional) consolidation, and references to an undertaking excluded from consolidation shall be construed accordingly;

"purchase price", in relation to an asset of a company or any raw materials or consumables used in the production of such an asset, includes any consideration (whether in cash or otherwise) given by the company in respect of that asset or those materials or consumables, as the case may be;

"qualified", in relation to an auditors' report, means that the report does not state the auditors' unqualified opinion that the accounts have been properly prepared in accordance with this Act or, in the case of an undertaking not required to prepare accounts in accordance with this Act, under any corresponding legislation under which it is required to prepare accounts;

"true and fair view" refers—

(a)   in the case of individual accounts, to the requirement of section 226(2), and

(b)   in the case of group accounts, to the requirement of section 227(3);

"turnover", in relation to a company, means the amounts derived from the provision of goods and services falling within the company's ordinary activities, after deduction of—

  (i)   trade discounts,
 (ii)   value added tax, and
(iii)   any other taxes based on the amounts so derived.

(2)   In the case of an undertaking not trading for profit, any reference in this Part to a profit and loss account is to an income and expenditure account; and references to profit and loss and, in relation to group accounts, to a consolidated profit and loss account shall be construed accordingly.

(3)   References in this Part to "realised profits" and "realised losses", in relation to a company's accounts, are to such profits or losses of the company as fall to be treated as realised in accordance with principles generally accepted, at the time when the accounts are prepared, with respect to the determination for accounting purposes of realised profits or losses.

This is without prejudice to—

(a)   the construction of any other expression (where appropriate) by reference to accepted accounting principles or practice, or

(b) any specific provision for the treatment of profits or losses of any description as realised.]¹

---

¹ Inserted by CA 1989, s 22 with effect from 1 April 1990 (SI 1990 No 355) subject to the transitional and saving provisions in Arts 6 to 9 of that Order.

[262A Index of defined expressions

The following Table shows the provisions of this Part defining or otherwise explaining expressions used in this Part (other than expressions used only in the same section or paragraph)—

accounting reference date and accounting reference period	section 224
accounting standards and applicable accounting standards	section 256
annual accounts	
(generally)	section 262(1)
(includes notes to the accounts)	section 261(2)
annual report	section 262(1)
associated undertaking (in Schedule 4A)	paragraph 20 of that Schedule
balance sheet (includes notes)	section 261(2)
balance sheet date	section 262(1)
banking group	section 255A(3)
capitalisation (in relation to work or costs)	section 262(1)
credit institution	section 262(1)
current assets	section 262(1)
fellow subsidiary undertaking	section 259(4)
financial year	section 223
fixed assets	section 262(1)
group	section 262(1)
group undertaking	section 259(5)
historical cost accounting rules (in Schedule 4)	paragraph 29 of that Schedule
included in the consolidation and related expressions	section 262(1)
individual accounts	section 262(1)
insurance group	section 255A(4)
land of freehold tenure and land of leasehold tenure (in relation to Scotland)	
—in Schedule 4	paragraph 93 of that Schedule
—in Schedule 9	paragraph 36 of that Schedule
lease, long lease and short lease	
—in Schedule 4	paragraph 83 of that Schedule
—in Schedule 9	paragraph 34 of that Schedule
listed investment	
—in Schedule 4	paragraph 84 of that Schedule
—in Schedule 9	paragraph 33 of that Schedule

Companies Act 1985

notes to the accounts	section 261(1)
parent undertaking (and parent company)	section 258 and Schedule 10A
participating interest	section 260
pension costs (in Schedule 4)	paragraph 94(2) and (3) of that Schedule
period allowed for laying and delivering accounts and reports	section 244
profit and loss account	
(includes notes)	section 261(2)
(in relation to a company not trading for profit)	section 262(2)
provision	
—in Schedule 4	paragraphs 88 and 89 of that Schedule
—in Schedule 9	paragraph 32 of that Schedule
purchase price	section 262(1)
qualified	section 262(1)
realised losses and realised profits	section 262(3)
reserve (in Schedule 9)	paragraph 32 of that Schedule
shares	section 259(2)
social security costs (in Schedule 4)	paragraph 94(1) and (3) of that Schedule
special provisions for banking and insurance companies and groups	sections 255 and 255A
subsidiary undertaking	section 258 and Schedule 10A
true and fair view	section 262(1)
turnover	section 262(1)
undertaking and related expressions	section 259(1) to (3).][1]

[1] Inserted by CA 1989, s 22 with effect from 1 April 1990 (SI 1990 No 355) subject to the transitional and saving provisions in Arts 6 to 9 of that Order.

Notes. The original provisions of Part VII above (Secs 221-262) were replaced by CA 1989, ss 1-22 which inserted new sections 221-262A above.

PART XIII   ARRANGEMENTS AND RECONSTRUCTIONS

425   Power of company to compromise with creditors and members

(1)   Where a compromise or arrangement is proposed between a company and its creditors, or any class of them, or between the company and its members, or any class of them, the court may on the application of the company or any creditor or member of it or, in the case of a company being wound up [or an administration order being in force in relation to a company, of the liquidator or administrator][1], order a meeting of the creditors or class of creditors, or of the members of the company or class of members (as the case may be), to be summoned in such manner as the court directs.

(2)   If a majority in number representing three-fourths in value of the creditors or class of creditors or members or class of members (as the case may be), present and voting either in person or by proxy at the meeting, agree to any compromise or arrangement, the compromise or arrangement, if sanctioned by the court, is binding on all creditors or the class of creditors or on the members or class of members (as the case may be), and also on the company or, in the case of a company in the course of being wound up, on the liquidator and contributories of the company.

(3)   The court's order under subsection (2) has no effect until an office copy of it has been delivered to the registrar of companies for registration; and a copy of every such order shall be annexed to every copy of the company's memorandum issued after the order has been made or, in the case of a company not having a memorandum, of every copy so issued of the instrument constituting the company or defining its constitution.

(4)   If a company makes default in complying with subsection (3), the company and every officer of it who is in default is liable to a fine.

(5)   An order under subsection (1) pronounced in Scotland by the judge acting as vacation judge [. . .][2] is not subject to review, reduction, suspension or stay of execution.

(6)   In this section and the next—

(a)   "company" means any company liable to be wound up under this Act, and

(b)   "arrangement" includes a reorganisation of the company's share capital by the consolidation of shares of different classes or by the division of shares into shares of different classes, or by both of those methods.

---

[1]   Substituted by IA 1985, s 109, 6 Sch 11 with effect from 29 December 1986 (see SI 1986 No 1924). Previously ', of the liquidator'.

[2]   Repealed by Court of Session Act 1988, s 52(2), 2 Sch with effect from 29 September 1988.

Companies Act 1985

PART XXVI INTERPRETATION

735 "Company", etc.

(1) In this Act—

    (a) "company" means a company formed and registered under this Act, or an existing company;

    (b) "existing company" means a company formed and registered under the former Companies Acts, but does not include a company registered under the Joint Stock Companies Acts, the Companies Act 1862 or the Companies (Consolidation) Act 1908 in what was then Ireland;

    (c) "the former Companies Acts" means the Joint Stock Companies Acts, the Companies Act 1862, the Companies (Consolidation) Act 1908, the Companies Act 1929 and the Companies Acts 1948 to 1983.

(2) "Public company" and "private company" have the meanings given by section 1(3).

(3) "The Joint Stock Companies Acts" means the Joint Stock Companies Act 1856, the Joint Stock Companies Acts 1856, 1857, the Joint Stock Banking Companies Act 1857 and the Act to enable Joint Stock Banking Companies to be formed on the principle of limited liability, or any one or more of those Acts (as the case may require), but does not include the Joint Stock Companies Act 1844.

(4) The definitions in this section apply unless the contrary intention appears.

[735A Relationship of this Act to Insolvency Act

(1) In this Act "the Insolvency Act" means the Insolvency Act 1986; and in the following provisions of this Act, namely, sections 375(1)(b), 425(6)(a), [. . .]⁴ 460(2), 675, 676, 677, 699(1), 728 and Schedule 21, paragraph 6(1), the words "this Act" are to be read as including Parts I to VII of that Act, sections 411, 413, 414, 416 and 417 in Part XV of that Act, and also the Company Directors Disqualification Act 1986.

(2) In sections 704(5), 706(1), 707(1), [707A(1),]² 708(1)(a) and (4), [709(1) and (3),]², [710A]³, 713(1), 729 and 732(3) references to the Companies Acts include Parts I to VII of the Insolvency Act, sections 411, 413, 414, 416 and 417 in Part XV of that Act, and also the Company Directors Disqualification Act 1986.

(3) Subsections (1) and (2) apply unless the contrary intention appears.]¹

---

¹   Inserted by IA 1986, s 439(1), 13 Sch Part II with effect from 29 December 1986 (see IA 1986, s 443 and SI 1986 No 1924).

²   Inserted by CA 1989, s 127 with effect from a date to be appointed.

³   Substituted by CA 1989, s 127 with effect from a date to be appointed. Previously '710(5)'.

⁴   Repealed by CA 1989, 24 Sch with effect from 21 February 1990 (SI 1990 No 142). Previously '140, 449(1)(a) and (d)'.

[735B Relationship of this Act to Parts IV and V of the Financial Services Act 1986

In sections 704(5), 706(1), 707(1), 707A(1), 708(1)(a) and (4), 709(1) and (3), 710A and 713(1) references to the Companies Acts include Parts IV and V of the Financial Services Act 1986.]¹

¹ Inserted by CA 1989, s 127 with effect from a date to be appointed.

[736 "Subsidiary", "holding company" and "wholly-owned subsidiary"

(1) A company is a "subsidiary" of another company, its "holding company", if that other company—

(a) holds a majority of the voting rights in it, or

(b) is a member of it and has the right to appoint or remove a majority of its board of directors, or

(c) is a member of it and controls alone, pursuant to an agreement with other shareholders or members, a majority of the voting rights in it,

or if it is a subsidiary of a company which is itself a subsidiary of that other company.

(2) A company is a "wholly-owned subsidiary" of another company if it has no members except that other and that other's wholly-owned subsidiaries or persons acting on behalf of that other or its wholly-owned subsidiaries.

(3) In this section "company" includes any body corporate.]¹

¹ Substituted by CA 1989, s 144 with effect from a date to be appointed. See below for the original provisions.

Cross references. See Secs 736A, 736B; CA 1989, s 144(2)(6).

[736A Provisions supplementing s 736

(1) The provisions of this section explain expressions used in section 736 and otherwise supplement that section.

(2) In section 736(1)(a) and (c) the references to the voting rights in a company are to the rights conferred on shareholders in respect of their shares or, in the case of a company not having a share capital, on members, to vote at general meetings of the company on all, or substantially all, matters.

(3) In section 736(1)(b) the reference to the right to appoint or remove a majority of the board of directors is to the right to appoint or remove directors holding a majority of the voting rights at meetings of the board on all, or substantially all, matters; and for the purposes of that provision—

(a) a company shall be treated as having the right to appoint to a directorship if—

(i) a person's appointment to it follows necessarily from his appointment as director of the company, or

(ii) the directorship is held by the company itself; and

(b) a right to appoint or remove which is exercisable only with the consent or concurrence of another person shall be left out of account unless no other person has a right to appoint or, as the case may be, remove in relation to that directorship.

(4) Rights which are exercisable only in certain circumstances shall be taken into account only—

(a) when the circumstances have arisen, and for so long as they continue to obtain, or

(b) when the circumstances are within the control of the person having the rights;

467

and rights which are normally exercisable but are temporarily incapable of exercise shall continue to be taken into account.

(5) Rights held by a person in a fiduciary capacity shall be treated as not held by him.

(6) Rights held by a person as nominee for another shall be treated as held by the other; and rights shall be regarded as held as nominee for another if they are exercisable only on his instructions or with his consent or concurrence.

(7) Rights attached to shares held by way of security shall be treated as held by the person providing the security—

    (a) where apart from the right to exercise them for the purpose of preserving the value of the security, or of realising it, the rights are exercisable only in accordance with his instructions;

    (b) where the shares are held in connection with the granting of loans as part of normal business activities and apart from the right to exercise them for the purpose of preserving the value of the security, or of realising it, the rights are exercisable only in his interests.

(8) Rights shall be treated as held by a company if they are held by any of its subsidiaries; and nothing in subsection (6) or (7) shall be construed as requiring rights held by a company to be treated as held by any of its subsidiaries.

(9) For the purposes of subsection (7) rights shall be treated as being exercisable in accordance with the instructions or in the interests of a company if they are exercisable in accordance with the instructions of or, as the case may be, in the interests of—

    (a) any subsidiary or holding company of that company, or

    (b) any subsidiary of a holding company of that company.

(10) The voting rights in a company shall be reduced by any rights held by the company itself.

(11) References in any provision of subsections (5) to (10) to rights held by a person include rights falling to be treated as held by him by virtue of any other provision of those subsections but not rights which by virtue of any such provision are to be treated as not held by him.

(12) In this section "company" includes any body corporate.][1]

---

[1]   Inserted by CA 1989, s 144 with effect from a date to be appointed.

Cross references. See Sec 736B.

Note. The provisions of Secs 736 and 736A above replaced the original Sec 736.

[736B Power to amend ss 736 and 736A

(1) The Secretary of State may by regulations amend sections 736 and 736A so as to alter the meaning of the expressions "holding company", "subsidiary" or "wholly-owned subsidiary".

(2) The regulations may make different provision for different cases or classes of case and may contain such incidental and supplementary provisions as the Secretary of State thinks fit.

(3) Regulations under this section shall be made by statutory instrument which shall be subject to annulment in pursuance of a resolution of either House of Parliament.

(4) Any amendment made by regulations under this section does not apply for the purposes of enactments outside the Companies Acts unless the regulations so provide.

(5) So much of section 23(3) of the Interpretation Act 1978 as applies section 17(2)(a) of that Act (effect of repeal and re-enactment) to deeds, instruments and documents other than enactments shall not apply in relation to any repeal and re-enactment effected by regulations made under this section.]¹

---

¹ Inserted by CA 1989, s 144 with effect from a date to be appointed.

---

737 "Called-up share capital"

(1) In this Act, "called-up share capital", in relation to a company, means so much of its share capital as equals the aggregate amount of the calls made on its shares (whether or not those calls have been paid), together with any share capital paid up without being called and any share capital to be paid on a specified future date under the articles, the terms of allotment of the relevant shares or any other arrangements for payment of those shares.

(2) "Uncalled share capital" is to be construed accordingly.

(3) The definitions in this section apply unless the contrary intention appears.

738 "Allotment" and "paid up"

(1) In relation to an allotment of shares in a company, the shares are to be taken for the purposes of this Act to be allotted when a person acquires the unconditional right to be included in the company's register of members in respect of those shares.

(2) For purposes of this Act, a share in a company is deemed paid up (as to its nominal value or any premium on it) in cash, or allotted for cash, if the consideration for the allotment or payment up is cash received by the company, or is a cheque received by it in good faith which the directors have no reason for suspecting will not be paid, or is a release of a liability of the company for a liquidated sum, or is an undertaking to pay cash to the company at a future date.

(3) In relation to the allotment or payment up of any shares in a company, references in this Act (except sections 89 to 94) to consideration other than cash and to the payment up of shares and premiums on shares otherwise than in cash include the payment of, or any undertaking to pay, cash to any person other than the company.

(4) For the purpose of determining whether a share is or is to be allotted for cash, or paid up in cash, "cash" includes foreign currency.

739 "Non-cash asset"

(1) In this Act "non-cash asset" means any property or interest in property other than cash; and for this purpose "cash" includes foreign currency.

(2)   A reference to the transfer or acquisition of a non-cash asset includes the creation or extinction of an estate or interest in, or a right over, any property and also the discharge of any person's liability, other than a liability for a liquidated sum.

740   "Body corporate" and "corporation"

References in this Act to a body corporate or to a corporation do not include a corporation sole, but include a company incorporated elsewhere than in Great Britain.

Such references to a body corporate do not include a Scottish firm.

741   "Director" and "shadow director"

(1)   In this Act, "director" includes any person occupying the position of director, by whatever name called.

(2)   In relation to a company, "shadow director" means a person in accordance with whose directions or instructions the directors of the company are accustomed to act.

However, a person is not deemed a shadow director by reason only that the directors act on advice given by him in a professional capacity.

(3)   For the purposes of the following provisions of this Act, namely—

section 309 (directors' duty to have regard to interests of employees),

section 319 (directors' long-term contracts of employment),

sections 320 to 322 (substantial property transactions involving directors), and

sections 330 to 346 (general restrictions on power of companies to make loans, etc., to directors and others connected with them),

(being provisions under which shadow directors are treated as directors), a body corporate is not to be treated as a shadow director of any of its subsidiary companies by reason only that the directors of the subsidiary are accustomed to act in accordance with its directions or instructions.

742   Expressions used in connection with accounts

[(1)   In this Act, unless a contrary intention appears, the following expressions have the same meaning as in Part VII (accounts)—

"annual accounts",

"accounting reference date" and "accounting reference period",

"balance sheet" and "balance sheet date",

"current assets",

"financial year", in relation to a company,

"fixed assets",

"parent company" and "parent undertaking",

"profit and loss account", and

"subsidiary undertaking".

(2) References in this Act to "realised profits" and "realised losses", in relation to a company's accounts, shall be construed in accordance with section 262(3).][1]

---

[1]   Substituted by CA 1989, 10 Sch 15 with effect from 1 April 1990 (SI 1990 No 355) subject to the transitional and saving provisions in Arts 6 to 9 of that Order reproduced above Sec 221 above.
Previously
'(1)   In this Act, unless the contrary intention appears—
  (a)   "accounting reference period" has the meaning given by sections 224 to 226;
  (b)   "accounts" includes a company's group accounts (within the meaning of section 229), whether prepared in the form of accounts or not;
  (c)   "balance sheet date", in relation to a balance sheet, means the date as at which the balance sheet was prepared;
  (d)   "financial year"—
    (i)   in relation to a body corporate to which Part VII applies, means a period in respect of which a profit and loss account under section 227 in that Part is made up, and
    (ii)   in relation to any other body corporate, means a period in respect of which a profit and loss account of the body laid before it in general meeting is made up,
    (whether, in either case, that period is a year or not);
  (e)   any reference to a profit and loss account, in the case of a company not trading for profit, is to its income and expenditure account, and references to profit or loss and, if the company has subsidiaries, references to a consolidated profit and loss account are to be construed accordingly.
(2)   Except in relation to special category accounts, any reference to a balance sheet or profit and loss account includes any notes to the account in question giving information which is required by any provision of this Act, and required or allowed by any such provision to be given in a note to company accounts.
(3)   In relation to special category accounts, any reference to a balance sheet or profit and loss account includes any notes thereon or document annexed thereto giving information which is required by this Act and is thereby allowed to be so given.
(4)   References to special category companies and special category accounts are to be construed in accordance with Chapter II of Part VII.
(5)   For the purposes of Part VII, a body corporate is to be regarded as publishing any balance sheet or other account if it publishes, issues or circulates it or otherwise makes it available for public inspection in a manner calculated to invite members of the public generally, or any class of members of the public, to read it.
(6)   Expressions which, when used in Schedule 4, fall to be construed in accordance with any provision of Part VII of that Schedule have the same meaning (unless the contrary intention appears) when used in any provision of this Act.'

---

743 "Employees' share scheme"

For purposes of this Act, an employees' share scheme is a scheme for encouraging or facilitating the holding of shares or debentures in a company by or for the benefit of—

(a) the bona fide employees or former employees of the company, the company's subsidiary or holding company or a subsidiary of the company's holding company, or

(b) the wives, husbands, widows, widowers or children or step-children under the age of 18 of such employees or former employees.

Cross references. See CA 1989, 18 Sch 37.

[743A Meaning of "office copy" in Scotland

References in this Act to an office copy of a court order shall be construed, as respects Scotland, as references to a certified copy interlocutor.][1]

---

[1]   Inserted by CA 1989, 19 Sch 19 with effect from 1 March 1990 (SI 1990 No 142).

Companies Act 1985

744   Expressions used generally in this Act

In this Act, unless the contrary intention appears, the following definitions apply—

"agent" does not include a person's counsel acting as such;

[. . .]⁷

"articles" means, in relation to a company, its articles of association, as originally framed or as altered by resolution, including (so far as applicable to the company) regulations contained in or annexed to any enactment relating to companies passed before this Act, as altered by or under any such enactment;

[. . .]⁵

[. . .]⁸

"bank holiday" means a holiday under the Banking and Financial Dealings Act 1971;

["banking company" means a company which is authorised under the Banking Act 1987;]⁶

"books and papers" and "books or papers" include accounts, deeds, writings and documents;

"the Companies Acts" means this Act, the Insider Dealing Act and the Consequential Provisions Act;

"the Consequential Provisions Act" means the Companies Consolidation (Consequential Provisions) Act 1985;

"the court", in relation to a company, means the court having jurisdiction to wind up the company;

"debenture" includes debenture stock, bonds and any other securities of a company, whether constituting a charge on the assets of the company or not;

"document" includes summons, notice, order, and other legal process, and registers;

"equity share capital" means, in relation to a company, its issued share capital excluding any part of that capital which, neither as respects dividends nor as respects capital, carries any right to participate beyond a specified amount in a distribution;

[. . .]⁹

"the Gazette" means, as respects companies registered in England and Wales, the London Gazette and, as respects companies registered in Scotland, the Edinburgh Gazette;

[. . .]¹

"hire-purchase agreement" has the same meaning as in the Consumer Credit Act 1974;

"the Insider Dealing Act" means the Company Securities (Insider Dealing) Act 1985;

"insurance company" means the same as in the Insurance Companies Act 1982;

[. . .]¹⁰

"memorandum", in relation to a company, means its memorandum of association, as originally framed or as altered in pursuance of any enactment;

"number", in relation to shares, includes amount, where the context admits of the reference to shares being construed to include stock;

"officer", in relation to a body corporate, includes a director, manager or secretary;

"official seal", in relation to the registrar of companies, means a seal prepared under section 704(4) for the authentication of documents required for or in connection with the registration of companies;

"oversea company" means—

(a)   a company incorporated elsewhere than in Great Britain which, after the commencement of this Act, establishes a place of business in Great Britain, and

(b)   a company so incorporated which has, before that commencement, established a place of business and continues to have an established place of business in Great Britain at that commencement;

"place of business" includes a share transfer or share registration office;

"prescribed" means—

(a)   as respects provisions of this Act relating to winding up, prescribed by general rules [. . .]², and

(b)   otherwise, prescribed by statutory instrument made by the Secretary of State;

"prospectus" means any prospectus, notice, circular, advertisement, or other invitation, offering to the public for subscription or purchase any shares in or debentures of a company;

"prospectus issued generally" means a prospectus issued to persons who are not existing members of the company or holders of its debentures;

[. . .]³

[. . .]⁴

"the registrar of companies" and "the registrar" mean the registrar or other officer performing under this Act the duty of registration of companies in England and Wales or in Scotland, as the case may require;

"share" means share in the share capital of a company, and includes stock (except where a distinction between shares and stock is express or implied); and

[. . .]¹¹.

---

1   Repealed by IA 1985, s 235(3), 10 Sch Part II with effect from 1 March 1986 in so far as relating to the making of general rules in England and Wales (SI 1986 No 185) and otherwise as from 29 December 1986 (SI 1986 No 1924).
Previously
' "general rules" means general rules made under section 663, and includes forms;'.

2   Repealed by IA 1985, s 235(3), 10 Sch Part II as ¹ above.
Previously 'under section 663'.

3   Repealed by Banking Act 1987, s 108(1), 6 Sch 18(8), 7 Sch Part I with effect from 1 October 1987 (see SI 1987 No 1664).
Previously
' "recognised bank" means a company which is recognised as a bank for the purposes of the Banking Act 1979;'.

4   Repealed by FSA 1986, s 212(3), 17 Sch Part I with effect from 29 April 1988 (see SI 1988 No 740).
Previously
' "recognised stock exchange" means any body of persons which is for the time being a recognised stock exchange for the purposes of the Prevention of Fraud (Investments) Act 1958;'.

5   Deleted by CA 1989, 10 Sch 16 with effect from 1 April 1990 (SI 1990 No 355) subject to the transitional and saving provisions in Arts 6 to 9 of that Order.
Previously '["authorised institution" means a company which is an institution authorised under the Banking Act 1987;]ᵃ'.

a   Inserted by Banking Act 1987, s 108(1), 6 Sch 18(8) with effect from 1 October 1987 (see SI 1987 No 1664).

6   Inserted by CA 1989, 10 Sch 16 with effect as in [5] above.

7   Repealed by CA 1989, 24 Sch with effect from a date to be appointed.
Previously
' "annual return" means the return to be made by a company under section 363 or 364 (as the case may be);'.

8   Repealed by CA 1989, 24 Sch with effect from a date to be appointed.
Previously
' "authorised minimum" has the meaning given by section 118;'.

9   Repealed by CA 1989, 24 Sch with effect from a date to be appointed.
Previously
' "expert" has the meaning given by section 62;
"floating charge" includes a floating charge within the meaning given by section 462;'.

10   Repealed by CA 1989, 24 Sch with effect from a date to be appointed.
Previously
' "joint stock company" has the meaning given by section 683;'.

11   Repealed by CA 1989, 24 Sch with effect from a date to be appointed.
Previously
' "undistributable reserves" has the meaning given by section 264(3).'.

Notes
(a)   The definition of "prospectus issued generally" is repealed by FSA 1986, s 212(3), 17 Sch Part I with effect from 29 April 1988 to the extent that it applies to a prospectus offering for subscription, or to any form of application for, units in a body corporate which is a recognised scheme (SI 1988 No 740).

[744A Index of defined expressions

The following Table shows provisions defining or otherwise explaining expressions for the purposes of this Act generally—

accounting reference date, accounting reference period	sections 224 and 742(1)
acquisition (in relation to a non-cash asset)	section 739(2)
agent	section 744
allotment (and related expressions)	section 738
annual accounts	sections 261(2), 262(1) and 742(1)
annual general meeting	section 366
annual return	section 363
articles	section 744
authorised minimum	section 118
balance sheet and balance sheet date	sections 261(2), 262(1) and 742(1)
bank holiday	section 744
banking company	section 744
body corporate	section 740
books and papers, books or papers	section 744
called-up share capital	section 737(1)
capital redemption reserve	section 170(1)
the Companies Acts	section 744
companies charges register	section 397
company	section 735(1)
the Consequential Provisions Act	section 744
corporation	section 740
the court (in relation to a company)	section 744
current assets	sections 262(1) and 742(1)

debenture	section 744
director	section 741(1)
document	section 744
elective resolution	section 379A
employees' share scheme	section 743
equity share capital	section 744
existing company	section 735(1)
extraordinary general meeting	section 368
extraordinary resolution	section 378(1)
financial year (of a company)	sections 223 and 742(1)
fixed assets	sections 262(1) and 742(1)
floating charge (in Scotland)	section 462
the former Companies Acts	section 735(1)
the Gazette	section 744
hire-purchase agreement	section 744
holding company	section 736
the Insider Dealing Act	section 744
the Insolvency Act	section 735A(1)
insurance company	section 744
the Joint Stock Companies Acts	section 735(3)
limited company	section 1(2)
member (of a company)	section 22
memorandum (in relation to a company)	section 744
non-cash asset	section 739(1)
number (in relation to shares)	section 744
office copy (in relation to a court order in Scotland)	section 743A
officer (in relation to a body corporate)	section 744
official seal (in relation to the registrar of companies)	section 744
oversea company	section 744
overseas branch register	section 362
paid up (and related expressions)	section 738
parent company and parent undertaking	sections 258 and 742(1)
place of business	section 744
prescribed	section 744
private company	section 1(3)
profit and loss account	sections 261(2), 262(1) and 742(1)
prospectus	section 744
public company	section 1(3)
realised profits or losses	sections 262(3) and 742(2)
registered number (of a company)	section 705(1)
registered office (of a company)	section 287
registrar and registrar of companies	section 744
resolution for reducing share capital	section 135(3)
shadow director	section 741(2) and (3)
share	section 744
share premium account	section 130(1)
share warrant	section 188
special notice (in relation to a resolution)	section 379
special resolution	section 378(2)
subsidiary	section 736
subsidiary undertaking	sections 258 and 742(1)

---

[1]   Inserted by CA 1989, 19 Sch 20 with effect from a date to be appointed.

SCHEDULE 4
(Sections 228, 230 and as amended by CA 1989, s 4(2), 1 Sch)

FORM AND CONTENT OF COMPANY ACCOUNTS

PART I   GENERAL RULES AND FORMATS

SECTION A   GENERAL RULES

1   (1)   Subject to the following provisions of this Schedule—

    (a)   every balance sheet of a company shall show the items listed in either of the balance sheet formats set out below in section B of this Part; and

    (b)   every profit and loss account of a company shall show the items listed in any one of the profit and loss account formats so set out;

    in either case in the order and under the headings and sub-headings given in the format adopted.

  (2)   Sub-paragraph (1) above is not to be read as requiring the heading or sub-heading for any item to be distinguished by any letter or number assigned to that item in the format adopted.

2   (1)   Where in accordance with paragraph 1 a company's balance sheet or profit and loss account for any financial year has been prepared by reference to one of the formats set out in section B below, the directors of the company shall adopt the same format in preparing the accounts for subsequent financial years of the company unless in their opinion there are special reasons for a change.

  (2)   Particulars of any change in the format adopted in preparing a company's balance sheet or profit and loss account in accordance with paragraph 1 shall be disclosed, and the reasons for the change shall be explained, in a note to the accounts in which the new format is first adopted.

3   (1)   Any item required in accordance with paragraph 1 to be shown in a company's balance sheet or profit and loss account may be shown in greater detail than required by the format adopted.

  (2)   A company's balance sheet or profit and loss account may include an item representing or covering the amount of any asset or liability, income or expenditure not otherwise covered by any of the items listed in the format adopted, but the following shall not be treated as assets in any company's balance sheet—

    (a)   preliminary expenses;

    (b)   expenses of and commission on any issue of shares or debentures; and

    (c)   costs of research.

  (3)   In preparing a company's balance sheet or profit and loss account the directors of the company shall adapt the arrangement and headings and sub-headings otherwise required by paragraph 1 in respect of items to which an Arabic number is assigned in the format adopted, in any case where the special nature of the company's business requires such adaptation.

  (4)   Items to which Arabic numbers are assigned in any of the formats set out in section B below may be combined in a company's accounts for any financial year if either—

      (a)   their individual amounts are not material to assessing the state of affairs or profit or loss of the company for that year; or

      (b)   the combination facilitates that assessment;

but in a case within paragraph (b) the individual amounts of any items so combined shall be disclosed in a note to the accounts.

(5)   Subject to paragraph 4(3) below, a heading or sub-heading corresponding to an item listed in the format adopted in preparing a company's balance sheet or profit and loss account shall not be included if there is no amount to be shown for that item in respect of the financial year to which the balance sheet or profit and loss account relates.

(6)   Every profit and loss account of a company shall show the amount of the company's profit or loss on ordinary activities before taxation.

(7)   Every profit and loss account of a company shall show separately as additional items—

      (a)   any amount set aside or proposed to be set aside to, or withdrawn or proposed to be withdrawn from, reserves; and

      (b)   the aggregate amount of any dividends paid and proposed.

4   (1)   In respect of every item shown in a company's balance sheet or profit and loss account the corresponding amount for the financial year immediately preceding that to which the balance sheet or profit and loss account relates shall also be shown.

(2)   Where that corresponding amount is not comparable with the amount to be shown for the item in question in respect of the financial year to which the balance sheet or profit and loss account relates, the former amount shall be adjusted and particulars of the adjustment and the reasons for it shall be disclosed in a note to the accounts.

(3)   Paragraph 3(5) does not apply in any case where an amount can be shown for the item in question in respect of the financial year immediately preceding that to which the balance sheet or profit and loss account relates, and that amount shall be shown under the heading or sub-heading required by paragraph 1 for that item.

5   Amounts in respect of items representing assets or income may not be set off against amounts in respect of items representing liabilities or expenditure (as the case may be), or vice versa.

SECTION B   THE REQUIRED FORMATS FOR ACCOUNTS

Preliminary

6   References in this Part of this Schedule to the items listed in any of the formats set out below are to those items read together with any of the notes following the formats which apply to any of those items, and the requirement imposed by paragraph 1 to show the items listed in any such format in the order adopted in the format is subject to any provision in those notes for alternative positions for any particular items.

7 A number in brackets following any item in any of the formats set out below is a reference to the note of that number in the notes following the formats.

8 In the notes following the formats—

(a) the heading of each note gives the required heading or sub-heading for the item to which it applies and a reference to any letters and numbers assigned to that item in the formats set out below (taking a reference in the case of Format 2 of the balance sheet formats to the item listed under "Assets" or under "Liabilities" as the case may require); and

(b) references to a numbered format are to the balance sheet format or (as the case may require) to the profit and loss account format of that number set out below.

Companies Act 1985

Balance Sheet Formats   Format 1

A.   Called up share capital not paid (1)

B.   Fixed assets

   I   Intangible assets
      1. Development costs
      2. Concessions, patents, licences, trade marks and similar rights and assets (2)
      3. Goodwill (3)
      4. Payments on account

   II   Tangible assets
      1. Land and buildings
      2. Plant and machinery
      3. Fixtures, fittings, tools and equipment
      4. Payments on account and assets in course of construction

   III Investments
      1. Shares in group [undertakings][1]
      2. Loans to group [undertakings][1]
      3. [Participating interests][2]
      4. Loans to [undertakings in which the company has a participating interest][3]
      5. Other investments other than loans
      6. Other loans
      7. Own shares (4)

C.   Current assets

   I   Stocks
      1. Raw materials and consumables
      2. Work in progress
      3. Finished goods and goods for resale
      4. Payments on account

   II   Debtors (5)
      1. Trade debtors
      2. Amounts owed by group [undertakings][1]
      3. Amounts owed by [undertakings in which the company has a partici-pating interest][3]
      4. Other debtors
      5. Called up share capital not paid (1)
      6. Prepayments and accrued income (6)

   III Investments
      1. Shares in group [undertakings][1]
      2. Own shares (4)
      3. Other investments

   IV   Cash at bank and in hand

D.   Prepayments and accrued income (6)

E.   Creditors: amounts falling due within one year

    1. Debenture loans (7)
    2. Bank loans and overdrafts
    3. Payments received on account (8)
    4. Trade creditors
    5. Bills of exchange payable
    6. Amounts owed to group [undertakings][1]
    7. Amounts owed to [undertakings in which the company has a partici-pating interest][3]
    8. Other creditors including taxation and social security (9)
    9. Accruals and deferred income (10)

F. Net current assets (liabilities) (11)

G. Total assets less current liabilities

H. Creditors: amounts falling due after more than one year
    1. Debenture loans (7)
    2. Bank loans and overdrafts
    3. Payments received on account (8)
    4. Trade creditors
    5. Bills of exchange payable
    6. Amounts owed to group [undertakings][1]
    7. Amounts owed to [undertakings in which the company has a partici-pating interest][3]
    8. Other creditors including taxation and social security (9)
    9. Accruals and deferred income (10)

I. Provisions for liabilities and charges
    1. Pensions and similar obligations
    2. Taxation, including deferred taxation
    3. Other provisions

J. Accruals and deferred income (10)

K. Capital and reserves

  I Called up share capital (12)

  II Share premium account

  III Revaluation reserve

  IV Other reserves
    1. Capital redemption reserve
    2. Reserve for own shares
    3. Reserves provided for by the articles of association
    4. Other reserves

  V Profit and loss account

---

[1] Substituted by CA 1989, 1 Sch 2 with effect from 1 April 1990 (SI 1990 No 355) subject to the transitional and saving provisions in Arts 6 to 9 of that Order.
Previously 'companies'.

[2] Substituted by CA 1989, 1 Sch 3 with effect as in [1] above.
Previously 'Shares in related companies'.

[3] Substituted by CA 1989, 1 Sch 4 with effect as in [1] above.
Previously 'related companies'.

Companies Act 1985

Balance Sheet Formats   Format 2

ASSETS

A.   Called up share capital not paid (1)

B.   Fixed assets

    I   Intangible assets
        1. Development costs
        2. Concessions, patents, licences, trade marks and similar rights and assets (2)
        3. Goodwill (3)
        4. Payments on account

    II   Tangible assets
        1. Land and buildings
        2. Plant and machinery
        3. Fixtures, fittings, tools and equipment
        4. Payments on account and assets in course of construction

    III Investments
        1. Shares in group [undertakings][1]
        2. Loans to group [undertakings][1]
        3. [Participating interests][2]
        4. Loans to [undertakings in which the company has a participating interest][3]
        5. Other investments other than loans
        6. Other loans
        7. Own shares (4)

C.   Current assets

    I   Stocks
        1. Raw materials and consumables
        2. Work in progress
        3. Finished goods and goods for resale
        4. Payments on account

    II   Debtors (5)
        1. Trade debtors
        2. Amounts owed by group [undertakings][1]
        3. Amounts owed by [undertakings in which the company has a participating interest][3]
        4. Other debtors
        5. Called up share capital not paid (1)
        6. Prepayments and accrued income (6)

    III Investments
        1. Shares in group [undertakings][1]
        2. Own shares (4)
        3. Other investments

    IV Cash at bank and in hand

D.   Prepayments and accrued income (6)

LIABILITIES

A.   Capital and reserves

I   Called up share capital (12)

II   Share premium account

III   Revaluation reserve

IV   Other reserves
      1. Capital redemption reserve
      2. Reserve for own shares
      3. Reserves provided for by the articles of association
      4. Other reserves

V   Profit and loss account

B.   Provisions for liabilities and charges
      1. Pensions and similar obligations
      2. Taxation including deferred taxation
      3. Other provisions

C.   Creditors (13)
      1. Debenture loans (7)
      2. Bank loans and overdrafts
      3. Payments received on account (8)
      4. Trade creditors
      5. Bills of exchange payable
      6. Amounts owed to group [undertakings][1]
      7. Amounts owed to [undertakings in which the company has a partici-
         pating interest][3]
      8. Other creditors including taxation and social security (9)
      9. Accruals and deferred income (10)

D.   Accruals and deferred income (10)

---

[1]   Substituted by CA 1989, 1 Sch 2 with effect from 1 April 1990 (SI 1990 No 355) subject to the transitional and saving provisions in Arts 6 to 9 of that Order.
Previously 'companies'.

[2]   Substituted by CA 1989, 1 Sch 3 with effect as in [1] above.
Previously 'Shares in related companies'.

[3]   Substituted by CA 1989, 1 Sch 4 with effect as in [1] above.
Previously 'related companies'.

Notes on the balance sheet formats

(1)   *Called up share capital not paid*
     (Formats 1 and 2, items A and C.II.5.)
     This item may be shown in either of the two positions given in Formats 1 and 2.

(2)   *Concessions, patents, licences, trade marks and similar rights and assets*
     (Formats 1 and 2, item B.I.2.)
     Amounts in respect of assets shall only be included in a company's balance sheet under this item if either—
     (a)   the assets were acquired for valuable consideration and are not required to be shown under goodwill; or
     (b)   the assets in question were created by the company itself.

(3)   *Goodwill*
     (Formats 1 and 2, item B.I.3.)

Amounts representing goodwill shall only be included to the extent that the goodwill was acquired for valuable consideration.

(4) *Own shares*
(Formats 1 and 2, items B.III.7 and C.III.2.)
The nominal value of the shares held shall be shown separately.

(5) *Debtors*
(Formats 1 and 2, items C.II.1 to 6.)
The amount falling due after more than one year shall be shown separately for each item included under debtors.

(6) *Prepayments and accrued income*
(Formats 1 and 2, items C.II.6 and D.)
This item may be shown in either of the two positions given in Formats 1 and 2.

(7) *Debenture loans*
(Format 1, items E.1 and H.1 and Format 2, item C.1.)
The amount of any convertible loans shall be shown separately.

(8) *Payments received on account*
(Format 1, items E.3 and H.3 and Format 2, item C.3.)
Payments received on account of orders shall be shown for each of these items in so far as they are not shown as deductions from stocks.

(9) *Other creditors including taxation and social security*
(Format 1, items E.8 and H.8 and Format 2, item C.8.)
The amount for creditors in respect of taxation and social security shall be shown separately from the amount for other creditors.

(10) *Accruals and deferred income*
(Format 1, items E.9, H.9 and J and Format 2, items C.9 and D.)
The two positions given for this item in Format 1 at E.9 and H.9 are an alternative to the position at J, but if the item is not shown in a position corresponding to that at J it may be shown in either or both of the other two positions (as the case may require).
The two positions given for this item in Format 2 are alternatives.

(11) *Net current assets (liabilities)*
(Format 1, item F.)
In determining the amount to be shown for this item any amounts shown under "prepayments and accrued income" shall be taken into account wherever shown.

(12) *Called up share capital*
(Format 1, item K.I and Format 2, item A.I.)
The amount of allotted share capital and the amount of called up share capital which has been paid up shall be shown separately.

(13) *Creditors*
(Format 2, items C.1 to 9.)
Amounts falling due within one year and after one year shall be shown separately for each of these items and their aggregate shall be shown separately for all of these items.

Profit and loss account formats   Format 1 (see note (17) below)

1.   Turnover
2.   Cost of sales (14)
3.   Gross profit or loss
4.   Distribution costs (14)
5.   Administrative expenses (14)
6.   Other operating income
7.   Income from shares in group [undertakings][1]
8.   Income from [participating interests][2]
9.   Income from other fixed asset investments (15)
10. Other interest receivable and similar income (15)
11. Amounts written off investments
12. Interest payable and similar charges (16)
13. Tax on profit or loss on ordinary activities
14. Profit or loss on ordinary activities after taxation
15. Extraordinary income
16. Extraordinary charges
17. Extraordinary profit or loss
18. Tax on extraordinary profit or loss
19. Other taxes not shown under the above items
20. Profit or loss for the financial year

---

[1]   Substituted by CA 1989, 1 Sch 2 with effect from 1 April 1990 (SI 1990 No 355) subject to the transitional and saving provisions in Arts 6 to 9 of that Order.
Previously 'companies'.

[2]   Substituted by CA 1989, 1 Sch 3 with effect as in [1] above.
Previously 'shares in related companies'.

Companies Act 1985

Profit and loss account formats   Format 2

1. Turnover
2. Change in stocks of finished goods and in work in progress
3. Own work capitalised
4. Other operating income
5. (a) Raw materials and consumables
    (b) Other external charges
6. Staff costs:
    (a) wages and salaries
    (b) social security costs
    (c) other pension costs
7. (a) Depreciation and other amounts written off tangible and intangible fixed assets
    (b) Exceptional amounts written off current assets
8. Other operating charges
9. Income from shares in group [undertakings][1]
10. Income from [participating interests][2]
11. Income from other fixed asset investments (15)
12. Other interest receivable and similar income (15)
13. Amounts written off investments
14. Interest payable and similar charges (16)
15. Tax on profit or loss on ordinary activities
16. Profit or loss on ordinary activities after taxation
17. Extraordinary income
18. Extraordinary charges
19. Extraordinary profit or loss
20. Tax on extraordinary profit or loss
21. Other taxes not shown under the above items
22. Profit or loss for the financial year

---

[1] Substituted by CA 1989, 1 Sch 2 with effect from 1 April 1990 (SI 1990 No 355) subject to the transitional and saving provisions in Arts 6 to 9 of that Order.
Previously 'companies'.

[2] Substituted by CA 1989, 1 Sch 3 with effect as in [1] above.
Previously 'shares in related companies'.

Profit and loss account formats   **Format 3** (see note (17) below)

A.   Charges
   1.   Cost of sales (14)
   2.   Distribution costs (14)
   3.   Administrative expenses (14)
   4.   Amounts written off investments
   5.   Interest payable and similar charges (16)
   6.   Tax on profit or loss on ordinary activities
   7.   Profit or loss on ordinary activities after taxation
   8.   Extraordinary charges
   9.   Tax on extraordinary profit or loss
   10. Other taxes not shown under the above items
   11. Profit or loss for the financial year

B.   Income
   1.   Turnover
   2.   Other operating income
   3.   Income from shares in group [undertakings][1]
   4.   Income from [participating interests][2]
   5.   Income from other fixed asset investments (15)
   6.   Other interest receivable and similar income (15)
   7.   Profit or loss on ordinary activities after taxation
   8.   Extraordinary income
   9.   Profit or loss for the financial year

---

[1]   Substituted by CA 1989, 1 Sch 2 with effect from 1 April 1990 (SI 1990 No 355) subject to the transitional and saving provisions in Arts 6 to 9 of that Order.
Previously 'companies'.

[2]   Substituted by CA 1989, 1 Sch 3 with effect as in [1] above.
Previously 'shares in related companies'.

Companies Act 1985

Profit and loss account formats   Format 4

A. Charges
1. Reduction in stocks of finished goods and in work in progress
2. (a) Raw materials and consumables
   (b) Other external charges
3. Staff costs:
   (a) wages and salaries
   (b) social security costs
   (c) other pension costs
4. (a) Depreciation and other amounts written off tangible and intangible fixed assets
   (b) Exceptional amounts written off current assets
5. Other operating charges
6. Amounts written off investments
7. Interest payable and similar charges (16)
8. Tax on profit or loss on ordinary activities
9. Profit or loss on ordinary activities after taxation
10. Extraordinary charges
11. Tax on extraordinary profit or loss
12. Other taxes not shown under the above items
13. Profit or loss for the financial year

B. Income
1. Turnover
2. Increase in stocks of finished goods and in work in progress
3. Own work capitalised
4. Other operating income
5. Income from shares in group [undertakings][1]
6. Income from [participating interests][2]
7. Income from other fixed asset investments (15)
8. Other interest receivable and similar income (15)
9. Profit or loss on ordinary activities after taxation
10. Extraordinary income
11. Profit or loss for the financial year

---

[1] Substituted by CA 1989, 1 Sch 2 with effect from 1 April 1990 (SI 1990 No 355) subject to the transitional and saving provisions in Arts 6 to 9 of that Order.
Previously 'companies'.

[2] Substituted by CA 1989, 1 Sch 3 with effect as in [1] above.
Previously 'shares in related companies'.

Notes on the profit and loss account formats

(14) *Cost of sales: distribution costs: administrative expenses*
(Format 1, items 2, 4 and 5 and Format 3, items A.1, 2 and 3.)
These items shall be stated after taking into account any necessary provisions for depreciation or diminution in value of assets.

(15) *Income from other fixed asset investments: other interest receivable and similar income*
(Format 1, items 9 and 10: Format 2, items 11 and 12: Format 3, items B.5 and 6: Format 4, items B.7 and 8.)
Income and interest derived from group [undertakings][1] shall be shown separately from income and interest derived from other sources.

(16) *Interest payable and similar charges*
(Format 1, item 12: Format 2, item 14: Format 3, item A.5: Format 4, item A.7.)
The amount payable to group [undertakings]¹ shall be shown separately.

(17) *Formats 1 and 3*
The amount of any provisions for depreciation and diminution in value of tangible and intangible fixed assets falling to be shown under items 7(a) and A.4(a) respectively in Formats 2 and 4 shall be disclosed in a note to the accounts in any case where the profit and loss account is prepared by reference to Format 1 or Format 3.

---

¹ Substituted by CA 1989, 1 Sch 2 with effect from 1 April 1990 (SI 1990 No 355) subject to the transitional and saving provisions in Arts 6 to 9 of that Order.
Previously 'companies'.

PART II ACCOUNTING PRINCIPLES AND RULES

SECTION A ACCOUNTING PRINCIPLES

9 Preliminary

Subject to paragraph 15 below, the amounts to be included in respect of all items shown in a company's accounts shall be determined in accordance with the principles set out in paragraphs 10 to 14.

Accounting principles

10 The company shall be presumed to be carrying on business as a going concern.

11 Accounting policies shall be applied consistently [within the same accounts and]¹ from one financial year to the next.

---

¹ Inserted by CA 1989, 1 Sch 5 with effect from 1 April 1990 (SI 1990 No 355) subject to the transitional and saving provisions in Arts 6 to 9 of that Order.

---

12 The amount of any item shall be determined on a prudent basis, and in particular—

(a) only profits realised at the balance sheet date shall be included in the profit and loss account; and
(b) all liabilities and losses which have arisen or are likely to arise in respect of the financial year to which the accounts relate or a previous financial year shall be taken into account, including those which only become apparent between the balance sheet date and the date on which it is signed on behalf of the board of directors in pursuance of [section 233]¹ of this Act.

---

¹ Substituted by CA 1989, 10 Sch 20 with effect from 1 April 1990 (SI 1990 No 355) subject to the transitional and saving provisions in Arts 6 to 9 of that Order.
Previously 'section 238'.

Companies Act 1985

13   All income and charges relating to the financial year to which the accounts relate shall be taken into account, without regard to the date of receipt or payment.

14   In determining the aggregate amount of any item the amount of each individual asset or liability that falls to be taken into account shall be determined separately.

15   **Departure from the accounting principles**

If it appears to the directors of a company that there are special reasons for departing from any of the principles stated above in preparing the company's accounts in respect of any financial year they may do so, but particulars of the departure, the reasons for it and its effect shall be given in a note to the accounts.

SECTION B   HISTORICAL COST ACCOUNTING RULES

16   **Preliminary**

Subject to section C of this Part of this Schedule, the amounts to be included in respect of all items shown in a company's accounts shall be determined in accordance with the rules set out in paragraphs 17 to 28.

Fixed assets

General rules

17   Subject to any provision for depreciation or diminution in value made in accordance with paragraph 18 or 19 the amount to be included in respect of any fixed asset shall be its purchase price or production cost.

18   In the case of any fixed asset which has a limited useful economic life, the amount of—

(a)   its purchase price or production cost; or

(b)   where it is estimated that any such asset will have a residual value at the end of the period of its useful economic life, its purchase price or production cost less that estimated residual value;

shall be reduced by provisions for depreciation calculated to write off that amount systematically over the period of the asset's useful economic life.

19   (1)   Where a fixed asset investment of a description falling to be included under item B.III of either of the balance sheet formats set out in Part I of this Schedule has diminished in value provisions for diminution in value may be made in respect of it and the amount to be included in respect of it may be reduced accordingly; and any such provisions which are not shown in the profit and loss account shall be disclosed (either separately or in aggregate) in a note to the accounts.

(2)   Provisions for diminution in value shall be made in respect of any fixed asset which has diminished in value if the reduction in its value is expected to be permanent (whether its useful economic life is limited or not), and the amount to be included in respect of it shall be reduced accordingly; and any such provisions which are not shown in the profit and loss account shall be disclosed (either separately or in aggregate) in a note to the accounts.

(3)   Where the reasons for which any provision was made in accordance with sub-paragraph (1) or (2) have ceased to apply to any extent, that provision shall be written back to the extent that it is no longer necessary; and any amounts written back in accordance with this sub-paragraph which are not shown in the profit and loss account shall be disclosed (either separately or in aggregate) in a note to the accounts.

Rules for determining particular fixed asset items

20   (1)   Notwithstanding that an item in respect of "development costs" is included under "fixed assets" in the balance sheet formats set out in Part I of this Schedule, an amount may only be included in a company's balance sheet in respect of development costs in special circumstances.

(2)   If any amount is included in a company's balance sheet in respect of development costs the following information shall be given in a note to the accounts—

(a)   the period over which the amount of those costs originally capitalised is being or is to be written off; and

(b)   the reasons for capitalising the development costs in question.

21   (1)   The application of paragraphs 17 to 19 in relation to goodwill (in any case where goodwill is treated as an asset) is subject to the following provisions of this paragraph.

(2)   Subject to sub-paragraph (3) below, the amount of the consideration for any goodwill acquired by a company shall be reduced by provisions for depreciation calculated to write off that amount systematically over a period chosen by the directors of the company.

(3)   The period chosen shall not exceed the useful economic life of the goodwill in question.

(4)   In any case where any goodwill acquired by a company is shown or included as an asset in the company's balance sheet the period chosen for writing off the consideration for that goodwill and the reasons for choosing that period shall be disclosed in a note to the accounts.

Current assets

22   Subject to paragraph 23, the amount to be included in respect of any current asset shall be its purchase price or production cost.

23   (1)   If the net realisable value of any current asset is lower than its purchase price or production cost the amount to be included in respect of that asset shall be the net realisable value.

(2)   Where the reasons for which any provision for diminution in value was made in accordance with sub-paragraph (1) have ceased to apply to any extent, that provision shall be written back to the extent that it is no longer necessary.

Miscellaneous and supplementary provisions

Excess of money owed over value received as an asset item

24   (1)   Where the amount repayable on any debt owed by a company is greater than the value of the consideration received in the transaction giving rise to the debt, the amount of the difference may be treated as an asset.

(2)   Where any such amount is so treated—

(a)   it shall be written off by reasonable amounts each year and must be completely written off before repayment of the debt; and

(b)   if the current amount is not shown as a separate item in the company's balance sheet it must be disclosed in a note to the accounts.

Assets included at a fixed amount

25   (1)   Subject to the following sub-paragraph, assets which fall to be included—

(a)   amongst the fixed assets of a company under the item "tangible assets"; or

(b)   amongst the current assets of a company under the item "raw materials and consumables";

may be included at a fixed quantity and value.

(2)   Sub-paragraph (1) applies to assets of a kind which are constantly being replaced, where—

(a)   their overall value is not material to assessing the company's state of affairs; and

(b)   their quantity, value and composition are not subject to material variation.

Determination of purchase price or production cost

26   (1)   The purchase price of an asset shall be determined by adding to the actual price paid any expenses incidental to its acquisition.

(2)   The production cost of an asset shall be determined by adding to the purchase price of the raw materials and consumables used the amount of the costs incurred by the company which are directly attributable to the production of that asset.

(3)   In addition, there may be included in the production cost of an asset—

(a)   a reasonable proportion of the costs incurred by the company which are only indirectly attributable to the production of that asset, but only to the extent that they relate to the period of production; and

(b)   interest on capital borrowed to finance the production of that asset, to the extent that it accrues in respect of the period of production;

provided, however, in a case within paragraph (b) above, that the inclusion of the interest in determining the cost of that asset and the amount of the interest so included is disclosed in a note to the accounts.

(4)   In the case of current assets distribution costs may not be included in production costs.

27   (1)   Subject to the qualification mentioned below, the purchase price or production cost of—

(a)   any assets which fall to be included under any item shown in a company's balance sheet under the general item "stocks"; and

(b)   any assets which are fungible assets (including investments);

may be determined by the application of any of the methods mentioned in sub-paragraph (2) below in relation to any such assets of the same class.

The method chosen must be one which appears to the directors to be appropriate in the circumstances of the company.

(2)　Those methods are—

    (a)　the method known as "first in, first out" (FIFO);
    (b)　the method known as "last in, first out" (LIFO);
    (c)　a weighted average price; and
    (d)　any other method similar to any of the methods mentioned above.

(3)　Where in the case of any company—

    (a)　the purchase price or production cost of assets falling to be included under any item shown in the company's balance sheet has been determined by the application of any method permitted by this paragraph; and
    (b)　the amount shown in respect of that item differs materially from the relevant alternative amount given below in this paragraph;

the amount of that difference shall be disclosed in a note to the accounts.

(4)　Subject to sub-paragraph (5) below, for the purposes of sub-paragraph (3)(b) above, the relevant alternative amount, in relation to any item shown in a company's balance sheet, is the amount which would have been shown in respect of that item if assets of any class included under that item at an amount determined by any method permitted by this paragraph had instead been included at their replacement cost as at the balance sheet date.

(5)　The relevant alternative amount may be determined by reference to the most recent actual purchase price or production cost before the balance sheet date of assets of any class included under the item in question instead of by reference to their replacement cost as at that date, but only if the former appears to the directors of the company to constitute the more appropriate standard of comparison in the case of assets of that class.

(6)　For the purposes of this paragraph, assets of any description shall be regarded as fungible if assets of that description are substantially indistinguishable one from another.

Substitution of original stated amount where price or cost unknown

28　Where there is no record of the purchase price or production cost of any asset of a company or of any price, expenses or costs relevant for determining its purchase price or production cost in accordance with paragraph 26, or any such record cannot be obtained without unreasonable expense or delay, its purchase price or production cost shall be taken for the purposes of paragraphs 17 to 23 to be the value ascribed to it in the earliest available record of its value made on or after its acquisition or production by the company.

SECTION C　ALTERNATIVE ACCOUNTING RULES

Preliminary

29　(1)　The rules set out in section B are referred to below in this Schedule as the historical cost accounting rules.

(2)　Those rules, with the omission of paragraphs 16, 21 and 25 to 28, are referred to below in this Part of this Schedule as the depreciation rules; and references below in this Schedule to the historical cost accounting rules do not include the depreciation rules as they apply by virtue of paragraph 32.

30   Subject to paragraphs 32 to 34, the amounts to be included in respect of assets of any description mentioned in paragraph 31 may be determined on any basis so mentioned.

31   Alternative accounting rules

(1)   Intangible fixed assets, other than goodwill, may be included at their current cost.

(2)   Tangible fixed assets may be included at a market value determined as at the date of their last valuation or at their current cost.

(3)   Investments of any description falling to be included under item B.III of either of the balance sheet formats set out in Part I of this Schedule may be included either—

    (a)   at a market value determined as at the date of their last valuation; or

    (b)   at a value determined on any basis which appears to the directors to be appropriate in the circumstances of the company;

but in the latter case particulars of the method of valuation adopted and of the reasons for adopting it shall be disclosed in a note to the accounts.

(4)   Investments of any description falling to be included under item C.III of either of the balance sheet formats set out in Part I of this Schedule may be included at their current cost.

(5)   Stocks may be included at their current cost.

32   Application of the depreciation rules

(1)   Where the value of any asset of a company is determined on any basis mentioned in paragraph 31, that value shall be, or (as the case may require) be the starting point for determining, the amount to be included in respect of that asset in the company's accounts, instead of its purchase price or production cost or any value previously so determined for that asset; and the depreciation rules shall apply accordingly in relation to any such asset with the substitution for any reference to its purchase price or production cost of a reference to the value most recently determined for that asset on any basis mentioned in paragraph 31.

(2)   The amount of any provision for depreciation required in the case of any fixed asset by paragraph 18 or 19 as it applies by virtue of sub-paragraph (1) is referred to below in this paragraph as the adjusted amount, and the amount of any provision which would be required by that paragraph in the case of that asset according to the historical cost accounting rules is referred to as the historical cost amount.

(3)   Where sub-paragraph (1) applies in the case of any fixed asset the amount of any provision for depreciation in respect of that asset—

    (a)   included in any item shown in the profit and loss account in respect of amounts written off assets of the description in question; or

    (b)   taken into account in stating any item so shown which is required by note (14) of the notes on the profit and loss account formats set out in Part I of this Schedule to be stated after taking into account any necessary provisions for depreciation or diminution in value of assets included under it;

may be the historical cost amount instead of the adjusted amount, provided that the amount of any difference between the two is shown separately in the profit and loss account or in a note to the accounts.

33 Additional information to be provided in case of departure from historical cost accounting rules

(1) This paragraph applies where the amounts to be included in respect of assets covered by any items shown in a company's accounts have been determined on any basis mentioned in paragraph 31.

(2) The items affected and the basis of valuation adopted in determining the amounts of the assets in question in the case of each such item shall be disclosed in a note to the accounts.

(3) In the case of each balance sheet item affected (except stocks) either—

(a) the comparable amounts determined according to the historical cost accounting rules; or

(b) the differences between those amounts and the corresponding amounts actually shown in the balance sheet in respect of that item;

shall be shown separately in the balance sheet or in a note to the accounts.

(4) In sub-paragraph (3) above, references in relation to any item to the comparable amounts determined as there mentioned are references to—

(a) the aggregate amount which would be required to be shown in respect of that item if the amounts to be included in respect of all the assets covered by that item were determined according to the historical cost accounting rules; and

(b) the aggregate amount of the cumulative provisions for depreciation or diminution in value which would be permitted or required in determining those amounts according to those rules.

34 Revaluation reserve

(1) With respect to any determination of the value of an asset of a company on any basis mentioned in paragraph 31, the amount of any profit or loss arising from that determination (after allowing, where appropriate, for any provisions for depreciation or diminution in value made otherwise than by reference to the value so determined and any adjustments of any such provisions made in the light of that determination) shall be credited or (as the case may be) debited to a separate reserve ("the revaluation reserve").

(2) The amount of the revaluation reserve shall be shown in the company's balance sheet under a separate sub-heading in the position given for the item "revaluation reserve" in Format 1 or 2 of the balance sheet formats set out in Part I of this Schedule, but need not be shown under that name.

[(3) An amount may be transferred from the revaluation reserve—

(a) to the profit and loss account, if the amount was previously charged to that account or represents realised profit, or

(b) on capitalisation;

and the revaluation reserve shall be reduced to the extent that the amounts transferred to it are no longer necessary for the purposes of the valuation method used.

Companies Act 1985

(3A) In sub-paragraph (3)(b) "capitalisation", in relation to an amount standing to the credit of the revaluation reserve, means applying it in wholly or partly paying up unissued shares in the company to be allotted to members of the company as fully or partly paid shares.

(3B) The revaluation reserve shall not be reduced except as mentioned in this paragraph.][1]

(4) The treatment for taxation purposes of amounts credited or debited to the revaluation reserve shall be disclosed in a note to the accounts.

---

[1] Substituted by CA 1989, 1 Sch 6 with effect from 1 April 1990 (SI 1990 No 355) subject to the transitional and saving provisions in Arts 6 to 9 of that Order.
Previously
'(3) The revaluation reserve shall be reduced to the extent that the amounts standing to the credit of the reserve are in the opinion of the directors of the company no longer necessary for the purpose of the accounting policies adopted by the company; but an amount may only be transferred from the reserve to the profit and loss account if either—
(a) the amount in question was previously charged to that account; or
(b) it represents realised profit.'

PART III   NOTES TO THE ACCOUNTS

35   Preliminary

Any information required in the case of any company by the following provisions of this Part of this Schedule shall (if not given in the company's accounts) be given by way of a note to those accounts.

Disclosure of accounting policies

36   The accounting policies adopted by the company in determining the amounts to be included in respect of items shown in the balance sheet and in determining the profit or loss of the company shall be stated (including such policies with respect to the depreciation and diminution in value of assets).

[36A   It shall be stated whether the accounts have been prepared in accordance with applicable accounting standards and particulars of any material departure from those standards and the reasons for it shall be given.][1]

---

[1] Inserted by CA 1989, 1 Sch 7 with effect from 1 April 1990 (SI 1990 No 355) subject to the transitional and saving provisions in Arts 6 to 9 of that Order.

Information supplementing the balance sheet

37   Paragraphs 38 to 51 require information which either supplements the information given with respect to any particular items shown in the balance sheet or is otherwise relevant to assessing the company's state of affairs in the light of the information so given.

Share capital and debentures

38   (1)   The following information shall be given with respect to the company's share capital—

(a)   the authorised share capital; and
(b)   where shares of more than one class have been allotted, the number and aggregate nominal value of shares of each class allotted.

496

(2)   In the case of any part of the allotted share capital that consists of redeemable shares, the following information shall be given—

    (a)   the earliest and latest dates on which the company has power to redeem those shares;

    (b)   whether those shares must be redeemed in any event or are liable to be redeemed at the option of the company or of the shareholder; and

    (c)   whether any (and, if so, what) premium is payable on redemption.

39   If the company has allotted any shares during the financial year, the following information shall be given—

    (a)   the reason for making the allotment;

    (b)   the classes of shares allotted; and

    (c)   as respects each class of shares, the number allotted, their aggregate nominal value, and the consideration received by the company for the allotment.

40   (1)   With respect to any contingent right to the allotment of shares in the company the following particulars shall be given—

    (a)   the number, description and amount of the shares in relation to which the right is exercisable;

    (b)   the period during which it is exercisable; and

    (c)   the price to be paid for the shares allotted.

(2)   In sub-paragraph (1) above "contingent right to the allotment of shares" means any option to subscribe for shares and any other right to require the allotment of shares to any person whether arising on the conversion into shares of securities of any other description or otherwise.

41   (1)   If the company has issued any debentures during the financial year to which the accounts relate, the following information shall be given—

    (a)   the reason for making the issue;

    (b)   the classes of debentures issued; and

    (c)   as respects each class of debentures, the amount issued and the consideration received by the company for the issue.

(2)   Particulars of any redeemed debentures which the company has power to reissue shall also be given.

(3)   Where any of the company's debentures are held by a nominee of or trustee for the company, the nominal amount of the debentures and the amount at which they are stated in the accounting records kept by the company in accordance with section 221 of this Act shall be stated.

Fixed assets

42   (1)   In respect of each item which is or would but for paragraph 3(4)(b) be shown under the general item "fixed assets" in the company's balance sheet the following information shall be given—

    (a)   the appropriate amounts in respect of that item as at the date of the beginning of the financial year and as at the balance sheet date respectively;

    (b)   the effect on any amount shown in the balance sheet in respect of that item of—

        (i)   any revision of the amount in respect of any assets included under that item made during that year on any basis mentioned in paragraph 31;

(ii) acquisitions during that year of any assets;
(iii) disposals during that year of any assets; and
(iv) any transfers of assets of the company to and from that item during that year.

(2) The reference in sub-paragraph (1)(a) to the appropriate amounts in respect of any item as at any date there mentioned is a reference to amounts representing the aggregate amounts determined, as at that date, in respect of assets falling to be included under that item on either of the following bases, that is to say—

(a) on the basis of purchase price or production cost (determined in accordance with paragraphs 26 and 27); or
(b) on any basis mentioned in paragraph 31,

(leaving out of account in either case any provisions for depreciation or diminution in value).

(3) In respect of each item within sub-paragraph (1)—

(a) the cumulative amount of provisions for depreciation or diminution in value of assets included under that item as at each date mentioned in sub-paragraph (1)(a);
(b) the amount of any such provisions made in respect of the financial year;
(c) the amount of any adjustments made in respect of any such provisions during that year in consequence of the disposal of any assets; and
(d) the amount of any other adjustments made in respect of any such provisions during that year;

shall also be stated.

43 Where any fixed assets of the company (other than listed investments) are included under any item shown in the company's balance sheet at an amount determined on any basis mentioned in paragraph 31, the following information shall be given—

(a) the years (so far as they are known to the directors) in which the assets were severally valued and the several values; and
(b) in the case of assets that have been valued during the financial year, the names of the persons who valued them or particulars of their qualifications for doing so and (whichever is stated) the bases of valuation used by them.

44 In relation to any amount which is or would but for paragraph 3(4)(b) be shown in respect of the item "land and buildings" in the company's balance sheet there shall be stated—

(a) how much of that amount is ascribable to land of freehold tenure and how much to land of leasehold tenure; and
(b) how much of the amount ascribable to land of leasehold tenure is ascribable to land held on long lease and how much to land held on short lease.

Investments

45 (1) In respect of the amount of each item which is or would but for paragraph 3(4)(b) be shown in the company's balance sheet under the general item "investments" (whether as fixed assets or as current assets) there shall be stated—

(a) how much of that amount is ascribable to listed investments; and

(b)   how much of any amount so ascribable is ascribable to investments as respects which there has been granted a listing on a [recognised investment exchange other than an overseas investment exchange within the meaning of the Financial Services Act 1986][1] and how much to other listed investments.

(2)   Where the amount of any listed investments is stated for any item in accordance with sub-paragraph (1)(a), the following amounts shall also be stated—

(a)   the aggregate market value of those investments where it differs from the amount so stated; and

(b)   both the market value and the stock exchange value of any investments of which the former value is, for the purposes of the accounts, taken as being higher than the latter.

[1]   Substituted by FSA 1986, s 212(2), 16 Sch 23(a) with effect from 29 April 1988 (see SI 1988 No 740). Previously 'recognised stock exchange'.

Reserves and provisions

46   (1)   Where any amount is transferred—

(a)   to or from any reserves; or

(b)   to any provisions for liabilities and charges; or

(c)   from any provision for liabilities and charges otherwise than for the purpose for which the provision was established;

and the reserves or provisions are or would but for paragraph 3(4)(b) be shown as separate items in the company's balance sheet, the information mentioned in the following sub-paragraph shall be given in respect of the aggregate of reserves or provisions included in the same item.

(2)   That information is—

(a)   the amount of the reserves or provisions as at the date of the beginning of the financial year and as at the balance sheet date respectively;

(b)   any amounts transferred to or from the reserves or provisions during that year; and

(c)   the source and application respectively of any amounts so transferred.

(3)   Particulars shall be given of each provision included in the item "other provisions" in the company's balance sheet in any case where the amount of that provision is material.

Provision for taxation

47   [The amount of any provision for deferred taxation shall be stated separately from the amount of any provision for other taxation.][1]

[1]   Substituted by CA 1989, 1 Sch 8 with effect from 1 April 1990 (SI 1990 No 355) subject to the transitional and saving provisions in Arts 6 to 9 of that Order.
Previously
'The amount of any provisions for taxation other than deferred taxation shall be stated'.

Details of indebtedness

48   (1)   In respect of each item shown under "creditors" in the company's balance sheet there shall be stated—

(a)   the aggregate amount of any debts included under that item which are payable or repayable otherwise than by instalments and fall due for payment or repayment after the end of the period of five years beginning with the day next following the end of the financial year; and

     (b)   the aggregate amount of any debts so included which are payable or repayable by instalments any of which fall due for payment after the end of that period;

and in the case of debts within paragraph (b) above the aggregate amount of instalments falling due after the end of that period shall also be disclosed for each such item.

(2)   Subject to sub-paragraph (3), in relation to each debt falling to be taken into account under sub-paragraph (1), the terms of payment or repayment and the rate of any interest payable on the debt shall be stated.

(3)   If the number of debts is such that, in the opinion of the directors, compliance with sub-paragraph (2) would result in a statement of excessive length, it shall be sufficient to give a general indication of the terms of payment or repayment and the rates of any interest payable on the debts.

(4)   In respect of each item shown under "creditors" in the company's balance sheet there shall be stated—

     (a)   the aggregate amount of any debts included under that item in respect of which any security has been given by the company; and
     (b)   an indication of the nature of the securities so given.

(5)   References above in this paragraph to an item shown under "creditors" in the company's balance sheet include references, where amounts falling due to creditors within one year and after more than one year are distinguished in the balance sheet—

     (a)   in a case within sub-paragraph (1), to an item shown under the latter of those categories; and
     (b)   in a case within sub-paragraph (4), to an item shown under either of those categories;

and references to items shown under "creditors" include references to items which would but for paragraph 3(4)(b) be shown under that heading.

49   If any fixed cumulative dividends on the company's shares are in arrear, there shall be stated—

(a)   the amount of the arrears; and
(b)   the period for which the dividends or, if there is more than one class, each class of them are in arrear.

Guarantees and other financial commitments

50   (1)   Particulars shall be given of any charge on the assets of the company to secure the liabilities of any other person, including, where practicable, the amount secured.

(2)   The following information shall be given with respect to any other contingent liability not provided for—

     (a)   the amount or estimated amount of that liability;
     (b)   its legal nature; and
     (c)   whether any valuable security has been provided by the company in connection with that liability and if so, what.

(3)   There shall be stated, where practicable—

(a)   the aggregate amount or estimated amount of contracts for capital expenditure, so far as not provided for; and

(b)   the aggregate amount or estimated amount of capital expenditure authorised by the directors which has not been contracted for.

(4)   Particulars shall be given of—

(a)   any pension commitments included under any provision shown in the company's balance sheet; and

(b)   any such commitments for which no provision has been made;

and where any such commitment relates wholly or partly to pensions payable to past directors of the company separate particulars shall be given of that commitment so far as it relates to such pensions.

(5)   Particulars shall also be given of any other financial commitments which—

(a)   have not been provided for; and

(b)   are relevant to assessing the company's state of affairs.

(6)   [. . .][1]

---

[1]   Repealed by CA 1989, 24 Sch with effect from 1 April 1990 (SI 1990 No 355) subject to the transitional and saving provisions in Arts 6 to 9 of that Order.
Previously
'Commitments within any of the preceding sub-paragraphs undertaken on behalf of or for the benefit of—
(a)   any holding company or fellow subsidiary of the company; or
(b)   any subsidiary of the company;
shall be stated separately from the other commitments within that sub-paragraph (and commitments within paragraph (a) shall also be stated separately from those within paragraph (b)).'

Miscellaneous matters

51   (1)   Particulars shall be given of any case where the purchase price or production cost of any asset is for the first time determined under paragraph 28.

(2)   Where any outstanding loans made under the authority of section 153(4)(b) [, (bb)][1] or (c) or section 155 of this Act (various cases of financial assistance by a company for purchase of its own shares) are included under any item shown in the company's balance sheet, the aggregate amount of those loans shall be disclosed for each item in question.

(3)   The aggregate amount which is recommended for distribution by way of dividend shall be stated.

---

[1]   Inserted by CA 1989, 1 Sch 9 with effect from 1 April 1990 (SI 1990 No 355) subject to the transitional and saving provisions in Arts 6 to 9 of that Order.

Information supplementing the profit and loss account

52   Paragraphs 53 to 57 require information which either supplements the information given with respect to any particular items shown in the profit and loss account or otherwise provides particulars of income or expenditure of the company or of circumstances affecting the items shown in the profit and loss account.

Separate statement of certain items of income and expenditure

53   (1)   Subject to the following provisions of this paragraph, each of the amounts mentioned below shall be stated.

(2)   The amount of the interest on or any similar charges in respect of—

  (a) bank loans and overdrafts, and loans made to the company (other than bank loans and overdrafts) which—

    (i) are repayable otherwise than by instalments and fall due for repayment before the end of the period of five years beginning with the day next following the end of the financial year; or

    (ii) are repayable by instalments the last of which falls due for payment before the end of that period; and

  (b) loans of any other kind made to the company.

This sub-paragraph does not apply to interest or charges on loans to the company from group [undertakings][1], but, with that exception, it applies to interest or charges on all loans, whether made on the security of debentures or not.

(3) The amounts respectively set aside for redemption of share capital and for redemption of loans.

(4) The amount of income from listed investments.

(5) The amount of rents from land (after deduction of ground rents, rates and other outgoings).

This amount need only be stated if a substantial part of the company's revenue for the financial year consists of rents from land.

(6) The amount charged to revenue in respect of sums payable in respect of the hire of plant and machinery.

(7) [...][2]

---

[1] Substituted by CA 1989, 1 Sch 2 with effect from 1 April 1990 (SI 1990 No 355) subject to the transitional and saving provisions in Arts 6 to 9 of that Order.
Previously 'companies'.

[2] Repealed by CA 1989, 24 Sch with effect as in [1] above.
Previously
'The amount of the remuneration of the auditors (taking "remuneration", for the purposes of this sub-paragraph, as including any sums paid by the company in respect of the auditors' expenses).'

Particulars of tax

54 (1) The basis on which the charge for United Kingdom corporation tax and United Kingdom income tax is computed shall be stated.

  (2) Particulars shall be given of any special circumstances which affect liability in respect of taxation of profits, income or capital gains for the financial year or liability in respect of taxation of profits, income or capital gains for succeeding financial years.

  (3) The following amounts shall be stated—

    (a) the amount of the charge for United Kingdom corporation tax;

    (b) if that amount would have been greater but for relief from double taxation, the amount which it would have been but for such relief;

    (c) the amount of the charge for United Kingdom income tax; and

    (d) the amount of the charge for taxation imposed outside the United Kingdom of profits, income and (so far as charged to revenue) capital gains.

These amounts shall be stated separately in respect of each of the amounts which is or would but for paragraph 3(4)(b) be shown under the following items in the profit and loss account, that is to say "tax on profit or loss on ordinary activities" and "tax on extraordinary profit or loss".

Particulars of turnover

55 (1) If in the course of the financial year the company has carried on business of two or more classes that, in the opinion of the directors, differ substantially from each other, there shall be stated in respect of each class (describing it)—

(a) the amount of the turnover attributable to that class; and

(b) the amount of the profit or loss of the company before taxation which is in the opinion of the directors attributable to that class.

(2) If in the course of the financial year the company has supplied markets that, in the opinion of the directors, differ substantially from each other, the amount of the turnover attributable to each such market shall also be stated.

In this paragraph "market" means a market delimited by geographical bounds.

(3) In analysing for the purposes of this paragraph the source (in terms of business or in terms of market) of turnover or (as the case may be) of profit or loss, the directors of the company shall have regard to the manner in which the company's activities are organised.

(4) For the purposes of this paragraph—

(a) classes of business which, in the opinion of the directors, do not differ substantially from each other shall be treated as one class; and

(b) markets which, in the opinion of the directors, do not differ substantially from each other shall be treated as one market;

and any amounts properly attributable to one class of business or (as the case may be) to one market which are not material may be included in the amount stated in respect of another.

(5) Where in the opinion of the directors the disclosure of any information required by this paragraph would be seriously prejudicial to the interests of the company, that information need not be disclosed, but the fact that any such information has not been disclosed must be stated.

Particulars of staff

56 (1) The following information shall be given with respect to the employees of the company—

(a) the average number of persons employed by the company in the financial year; and

(b) the average number of persons so employed within each category of persons employed by the company.

(2) The average number required by sub-paragraph (1)(a) or (b) shall be determined by dividing the relevant annual number by the number of weeks in the financial year.

(3) The relevant annual number shall be determined by ascertaining for each week in the financial year—

(a) for the purposes of sub-paragraph (1)(a), the number of persons employed under contracts of service by the company in that week (whether throughout the week or not);

(b) for the purposes of sub-paragraph (1)(b), the number of persons in the category in question of persons so employed;

and, in either case, adding together all the weekly numbers.

Companies Act 1985

(4) In respect of all persons employed by the company during the financial year who are taken into account in determining the relevant annual number for the purposes of sub-paragraph (l)(a) there shall also be stated the aggregate amounts respectively of—

(a) wages and salaries paid or payable in respect of that year to those persons;
(b) social security costs incurred by the company on their behalf; and
(c) other pension costs so incurred;

save in so far as those amounts or any of them are stated in the profit and loss account.

(5) The categories of persons employed by the company by reference to which the number required to be disclosed by sub-paragraph (1)(b) is to be determined shall be such as the directors may select, having regard to the manner in which the company's activities are organised.

Miscellaneous matters

57 (1) Where any amount relating to any preceding financial year is included in any item in the profit and loss account, the effect shall be stated.

(2) Particulars shall be given of any extraordinary income or charges arising in the financial year.

(3) The effect shall be stated of any transactions that are exceptional by virtue of size or incidence though they fall within the ordinary activities of the company.

58 General

(1) Where sums originally denominated in foreign currencies have been brought into account under any items shown in the balance sheet or profit and loss account, the basis on which those sums have been translated into sterling shall be stated.

(2) Subject to the following sub-paragraph, in respect of every item stated in a note to the accounts the corresponding amount for the financial year immediately preceding that to which the accounts relate shall also be stated and where the corresponding amount is not comparable, it shall be adjusted and particulars of the adjustment and the reasons for it shall be given.

(3) Sub-paragraph (2) does not apply in relation to any amounts stated by virtue of any of the following provisions of this Act—

[(a) paragraph 13 of Schedule 4A (details of accounting treatment of acquisitions),
(b) paragraphs 2, 8(3), 16, 21(1)(d), 22(4) and (5), 24(3) and (4) and 27(3) and (4) of Schedule 5 (shareholdings in other undertakings),
(c) Parts II and III of Schedule 6 (loans and other dealings in favour of directors and others), and
(d) paragraphs 42 and 46 above (fixed assets and reserves and provisions).][1]

---

[1] Substituted by CA 1989, 1 Sch 9 with effect from 1 April 1990 (SI 1990 No 355) subject to the transitional and saving provisions in Arts 6 to 9 of that Order.
Previously
'(a) section 231 as applying Parts I and II of Schedule 5 (proportion of share capital of subsidiaries and other bodies corporate held by the company, etc.),
(b) sections 232 to 234 and Schedule 6 (particulars of loans to directors, etc.), and
(c) paragraphs 42 and 46 above.'

[PART IV SPECIAL PROVISIONS WHERE COMPANY IS A PARENT COMPANY OR SUBSIDIARY UNDERTAKING

59 Dealings with or interests in group undertakings

Where a company is a parent company or a subsidiary undertaking and any item required by Part I of this Schedule to be shown in the company's balance sheet in relation to group undertakings includes—

(a) amounts attributable to dealings with or interests in any parent undertaking or fellow subsidiary undertaking, or

(b) amounts attributable to dealings with or interests in any subsidiary undertaking of the company,

the aggregate amounts within paragraphs (a) and (b) respectively shall be shown as separate items, either by way of subdivision of the relevant item in the balance sheet or in a note to the company's accounts.][1]

---

[1] Substituted by CA 1989, 1 Sch 11 with effect from 1 April 1990 (SI 1990 No 355) subject to the transitional and saving provisions in Arts 6 to 9 of that Order.
Previously
'PART IV SPECIAL PROVISIONS WHERE THE COMPANY IS A HOLDING OR SUBSIDIARY COMPANY

Company's own accounts

59 Where a company is a holding company or a subsidiary of another body corporate and any item required by Part I of this Schedule to be shown in the company's balance sheet in relation to group companies includes—

(a) amounts attributable to dealings with or interests in any holding company or fellow subsidiary of the company; or

(b) amounts attributable to dealings with or interests in any subsidiary of the company;

the aggregate amounts within paragraphs (a) and (b) respectively shall be shown as separate items, either by way of subdivision of the relevant item in the balance sheet or in a note to the company's accounts.'

[59A **Guarantees and other financial commitments in favour of group undertakings**

Commitments within any of sub-paragraphs (1) to (5) of paragraph 50 (guarantees and other financial commitments) which are undertaken on behalf of or for the benefit of—

(a) any parent undertaking or fellow subsidiary undertaking, or

(b) any subsidiary undertaking of the company,

shall be stated separately from the other commitments within that sub-paragraph, and commitments within paragraph (a) shall also be stated separately from those within paragraph (b).][1]

---

[1] Inserted by CA 1989, 1 Sch 11 with effect from 1 April 1990 (SI 1990 No 355) subject to the transitional and saving provisions in Arts 6 to 9 of that Order.

60-70 [. . .][1]

---

[1] Repealed by CA 1989, 24 Sch with effect from 1 April 1990 (SI 1990 No 355) subject to the transitional and saving provisions in Arts 6 to 9 of that Order.

PART V   SPECIAL PROVISIONS WHERE THE COMPANY IS AN INVESTMENT COMPANY

71   (1)   Paragraph 34 does not apply to the amount of any profit or loss arising from a determination of the value of any investments of an investment company on any basis mentioned in paragraph 31(3).

(2)   Any provisions made by virtue of paragraph 19(1) or (2) in the case of an investment company in respect of any fixed asset investments need not be charged to the company's profit and loss account provided they are either—

(a)   charged against any reserve account to which any amount excluded by sub-paragraph (1) from the requirements of paragraph 34 has been credited; or

(b)   shown as a separate item in the company's balance sheet under the sub-heading "other reserves".

(3)   For the purposes of this paragraph, as it applies in relation to any company, "fixed asset investment" means any asset falling to be included under any item shown in the company's balance sheet under the subdivision "investments" under the general item "fixed assets".

72   (1)   Any distribution made by an investment company which reduces the amount of its net assets to less than the aggregate of its called-up share capital and undistributable reserves shall be disclosed in a note to the company's accounts.

(2)   For purposes of this paragraph, a company's net assets are the aggregate of its assets less the aggregate of its liabilities (including any provision for liabilities or charges within paragraph 89); and "undistributable reserves" has the meaning given by section 264(3) of this Act.

73   A company shall be treated as an investment company for the purposes of this Part of this Schedule in relation to any financial year of the company if—

(a)   during the whole of that year it was an investment company as defined by section 266 of this Act, and

(b)   it was not at any time during that year prohibited under section 265(4) of this Act (no distribution where capital profits have been distributed, etc.) from making a distribution by virtue of that section.

74   [. . .]¹

---

¹   Repealed by CA 1989, 24 Sch with effect from 1 April 1990 (SI 1990 No 355) subject to the transitional and saving provisions in Arts 6 to 9 of that Order.

PART VI   SPECIAL PROVISIONS WHERE THE COMPANY HAS ENTERED INTO ARRANGEMENTS SUBJECT TO MERGER RELIEF

75   [. . .]¹

---

¹   Repealed by CA 1989, 24 Sch with effect from 1 April 1990 (SI 1990 No 355) subject to the transitional and saving provisions in Arts 6 to 9 of that Order.

PART VII   INTERPRETATION OF SCHEDULE

76   The following paragraphs apply for the purposes of this Schedule and its interpretation.

77-81 [. . .][1]

---

[1]   Repealed by CA 1989, 24 Sch with effect from 1 April 1990 (SI 1990 No 355) subject to the transitional and saving provisions in Arts 6 to 9 of that Order.

Historical cost accounting rules

82   References to the historical cost accounting rules shall be read in accordance with paragraph 29.

Leases

83   (1)   "Long lease" means a lease in the case of which the portion of the term for which it was granted remaining unexpired at the end of the financial year is not less than 50 years.

(2)   "Short lease" means a lease which is not a long lease.

(3)   "Lease" includes an agreement for a lease.

Listed investments

84   "Listed investment" means an investment as respects which there has been granted a listing [on a recognised investment exchange other than an overseas investment exchange within the meaning of the Financial Services Act 1986 or on any stock exchange of repute outside Great Britain][1].

---

[1]   Substituted by FSA 1986, s 212(2), 16 Sch 23(b) with effect from 29 April 1988 (see SI 1988 No 740). Previously 'on a recognised stock exchange, or on any stock exchange of repute (other than a recognised stock exchange) outside Great Britain'.

Loans

85   A loan is treated as falling due for repayment, and an instalment of a loan is treated as falling due for payment, on the earliest date on which the lender could require repayment or (as the case may be) payment, if he exercised all options and rights available to him.

Materiality

86   Amounts which in the particular context of any provision of this Schedule are not material may be disregarded for the purposes of that provision.

87   [. . .][1]

---

[1]   Repealed by CA 1989, 24 Sch with effect from 1 April 1990 (SI 1990 No 355) subject to the transitional and saving provisions in Arts 6 to 9 of that Order.

Provisions

88   (1)   References to provisions for depreciation or diminution in value of assets are to any amount written off by way of providing for depreciation or diminution in value of assets.

(2)   Any reference in the profit and loss account formats set out in Part I of this Schedule to the depreciation of, or amounts written off, assets of any description is to any provision for depreciation or diminution in value of assets of that description.

89   References to provisions for liabilities or charges are to any amount retained as reasonably necessary for the purpose of providing for any liability or loss which is either likely to be incurred, or certain to be incurred but uncertain as to amount or as to the date on which it will arise.

90-92 [. . .]¹

¹   Repealed by CA 1989, 24 Sch with effect from 1 April 1990 (SI 1990 No 355) subject to the transitional and saving provisions in Arts 6 to 9 of that Order.

Scots land tenure

93   In the application of this Schedule to Scotland, "land of freehold tenure" means land in respect of which the company is the proprietor of the *dominium utile* or, in the case of land not held on feudal tenure, is the owner; "land of leasehold tenure" means land of which the company is the tenant under a lease; and the reference to ground-rents, rates and other outgoings includes feu-duty and ground annual.

Staff costs

94   (1)   "Social security costs" means any contributions by the company to any state social security or pension scheme, fund or arrangement.

(2)   "Pension costs" includes any other contributions by the company for the purposes of any pension scheme established for the purpose of providing pensions for persons employed by the company, any sums set aside for that purpose and any amounts paid by the company in respect of pensions without first being so set aside.

(3)   Any amount stated in respect of either of the above items or in respect of the item "wages and salaries" in the company's profit and loss account shall be determined by reference to payments made or costs incurred in respect of all persons employed by the company during the financial year who are taken into account in determining the relevant annual number for the purposes of paragraph 56(1)(a).

95   [. . .]¹

¹   Repealed by CA 1989, 24 Sch with effect from 1 April 1990 (SI 1990 No 355) subject to the transitional and saving provisions in Arts 6 to 9 of that Order.

SCHEDULE 4A
(Section 5(2), CA 1989)

FORM AND CONTENT OF GROUP ACCOUNTS

Note. This Schedule inserted by CA 1989, s 5(2), 2 Sch with effect from 1 April 1990 (SI 1990 No 355) subject to the transitional and saving provisions in Arts 6 to 9 of that Order.

General rules

1   (1)   Group accounts shall comply so far as practicable with the provisions of Schedule 4 as if the undertakings included in the consolidation ("the group") were a single company.

   (2)   In particular, for the purposes of paragraph 59 of that Schedule (dealings with or interests in group undertakings) as it applies to group accounts—

      (a)   any subsidiary undertakings of the parent company not included in the consolidation shall be treated as subsidiary undertakings of the group, and

      (b)   if the parent company is itself a subsidiary undertaking, the group shall be treated as a subsidiary undertaking of any parent undertaking of that company, and the reference to fellow-subsidiary undertakings shall be construed accordingly.

   (3)   Where the parent company is treated as an investment company for the purposes of Part V of that Schedule (special provisions for investment companies) the group shall be similarly treated.

2   (1)   The consolidated balance sheet and profit and loss account shall incorporate in full the information contained in the individual accounts of the undertakings included in the consolidation, subject to the adjustments authorised or required by the following provisions of this Schedule and to such other adjustments (if any) as may be appropriate in accordance with generally accepted accounting principles or practice.

   (2)   If the financial year of a subsidiary undertaking included in the consolidation differs from that of the parent company, the group accounts shall be made up—

      (a)   from the accounts of the subsidiary undertaking for its financial year last ending before the end of the parent company's financial year, provided that year ended no more than three months before that of the parent company, or

      (b)   from interim accounts prepared by the subsidiary undertaking as at the end of the parent company's financial year.

3   (1)   Where assets and liabilities to be included in the group accounts have been valued or otherwise determined by undertakings according to accounting rules differing from those used for the group accounts, the values or amounts shall be adjusted so as to accord with the rules used for the group accounts.

   (2)   If it appears to the directors of the parent company that there are special reasons for departing from sub-paragraph (1) they may do so, but particulars of any such departure, the reasons for it and its effect shall be given in a note to the accounts.

(3)   The adjustments referred to in this paragraph need not be made if they are not material for the purpose of giving a true and fair view.

4   Any differences of accounting rules as between a parent company's individual accounts for a financial year and its group accounts shall be disclosed in a note to the latter accounts and the reasons for the difference given.

5   Amounts which in the particular context of any provision of this Schedule are not material may be disregarded for the purposes of that provision.

6   Elimination of group transactions

(1)   Debts and claims between undertakings included in the consolidation, and income and expenditure relating to transactions between such undertakings, shall be eliminated in preparing the group accounts.

(2)   Where profits and losses resulting from transactions between undertakings included in the consolidation are included in the book value of assets, they shall be eliminated in preparing the group accounts.

(3)   The elimination required by sub-paragraph (2) may be effected in proportion to the group's interest in the shares of the undertakings.

(4)   Sub-paragraphs (1) and (2) need not be complied with if the amounts concerned are not material for the purpose of giving a true and fair view.

Acquisition and merger accounting

7   (1)   The following provisions apply where an undertaking becomes a subsidiary undertaking of the parent company.

(2)   That event is referred to in those provisions as an "acquisition", and references to the "undertaking acquired" shall be construed accordingly.

8   An acquisition shall be accounted for by the acquisition method of accounting unless the conditions for accounting for it as a merger are met and the merger method of accounting is adopted.

9   (1)   The acquisition method of accounting is as follows.

(2)   The identifiable assets and liabilities of the undertaking acquired shall be included in the consolidated balance sheet at their fair values as at the date of acquisition.

In this paragraph the "identifiable" assets or liabilities of the undertaking acquired means the assets or liabilities which are capable of being disposed of or discharged separately, without disposing of a business of the undertaking.

(3)   The income and expenditure of the undertaking acquired shall be brought into the group accounts only as from the date of the acquisition.

(4)   There shall be set off against the acquisition cost of the interest in the shares of the undertaking held by the parent company and its subsidiary undertakings the interest of the parent company and its subsidiary undertakings in the adjusted capital and reserves of the undertaking acquired.

For this purpose—

"the acquisition cost" means the amount of any cash consideration and the fair value of any other consideration, together with such amount (if any) in respect of fees and other expenses of the acquisition as the company may determine, and

"the adjusted capital and reserves" of the undertaking acquired means its capital and reserves at the date of the acquisition after adjusting the identifiable assets and liabilities of the undertaking to fair values as at that date.

(5) The resulting amount if positive shall be treated as goodwill, and if negative as a negative consolidation difference.

10 (1) The conditions for accounting for an acquisition as a merger are—

    (a) that at least 90 per cent. of the nominal value of the relevant shares in the undertaking acquired is held by or on behalf of the parent company and its subsidiary undertakings,

    (b) that the proportion referred to in paragraph (a) was attained pursuant to an arrangement providing for the issue of equity shares by the parent company or one or more of its subsidiary undertakings,

    (c) that the fair value of any consideration other than the issue of equity shares given pursuant to the arrangement by the parent company and its subsidiary undertakings did not exceed 10 per cent. of the nominal value of the equity shares issued, and

    (d) that adoption of the merger method of accounting accords with generally accepted accounting principles or practice.

(2) The reference in sub-paragraph (1)(a) to the "relevant shares" in an undertaking acquired is to those carrying unrestricted rights to participate both in distributions and in the assets of the undertaking upon liquidation.

11 (1) The merger method of accounting is as follows.

(2) The assets and liabilities of the undertaking acquired shall be brought into the group accounts at the figures at which they stand in the undertaking's accounts, subject to any adjustment authorised or required by this Schedule.

(3) The income and expenditure of the undertaking acquired shall be included in the group accounts for the entire financial year, including the period before the acquisition.

(4) The group accounts shall show corresponding amounts relating to the previous financial year as if the undertaking acquired had been included in the consolidation throughout that year.

(5) There shall be set off against the aggregate of—

    (a) the appropriate amount in respect of qualifying shares issued by the parent company or its subsidiary undertakings in consideration for the acquisition of shares in the undertaking acquired, and

    (b) the fair value of any other consideration for the acquisition of shares in the undertaking acquired, determined as at the date when those shares were acquired,

the nominal value of the issued share capital of the undertaking acquired held by the parent company and its subsidiary undertakings.

(6) The resulting amount shall be shown as an adjustment to the consolidated reserves.

(7)   In sub-paragraph (5)(a) "qualifying shares" means—

    (a)   shares in relation to which section 131 (merger relief) applies, in respect of which the appropriate amount is the nominal value; or

    (b)   shares in relation to which section 132 (relief in respect of group reconstructions) applies, in respect of which the appropriate amount is the nominal value together with any minimum premium value within the meaning of that section.

12   (1)   Where a group is acquired, paragraphs 9 to 11 apply with the following adaptations.

    (2)   References to shares of the undertaking acquired shall be construed as references to shares of the parent undertaking of the group.

    (3)   Other references to the undertaking acquired shall be construed as references to the group; and references to the assets and liabilities, income and expenditure and capital and reserves of the undertaking acquired shall be construed as references to the assets and liabilities, income and expenditure and capital and reserves of the group after making the set-offs and other adjustments required by this Schedule in the case of group accounts.

13   (1)   The following information with respect to acquisitions taking place in the financial year shall be given in a note to the accounts.

    (2)   There shall be stated—

    (a)   the name of the undertaking acquired or, where a group was acquired, the name of the parent undertaking of that group, and

    (b)   whether the acquisition has been accounted for by the acquisition or the merger method of accounting;

and in relation to an acquisition which significantly affects the figures shown in the group accounts, the following further information shall be given.

    (3)   The composition and fair value of the consideration for the acquisition given by the parent company and its subsidiary undertakings shall be stated.

    (4)   The profit or loss of the undertaking or group acquired shall be stated—

    (a)   for the period from the beginning of the financial year of the undertaking or, as the case may be, of the parent undertaking of the group, up to the date of the acquisition, and

    (b)   for the previous financial year of that undertaking or parent undertaking;

and there shall also be stated the date on which the financial year referred to in paragraph (a) began.

    (5)   Where the acquisition method of accounting has been adopted, the book values immediately prior to the acquisition, and the fair values at the date of acquisition, of each class of assets and liabilities of the undertaking or group acquired shall be stated in tabular form, including a statement of the amount of any goodwill or negative consolidation difference arising on the acquisition, together with an explanation of any significant adjustments made.

    (6)   Where the merger method of accounting has been adopted, an explanation shall be given of any significant adjustments made in relation to the amounts of the assets and liabilities of the undertaking or group acquired, together with a statement of any resulting adjustment to the consolidated reserves (including the re-statement of opening consolidated reserves).

(7)   In ascertaining for the purposes of sub-paragraph (4), (5) or (6) the profit or loss of a group, the book values and fair values of assets and liabilities of a group or the amount of the assets and liabilities of a group, the set-offs and other adjustments required by this Schedule in the case of group accounts shall be made.

14   (1)   There shall also be stated in a note to the accounts the cumulative amount of goodwill resulting from acquisitions in that and earlier financial years which has been written off.

        (2)   That figure shall be shown net of any goodwill attributable to subsidiary undertakings or businesses disposed of prior to the balance sheet date.

15   Where during the financial year there has been a disposal of an undertaking or group which significantly affects the figures shown in the group accounts, there shall be stated in a note to the accounts—

    (a)   the name of that undertaking or, as the case may be, of the parent undertaking of that group, and

    (b)   the extent to which the profit or loss shown in the group accounts is attributable to profit or loss of that undertaking or group.

16   The information required by paragraph 13, 14 or 15 above need not be disclosed with respect to an undertaking which—

    (a)   is established under the law of a country outside the United Kingdom, or

    (b)   carries on business outside the United Kingdom

if in the opinion of the directors of the parent company the disclosure would be seriously prejudicial to the business of that undertaking or to the business of the parent company or any of its subsidiary undertakings and the Secretary of State agrees that the information should not be disclosed.

17   **Minority interests**

    (1)   The formats set out in Schedule 4 have effect in relation to group accounts with the following additions.

    (2)   In the Balance Sheet Formats a further item headed "Minority interests" shall be added—

        (a)   in Format 1, either after item J or at the end (after item K), and

        (b)   in Format 2, under the general heading "LIABILITIES", between items A and B;

    and under that item shall be shown the amount of capital and reserves attributable to shares in subsidiary undertakings included in the consolidation held by or on behalf of persons other than the parent company and its subsidiary undertakings.

    (3)   In the Profit and Loss Account Formats a further item headed "Minority interests" shall be added—

        (a)   in Format 1, between items 14 and 15,

        (b)   in Format 2, between items 16 and 17,

        (c)   in Format 3, between items 7 and 8 in both sections A and B, and

        (d)   in Format 4, between items 9 and 10 in both sections A and B;

and under that item shall be shown the amount of any profit or loss on ordinary activities attributable to shares in subsidiary undertakings included in the consolidation held by or on behalf of persons other than the parent company and its subsidiary undertakings.

(4) In the Profit and Loss Account Formats a further item headed "Minority interests" shall be added—

(a) in Format 1, between items 18 and 19,

(b) in Format 2, between items 20 and 21,

(c) in Format 3, between items 9 and 10 in section A and between items 8 and 9 in section B, and

(d) in Format 4, between items 11 and 12 in section A and between items 10 and 11 in section B;

and under that item shall be shown the amount of any profit or loss on extraordinary activities attributable to shares in subsidiary undertakings included in the consolidation held by or on behalf of persons other than the parent company and its subsidiary undertakings.

(5) For the purposes of paragraph 3(3) and (4) of Schedule 4 (power to adapt or combine items)—

(a) the additional item required by sub-paragraph (2) above shall be treated as one to which a letter is assigned, and

(b) the additional items required by sub-paragraphs (3) and (4) above shall be treated as ones to which an Arabic number is assigned.

18 Interests in subsidiary undertakings excluded from consolidation

The interest of the group in subsidiary undertakings excluded from consolidation under section 229(4) (undertakings with activities different from those of undertakings included in the consolidation), and the amount of profit or loss attributable to such an interest, shall be shown in the consolidated balance sheet or, as the case may be, in the consolidated profit and loss account by the equity method of accounting (including dealing with any goodwill arising in accordance with paragraphs 17 to 19 and 21 of Schedule 4).

19 Joint ventures

(1) Where an undertaking included in the consolidation manages another undertaking jointly with one or more undertakings not included in the consolidation, that other undertaking ("the joint venture") may, if it is not—

(a) a body corporate, or

(b) a subsidiary undertaking of the parent company,

be dealt with in the group accounts by the method of proportional consolidation.

(2) The provisions of this Part relating to the preparation of consolidated accounts apply, with any necessary modifications, to proportional consolidation under this paragraph.

Associated undertakings

20 (1) An "associated undertaking" means an undertaking in which an undertaking included in the consolidation has a participating interest and over whose operating and financial policy it exercises a significant influence, and which is not—

(a) a subsidiary undertaking of the parent company, or

(b) a joint venture dealt with in accordance with paragraph 19.

(2) Where an undertaking holds 20 per cent. or more of the voting rights in another undertaking, it shall be presumed to exercise such an influence over it unless the contrary is shown.

(3) The voting rights in an undertaking means the rights conferred on shareholders in respect of their shares or, in the case of an undertaking not having a share capital, on members, to vote at general meetings of the undertaking on all, or substantially all, matters.

(4) The provisions of paragraphs 5 to 11 of Schedule 10A (rights to be taken into account and attribution of rights) apply in determining for the purposes of this paragraph whether an undertaking holds 20 per cent. or more of the voting rights in another undertaking.

21 (1) The formats set out in Schedule 4 have effect in relation to group accounts with the following modifications.

(2) In the Balance Sheet Formats the items headed "Participating interests", that is—

(a) in Format 1, item B.III.3, and

(b) in Format 2, item B.III.3 under the heading "ASSETS",

shall be replaced by two items, "Interests in associated undertakings" and "Other participating interests".

(3) In the Profit and Loss Account Formats, the items headed "Income from participating interests", that is—

(a) in Format 1, item 8,

(b) in Format 2, item 10,

(c) in Format 3, item B.4, and

(d) in Format 4, item B.6,

shall be replaced by two items, "Income from interests in associated under-takings" and "Income from other participating interest. ".

22 (1) The interest of an undertaking in an associated undertaking, and the amount of profit or loss attributable to such an interest, shall be shown by the equity method of accounting (including dealing with any goodwill arising in accordance with paragraphs 17 to 19 and 21 of Schedule 4).

(2) Where the associated undertaking is itself a parent undertaking, the net assets and profits or losses to be taken into account are those of the parent and its subsidiary undertakings (after making any consolidation adjustments).

(3) The equity method of accounting need not be applied if the amounts in question are not material for the purpose of giving a true and fair view.

Companies Act 1985

SCHEDULE 5
(Section 6(2), CA 1989)

DISCLOSURE OF INFORMATION: RELATED UNDERTAKINGS

Note. This Schedule substituted by CA 1989, s 6(2), 3 Sch with effect from 1 April 1990 (SI 1990 No 355) subject to the transitional and saving provisions in Arts 6 to 9 of that Order. See after end of Schedule for the previous provisions of 5 Sch.

Cross references. See 4 Sch 63.

PART I   COMPANIES NOT REQUIRED TO PREPARE GROUP ACCOUNTS

1   Subsidiary undertakings

(1)   The following information shall be given where at the end of the financial year the company has subsidiary undertakings.

(2)   The name of each subsidiary undertaking shall be stated.

(3)   There shall be stated with respect to each subsidiary undertaking—

   (a)   if it is incorporated outside Great Britain, the country in which it is incorporated;
   (b)   if it is incorporated in Great Britain, whether it is registered in England and Wales or in Scotland;
   (c)   if it is unincorporated, the address of its principal place of business.

(4)   The reason why the company is not required to prepare group accounts shall be stated.

(5)   If the reason is that all the subsidiary undertakings of the company fall within the exclusions provided for in section 229, it shall be stated with respect to each subsidiary undertaking which of those exclusions applies.

2   Holdings in subsidiary undertakings

(1)   There sh ll be stated in relation to shares of each class held by the company in a subsidiary undertaking—

   (a)   the identity of the class, and
   (b)   the proportion of the nominal value of the shares of that class represented by those shares.

(2)   The shares held by or on behalf of the company itself shall be distinguished from those attributed to the company which are held by or on behalf of a subsidiary undertaking.

3   Financial information about subsidiary undertakings

(1)   There shall be disclosed with respect to each subsidiary undertaking—

   (a)   the aggregate amount of its capital and reserves as at the end of its relevant financial year, and
   (b)   its profit or loss for that year.

(2)   That information need not be given if the company is exempt by virtue of section 228 from the requirement to prepare group accounts (parent company included in accounts of larger group).

(3)   That information need not be given if—

  (a)   the subsidiary undertaking is not required by any provision of this Act to deliver a copy of its balance sheet for its relevant financial year and does not otherwise publish that balance sheet in Great Britain or elsewhere, and

  (b)   the company's holding is less than 50 per cent. of the nominal value of the shares in the undertaking.

(4)   Information otherwise required by this paragraph need not be given if it is not material.

(5)   For the purposes of this paragraph the "relevant financial year" of a subsidiary undertaking is—

  (a)   if its financial year ends with that of the company, that year, and

  (b)   if not, its financial year ending last before the end of the company's financial year.

4   Financial years of subsidiary undertakings

Where the financial year of one or more subsidiary undertakings did not end with that of the company, there shall be stated in relation to each such undertaking—

  (a)   the reasons why the company's directors consider that its financial year should not end with that of the company, and

  (b)   the date on which its last financial year ended (last before the end of the company's financial year).

Instead of the dates required by paragraph (b) being given for each subsidiary undertaking the earliest and latest of those dates may be given.

5   Further information about subsidiary undertakings

(1)   There shall be disclosed—

  (a)   any qualifications contained in the auditors' reports on the accounts of subsidiary undertakings for financial years ending with or during the financial year of the company, and

  (b)   any note or saving contained in such accounts to call attention to a matter which, apart from the note or saving, would properly have been referred to in such a qualification,

in so far as the matter which is the subject of the qualification or note is not covered by the company's own accounts and is material from the point of view of its members.

(2)   The aggregate amount of the total investment of the company in the shares of subsidiary undertakings shall be stated by way of the equity method of valuation, unless—

  (a)   the company is exempt from the requirement to prepare group accounts by virtue of section 228 (parent company included in accounts of larger group), and

  (b)   the directors state their opinion that the aggregate value of the assets of the company consisting of shares in, or amounts owing (whether on account of a loan or otherwise) from, the company's subsidiary undertakings is not less than the aggregate of the amounts at which those assets are stated or included in the company's balance sheet.

(3)   In so far as information required by this paragraph is not obtainable, a statement to that effect shall be given instead.

6   Shares and debentures of company held by subsidiary undertakings

(1)   The number, description and amount of the shares in and debentures of the company held by or on behalf of its subsidiary undertakings shall be disclosed.

(2)   Sub-paragraph (1) does not apply in relation to shares or debentures in the case of which the subsidiary undertaking is concerned as personal representative or, subject as follows, as trustee.

(3)   The exception for shares or debentures in relation to which the subsidiary undertaking is concerned as trustee does not apply if the company, or any subsidiary undertaking of the company, is beneficially interested under the trust, otherwise than by way of security only for the purposes of a transaction entered into by it in the ordinary course of a business which includes the lending of money.

(4)   Schedule 2 to this Act has effect for the interpretation of the reference in sub-paragraph (3) to a beneficial interest under a trust.

Significant holdings in undertakings other than subsidiary undertakings

7   (1)   The information required by paragraphs 8 and 9 shall be given where at the end of the financial year the company has a significant holding in an undertaking which is not a subsidiary undertaking of the company.

(2)   A holding is significant for this purpose if—

(a)   it amounts to 10 per cent. or more of the nominal value of any class of shares in the undertaking, or

(b)   the amount of the holding (as stated or included in the company's accounts) exceeds one-tenth of the amount (as so stated) of the company's assets.

8   (1)   The name of the undertaking shall be stated.

(2)   There shall be stated—

(a)   if the undertaking is incorporated outside Great Britain, the country in which it is incorporated;

(b)   if it is incorporated in Great Britain, whether it is registered in England and Wales or in Scotland;

(c)   if it is unincorporated, the address of its principal place of business.

(3)   There shall also be stated—

(a)   the identity of each class of shares in the undertaking held by the company, and

(b)   the proportion of the nominal value of the shares of that class represented by those shares.

9   (1)   Where the company has a significant holding in an undertaking amounting to 20 per cent. or more of the nominal value of the shares in the undertaking, there shall also be stated—

(a)   the aggregate amount of the capital and reserves of the undertaking as at the end of its relevant financial year, and

(b)   its profit or loss for that year.

(2)   That information need not be given if—

   (a)   the company is exempt by virtue of section 228 from the requirement to prepare group accounts (parent company included in accounts of larger group), and

   (b)   the investment of the company in all undertakings in which it has such a holding as is mentioned in sub-paragraph (1) is shown, in aggregate, in the notes to the accounts by way of the equity method of valuation.

(3)   That information need not be given in respect of an undertaking if—

   (a)   the undertaking is not required by any provision of this Act to deliver a copy of its balance sheet for its relevant financial year and does not otherwise publish that balance sheet in Great Britain or elsewhere, and

   (b)   the company's holding is less than 50 per cent. of the nominal value of the shares in the undertaking.

(4)   Information otherwise required by this paragraph need not be given if it is not material.

(5)   For the purposes of this paragraph the "relevant financial year" of an undertaking is—

   (a)   if its financial year ends with that of the company, that year, and

   (b)   if not, its financial year ending last before the end of the company's financial year.

10   Arrangements attracting merger relief

(1)   This paragraph applies to arrangements attracting merger relief, that is, where a company allots shares in consideration for the issue, transfer or cancellation of shares in another body corporate ("the other company") in circumstances such that section 130 of this Act (share premium account) does not, by virtue of section 131(2) (merger relief), apply to the premiums on the shares.

(2)   If the company makes such an arrangement during the financial year, the following information shall be given—

   (a)   the name of the other company,

   (b)   the number, nominal value and class of shares allotted,

   (c)   the number, nominal value and class of shares in the other company issued, transferred or cancelled, and

   (d)   particulars of the accounting treatment adopted in the company's accounts in respect of the issue, transfer or cancellation.

(3)   Where the company made such an arrangement during the financial year, or during either of the two preceding financial years, and there is included in the company's profit and loss account—

   (a)   any profit or loss realised during the financial year by the company on the disposal of—

     (i)   any shares in the other company, or

     (ii)   any assets which were fixed assets of the other company or any of its subsidiary undertakings at the time of the arrangement, or

(b)   any part of any profit or loss realised during the financial year by the company on the disposal of any shares (other than shares in the other company) which was attributable to the fact that there were at the time of the disposal amongst the assets of the company which issued the shares, or any of its subsidiary undertakings, such shares or assets as are described in paragraph (a) above,

then, the net amount of that profit or loss or, as the case may be, the part so attributable shall be shown, together with an explanation of the transactions to which the information relates.

(4)   For the purposes of this paragraph the time of the arrangement shall be taken to be—

(a)   where as a result of the arrangement the other company becomes a subsidiary undertaking of the company, the date on which it does so or, if the arrangement in question becomes binding only on the fulfilment of a condition, the date on which that condition is fulfilled;

(b)   if the other company is already a subsidiary undertaking of the company, the date on which the shares are allotted or, if they are allotted on different days, the first day.

11   Parent undertaking drawing up accounts for larger group

(1)   Where the company is a subsidiary undertaking, the following information shall be given with respect to the parent undertaking of—

(a)   the largest group of undertakings for which group accounts are drawn up and of which the company is a member, and

(b)   the smallest such group of undertakings.

(2)   The name of the parent undertaking shall be stated.

(3)   There shall be stated—

(a)   if the undertaking is incorporated outside Great Britain, the country in which it is incorporated;

(b)   if it is incorporated in Great Britain, whether it is registered in England and Wales or in Scotland;

(c)   if it is unincorporated, the address of its principal place of business.

(4)   If copies of the group accounts referred to in sub-paragraph (1) are available to the public, there shall also be stated the addresses from which copies of the accounts can be obtained.

12   Identification of ultimate parent company

(1)   Where the company is a subsidiary undertaking, the following information shall be given with respect to the company (if any) regarded by the directors as being the company's ultimate parent company.

(2)   The name of that company shall be stated.

(3)   If known to the directors, there shall be stated—

(a)   if that company is incorporated outside Great Britain, the country in which it is incorporated;

(b)   if it is incorporated in Great Britain, whether it is registered in England and Wales or in Scotland.

(4)   In this paragraph "company" includes any body corporate.

13   Constructions of references to shares held by company

(1)   References in this Part of this Schedule to shares held by a company shall be construed as follows.

(2)   For the purposes of paragraphs 2 to 5 (information about subsidiary undertakings)—

    (a)   there shall be attributed to the company any shares held by a subsidiary undertaking, or by a person acting on behalf of the company or a subsidiary undertaking; but

    (b)   there shall be treated as not held by the company any shares held on behalf of a person other than the company or a subsidiary undertaking.

(3)   For the purposes of paragraphs 7 to 9 (information about undertakings other than subsidiary undertakings)—

    (a)   there shall be attributed to the company shares held on its behalf by any person; but

    (b)   there shall be treated as not held by a company shares held on behalf of a person other than the company.

(4)   For the purposes of any of those provisions, shares held by way of security shall be treated as held by the person providing the security—

    (a)   where apart from the right to exercise them for the purpose of preserving the value of the security, or of realising it, the rights attached to the shares are exercisable only in accordance with his instructions, and

    (b)   where the shares are held in connection with the granting of loans as part of normal business activities and apart from the right to exercise them for the purpose of preserving the value of the security, or of realising it, the rights attached to the shares are exercisable only in his interests.

PART II   COMPANIES REQUIRED TO PREPARE GROUP ACCOUNTS

14   Introductory

In this Part of this Schedule "the group" means the group consisting of the parent company and its subsidiary undertakings.

15   Subsidiary undertakings

(1)   The following information shall be given with respect to the undertakings which are subsidiary undertakings of the parent company at the end of the financial year.

(2)   The name of each undertaking shall be stated.

(3)   There shall be stated—

    (a)   if the undertaking is incorporated outside Great Britain, the country in which it is incorporated;

    (b)   if it is incorporated in Great Britain, whether it is registered in England and Wales or in Scotland;

    (c)   if it is unincorporated, the address of its principal place of business.

(4)   It shall also be stated whether the subsidiary undertaking is included in the consolidation and, if it is not, the reasons for excluding it from consolidation shall be given.

(5)   It shall be stated with respect to each subsidiary undertaking by virtue of which of the conditions specified in section 258(2) or (4) it is a subsidiary undertaking of its immediate parent undertaking.

That information need not be given if the relevant condition is that specified in subsection (2)(a) of that section (holding of a majority of the voting rights) and the immediate parent undertaking holds the same proportion of the shares in the undertaking as it holds voting rights.

16   Holdings in subsidiary undertakings

(1)   The following information shall be given with respect to the shares of a subsidiary undertaking held—

(a)   by the parent company, and
(b)   by the group;

and the information under paragraphs (a) and (b) shall (if different) be shown separately.

(2)   There shall be stated—

(a)   the identity of each class of shares held, and
(b)   the proportion of the nominal value of the shares of that class represented by those shares.

17   Financial information about subsidiary undertakings not included in the consolidation

(1)   There shall be shown with respect to each subsidiary undertaking not included in the consolidation—

(a)   the aggregate amount of its capital and reserves as at the end of its relevant financial year, and
(b)   its profit or loss for that year.

(2)   That information need not be given if the group's investment in the undertaking is included in the accounts by way of the equity method of valuation or if—

(a)   the undertaking is not required by any provision of this Act to deliver a copy of its balance sheet for its relevant financial year and does not otherwise publish that balance sheet in Great Britain or elsewhere, and
(b)   the holding of the group is less than 50 per cent. of the nominal value of the shares in the undertaking.

(3)   Information otherwise required by this paragraph need not be given if it is not material.

(4)   For the purposes of this paragraph the "relevant financial year" of a subsidiary undertaking is—

(a)   if its financial year ends with that of the company, that year, and
(b)   if not, its financial year ending last before the end of the company's financial year.

18   Further information about subsidiary undertakings excluded from consolidation

(1)   The following information shall be given with respect to subsidiary undertakings excluded from consolidation.

(2)   There shall be disclosed—

(a)   any qualifications contained in the auditors' reports on the accounts of the undertaking for financial years ending with or during the financial year of the company, and

(b)   any note or saving contained in such accounts to call attention to a matter which, apart from the note or saving, would properly have been referred to in such a qualification,

in so far as the matter which is the subject of the qualification or note is not covered by the consolidated accounts and is material from the point of view of the members of the parent company.

(3)   In so far as information required by this paragraph is not obtainable, a statement to that effect shall be given instead.

19   Financial years of subsidiary undertakings

Where the financial year of one or more subsidiary undertakings did not end with that of the company, there shall be stated in relation to each such undertaking—

(a)   the reasons why the company's directors consider that its financial year should not end with that of the company, and

(b)   the date on which its last financial year ended (last before the end of the company's financial year).

Instead of the dates required by paragraph (b) being given for each subsidiary undertaking the earliest and latest of those dates may be given.

20   Shares and debentures of company held by subsidiary undertakings

(1)   The number, description and amount of the shares in and debentures of the company held by or on behalf of its subsidiary undertakings shall be disclosed.

(2)   Sub-paragraph (1) does not apply in relation to shares or debentures in the case of which the subsidiary undertaking is concerned as personal representative or, subject as follows, as trustee.

(3)   The exception for shares or debentures in relation to which the subsidiary undertaking is concerned as trustee does not apply if the company or any of its subsidiary undertakings is beneficially interested under the trust, otherwise than by way of security only for the purposes of a transaction entered into by it in the ordinary course of a business which includes the lending of money.

(4)   Schedule 2 to this Act has effect for the interpretation of the reference in sub-paragraph (3) to a beneficial interest under a trust.

21   Joint ventures

(1)   The following information shall be given where an undertaking is dealt with in the consolidated accounts by the method of proportional consolidation in accordance with paragraph 19 of Schedule 4A (joint ventures)—

(a)   the name of the undertaking;

(b)   the address of the principal place of business of the undertaking;

(c)   the factors on which joint management of the undertaking is based; and

(d)   the proportion of the capital of the undertaking held by undertakings included in the consolidation.

(2)   Where the financial year of the undertaking did not end with that of the company, there shall be stated the date on which a financial year of the undertaking last ended before that date.

Companies Act 1985

22 Associated undertakings

(1) The following information shall be given where an undertaking included in the consolidation has an interest in an associated undertaking.

(2) The name of the associated undertaking shall be stated.

(3) There shall be stated—

(a) if the undertaking is incorporated outside Great Britain, the country in which it is incorporated;

(b) if it is incorporated in Great Britain, whether it is registered in England and Wales or in Scotland;

(c) if it is unincorporated, the address of its principal place of business.

(4) The following information shall be given with respect to the shares of the undertaking held—

(a) by the parent company, and

(b) by the group;

and the information under paragraphs (a) and (b) shall be shown separately.

(5) There shall be stated—

(a) the identity of each class of shares held, and

(b) the proportion of the nominal value of the shares of that class represented by those shares.

(6) In this paragraph "associated undertaking" has the meaning given by paragraph 20 of Schedule 4A; and the information required by this paragraph shall be given notwithstanding that paragraph 22(3) of that Schedule (materiality) applies in relation to the accounts themselves.

Other significant holdings of parent company or group

23 (1) The information required by paragraphs 24 and 25 shall be given where at the end of the financial year the parent company has a significant holding in an undertaking which is not one of its subsidiary undertakings and does not fall within paragraph 21 (joint ventures) or paragraph 22 (associated undertakings).

(2) A holding is significant for this purpose if—

(a) it amounts to 10 per cent. or more of the nominal value of any class of shares in the undertaking, or

(b) the amount of the holding (as stated or included in the company's individual accounts) exceeds one-tenth of the amount of its assets (as so stated).

24 (1) The name of the undertaking shall be stated.

(2) There shall be stated—

(a) if the undertaking is incorporated outside Great Britain, the country in which it is incorporated;

(b) if it is incorporated in Great Britain, whether it is registered in England and Wales or in Scotland;

(c) if it is unincorporated, the address of its principal place of business.

(3) The following information shall be given with respect to the shares of the undertaking held by the parent company.

(4)   There shall be stated—

    (a)   the identity of each class of shares held, and
    (b)   the proportion of the nominal value of the shares of that class represented by those shares.

25   (1)   Where the company has a significant holding in an undertaking amounting to 20 per cent. or more of the nominal value of the shares in the undertaking, there shall also be stated—

    (a)   the aggregate amount of the capital and reserves of the undertaking as at the end of its relevant financial year, and
    (b)   its profit or loss for that year.

    (2)   That information need not be given in respect of an undertaking if—

    (a)   the undertaking is not required by any provision of this Act to deliver a copy of its balance sheet for its relevant financial year and does not otherwise publish that balance sheet in Great Britain or elsewhere, and
    (b)   the company's holding is less than 50 per cent. of the nominal value of the shares in the undertaking.

    (3)   Information otherwise required by this paragraph need not be given if it is not material.

    (4)   For the purposes of this paragraph the "relevant financial year" of an undertaking is—

    (a)   if its financial year ends with that of the company, that year, and
    (b)   if not, its financial year ending last before the end of the company's financial year.

26   (1)   The information required by paragraphs 27 and 28 shall be given where at the end of the financial year the group has a significant holding in an undertaking which is not a subsidiary undertaking of the parent company and does not fall within paragraph 21 (joint ventures) or paragraph 22 (associated undertakings).

    (2)   A holding is significant for this purpose if—

    (a)   it amounts to 10 per cent. or more of the nominal value of any class of shares in the undertaking, or
    (b)   the amount of the holding (as stated or included in the group accounts) exceeds one-tenth of the amount of the group's assets (as so stated).

27   (1)   The name of the undertaking shall be stated.

    (2)   There shall be stated—

    (a)   if the undertaking is incorporated outside Great Britain, the country in which it is incorporated;
    (b)   if it is incorporated in Great Britain, whether it is registered in England and Wales or in Scotland;
    (c)   if it is unincorporated, the address of its principal place of business.

    (3)   The following information shall be given with respect to the shares of the undertaking held by the group.

    (4)   There shall be stated—

    (a)   the identity of each class of shares held, and

      (b)   the proportion of the nominal value of the shares of that class represented by those shares.

28   (1)   Where the holding of the group amounts to 20 per cent. or more of the nominal value of the shares in the undertaking, there shall also be stated—

      (a)   the aggregate amount of the capital and reserves of the undertaking as at the end of its relevant financial year, and

      (b)   its profit or loss for that year.

    (2)   That information need not be given if—

      (a)   the undertaking is not required by any provision of this Act to deliver a copy of its balance sheet for its relevant financial year and does not otherwise publish that balance sheet in Great Britain or elsewhere, and

      (b)   the holding of the group is less than 50 per cent. of the nominal value of the shares in the undertaking.

    (3)   Information otherwise required by this paragraph need not be given if it is not material.

    (4)   For the purposes of this paragraph the "relevant financial year" of an outside undertaking is—

      (a)   if its financial year ends with that of the parent company, that year, and

      (b)   if not, its financial year ending last before the end of the parent company's financial year.

29   **Arrangements attracting merger relief**

    (1)   This paragraph applies to arrangements attracting merger relief, that is, where a company allots shares in consideration for the issue, transfer or cancellation of shares in another body corporate ("the other company") in circumstances such that section 130 of this Act (share premium account) does not, by virtue of section 131(2) (merger relief), apply to the premiums on the shares.

    (2)   If the parent company made such an arrangement during the financial year, the following information shall be given—

      (a)   the name of the other company,

      (b)   the number, nominal value and class of shares allotted,

      (c)   the number, nominal value and class of shares in the other company issued, transferred or cancelled, and

      (d)   particulars of the accounting treatment adopted in the parent company's individual and group accounts in respect of the issue, transfer or cancellation, and

      (e)   particulars of the extent to which and manner in which the profit or loss for the financial year shown in the group accounts is affected by any profit or loss of the other company, or any of its subsidiary undertakings, which arose before the time of the arrangement.

    (3)   Where the parent company made such an arrangement during the financial year, or during either of the two preceding financial years, and there is included in the consolidated profit and loss account—

      (a)   any profit or loss realised during the financial year on the disposal of—
          (i)   any shares in the other company, or
         (ii)   any assets which were fixed assets of the other company or any of its subsidiary undertakings at the time of the arrangement, or

(b) any part of any profit or loss realised during the financial year on the disposal of any shares (other than shares in the other company) which was attributable to the fact that there were at the time of the disposal amongst the assets of the company which issued the shares, or any of its subsidiary undertakings, such shares or assets as are described in paragraph (a) above,

then, the net amount of that profit or loss or, as the case may be, the part so attributable shall be shown, together with an explanation of the transactions to which the information relates.

(4) For the purposes of this paragraph the time of the arrangement shall be taken to be—

(a) where as a result of the arrangement the other company becomes a subsidiary undertaking of the company in question, the date on which it does so or, if the arrangement in question becomes binding only on the fulfilment of a condition, the date on which that condition is fulfilled;

(b) if the other company is already a subsidiary undertaking of that company, the date on which the shares are allotted or, if they are allotted on different days, the first day.

30 Parent undertaking drawing up accounts for larger group

(1) Where the parent company is itself a subsidiary undertaking, the following information shall be given with respect to that parent undertaking of the company which heads—

(a) the largest group of undertakings for which group accounts are drawn up and of which that company is a member, and

(b) the smallest such group of undertakings.

(2) The name of the parent undertaking shall be stated.

(3) There shall be stated—

(a) if the undertaking is incorporated outside Great Britain, the country in which it is incorporated;

(b) if it is incorporated in Great Britain, whether it is registered in England and Wales or in Scotland;

(c) if it is unincorporated, the address of its principal place of business.

(4) If copies of the group accounts referred to in sub-paragraph (1) are available to the public, there shall also be stated the addresses from which copies of the accounts can be obtained.

31 Identification of ultimate parent company

(1) Where the parent company is itself a subsidiary undertaking, the following information shall be given with respect to the company (if any) regarded by the directors as being that company's ultimate parent company.

(2) The name of that company shall be stated.

(3) If known to the directors, there shall be stated—

(a) if that company is incorporated outside Great Britain, the country in which it is incorporated;

(b) if it is incorporated in Great Britain, whether it is registered in England and Wales or in Scotland.

527

(4)   In this paragraph "company" includes any body corporate.

32   Construction of references to shares held by parent company or group

(1)   References in this Part of this Schedule to shares held by the parent company or the group shall be construed as follows.

(2)   For the purposes of paragraphs 16, 22(4) and (5) and 23 to 25 (information about holdings in subsidiary and other undertakings)—

   (a)   there shall be attributed to the parent company shares held on its behalf by any person; but
   (b)   there shall be treated as not held by the parent company shares held on behalf of a person other than the company.

(3)   References to shares held by the group are to any shares held by or on behalf of the parent company or any of its subsidiary undertakings; but there shall be treated as not held by the group any shares held on behalf of a person other than the parent company or any of its subsidiary undertakings.

(4)   Shares held by way of security shall be treated as held by the person providing the security—

   (a)   where apart from the right to exercise them for the purpose of preserving the value of the security, or of realising it, the rights attached to the shares are exercisable only in accordance with his instructions, and
   (b)   where the shares are held in connection with the granting of loans as part of normal business activities and apart from the right to exercise them for the purpose of preserving the value of the security, or of realising it, the rights attached to the shares are exercisable only in his interests.

Note. The above Schedule was substituted by CA 1989, 3 Sch with effect from a date to be appointed.

SCHEDULE 7
(Section 235 and as amended by CA 1989, s 8(2), 5 Sch)

MATTERS TO BE DEALT WITH IN DIRECTORS' REPORT

PART I   MATTERS OF A GENERAL NATURE

6   Miscellaneous

The directors' report shall contain—

(a)   particulars of any important events affecting the company or any of its
       [subsidiary undertakings][1] which have occurred since the end of the financial
       year,
(b)   an indication of likely future developments in the business of the company and
       of its [subsidiary undertakings][1], and
(c)   an indication of the activities (if any) of the company and its [subsidiary
       undertakings][1] in the field of research and development.

---

[1]   Substituted by CA 1989, 5 Sch 2 with effect from 1 April 1990 (SI 1990 No 355) subject to the transitional
      and saving provisions in Arts 6 to 9 of that Order.
      Previously 'subsidiaries'.

PART II   DISCLOSURE REQUIRED BY COMPANY ACQUIRING ITS OWN
SHARES, ETC.

7   This Part of this Schedule applies where shares in a company—

(a)   are purchased by the company or are acquired by it by forfeiture or surrender
       in lieu of forfeiture, or in pursuance of section 143(3) of this Act (acquisition
       of own shares by company limited by shares), or
(b)   are acquired by another person in circumstances where paragraph (c) or (d)
       of section 146(1) applies (acquisition by company's nominee, or by another
       with company financial assistance, the company having a beneficial interest),
       or
(c)   are made subject to a lien or other charge taken (whether expressly or otherwise)
       by the company and permitted by section 150(2) or (4), or section 6(3) of the
       Consequential Provisions Act (exceptions from general rule against a company
       having a lien or charge on its own shares).

8   The directors' report with respect to a financial year shall state—

(a)   the number and nominal value of the shares so purchased, the aggregate amount
       of the consideration paid by the company for such shares and the reasons for
       their purchase;
(b)   the number and nominal value of the shares so acquired by the company,
       acquired by another person in such circumstances and so charged respectively
       during the financial year;
(c)   the maximum number and nominal value of shares which, having been so
       acquired by the company, acquired by another person in such circumstances
       or so charged (whether or not during that year) are held at any time by the
       company or that other person during that year;
(d)   the number and nominal value of the shares so acquired by the company,
       acquired by another person in such circumstances or so charged (whether or
       not during that year) which are disposed of by the company or that other person
       or cancelled by the company during that year;

Companies Act 1985

    (e)   where the number and nominal value of the shares of any particular description are stated in pursuance of any of the preceding sub-paragraphs, the percentage of the called-up share capital which shares of that description represent;

    (f)   where any of the shares have been so charged the amount of the charge in each case; and

    (g)   where any of the shares have been disposed of by the company or the person who acquired them in such circumstances for money or money's worth the amount or value of the consideration in each case.

SCHEDULE 8
(Section 13(2), CA 1989)

EXEMPTIONS FOR SMALL AND MEDIUM-SIZED COMPANIES

Note. This Schedule is substituted by CA 1989, s 13(2), 6 Sch with effect from 1 April 1990 (SI 1990 No 355) subject to the transitional and saving provisions in Arts 6 to 9 of that Order.

PART I   SMALL COMPANIES

3   Disclosure of information in notes to accounts

(1)   Of the information required by Part III of Schedule 4 (information to be given in notes to accounts if not given in the accounts themselves) only the information required by the following provisions need be given—

paragraph 36 (accounting policies),

paragraph 38 (share capital),

paragraph 39 (particulars of allotments),

paragraph 42 (fixed assets), so far as it relates to those items to which a letter or Roman number is assigned in the balance sheet format adopted,

paragraph 48(1) and (4) (particulars of debts),

paragraph 58(1) (basis of conversion of foreign currency amounts into sterling),

paragraph 58(2) (corresponding amounts for previous financial year), so far as it relates to amounts stated in a note to the company's accounts by virtue of a requirement of Schedule 4 or under any other provision of this Act.

(2)   Of the information required by Schedule 5 to be given in notes to the accounts, the information required by the following provisions need not be given—

paragraph 4 (financial years of subsidiary undertakings),

paragraph 5 (additional information about subsidiary undertakings),

paragraph 6 (shares and debentures of company held by subsidiary undertakings),

paragraph 10 (arrangements attracting merger relief).

(3)   Of the information required by Schedule 6 to be given in notes to the accounts, the information required by Part I (directors' and chairman's emoluments, pensions and compensation for loss of office) need not be given.

Companies Act 1985

PARENT AND SUBSIDIARY UNDERTAKINGS: SUPPLEMENTARY PROVISIONS

Note. This Schedule inserted by CA 1989, s 21(2), 9 Sch with effect from 1 April 1990 (SI 1990 No 355) subject to the transitional and saving provisions in Arts 6 to 9 of that Order.

1 Introduction

The provisions of this Schedule explain expressions used in section 258 (parent and subsidiary undertakings) and otherwise supplement that section.

2 Voting rights in an undertaking

(1) In section 258(2)(a) and (d) the references to the voting rights in an undertaking are to the rights conferred on shareholders in respect of their shares or, in the case of an undertaking not having a share capital, on members, to vote at general meetings of the undertaking on all, or substantially all, matters.

(2) In relation to an undertaking which does not have general meetings at which matters are decided by the exercise of voting rights, the references to holding a majority of the voting rights in the undertaking shall be construed as references to having the right under the constitution of the undertaking to direct the overall policy of the undertaking or to alter the terms of its constitution.

3 Right to appoint or remove a majority of the directors

(1) In section 258(2)(b) the reference to the right to appoint or remove a majority of the board of directors is to the right to appoint or remove directors holding a majority of the voting rights at meetings of the board on all, or substantially all, matters.

(2) An undertaking shall be treated as having the right to appoint to a directorship if—

(a) a person's appointment to it follows necessarily from his appointment as director of the undertaking, or

(b) the directorship is held by the undertaking itself.

(3) A right to appoint or remove which is exercisable only with the consent or concurrence of another person shall be left out of account unless no other person has a right to appoint or, as the case may be, remove in relation to that directorship.

4 Right to exercise dominant influence

(1) For the purposes of section 258(2)(c) an undertaking shall not be regarded as having the right to exercise a dominant influence over another undertaking unless it has a right to give directions with respect to the operating and financial policies of that other undertaking which its directors are obliged to comply with whether or not they are for the benefit of that other undertaking.

(2) A "control contract" means a contract in writing conferring such a right which—

(a) is of a kind authorised by the memorandum or articles of the undertaking in relation to which the right is exercisable, and

(b)   is permitted by the law under which that undertaking is established.

(3)   This paragraph shall not be read as affecting the construction of the expression "actually exercises a dominant influence" in section 258(4)(a).

5   Rights exercisable only in certain circumstances or temporarily incapable of exercise

(1)   Rights which are exercisable only in certain circumstances shall be taken into account only—

(a)   when the circumstances have arisen, and for so long as they continue to obtain, or

(b)   when the circumstances are within the control of the person having the rights.

(2)   Rights which are normally exercisable but are temporarily incapable of exercise shall continue to be taken into account.

Rights held by one person on behalf of another

6   Rights held by a person in a fiduciary capacity shall be treated as not held by him.

7   (1)   Rights held by a person as nominee for another shall be treated as held by the other.

(2)   Rights shall be regarded as held as nominee for another if they are exercisable only on his instructions or with his consent or concurrence.

8   Rights attached to shares held by way of security

Rights attached to shares held by way of security shall be treated as held by the person providing the security—

(a)   where apart from the right to exercise them for the purpose of preserving the value of the security, or of realising it, the rights are exercisable only in accordance with his instructions, and

(b)   where the shares are held in connection with the granting of loans as part of normal business activities and apart from the right to exercise them for the purpose of preserving the value of the security, or of realising it, the rights are exercisable only in his interests.

9   Rights attributed to parent undertaking

(1)   Rights shall be treated as held by a parent undertaking if they are held by any of its subsidiary undertakings.

(2)   Nothing in paragraph 7 or 8 shall be construed as requiring rights held by a parent undertaking to be treated as held by any of its subsidiary undertakings.

(3)   For the purposes of paragraph 8 rights shall be treated as being exercisable in accordance with the instructions or in the interests of an undertaking if they are exercisable in accordance with the instructions of or, as the case may be, in the interests of any group undertaking.

10   Disregard of certain rights

The voting rights in an undertaking shall be reduced by any rights held by the undertaking itself.

Companies Act 1985

11 Supplementary

References in any provision of paragraphs 6 to 10 to rights held by a person include rights falling to be treated as held by him by virtue of any other provision of those paragraphs but not rights which by virtue of any such provision are to be treated as not held by him.

TABLE OF LEGISLATION AND OF OTHER REGULATIONS

TABLE OF COMPANIES

References are to paragraph numbers of this book where extracts from the financial statements of these companies are reproduced.

Metal box	8.40
Pearsons	11.13,11.30
Reed International	7.58
Reuters Holdings	4.43,10.16
RTZ Corporation	4.64,10.16,11.27,11.32,11.62
Saatchi & Saatchi	8.35,8.53
Sketchley	3.76
Stakis	10.4
Tesco	7.93
Thorn EMI	4.22,8.21,8.42,10.19
Tootal Group	4.11
Trafalgar House	6.14
Trusthouse Forte	3.15
Ultramar	7.121
Willis Faber	3.80

Index

References are to paragraph numbers of this book.

Notes

Notes

Notes

Notes

Tolley
HOTLINE

081-686 0115

The above Hotline number is a direct line to our Customer Liaison staff and can be used for a faster, more convenient service when ordering any Tolley publication.

(Outside office hours an answering machine is in operation)

Tolley Publishing Co. Ltd.,
Tolley House, 2 Addiscombe Road, Croydon, Surrey, CR9 5AF

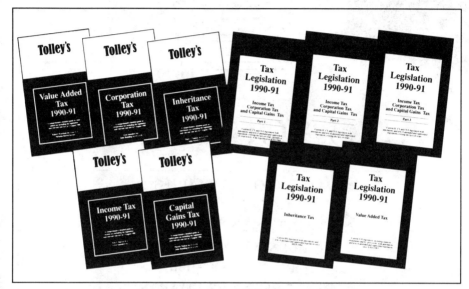

Tolley Publications

TAXATION PUBLICATIONS

Tax Reference Annuals
Available September 1990

Tolley's Income Tax 1990-91 £22.95
Tolley's Corporation Tax 1990-91 £18.95
Tolley's Capital Gains Tax 1990-91 £19.95
Tolley's Inheritance Tax 1990-91 £16.95
Tolley's Value Added Tax 1990-91 £19.95
Tolley's National Insurance Contributions 1990-91 £23.95

Tolley's Tax Legislation Series
Available August 1990

Income Tax, Corporation Tax and Capital Gains Tax Legislation 1990-91 (in 2 parts) £25.95
Inheritance Tax Legislation 1990-91 £10.95
Value Added Tax Legislation 1990-91 £14.95
NIC Legislation 1990-91 £13.95

Tolley's Looseleaf Tax Service
Available September 1990

Tolley's Tax Service *Income Tax, Corporation Tax and Capital Gains Tax* (3 binders) £tba
Tolley's Inheritance Tax Service £tba
Tolley's Value Added Tax Service (2 binders) £tba

Other Annual Tax Books

Taxwise Taxation Workbook No 1 (IT/CT/CGT) 1990-91 £18.95
Taxwise Taxation Workbook No 2 (IHT/VAT/Trusts/Planning/Management 1990-91 £15.95
Tolley's Capital Allowances 3rd Edition £21.95
Tolley's Estate Planning 2nd Edition £19.95
Tolley's Official Tax Statements 1989-90 £24.95
Tolley's Tax Cases 1990 £21.95
Tolley's Tax Computations 1989-90 £23.75
Tolley's Tax Data 1990-91 £9.95
Tolley's Tax Guide 1990-91 £16.95 (to 15/9/90)
Tolley's Tax Office Addresses 1990 £5.95
Tolley's Tax Planning 1990 (2 volumes) £42.50
Tolley's Tax Tables 1990 £6.95
Tolley's Taxation in the Channel Islands and Isle of Man 1990 £tba
Tolley's Taxation in the Republic of Ireland 1990-91 £tba
Tolley's VAT Planning 1990 £19.95
Tolley's VAT Cases 1990 £44.95

Other Tax Books

Tolley's Capital Gains Tax Base Date Prices 31st March 1982 (Revised Issue 1989) £25.00
Tolley's Guide to the VAT Compliance and Penalty Provisions 2nd Edition £12.95
Tolley's Guide to the New VAT Partial Exemption Rules 2nd Edition £15.95
Tolley's Property Taxes 3rd Edition £24.95
Tolley's Retirement Relief £12.95
Tolley's Roll-over and Hold-over Reliefs £19.95
Tolley's Schedule E: Taxation of Employments £tba
Tolley's Stamp Duties and Stamp Duty Reserve Tax £tba (3rd Edition includes legislation)
Tolley's Personal Tax and Investment Planning £tba
Tolley's Tax Havens £tba
Tolley's Tax Investigations £tba

Tolley's Tax Planning for New Businesses 3rd Edition £15.95
Tolleys Taxation of UK Trusts £24.95
Tolley's Taxation of Insolvent Companies £9.95
Tolley's Taxation of Lloyd's Underwriters £29.95
Tolley's Taxation of Marriage and Marriage Breakdown £14.95
Tolley's VAT Investigations £tba
Tolley's VAT on Construction, Land and Property £16.95
Tolley's Purchase and Sale of a Private Company's Shares 3rd Edition £19.95

LEGAL PUBLICATIONS

Company Law and Practice

Tolley's Company Law (looseleaf) £49.95
Tolley's Companies Legislation £19.95
Tolley's Index to Companies Legislation 4th Edition £9.95
Tolley's Practical Guide to Company Acquisitions £23.00
Tolley's Duties and Responsibilities of a Company Secretary £tba

Employment Law and Social Security

Tolley's Employment Handbook 7th Edition £19.95
Tolley's Health and Safety at Work Handbook 3rd Edition £tba
Tolley's Payroll Handbook 4th Edition £tba
Tolley's Social Security and State Benefits 1990-91 £24.95

Insolvency

The Bankruptcy (Scotland) Act 1985 - A Practical Guide £17.95
Tolley's Receivership Manual 3rd Edition £21.95
Tolley's Corporate Insolvency Handbook £tba

BUSINESS PUBLICATIONS

Accounting and Finance

Tolley's Charities Manual (looseleaf) £tba
Tolley's Companies Accounts Check List 1990 £tba per pack of 5 (inc VAT)
Tolley's Government Assistance for Businesses 2nd Edition £14.95
Tolley's Workbook on Financial Accounting £10.95
Tolley's Workbook on Statistics £9.95
Tolley's Commercial Loan Agreements £29.95
Tolley's Sources of Corporate Finance £tba
Tolley's Accounting for Pension Costs £tba

Pensions

Tolley's Personal Pensions and Occupational Pension Schemes: An Employer's Guide £10.95
Tolley's Pension Scheme Model Annual Report £7.00
Tolley's Small Self-Administered Pension Schemes £16.95
Pension Fund Surpluses £7.50
The Actuary in Practice £14.95
Your New Pensions Choice 3rd Edition £3.50

Survey

CSR Survey of Company Car Schemes 1990 £tba

You may order any of these titles, or obtain a copy of the Tolley catalogue, by telephoning 081-686 0115

Tolley's Journals and Newsletters

Tolley's Journals

Taxation
Founded in 1927, *Taxation* is the only weekly tax magazine for the professional. It contains leading and feature articles on major items of interest, a news digest section, reports of tax cases, and, of course, the ever-popular readers' queries section.

Pensions World
Established since 1972, Pensions World is widely regarded as the authoritative monthly for all those involved in pensions planning. Accepted by the National Association of Pension Funds Ltd, it is distributed to all members as the Association's official journal.

Tolley's Newsletters
All are designed to save valuable time and offer practical help in complex fields.

Company Secretary's Review
An eight page business fortnightly that covers the entire field of work of the company secretary/administrator.

Tolley's Practical Tax
A fortnightly eight page bulletin that concentrates solely on taxation matters for the busy accountant and taxation practitioner.

Tolley's Practical VAT
An eight page monthly for VAT specialists giving full coverage of all VAT matters via articles, tribunal reports, updating section and points of VAT Practice.

Payroll Manager's Review
This monthly newsletter provides practical advice and updating information on all subjects affecting payroll, via news, articles and features including case studies and answers to readers' problems.

Compliance Monitor
Monthly updating information and guidance for Compliance Officers and others involved with implementing the financial services regulatory system.

Single Market Monitor
Monthly updating newsletter for senior managers on EC and UK legislation and other developments in the EC.

Multinational Employer
Monthly periodical for those involved in the management of overseas operations and personnel anywhere in the world.

Audit Briefing
Monthly publication presenting advice, guidance and updating on audit-related matters, plus other business information of value to auditors.

For sample copies or information please ring 081-686 0115

Any new subscribers cancelling their subscriptions to Tolley periodicals within eight weeks will obtain a full refund.

Order form

To: Tolley Publishing Company Ltd., Tolley House, 2 Addiscombe Road, Croydon, Surrey CR9 5AF England.　　　　Telephone: 081-686 9141

Please send me the following book(s), as shown below. I understand that if, for any reason, I am not satisfied with my order and return the book(s) in saleable condition within 21 days, Tolley will refund my money in full.

If you wish to place a standing order for any book(s) and obtain the benefits of the Tolley Subscriber Service, please tick the relevant standing order box(es). All books placed on standing order are sent post-free within the U.K. Please add 5% towards postage and packing if not placed on standing order.

Title	Price per copy	No. of copies	Standing order	Amount £
			☐	
			☐	
			☐	
			☐	
			☐	
			☐	

Plus VAT (if applicable) _____

Plus 5% postage and packing (if applicable) _____

Total £ _____

Cheque is enclosed for total amount of order £ _____
Please debit Access/Visa* account number

[_____]　ACCESS　VISA　Signature _____

*Please delete as necessary

Please send me a copy of the full Tolley catalogue ☐

Name† _____

Firm _____

Position _____

Address† _____

_____

_____ Post Code _____

Telephone No _____ Date _____
†If paying by credit card, please enter name and address of cardholder

Registered No. 729731 England VAT No. 243 3583 67　　　　　　　　　Code 262